designing and maintaining

YOUR EDIBLE LANDSCAPE
NATURALLY

by

Robert Kourik

Foreword by Rosalind Creasy
Edited by Mark Kane
Illustrations by Maia Massion

Additional illustrations by
Heidi Schmidt, Amie Hill, Linda Parker

Metamorphic Press

Library of Congress Catalog Card Number: 85-63207

ISBN 0-9615848-0-7 (pbk.)

Cover design by Sandra Farkas
Book design by Sandra Farkas
Layout by Heidi Schmidt

All photographs by Robert Kourik unless otherwise noted. The back-cover photographs entitled "A Fall Harvest" and "'Pink Pearl' Apple Tart" are © Doug Gosling, 1984.

Distribution to bookstores, libraries, and retail nurseries, contact: Rodale Press, Inc., 33 E. Minor, Emmaus, PA 18049.

Distribution to mail order companies, contact: The Edible Landscape Book Project, P.O. Box 1841, Santa Rosa, CA 95402.

Metamorphic Press
P.O. Box 1841
Santa Rosa, CA 95402

Printed in the United States of America

10 9 8 7 6 5 4 3 2

Grateful acknowledgments are made to the following for permission to reprint previously published material:

Acres, U.S.A., for passages from *An Acres U.S.A. Primer*, by Charles Walters and C. J. Fenzau. Acres, U.S.A., 1979.

Creative Think, for passages from *A Whack On the Side of the Head*, by Roger von Oech. Creative Think, 1983.

Faber and Faber, for passages from *Intensive Gardening*, by R. Dolziel O'Brien. Faber & Faber, 1956.

Faber and Faber, for passages from *Practical Organic Gardening*, by Ben Easey. Faber & Faber, 1955.

Hilltop Orchards & Nurseries, for pollination charts and tree spacing guides from the *Hilltop Catalogs*. Hilltop Orchards & Nurseries, Hartford, MI 49057.

Institute for Local Self-Reliance, for the poster *Gardening for Health*. 1717 18th St. NW, Washington, DC 20009.

Kiwi Fence Systems, Inc., for diagrams from *How-to-Build Orchard and Vineyard Trellises*. R.D. 2, Box 51A, Waynesburg, PA 15370.

Longman Publishing Group, for passages from *Soil Conditions and Plant Growth*, by E. W. Russell. Longman Group, 1974.

McGraw-Hill, for passages from *Root Development of Vegetable Crops*, by John Weaver. McGraw-Hill, 1927.

Mitchell Beazley Publishers, for passages from *The Principles of Gardening*, by Hugh Johnson. Simon & Schuster, 1979.

Necessary Trading Company, for the chart "Necessary Bio-Selector™ for Insect Pest Control," from *The Necessary Catalogue*, Vol. 3. Necessary Trading, 1982, New Castle, VA 24127.

Netafim™ Irrigation, Inc., for the illustration of irrigation parts. 4450 No. Brawley, #121, Fresno, CA 93711.

Permaculture Institute, for passages from *Permaculture I*, by Bill Mollison and David Holmgren. Bill Mollison, 1981.

Rodale Press, for passages from "Soil Tests" series in *New Farm* magazine. Rodale Press, Jan.- Aug. 1983.

John Muir Publications, for passages from *The Food and Heat Producing Solar Greenhouse*, by Bill Yanda and Rick Fisher. John Muir Pub., 1980.

John Wiley & Sons, for charts from *Design-Data Book for Civil Engineers*, by Elwyn Seelye. John Wiley & Sons, 1981.

Sierra Club Books, for carbon/nitrogen ratio charts in *The Integral Urban House*, by the Farallones Institute. Sierra Club Books, 1979.

Sierra Club Books, for the nitrogen content chart in *Other Homes and Garbage*, by Jim Leckie, Gil Masters, Harry Whitehouse, and Lily Young. Sierra Club Books, 1975.

Sierra Club Books, for passages from *The Unsettling of America*, by Wendell Berry. Sierra Club Books, 1977.

Speedling, Inc., for the photograph of a TODD® Planter Flat. c/o Altman & Co., 5444 Bay Center Dr., #224, Tampa, FL 33609.

Storey Communications, for passages from *Improving Garden Soil with Green Manures*, by Richard Alther and Richard Raymond. Garden Way Publishing, 1979.

Ten Speed Press, for passages from *How to Grow More Vegetables*, by John Jeavons. Ten Speed Press, 1977. Box 7123, Berkeley, CA 94707.

"Robert Kourik's new book is a fine addition to the literature on landscaping with food plants. He presents a realistic look at what this sort of gardening requires, noting both advantages and limitations . . . it is based on extensive research plus his own experiences working with clients and their plantings. The sections on planting and caring for trees are especially impressive, including new information that has not been widely circulated. The many charts and the sources at the end of each chapter make this an excellent general gardening reference."

Kit Anderson, editor
***Gardens for All* magazine**

"I'm really impressed with your book. It's a pleasure to read in addition to being very informative. The holistic approach, including aesthetics and design techniques in addition to environmentally sensitive horticultural techniques, makes the book quite valuable to anyone involved with growing edibles."

James Zanetto, architect/environmental planner
Davis Design Research

"This book's sensible and non-dogmatic advice will guide you into a kind of ecologically conscious gardening that will remain beautiful but that also follows the example of productive natural systems – good for your soil, your plants, and yourself. I was particularly surprised by the scope and depth of root systems – and I've been gardening since I was about six."

Ernest Callenbach, author of
Ecotopia* and *Ecotopia Emerging

"This highly original and eminently readable work will be very useful to novice as well as experienced gardeners and professionals interested in edible landscaping. The numerous unique plant lists and tables of support information – drawn from extremely diverse sources – are alone worth the price of the book. Reviewing the manuscript inspired me to sheet compost 100 square feet outside our kitchen for planting various herbs and vegetables."

Robert Woolley, manager
Dave Wilson Nursery

TABLE OF CONTENTS

xi   List of Figures

xv   Foreword by Rosalind Creasy

xvi   Preface

xix   Acknowledgments

PART ONE

1

THE BASICS OF EDIBLE LANDSCAPING

Introduction to Edible Landscaping

1   Why Edible Landscaping?

5   The New Approach to Edible Landscapes: Synergy

9   In Praise of the Suburbs

Organic Gardening — Myths and Facts

15   The "Organic" Concept

19   Of Pests and Poisons

Understanding Your Property

23   The Climate in Your Yard

29   Your Soil

35   Existing Vegetation: What It Means, What It Offers

PART TWO

2

DESIGNING YOUR EDIBLE LANDSCAPE

Plan Before You Plant

41   Blending Aesthetics and Function

49   Defining and Planning Your Goals

57   Zones of Use, Multiple Use

63   Making Use of Local Wisdom

Energy-Conserving Landscaping

67 Shaping the Wind: Shelter for the Home and Garden

73 Shaping Sunlight

77 Shaping Water

Putting It All Together

83 Synergy

87 Creating Your Design

91 The Golden Rules of Edible Landscaping

PART THREE

3

GROWING VEGETABLES

No-Till Gardening: Less Work, Good Yields

95 Sheet Composting for "Wild" and "Tame" Plants

101 Sink or Swim: Self-Seeding Vegetables

105 Hay Bale Vegetables: Soil Building from the Top Down

107 Surface Cultivation: Good Yields without Digging

Tillage: A Little More Work, Greater Yields

113 Sod Culture: Vegetables in the Lawn

115 Double-Digging: A Balanced Review

Growing Healthier Vegetables

125 Soil Inoculants

127 Seedlings the Speedling® Way

129 Drip Irrigation

133 Intercropping

cp **COLOR PLATES**

PART FOUR

4

GROWING TREE CROPS

Choosing the Best Trees for Your Climate

139 Special Trees for Special Climates

147   Fruit for All Seasons

151   Ensuring Good Pollination

155   Disease-Resistant Trees

Roots, Soil, and Rootstocks

161   Deep-Rooted Myths

165   The Best Rootstocks for Your Soil

Trees of All Sizes

179   Standard, Semi-Dwarf, and Dwarf Trees

183   Genetic Dwarf (Miniature) Fruit and Nut Trees

191   Spacing Fruit and Nut Trees

Planting Trees

193   To Amend or Not To Amend

197   Preparing the Hole, Planting the Tree

Pruning Fruit and Nut Trees

203   The Basics of Tree Growth and Pruning

211   The No-Pruning Style

213   Open Center Pruning

217   Central Leader Pruning

221   Special Effects: Espalier, Oblique Cordon, and Miniature Trees

Caring for Your Fruit and Nut Trees

225   Drip Irrigation, Mulching, and Frost Protection

229   Fertilizing Tree Crops

PART FIVE

5

BIOLOGICAL BALANCE WITH INSECTS

235   Companion Planting: Sometimes Fact, Sometimes Fiction

237   Companion Plants that Repel Pests

245   Nature's Balance: Good Bugs and Bad Bugs

251   Attracting Good Bugs

255   Integrated Pest Management

PART SIX

6

SOIL IS HEALTH — IMPROVING SOILS, FREE FERTILIZERS

261 Feeding the Soil

265 Nature's Nutrients and Dynamic Accumulators

273 Grow Your Own Fertilizers: Cover Crops and Green Manures

277 A Five-Year Plan for Soil Improvement

PART SEVEN

7

MIXING TREES, LAWNS, FLOWERS, HERBS, VINES, AND VEGETABLES

283 Competition for Sun, Water, and Fertilizer

287 Diversity, Pests, and Diseases

291 Finishing Touches:
Perennial Legumes, Edible Flowers, and Mulches

PART EIGHT

8

THE EDIBLE LANDSCAPE COOKBOOK™

295 The Golden Hits of Edible Landscaping

APPENDIXES

311 **1** Climate Zones

313 **2** Solar Charts

317 **3** Site Analysis Survey

321 **4** Deciduous and Evergreen Vines

325 **5** Carbon-to-Nitrogen Ratios
and the N-P-K of Compostable Materials

327 **6** Liquid Measure Conversions

329 **7** Sizing Materials for Landscaping

331 **8** Mail-Order Suppliers of Plants, Seeds,
and Gardening Tools

341 **9** Producers and Suppliers
of Biological Pest Control Agents

345 **10** "Edible" Organizations and Periodicals

351 **INDEX**

LIST OF FIGURES

PAGE NUMBER

Figure 1.1   Ornamental kale (color plate)   cp 1

Figure 1.2   'Romanesco' broccoli, sometimes called 'Green Point' (color plate)   cp 1

Figure 1.3   Oriental persimmons (color plate)   cp 2

Figure 1.4   'Garden Beauty' nectarine (color plate)   cp 2

Figure 1.5   A patio planting of red and green chard, red-leaved lettuce, and a miniature 'Garden Prince' almond with ornamentals (color plate)   cp 3

Figure 1.6   The range of production methods and energy expended to produce food (chart)   2

Figure 1.7   Growing your own food saves millions of BTUs of fossil fuels each year (chart)   3

Figure 1.8   An aerial view of the Kelleys' edible landscape (illustration)   5

Figure 1.9   Cross section of the Kelleys' terraced landscape, showing underground drainage (illustration)   6

Figure 1.10   The Kelleys' landscape (color plate)   cp 3

Figure 1.11   The Kelleys' kitchen door leads directly to the landscape and compost bins (color plate)   cp 4

Figure 1.12   The three 100-square-foot vegetable terraces are planted intensively (color plate)   cp 4

Figure 1.13   An informal border eases the transition from the geometric beds (color plate)   cp 5

Figure 1.14   Flagstones are set in packed gravel (color plate)   cp 5

Figure 1.15   This edible landscape bears earlier and longer (color plate)   cp 5

Figure 1.16   A greenbelt of almond trees in Village Homes (photograph)   9

Figure 1.17   A community lawn and gazebo in Village Homes (photograph)   9

Figure 1.18   A dry creekbed serves as a catch basin in winter (photograph)   10

Figure 1.19   A lawnlike ground cover of Dutch white clover (photograph)   10

Figure 1.20   A small, efficient edible landscape is close to the kitchen and patio (photograph)   11

Figure 1.21   A miniature peach tree, herbs, ornamentals, and a lawn surround a solar home (photograph)   11

Figure 1.22   Miniature peach trees make a leafy hedge (photograph)   11

Figure 1.23   Rosemary and ornamental perennials protect the soil from runoff (photograph)   11

Figure 1.24   Village Homes has an abundance of beneficial insects such as this praying mantid (photogaph)   12

Figure 1.25   The diversity and productivity of urban, suburban, and rural areas (chart)   13

Figure 2.1   The toxicity of chemical and organic insecticides (chart)   20

Figure 3.1   Sources of information about local weather (chart)   23

Figure 3.2   Wind roses (illustration)   24

Figure 3.3   Flagged treetops reveal the prevailing winds (photograph)   25

Figure 3.4   Homemade solar and shade prospector (illustration)   26

Figure 3.5   The Solar Site Selector (photograph)   27

Figure 3.6   Looking through the Solar Site Selector (illustration)   28

Figure 3.7   Sketching the shade cast by trees and buildings (illustration)   28

Figure 3.8   Recording the bloom sequence of fruit trees (illustration)   28

Figure 3.9   Soil horizons (illustration)   30

Figure 3.10   Soil bacteria live at specific depths (illustration)   31

Figure 3.11   Results of a soil survey (illustration)   32

Figure 3.12   Soil indicators (chart)   36

Figure 4.0   Low-effort perennial edibles (chart)   45

Figure 4.1   A multi-layer planting (illustration)   47

Figure 4.2   Redwood rounds and flagstones with Dutch white clover (color plate)   47, cp 6

Figure 4.3   Area needed for growing vegetables (chart)   52

Figure 4.4   The yields of trees, vines, and shrubs (chart)   53

Figure 4.5   Maintenance time for ground covers, shrubs, and trees (chart)   55

Figure 4.6   The Kelleys' edible landscape is compact and close to the kitchen (color plate)   cp 6

Figure 4.7   A stone wall warms a garden (photograph)   58

Figure 4.8   Multi-purpose edibles (chart)   59

Figure 4.9   A multi-grafted "fruit salad" tree (photograph and color plate)   63, cp 6

Figure 5.1   Wind speed and chill factor (chart)   67

Figure 5.2   A windbreak's zone of protection (illustration)   68

Figure 5.3   Curving a driveway through a windbreak; a windbreak's height (illustration)   68

Figure 5.4   Shrubs slow winds, reducing the chill factor (illustration)   68

Figure 5.5   A windbreak may shade vegetable areas (illustration)   68

Figure 5.6   A windbreak's roots extend far into your landscape (illustration)   70

Figure 5.7   Planning for immediate and long-term wind protection (illustration)   71

Figure 5.8   Trellised vines and misted shrubs cool the house (illustration)   74

Figure 5.9   Funneling a breeze past cool, moist bricks and shrubs (illustration)   74

Figure 5.10   Trees on the south side can give unwanted shade in winter (illustration)   75

Figure 5.11   Bare winter branches cast a surprising amount of shadow (illustration)   75

Figure 5.12   Calculating which branches to remove for more winter sunlight (illustration)   76

Figure 5.13   Creating a natural-looking creekbed (illustration)   78

Figure 5.14   Plants for a riparian habitat (chart)   79

Figure 5.15   A drywell prevents erosion at a downspout (illustration)   80

Figure 5.16   Calculating the maximum runoff from a roof (chart)   80

Figure 5.17   One-hour rainfall maps (illustration)   81

Figure 6.1   The eaves of your house can shelter tender edibles (illustration)   83

Figure 6.2   Espaliered miniature 'Garden Delicious' apple trees (photograph)   84

Figure 6.3   Estimating the future impact of a tree on a view (photograph)   87

Figure 7.1   Many wild edibles are far more nutritious than lettuce (chart)   96

Figure 7.2   No-till edibles for leafy greens (chart)   96

Figure 7.3   The layers of a sheet-composted garden (illustration)   97

Figure 7.4   Windbreaks trap invasive seeds (illustration)   98

Figure 7.5   A raised bed for ornamentals, built with sheet composting (color plate)   cp 7

Figure 7.6   Plants for no-till gardens (chart)   101

Figure 7.7   Preventing cross-pollination of vegetables (chart)   102

Figure 7.8   A grid tests edibles for a self- seeding plot (illustration)   102

Figure 7.9   The layers of a hay bale garden (illustration)   105

Figure 7.10   Squash vines shade and camouflage a hay bale garden (photograph)   106

Figure 7.11   Bastard-trenching with buried kitchen scraps or compost (illustration)   107

Figure 7.12   Hand tools for surface cultivation (illustration)   109

Figure 7.13   The average yields of a surface-cultivated garden (chart)   110

Figure 8.1   Mowing legumes increases nitrogen in the soil (illustration)   114

Figure 8.2   The soil layers in a double-dug bed (illustration)   115

Figure 8.3   Inverting the soil without disturbing it (illustration)   116

Figure 8.4   The roots of an 11-week-old squash plant (illustration)   119

Figure 8.5   The midsummer root development of Swiss chard (illustration)   120

Figure 8.6   The roots of a cabbage 75 days after transplanting (illustration)   120

Figure 8.7   The first 12 inches of roots of mature sweet corn (illustration)   120

Figure 8.8   The mature root system of kohlrabi (illustration)   121

Figure 8.9   The root system of a garden beet (illustration)   121

Figure 8.10   Double-digging without straining the back (photograph)   122

Figure 8.11   The double-digging technique (photograph)   122

Figure 8.12   The double-digging technique (photograph)   122

Figure 9.1   A cross section of the TODD® planter (photograph)   127

Figure 9.2   A TODD® planter reinforced with bender board (photograph)   127

Figure 9.3   The major components of a drip irrigation system (illustration)   131

Figure 9.4   A grapevine protects a kale plant (photograph)   133

Figure 9.5   Vegetable root zones compared (illustration)   134

Figure 9.6   Shallow-rooted vegetables (chart)   135

Figure 9.7   Vegetables with roots from 4 to 6 feet deep (chart)   135

Figure 9.8   Vegetables with roots deeper than 6 feet (chart)   135

Figure 9.9   The root zone of a lima bean plant (illustration)   135

Figure 9.10   The root zone of a parsnip (illustration)   135

Figure 9.11   The root zone of a carrot (illustration)   136

Figure 9.12   The root zone of a radish (illustration)   136

Figure 9.13   The root zone of a cauliflower (illustration)   136

Figure 9.14   The root zone of an onion (illustration)   136

Figure 9.15   The root zone of spinach (illustration)   137

Figure 9.16   The root zone of a pepper plant (illustration)   137

Figure 9.17   The root zone of lettuce (illustration)   137

Figure 9.18   Fast-growing plants for intercropping (chart)   138

Figure 9.19   Slow-growing plants for intercropping (chart)   138

Figure 10.1   The three main zones of low-chill winters (illustration)   141

Figure 10.2   Chill requirements for fruit and nut trees (chart)   142

Figure 10.3   Low-chill fruit and nut trees (chart)   142

Figure 10.4   Ripening dates for fruit and nut tree varieties (chart)   147

Figure 10.4A   Self-fruitful trees (chart)   147

Figure 10.4B   Trees requiring pollinizers (chart)   151

Figure 10.4C   Self-fruitful trees that are exceptions (chart)   151

Figure 10.5   Pollinizers for apple tree varieties (chart)   152

Figure 10.6   Pollinizers for sweet cherry, European plum, pear, and Japanese plum trees (chart)   153

Figure 10.7   Disease-resistant edible trees and shrubs (chart)   155

Figure 10.8   Pears resistant to fire blight (chart)   156

Figure 10.9   Apples resistant to fire blight (chart)   156

Figure 10.10   Peaches resistant to peach leaf curl (chart)   157

Figure 10.11   Peaches resistant to brown rot (chart)   158

Figure 10.12   Peaches resistant to gummosis (chart)   158

Figure 10.13   Peaches resistant to bacterial leaf spot (chart)   158

Figure 10.14   Apples resistant to scab (chart)   158

Figure 10.15   Disease-resistant apples (chart)   159

Figure 10.16   Walnuts resistant to blight (chart)   160

Figure 11.0   The width of tree roots compared to the width of the canopies (illustration)   161

Figure 11.1   The roots of a pear tree compared to its canopy (illustration)   162

Figure 11.2   The roots of a 20-year-old apple tree (illustration)   162

Figure 11.3   The root zones of vegetables and of a fruit tree (illustration)   162

Figure 11.4   The roots of two apple trees avoid compacted soil and each other (illustration)   163

Figure 11.5   Tree roots in hardpan soil (illustration)   163

Figure 11.6   Tree roots growing on a slope (illustration)   163

Figure 11.7 - 11.17   Rootstocks for fruit and nut trees (charts)   **166 to 177**

Figure 12.1   There is a tree size to fit any landscape (illustration)   179

Figure 12.2   Heights and widths of standard-size trees (chart)   180

Figure 12.3   Miniature peach trees in a raised bed (photograph)   183

Figure 12.4   A miniature tree has more buds in the same space (illustration)   183

Figure 12.5   The roots of a miniature tree take much more space than its top (illustration)   184

Figure 12.6   A low wall of stone helps fruit to ripen (photograph)   184

Figure 12.7   A 14-year-old miniature peach tree (photograph)   186

Figure 12.8   Miniature tree varieties (chart)   188

Figure 12.9   Slowing and stimulating tree growth (chart)   191

Figure 13.1   Planting a fruit tree (illustration)   197

Figure 13.2   Planting a tree in clay soils (illustration)   198

Figure 13.3   Planting a grafted tree (illustration)   199

Figure 13.4   Turning a dwarf tree into a full-size tree (illustration)   199

Figure 13.5   Sand keeps a young tree from "walking" (illustration)   200

Figure 14.1   A young apple flower bud (photograph)   203

Figure 14.2   A peach flower bud (photograph)   204

Figure 14.3   A narrow fork forms a weak attachment to the trunk (illustration)   204

Figure 14.4   The most fruitful part of an arched limb (illustration)   205

Figure 14.5   The most vertical growth occurs near the peak of an arched limb (photograph)   205

Figure 14.6   Clothespins spread young branches (illustration)   206

Figure 14.7   Toothpicks make fast, inexpensive branch spreaders (photograph)   206

Figure 14.8   Notching to promote fruit buds or branches (illustration)   206

Figure 14.9   A notch that produced a flower bud (photograph)   207

Figure 14.10   Making a fast-healing pruning cut (illustration)   208

Figure 14.11   A dead oak limb slowly decays (photograph)   209

Figure 14.12   A callus not yet healed over (photograph)   209

Figure 14.13   An oak tree's fully healed callus (photograph)   210

Figure 14.14   Yields per tree with different pruning styles (illustration)   211

Figure 14.15   Training an open center tree (illustration)   213

Figure 14.16   The spreading main branches of an open center tree (illustration)   213

Figure 14.17   The open center style can create too many narrow forks (illustration)   214

Figure 14.18   Early training in the delayed open center style (illustration)   214

Figure 14.19   A mature delayed open center tree (illustration)   214

Figure 14.20   A century-old pear trained in the delayed open center style (photograph)   215

Figure 14.21   Open center trees gain support from "pleached" branches (photograph)   215

Figure 14.22   Young branches twisted together to form a living guy wire (photograph)   215

Figure 14.23   Interior shade causes fruit spurs to die (illustration)   217

Figure 14.24   Summer pruning encourages more fruit buds (illustration)   218

Figure 14.25   A palmette verrier espalier (illustration)   221

Figure 14.26   An oblique cordon espalier (illustration)   221

Figure 14.27   A horizontal palmette, or cordon, espalier (illustration)   221

Figure 14.28   A fan-shaped "solar" miniature fruit tree (illustration)   223

Figure 15.1   Most of the water that affect yields comes from the top 2 to 3 feet of soil (illustration)   226

Figure 15.2   The interior of a complex, or tortuous path, emitter (illustration)   226

Figure 15.3   The annual sequence and layers of a perennial mulch (illustration)   227

Figure 15.4   Colorful ground covers soften the effect of an expanse of mulch (color plate)   227

Figure 15.5   A field of snow-white perlite in bloom (photograph)   224

Figure 15.6   Terminal-bearing edibles (chart)   228

Figure 15.7   Seasonal growth indicating adequate nitrogen (chart)   229

Figure 15.8   Nitrogen requirements of fruit and nut trees (chart)   230

Figure 15.9   Converting nitrogen to organic amendments (chart)   230

Figure 15.10   The nitrogen needs of tree crops and vegetables (chart)   231

Figure 15.11   Cover crops with deep taproots (chart)   233

Figure 16.1   Companion planting research summaries (chart)   239

Figure 16.2   Successful intercropping tests (chart)   241

Figure 16.3   A beneficial wasp parasitizing an aphid (illustration)   245

Figure 16.4   The stages of a ladybug (illustration)   246

Figure 16.5   An adult tachinid fly (illustration)   246

Figure 16.6   An adult soldier beetle (illustration)   246

Figure 16.7   An adult snakefly (illustration)   247

Figure 16.8   A syrphid fly larva on a flower bud (illustration)   248

Figure 16.9   Potential insectary plants (chart)   252

Figure 16.10   Insect pest controls (chart)   258

Figure 16.11   Pest-resistant vegetable varieties (chart)   260

Figure 16.12   The umbel flower buds of anise (color plate)   **cp 8**

Figure 17.1   The availability of nitrogen in legumes (illustration)   **265**

Figure 17.2   Amounts of nitrogen gathered by legumes (chart)   **266**

Figure 17.3   Cover crops suited to your soil and climate (chart)   **267**

Figure 17.4   Dynamic accumulator plants (chart)   **269**

Figure 17.5   A five-year plan for gradual soil development (illustration)   **277**

Figure 17.6   Five-year soil development in a yard (illustration)   **278**

Figure 17.7   A seven-step crop rotation plan (illustration)   **279**

Figure 18.1   Edibles that grow in shade (chart)   **283**

Figure 18.2   Trees that prefer not to grow in a lawn (chart)   **284**

Figure 18.3   Citrus trees flourish in a lawn (photograph)   **285**

Figure 18.4   Trees and other edibles that may grow well in or near lawns (chart)   **285**

Figure 18.5   Watering trees with overhead spinklers can aggravate diseases (photograph)   **286**

Figure 18.6   The alternate-row method of pruning cane fruits (illustration)   **286**

Figure 18.7   Host plants for diseases (chart)   **287**

Figure 18.8   Disease vectors (chart)   **288**

Figure 18.9   Legume family trees and shrubs (chart)   **291**

Figure 18.10   Non-leguminous nitrogen-fixing trees and shrubs (chart)   **291**

Figure 18.11   A mullein stalk blooms over many months for a wonderful border accent (color plate)   **cp 8**

Figure 18.12   The blossoms of pineapple guava are succulent and tropical tasting (color plate)   **cp 8**

Figure 18.13   Edible flowers (chart)   **292**

Figure 18.14   To mulch or not to mulch (chart)   **292**

FOREWORD

When I wrote my book on edible landscaping, people's attitudes about food plants were very different from what they are today. Planting edibles in an ornamental setting was unthinkable; vegetable gardens and orchards were considered functional, unattractive areas to be screened from view. Given this prejudice, I went to great lengths to demonstrate how ornamental edibles fit into classic styles of landscape design. Now that people are more acccepting of beautiful foodscapes, the way has been paved for Robert's book, which expands the frontiers of edible landscaping.

Robert and I first became aware of the synchronistic nature of our work in 1978 when I was invited to speak at a workshop he was sponsoring. Since then, we have taught together, exchanged information, and shared dreams about the impact our work will have on landscape design and on suburban America.

When we co-teach, the information we cover divides naturally into two categories – I present an overview of edible landscaping and the principles of ornamental, edible design; Robert provides the details of time-saving strategies, organic pest control, soil building, and labor-saving methods.

Robert's knowledge of landscape techniques and data is encyclopedic. When designing, I have often wished I had his knowledge at my fingertips; so much of what he covers is not available or is hopelessly scattered in many different resources. With his book, we now have at hand a complete guide to plants that attract beneficial insects and extensive lists of disease-resistant tree crop varieties. No longer do I have to sift through my notes for information on rootstocks – it's all here in his comprehensive charts, as are recommendations of fruit tree varieties for mild-winter areas, and comprehensive data on cover crops.

Home gardeners will appreciate the way this book gently leads one toward a stewardship of the landscape, instead of declaring war against nature. They will be relieved to know that they don't have to assault the insects in their gardens, but, rather, can manage some and live in harmony with the rest. Novice pruners will feel confident, knowing they are well informed. And the emphasis on low-maintenance edibles reassures them that their landscapes will be productive friends.

Too many horticulture books seem to make gardening a chore, about as much fun as changing the oil in your car or cleaning your oven. As you use this book, let Robert's engaging humor and love of gardening inspire you once more to go out to experience its wonders. As he says, "If your landscape is just drudgery, you're doing something wrong."

Rosalind Creasy
Los Altos, California
16 November 1985

PREFACE

My interest in edible landscaping really began with my appetite – I've always loved good food. My enjoyment of good cooking began when I was young, during visits to relatives in rural Missouri (pronounced *Muh-ZUR-uh*). Their table was heaped with the finest homegrown foods that the Midwest can serve up: fresh vegetables from the "kitchen garden"; strawberries misted with morning dew bobbing in cream so rich it would float a spoon; platters of sweet corn on the cob picked minutes ago; home-churned golden butter pressed in wooden molds; bacon cured over hickory smoke in a little shed 20 feet from the kitchen; a wide assortment of the tastiest meat I've ever sampled; pies of all persuasions (I especially looked forward to my Aunt Jack's "pea pie," made from wild gooseberries); fragrant homemade jams; steaming mountains of mashed potatoes; warm, moist bread fresh from the wood-fired oven; and eggs whose orange yolks rivaled the setting sun – all preceded by a prayer to thank the Lord for the bounties of this earth.

I struggled through years of living on my own without the good cooking I'd come to love, but finally I found a place to live where I could grow some of my own food. At the same time, I started maintaining landscapes for a living. Though I had surrounded my home with intensive beds of vegetables and had arranged an area beneath the porch for a tiny coop for Bantam chickens, thereby providing much of my food, the people whose landscapes I maintained bought all their food at the supermarket. The contrast was puzzling.

In 1975 vegetable gardens were finally in vogue. My clients got on the bandwagon and had me build vegetable beds, generally situated out back where they couldn't be seen. It was a false start. Within a year most of the gardens had been abandoned. (I ate most of the produce harvested from one thousand-dollar garden on my lunch breaks!) The only garden that remained in use had two important things going for it – the vegetable beds were visible from the kitchen, and the brick wall, stone path, and railroad-tie steps were visually integrated with the rest of the landscape. This good-looking, easy-to-harvest garden was flourishing.

Soon I was designing more and more good-looking edible landscapes. For years the term *edible landscape* confused people – some imagined plodding cows, and others assumed I wanted to be like Euell Gibbons. Now, because of Rosalind Creasy's book and my work, edible landscaping has caught on – the term and the practice are recognized nationwide.

Why I Wrote and Published This Book

There were three compelling reasons for publishing a book on edible landscaping. First, many of my workshop students asked me to. Second, my research files were expanding at an exponential rate and a book seemed to be an excellent place to collate all the facts I can't keep in the ol' brainbox. And last, after a decade of certified, self-imposed non-profit living, I was ready to pursue a business that combined right livelihood with profit.

It was apparent early on that authoring and self-publishing (through a limited partnership) was the best way to ensure the integrity and quality of the book. Yet, self-publishing is a tumultuous journey, with many risks and rewards along the path. The "edible book" was nursed through a long, troubled, and exciting germination and has finally come to fruition. It summarizes my eight years of experience in this relatively new field of horticulture. Not wanting to waste trees on the same old information, I restricted my text for the most part to ideas, techniques, strategies, and plants that are covered little or not at all in other gardening books.

For Every Gardener and Landscaper

This reference is intended for people at any level of horticultural experience, from beginners to landscape architects. For the beginner I have attempted to give a balanced view of the latest information about your yard's environment and plants, avoiding old myths and previously misunderstood ecological dynamics. For the experienced gardener, landscaper, and landscape architect (as well as for the beginner), I have included dozens of illustrations and charts that jog the memory, give new options, and speed the design process.

Most important, I have tried to write a book that will encourage every reader to experiment – an enjoyable, productive way to learn about and to grow with your landscape.

For Every Climate

The text was written for virtually all temperate-zone climates. I have used many examples from California because that is the region I know best, but most of the design guidelines and techniques are appropriate to any non-tropical climate.

How to Use This Book

First, find a comfortable chair and leaf through the book. Notice how it is divided between chapters on design guidelines and chapters on the more nuts-and-bolts aspects of edible landscaping. I suggest that you read the entire section on integrated design before studying any of the techniques chapters. Though each section is a self-contained unit, I recommend you read them in the order in which they appear.

The annotated references at the end of each chapter are my favorite books on the chapter's subject. Instead of repeating another author's excellent discussions, I refer the reader to the best book on the subject. There is an extensive index, one of the most complete to be found, and a list of figures to help you quickly find any topic or plant described in the book. After you have read the book from cover to cover, I hope it will live on your gardening bookshelf for years as a trusted reference.

Life Renews Itself

In nature, when one entity comes to an end, within it are seeds or sustenance for the future. This book is the first seed I have sown in what I hope will become a diverse program to nurture and promote edible landscaping. The future holds more self-published books, articles, workshops, good eating, and good friendships; all will have grown from this initial project.

I'd like to tell you a true story of how book projects gave birth to more book projects. When Larry Korn's grandfather, Morris Galler, died, he willed a sum of money "to be used to promote and educate people about natural farming." With that seed money, Larry traveled to Japan and worked with Masanoba Fukuoka. From that experience came the inspirational book *The One-Straw Revolution*, which Larry edited. With the return from that book, Larry loaned money for the production and publication of *The Future Is Abundant*. When the money was repaid, Larry had enough trust and

faith to invest in my book the amount his grandfather had originally willed him. The seed, his grandfather's wish to promote sustainable food production, has been renewed many times over. This book, therefore, is dedicated to all who strive to work as partners with nature for a healthier life and for a better world.

Robert Kourik

Robert Kourik
Occidental, California
24 December 1985

ACKNOWLEDGMENTS

Technical Reviewers, by Chapter or Part

"Why Edible Landscaping"

Rosalind Creasy – author, consultant, and designer

"The New Approach to Edible Landscapes"

Rosalind Creasy

"In Praise of the Suburbs"

Rosalind Creasy

Mike Corbett – developer, Village Homes; and solar community designer

Marc Rubald – land manager, Village Homes

"Your Soil"

Richard Merrill – instructor, Cabrillo Junior College; designer and consultant, solar greenhouses and small-scale agricultural systems

"Existing Vegetation"

Ron Whitehurst – author and consultant

"Blending Aesthetics and Function"

Carol Hannum, ASLA – landscape architect, designer, and consultant

No-Till Gardening"

Larry Korn – editor, *The One-Straw Revolution*, and author

"Sheet Composting for 'Wild' and 'Tame' Plants"

James Duke, Ph.D. – Germplasm Resources Laboratory, USDA (for nutritional data on weeds)

"Sink or Swim – Self-Seeding Vegetables"

Jamie Jobb – director, Howe Homestead Park; and author, gardener, and consultant

"Double-Digging – A Balanced Review"

John Jeavons – founder and director, Ecology Action Bio-Intensive Mini-Farming Program; researcher, educator, author, and consultant

Michael Stusser – former director, Farallones Institute Rural Center garden program; and owner of Osmosis, Inc.

"Seedlings the Speedling® Way"

Kate Burroughs – entomologist, co-owner of Harmony Farm Supply, and IPM consultant

"Drip Irrigation"

David Henry – co-owner of Harmony Farm Supply, and consultant in irrigation systems design

"Growing Tree Crops" (Part Four)

Larry Geno – co-owner, Bear Creek Nursery

Robert Woolley – manager, Dave Wilson Nursery

"Special Trees for Special Climates"

Bill Nelson – owner, Pacific Tree Farms

"The Best Rootstocks for Your Soil"

Paul Vossen – extension agent, U.C. Cooperative Extension Service, Sonoma County, CA

"Pruning Fruit and Nut Trees"

Molly Breen – owner/manager, Pike Mountain Apples

"Biological Balance with Insects" (Part Five)

Miguel Altieri – instructor, researcher, and author, Division of Biological Control, U.C. Berkeley Albany Station

Robert Bugg, Ph.D. – entomologist, researcher, and author

Steve Gliessman – director, Agroecology Program, U.C. Santa Cruz; and instructor, author, and researcher

"Nature's Balance"

Kate Burroughs

Richard Merrill

"Integrated Pest Management"

Kate Burroughs

"Finishing Touches"

Rosalind Creasy (the list of edible flowers)

"The Golden Hits of Edible Landscaping"

Doug Gosling – co-manager, Farallones Institute Rural Center market gardens; and culinary genius, food stylist, and professional photographer

Myra Portwood – owner, The Bakery

Appendix 8

Rosalind Creasy

Appendix 9

Sheila Daar – Bio-Integral Resource Center

Reviewers of Botanical Names

Lee Slimp – Botany Department, U.C. Davis

Marshall Olbrick – owner, Western Hills Nursery

Nominations for Moral Support

Molly Sterling – my gentle but firm therapist during the highest points and darkest hours of the book's production.

Shery Litwin – former intern; current friend, associate, and ace edible landscape designer. Shery was the first person to suggest I write this book, and she helped put the process in motion by initiating a meeting with Rodale Press in January 1982.

Laura Goldman – provider of supportive coffee and bagels, and of neck massages supreme; queen of the mailing list madness, and a cornerstone of my friendly neighborhood.

Betsy Timm – fellow M.A.S.H. and hamburger fanatic, my trusted public relations director, and a warm, dear friend for life.

Bruce Neeb – fellow edible landscape enthusiast who has been a perennial source of professional and emotional support. As my host at the Esalen Institute, he has helped me relax, recuperate, and re-create when I needed it most.

Rosalind Creasy – she taught me new lessons in mixing business and pleasure, friendliness and professionalism. I am grateful for all the occasions we have had to teach edible landscaping together and for our conversations late into the night about the latest edible trends, life, friendship, and our mutual need to do good work to change the world, without giving up ourselves. I am pleased we are friends, colleagues, co-teachers, and fellow M.A.S.H. fanatics.

Nominations for Indispensable Assistance

The Investors – they had an enormous amount of faith and trust in my professional and personal skills for the three years it took to complete this book. They exhibited amazing understanding when the project took much longer than anticipated (Murphy's Law works overtime at my house). Each person offered emotional, professional, and moral support at different times during the project. I am truly grateful and indebted (figuratively speaking!) for their confidence in a vision, their desire to see the "edible word" disseminated, and for their financial support. These people will recycle the profits from this venture into right livelihood and socially appropriate investments.

Mark Kane – Mark's mastery of the English language and enthusiasm for edible landscaping is impressive. He skillfully reduced my wordy rough drafts by over one-half. A special thanks to his concise and articulate use of the blue pen.

Bart Johnson – fellow edible landscaper and seeker of truth, who provided moral support when I thought there was no light at the end of the book/tunnel (much less a tunnel!). Bart read most of the roughest drafts of the entire manuscript, as well as the edited versions. He provided indispensable critiques of the content, gently questioned many of my underlying assumptions, probed for background facts and experiences, provided valuable experience and data that I lacked, helped improve my grammar and sentence construction, and

shared his time, beer, and heart late into many evenings.

Mom and Dad – they have stood by throughout my professional and emotional changes, rarely doubting and always ready to be supportive. They provided very necessary financial assistance during the project's intermittent cash-flow droughts. Their excitement about my work has been an important source of support over the years.

Nominations for Technical Support

Robert Woolley – for many years Robert has been the tree crops expert whom I trust the most. He is a warm, relaxed, and witty lover of horticulture – especially fruit and nut trees – and one of the most thorough and level-headed experts in the field. I enjoy his gentle critique of organic methods that looks for objective facts.

Dwan Typography – Special thanks to Kevin and Rebecca Dwan, and John Pielaszczyk, for their careful and speedy work. They made the monumental leap into typesetting over halfway through the project with grace and accuracy.

Sandy Farkas – the graphic artist who designed the book's cover, color plate section, and page layout. She taught us some remarkable techniques for paste-up. Her incredible attention to detail and clear sense of design are sources of inspiration. Without her, the book would not have its crisp Shakerlike style.

Heidi Schmidt – the gifted artist and patient craftswoman behind the paste-up of the book, who also created many of the illustrations. Her relaxed, thorough approach to this most tedious task was essential to the book's quality. A great friend and neighbor.

Heidi Schmidt's illustrations appear on pages 27, 31, 68, 74–76, 131, 141, 184, 204, 205, 211, 217, 221, 226, 265, 277, 278, 286, and appendix drawings.

Neil Wilkinson – my contact at Delta Press, Neil brings new meaning to the word service. He offered volumes of information and advice and put up with my many calls about the confusing world of the web press.

Doug Gosling – a culinary and gardening friend who spent long afternoons and late nights helping to invent, adapt, and improve the recipes in the last chapter of the book. Doug is a genius in the kitchen, a master of torts and desserts; he also grows delectable gourmet vegetables, and provided the back-cover photographs "'Pink Pearl' Tart" and "A Fall Harvest." He really helped put the "edible" into this book.

Charlie Judson – a computer genius who fearlessly treads the mysterious realm of programming.

Without Charlie we would not have a functional database program nor the skill to use it. He patiently wrote and rewrote the software and even de-bugged the "canned" software that was supposed to make life easier. I hope our friendship has survived my many requests for help with these infernal electronic gadgets.

Chris Judson – Chris, Charlie's wife, who graciously put up with the two-guys-with-beers trying to untangle many computer nightmares; and who shares with me her knowledge about and enthusiasm for gardening.

Barbara Youngblood – she provided the very important service of grammatically proofing the entire manuscript and editing the style of the front matter. Barbara's editorial experience and personal interest in gardening was a great professional and moral support.

Reference librarians, Santa Rosa Main Library – they were always patient and helpful no matter how obscure the question or how incomplete the citation.

Amie Hill – One of the gentlest people I know. I look forward to her yearly "sabbatical" in California. Her delightful style of drawing adds a wonderful touch to the *Golden Rules* in this book.
Amie Hill's illustrations appear on pages 91–94, inclusive.

Janet Shanahan, Mary Johnson, and the staff at Alpha Color – Jan and Mary's patience with processing my work orders was exemplary. The entire staff provided excellent service, PMTs, slides, and prints.

Ron and Diane Hudelson, Sprint Instant Print – Ron and Diane lived up to the name of their business when printing our promotional brochures. Their flexibility with billing was most helpful during cash-flow crunches.

Art Summerfield, Summerfield Graphics – Art's precision and knowledge of color separations resulted in the excellent color on the cover and in the color plate section.

Carol Pladsen and Kate Miller, Nolo Press – these generous folks were a great source of support and enthusiasm, offering wonderful advice on the cover design and text, and on various contracts.

Elinor Lindheimer – she performed a thorough and speedy preparation of the index. Elinor excels in the obscure but essential art of indexing, as well as being an excellent copy editor.

Maia Massion – she did most of the line drawings, and I feel privileged to have the clean, delightful style of her illustrations in my book.

Linda Parker – she brings to her scientific illustrations the same focused intensity that she exhibits in her daily life. The small reproductions of her drawings in the book do not do them justice – they are truly art.
Linda Parker's illustrations appear on pages 245, 246, 247, and 248.

Nominations for General Support and Assistance

Jan Aanstoos, Chester Aaron, Kit Anderson, Jane Alexander, Greg Archbald, Ann Cameron, Michael Coblentz, David Dillman, Matthew Farrugio, Shirley Foster, Anne Halpin, Barbara Hoffmann, Patti Holden, John Kelley, Pat Kilkinney, David Lee, Marshia Loar, Helen Malcomb-Neeb, Susan McDowell, Casey McVuy, Eileen Mulligan, Lisa Nalbone, Clara Rosemarda, Pierre Stephens, Madeline Schnapp, Michael Stusser, Linda Taber, Pam Tappen, Clayton Ward, Tom Woll, Craig Zaffe, Peter Zweig.

and the envelope, please ... the winner, for Best Leading Role, is ...

Leanne Clement. Every author mentions the person without whom the book would not be possible. Well, Leanne is that person. We never came up with an official title that would do justice to her range of responsibilities: editing all excerpts for publication in magazines, coding and tracking copy for the typesetter, securing permission to reprint copyright materials, designing project management systems, coordinating the package-insert marketing program, designing parameters of the mailing-list software, and providing comic relief with her own brand of "pun-ishment." She is an *excellent* copy and rewrite editor, and was able to blend the many technical reviewers' changes into the manuscript while preserving its cohesiveness. She was also the only editor and proofreader for many segments of the book. Leanne provided a fresh insight into edible landscaping; many of her own inspired ideas are added to the text.

It would have taken an extra year or more without Leanne, and there would have been hundreds of errors in the final book. For accuracy, attention to detail, and perseverance, she has no match. She was able to take a broad overview, as well, of the ideas, content, order, and presentation of each topic. I marveled at the many times she spotted thematic and semantic glitches; she also found several important inconsistencies that spanned the entire manuscript, and which had escaped the notice of other reviewers.

More important, Leanne has helped me bridge the gap between friendship and work. We have gone a few rounds, it's true, but we have emerged close friends and more effective professionals. I cannot dream of a better match of personalities for working together.

1

THE BASICS OF EDIBLE LANDSCAPING
Introduction to Edible Landscaping

WHY EDIBLE LANDSCAPING?

Roll back part of your lawn and renew the age-old tradition of surrounding a home with a productive landscape. Using designs that suit your spare time, edible landscaping is a convenient way to grow vegetables, berries, herbs, fruits, nuts, and ornamental plants in attractive and harmonious groupings, without the use of dangerous chemicals. As you nurture your edible landscape, it will sustain you and your family with benefits that go far beyond good food.

Pleasure . . .

Many otherwise useful gardening books forget that you, the gardener, are the most important living thing in the garden. Often, they focus only on the plants, omitting the ways you can garden with pleasure in a busy life. If gardening isn't fun, why bother? Most of us aren't growing food for survival. It shouldn't be a chore. Find pleasure in your landscape; play with the plants. Experiment. Break some of the rules. With each passing season, you will find more beautiful and more fruitful ways for you and your landscape to grow.

. . . and Beauty

I started experimenting early on with unusual gardening and landscaping techniques, colorful vegetables, and exotic food plants. My work and the work of other edible landscapers is proving that landscapes can be ornamental *and* tasty, colorful *and* useful.

When my landscape maintenance business first began, I took care of landscapes that were completely ornamental. Over time, more and more clients wanted vegetable gardens, but I noticed that too often the vegetable garden was treated like a second-class landscape, hidden away behind the dog pen or garage. I soon realized there is nothing second-class about food plants and that I could design and plant an edible *and* gorgeous landscape. The beauty and variety of a well-designed edible landscape really impress my clients, their friends, and visitors.

A traditional ornamental landscape combines colors, textures, smells, and sounds but usually neglects flavors. Your edible landscape will stimulate all the senses—fragrant day lilies for the flower border that can be used in salads or stuffed with herb cheeses, a colorful ground cover of a variegated gold and green thyme for soups and casseroles, a soft herbal sitting bench planted with chamomile that can be harvested for tea, a cool, relaxing arbor laden with the fruits of grape and kiwi vines—the possibilities are endless.

Colorful Edibles

There are hundreds of examples of food plants that add color to your landscape. It's time for the prejudice against edibles as ornamentals to wither and be replaced by the respect they deserve as landscape plants.

"Ornamental" kale provides a spectacular display of fall and spring color (see Fig. 1.1 in color plates), and it has the same taste as garden kale. In the photograph, the ornamental kale is planted among lettuce for a beautiful contrast in color and form. Ruby chard, 'Romanesco' broccoli (see Fig. 1.2 in color plates), nasturtiums, and 'Radicchio' (an Italian red-leafed chicory) are all true ornamentals, and edible too. Liberated from the conventional garden, colorful vegetables have a place in the edible landscape.

Many perennial edibles have as much color as ornamentals. The silver-grey highlights of artichokes and the bold pattern of their leaves are as dramatic a show as any plant makes. The fiery fall colors of an Oriental chestnut, Asian pear, cherry, or peach are as impressive as those of virtually any ornamental shade tree. Ripe Oriental persimmons hanging on the bare branches of a fog-shrouded tree are a magical view (see Fig. 1.3 in color plates). The glossy green leaf and spectacular fall color add their highlights in season.

If you like the formal look, both rosemary and the silver-grey-leaved pineapple guava (for warm-winter climates) are easily sheared to almost any form. The genetic dwarf peaches and nectarines are well-behaved, dense shrub-like fruit trees. The hot pink, double flowers of the genetic dwarf 'Garden Beauty' nectarine (see Fig. 1.4 in color plates) are some of the most dazzling to be found.

An edible landscape can be small, but elegant

and picturesque. Consider the appeal of the landscape planted by Helen Malcolm-Neeb near Big Sur, California (see Fig. 1.5 in color plates). Colorful red chard, two kinds of lettuce, narrow-leaved chives, and edible violas mingle with the ornamental blossoms of alyssum. They are arranged like a bouquet beneath a young miniature "Garden Prince" almond that displays delicate pink blossoms each spring.

Taste Appeal

My garden is beautiful, but it is also designed for flavor: different, better tastes, the kind no grocery store could possibly offer. To me, there is no question. If you want *real* flavor, you have to grow your own.

I learned about really good food on family visits to relatives "up in the country." I was fortunate—two aunts lived on different farms in rural Missouri. I explored field, forest, pond, and garden with inquisitive delight, but my strongest recollections are of the flavors, colors, and textures of home-grown foods. Home-grown produce tastes best. My reason for starting to garden was to have those home-grown tastes no money can buy. A store-bought 'Granny Smith' apple is good, but one freshly picked from the tree and fully ripe is superb.

I can grow flavors not to be found in any market. 'Anoka,' an obscure apple, unfamiliar to commercial production, has more crispness than a crackling watermelon and great flavor. The Asian pear called 'Hosui' is even more exotic. You would be able to smell the fragrance, laced with the aroma of allspice, from several feet away as I bit into the extra crunchy, juicy fruit.

In the store, lemon and basil are sold as separate flavors. The lemon basil I grow in my landscape provides a delightful, unique blend of both tastes when added to sauces or salads.

Independence

Though food is basic, it has become just another service. Shopping at a supermarket, the buyer is dependent upon the limitations of modern agriculture. Supermarket produce is often mediocre—bland and travel-worn. Recently, I wandered among the produce stands of New York City's West Side and looked through the shipping cartons behind each shop. Though it was mid-May, I was amazed to find nothing from the eastern seaboard and very little from the United States mainland. The airplane, the truck, and the train have made it possible to soothe cosmopolitan palates with almost any food, regardless of the season. But the cost is high—huge amounts of energy, mainly from irreplaceable fossil fuels, are used to ship our produce, not to mention grow it.

Our country's agriculture expends more energy to grow our food than it gets back in the form of calories (see Fig. 1.6). By the time food gets to the table, its calories are dwarfed by the energy that was burned to process and deliver it (Fig. 1.7). Most of the foods we eat are black holes for energy. The oil that provides us a pale, tasteless tomato in January probably comes from the Middle East. As oil prices escalate, food prices rise too. An incident in the Middle East could break your household food budget.

Figure 1.6 Food production methods range from 50 calories of food produced for every calorie of hand energy used, to only one calorie of food for every 20 calories of machine energy.

If you grow a percentage of your own food, you have a measure of independence, and the skill to grow more if need be. An edible landscape produces more calories than it consumes and can make suburban lawns into food-producing areas, and suburban dwellers into growers, not just consumers. An edible landscape can add to the value of your property and improve your family's balance of payments, as well as the nation's.

Health

The agricultural practices of harvesting green fruit and immature vegetables and long-distance shipping have done a lot to reduce the nutritional value of supermarket food. Just as lost nutrients erode our chances for a healthy diet, so do agricultural chemicals. The arsenal of weapons used to eradicate pests and weeds in our amber waves of grain is frightening. Chemicals like 2,4-D and 2,4,5-T (which can contain dioxin) are still used on pastures, rice fields, and cotton fields. Methoxychlor, EDB, Captan ... the list goes on and on. What this means to our health is at best uncertain, at worst disastrous.

The standards set by the World Health Organization for the amount of "allowable" poisons (called the "practical residue limit") in our food is based on a statistical, abstract average 50 kilogram adult – not a baby, whose natural defenses are fewer and whose weight is much less than 50 kilograms.

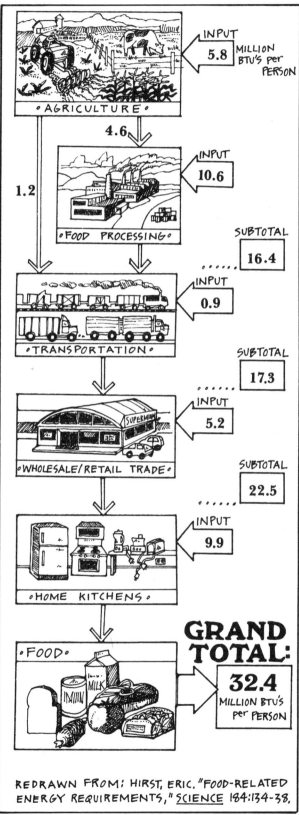

REDRAWN FROM: HIRST, ERIC. "FOOD-RELATED ENERGY REQUIREMENTS," SCIENCE 184:134-38.

Figure 1.7 Growing your own food saves millions of BTUs of fossil fuels each year.

So it is not surprising that a study published in *Environment* found:

The allowable daily intakes for infants might be exceeded for dieldrin by 10.2 times, for heptachlor epoxide by 2 times, and for HCB by 2.8 times their maximum tolerance levels. If the allowable level of pesticide residues were found in cow's milk [at the manufacturer's], the allowable daily intake [of an infant] could easily be legally exceeded. (Vol. 22, no. 7, pp. 6-13)

Both dieldrin and heptachlor are on the Rachel Carson Trust list of suspected cancer-causing chemicals. It is sad, but too often true that the sins of the fathers shall be visited upon the children. Growing as much of your own food as you can without chemicals is the one sure way to protect your family's health, but don't stop with the vegetables: use safe, non-toxic methods for your entire yard.

Variety

If agriculture were a true service to consumers, the variety of food it offered would be increasing, not narrowing. There are 3,000 to 10,000 edible plants in the world (depending on who is doing the estimating), but the National Academy of Science estimated in 1975 that only 150 edible plants have had any large-scale commercial use worldwide. Worse still, the diet of most of the world's people consists of about 20 basic foods. The report cautions, "These plants are the main bulwark between mankind and starvation. It is a very small bastion."

Gazing from my desk out the window, I count over 60 types of vegetables, fruits, and nuts growing in my newest edible landscape. By next year, the variety it offers me will have doubled. That's my kind of landscape—one I can count on to provide me with plentiful, healthy food.

Berry, Wendell. **The Unsettling of America: Culture & Agriculture.** San Francisco: Sierra Club Books, 1977. This book strongly influenced my early development as an ecological landscaper. An excellent review of the cultural, personal, and family disruptions caused by modern agriculture. Provides a good case for growing as much of your own food as possible. Required reading.

Carson, Rachel. **Silent Spring.** Boston: Houghton-Mifflin, 1962. Humans are one of the species threatened with genetic deformities, stillbirths, and other medical nightmares due to the proliferation of chemical insecticides and poisons. This book is just as relevant now as the day it was published. The daily news substantiates what Carson boldly warned of 23 years ago.

Creasy, Rosalind. **The Complete Book of Edible Landscaping**. San Francisco: Sierra Club Books, 1982. The "other" edible landscaping book, by a good friend and collaborator. The plant encyclopedia section is an essential reference. The prerequisite, and perfect companion, to my book!

Farallones Institute. **The Integral Urban House**. San Francisco: Sierra Club Books, 1979. A classic guide for developing a holistic home and garden in the suburbs or city. Covers solar heating better than vegetable culture, and is very weak on tree crops and perennial food plants. Good ideas on raising rabbits and chickens in small areas and integrating them with garden and kitchen.

Howard, Sir Albert. **An Agricultural Testament**. Rev. ed. Emmaus, PA: Rodale Press, 1972. A classic discourse on how to stop the erosion of valuable topsoil and rejuvenate our farmlands, using organic methods and composting.

Hyams, Edward. **Soil and Civilization**. New York: Harper Colophon, 1976. An interesting history of agricultural erosion. Hyam makes the case that poor agricultural practices erode both soil and civilizations.

Jabs, Carolyn. **The Heirloom Gardener**. San Francisco: Sierra Club Books, 1984. The only quality book on this important subject. The losses from our edible plant gene pool are a biological tragedy; Jabs shows how each of us can help reverse the alarming trend. Includes interviews with collectors of heirloom varieties, how to secure seeds of heirlooms, and a thorough list of catalogs, exchanges, farms, museums, and books. Buy this book and put it to use.

Jackson, Wes; Berry, Wendell; and Coleman, Bruce, eds. **Meeting the Expectations of the Land**. Berkeley: North Point Press, 1985. The most current collection of essays on the biological and cultural degradation caused by corporate, chemical agriculture. Many of the writings, by researchers, land use planners, farmers, and poets, show how organic agriculture can create a healthy, sustainable stewardship of the land. A good update on issues originally discussed in Berry's *Unsettling of America*, and in Merrill's *Radical Agriculture*.

Margolin, Malcolm. **The Earth Manual**. Boston: Houghton-Mifflin, 1975. A basic review of ecologically sane ways to treat landscapes, revegetate bare soil, and repair man's damage to the environment.

Merrill, Richard, ed. **Radical Agriculture**. New York: Harper & Row, 1976. An early-contemporary discourse on the need for and viability of organic farming. Good background reading; see how far we have to go to reach the goals outlined in the essays.

National Academy of Science. **Underexploited Tropical Plants of Promising Economic Value**. Washington, DC: N.A.S., 1975. The first book to get me excited about the loss of genetic diversity in food plants. Describes the virtues of many unusual edible plants such as grain amaranth and winged beans. The inspirational text gives seed resources and contact people at the end of each chapter.

Vilmorin-Andrieux, MM. **The Vegetable Garden**. Berkeley: Ten Speed Press, 1981. A reproduction of a seed catalog originally published in France in 1885. The details make this a good reference for organic vegetable culture, since it was written well before chemical agriculture got started. It is startling to read of the many varieties that do not exist today (there are 50 *pages* of pea varieties, including several like the "new" Sugar Snap™).

THE NEW APPROACH TO EDIBLE LANDSCAPES: SYNERGY

Landscaping, like so much of our modern life-style, has been shattered into separate pieces: a single row of junipers along the driveway, a vegetable patch here, a few flowers over there, a lone fruit tree neglected in the backyard. But nature works as a whole, as a community—not pieces cast asunder. We can follow nature's example in planning an edible landscape. My approach to edible landscaping aims to arrange all the plants and structures into a unified, biologically dynamic whole.

An active, interdependent system is more effective than the sum of its parts—a benefit called synergy. Properly designed, the edible landscape produces synergy; this book reviews many of the examples of synergy I have observed, discovered, or borrowed in the course of my work as an edible landscaper. For now, here are a few examples from an edible landscape I designed and installed in 1978 for Mr. and Mrs. John Kelley. Figures 1.8 and 1.9 show the plans for this landscape.

The Kelleys' landscape, cascading down the south side of their hillside property, was designed to be viewed from their dining room and summer veranda. (See Fig. 1.10 in color plates.) The 1,000-square-foot landscape includes vegetables, culinary herbs, fruit and nut trees, ornamental flowers, composting bins, medicinal plants, and erosion-controlling ground covers. The upper vegetable area is very close to the back door, for convenient harvesting. A short path leads from the kitchen to a discreet, fully enclosed set of compost bins. (See Fig. 1.11 in color plates.)

Three 100-square-foot beds of intensive vegetable culture are terraced down the slope. They provide more fresh produce than the Kelleys can eat—much is given to relatives and friends. (See Fig. 1.12 in color plates.)

The vegetable beds are framed by colorful herbaceous borders (see Fig. 1.13 in color plates), with plants chosen for a variety of characteristics and functions: drought resistance, for use as herbal teas, for cut flowers, for edible flowers, and to provide as many types of pollen and nectar as possible. The pollens and nectars lure beneficial insects to the garden throughout the year. The beneficial insects—among them hover flies, green lacewings, aphid wasps, snakeflies, tachinid flies, and braconid wasps—help control aphids, tomato hornworms, mealybugs, and various caterpillars within the edible landscape. Some of the plants that attract beneficial insects are white clover, yarrow, and fennel.

Other flowers were included to attract bees and ensure that the fruits, nuts, and vegetables were pollinated. These include borage, white clover, and creeping and common thyme. Some of the flowers

Figure 1.8 An aerial view of the Kelleys' edible landscape.

are edible, and more are useful as spices and herbal teas. (For more on this subject, see "Attracting Good Bugs.")

Multi-Purpose Elements

Multi-purpose plants are only part of a synergistic landscape. Multi-purpose structures can be employed, as well. Surrounding the vegetable terraces of the Kelleys' landscape are flagstone paths set in packed, crushed rock. (See Fig. 1.14 in color plates.) The crushed rock allows rain and irrigation water to percolate into the soil below, where it is stored for the plants' use. And the crushed rock discourages runoff, reducing erosion.

Extensive use of stone helps warm the landscape, which is located in a mild, coastal climate. The grey flagstones absorb the sun's warmth, yet reflect some sunlight upward to enhance the growth of the vegetables. The heat absorbed by the stones each day radiates into the garden at night. These vegetable terraces ripen food one to two weeks earlier and the plants continue bearing several weeks longer in the fall than nearby vegetable gardens without stone paths. (See Fig. 1.15 in color plates.)

... The Subtle Difference

As you proceed through this book, you will probably come up with many ideas of your own for em-

ploying synergy in your landscape. Though it may take more planning, I believe it is well worth the effort to design not just a beautiful edible landscape, but one where the harmonious association of all living and structural parts is a beauty unto itself. With nature as a source of inspiration – using non-poisonous gardening methods, working to find new ways to make everything function as a coordinated whole – you will be healthier and your surroundings more beautiful.

Creasy, Rosalind. **The Complete Book of Edible Landscaping**. San Francisco: Sierra Club Books, 1982. The "other" edible landscaping book, by a good friend and collaborator. The plant encyclopedia section is an essential reference. The prerequisite, and perfect companion, to my book!

Howard, Sir Albert. **The Soil and Health**. New York: Schocken Books, 1972. This classic by the father of modern composting describes the origin and process of the Indore method, the prototype of today's fast/hot compost method.

Kern, Barbara and Ken. **The Owner-Built Homestead**. New York: Charles Scribner's Sons, 1977. A classic for the homesteading movement. Very useful in considering

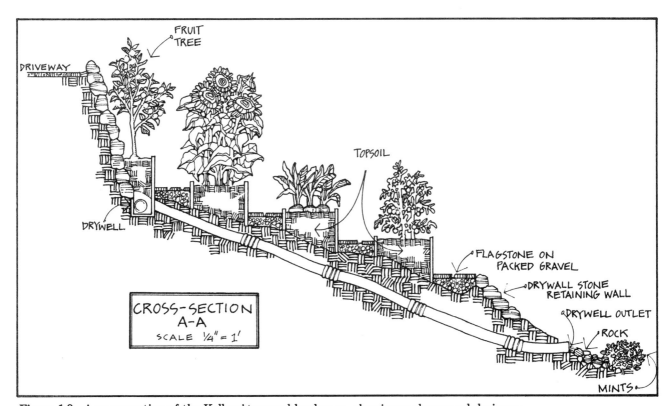

Figure 1.9 A cross-section of the Kelleys' terraced landscape, showing underground drainage.

ways to integrate energy, food, water, and waste systems for your home and yard. Though intended for rural settings, many of the examples can be adapted to the code restrictions and style of the suburbs. The most accurate information is contained in the chapters on site analysis, planning, and alternative construction techniques.

King, F. H. **Farmers of Forty Centuries**. Emmaus, PA: Rodale Press, 1911. A travelog through turn-of-the-century China when all farming was done by hand. A wonderful, though rambling, review of another culture's raised bed gardening methods.

Leckie, Jim; Masters, Gil; Whitehouse, Harry; and Young, Lily. **More Other Homes and Garbage.** Rev. ed. San Francisco: Sierra Club Books, 1975. This updated classic on integrated, sustainable homes and gardens has much more on wind power, methane generation, and hydropower than does the Farallones Institute's *Integral Urban House;* but similarly, is very weak on perennial food plants and tree crops.

Mollison, Bill, and Holmgren, David. **Permaculture One**. Stanley, Tasmania: Tagari Books, 1978. A good introduction to the Australian equivalent of sustainable/holistic/integrated farms and gardens. The theories were an inspiration to me 7 years ago, but most of the examples are inappropriate for U.S. climates, property sizes, and lifestyles.

Mollison, Bill. **Permaculture II**. Stanley, Tasmania: Tagari Books, 1981. Further development of the permaculture theories, with a big section appropriate only where it rains less than 10 inches a year.

Olkowski, Helga and William. **The City People's Book of Raising Food**. Emmaus, PA: Rodale Press, 1975. One of the few level-headed books about the practical, and impractical, ways to grow food in urban areas. Every urban gardener should have a copy. Out of print, unfortunately; grab any copy you see in a used book store.

IN PRAISE OF THE SUBURBS

Suburbs have a lot to offer – they have affordable, manageable housing; they're neighborly; they can be energy efficient, and some are biologically exciting. Unfortunately, many suburban yards are locked into non-productive and unrewarding forms of landscaping. We can make the suburbs even better places to live – with landscapes that revitalize both property and people. In an edible landscape, where plants do double duty, the effect amounts to a renaissance of the suburbs.

An Edible Suburb

Ecological productivity and edible abundance are on display in Village Homes, a small subdivision in Davis, California, which is probably the most solarized and edibly landscaped suburb in the world. The founders of Village Homes, Mike and Judy Corbett, set out to develop a suburb that would be as self-sufficient as possible in both energy and food. Now, with 240 homes on 63 acres of former farmland, their dream has become reality.

Sixty to 75 percent of the hot water in each home is provided by a solar system, and solar provides a good percentage of space heating and cooling in all homes. Most of these solar systems are passive, meaning there are no moving parts. In addition, the landscaping at Village Homes is both instructive and inspirational – let's take a short walking tour.

An Edible Border

You enter Village Homes through a greenbelt of almonds, pineapple guavas, figs, and plums (see Fig. 1.16). Since the beginning, the greenbelt has been managed by a crew that works for the homeowner's association. Initially the crew's wages were

Figure 1.16 A greenbelt of almond trees borders one side of Village Homes. The almonds are harvested as a cash crop for the homeowners' association.

Figure 1.17 The gazebo houses a weekend "farm market" for produce raised in Village Homes. A spacious community lawn is seen in the distance.

paid in part by the developers and in part from dues collected by the homeowners' association. Now, as the trees and grapevines mature and crops increase, the income from the sale of fruits and nuts helps pay the crew. The goal is to at least stabilize the homeowners' monthly dues. Imagine a subdivision where the dues escape inflation!

There are mini-orchards in each neighborhood. Next to a house you might see a vineyard – the smallest is only a fifth of an acre. There are plantings of Asian pears, persimmons, plums, apricots, pears, figs, pineapple guavas, peaches, nectarines, and almonds.

With mini-orchards so close to houses, herbicides and chemical pesticides are banned. The mandate to the crew is to care for all the subdivision's plantings with organic, non-toxic means. Not only are families free from exposure to poisonous chemicals, but the produce fetches a premium price on the market. So far the crew has been successful in maintaining acceptable yields while using organic methods. They even use all-organic methods and non-chemical fertilizers to maintain the picture-perfect lawn for sports and family recreation shown in Fig. 1.17.

Community Recreation

Beyond the turf area is the community center, which offers meeting space, a nursery school in the mornings, a solar-heated swimming pool, a dance hall, and a patio. Nearby is a small amphitheater for summertime use. Each seating tier is edged with concrete and covered with turf for comfort and coolness. Because Davis gets occasional heavy rains in the winter, the architects designed the lowest part of the amphitheater, which looks like a dry creek bed in the summer, to act as a catch basin (see Fig. 1.18). After the storm has passed, the

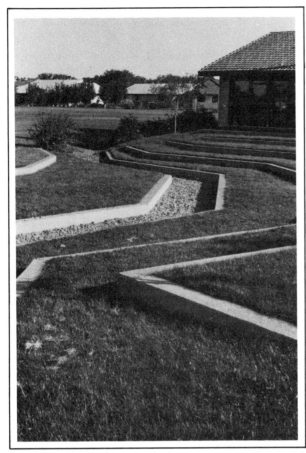

Figure 1.18 The dry creekbed that traverses the amphitheatre serves as a catch basin in winter, preventing erosion and storing rainwater in the soil.

ponded water slowly seeps into the soil. The design prevents erosion and stores 90 percent of the winter's rain in the top 20 feet of soil for use by plants during the dry summer.

Appropriate Lawns

Fledgling environmentalists are prone to condemn lawns. Though the typical lawn certainly wastes fossil fuels in the form of herbicides and fertilizers and gas and oil for power mowers, there are appropriate uses for turf—uses for which there are no acceptable substitutes. And I believe lawns need not waste fossil fuels.

The best use of lawns is for abuse: no other surface is as suitable as turf for daily foot traffic or sports. Blacktop is costly, ugly, and hard on the falling body. Mulches do not stay around, and usually do not provide much real softness for sports. Some—such as the various wood-chip mulches—add splinters to rambunctious kids.

Some critics of turf recommend herbal lawns—combinations of clovers, chamomile, thymes and bird's foot trefoil—meant to match the look of a classic green lawn. While an herbal lawn can be

lush and green and does need less mowing than turf, in my experience it is practical only for small areas. An herbal lawn takes as much time to care for as turf, perhaps more. What is saved in reduced mowing is more than spent in weeding, watering, and repairing worn areas.

As a ground cover, clovers are useful only where one intends to look and not play. The leaf is easily bruised, producing a very stubborn stain on clothing. And the flowers attract bees, which don't appreciate being stepped on or rolled on. Dutch white clover works well at Village Homes in some of the tree plantings, where it gives a lawn-like look. For the plum tree planting in Fig. 1.19, clover is used appropriately as a low-maintenance cover.

At Village Homes, the sports field is the main area of turf, and it is cared for without chemicals. The plot was seeded heavily to get a solid stand of turf established quickly and to choke out weeds, eliminating any need for toxic herbicides. (An easier, more reliable method is to place sod directly on the prepared soil. Of course, the supplier uses toxic chemicals to produce weed-free sod, and the price of sod is quite high.) To keep the lawn looking plush, the crew waters regularly, leaves all clippings in place, makes a yearly application of poultry manure, and aerates the lawn once each winter. They have found their method to be more cost-effective than the use of chemical fertilizers. I have maintained lawns with periodic applications of sifted compost, blood meal, rock powders, and Clod-Buster™ (a type of naturally deposited, ancient compost that acts to stimulate the soil's bacterial life and loosen up the soil structure). I consider the extra effort to be justified. The alternative is allowing kids to roll around on turf sprayed with known toxins and carcinogens.

Figure 1.19 A lawnlike ground cover of Dutch white clover works well under plum trees, where there is little foot traffic.

Lawns improve the weather. Studies have shown that lawn-covered areas are 10° to 14° cooler than bare soil. A freshly watered lawn acts as an air conditioner. When the breeze crosses a moist lawn and sweeps through the house, the cooling effect can be substantial. The homeowners on the north end of the field can really feel the free air conditioning with each southerly breeze. (See "Energy-Conserving Landscaping" for more on cooling with plants.)

Still, compared to wildflower meadows and some types of shrubbery, lawns are costly. While it is important to roll back as much lawn as possible to save money and effort, we will never be able, nor should we want, to eliminate all the lawns in America. The limited and thoughtful use of lawns in Village Homes is an excellent model.

Edible Landcapes

At Village Homes, edible landscapes prevail—at least 80 percent of the homes have food gardens as well as ornamentals (see Figs. 1.20, 1.21, and 1.22). Some homeowners design and install their own landscapes, while others hire professionals. The variety of plants and designs in use is astounding. The lots, averaging 55 feet by 85 feet, are too small for large-scale production of such space-hogging vegetables as corn and winter squashes. The developers reserved plots of land where homeowners grow vegetables in quantity. A homeowner need only sign up each spring and pay a refundable deposit, promising to clean up the plot in the fall. I have seen large plantings of corn, beans, winter squashes, sunflowers, hot peppers, and even one plot of Jerusalem artichokes.

More Than Just Edible

While there is more food growing in this subdivision than in any other housing tract in America,

Figure 1.20 A small, efficient edible landscape is close to the kitchen and patio.

Figure 1.21 A miniature peach tree, herbs, ornamentals, and lawn surround a solar home.

Figure 1.22 Miniature peach trees make a leafy hedge along a common pathway.

the ornamental plantings hold their own. Figure 1.23 shows a street-side planting designed to protect the soil from runoff where the gutter dumps into a creek bed, without the use of lots of ugly and costly concrete. A few stones create turbulence in the water rushing off the curb, releasing much of the energy built up as the water runs down the gutter. The plants also slow the water and bind the soil with their roots. The water tumbles into a small pool, sculpted there to catch the overflow of a heavy rain. From the pool, the creek meanders along a rocky bottom between plantings of rushes, cattails, wild cherries, *Myoporum parvifolium* (a low-maintenance ground cover that provides lots of nectar to bees in the summer), clover (a nitrogen-accumulating plant), and various ornamental shrubs and flowers. In summer, kids and adults can be seen casually nibbling on the wild cherries within reach. Since there are so many edibles in the neighborhood, nobody goes to the trouble to use a ladder for the fruits out of reach. The birds get a welcome feast.

Figure 1.23 Rosemary and ornamental perennials protect the soil where the curb's runoff spills into a natural-looking swale.

A Haven for Good Bugs

For me, the most remarkable feature of Village Homes is the abundance of beneficial bugs – good bugs that bother and kill the ones we call pests. The housing tracts that border Village Homes are biological dead zones by comparison.

The amazing diversity of ornamental and food plants in Village Homes and the non-toxic maintenance make this suburb a biologically rich oasis. On a short stroll, I have always been able to spot a dozen or more praying mantids, clever stalkers that do a lot to reduce flying and crawling pests. The praying mantids are so at home that I have seen these imposing, yet beneficial, critters calmly sitting on the mailboxes waiting to catch their next meal (see Fig. 1.24). Village Homes also harbors thousands of green lacewings. The larvae of these small, delicate creatures satisfy their tremendous appetites with meals of aphids. Ladybugs, also predators of aphids in both the adult and larval stage, are more numerous here than in nearby neighborhoods.

Flowers for Bugs and for People

Many adult beneficial insects need a constant source of food – usually pollen or nectar – to fuel their incessant search for host insects to lay eggs on or near. I believe that the abundance of beneficial insects at Village Homes is due in great part to the subdivision's amazing variety of flowering plants. (See "Biological Balance with Insects" for more on this subject.)

Suburbs Offer Ecological Wealth

That a suburb can harbor a rich collection of plants and animals has been documented by several researchers. Figure 1.25 summarizes two surveys. Notice how the number of bird species in older suburbs and landscaped parks approaches that of native ecosystems, while the total bird population equals or surpasses that of the undisturbed ecosystem. By mingling exotic and native plants, older suburbs can also approach or equal the diversity in a natural ecosystem.

In Fig. 1.25, biomass denotes the gross weight of plant tissue. The greater the biomass, the greater the storage and cycling of nutrients. When growth and decay are equal, the ecosystem is said to be stable, not accumulating more biomass. The growth of civilization has been dependent upon the cultivation and management of ecological zones where biomass is increasing, outstripping decay. These zones of increasing fertility are found in agricultural and abandoned fields, and in all but the oldest suburbs.

In short, the suburbs can offer a biologically rich blending of exotic and native plants and animals, a diversity that ensures the ongoing ecological vitality of the suburbs and the delight of its inhabitants. Edible landscapes enrich the diversity of a healthy suburb, using gardening methods that cooperate with, rather than subdue, nature.

Figure 1.24 Village Homes has an abundance of beneficial insects such as this praying mantid, because insecticides are rarely used.

BIOLOGICAL ZONES	AGRICULTURE	NATURAL ECOSYSTEM (REMNANTS)	WEEDY GRASSLAND (Abandoned Croplands)	CONSTRUCTION ZONE (WEEDY)	NEW SUBURB (0-15 YRS.)	LANDSCAPED PARKLAND	OLDER SUBURB (15-50 YRS.)	OLDEST SUBURB (>50 YRS.)	CITY CORE
NET PRODUCTIVITY	HIGH $P > R$**	STABLE $P = R$*	LOW $P > R$	MINIMAL	LOW $P > R$	VARIABLE	HIGH $P > R$	LOW $P = R$	MINIMAL
BIOMASS	LOW	HIGH	LOW	VERY LOW	LOW	LOW-HIGH	MEDIUM	MEDIUM-HIGH	LOW
PLANT DIVERSITY	LOW	HIGH	HIGH	LOW	LOW	LOW-MEDIUM	HIGH	MEDIUM	LOW
TYPES OF PLANTS	CULTIVARS	NATIVE	NATIVE/ EXOTIC	WEEDS	EXOTICS	NATIVE/ EXOTIC	NATIVE/ EXOTIC	NATIVE/ EXOTIC	WEEDS/ EXOTIC
NO. OF BIRD SPECIES	N.A. ☆☆	25-31	5	N.A.	5	24	19	13	13
NO. OF BIRDS per 247 ACRES	N.A.	381-438	247	N.A.	158	626	742	162	796

REDRAWN FROM: "Ecology and Mgmt. of Disturbed Urban Land," R.S. DORNEY, LANDSCAPE ARCHITECTURE, MAY 1979.
** $P > R$: BIOMASS accumulates/growth > decay.   * $P = R$: decay = growth.   ☆☆ NOT AVAILABLE.

Figure 1.25 An ecologist's study of the diversity and productivity of urban, suburban, and rural areas. When photosynthesis (P) is greater than respiration (R), more plant tissue is accumulating than decaying.

Bainbridge, David; Corbett, Judy; and Hoffacre, John. **Village Homes' Solar House Designs**. Emmaus, PA: Rodale Press, 1979. The only book on Village Homes. The first few pages provide a general overview of the reasons behind the world's most edibly-landscaped and solarized subdivision, and its impacts on our culture. The rest of the book features design details of some of the best solar homes.

Olkowski, Helga and William. **The City People's Book of Raising Food**. Emmaus, PA: Rodale Press, 1975. One of the few level-headed books about the practical, and impractical, ways to grow food in urban areas. Every urban gardener should have a copy. Out of print, unfortunately; grab any copy you see in a used book store.

1 THE BASICS OF EDIBLE LANDSCAPING
Organic Gardening – Myths and Facts

THE "ORGANIC" CONCEPT

The revival of a more natural, less toxic form of horticulture goes by many names – organic gardening, biological husbandry, biodynamics, sustainable agriculture, ecological gardening, natural farming, self-sufficient gardening, permaculture, eco-agriculture, and many more. Whatever the name (and, believe it or not, people waste their time trying to decide which is the best), one basic concept underlies the revival. The intent of organic food gardeners is to bring a feast of fresh, healthy food to the table without slapping mother nature in the face. While modern farming tries to man-handle nature, organic gardeners walk a much softer path from soil to harvest to the kitchen table.

Careful and productive use of nature is what Wendell Berry calls "kindly use." In *The Unsettling of America* he writes,

By understanding, imagining, and living out the possibilities of "kindly use" [we can] dissolve the boundaries that divide people from the land and its care, which together are the source of human life.

We are part of nature and deserve the enjoyment of forest, field, and meadow. We also bear the responsibility of caring for nature. As Berry continues:

But kindly use is a concept that of necessity broadens, becomes more complex and diverse, as it approaches action. To treat every field, or every part of every field, with the same consideration is not farming but industry. Kindly use depends upon intimate knowledge, the most sensitive responsiveness and responsibility.

A Definition

Of the many definitions I have read, the one that comes closest to embracing all the ideals of organic gardening is by M. Kiley-Worthington of the University of Sussex, England. I have adapted it slightly to the home scale. A natural or organic garden or edible landscape is stewardship of nature's cycles and should:

- Strive to make good use of locally available materials while promoting a biologically renewable environment.

- Be as diversified as possible.

- Be scaled to the homeowner's needs, while being well-adapted to the place (the nuances and details of the property and environment).

- Produce maximum yields without interrupting the natural processes of the environment.

- Be within the reach of the homeowner's budget and suited to their available time for maintenance.

- Have all the garden's produce fully utilized by the family. What isn't eaten should be recycled to promote the fertility of the soil.

- Be good looking, comfortable, pleasurable, and rewarding to each member of the family.

The best gardens are personal ones, suited to the gardener. My own approach is edible landscaping, which is a "species" of the "genus" of organic gardening. Good landscapes are places for living, working, playing, and relaxing. You step out the back door and feel nature's patterns, receiving emotional and bodily strength.

It is tragic that chemical gardening seems so much simpler than the organic approach. People attracted by the illusion of simplicity endanger their families' health and damage the environment. Organic gardening may be more complex, but it is also thoughtful, creative, and resourceful.

Second Nature

Organic gardening takes work, study, and a willingness to enjoy the ups and downs. Satisfied gardeners are inclined to say, without discouragement, "Well, I just didn't have any luck with those yellow tomatoes this year; I'll try out a different kind next year." Each season adds to a gardener's understanding and to a deeper kind of knowledge, the type that one feels in the bones, that can be passed on to others—especially to children. I am happy to watch the landscape mature, evolve, and become both more stable and more limber, more able to respond to change with growth and fruitfulness. I am even happier to match wits with nature, to try to perceive her "reasoning," her patterns, her inner workings. One part of me enjoys watching the season unfold, the other wants to know why.

Many a gardener will say a lush crop of corn was "good luck." With some folks it really was good luck, but with others it was wisdom gained by patient observation. Acting on intuition is great fun, especially when you get good results. I often plant my vegetable seeds on a whim. The time seems right, so I plant. From friends who plant by phases of the moon, I learned that the timing of my planting often corresponded with theirs. I do not believe that planting by the moon is essential to good plant growth, but the coincidence was fascinating. Most of those spontaneous seedings were soon followed by a helpful shower—no need to check the weather report to see if I should water the garden.

People Power

In farming and gardening, people are more efficient than machines. The energy cost of an orange includes the energy in the fertilizer, the fuel to plow the weeds under, the fuel to make and spray pesticides, and the energy to process and ship it. In Fig. 1.6, note how food grown by people stacks up against crops produced by machines. Everything listed below the middle of the chart (the break-even point, where as much energy is harvested as was expended) is on the losing end. If you lived in a poor country, the bottom half of the chart would mean higher food bills or eventual starvation. And the bottom half is where most modern, mechanical agriculture would be found. Even in cases where mechanized cropping produces net energy, there are hand-labor methods that can do even better. The potatoes grown in the mountains of Chile return over 20 times more calories than were exerted to produce them. Far from "primitive," the Andean farmers show more wisdom than modern agriculturists because they reap much more than they spend. Our agriculture's reliance on machinery and chemicals puts us in debt for fuel, soil fertility, and bounty, and makes us dependent, not free.

Edible landscaping and organic gardening should take advantage of human efficiency and not rely upon machines. This does not mean that I vehemently reject machines—I find tillers useful on occasion, such as when I first start a garden. But by using what I call "inspired laziness," I grow most of my food without a lot of effort, without machinery, without lower-back pain, yet with abundant yields.

Least Is Best

A vital attitude in organic gardening is to use the simplest strategy or technique first, then wait and see what happens. I once spotted several cater-pillars feasting on an anise plant near my porch. I knew there was a nest of paper wasps on the porch, and I knew that they feed upon caterpillars. I let the caterpillars be. Sure enough, within three weeks, before much of the anise foliage had been eaten, the paper wasps carved up all the caterpillars to feed their larvae. All I needed to "control" those pesty caterpillars was patience and a bit of care as I crossed the porch—as simple a technique as possible.

Carson, Rachel. **Silent Spring.** Boston: Houghton-Mifflin, 1962. Humans are one of the species threatened with genetic deformities, stillbirths, and other medical nightmares due to the proliferation of chemical insecticides and poisons. This book is just as relevant now as the day it was published. The daily news substantiates what Carson boldly warned of 23 years ago.

Hills, Lawrence D. **Grow Your Own Fruit and Vegetables.** Rev. ed. Thetford, England: Faber & Faber, 1979. An English manual with an organic bias that is better than most American books on organic gardening.

Howard, Sir Albert. **An Agricultural Testament.** Rev. ed. Emmaus, PA: Rodale Press, 1972. A classic discourse on how to stop the erosion of valuable topsoil and rejuvenate our farmlands, using organic methods and composting.

King, F. H. **Farmers of Forty Centuries.** Emmaus, PA: Rodale Press, 1911. A travelog through turn-of-the-century China when all farming was done by hand. A wonderful, though rambling, review of another culture's raised bed gardening methods.

Margolin, Malcolm. **The Earth Manual.** Boston: Houghton-Mifflin, 1975. A basic review of ecologically sane ways to treat landscapes, revegetate bare soil, and repair man's damage to the environment.

Merrill, Richard, ed. **Radical Agriculture.** New York: Harper & Row, 1976. An early-contemporary discourse on the need for and viability of organic farming. Good background reading; see how far we have to go to reach the goals outlined in the essays.

Mollison, Bill, and Holmgren, David. **Permaculture One.** Stanley, Tasmania: Tagari Books, 1978. A good introduction to the Australian equivalent of sustainable/holistic/integrated farms and gardens. The theories were an inspiration to me 7 years ago, but most of the examples are inappropriate for U.S. climates, property sizes, and lifestyles.

Mollison, Bill. **Permaculture II.** Stanley, Tasmania: Tagari Books, 1981. Further development of the permaculture theories, with a big section appropriate only where it rains less than 10 inches a year.

Odum, Eugene. **Ecology**. 2nd ed. New York: Holt, Reinhardt & Winston, 1975. A good, technical overview of the science of ecology.

Rateaver, Bargyla and Gylver. **The Organic Method Primer**. Pauma Valley, CA: Bargyla and Gylver Rateaver, 1973. The first good reference for patterning organic gardening after nature's dynamics. A true classic of organic gardening, though some of the sources remain obscure. Out of print; look for a used copy.

Rodale Press. **The Encyclopedia of Organic Gardening**. Emmaus, PA: Rodale Press, 1978. *The* bible for organic gardeners. Sometimes too wordy, sometimes too lean; still, a must for every edible landscaper's library.

Walters, Charles, Jr., and Fenzau, C. J. **An Acres U.S.A. Primer**. Raytown, MO: Acres, U.S.A., 1979. A long-winded but interesting survey of a genre of organic farming found throughout the Midwest. Though some of their conclusions are hard to accept, these farmers get good results and yields.

Whittaker, Robert. **Communities and Ecosystems**. 2nd ed. New York: MacMillan, 1975. A textbook review of the science of ecosystem research. The most readable of the ecosystem textbooks, for only the most studious reader.

1

OF PESTS AND POISONS

Myth: "Organic Pesticides Can't Hurt People"

> *Pyrethrum insecticide is . . . regarded as the least toxic to man and animals of all insecticides.*
>
> *Rotenone . . . is a contact and stomach poison . . . and is of very low toxicity to man and animals.*
>
> (Encyclopedia of Organic Gardening, 1971, Rodale Press)

While the guideline "least is best" should be foremost in the mind of an organic gardener, many end up using sprays to attack insects in the belief that "organic" insecticides are completely safe. *Organic insecticide* is a confusing term, but the common assumption is that a spray made from natural materials (roots, bark, flowers, and so on) is a safe way to kill pests. All pesticides are toxic. They are toxic by degrees; some are more harmful than others. Pyrethrum, derris or rotenone, ryania, and sabadilla—all plant-derived insecticides—are poisonous compounds.

Insecticides are ranked for immediate toxicity by the LD^{50}, the dose that kills 50 percent of the animals exposed. There are four categories of LD^{50}, category IV being the least harmful. Each successive category is 10 times more toxic than the previous category. Thus, category I is 1,000 times more toxic than category IV. As Figure 2.1 shows, organic or botanical insecticides are not less toxic than synthetic insecticides.

Nicotine, or more accurately, nicotine sulfate, an extract of tobacco plants, is more toxic than the infamous DDT. Pyrethrum is slightly more poisonous than malathion, notorious as the dreaded ingredient of the aerial spraying in northern California for Mediterranean fruit fly.

Pyrethrum, ryania, and nicotine sulfate are contact poisons. If they land on a person's skin or are inhaled, a toxic reaction may follow. Even rotenone, a stomach poison, can cause headaches if inhaled. Nausea and fever are other possible symptoms of exposure to botanical insecticidal sprays. If you resort to botanical sprays, protect yourself. Wear a long-sleeved shirt, full-length pants, and a respirator. Wash all tools and your arms and face thoroughly afterward.

Botanical insecticides differ from most synthetic pesticides in one important respect. The long-term toxicity of botanical insecticides is generally low. They do not accumulate in the environment. In a mere 12 hours or less of sunlight, Pyrethrum degrades into harmless residues. Because of their rapid breakdown, botanical sprays require more frequent application to achieve the desired control. Even though it is a man-made chemical, malathion also is short-lived; it breaks down in three days into harmless compounds.

Many synthetic poisons have a staying power that disables or kills insects or animals long after spraying. The ability of a persistent chemical to travel higher in the food chain, increasing its concentration and spreading its lethal effect, is called biological magnification. Humans, birds, animals, insects, and future generations bear traces of DDT that was sprayed in the 1940s and '50s. This is the unforgivable, tragic aspect of some chemical insecticides. Botanical sprays have none of that impact.

I prefer a cautionary definition of organic pesticide: *A toxic compound derived or extracted from plants, not fabricated from petrochemicals, that has insecticidal properties but that rapidly degrades in the open environment into harmless ingredients.* Never forget to treat *all* insecticides with respect.

Myth: All Pests Are All Bad

Be wary of condemning an insect. Aphids are on everyone's list of dreaded pests, and gardeners often wage war against aphids at any cost. Yet some open-minded scientists have documented benevolent influences of this besieged bug. In a paper published in *New Scientist* (Oct. 13, 1977), Dennis Owen and Richard Wiegert discuss how aphids may help fertilize lime trees! If you have ever parked under a tree laden with aphids, you will vividly recall the sticky mess of honeydew, or aphid excrement, that dropped onto your windshield. Aphids insert their pointed mouth parts, called stylets, into the phloem, the active cells of transport for plant nutrients, to feed upon the sugars and amino acids in the sap. Some passes through their bodies unused, making sticky honeydew. The quantities of honeydew excreted are remarkable, the equivalent of one kilogram (2.25 pounds) of sugar per square meter of soil beneath a single 46-foot-tall lime tree.

"The aphids' activity would seem to represent a loss for the lime tree, but ecology involves a myriad of cycles and interactions. A little-known bacterium, azotobacter, lives in the soil where it converts nitrogen from the air into solid nitrogen. Azotobacter has a sweet tooth. A mere gram of glucose in 100 grams of soil increases these bacteria by a factor of 1,000. The report reads, "By releasing sugar [from the sap as honeydew] the gain in nitrogen [via the Azotobacter-to-citrus roots path] may exceed the loss [of the sap's carbohydrates and sugars]." The net impact of a certain population level of aphids on the citrus is beneficial. Of course, the aphid colony can grow to

RELATIVE TOXICITY OF INSECTICIDES

Chemical	Organic (plant extract)	Toxicity (LD$_{50}$ in mg./kg.)	Class	Signal Word Required by EPA
Aldrin		36–90	I	Danger – Poison
Dieldrin		46	I	Danger – Poison
	Nicotine	**50–91**	**II**	**Warning**
Lindane		76–200	II	Warning
DDT		87–500	II	Warning
	Rotenone	**100–132**	**II**	**Warning**
Chlordane		283–590	II	Warning
	Ryania	**750–1,200**	**III**	**Caution**
	Pyrethrum	**820–1,870**	**III**	**Caution**
Malathion		885–2,800	III	Caution
Ronnel		906–3,025	III	Caution
TDE		4,000	III	Caution
	Sabadilla	**4,000**	**III**	**Caution**
Methoxychlor		5,000–7,000	IV	None
Perthane		6,600–8,170	IV	None
Phoxim		8,500–8,800	IV	None
Acarol		5,000–34,600	IV	None

Figure 2.1 The smaller the Roman numeral, the more toxic the class of poison; the smaller the Arabic numeral, the more toxic the material. For example, it takes approximately 100 times more sabadilla (LD$_{50}$ = 4,000) to equal the toxic effect of dieldrin (LD$_{50}$ = 46).

be so big that the cycle becomes counterproductive. The balance is delicate.

There are studies that show increases in yields due to aphids. C. J. Banks and E. D. Macauley, in *The Journal of Experimental Botany*, reported:

Colonies of 400-800 aphids per plant lasting for 3 weeks in the early life of field bean did not significantly reduce the yield of . . . seeds; on the contrary, the results show slightly increased yields as if small colonies had in some way stimulated the plants.

The work of E. A. Wood in England revealed that "wheat kept free of . . . aphid[s] . . . averaged .9 bu/acre less than the plots with around 200 aphids per lineal foot." Now, that is specific.

Caterpillars Help Trees . . .

To conserve soil moisture during the dry summer months, most trees in California drop a large number of leaves. (The California buckeye even goes naked in mid- to late summer.) The oaks have a different method – they rely on the oak leaf caterpillar. In spring and summer, three to four generations of the oak leaf caterpillar eat oak foliage, reducing the leaf surface area and the oak's demand for water. Periodically, often on seven year intervals in California coastal areas, very large populations of oak leaf caterpillars emerge. The heavy feeding will totally defoliate some trees for part of the summer. Even this will not kill most trees; the reserve of food energy in the trunk and root system provides for new growth. Though repeated defoliation and other extreme stresses may kill a few trees, the forest lives on. The system works.

Tampering with the oak-caterpillar symbiosis can be disastrous. During the famous California drought of 1977-78, some oak trees were killed by the well-meaning eradication of caterpillars. With no protective partial defoliation and a crippling, severe drought, some majestic oaks were killed. Homeowners with oaks on their property often loathe the caterpillar droppings that cover their sidewalks, and for that reason alone, spray their trees to eradicate the "pest." It is sad to see a 300-year-old gnarled, regal oak die so quickly from a few years of human misunderstanding. Who is the real pest?

... and Increase Yields

Edible crops as well can benefit from some defoliation. Dr. P. Harris quotes research from Czechoslovakia:

Skukray (1968) reported that 50% defoliation of late potatoes from mid-June to the end of July increased tuber yields by 13.2-26.2%. Other researchers found that indiscriminate feeding on the leaves of turnips by five larvae of two types of pests slightly increased yields. Beyond the five, each additional larva reduced the yields by 2.6%. ("A Possible Explanation of Plant Yield Increases Following Insect Damage")

Rice responded to defoliation even more dramatically:

Taylor (1972) found ... that removal of half, two-thirds or all the foliage from upland rice before tillering [formation of the seed head] ... increased yield by 32, 28 and 9% respectively.

The Lesson

Though the practical implications of these examples are obscure, we should pause and reflect. They illustrate my favorite insect axiom: *One bug does not a problem make.* We are not as perceptive or fully understanding of nature's complexity as we would like to believe. Good stewardship of our land and forests demands that we try hard to perceive nature's interactions. To maintain nature's intended balance, we need bugs – good and bad alike. No book can delineate the healthiest population densities for your landscape. Explore and experience in your own backyard.

Organic gardening is complex and simple, a blend of good science, fact, experience, intuition, experiments, play, and speculation. The proportions change with each day and season, keeping the gardener's mind alert and body active. The oldest gardeners I know are the most limber – in mind, if not in body. Gardening keeps us healthy and young at heart, and organic gardening does so even more. Organic gardens help raise healthy people.

Abraham, George and Katy. **Organic Gardening Under Glass**. Emmaus, PA: Rodale Press, 1975. The first book on the subject. Not up to date, but still a good general reference. For indoor use of beneficial insects, see William Jordan's *Windowsill Ecology*.

Jordan, William, Jr. **Windowsill Ecology**. Emmaus, PA: Rodale Press, 1977. The most detailed of the non-technical references on the use of beneficial insects in greenhouses, atriums, and homes.

New Alchemy Institute. **Gardening for All Seasons**. Andover, MA: Brick House Publishing, 1983. An excellent book based on New Alchemy's thorough research and testing. Their integrated systems for food production and preservation are more current than those described in the Farallones Institute's *Integral Urban House*. Covers vegetable cultivation, greenhouse production, aquaculture, raising chickens, tree crops, recycling, and community gardens. Especially good for people living in colder winter climates of the U.S.

Olkowski, Helga and William. **The City People's Book of Raising Food**. Emmaus, PA: Rodale Press, 1975. One of the few level-headed books about the practical, and impractical, ways to grow food in urban areas. Every urban gardener should have a copy. Out of print, unfortunately; grab any copy you see in a used book store.

Rodale Press. **The Encyclopedia of Organic Gardening**. Emmaus, PA: Rodale Press, 1978. *The* bible for organic gardeners. Sometimes too wordy, sometimes too lean; still, a must for every edible landscaper's library.

1

THE BASICS OF EDIBLE LANDSCAPING
Understanding Your Property

THE CLIMATE IN YOUR YARD

Understanding local climate and the climate in your yard can help you reap a more abundant harvest. Though the evening news includes a weather report, you have to discover the nuances of local weather on your own, becoming a sort of weather detective. The search is fun, and you will be surprised how much of it can be done on the phone.

Figure 3.1 is a flow chart that is meant to streamline your work and save time. Let me show you how I used the chart to gather all the information I needed, including the data shown in Figs. 3.2 and 3.11, for a site located on the University of California campus at Santa Barbara. (The Client was the American Institute of Wine and Food, a non-profit organization founded "for the gathering, preservation, and dissemination of gastronomic knowledge.") I am cheating a little bit: I used not only the vast resources of the University for this study, but also weather data from a small airport just 3 miles from the site. But I will explain how you can get virtually all the same information wherever you live.

Rain and Temperature

I usually contact the local TV station or newspaper for rainfall and temperature data, but the proximity of an airport to this site meant they got my first call. In addition to average temperatures, an airport provides the bonus of actual highs and lows, information that is very useful in deciding which cold-sensitive plants to experiment with, as well as which times of the year you may need plantings to cool or to warm the house, patio, or play area.

Wind

The charts in Fig. 3.2 are called wind roses. Airports are the only source of wind rose data; other sources will give you only the average wind speed and prevailing direction. On a wind rose chart, the width of each little spoke indicates the wind's speed. The direction of the wind is indicated by the angle at which the spoke radiates from the circle (like a compass with North at the top). The average percentage of time that the wind blows in a certain direction is indicated by the length of the spoke.

For each quarter of the year, there is an average for both day and night. This information is vital for deciding where to place windbreaks and windmills and how to put cooling breezes to work in the summer.

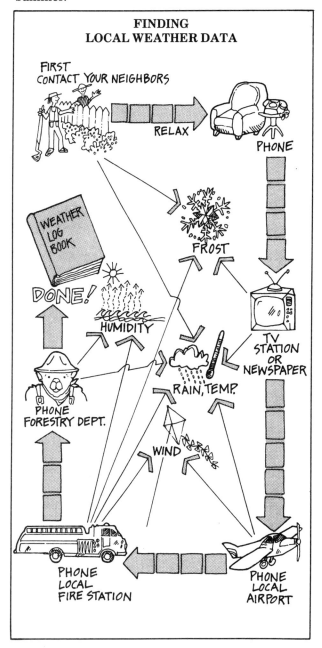

Figure 3.1 There are many sources of information about the weather in your area.

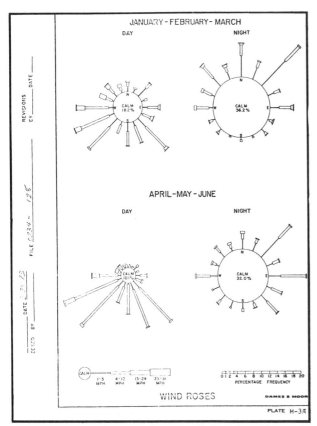

Figure 3.2 Wind roses show wind direction (the ray's location), wind speed (the ray's width), and wind frequency (the ray's length).

Frost

When you contact the sources in Fig. 3.1, be sure to gather the average length of the growing season and the average last day of frost. For the Santa Barbara site, the growing season is 342 days and the last date on which there is a 50 percent chance of frost is January 23. Eat your heart out, Michigan (and most other states, for that matter).

Finding Weather Data

Now it's your turn. My favorite way to find weather data is to talk to a neighbor who records the weather. In many locales there are backyard weather stations as well-tended and thorough as any official weather station. Ask around your neighborhood for amateur weather recorders.

If you can't turn up someone, the next step is to situate a comfortable chair next to the phone. Have plenty of paper, a pen, a copy of the flow chart, some refreshments, and a chunk of time. Call the nearest television and radio stations and talk to the weather reporters or the employees who have been around the longest. Also call the closest newspaper. In both cases, ask for weather records and where to find hobby weather stations. Call the nearest fire station (make sure you are calling the business number, not the emergency number) and ask what kind of weather records they keep. Unfortunately, local fire stations are not able to keep as many records as they used to. Try to fill in your chart with the daily and monthly averages (minimum and maximum) for temperature, rainfall, humidity, wind speed and direction, and the first and last average dates for frost.

In rural areas, contact the county or regional forestry department. The director of my county's office was very helpful. I learned the maximum and minimum for humidity and temperature, the wind's speed and direction, and the amount and duration of rainfall—but only for the fire season, which runs from June through October. The fire season corresponds closely with my area's watering season but does not cover frost dates. The director said I could come in and photocopy the records, and he referred me to five other possible sources of weather information. The first was the National Weather Service. Its stations are widely scattered—California has only five. Perhaps there is a station near your home. The telephone number is listed under the National Oceanic and Atmospheric Administration (a fact it had taken the forestry director years to discover). The other sources were the State Park Service, Bureau of Land Management, and the State Air Pollution Control agencies. That was plenty, considering the quagmire of governmental agencies.

Be Your Own Weather Station

Collecting your own weather information is useful and fun. The more I watch the weather, the more accurate I get in making predictions and the better my edible landscape works. Anticipating weather changes is especially helpful when cultivating soil and transplanting. Often, I have prepared the soil just in time to benefit from a rainstorm that arrived earlier than the weatherman predicted.

Rain Gauge

Every edible landscape should have two rain gauges. While your local retail nursery may offer several, I recommend looking in the Ben Meadows Company catalog, which specializes in the tools of the survey, forestry, tree surgery, and forest firefighting professions. The choices range from a $2.70 plastic gauge to $50 and $150 professional models. (The mailing address is listed at the end of this chapter.)

If most of your edible landscape is in the open, your rain gauge should also be in an open area. If a good percentage of your landscape is under the foliage of trees, place another rain gauge under the trees to register the difference that fog and dew make. In my local redwood and Douglas fir forests, the water that reaches the ground can be 50 percent greater under the trees than in a nearby meadow. The foliage acts as a rain scoop, condensing moisture from fog and shedding it onto the ground.

Thermometer

Use a maximum-minimum thermometer. It shows you the day's hottest and coldest temperatures at one reading, and what it shows may be amazingly different from what you hear on the evening news. Since a yard can have several microclimates, you might want to use several maximum-minimum thermometers. One placed beneath the eave of the house will reveal how much warmer that protected microclimate is than an open area. If you have a sloped yard, there may be a frost pocket at the bottom. A maximum-minimum thermometer will show how much cold settles there.

Unfortunately, these helpful tools pinch the wallet. The most readily available model in my area is $19.95. The Ben Meadows catalog has a less accurate type for $11.80, still steep if you want more than one.

A small box, with a top and three sides but no bottom, is the standard shelter for maximum-minimum thermometers. The open side faces north. If the sun hits the bulb directly you will get a false reading. Check with your local Cooperative Extension Service for plans on how to build an inexpensive thermometer shelter.

There are fancier ways to record temperatures. One is using an automatic pen. The cheapest, a spring-wound model, is $160. Another is a kit that hooks into a Vic 20™ or Commodore 64™ computer. The sensor tracks dew point, temperature, humidity, and atmospheric pressure. The software plots historical data, graphically displays weather trends, forecasts the weather, and compares the predictions with those of the local weatherman. While these extravagant tools are not necessary for most edible landscapes, they help you undertake a monitoring and spray program for the organic control of fruit and nut tree pests and diseases such as codling moth on apples and pears, San Jose scale, omnivorous leaf roller, and scab. In the case of codling moth control, knowing the temperature at dusk makes for a more accurate spray program and better control than using just the maximum and minimum temperatures.

Wind

The directions of the prevailing wind and the heaviest winds on your property will very likely differ from those at the nearest official recording station. Check them yourself. For the prevailing winds, take a look at the tallest trees in your neighborhood. Some will exhibit flagging, as in

Figure 3.3 Treetops reveal the direction of prevailing winds. Flagging can be dramatic, as in the case of the desperately staked young cypress (top); or subtle, as shown by the cypress in the lower photograph.

Fig. 3.3. Their tips make growth only on the downwind side. The most intense gusts and storms—the winds that can damage your fruit trees—probably arrive from a different direction.

During storms, I get out in the garden and watch. I also use the wooden windmills that have clackers (sold at retail nurseries for gopher control) to observe storm winds. I remove the clackers and put the windmills in the garden where I can watch them from the house. They also indicate something about the winds that occur when you are not home. Being heavier than most weather vanes, they come to rest pointing in the direction of the last gusting wind. Knowing the storm winds helps you know in which direction to face the graft of a fruit tree when planting and how to protect fruit-laden trees.

Sunshine and Shade Patterns

To make the best use of your property – and when yards are small – you will need to know the seasonal patterns of where the sun does and does not shine. Since the sun's position in the sky changes throughout the year, the shade in the early spring will be in very different places than in midsummer. For planting winter vegetables, encouraging early spring blossoming of fruit and nut trees, and early planting of summer vegetables, knowing the exact boundaries of shade is very helpful. There are three types of devices that can be used to analyze shade patterns directly at any time of the year, for whatever month you need information.

A Straw Poll of the Sun

The first device (see Fig. 3.4) can be built with things you already have at home – a drinking straw, a protractor, a directional compass, a short piece of string, a small heavy object – and the solar altitude and azimuth charts in Appendix 2. Tape the straw to the straight part of the protractor. Tie the small weight to the string and hang it from the hole in the middle of the protractor to serve as a plumb bob.

Use the compass to locate solar south. True solar south differs from magnetic south by an angle given in the Magnetic Deviation Chart (or isogonic chart) that appears in Appendix 2. Once you have determined solar south, face that direction.

From the solar altitude and azimuth chart for your latitude, pick the month that you are curious about, say December 21 at 40° latitude. Follow the curved line to 0° (true south) and read the altitude of the sun at noon from the concentric arcs, 27°.

With the string hanging down from the protractor, tilt the protractor to an angle of 27° above level – the string will cross the grid on the protractor at 63° (90° minus 27°). Looking through the straw you will be able to see if any trees or buildings are in the way by noting any obstructions *above* the line of view. Make a note of the location of any branches that need to be removed in order to

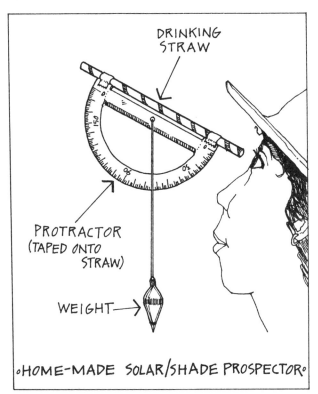

Figure 3.4

allow full sunlight through to your garden or house.

Repeat these steps for several angles to the east and west of true south. Use the degree markings on the compass to orient your body for each measurement. In this example, on December 21 at 8 A.M., the sun is 45° to the east of south and 10° to 12° above the horizon.

A Window on the Sun

A ready-made and more accurate device, the Solar Card ($12.95 from Solar Card, 7 Church Hill Rd., Harrisville, NH 03450), gives the sun's paths from September 21 through March 21 for your latitude as a curved grid on transparent plastic. Hold the Solar Card several inches from your nose, making sure it is level, and sight through the grid. This method takes some eyeball gymnastics, but it does allow you to see where existing plants or buildings block the sun. Pick the path that represents the month you want to know about – anything that crosses the path will cast a shadow where your eye is, not at your feet. For an accurate reading of low plants, squat down near the ground.

The Solar Site Selector

The Solar Site Selector is my favorite and most-used tool when I am consulting. It is more expensive than the others but much handier and more accurate. (The latest version, which includes a visor for the summer sun, is $89.50 plus $4 shipping from Lewis and Associates, 105 Rockwood Dr., Grass Valley, CA 95945-5690.) Figs. 3.5 and 3.6 show how easy the Solar Site Selector is to use. In my county, a local non-profit organization purchased one of these devices and rents it out for only $5 a day. It is a valuable service, one worth establishing in every city or county.

Figure 3.5 The Solar Site Selector can be hand-held or mounted on a tripod. This version includes two gridded "masks," one for winter and one for summer. (Photograph by Lewis and Associates.)

The Site Selector comes with a 200° lens (the same as the peeper used in doors to allow you to see who is knocking) that makes it simple to see the entire grid, bubble level, and compass at once and to carefully view the skyline. Mount the Site Selector to a camera tripod for easy adjusting and hands-free viewing—a real bonus for charting a permanent record of the solar shade pattern.

For an accurate reading in the vegetable garden, put the viewer as close to the ground as is comfortable, since you are concerned with how much light the plants will get. Before putting my solar site selector together, I made a number of photocopies of the grid. Wherever a reading is taken, I sketch the location of obstacles and their subsequent shade patterns onto one of the paper copies. Figure 3.7 shows an example of the permanent record I made while siting for my vegetable area.

These same devices can be used to find the best location for a solar water or space heater, a photovoltaic panel, or to anticipate the impact of any tree you are considering planting.

Bloom Sequence

I record the spring and summer bloom cycle and use the data to schedule landscaping work. I get an extra calendar from an insurance company or feed store each fall, and next spring, I mark down what blooms when, as in Fig. 3.8. After a few seasons, I know that once the acacia trees begin blooming I had better get to pruning the almonds, apricots, and plums. I know, for example, that the plum on the top of Grandview Drive blooms 10 to 14 days before my plum. When I see that Grandview Drive plum blooming, I know I cannot put off pruning my tree any longer. After keeping a record for several years, you will find that the dates in most gardening books are inaccurate for your yard. You will be able to time planting and pruning more accurately, as well as know how much earlier or later the season is compared to last year.

Leaf Fall Sequence

Observing when trees lose their leaves lets you pick the best species to plant on the south side of a house. In my area, many species still hold their

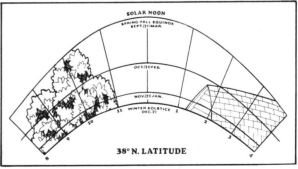

Figure 3.6 Top: a view through the 200° lens. Bottom: the same view through the plastic grid.

leaves when the heating season begins. The sweetgum (*Liquidambar styraciflua*) holds its leaves into December and even January, depending on the weather. Many fruit trees drop their leaves before the native trees. Also, an unirrigated tree drops its leaves before the same tree under irrigation. At the Farallones Institute Rural Center (in Occidental, California), the only tree to be leafless by the beginning of the heating season is an unirrigated "Rio Oso Gem" peach.

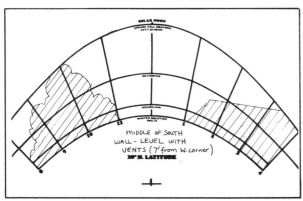

Figure 3.7 On a photocopy of the grid, sketch the pattern of shade cast by trees and buildings.

Figure 3.8 Recording the sequence of early spring bloom can help you anticipate when to prune.

Observing While Gardening

Another way to understand the sunlight patterns and the microclimates of your yard is simply to grow vegetables. Instead of designing a landscape just after moving into your new home, wait and observe the yard through a complete cycle of seasons. For at least a year, grow edibles in a number of spots that seem to have beneficial sunlight and climate. You will probably get a very

good feel for the nuances of sunshine patterns, frost pockets, windy spots, wet soils, rocky soils, and other important information before designing your edible landscape. The placement of your first edibles may turn out to be ill-advised or just right.

Reading About Weather

To keep up with the latest in meteorology, consider subscribing, or ask your library to subscribe, to the periodicals listed below.

Weatherwise

Six issues per year for $25. Write 4000 Albemarle St. N.W., Washington, DC 20016. Expensive and a little technical, but has full-color illustrations, which come in handy for an article such as "Supernumerary Rainbows."

The New Weather Observer

"A year's worth of sporadic publications" for $10. Write Box 485, Inverness, California 94937. A black-and-white, home-produced journal that makes meteorology understandable and entertaining. Topics have included volcanoes and the weather, eclipses, lightning, and El Niño.

Geisner, Rudolph. **The Climate Near the Ground**. Cambridge, MA: Harvard University Press, 1965. A classic textbook on microclimates. Highly technical, and expensive.

Simonds, Calvin. **The Weather-Wise Gardener**. Emmaus, PA: Rodale Press, 1983. A recent book on how to study your local climate and predict the weather.

Ben Meadows Company, 2601-B West 5th Ave., P. O. Box 2781, Eugene, OR 97402. Write for the price of their catalog.

The earth is the mother of us all—plants, animals, and men. The phosphorus and calcium of the earth build our skeletons and nervous systems. Everything else our bodies need except air and sun comes from the earth.

Nature treats the earth kindly. Man treats her harshly. He overplows the cropland, overgrazes the pasturelands, and overcuts the timberland. He destroys millions of acres completely. He pours fertility year after year into the cities, which in turn pour what they do not use down the sewers into the rivers and the oceans. The social lesson of soil waste is that no man has the right to destroy soil even if he does own it in fee simple.

Pretty strong words. I wish I had written them. Remarkably, these thoughts of a former U.S. Secretary of Agriculture, Henry Wallace, are expressed in the 1938 U.S. Department of Agriculture Yearbook, *Soils and Men*. The words are as true today as they were over 45 years ago.

Soil may seem like a fixed element in our gardens, but it is actually malleable. You can change it for the better and improve the yields of your edible landscape. But you will need to know what you are starting with. The foundation of a good edible landscape design is an understanding of soil and a survey of your home's soil.

The Four Components of Good Soil

The four most important non-living elements of a soil are air, water, minerals, and organic matter.

Air

Air space is vital to good growth. The microscopic channels that meander through a soil are called pore spaces. They are like tiny conduits for air and water. Air provides roots with the breath of life, and pore space allows the soil to breathe. The proportion of pore space and water in the soil largely determines the growth of plants. Too much oxygen quickly reduces the organic matter to a much less useful ash. Too little air, due to a heavy soil or too much water, and the soil life deteriorates, reducing fertility.

Water

When there is too much water in the soil, the roots are likely to rot or drown. Too little water, and the plant withers. Water is the medium of transport for nutrients. It coats the particles of soil, organic matter, and humus, so their nutrients dissolve and are absorbed by the plant.

Mineral

The mineral component of soil is a reserve of different nutrients. A very small percentage is directly soluble for immediate use by roots. Most of the reserve must first be altered by the soil's slightly acid water solution, or by bacteria and other soil life, and incorporated into the colloidal strands of humus before it can be used by plants.

Organic Matter

Organic matter is the fiber of the soil, as important to soil health as dietary fiber is important to our health. Once any form of life—plant, animal, or single cell—dies, its remains begin to decompose, releasing nutrients back into the web of life to be recombined as new life. Organic matter, through the action of the soil's bacteria, eventually releases nutrients to plants. In the meantime, the organic matter keeps the soil loose and spongy and holds onto nutrients that would otherwise leach away. With further decomposition, organic matter becomes humus. This wonderful ingredient of soil does everything organic matter does, only better.

The Importance of Humus

The goal of all good soil-building techniques is to increase the soil's humus content. Humus is the by-product of soil life—bacteria, worms, animals, algae, fungi, and other critters of decomposition—and it is the end product of the decomposition of organic matter. Defined another way in *Nature and Properties of Soils*, humus is "a complex and rather resistant mixture of brown or dark brown amorphous and colloidal substances that have been modified from the original tissues or have been synthesized by the various soil organisms."

Humus is considered to be relatively stable, but if it were, we would be over our heads in humus. In fact, it does eventually break down. It oxidizes (a process of flameless decomposition promoted by the oxygen in the soil). Upon oxidation, the humus is dismantled into carbon dioxide and water, releasing energy or heat in the process. Since the source of humus is dead plants and animals, it is constantly being renewed. Like the rest of nature, it is always in a state of dynamic equilibrium.

The colloidal nature of humus is responsible for its ability to hold onto water and nutrients, to keep the soil light and fluffy, and to release nutrients to plant roots. Colloids are much like a sticky glue—elastic and strong, with tremendous holding capacity. Colloids act as "granulators" in heavy soils.

The microscopic strands of sticky, colloidal compounds coat tiny clay particles and bind them together, opening pores that allow air and water to easily penetrate.

Humus is beneficial to all soils. The loose, crumbly nature of ideal soil is created in great part by humus and its colloidal nature. With sufficient humus, heavy clay soils have better drainage and aeration. In sandy soils, the humus holds onto water and nutrients that might otherwise leach away.

Humus is also important to soil fertility. It holds more moisture, releases more nutrients, and provides a better soil structure than an equivalent amount of organic matter. Since organic matter is the source of humus, every soil-improvement strategy in this book is geared toward increasing the organic matter, and thereby, the humus content.

In an ideal silty loam soil, the proportions of elements are: air, 25 percent; water, 25 percent; minerals, 45 percent, and organic matter, 5 percent. I mention these figures to impress you with how tiny the percentage of organic matter is when compared to its vital role.

Figure 3.9 As edible landscapers, we are most concerned with the quality of soil in horizon "A."

Soil Texture and Structure

Knowing your soil's makeup will help you anticipate trouble. The two extremes are sand and clay. A soil high in clay drains slowly, while a soil high in sand drains quickly. Clay has more inherent nutrition than sand, but that nutrition is usually unavailable to the roots because of the heavy, or tight, nature of clay. Sand is the least fertile of soils because it has less of a physical and chemical capacity for holding nutrients.

A quick way to get a feel for your soil's texture involves getting your hands dirty. Take a small amount of soil in your palm and add enough water to thoroughly moisten the soil, without making it runny. After the soil and water are fully mixed, rub some of the mixture between two fingers. Clay feels and looks slippery. A gritty feeling, without a shiny look, indicates soil that is high in sand. Silt, which is intermediate between sand and clay, almost feels greasy, but has less of the sticky or plastic feel of clay.

There are fancier methods. One involves rolling a coil of moistened soil between the palms and seeing how long the "snake" gets before breaking—the longer the snake, the more clay the soil has. The most complicated method involves measuring the sand, silt, and clay after they settle out of solution by using a hydrometer. (For a full description of these two tests, see pages 193 to 195 of *The Integral Urban House—Self-Reliant Living in the City*, Sierra Club Books.)

Tilth

The structure of a soil is the arrangement of soil particles into groups or aggregates. Structure depends only in part on texture. Tilth, the sum of texture and structure, is the usual word for the workability of soil. Good tilth, the sometimes-elusive goal of every gardener, is the perfect, loamy, easily crumbled soil so prevalent in an undisturbed forest floor or where many earthworms have been active.

Organic Matter—A Panacea

In almost any soil, from heavy clay to pure sand, soil deficiencies are greatly relieved by the addition of organic matter. The old axiom of organic gardening is basically sound advice: When in doubt, add more organic matter. (The form scarcely matters—compost, humus, raw organic matter.) For farmers, this carefree adage could easily lead to economic ruin, but as home gardeners, we can almost always acquire more organic matter.

Soil Survey—It's the Pits

Knowing the depth, fertility, texture, structure, organic matter, and humus content of your soil is vital to planting and nurturing a productive edible landscape. By digging trenches or pits in several places around your property, you can study your soil's profile; the lowest layers affect which plants will grow easily and which plants will grow only with continued nurturing.

I dig a pit or trench wide enough to climb in, and have found myself up to my waist in order to view the lower layers. Before tackling the strenuous task of digging trenches, take a look at a recently made road-cut nearby. Soil scientists have an amazing collection of obscure codes and fancy words for the layers you will see, but let's keep things simple. The topmost layer is composed of raw and rotted plant debris. There, we find nature's mulch, plant and animal remains that have just begun to decompose, beginning the grand cycle of living tissue to soil nutrient to be reborn as more living tissue.

Topsoil: Alive, Fertile and Valuable

Over time, through the action of rain and an amazing variety of soil life, nature's mulch decomposes into a rich brown, loamy material (see "A" horizon in Fig. 3.9) enriching the layer commonly referred to as topsoil. Here we find well-rotted, composted organic matter mixed with the native soil. Here, humus is found. Clay particles, minerals, organic matter, and good aeration make this the most biologically active zone of the soil.

Because topsoil is so aerobic (full of air), soil life gets plenty of oxygen for growth. Also, its open structure allows toxic gases produced by respiration – for example, carbon dioxide and sulfur dioxide – to escape the soil quickly and relatively harmlessly.

We should think of soils as alive and breathing. Alan Chadwick, the first proponent of raised-bed gardening in the United States, went so far as to state, "We are actually cultivating the air – a distance of approximately two inches above the soil surface – and reaching perhaps one-half inch below it. We are [by proper cultivation] inducing the soil to breathe." The better the soil breathes, the more fruitful the plant life. Roots are dependent upon air for life and nutrition, and so are the soil organisms that liberate nutrients from the colloidal humus and make them available to plants.

Many gardeners assume that a tree's deeper roots allow it to forage water and nutrients from levels of the soil untouched by herbs, grasses, and broadleaf weeds. In fact, the most aerobic layers of the soil provide the majority of the water and nutrients for healthy growth and yields. (See "Deep-Rooted Myths.")

Subsoil

Usually, a lighter color and less friable texture mark the start of the subsoil. Subsoils are younger soils, more recently derived from the raw rock below them than topsoil is, and have much less soil life. Figure 3.10 reveals how rapidly the number of soil organisms declines in deeper levels of the soil. The first foot of soil may have 7 to 50 times more soil life than the next 3½ feet. Merely mixing topsoil with subsoil will not make the deeper levels more biologically active. The surface-loving bacteria simply die.

Often the subsoil is composed of clay, ranging from red to orange to bluish in color. The red-orange clays reveal that enough air is present to

oxidize the iron so prevalent in clays. A yellow color indicates a lower level of oxygen. Blue clays are without oxygen, usually because of great depth or a high water table. Blue clays won't support plant roots – in fact, it is hard enough to support good growth with red-orange clays.

If the duff and mulch layer above the topsoil is thin or if the climate is very rainy, nutrients leach down to the clay subsoil, bind to the clay and become basically unavailable to most roots. The few roots that do manage to live in subsoils get more water and anchorage than food, proportionally, than roots in the topsoil.

Figure 3.10 The soil's bacteria live at specific depths. When soil is tilled under, surface-loving bacteria die.

Bedrock

If you are persistent – maybe too persistent – your test pit will hit a rocky layer. In some areas, the bedrock (or parent material, as it is called by soil scientists) is rather close to the surface. If the subsoil is deep, don't bother to keep digging – your back will probably give out first. The parent material is basically rock, ready to begin the evolution to subsoil and eventually, topsoil. Time heals all, but the bedrock layer is basically useless to us as edible landscapers. It is the final limit to root growth. The rugged, gnarled pine, clinging by several twisted roots to the fractured rock cliff, is a marvel of nature; most plants grown as food would wither in such a setting.

Soil Tests and Surveys

Soil tests are a good tool to use when you suspect an extreme deficiency or toxic surplus of some mineral in your soil. However, soil testing basically provides a general assay, not a complete picture (until you have done a series of tests over many years). Call your local university cooperative extension to see if you can get a free soil test. If you must pay, expect costs in a range from $6 to $20 for each sample, depending on the lab and the number of nutrients tested for. The lab will tell you how to take a sample and will send fertilizer recommendations with the test results.

It is possible to get a general idea of your soil's type and potential for free. The federal government has spent millions of dollars to do aerial surveys of soil types and classifications. These surveys are available to everyone. First call the regional office of the U.S.D.A. Soil Conservation Service. Ask if they have an index map for locating your property. With the information, the soil conservation staff can refer to another map to determine your soil type and classification and explain their implications. Other sources of information about your soil type and classification include the county library, the local college or junior college library, and any soil engineering office.

Figure 3.11 shows a portion of the soil surveys done for the Santa Barbara site mentioned in the previous chapter. An archeological kitchen midden (the remains of an Indian dump heap or ancient compost heap) were found at "S Ba 51" (top) and "A" (bottom). The tiny 3-digit numbers (top) show where the soil samples were taken. The different patterns (bottom) show the different soil types, based on the soil survey.

Soil Tests for Commercial Reasons

The figures offered by a lab as recommended fertilizer rates are critical to farmers but not to gardeners. For one thing, farmers do not have any margin for error: they are too close to bankruptcy to guess or gamble with fertilizer rates. Home gardeners are not nearly as penny-wise, nor are they gardening for a living. Secondly, farmers test on a frequent basis. They learn, over the years, the correlation between what the lab recommends and how the crops respond.

Instead of a soil test, I prefer to judge a soil by the existing vegetation (see the next chapter). I find it satisfying to have the knowledge necessary to understand a soil's virtues and limitations, to be independent of soil labs, the mail, bags, labels, and all the paraphernalia needed for soil testing. Also, I routinely add large amounts of amendments and do extensive soil preparation for the landscapes I develop, and this usually compensates for any mineral deficiencies or imbalances.

Figure 3.11 This soil survey revealed three soil types and a rare problem: an archeological site, protected by state law from development.

Brooklyn Botanical Gardens. **Handbook on Soils**. Garden Series, #12. Brooklyn, NY: Brooklyn Botanical Gardens, 1966. A brief introduction that seems almost biased against organic methods.

Buckman, H. O., and Brady, N. C. **The Nature and Properties of Soils**. New York: MacMillan, 1974. Rev. ed. My second choice of technical soil books, after E. W. Russell's *Soil Conditions and Plant Growth*. Buckman's text is better on conventional soil chemistry. Seek a library copy before buying this expensive manual.

Howard, Sir Albert. **The Soil and Health.** New York: Schocken Books, 1972. This classic from the father of modern composting describes the origin and process of the Indore method, the prototype of today's fast/hot compost method.

Russell, E. W. **Soil Conditions and Plant Growth.** 10th ed. New York: Longman, 1974. The only book I know of that combines a very scientific review of soil chemistry with an emphasis on organic methods. Extensive footnotes and citations from international literature. Often refers to the important research on organic farming by the Rothamsted Agricultural Station in England. Superior book for frequent referral by designers, students of organic methods, and researchers.

Wright, David. **Fruit Trees and the Soil.** London: Faber and Faber, 1960. A short, succinct manual on the organic care of fruit trees. Presents the most understandable discussion I have read on the biochemistry of soil as it relates to organic home gardening. Demystifies soil fertility and how it influences fruit tree growth and production.

EXISTING VEGETATION: WHAT IT MEANS, WHAT IT OFFERS

Weeds are more useful than most of us realize. I love to eat certain weeds, but the first use I make of weeds is to read the story they tell about the soil. By the way, I won't be using the word weed, since it connotes a worthless plant. I prefer the word plant.

Plants as Indicators of Soil Type

Before the advent of soil tests, farmers developed a lore about the significance of wild plants in their fields. Some of that lore found its way into books. In 1920, the botanist Fredrick Clements stated, "Each plant is an indicator . . . the product of the conditions under which it grows, and is thereby a measure of these conditions . . . a plant furnishes a clue to the factors at work upon it." E.E. Pfeiffer, one of the primary practitioners of biodynamic farming, viewed plants as great teachers and stated, "[Weeds are] indicating through their mere presence and multiplication what is wrong." Of course, plants also indicate what is right with a soil.

From *An Acres U.S.A. Primer* by Charles Walters, Jr., and C.J. Fenzau, come two very good examples of indicator plants. The first is tumbleweed, also known as Russian thistle (*Salsola kali L.* var. *tenuifolia Tausch*): "Russian thistle likes an environment . . . low [in] iron, low [in] calcium, and a poor organic matter structure in the soil." The second is lamb's-quarters (*Chenopodium album*).

*Lambsquarters sometimes grows five feet tall. It harbors a lot of nutrition for certain insects and stores a high quality of phosphate. It reflects the availability of good nutrition in the soil. Used in silage, it supplies needed nutrients. As a matter of fact, both pigweed (*Amaranthus retroflexus*) and lambsquarters can become excellent silage. Both have a high protein content [which also means, high nitrogen content]. Lambsquarters grows in a soil that has an appropriate decay system [loose, friable soil with plenty of air and healthy decomposing soil life].*

There are limitations to indicator lore. For the plants in Fig. 3.12, based on my experience, the most dependable uses in descending order are for estimating moisture levels, for judging whether the soil has ever been cultivated or disturbed, for gauging the tilth of the soil, for estimating nutrient content, and for estimating pH.

Choosing the Best Indicators

One plant is not a practical indicator of any-thing. Single plants may grow in atypical situations, and many species have wide tolerances of soil and water conditions. Use plant communities, not just a few plants, as indicators.

In one of my gardens, a dock plant (*Rumex crispus*) appeared among the carrots. Though the indicator list shows dock to be an indicator of acid soil, I knew the soil in the carrot patch was not acidic. A broken piece of dock root probably survived composting and sprouted once the compost was added to the carrot patch. In other yards, where dock grew abundantly in low areas, it told me the extent of poorly drained and acidic soil. I reserved such spots for a bench or a toolshed—anything but vegetables and fruit trees, which require good drainage.

Use the lushest, healthiest-looking plants as indicators. If a plant appears stunted, it may be wise not to use it as an indicator. It is probably growing in marginal conditions.

Since annual plants cast their seeds far and wide, they are likely to appear over a wider range of conditions than perennials. And since annuals die each year, it is hard to tell if the cause is a hostile situation or old age. Because perennials live for a longer time in one place, they are more reliable indicators.

Just as one point on a graph does not make a line, and one fact does not make a trend, so one group of plants does not provide surefire indication of soil type. Always use more than one indicator to understand your site. For example, dock, dandelion, chicory, and plantain all show up under the column for clay soil. One of these plants is a likely indicator, but two provide a confirmation.

A single species does not reliably indicate two conditions at once. The list has 19 plants for acidic conditions and 19 for wet soils, but only 8 plants that indicate both wet and acidic soils. If you suspect a wet and acidic soil, look for plants that prefer both conditions, as well as plants for each condition.

Spotting Soil Problems

The most reliable and noticeable indicators are those for the soil's water level or moisture content. Waterlogged soils are easy to spot when it is raining, but indicators allow you to spot poorly drained soils at any time of the year. They can also reveal what the water content is like deeper than you may want to dig.

The best indicators in my area for soils too wet for most fruit trees and many vegetables are curly dock (*Rumex crispus*), horsetail (*Equisetum* sp.), cattails (*Typha* sp.), and wiregrass (*Heleocharis palustris*). Willows often grow where it is too wet in the winter and spring for vegetables, but where the soil has usually dried out enough by midsummer for a planting of quick-ripening vegetables.

Figure 3.12

SOIL INDICATORS

Common Name	Botanical Name	Dry	Wet	Cultivated/Tilled	Uncultivated/Neglected	Low N	High N	Low K	High K	Low P	High P	Sand	Clay	Hardpan/Crusty	Acid	Alkaline	Low Fertility	High Fertility	Salty
Agrimony		X																	
Artemisia maritima	*Artemisia maritima*																		X
Aster, sea																			X
Aster, swamp			X																
Bellflower	*Campanula sp.*														X				
Bindweed, field	*Convolvulus arvensis*												X	X					
Bindweed, hedge	*Convolvulus sepium*		X																
Bracken, eastern	*Pteridium aquifolium*						X		X						X				
Buttercups	*Ranunculus acris*		X	X									X						
Buttercup, creeping	*Ranunculus repens*		X										X						
Campion	*Lychnis alba*														X				
Carpetweed	*Mollugo verticillata*			X															
Carrot, wild	*Daucus carota*				X								X			X	X		
Catchfly, night-flowering	*Silene noctiflora*	X																	
Cattail	*Typha latifolia*		X																
Celandine			X																
Chamomile, corn	*Anthemis arvensis*		X					X						X		X			
Chamomile, German	*Chamomilla pecutita*													X	X				
Chickweed	*Stellaria media*			X														X	
Chicory	*Cichorium intybus*			X									X					X	
Cinquefoil, silvery	*Potentilla argentea*	X												X					
Clovers	*Trifolium sp.*					X													
Clover, hop	*Medicago lupulina*														X				
Clover, rabbit foot		X								X				X					
Clover, red	*Trifolium protense*							X											
Clover, white	*Trifolium repens*	X			X														
Cockle, white	*Lychnis alba*												X						
Coltsfoot			X											X	X				
Cornflower	*Centaurea cyanus*												X						
Corn marigold													X		X				
Cotton grasses	*Eriophorum sp*		X																
Cudweed, low	*Gnaphalium sp.*		X																
Daisy, English	*Bellis perennis*													X	X				
Daisy, ox eye	*Chrysanthemum leucanthemum*			X	X														
Dandelion	*Taraxacum vulgare*			X										X	X				
Docks	*Rumex sp.*		X												X				
Dock, broad leaved	*Rumex obtusifoias*		X											X					
Fat hen	*Atriplex hastata*																	X	
Fingerleaf														X					
Foxtail, short awned	*Hordeum jubatum*		X																
Fumitory	*Fumaria officinalis*							X											
Goldenrods	*Solidago sp.*		X										X						
Goosefoot, oak leaved				X															
Grass, quack	*Agropyron repens*													X					
Groundsel	*Senecio vulgaris*		X															X	
Hawkweeds	*Hieracium sp.*														X				
Hedge-nettle, marsh			X																
Hellebore, false	*Veratrum californicum*		X																
Hemlock, poison	*Conium maculatum*		X																

continued

Figure 3.12   continued

SOIL INDICATORS

Common Name	Botanical Name	Dry	Wet	Cultivated/Tilled	Uncultivated/Neglected	Low N	High N	Low K	High K	Low P	High P	Sand	Clay	Hardpan/Crusty	Acid	Alkaline	Low Fertility	High Fertility	Salty
Henbame, black	*Hyscyamus niger*															X			
Henbit	*Camium amplexicaule*			X													X		
Horehound	*Marrubium vulgare*			X															
Horsenettle	*Solanum carolinense*			X			X					X							
Horsetails	*Equisetum sp.*		X										X		X				
Horsetail, field	*Equisetum arvense*		X									X							
Horsetail, marsh			X																
Joe-pye weed			X																
Knapweeds	*Centaurea nigra*								X						X				
Knawel	*Scleranthus annuus*														X				
Knotweed, prostrate	*Polygonum aviculare*			X											X				
Lady's thumb	*Polygonum periscaria*		X												X				
Lamb's quarters	*Chenopodium album*			X														X	
Lettuce, prickly	*Lactuca scariola*			X															
Lupine	*Lupinus sp.*					X													
Mallow, musk	*Malva moschata*			X															
Mare's tail	*Erigeron canadensis*		X																
Mayweed	*Anthemis cotula*												X		X				
Meadow sweet	*Astilbe sp.*		X																
Medic, black	*Medicago lupulina*					X													
Milkweed	*Asclepius syriaca*												X						
Mosses	*Bryophyta sp.*		X																
Mugwort	*Artemesia vulgaris*				X														
Mullein, common	*Verbascum sp.*				X										X		X		
Mustards	*Brassica sp.*													X	X				
Nettles, stinging	*Urtica urens*	X	X												X				
Pansy, wild	*Viola sp.*														X				
Parsnip, wild	*Sium suave*					X										X			
Peppergrass, field	*Cardaria draba*														X				
Pennycress	*Thlaspi arvense*												X		X				
Pigweed, prostrate	*Amaranthus retroflexus*	X																	
Pigweed, red root	*Amaranthus retroflexus*				X														
Pineapple weed	*Matricaria matricarioides*												X						
Pinks	*Dianthus sp.*					X													
Plantains	*Plantago sp.*	X	X										X		X				
Radish, wild	*Rapranus raphanistrum*				X										X		X		
Ragwort, tansy	*Senecio jacobaea*		X																
Rape	*Brassica hapus*					X													
Rape, bird													X						
Redshank	*Polygonum periscaria*		X																
Robin, ragged			X																
Rose family	*Rosa sp.*					X													
Rushes			X																
Salad burnet	*Poterium sanguisorba*															X			
Salep																X			
Scarlet Pimpernel	*Anagallis arvensis*															X			
Sea Plantain																			X
Sedges	*Cyperaceae sp.*		X																
Shepherd's purse	*Capsella bursa-pastoris*											X							X

continued

continued

SOIL INDICATORS

Common Name	Botanical Name	Dry	Wet	Cultivated/Tilled	Uncultivated/Neglected	Low N	High N	Low K	High K	Low P	High P	Sand	Clay	Hardpan/Crusty	Acid	Alkaline	Low Fertility	High Fertility	Salty
Silverweed			X																
Smartweeds	*Polyogonum scabrum*		X																
Sorrel, garden	*Rumex sp.*		X												X				
Sorrel, sheep	*Rumex acetosella*											X			X				
Sow thistle	*Sonchus arvensis*												X		X				
Speedwell	*Veronica sp.*	X		X															
Spruge, leafy	*Euphorbia esula*	X																	
Spurges	*Euphorbia sp.*			X															
Spurry, corn	*Spergula arvensis*											X			X				
Stinkweed	*Thlaspi arvense*													X		X			
Strawberry, wild	*Fragaria sp.*														X				
Sundews															X				
Thistle, Canada	*Cirsium arvense*												X						
Thistle, nodding	*Carduus nutans*															X			
Thistle, Russian	*Salsola pestifer*	X																	X
Toadflax	*Linaria vulgaris*												X						
Vetches	*Vicia sp.*					X													
Water hemlock, spotted	*Cicuta maculata*		X																
Watercress	*Nasturtium officinale*		X																
Willow, black	*Salix sp.*		X																
Wormwood, biennial	*Artemisia biennis*				X			X									X		
Yarrow	*Achilea millefolium*											X							

Figure 3.12 For sources of information, see footnotes at bottom of Figure 17.4, page 270.

The plants listed in the Cultivated/Tilled column are rapid invaders of freshly aerated soil. Though open soil usually indicates high fertility, remember that there are also heavy, fertile soils. Double-check fertility with other indicators. A tilled soil does not always mean good tilth. For the best indication of tilth, use the columns labeled clay, sand, and hardpan.

Some plant indicators reveal good places to garden. If you see chickweed (*Stellaria media*) on your property, rejoice. It is a very good indicator of loamy, fertile soils.

If there are any severe nutrient deficiencies in your soil, they will be revealed by discolored leaves. I do not often see a yard where the plants show visible symptoms of severe mineral deficiency. In such cases, a soil sample, or a leaf tissue sample, can distinguish the problem. Or simply use plenty of compost and organic matter to amend the soil. Compost is a great buffer. In general, it corrects nutrient deficiencies with less fuss than using a soil test and following its recommendations.

Develop Your Own List

Information based on personal experience often varies considerably from person to person. For example, in my area a local apple grower is almost proud of the red-stem filaree (*Erodium cicutarium*) in his orchard. "It means a rich soil," he says. I believe, however, that filaree is more indicative of tilled or disturbed soils than of fertility. Sarah Kidd, a local expert horticulturist, uses filaree as a *relative* indicator of fertility. In poor soils, filaree grows only a few inches tall, while in rich soils it can be over two feet tall. If you know reliable plant indicators that are not on this list, I would appreciate hearing from you.

pH Analysis

The range of pH tolerance of many food crops is rather narrow, and small changes in the soil will have rather dramatic effects upon which crops will grow well. Since plant indicators may be unreliable in a highly acidic or alkaline setting, use a soil test to check pH for critical crops, especially when growing acid-loving plants such as blueberries, cranberries, potatoes, and tomatoes. You can quickly modify pH with amendments: lime to make soil less acidic and sulfur to reduce alkalinity.

Indicators and Soil-Building Programs

A "weed" problem can often be corrected by applying the correct fertilizer and improving the tilth of the soil. If, for example, you have a lawn full of dandelions, aerating and liming to make the soil less acidic will probably greatly reduce the number of dandelions. As another example, consider broom sedge (*Andropogon virginicus L.*), a common wild grass in farmlands of the East and Southeast. From *An Acres U.S.A. Primer*, we read how management of the soil's nutrients can eliminate a weed problem:

Broom sedge is what it is—a poverty crop for depleted, degenerative soil. It reigns supreme when a soil system has reached a depression of depletion, and stands as a flag waving its signal [of] worn out, burned out, oxidized soil ... without calcium ... How can a farmer get rid of this weed? First it will be necessary to bring the pH back into better equilibrium. The calcium level must be brought up. This will change the hormone and biological processes in the soil. At first these adjustments will do little more than keep the broom sedge seed dormant and allow a better quality weed to grow so that it can return more humus to the soil ... The comeback trail will permit other crops to grow and sustain the repair job at the same time.

Beyond Indicators—Using the Plants That Come with the Property

The plants that naturally inhabit your property have many uses. They may help improve the fertility of your edible landscape. Some can be cut and composted—a good way to gather nutrients from the plants in a large area and concentrate their nutrients in the smaller area of a vegetable plot. (See "Cover Crops—Growing Your Own Fertilizers.") Here are some possibilities.

Potential Use	Examples
Compost material	Stinging nettle, oak leaves, wild sweet peas, lawn clippings, scotch broom, and virtually any green or dead plant tissue except for tenacious

Potential Use	Examples
	plants that spread by underground runners, such as bamboo, crabgrass, Bermuda grass, and quack grass.
Firewood	Clippings and prunings from trees and shrubs.
Edibles	Wild edibles like lamb's-quarters, amaranth, purslane, dock, and many others.
Herb tea/medicine	Plantain for poultices, dandelion as a diuretic, mint teas and burdock as blood tonics, and juniper berries to tone the digestive tract.
Wildlife habitat	Wild cherries and plums, osage orange, cattails, rushes, elderberries, and many weed seeds for birds.
Insectary plants	Wild fennel, California buckwheat, rue, and other plants with small flowers. (See "Attracting Good Bugs.")
Mushrooms, edible	If you have edible mushrooms, save the duff, or natural mulch, where they sprout. Spread some of the duff around elsewhere to inoculate for mushrooms.
Materials	Willow for baskets and wattling, limbs for posts, trunks for edging paths, vines for baskets and other handcrafted items.
Mulch	Leaves, branches, chips from the local tree services; conifer needles and other mulching materials.
Decorations	Pine cones, dried flowers, and seed pods make excellent materials for holiday crafts and flower arrangements.

There are hundreds of uses for the plants that grow all around you. It is good fun to discover as many uses as possible. Don't curse the mess in your backyard; turn it into something useful.

Cocannouer, Joseph. **Weeds: Guardians of the Soil**. New York: Devin-Adair, 1950. One of the few books on the beneficial role of weeds, weeds as indicators of soil fertility, and dynamic accumulators. Much of the information appears to be gleaned from the oral history of farmers, rather than from scientific studies, but it provides a good introduction to the topics.

Pfeiffer, Ehrenfried. **Weeds and What They Tell**. Springfield, IL: BioDynamic Farming and Gardening, n.d. An early reference for weeds as soil indicators. The index and list of plant groups make it is easier to use than Cocannouer's *Weeds: Guardians of the Soil*. Both references are based primarily on folklore.

Rateaver, Bargyla and Gylver. **The Organic Method Primer**. Pauma Valley, CA: Bargyla and Gylver Rateaver, 1973. The first good reference for patterning organic gardening after nature's dynamics. A true classic of organic gardening, though some of the sources remain obscure. Out of print; look for a used copy.

BLENDING AESTHETICS AND FUNCTION

The Origins of Landscape Design

For centuries, only the rich had the time and money to alter natural landscapes solely for sensual pleasure. Their estates opened a split in the history of horticulture—a separation of productive, utilitarian gardens from landscapes for pleasure. Gardens were for the common folk, landscapes for the rich. A French king would have a potted orange tree brought to the table so he could pluck a perfectly ripe orange for breakfast.

The appreciation of paintings and traditional landscapes is similar. Henry Hubbard, a professor of landscape architecture at Harvard, wrote in 1917:

Landscape composition is to the landscape architect, as it is to the landscape painter, the arrangement of the elements of his design into an ordered whole. The success of the landscape designer ... will depend on his skill in combining the shapes and textures and colors at his disposal in a pleasant and orderly fashion. (From *An Introduction to the Study of Landscape Design*)

In fact, many landscapes were designed as a collection or sequence of views, much like a gallery of paintings. The stroller was encouraged to linger at each scenic vista much as one would before paintings in a museum.

Landscape Architecture: An Art Gone Stale

Besides the tradition of landscape-as-painting, which continues to the present, today's landscapers are influenced by the urge to build. The term landscape architect is a recent creation. It reveals the tendency of landscape designers to be more intent on structure and form than on plants and nature. But even before landscape designers became landscape architects, there was a tendency to "architecturalize" and control nature, designing landscapes dominated by structures, not plants.

For one thing, structures are easier to plan than living plants. Lumber and concrete are not as likely to move around, change, or act peculiarly. It is much easier to teach the engineering of objects in the classroom and at the drafting table than to teach the nuances of living plants.

In addition, structures create an immediate effect—people are likely to be impressed. Because plants look best after some time has elapsed, they make a gradual, less visible impact. I have often labored on a job all day, improving the soil and planting. When the homeowners returned, they took little notice of the changes. The full effect takes years. But after a day of brickwork, I have seen homeowners excited about the noticeable change in their landscape.

Finally, structures prevail because they are simpler to design than an arrangement of plants. The myriad needs of plants—for proper climate, soil, light, water, and nutrition, just to name a few elements—add complexity to the design process. If the plants are to be well-adapted to the site and achieve an expected visual impact, much time should be spent choosing the best plants for the situation. Landscape architects who have not worked extensively in the field, that is, with many real plants, apparently find structures more convenient to design.

Making Landscapes Local

Many landscapes ignore the natural environment. There are swimming pools and lawns in the deserts of Arizona, lawns carved out of the lush forest of the Northeast, and tropical, humidity-loving plants in the arid climates of California. Fortunately, many landscape architecture textbooks now stress environmental design, encouraging the designer to match the landscape to its locale. We can hope for the best.

Making Landscapes Personal

Though landscape architecture is a service, designers often succumb to personal fascinations with a particular element or design theme. From my perspective, the worst designers are those who have one narrow style. As a trademark, this may be a distinction, but it usually leads to designs imposed on unsuspecting clients and unsuitable environments. The challenge for the designer is to shape a landscape to match the client's own desires, lifestyle, and budget—while adapting to the environmental context. (Of course, by designing and installing your own personal edible landscape, you can avoid this pitfall.)

Making Landscapes Flexible

Another questionable practice of landscape architecture is the package deal, with the garden treated as a fixed product. I think Hugh Johnson was right when he wrote in *The Principles of Gardening:*

The conventional wisdom of gardening books tells us to make a decision about the lay-out, commit it to paper, and then follow it ... It is a counsel of perfection that few people follow. In the U.S. it is common practice to have the place "landscaped" once and for all, but in Europe most gardens emerge over time.

The best landscapes are constantly evolving. Again from Hugh Johnson:

Without constant watchful care a garden—any garden—rapidly returns to the state of the country round it. It is or ought to be, the gardener's pleasure to be constantly adjusting, correcting, editing.

Landscapes for Living In

Another fault is failing to bring the home and homeowners into contact with nature. The best landscapes encourage one to spend leisure time in them. Without benches, picnic tables, barbecues, feeders and shrubs for wild birds, private areas, or grassy sitting areas, a landscape delights the eye only—it does not promote participation or recreation.

Making Landscapes Useful

A designer preoccupied with composition ignores function. Too many designs neglect, for example, the cooling and sheltering benefit of trees. Landscaping for energy conservation deserves consideration in most designs.

The time has come to correct the bias that food plants are unattractive. Not every landscape should be edible, and not every plant in an edible landscape need be edible. But there are plenty of beautiful ways to incorporate food plants into landscapes. We must welcome food plants back into our homes and our landscapes.

Design as Art, for Beauty and Form

Simon Rodia spent 33 years slowly piecing together the monumental spires now known as the Watts Towers. Each day, Rodia took satisfaction from his craft. To others, the towers became a symbol of the power and vision of an individual breaking conventions to pursue pure, spontaneous art. But Rodia was not an artist. He said, "I had in mind to do something big and I did." Nothing lofty and complex, just a simple personal challenge for a common man.

I shy away from discussions about what constitutes an "artful" landscape. I think everyone can grow their own Watts Tower of an edible landscape. Satisfaction, not high art, should be your goal.

Nonetheless, good landscapes have many similarities. My own designs, done by instinct, often match the guidelines of landscape architecture. I'm a firm believer in intuition and gut feelings, but I also respect the traditional guidelines. Here is my condensation of the classic components and goals of tasteful landscape design.

- **Accent**
  A plant or element of a striking texture, shape, or color used in a limited number so as to stand out from its surroundings.

- **Association**
  Two plants together that produce a noticeable contrast, such as a dark green glossy leaf and a silver-grey leaf.

- **Asymmetry**
  Elements arranged not as mirror reflections of a central point. Important for a more natural-looking landscape.

- **Balance**
  Having the visual weight of one part of a composition matched or countered by another part. The goal is to produce an equilibrium of attention throughout the garden.

- **Color**
  Best used as an accent to increase richness. Can easily detract from composition, unity, and balance. Greatly overused in modern landscapes.

- **Composition**
  The arrangement of all elements, living and structural, into a pleasing presentation. Space is as important as solid form in composition.

- **Density/Mass**
  The apparent bulk or visual weight of an object. A visual "feeling" that is important in achieving balance.

- **Harmony**

  A goal of classical design. The use of repetition for a calm, symmetrical balance. Also emphasizes the commonality of unrelated things.

- **Proportion**

  The relative arrangement or relationship of one part of the composition to another.

- **Repetition**

  The repeated but limited or restrained use of elements with the same interest, density, or scale. The careful recurrence of an object or plant throughout a design enhances a theme and furthers harmony. Can lead to monotony. Can lead to monotony. Can lead to . . .

- **Rhythm**

  Produced by regular breaks in continuity or by recurring accents. Used classically to refer to regular alternations of form, space, light, or color.

- **Richness**

  A certain amount of variety, not to be overdone. A rich landscape is one with depth and nuance. A combination of richness and simplicity is an ideal goal, often unrealized.

- **Scale**

  Elements in proportion with the overall size of the landscape. Useful in revealing perspective.

- **Sequence**

  Elements placed to guide the eye.

- **Simplicity**

  A reduction of nature's diversity to reveal a select beauty. Limiting elements helps to accentuate their distinctive virtues. For me, a paramount and difficult goal.

- **Structure**

  The inanimate framework of the landscape. Composed of rocks, paths, fences, water, trees, buildings, and so on.

- **Symmetry**

  Matching geometry, where both sides of an axis are similar or exactly balanced. A common motif among the formal gardens of Europe.

- **Tension**

  The use of contrasting elements to produce a kind of creative balance of the expected and unexpected. Too much variety or accent generates unproductive tension.

- **Texture**

  An important element for adding richness to compositions. The landscaper has far more options for texture than does the painter or even the sculptor of stone.

- **Unity**

  The synthesis of all elements to reveal a common theme.

- **Variety**

  Commonly overdone. A certain amount of variety furthers harmony between contrast and tension. Too much appears chaotic.

Use this list as a source of ideas, inspiration, and reflection, not as a scorecard for your own landscape. You have years to build a landscape that exhibits the virtues of unity, simplicity, harmony, and balance. It is a goal worth reaching for.

Aesthetics – Wild Versus Proper

Both my grandmothers were avid gardeners, with very different styles. Grandma Kourik clipped and pampered her small, proper garden. Grandma Tevis, a few miles away, but light years away in style, maintained a small lawn bordered by a thicket of herbaceous plants and shrubs. Both gardens were designed while working in the garden, not on paper.

In Grandma Tevis's backyard, the riot of seasonal color seemed to spring forth from a wilderness of natural beauty. Yet she had chosen and placed each plant. I enjoyed the hidden alcoves, the secret enclosure beneath the forsythia bush. Grandma Tevis, who let nature run her course, would say, "I wonder if I'll have any luck with that yellow lily this year."

On the other hand, Grandma Kourik's garden made her intentions visible, displaying color and pattern like a framed painting. I learned about specific plants, their growth habits, and cultural needs in the visible order in her garden. Grandma Kourik struggled with nature. Trying to compensate for weather, she was likely to say, "I planted the pansies three weeks later than last year."

There is no need to argue which is better, for the best style is the one that fits the temperament of the gardener. In fact, these seemingly divergent styles can be combined within one landscape. In planning a landscape, I often place areas that appear wild near more formal plantings. I tend to develop naturalized areas around the perimeters of the landscape, softening the transition from a more stylized form to the edge of the yard. This "moat" of rambunctious shrubbery makes the garden appear as an island separate from nearby yards. Finding tasty, self-sown lettuce seedlings tucked away among a chaotic border is one of the delights of natural landscaping. But highly visible patterns and cycles in a landscape are easiest for beginning gardeners. A formal design simplifies the care and maintenance of annual plantings. The seeding and transplant sequence is more apparent.

I resent the tendency toward a "school of thought" in garden design. I certainly can't outline the best style for you. How the arrangement of plants affects your eye and heart is an exciting discovery. The truest art is a dialogue. The landscape you shape will reveal much of your personality, and the landscape will shape you.

The Aesthetics of Edibles

I will never understand how food plants got labeled as unaesthetic for a landscape. Perhaps people found the rigid rows of a typical vegetable garden unattractive. Yet suburbia is filled with regimented junipers and yews along many a straight wall or drive. And an orderly arrangement of fruit trees is no more geometric than a privet hedge or a formal arbor. Some people dislike the unplanted areas that occur during the year in a vegetable garden. Yet the most classic of English gardens always have bare areas where annual bedding plants are grown for transplanting. As in many vegetable gardens, the annual beds are often mulched for winter. In any event, edibles are beyond argument good-looking.

Low Maintenance

A real concern is fitting a food-producing landscape into our busy lives. In my experience, the single greatest cause for the demise of an edible landscape is the burden it imposes on the homeowner. The amount of effort needed to sustain a landscape or garden is, perhaps, the single most important design consideration. Planting happens quickly, at the peak of the gardener's enthusiasm. Maintenance usually ends up being crammed into busy, everyday life. It is tragic to watch someone's source of joy and wholehearted passion turn into drudgery and become a burden. So often, ambitious gardens that have become too difficult to be properly maintained are neglected, rather than scaled back to a manageable size.

In my enthusiasm to design a landscape that mimicked the forest, I once planted lemon trees slightly beneath a large, evergreen California bay laurel, then planted herbs and ground cover plants under the lemons. I intended to show complex productivity patterned after the multi-layered forest canopy.

The canopy of the bay laurel provided needed frost protection during the winter, but also shaded the lemons. While lemons bear well in considerable shade, I tried to boost the lemon crop by thinning some of the branches of the bay each year. This proved to be a troublesome task that required three people — one person high within the bay to cut limbs, one to carefully lower each limb with a rope, and one to protect the lemon trees from the lowered limbs. During the pruning, the workers had to tiptoe among the plants growing under the citrus. After several seasons of frustrating effort, I now feel the tediousness of pruning far outweighs the benefits of the association of the bay and lemon. However, the problem remained: lemons planted in the open, a mere 20 feet away from the bay laurel, suffer frost damage each winter. To meet the goal of low maintenance, I would now recommend planting dwarf lemon trees along the south wall and under the eaves of the nearby house. They would bear well, be untouched by frost and be easy to maintain.

Some of the most important factors influencing maintenance are the proportion of edible plants in the garden, the size of the garden, and the size of your budget. The question of size will be discussed at length in the next chapter. But first, a discussion of the maintenance of ornamentals versus edibles.

High and Low Maintenance Are Relative Terms

It is inaccurate to say that ornamentals, as a rule, require less maintenance than edibles. For example, cut flowers, both annual and perennial, are very labor intensive. For maximum beauty and production, any dead flowers should be cut away. With Shasta daisies, marguerites, and coreopsis, this is a considerable task. (Still, if you really love the beauty of these flowers, the work is not a burden.) Evergreen shrubs are considered low maintenance plants. Yet, even the juniper requires spraying for bagworms (*Thyridopteryx ephemeraeformis*) in the Midwest and elsewhere. There are edible shrubs and trees that require less spraying for pests than junipers — the quince, papaw, persimmon, strawberry tree, loquat, and pineapple guava are good examples. A common street tree, the London plane sycamore (*Platanus acerifolia*) is prone to a blight (anthracnose) that distorts leaves and covers them with an unsightly white powder. An extensive spraying program is necessary to control the disease. What's more, a sycamore's leaf fall is enormous, demanding lots of raking. By contrast, a pineapple guava (*Feijoa sellowiana*) is an evergreen that can be shaped into a small shade tree. It drops only a few leaves throughout the year. The small, firm fruits don't splatter when they fall, and require little or no cleanup. Virtually free of diseases and pests, the pineapple guava is a good example of an edible that takes less work than an ornamental. (See Fig. 4.5 — avocado and citrus trees, though not necessarily good street trees, also require less maintenance than sycamores.)

In spite of such examples, I can more easily plan a low maintenance ornamental landscape than an edible one, and even the best edible landscapes are still much more effort than the best-planned ornamental ones. Start small with edibles. Each year you can add more area for food production if last year's garden was easy for you to maintain.

Low Effort Edibles

By carefully selecting the edibles you plant, you can greatly reduce your maintenance efforts. Some gardeners will do anything to produce a succulent, tree-ripened apricot. (I do not recommend planting apricots in northern California because they are prone to many serious disease problems there.) An uncommon, but more prudent approach would be to first make choices about effort, and then about taste.

The following is a list of perennial fruits and nuts that are on the low end of the effort scale, provided they are planted where the falling fruits will not need frequent clean-up.

Figure 4.0

Common Name	Botanical Name	*Zone
Strawberry tree	*Arbutus unedo*	8–9
Walnut, black	*Juglans nigra*	3–9
Western sand cherry	*Prunus besseyi*	3–5

*See climate zone maps, Appendix 1.

Figure 4.0

This list should be used as a point of departure. While these plants are likely to escape the ravages of seasonal disease and pestilence, there may be special considerations in your area. Check with local nurseries and landscapers for details.

Invest in Low Maintenance

I'm fond of saying, "You have to spend money to save time and money." I have seen cases where doubling the initial cost has reduced the ongoing maintenance by much more than half. The difficulty with this approach is the savings in effort and time are not initially as tangible as the lighter wallet.

I usually encourage people to spend more money and apply greater effort at the beginning, because I have seen too many edible landscapes crumble under the weight of daily maintenance. Weeds in pathways are a good example. Some people mulch paths to reduce weeds. In my area, sawdust is a common material. But it takes a lot of sawdust to cover a path with a 6-inch layer, and still, the most tenacious weeds pop through. I prefer to lay down strips of discarded or scrap carpet and then cover them with a much thinner layer of sawdust. That way, weeding the paths is virtually eliminated for the first season, less sawdust has to be trucked into the garden, and even more moisture is conserved in the soil. Periodically, I must add sawdust to thin spots to hide the carpet. Some wind-blown seeds sprout in the sawdust, but removal is easy because there is not much for the roots to grab onto. I hate to waste time weeding paths, and this approach eliminates many hours of work. It is time and money well spent.

Sometimes, small details make a big difference. I once installed some vegetable terraces where there previously had been no garden. I argued strongly that summertime watering would attract gophers, but the client did not want the extra cost of putting aviary wire beneath the wooden boxes. By the second year, gophers were so numerous that the client dug out an entire 100-square-foot terrace, 2½ feet deep, put in aviary wire, and refilled it. Hundreds of dollars worth of time were lost to make up for not spending $25 and less than an hour of labor.

Figure 4.0

LOW EFFORT PERENNIAL EDIBLES		
Common Name	**Botanical Name**	***Zone**
Alpine strawberry	*Fragaria alpina semperflorens*	3–10
Beach plum	*Prunus maritima*	5–7
Blueberry	*Vaccinium* sp.	3–9
Carob	*Ceratonia siliqua*	9–10
Chayote	*Sechium edule*	8–10
Chestnut	*Castanea* sp.	5–9
Elderberry	*Sambucus canadensis*	2–9
Fig	*Ficus carica*	8–10
Japanese bush plum	*Prunus japonica*	3–5
Jujube	*Zizyphus jujube*	6–10
Kiwi	*Actinidia chinensis, A. arguta*	9–10 / 6–10
Lemon guava	*Psidium littorale longipes*	10
Loquat	*Eriobotrya japonica*	8–10
Mulberry	*Morus nigra*	5–10
Nanking cherry	*Prunus tomentosa*	3–5
Natal plum	*Carissa grandiflora*	10
Olive	*Olea europaea*	9–10
Papaw	*Asimina triloba*	5–9
Pecan	*Carya illinoiensis*	6–9
Persimmon, American	*D. virginiana*	5–9
Persimmon, Oriental	*Diospyros kaki*	6–10
Pineapple guava	*Feijoa sellowiana*	9–10
Pine nut	*Pinus* sp.	3–10
Pistachio	*Pistacia vera*	7–9
Pomegranate	*Punica granatum*	9–10
Prickly pear	*Opuntia* sp.	5–10
Quince	*Cydonia oblonga*	5–9
Rose hips	*Rosa rugosa*	2–9
Salal	*Gaultheria shallon*	6–9
Sapote	*Casimiroa edulis*	10
Strawberry guava	*Psidium littorale littorale*	10

continued

At times, low maintenance is costly. A couple hired me to install a low maintenance edible landscape in a backyard overrun with Bermuda grass. I had my crew remove the top 6 to 12 inches of soil from most of the area. Then we brought in over 20 cubic yards of topsoil. For the patio area, a layer of plastic was covered with 8 inches of topsoil. Redwood rounds were placed like flagstones and the spaces between planted with clover and thyme. The rest of the yard was covered with 6 inches of topsoil and planted extra dense. The plantings quickly shaded the soil and stunted the regrowth of any Bermuda grass. The clients were very good about touring their landscape weekly to spot and pull the first sprouting shoots of Bermuda grass. Now, five years later, there is still no significant occurence of bermuda grass. Meanwhile, neighboring gardens that were simply weeded and planted less densely are well infested with Bermuda grass. The clients took an expensive approach because it suited them—they wanted no toxic chemicals, few weeds, and a low maintenance edible landscape.

Guidelines for Functional Edible Landscape Design

I think that the best edible landscapes keep maintenance sensibly low by giving a slightly greater priority to function than form. I can explain what I mean in a few guidelines. The first three are often ignored by novices. The remainder are important to consider, though not by any means ironclad rules.

Streamline Your Landscape.

Not every plant need be edible. In my experience, it is best to have no more than 50 percent of the perennial plants be edibles, and no more than 50 percent of the whole yard planted to edibles (unless it is smaller than 2,400 square feet). It takes an exceptional person, or special circumstances, to make a success of a landscape that is bigger than 1,200 square feet and almost 100 percent edible. If your yard is greater than 2,400 square feet, you should consider planting as much as 80 percent of the area in wildflower meadow and very carefree, ornamental shrubs, which are low maintenance alternatives to lawns.

Plan to have your vegetables very close to the kitchen.

For many gardeners, the first instinct is to put the vegetables "way out back," but the farther they are from the kitchen, the sooner you will tire of running out to get a salad for supper, and the sooner you will neglect the garden. You don't have to hide the vegetables—edible landscaping looks pleasing.

Keep the vegetable area small at first.

While fruit and nut trees are an important part of any edible landscape, the most frequently used and nutritionally important foods are vegetables. Start small, and lay out an area of only 100 square feet for the first year's garden. For a family of four, leave room in the plans for the area to grow to 600 square feet.

Make the central vegetable area rectangular.

A rectangle uses garden space efficiently and is the best shape for watering by hose and sprinkler. (The paths around a rectangle can be curved to soften the transition to less formal plantings.) If you use drip irrigation, other shapes can be considered. But remember that odd-shaped beds and paths are more tedious to care for. Curves are pretty, but straight paths help get the job done.

Plan the garden in blocks of 100 square feet. This makes it easy to calculate the amount of fertilizers needed—recommendations are usually listed in pounds per 100 square feet. For intensive beds of vegetables, make the beds no more than 4 feet wide. Shorter people will need to limit the width to 3 or 3½ feet. Beds that are too wide stress the lower back.

At first, choose low care plants.

Consider a common requirement in an ornamental landscape – ground cover plantings. Periwinkle (*Vinca* sp.) is a vigorous, easily established ground cover, but it is invasive and must be controlled by weeding. As a ground cover, strawberries should not be given as large an area as periwinkle. They take more water, fertilizer, and effort for good fruiting and a similar amount of effort to control spreading. The Alpine strawberry, also called *fraises des bois* by the French, may be planted in a bigger area than either periwinkle or regular strawberries. It grows in clumps that do not make troublesome runners. As a ground cover it still requires more water and fertilizer than periwinkle, but less maintenance. It is a good edible to start with.

Place herbs and perennial flowers near, but not in, the vegetable beds.

Perennial herbs and flowers should be grouped by similar water and fertilizer needs and planted in their own beds or borders, not randomly within the main vegetable plantings. Growing perennial plants with annual vegetables usually makes the maintenance more difficult. It is especially awkward to turn the soil for a new planting.

Though there are plants that have a beneficial effect on each other, there is rarely any reason for these so-called companion plants to be close together. Most of the helpful influence of flowers and herbs lies in their ability to attract beneficial insects, so these plants can be many feet away from the vegetable garden and still have a positive impact.

Plant fruit and nut trees in clusters of similar kinds.

Grouping fruit trees according to similar needs for water, fertilizer, and sprays simplifies their care. When peaches, for example, are scattered throughout the landscape it makes spraying for peach leaf curl more of a chore. Peaches require much more water and fertilizer than apples for healthy yields. If the two are interplanted, the apples are likely to grow more spindly and be more prone to pests because of the fertilizer and water given to the peaches.

Where possible, place fruit and nut trees at least four times their mature height away from the perimeter of the vegetable area so that their roots do not invade the vegetable beds. The trees can become weakened or diseased by the quantities of water and fertilizer needed to keep vegetables happy.

Make it compact.

The less distance you have to walk, the easier it is to manage your edible landscape. Compact plantings mean more variety in less area and less running around to care for everything. Use as many dwarf and miniature (genetic dwarf) fruit trees as possible. Not only are they easier to prune and harvest, but they take less space than full-size trees, letting you grow more types in a smaller area.

There are more compact vegetable varieties available every year. Now you can buy more than half a dozen types of winter squashes in a bush or semi-bush form. A number of tomato varieties are compact enough to grow in containers. Cucumbers also come in bush form, needing only one-third the usual garden space and no trellises.

Plan as many permanent paths as possible.

Permanent paths are vital in reducing maintenance. Note, however, that you must plan your landscape with forethought to avoid having to tear them out one day. Make the paths 2½ to 3 feet wide for easy wheelbarrow access. This is especially helpful for applying manure or compost and for harvesting. Use carpet covered by gravel or weed-free mulch, masonry, cobblestones, cement, mowed perennial clovers, or whatever cheap material you can find.

Use only ornamentals for multiple layered plantings.

The effect of many different types of foliage at three or four levels, grouped in the same planting, is quite striking, but edibles are usually too difficult to care for and harvest in such plantings.

Figure 4.1 shows one of my plantings. Because it is very narrow, only as wide as the genetic dwarf fruit tree, it is easy to harvest. Were I to plant more trees, I would need to make the clover patch near the plum tree and between the genetic dwarfs much wider in order to harvest without stepping on plants. If you want to have several sizes of fruit or nut trees growing near each other, make sure there is space for walking between each.

Use gravity to your advantage.

Gravity is a free and continuous source of energy—use it wisely and save your back. Where the ground is sloped, always move heavy objects downhill. Store topsoil and the raw materials for compost uphill from their eventual place of use. It is much easier to bring the produce of the edible landscape uphill than the raw materials. If it is not possible to store the heaviest objects uphill, then try to place them so they can be moved horizontally across the slope to their destination.

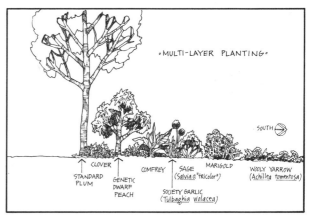

Figure 4.1 In a multi-layer planting, make paths between edibles for easier care and harvesting.

Alexander, Christopher; Ishikawa, Sara; and Silverstein, Murray. **A Pattern Language.** New York: Oxford University Press, 1977. This remarkable (and expensive) book is a must for designers, landscapers, and landscape architects. My favorite source of inspiration for composing more complex, creative landscape designs.

Clouston, Brian. **Landscape Design With Plants**. New York: Van Nostrand Reinhold, 1979. This hefty manual on the English approach to landscape design offers many photos of quality landscapes. One of the few books to give mathematical guidelines for the layout of flower borders, ground covers, shrubs, and trees.

Creasy, Rosalind. **The Complete Book of Edible Landscaping**. San Francisco: Sierra Club Books, 1982. The "other" edible landscaping book, by a good friend and collaborator. The plant encyclopedia section is an essential reference. The prerequisite, and perfect companion, to my book!

Creasy, Rosalind. **Earthly Delights**. San Francisco: Sierra Club Books, 1985. The newest release by the author of *The Complete Book of Edible Landscaping*. Covers a variety of gardens, from orchid collections to wildflower meadows, with examples of how to garden with an ecological perspective. There are three "edible" chapters: The Heirloom Vegetable Garden, The Gourmet Garden, and The Cottage Garden.

Damrosch, Barbara. **Theme Gardens**. New York: Workman Publishing, 1982. The helpful lists of plants appropriate for each theme make it a favorite for design inspiration. Not oriented toward edibles, but useful for choosing plants for visual pleasure.

Garland, Sarah. **The Herb Garden**. New York: Viking Penguin, 1984. My favorite book for ideas on using herbs in the landscape. Beautiful color photos cover the full range of styles, from classical knot gardens to wild, rambling plantings. Includes an excellent cultural encyclopedia that lists uses of the herbs.

Gessert, Kate. **The Beautiful Food Garden: The Encyclopedia of Attractive Food Plants**. New York: Van Nostrand, 1983. Primarily an encyclopedia of the "most attractive" edible annual vegetables and flowers, based on a limited, informal survey. Ignores the extent to which "most attractive" is based on personal taste. The chapter on bubble drawings and master planning strategies is one of the best descriptions in print of this important step in the design process. Review all the chapters on design before you begin your own. Out of print.

Johnson, Hugh. **The Principles of Gardening**. New York: Simon and Schuster, 1979. A well-designed, colorful book with lots of visual inspiration and step-by-step details on installation. Not much about edibles, but excellent for overall landscape design. While some examples are of aristocratic English gardens, many of the designs can be duplicated by the industrious home gardener.

Larkcom, Joy. **The Salad Garden**. New York: Viking Press, 1984. The best book on gardening with colorful, gourmet vegetables. Exquisite color photographs of gardens as well as a color close-up of each edible mentioned. A fair amount of space is given to edible weeds, edible flowers, and unusual leafy greens. Good cultural information. A book to buy.

Lathrop, Norma Jean. **Herbs — How to Select, Grow and Enjoy**. Tucson, AZ: HPBooks, 1981. Shows several herb farms and both formal and informal ways to design her-bal plantings. A mini-encyclopedia gives a good general overview of the cultural needs of herbs. The recipe section includes instructions for herbal vinegars, beauty aids, and wreaths.

Lees-Milne, Alvilde, and Verey, Rosemary. **The Englishwoman's Garden**. London: Chatto and Windus, 1983. As this book shows, the role and accomplishments of women in landscape architecture is vastly underrated. The English landscapes shown are very classic, with an aristocratic overtone. The color plates are not as vibrant as the ones in Verey and Samuel's *The American Woman's Garden*. See a copy in your library.

Podens, Marc, and Bortz, Brenda. **Ornamentals for Eating**. Emmaus, PA: Rodale Press, 1975. An obscure, out-of-print booklet that was one of the first to note the ornamental value of edible perennials. Emphasizes native edible shrubs and trees, and unusual tropical tree crops.

Rose, Graham. **The Low-Maintenance Garden**. New York: Viking Press, 1983. This good book on an often-neglected subject includes a mini-encyclopedia, labor-saving designs, and tips on techniques.

Stevenson, Violet. **The Wild Garden**. New York: Viking Press, 1985. Excellent coverage of gardens that are more rough-and-tumble, though most still appear designed and cultivated. Covers heath, fern, herb, water, and rock gardens, and wildflower meadows and woodlands. Superb color.

Tilth. **The Future is Abundant**. Arlington, WA: Tilth, 1982. An excellent reference for people interested in permaculture designs and theories, edible landscaping, and sustainable agriculture. A good collection of bibliographies, seed and plant sources, addresses of like-minded people, and short summaries of alternative gardening and farming techniques. The best feature is a 300-species index of edible and useful plants for the Pacific Northwest — every region needs an index like this one. Out of print.

Verey, Rosemary, and Samuels, Ellen. **The American Woman's Garden**. Boston, MA: New York Graphic Society, 1984. The important contributions that women have made to landscape architecture and horticulture are probably more neglected in the U.S. than in Europe. An inspiring display of 15 exceptional landscapes designed by American women, with better color plates than Lees-Milne and Verey's *The Englishwoman's Garden*.

Wilkinson, Elizabeth, and Henderson, Marjorie, eds. **The House of Boughs**. Covelo, CA: Yolla Bolly Press, 1985. My favorite collection of visual inspirations for designing garden and landscape structures — from pathways and arbors to ponds and rock grottos. Unlike similar books from England, there is no tedious text about the history of some chalet or castle, and most examples are more applicable to the home landscape.

DEFINING AND PLANNING YOUR GOALS

Beginner's Excitement

Over the years, my toughest challenge as a consultant and instructor has been to temper the beginning gardener's enthusiasm without suppressing his or her spirit. All beginners are propelled by a great sense of wonder and excitement. Unfortunately, this excitement often wanes—for some, just as the first seedling is eaten by a gopher; for others, after the second year of muscling an enormous tiller through the garden. Untempered enthusiasm can lead to a landscape too complex or too big to be sustained and nurtured throughout the season. When the results fall short of the gardener's expectations, frustration sets in. A feeling that you are the servant of your landscape turns normally rewarding tasks such as sprinkling and transplanting in chores. After a busy day at work, no one needs an onerous responsibility waiting at home.

Planning makes it possible to nestle the garden into your daily routine. And planning is especially important if you are trying to greatly increase the self-reliance of your home and provide a measure of food security for your family. If planning is a word that scares you, relax. There will be many seasons for experimenting. With each seasonal attempt at planning, my garden and I develop a more harmonious relationship. So will yours.

Planning with a Winning Attitude

For me, the creative aspect of planning is finding workable compromises. Parts of your design may seem at odds with each other, but you can find a way for them to work together.

Consider the edible landscape I designed for the Kelleys. The site was steep. John Kelley could not negotiate stairs very well because of poor blood circulation. At first the slope looked too difficult for John to garden.

I saw that, with careful grading, I could make sloped pathways that would be easier than steps for John. And I took advantage of the slope by building raised, boxed beds so John would not have to bend over to harvest small vegetables such as lettuce, or to plant seeds, and so he could harvest tall crops such as corn and tomatoes by walking along the path above each bed. John's edible landscape proved to be almost as easy to walk in as a flat garden, yet far more useful and comfortable for harvesting and seeding.

Consider the difficulty of fitting vining winter squashes into a tiny edible landscape. These rambunctious plants often cover 200 square feet or more of valuable garden space when left to ramble.

I make the squash plants do more for me than just grow squashes, or I find out-of-the-way places to turn them loose. I trellis them near west walls to keep the house cooler in the summer, or grow them up trees, over carports, into vacant lots, and along the fence for extra privacy. Try to turn limitations into virtues. Take an anticipated problem and turn it inside-out.

Priorities and Realities

There is never enough room or time for me to include all the things I would like in my edible landscape. I compromise between passion and practicality, dreams and reality—I find the deeper passions and weave them together with the realities of budget, time, and property. I encourage you to do the same at the start. First, list your landscaping desires and dreams, from the most important to the least. Examples are:

- We want a safe, clean path from the carport to the house.

- I have a passion for vine ripened tomatoes, we must grow them at any cost.

- We want to freeze plenty of pesto made with fresh basil.

- The fragrance of honeysuckle is a favorite.

- An automated watering system is our idea of practical convenience.

Now list the limitations or realities. The largest constraints are generally money, time, and skill. Include any limitations revealed when surveying your property. Your list might read as follows:

- I have a black thumb, even ivy wilts in my presence.

- If that low spot in the back yard were a little deeper we'd have a free swimming pool.

- The kids hate carrots.

- Our neighbor's garage sure casts a long shadow where the soil is best for vegetables.

- We have only four hours each weekend to work together in the garden.

- The path from the carport to the house would be a great place for mud wrestling.

- I feel like a klutz with a tiller.

- I hate sprinkling by hand.

- Pruning makes as much sense to me as international economics.

Now comes the difficult part—figuring out which items on the wish list are within grasp. Refer to the list of limitations to make sure your strongest desires are not curtailed by any strong constraints. You may have to put this list aside many times, reflect upon it, and return to adjust the priorities.

I love to prune. For me, a large number of fruit trees is no problem. The situation might be very different for you. Mull over your constraints. Get the family involved and make a party out of it. Above all, give yourself the option to change your mind and revise your list of priorities each year.

The Path of Decision Making: Working Toward Goals

Start with a single goal. (I generally wrestle with the toughest part of the design, or the greatest constraint, first. For me, this makes the rest of the design process much easier, especially since I will not have to re-work decisions made earlier that later create conflicts.) Say you have decided a path from the carport to the house is a top priority. The best paths are based on the most natural patterns of movement. The existing, muddy path is probably the best route. The usual next question is: "Will the path be a permanent one of brick or concrete, or a path easily adapted to change, one made of mulch or sod?" Examine the attributes of each major choice.

Paths

Fixed/Permanent	Flexible/Seasonal
• Looks more like landscape architecture	• Looks more like a corn patch
• Limits compaction of soil	• Encourages compaction around crops
• Requires a long-range plan; not easily changed	• Easily changed
• More costly, more effort	• Low cost and effort
• Lowest ongoing maintenance	• Higher maintenance
• Less likely to grow weeds	• Prone to grow weeds
• Increases property value	• No effect on property
• Able to take lots of traffic/abuse	• Best for light traffic
• Can be considered more beautiful	• Can be considered unaesthetic

Next comes the choice between straight and curved paths. I avoid straight paths except in the primary vegetable bed area. Otherwise, I use them only when the site allows for no other option or when efficiency of movement is essential. I see too many rigid lines in our subdivisions and towns; I would rather use curves to soften the edges and calm the eye. The design manual *Pattern Language* says: "Most every landscape will utilize both rigid and curved lines, each suited to a particular need." Meandering paths encourage relaxation and serenity, while a straight line may be best to connect two points of high activity, such as a carport and a front door.

Straight	Curved
• Uses less material	• Uses more material
• More direct and efficient for frequent travel	• Less direct and more relaxing
• Continues many straight architectural lines	• Counterbalances or softens rigid lines
• Forthright, linear	• Subtle, graceful
• Easier, less costly to construct	• More difficult, more costly to construct

Another choice is the width of the path. Be sure to consider the following questions. Is it to be used for a footpath only or for wheelbarrows too? for occasional use or frequent use? for leisure or for ease of production? for one person or for several walking side by side? for gathering, for access, or for traffic? If you want the minimum room for walking between vegetable beds, you need only a 1-foot-wide pathway. If you want to accommodate a wheelbarrow, you need 2½ to 3 feet. Wheelchair-accessible gardens need paths that are at least 3 feet wide with firm surfaces and grades of no more than 1:12 (a 1-foot rise in 12 feet of length). For two people to walk side by side, provide at least 4½ feet. For a soothing visual touch, make the path wider as it reaches its goal; this takes more material, but the walker feels invited.

Finally, choose the material.

Cheap Paths	Costly Paths
• Dirt	• Bricks in sand
• Grass or clover sod	• Bricks in mortar
• Mulched, straw or wood chips	• Poured concrete
• Carpet covered with wood chips	• Flagstone
• Soil-crete, stabilized soil	• Slate
• Crushed rock	• Cobblestone
• Sawdust	• Railroad ties
• Broken concrete "flagstone"	• Wood
• Sand	• Asphalt
• Wooden rounds	• Marble

Fixed, or permanent, paths are the most costly, but the easiest to maintain. They can be enchanting – for example, well-spaced log rounds or flagstones with plants between them. Figure 4.2 in the color plates shows how warm and inviting such a surface can be. Quality costs money, but money spent at the beginning for good looking and low maintenance pathways will be an asset for years to come.

As with paths, so with each aspect of an edible landscape. Once you define a goal in detail, outline the steps to realize it, and list the costs in time and money.

Sizing Your Landscape

First, do not get carried away with self-reliance. We are not islands unto ourselves. It is unreasonable to expect to grow all your food and hold down a full-time job at the same time.

Second, find out what is available free or cheap in your neighborhood. Most neighborhoods have a vast supply of unused food going to waste. On the campus of a local junior college, I once found five chestnut trees, planted long ago as part of an old estate. Early each morning in the fall, I would stroll beneath the chestnuts and gather 2 to 5 pounds of nuts. Recently, in a nearby backyard, I found a few trees with more nuts than the homeowners can possibly eat themselves. All this saves me time and a lot of garden space. Chestnut trees become enormous—up to 80 feet high and just as wide. It is difficult to squeeze such a large tree into most yards and still have room for sun-loving vegetables.

Harvesting wild edible weeds is another way to garden less. I gather stinging nettle from wild places near my home, and mushrooms and chickweed from a neighbor's backyard.

Third, share some fruit trees with your neighbors. In our county there are hundreds of acres of neglected orchards (waiting to sprout houses). The owners are often glad to have someone care for a few trees, which will yield plenty of fruit. If the neighborhood has no apricot or lime tree, plant one in your yard—perhaps you will be able to swap the fruit for types you don't have.

Sizing for Vegetables

Although you may choose to integrate edible plants throughout your edible landscape, it is useful in the planning stages to consider how much total area should be devoted to edibles. A good study of the average size of American gardens was done by the Harris Poll for Gardens for All (180 Flynn Ave., Burlington, VT 05401). You and I are not average, but the study has its uses, nevertheless. During the past three years the average area for a household vegetable garden has been between 500 and 600 square feet. These figures are for the 10 most popular vegetables, which are, in order of preference, tomatoes, peppers, green beans, cucumbers, onions, lettuce, summer squashes, carrots, radishes, and corn.

The average garden may be larger than necessary. It is sometimes surprising to beginners how

little space it takes to grow plenty of vegetables. The Kelleys used to live on a 500-acre ranch. When they bought a house in town, they found it hard to believe that 300 square feet of vegetable beds would satisfy their fresh vegetable needs. I stuck firm to my recommendation and refused to scale it up to 400 square feet. The vegetable beds in their edible landscape were well-amended, heavily fertilized, and intensively planted. By the end of the first season they were eating quantities of fresh vegetables and still could not give away all the extra produce. The following season, they planted each bed less densely.

Another possibility is to size your garden with a list of your family's favorite foods. From Fig. 4.3 (published by the Institute for Local Self-Reliance), you can calculate the space needed to grow what the average person consumes. This chart is based on U.S.D.A. information and conventional vegetable gardening.

Technique Affects Size

However you try to size your garden, take into account the way growing techniques affect the room you need. No-till gardening (see "Growing Vegetables") requires very little effort, but a large area because of the lower yields. Using a tiller for soil preparation and for weed control between each row of plants requires an even larger area. On the other hand, methods that require "elbow grease" are often highly productive in a small area. The highest yields per area result from the biodynamic/French intensive method, described in John Jeavons's book *How to Grow More Vegetables*. Jeavons lists the yields that may be obtained by gardeners of different experience: for tomatoes, a beginner could expect to grow 100 pounds per square foot of garden space; an intermediate, 194 pounds, and an advanced gardener, 418 pounds. If you are just starting out, your yields will just approach the lower figure. Even with a great deal of experience, it is hard to get the yields that Jeavons lists, and then only after a number of years of soil development. The fertility of your soil influences the size of your vegetable beds. The poorer your soil, the lower your yields will be and the more area you will need to have plenty of food.

Water equals yields, up to a point. If you are not going to water, you need more room. Irrigated gardens and landscapes, where no dry spells check the growth, usually out-perform unirrigated plots. In much of North America the summer rains are frequent enough to sustain vegetables without extra watering, but yields will be less per square foot of surface area.

AREA FOR FRESH VEGETABLES

Crop	Consumption (lbs./person/year)	Yield/10 sq. ft. (pounds)	Area Needed (sq. ft.)
Potatoes	55	6.7	82
Lettuce	23.5	11.6	20
Melons	21.8	3.5	62
Tomatoes	12.5	6.7	19
Onions	9.3	12.8	7
Cabbage	9	7.5	12
Corn	7.9	4	20
Celery	7.7	11	7
Carrots	6.9	15	5
Cucumbers	3.1	2.8	11
Peppers	2.8	4	7
Beans	1.8	7.5	2
Other brassicas	1.3	4	3
Other leafy vegetables	.6	6	1
Other misc.	10.6	4.2	25
TOTAL	**173.8**		**283**

AREA FOR PROCESSED VEGETABLES

Crop	Consumption (lbs./person/year)	Yield/10 sq. ft. (pounds)	Area Needed (sq. ft.)
Potatoes	62	6.7	93
Tomatoes	56.2	6.7	84
Corn	21.6	4	54
Peas	12.5	3.3	38
Beans	7	7.5	9
Cucumbers	6	2.8	21
Sweet potatoes	5.3	3.1	17
Brassicas	4.6	5.8	8
Root crops	3.8	15	3
Other misc.	10.1	3.4	30
TOTAL	**189.1**		**357**
FRESH VEGETABLES			**283**
GRAND TOTAL			**640 sq. ft.**

Adapted from *Gardening for Health*, a poster copyrighted by and available from the Institute for Self-Reliance, 1717 18th St. NW, Washington DC 20009. Enclose $3.25 for poster and handling.

Figure 4.3 Your consumption of vegetables may vary considerably from the national averages. (According to this chart, my yearly use of onions is equal to that of a small town!)

Some for the Bugs

Pests and disease influence yields. For the sake of my mental health, I always anticipate sacrificing 10 to 20 percent of my produce to the critters. By planting an area a little larger than I need, I can allow a share to bugs, gophers, birds, and disease, and avoid time-consuming pest controls.

For Fruits and Nuts

Sizing a mini-orchard is more chancy. The yields of tree crops, berries, and vines are dependent on soil texture and structure, pruning style, and watering and fertilization rates. With vegetables it is almost unthinkable not to water and fertilize, but there are tree crops that can survive and bear without watering and fertilizing, although the yields will be greatly reduced. In my area, unirrigated apple orchards yield two-thirds less than those with supplemental watering. (Where it rains in the summer, the difference would not be as great.) The heavier the soil, the lower the yields. Regular winter pruning usually encourages more leafy growth and less fruit production. Too much nitrogen fertilizer has much the same result. Keep all this variability in mind as you check the range of production for different types of fruit trees, berries, and vines in Fig. 4.4. Notice how quickly a few trees and vines can produce more fruit than you can eat.

To avoid a crop surplus, and the labor of canning and freezing, you can plant a number of trees, each for a different time of ripening. It is possible to eat ripe apples over a period of six months (in my area, as much as nine months). There are apples and pears that can be stored for an additional two to three months by simply wrapping them in newspaper and storing them in a cool, dry place. Using dwarf trees also helps limit the crop—reducing the pounds of fruit per tree to a more manageable amount, and also reducing the effort required to care for the extra number of trees.

Plan for the weather to ruin a percentage of each year's fruit. In spring, some blossoms and young fruit will be lost to frost, wind, and rain damage. In summer, hail can destroy fruit. Planting trees that bloom and ripen in sequence partially protects you from erratic weather. To get a peach crop every year in my climate, I recommend planting at least four types of peach trees (five is even safer). My father lives in St. Louis, where cold winters and erratic spring weather often ruins his peach crop. The 1984 winter saw temperatures so low that the fruit buds on the dormant peach trees died. Apples bloom much later than peaches, so fewer trees are needed to ensure a crop. What you learned from older neighbors about the local climate's eccentricities should have a part in deciding which fruit and nut trees to plant.

Make careful decisions about fruit and nut trees, or you may soon have a small orchard that is a burden to care for. See "Genetic Dwarf (Miniature) Fruit and Nut Trees" to learn how to get the most fruit with the least effort.

Figure 4.4

THE YIELDS OF FRUIT AND NUT TREES, VINES, AND SHRUBS

Crop	Yield
ALMOND	2.8 lbs. per 100 sq. ft.[1]
APPLE	
Dwarf	6 lbs. per tree[4]
	54.1 lbs. per 100 sq. ft.[1]
	100–300 lbs. per tree[3]
	on EM 9, 45–65 lbs. per tree[5]
	on EM 7, 47 lbs. per tree[5]
	on EM 26, 75 lbs. per tree[5]
Semi-Dwarf	54.1 lbs. per 100 sq. ft.[1]
	25 lbs. per tree[6]
	30–50 lbs. per tree[7]
	100 lbs. per tree[6]
	60–120 lbs. per tree[7]
	on MM 111, 175 lbs. per tree[5]
	on MM 106, 42 lbs. per tree[5]
Standard	54.1 lbs. per 100 sq. ft.[1]
	25 lbs. per tree[4]
	40 lbs. per tree[6]
	100–400 lbs. per tree[7]
	220–257 lbs. per tree[5]
APRICOT	
Dwarf	24.3 lbs. per 100 sq. ft.[1]
Semi-Dwarf	24.3 lbs. per 100 sq. ft.[1]
Standard	24.3 lbs. per 100 sq. ft.[1]
	30–120 lbs. per tree[7]
BLACKBERRY	23.8 lbs. per 100 sq. ft.[1]
	10–30 lbs. per plant[7]
CHERRY	
Dwarf	16.5 lbs. per 100 sq. ft.[1]
	30–40 lbs. per tree[7]
Standard	16.5 lbs. per 100 sq. ft.[1]
	100 lbs. per tree[6]
	30–120 lbs. per tree[7]
CHESTNUT	400 lbs. per tree[2]
CURRANT	10–12 lbs. per bush[7]
FIG	11.9 lbs. per 100 sq. ft.[1]
	15–20 lbs. per tree[7]
GRAPE	37.6 lbs. per 100 sq. ft.[1]
LEMON	74.6 lbs. per 100 sq. ft.[1]
NECTARINE	39.9 lbs. per 100 sq. ft.[1]
QUINCE	50 lbs. per tree[6]
PEACH	
Miniature	14–31 lbs. per tree[8]
Dwarf	60.1 lbs. per 100 sq. ft.[1]
	30–60 lbs. per tree[7]
	3–4 bushels per tree[9]
Standard	38–60.1 lbs. per 100 sq. ft.[1]
	30–120 lbs. per tree[7]
	200 lbs. per tree[6]
PEAR	
Dwarf	35.8 lbs. per 100 sq. ft.[1]
	6 lbs. per tree[4]
	25 lbs. per tree[6]
	40–120 lbs. per tree[7]

continued

Crop	Yield
Standard	35.8 lbs. per 100 sq. ft.[1]
	25 lbs. per tree[4]
	150 lbs. per tree[6]
	80–240 lbs. per tree[7]
PLUM	
Dwarf	30–60 lbs. per tree[7]
Standard	11.4–19.2 lbs. per 100 sq. ft.[1]
	100 lbs. per tree[6]
	30–120 lbs. per tree[7]
RASPBERRY	12.3 lbs. per 100 sq. ft.[1]
	1.5 lbs. per foot of row[7]
STRAWBERRY	16.7 lbs. per 100 sq. ft.[1]
	8–10 oz. per plant[7]
WALNUT	4.7 lbs. per 100 sq. ft.[1]

[1] Jeavons, John. *How to Grow More Vegetables*. Berkeley, CA: Ten Speed Press, 1982.

[2] Dave Wilson Nursery. *Catalog* (out of print).

[3] Kraft, Pat and Ken. *Grow Your Own Dwarf Fruit Trees*. New York, NY: Walker Publishing, 1974.

[4] Seymour, John. *The Self-Sufficient Gardener*. Garden City, NY: Doubleday Books, 1978. (Data is from England.)

[5] Tukey, Harold. *Dwarfed Fruit Trees*. Ithaca, NY: Comstock Publishing, 1964.

[6] Rodale, J.I. *How to Grow Vegetables and Fruits by the Organic Method*. Emmaus, PA: Rodale Press, 1961.

[7] Baker, Harry. *Fruit*. New York, NY: Simon and Schuster, 1980. (Data is from England.)

[8] Hansche, Hesse, Beutel, Beres, and Doyle, R. "The Commercial Potential of Dwarf Fruit Trees," *California Agriculture*. September, 1979.

[9] Stark Bros. Nursery. *Bear Facts*. Vol. 4, No. 9.

Figure 4.4

For Flowers and Herbs

Though herbs cost dearly in the store, it does not take very many plants to satisfy the seasoning needs of a family. For most herbs, a single plant is plenty for the first year. Among the exceptions are basil, garlic, onions, dill (for pickling), and scallions, which tend to be used in large quantities.

Flower beds are a wonderful addition to any edible landscape. To be kept up properly, however, they require a lot of time for "dead-heading"—cutting out the withered flowers so that more will form and so that the bed will continue to look beautiful. The time required for this is easy to underestimate. I once spent more than five hours cutting out the dead flowers in a 4-foot-by-20-foot bed of calendulas. It was relaxing work, but two weeks later the bed looked unkempt again. Keep plantings small. Just a few of your favorite perennials will provide plenty of cut flowers. Some flowers—such as anemones, hyacinths, gladiolas, daffodils, lilies, yarrows, delphiniums, asters, Dutch iris, and foxglove—you can plant in quantity, since they usually produce only one spike of flowers per plant and are easier to care for. Some annual flowers—such as petunias, zinnias, marigolds, and snapdragons—bloom so prolifically that dead-heading can be ignored or put off. Also, by planting small patches in succession, you can ensure a blaze of color without as much dead-heading effort.

Cost

Supermarket food is really cheaper than it seems at the checkout stand. While growing some of your own food can save you money at the market, a hard-nosed look at all the real costs of an edible landcape may show that purchasing food at the grocery store is cheaper than growing it. There are real expenses to an edible landscape – topsoil, soil amendments, plumbing for irrigation, structural improvements, fencing, tools, seeds, water, and your valuable time. If your main interest is in saving money, then keep it simple and fast – just dig up a plot of dirt, plant some seeds in rows, water, harvest, and eat.

Spend Money to Save Time

Since I believe you often have to spend money to save money and time, I encourage gardeners not to skimp on the start-up costs of an edible landscape. As a small example, consider the Gardena series of speed couplings for hoses. This watering system does away with the tedious and time-consuming effort of twisting each threaded hose fitting on and off. The system uses "click on" fittings. I wouldn't be without them. The speed hose connector is $2.20, and a tap, or accessory, connector is $1.10 for each accessory. The initial cost of these parts may seem high if you have more than several hose bibs and sprinklers. But the time saved over the season, because of the ease of moving hoses around, is considerable.

One of the highest initial costs for installing my designs is topsoil or amendments and fertilizers. I believe in extensive soil preparation before planting. A healthy and fertile soil is the foundation for good growth and low maintenance. One maintenance job I took, after another landscaper had finished the installation, had a hedge of English laurel (*Prunus laurocerasus*) that needed monthly spraying for shot-hole fungus. I spent four years improving the soil from the top down. Finally, the client remarked how nice it was to have a healthy hedge that rarely required spraying. Had the client initially undertaken the expense of soil preparation, the hedge would have been healthy from the beginning and, overall, a lot of money would have been saved.

Time

Time is definitely a non-renewable resource, to be treasured and used wisely, but if you are like me, it seems to be of no concern in the midst of gardening. But as a landscaper, I had to keep track of time in order to get paid, to stay within the client's budget, and to develop layouts, techniques, and strategies that save time for the client. For beginning gardeners I recommend the formula: It will take two to four times longer than expected and cost two to three times more than anticipated.

Save Time with Ornamentals

One way to save time is to use as many low maintenance ornamentals as possible. Most edibles demand more time to look truly spectacular than the lowest maintenance ornamentals. Figure 4.5 shows the range of time required to keep up 100 square feet of different types of ground covers, shrubs, and trees.

This kind of information is very difficult to find. The best way to find out about the maintenance time required for specific plants is to talk to local landscapers. Though skill and speed differ from one person to the next, an estimate is more helpful than just guessing.

Another way of adding color to your landscape without subtracting time from your maintenance schedule is to plant evergreen perennials that have interesting and colorful foliage. Some of my favorite plants are the silver, steel-blue, and grey-green perennials. Many require only a single shearing for dead flowers and a once-a-year shearing for shape.

Time for Edibles

Keep the edibles in small compact plantings to reduce the effort of cultivation. The Kelleys' edible landscape (see Fig. 4.6 in color plates) is the most time-saving and productive design I have done. After the project was installed, the amount of time spent on care, transplanting vegetables (most transplants were purchased), and planting some new flower borders and an occasional fruit tree, averaged only five to six hours per week. That is not much, especially considering the surplus of food that poured from the garden. This total does not include watering, but drip irrigation for the trees and perennials and oscillating sprinklers for the vegetables did much of the work.

John Jeavons is one of the few people who keep

detailed records of the time required to cultivate a garden. His recommendation is to allow for 6 to 12 hours for the first-time cultivation of each 100 square feet of biointensive bed. The next time will take you only 4 to 6 hours because of the improved soil. According to Jeavons, caring for each bed will take only 5 to 10 minutes each day. While some methods of cultivation, such as those described in the no-till section, take much less time than double-digging, they are not aesthetically pleasing. Convenience and elegance are not always compatible. Sometimes you will have to sacrifice the beauty of portions of your edible landscape in order to have an easy harvest.

Institute for Local Self-Reliance. **Gardening for Health**. Washington, DC: Institute for Local Self-Reliance, 1976. The source for the information in Fig. 4.3. An excellent chart ranks the most nutrient-productive vegetables by nutrients produced in a square foot each month. Also gives a nutritional analysis of three dozen vegetables.

National Gardening Association. **Gardening: The Complete Guide to Growing America's Favorite Fruits and Vegetables**. Boston: Addison-Wesley, 1986. An excellent guide to organic cultivation of the U.S.'s 40 favorite vegetables and fruits, and control of 40 common pests and diseases. Lots of color in this comprehensive 384-page reference. Buy it for your gardening bookshelf.

Swanson, Faith. **Herb Garden Design**. Hanover, NH: University Press of New England, 1984. Black and white designs for dozens of herb gardens, by type or by function. Most designs are formal or very formal. Good ready-to-use "blueprints" for gardeners who don't want to create their own design.

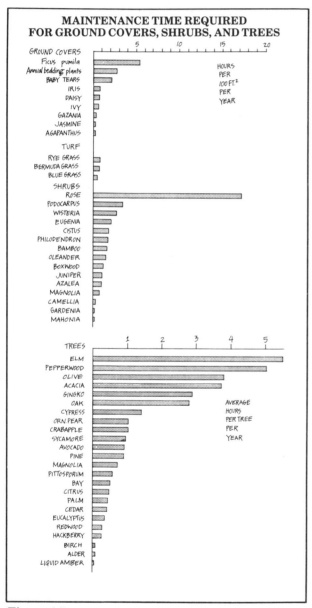

Figure 4.5

2

ZONES OF USE, MULTIPLE USE

Designing by Zones

The vast range of vegetables requires a wide range of care. Some, like lettuce and spinach, need more attention and frequent picking (if you eat as much of these as I do). Others, like eggplant and winter squash, need less care during most of the growing season – followed by a short burst of attention at harvest time. Considering such patterns is like a time-and-motion study of your garden. If you can lay out a path that saves a few steps with each visit to the lettuce bed, the time you will save over the coming years is considerable. Salad greens picked daily throughout the gardening season should be planted as close to the kitchen door as possible. Sounds obvious, but so many people disregard this fundamental point. Similarly, your favorite perennial herbs for salad dressings and seasonings should be planted very near the salad area. As an ornamental border along the path from the kitchen door to the salad plantings, these frequently used herbs can be quickly gathered as you return to the kitchen with fresh greens.

Since edible landscaping represents the dissolution of the boundaries between vegetable and ornamental gardens, we have more freedom to place elements where they best serve us. If time is money, then a landscape design that requires running around in circles will surely short-change you. As you care for and harvest your edible landscape, your patterns of movement will be largely determined by its overall design.

Group plants by "zones of use" in a particular proximity to the house based upon how frequently the plants are visited.

Low-Care Plants Farther from Home

Vegetables such as Jerusalem artichokes (*Helianthus tuberosus*) are self-reliant and hardy. They can be planted in large patches far from the house and harvested all at once. (In fact, this particular plant is so prone to spread and so difficult to eradicate, it *must* be planted far from other cultivated vegetables.) For convenience, make sure the sprinkler or drip system for watering Jerusalem artichokes is attached to a spigot close to the house. Then you can do periodic watering without having to even walk back to the patch of "sun chokes." Certain fruit trees unlikely to have pest and disease problems can also be placed far from the house. (The best candidates are listed in "Disease Resistant Trees.")

Compost piles made from the vegetable wastes of the garden are another element that can be placed farther from the home. Convenience would seem to indicate that if you add kitchen scraps to the compost, the pile should be close to the kitchen. But sometimes compost piles or bins can get a bit smelly, especially if they are not properly maintained. A slightly more distant location of the compost pile or bins will protect the kitchen from any drifting odors. (A good alternative for recyling just the kitchen scraps is a worm bin close to the kitchen door. The covered bin is inconspicuous, easy to maintain, and seldom creates an odor problem as red manure worms quickly digest high-nitrogen kitchen scraps. For more information, see the references at the end of the chapter.)

Exceptions to Zones

As the compost example illustrates, the zones-of-use guideline is not hard and fast. Not every element that needs daily care should be close to the house. Chickens are a good example. While they need daily feeding and frequent visits for egg collecting, the potential for dust, mites, and smell is great. It is best to locate chickens farther from the house, screening them to reduce the dust problem.

Rampant winter squash vines, needing little care during the growing season, make good choices for the perimeters of the property. However, these same vines could be planted close to the house and trained up a trellis to provide summer shade.

Concurrent Use and Density

Many parts of your landscape will need frequent attention—culinary herbs, salad greens, greenhouses, cold frames, fruit trees that require frequent spraying, chickens, rabbits, compost bins, and sprinkler or drip irrigation valves. Many will need to be designed into the relatively small area near the house. There are ways to combine them, to "layer" them together, for good use of space. In *Pattern Language*, Alexander says:

The compression of patterns . . . is the most ordinary economy of space. Every building, every room, every garden is better, when all the patterns which it needs are compressed as far as possible . . . The building [or garden] will be cheaper; and the meanings in it will be denser.

A solar greenhouse is an ideal example of density. It can heat your home while providing food throughout the year. It can also be a mudroom where you can remove dirty shoes and clothing before entering the house, act as a double entry to prevent heat loss from the house, provide an extra room for leisure activities, function as a humidifier in dry winter climates, and provide a place to experiment with exotic plants that would not ordinarily grow in your climate.

A landscape designed with dense zones of concurrent use will be more compact, easier to care for, and easier to enjoy. The north side of the Kelley site (Fig. 4.7) already had a large stone retaining wall along the driveway. I installed a narrow raised bed along the wall. There, fruit trees are encouraged to fully ripen their fruit by the heat generated by the wall. The trees are deciduous, and winter vegetables grow beneath them. The Kelleys train snow peas up the southern face of the wall and grow salad greens in the rest of the planter, harvesting peas and greens weeks ahead of more exposed plantings.

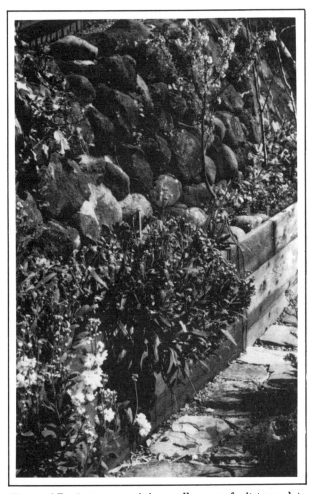

Figure 4.7 A stone retaining wall warms fruit trees, lettuce, and beets that grow in a narrow terrace at its base.

For Each Function, Several Elements

As insurance against the vagaries of climate, disease, and pests, grow several types of plants for each desired function. For example, to lure bees to your edible landscape, grow several types of blue-flowering plants (bees see blue more readily than other colors) that will bloom during the peak of spring fruit tree blossoming and throughout the summer.

For Each Element, Several Functions

A great way to get more variety in a limited space is to use plants that have a variety of uses. Just as a greenhouse can be used to propagate seedlings in the spring, dry fruits and nuts for storage in late summer, and warm the house in winter, so certain plants can serve several purposes at once. The hollyleaf cherry (*Prunus ilicifolia*), for example, makes a dense privacy hedge, has edible fruits, increases the bird population, and attracts beneficial insects with its blossoms.

Multi-Purpose Edibles

The simplest way to add variety to your food supply is to plant multi-purpose annual vegetables. Figure 4.8 lists examples that have more than one edible portion. Notice that some serve other useful functions as well.

I like to grow many of the ornamentals that have edible flowers or leaves. Any salad is more exciting sprinkled with a rainbow of colorful petals from nasturtiums, chives, and petunias. Other examples of edible flowers are day lilies, calendulas, violas, and roses. For a more complete list, see Fig. 18.13 in "Finishing Touches."

There are multi-purpose perennials, too. One of my favorites is the chayote (*Sechium edule*). An expert on rare fruits, Paul Jackson taught me the uses of this champion of multi-purpose plants. The fruit of a chayote ranges from smooth skinned to spiny, light to dark green, weighs up to a pound, and resembles a pear-shaped squash. The flesh is crisp, moist, and rather bland, much like a zucchini. I think the single soft seed, with its nut-like flavor, is the tastiest part. A three-year-old vine in Southern California can produce 200 to 300 fruits. That's a lot of fruit and seeds! The first 4 to 6 inches of any leading tip of the vine can be steamed and eaten as a vegetable. Since the vine can cover a 400-square-foot area in a single season, that's a huge amount of steamed greens, too. With Paul's help and through our own experimentation, my friends and I have sampled almost two dozen dishes using chayote as a major ingredient. My two favorite recipes are an eggplant Parmigiana, substituting chayote for the eggplant, and marinating the soft seeds in an herbal vinaigrette sauce. (See recipes in final chapter.)

I like perennial alternatives to some of the annuals. I grow Oriental garlic chives as a substitute for garlic, Egyptian top-set onions and chives for an onion flavor, comfrey for salad greens, day lilies for their colorful blossoms and edible tubers (tasting somewhat like a potato), dock and dandelion greens, salad burnet for garnishing salads, chayote for a zucchini substitute and for the steamed greens, and nasturtiums (which grow like perennials in our moderate California coastal climate) for a spicy flavor and a colorful highlight. All of these perennials are useful in themselves and can serve as substitutes if an annual equivalent fails.

More Than Just Edible

The multi-purpose plants in an edible landscape can have a broad range of influences. The "Other" column in Fig. 4.8 lists some of these attributes —plants that can shape the wind and sunlight (Russian olive and Siberian peashrub) or improve the soil (fava bean, chicory, and dandelion); plants to be cut as mulch or added to the compost pile (comfrey and fava bean); plants for wildlife (Russian olive and rose hips); trees and shrubs for fuel (if there is plenty of room, black locust); plants that attract beneficial predators and lure pollinating bees; plants that can be used in home-made concoctions to repel pests; and plants for feeding small animals such as rabbits or chickens (comfrey, Siberian peashrub, and rose hips). Most of these less frequently considered uses are discussed elsewhere in this book; look up each in the Index.

Figure 4.8

MULTI-PURPOSE EDIBLES COMMON NAME (Botanical name)	Annual, Perennial, Biennial	Root	Bulb	Tuber	Young Shoots	Stem	Seed	Spice	Leaf	Tea	Flower	Fruit	Attracts Beneficial Insects	Attracts Bees	OTHER
AMARANTH (Amaranthus sp.)	A						X		X		X		X		High in iron, calcium, potassium, and Vitamin C
ANGELICA (Angelica archangelica)	P				X						X				
ANISE (Pimpinella anisum)	A						X		X		X		X		Invasive
BEE BALM (Monarda didyma)	A								X	X	X			X	
BLACK LOCUST (Robinia pseudoacacia)	P										X			X	Fixes nitrogen, long-lasting fence posts, pods feed livestock
BORAGE (Borago officinalis)	A								X	X	X			X	Very good bee "food"
CARAWAY (Carum carvi)	A						X		X		X		X		
CELTUCE (the Composite Family)	A					X			X						
CHAYOTE (Sechium edule)	P			X	X		X						X		Fast vine for shade
CHICORY (Cichorium sp.)	P	X							X	X	X			X	Deep rooted
CHIVES (Allium sp.)	P				X			X	X		X				
COMFREY (Symphytum officinale)	P	X							X	X					Deep rooted; high in vitamins
CORIANDER (Coriandrum sativum)	A						X		X		X		X		
DANDELION (Taraxacum officinale)	P	X						X	X	X	X		X		Invasive
DAY LILY (Hemerocallis fulva)	P				X						X				
DILL (Anethum graveolens)	A				X		X	X	X		X		X		Deep rooted
EGYPTIAN TOP-SET ONION (Allium cepa var. viviprium)	P		X		X		X	X	X		X				

KEY: LIFE CYCLE (LC): A = annual P = perennial, B = biennal EDIBLE PARTS, USES: R = root, B = bulb, TB = tuber, Y = young shoots, S = stem, SD = seed, SP = spice, L = leaf, T = tea, FL = flower, F = fruit INSECTS: PR = attracts predatory insects, P = attracts pollinating bees

continued

COMMON NAME (Botanical name)	Annual, Perennial, Biennial	Root	Bulb	Tuber	Young Shoots	Stem	Seed	Spice	Leaf	Tea	Flower	Fruit	Attracts Beneficial Insects	Attracts Bees	OTHER
FAVA BEAN (Vicia faba)	A						X		X		X				Fixes 200 lb.of nitrogen per acre per year
FLORENCE FENNEL (Foeniculum vulgare var. azoricum)	A	X			X	X	X	X			X		X		Invasive
GARLIC (Allium sativum)	P		X		X		X	X	X		X				
HAMBURG PARSLEY (Petroselinum crispum)	B	X						X	X				X		
HYSSOP (Hyssopus officinalis)	P								X	X	X			X	
LEMON BALM (Melissa officinalis)	A								X	X	X			X	Invasive
LUFFA (Luffa cylindrica)	A			X	X				X		X	X			Good shade vine; sponges
LOVAGE (Leviticum officinale)	P				X	X	X		X				X		
MALLOW (Malva neglecta)	A								X		X				Invasive
MINER'S LETTUCE (Claytonia perfoliata)	A			X	X				X		X				
MUSTARDS (Brassica sp.)	A								X		X			X	
NASTURTIUM (Tropaeolum sp.)	A			X			X	X	X		X				Nurse crop for beneficial insects
ROSE HIPS (Rosa rugosa)	P						X	X		X	X	X			High vitamin C; barrier plant
ROSEMARY (Rosmarinus officinalis)	P						X	X	X					X	
RUSSIAN OLIVE (Elaeagnus angustifolia)	P											X			Fixes nitrogen; good wildlife habitat; good windbreak shrub
SIBERIAN PEA-SHRUB (Caragana arborescens)	P						X								Fixes nitrogen; good livestock food
SOCIETY GARLIC (Tulbaghia violacea)	P		X		X		X	X	X						
SWEET VIOLET (Viola odorata)	P								X		X				High vitamin A; shade-loving
VIOLA (Viola cornuta)	A								X		X				

Figure 4.8

KEY: LIFE CYCLE (LC): A = annual P = perennial, B = biennial EDIBLE PARTS, USES: R = root, B = bulb, TB = tuber, Y = young shoots, S = stem, SD = seed, SP = spice, L = leaf, T = tea, FL = flower, F = fruit INSECTS: PR = attracts predatory insects, P = attracts pollinating bees

Douglas, J. Sholto, and Hart, Richard. **Forest Farming**. London: Watkins Publishing, 1976. A source of inspiration for multi-story agriculture when I first became interested in alternatives to orchards. An excellent review of the principles of mixing tree crops and cattle. Unlike J. Russell Smith's *Tree Crops*, Douglas and Hart describe contemporary, working examples from around the world. Not relevant to small-scale, suburban settings.

Halpin, Anne. **Unusual Vegetables**. Emmaus, PA: Rodale Press, 1978. An excellent book on the topic, and one of the few to discuss the culture of chayote. One of Rodale's better books.

Hedrick, U. P., ed. **Sturtevent's Edible Plants of the World**. New York: Dover Publications, 1972. The most extensive listing of the edible characteristics of thousands of unusual and obscure plants. For unfamiliar plants, use this book with caution; many references are based on old citations and were not personally tested by the author. Many cold-sensitive, tropical plants are included.

Hills, Lawrence. **Comfrey**. New York: Universe Books, 1976. The definitive book on this important, though tenacious, herb.

Kern, Barbara and Ken. **The Owner-Built Homestead**. Charles Scribner's Sons, 1977. A classic for the homesteading movement. Very useful in considering ways to integrate energy, food, water, and waste systems for your home and yard. A major inspiration for me 12 years ago. Though intended for rural settings, many of the examples can be adapted to the code restrictions and style of the suburbs. The most accurate information is contained in the chapters on site analysis, planning, and alternative construction techniques.

King, F. H. **Farmers of Forty Centuries**. Emmaus, PA: Rodale Press, 1911. A travelog through turn-of-the-century China when all farming was done by hand. A wonderful, though rambling, review of another culture's raised bed gardening methods.

Leckie, Jim; Masters, Gil; Whitehouse, Harry; and Young, Lily. **More Other Homes and Garbage**. Rev. ed. San Francisco: Sierra Club Books, 1975. This updated classic on integrated, sustainable homes and gardens has much more on wind power, methane generation, and hydropower than does the Farallones Institute's *Integral Urban House;* but similarly, is very weak on perennial food plants and tree crops.

Mollison, Bill, and Holmgren, David. **Permaculture One**. Stanley, Tasmania: Tagari Books, 1978. A good introduction to the Australian equivalent of sustainable/holistic/integrated farms and gardens. The theories were an inspiration to me 7 years ago, but most of the examples are inappropriate for U.S. climates, property sizes, and lifestyles.

Mollison, Bill. **Permaculture Two**. Stanley, Tasmania: Tagari Books, 1981. Similar to its predecessor, with a big section appropriate only to gardeners who live where it rains less than 10 inches a year.

National Academy of Science. **Underexploited Tropical Plants of Promising Economic Value**. Washington, DC: N.A.S., 1975. The first book to get me excited about the loss of genetic diversity in food plants, and unusual edible plants such as amaranth and winged beans. The inspirational text gives seed resources and contact people at the end of each chapter.

Tilth. **The Future is Abundant**. Arlington, WA: Tilth, 1982. An excellent reference for people interested in permaculture designs and theories, edible landscaping, and sustainable agriculture. A good collection of bibliographies, seed and plant sources, addresses of like-minded people, and short summaries of alternative gardening and farming techniques. The best feature is a 300-species index of edible and useful plants for the Pacific Northwest—every region needs an index like this one. Out of print.

Yanda, Bill, and Fisher, Rick. **The Food and Heat Producing Solar Greenhouse**. Rev. ed. Santa Fe: John Muir, 1980. The classic book for designing and building your own solar greenhouse, though it does not mention that solar greenhouses can cause moisture problems where winters are wet and humid; also, the recommended vent sizes are too small.

MAKING USE OF LOCAL WISDOM

A great source of reliable local information is old-timers—people who have gardened in your community for decades and who are intimately aware of what grows well there. They are my favorite source of practical advice. Many were born on farms, moved to urban areas, and sustain a healthy connection with their childhood by caring for edible landscapes. They are vividly aware of the dreadful decline in the flavor and quality of food caused by "modern" agriculture.

In many edible landscapes, old-timers cultivate the customs of their homelands. I love to visit the Oriental gardens of large cities to get design ideas. In downtown Boston, I saw tidy and efficient Oriental gardens featuring unique ways of trellising, thereby making good use of vertical space. The older, master oriental gardeners are my best instructors for how to plant a variety of vegetables close together, getting the maximum use of tiny spaces. Mexican gardeners delight me with their relaxed, social approach to gardening. In Santa Rosa and at the Mexican-American community gardens of San Jose, garden designs always include a barbecue pit, a shaded arbor, and plenty of chairs and benches. In their gardens, an arbor's welcome shade is often cast by chayote vines. These garden designs remind me of the satisfying social aspects of gardening—that an edible landscape can be as much for friendship as for food.

Elderly gardeners can help you forecast the weather. They can tell the coming weather by a single cloud pattern or the activity of a squirrel. I enjoy hearing their perspectives on the patterns they have observed over the decades. They also have good insights about long-term trends in local weather patterns—changes in first and last frost dates, rainfall, and so on.

Old-timers can also help you plan your landscape maintenance routine. Like many people, I am always squeezing in my tree pruning at the last minute. Being stubbornly independent in my youth, I didn't often ask advice and had to learn for myself which ornamental flowers precede the blossom of which fruit trees. Had I talked to the most observant, older residents, I would have learned about the bloom sequence long ago. Gems of gardening wisdom can save you years of experimentation. Though it seems that most new gardeners must "re-invent the wheel" to some extent in order to get a solid personal understanding of gardening, talking first to wiser gardeners can save valuable time and energy.

Pioneers of New Varieties

Some traditional gardeners boldly try new foods, new techniques. Joe Massida, an 80-year-old Italian farmer, had a solar greenhouse heating his home long before the phrase solar greenhouse existed. He built the greenhouse against the south side of his home to shelter the tender trees—cherimoya, the true guava, coffee, and Surinam cherry. A window into the house admits the tropical warmth and fragrance. He has proven that dozens of types of exotic fruits will bear in an area where agricultural advisors shun recommending them. He has perhaps one of the oldest bearing kiwi vines outside of botanical gardens. Secured from the University of California at Davis 35 years ago, when the kiwi was just an obscure fruit, his plants now cover an arbor 12 feet wide and 30 feet long, laden (beyond belief) with tasty fruit. His avocado trees number more than a dozen, with six varieties. While his desire is rooted in the old country, he has come to grow varieties of edibles that many Italian gardeners have never heard of.

Quietly, every year in each community, these wise gardeners test new varieties. Before rushing to experiment with an exotic plant, ask around at the local garden clubs and talk to these experienced gardeners. Chances are you will find someone who has already worked with the plant you are interested in and who can give you good advice.

Many of the old-timers grow "foreign" plants—special edibles for ethnic recipes—and use methods that you may have never considered for your edible landscape. It is inspiring to talk with them—often, they are sources of information on how to grow the "impossible," or how to combine plants in ways not commonly seen in your region. Best of all, these old-timers have been conducting their gardening experiments for decades and have a wealth of information to share with you. Although the examples that follow are from California, the lessons to be learned apply anywhere.

Figure 4.9 Apricots, almonds, and nectarines can be grafted onto a plum tree to make a "fruit salad" tree with a long season of harvest. (In this photograph, each type of fruit is a different shade of grey.)

The "Edible" Apartments—
A Heritage of Gardening

Hidden away in Marin County—known mostly for its hot tubs and laid-back eccentrics—is perhaps the country's most "edible" apartment housing. This remarkable example of the potentials of edible landscaping has been nurtured for 44 years by a Portuguese couple, Angelina and Frank Flores. The apartment complex bears their last name, which means "flowers" in their native tongue. The cultivation of flowers, food, family, and tradition—that's what the Floreses' garden is all about. They were nurturing ornamental, edible plantings long before the phrase edible landscaping came into being.

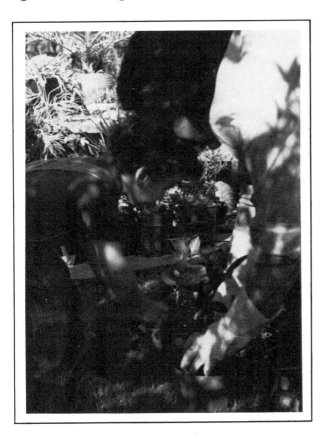

Lots of Food . . .

As Angelina walks me through the tidy yet rambling gardens, she shows me more and more kinds of food. Fruit trees stand out as major elements and appear everywhere. The list includes almonds, apples, apricots, bananas, cherries, figs, grapes, guavas (a small, but very tasty kind called strawberry guava—*Psidium littorale*), kumquats, lemons, lemquats (a cross between a lemon and a kumquat), loquats, nectarines, olives, oranges, peaches (including some red-fleshed types), pears, plums, pomegranates, quinces, and tangerines.

Along the driveway, I spot a rare example of grafting, one that many gardeners would not think

possible—peaches and almonds on the same tree. The Floreses know that nearly all stone fruits can be grafted together if you have enough skill, patience, and perseverance. The most impressive example of their grafting work is a tree with three types of plums, almonds, nectarines, and apricots—a fruit salad tree. (See Fig. 4.9, page 63 and in color plates.) Multiple-grafted trees allow the Floreses to have variety and choice in a small space.

There are other perennial edibles—passion fruit vines, taro (for its edible tuber), strawberries, chives, and garlic chives. Then there are the herbs: oregano and thyme for seasoning, chamomile and lemon verbena for teas that soothe the stomach, and rosemary—Angelina doesn't like its flavor but cultivates quite a few plants just for their beauty.

Near the house, the vegetables are harder to spot. They are tucked into little nooks and crannies throughout the perennial edible and ornamental plantings. Beet greens grow through a ground cover of chamomile. Cucumber vines twine up through a bed of dahlias. Kale peeks out from under a grapevine. The day's salad fixings are close to the house, nestled among shrubs, annual flowers, and under trees.

. . . and Lots of Flavor

And why, I ask, do you grow so many types of food? Angelina Flores replies, "For the fresh taste and for the recipes from the old country."

Though I personally love quinces when they are baked like apples, the Floreses have a fondness for quinces cooked with olive oil, garlic, onions, and tomatoes. (See recipes in final chapter.) Local markets don't carry quinces so the Floreses have several of these trees. I was flattered when Angelina offered to prepare their special quince dish for my next visit. This is how she described her recipe:

Take three or four big onions, peel them, slice them in small pieces and put in a pan with a little olive oil. Fry until the onion is almost fried. Put in a little bit fresh garlic, two or three—how you say in English—cloves. The time you fry the onion, you peel four or five big quince and slice like apples and cut them in half. As soon as you peel the quince, you peel the tomato. In five quince you can put three or four pretty good size tomato. Peel and cut them in pieces. As soon as the onion is ready, put water and put the quince and the tomato in a pot. Everything cook together. Not too much water, just part way. Cover the pot and don't let them boil too high. As soon as the water starts to boil, in fifteen minutes is ready. You don't want to let them cook too much. If fifteen minutes is not enough, cook two or three minutes more. A little salt and sugar is the taste. You like a little more, you put a little more. So is done—simple as can be.

As a proud Angelina led me through her edible paradise, she kept collecting samples. By the time I left, my arms were laden with yellow and red guavas, figs, lemon verbena tea, live seedlings, and from her kitchen, freshly baked zucchini bread. She can't be in the garden without offering up the bounty to visitors.

As she knelt to dig up the guavas, her grandson came over to look and to help. I watched the two of them together, their eyes sparkling from the friendship and the gardening. When we parted company, Angelina's final comment was, "I love to garden, I'm glad to know I can help others grow food." I left inspired and confident about the future of families and the heritage of edible landscaping.

Emil's Urban Orchard of Rare Fruits

A master of fruit tree care, Emil Linquist is a grandfatherly man with rough country charm. This professional tree surgeon, who has always had a special passion for fruit trees, is on a mission to save rare fruit varieties from extinction. The apple is his favored fruit. For Emil, the choice of apples in the local supermarket "isn't worth the powder to blow them to the hot place." With near-religious fervor, Emil has searched high and low for unusual and nearly extinct apple varieties, and in his urban backyard there are 120 varieties. His living heritage of fruit offers more flavor, texture, color, shape, and season of harvest than his visitors have ever dreamed of. Emil's urban orchard, which he calls a holding ground, is a one-man gene bank, a refuge for fruit varieties that might otherwise be lost because of the practices of commercial agriculture.

You might expect Emil's backyard to be quite large, but it is only 50 feet by 100 feet. There are more than a dozen types of fruits and berry vines besides the 120 varieties of apples, partly because

of his skill in grafting and pruning. Many of the trees are planted as close together as 18 inches, within rows only 3 feet apart. In order to plant so densely, Emil grafts his varieties onto special dwarf rootstocks. (Emil is my mentor for grafting. His preferred method is either the cleft or whip-and-tongue technique. He uses both when the trees are dormant.) Although his main purpose for growing so many trees is to provide grafting wood for other apple enthusiasts, the trees are very fruitful. And Emil is more interested in their flavor than in size or quantity.

Apples for Flavor

The desire for better flavor drives Emil's pursuit of unusual apple varieties. When pressed to name his favorites, he'll hem and haw, not wanting to be pinned down to selecting just a few. But his eyes light up when he mentions "the best doggone apple you ever sunk your teeth into"—the 'Fireside.' Some of his other favorites are 'Signe Tillisch,' 'Sweet Delicious,' 'Connell Red' (a mutation of 'Fireside'), and the 'Anoka' ("You have to take your glasses off when you bite into it and shut your eyes at the same time or she'll squirt in your face!").

For the best "keepers," he recommends 'Hudson's Golden Gem,' 'Connell Red,' 'Fireside,' and 'Sweet Delicious.' On the second day of February I've seen these keepers (plus 'Winter Banana,' 'Alexander,' 'Pearmain,' and 'Mulhall' apples) still in good shape while hanging on the tree. Emil's favorite cider apples are the 'Smith #1' and the 'Smith #2.'

Virtuous Apples

Emil is often inclined to tell all who will listen about the virtues of each apple. Each has a special trait and a spot in his heart. And the virtues he describes are incredible.

Of the 'Whitney' crabapple he exclaims, "You can plant that one up in Winnipeg, Canada and in Florida. You can plant it in a mud hole. My cousin has one that's planted in a low spot and has 2 or 3 inches of water standing in there all summer long, and that 'Whitney,' she's happy as a lark. It's the only crab that's fit to eat from the hand."

"This 'Wolf River' apple," he continues, "is next to a 'Spokane Beauty' for size. A nice-colored apple, runs a pound and a quarter, a pound and a half." And these are not the soft, pulpy apples that we associate with large size.

The 'Sweet Delicious' has nothing to do with the dreadful, modern 'Red Delicious' and is one of my favorite varieties. Emil is quick to explain why this apple never became a commercial variety: "These commercial growers got the stinking idea that water core (when the apple core turns slushy and translucent) is a bad thing. I like to call it sugar core. It never gets into the flesh, just stays transparent in the core. And it is a good keeper — still crispy and juicy after hanging onto the tree most of the winter!"

Evangelist for Heritage Fruit

In the last five years, Emil has devoted much time to passing on his wealth of knowledge. He now teaches year-round the virtues of heritage fruit and the care of home orchards. While I worked at the Farallones Institute, he gave workshops on how to graft fruit trees. He would trundle in with a small box of grafting tools and *enormous* bundles of scion wood for grafting. People fell silent as his folksy parables of tree culture unfolded. They watched transfixed as his large, callused hands made deft grafts of scions, not fingers. Hours later, Emil would still be talking to captivated folks, his eyes sparkling late into the night as he promoted the virtues of delicious, homegrown fruit.

Gardening with a Grain of Salt

In the pursuit of local gardening wisdom, it is helpful to keep in mind that some folk ways are just folk tales, not well-grounded in fact, and traditional, handed-down information can suffer in the translation. To sort out fact from fiction, I compare the recommendations of several local gardeners.

When questioned, many of my older gardening friends can recall who recommended a technique, but are often at a loss to explain the how or why of it. If it works, fine. But it is even better if you understand why. Knowing the inner workings of a technique will tend to make you a more thoughtful gardener, better able to design and care for your edible landscape. When questioning your local old-time gardeners, try to learn the whys as well as the whats that work for them.

DESIGNING YOUR EDIBLE LANDSCAPE
Energy-Conserving Landscaping

SHAPING THE WIND: SHELTER FOR HOME AND GARDEN

A hedge or row of shrubs and trees can sculpt the wind to the benefit of people and plants. Such plantings, called hedgerows, windbreaks, or shelterbelts, can save you as much as 50 percent on your heating and cooling bills. They can also make your edible landscape more productive.

Windbreaks shelter both field and house, reduce chilling by the wind, and thus provide energy savings in winter. Figure 5.1 shows how windchill increases with wind speed. At 0° F, reducing a 20 MPH wind to 5 MPH cuts the chill factor by more than one-third. Windbreaks can also funnel cooling winds in summer, filter dust from the air, raise temperature of soil and air (providing for earlier spring growth and increasing yields), protect the flower and fruit of trees, provide a habitat for wildlife, protect soil from wind and water erosion, increase the soil's water-holding capacity, protect property from drifting snow, and create privacy.

Designing Windbreaks for the Home

The starting point for designing a windbreak is straightforward geometry. As a brief summary, review Figs. 5.2 and 5.3. (For more detail, see the references at the end of this chapter.)

There is a minimum size for an effective windbreak. The length of a windbreak should be 11 times its mature height. Another rule of thumb states that the windbreak should be 50 feet longer, on both ends, than the area to be protected. This may seem awfully long, but there is a reason: as the wind is forced around the ends of the windbreak, its speed increases, creating a turbulent eddy that negates the value of all but the midsection of the windbreak.

Suburban properties often lack room for a long enough windbreak. To protect a single story home, the windbreak must be at least 14 to 20 feet high if close to the house, and even higher if away from the house. A windbreak 20 feet tall should be 220 feet long. If your yard can't accommodate a long windbreak, try foundation plantings of shrubs or trellised vines. Figure 5.4 gives the standard formula for planting shrubs near walls.

Figure 5.1 Reducing wind speed cuts the chill factor, lowering your home heating costs.

Figure 5.2 Windbreaks offer the most protection within a distance 10 to 15 times the height of the trees.

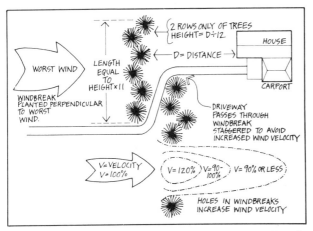

Figure 5.3 A driveway straight through a windbreak can negate the windbreak effect. Instead, curve a driveway through an offset opening. A windbreak must be at least 11 times longer than its height.

Sunlight Versus Shelter from the Wind

A conflict can arise between the windbreak and the garden. If the strongest winter winds blow from the south, the windbreak needed to shelter the house may cast a shadow over valuable garden space. Placing the windbreak farther away will reduce its influence on energy conservation, but the gain in sunny garden space is a healthy compromise for those who garden in the winter. Where space is limited, carefully plan areas of annual edibles so that successive plantings follow the movement of the sun. (See Fig. 5.5.)

To determine a windbreak's shade pattern, draw the windbreak and house to scale in a side view (an east or west elevation). Be accurate about the height of the windbreak, its distance from the house and garden area, and the slope of your property. Using the solar charts in Appendix 2, look up your latitude and the sun's angle above the horizon

(altitude) at noon for each of several months. Use a protractor to plot the angle from the ground to the top of the windbreak. The area below the line represents the shadow that will be cast by your proposed windbreak. (See "The Climate in Your Yard" for a method using solar siting devices.)

Increase Yields with Windbreaks

Windbreaks increase yields under certain conditions. A field previously planted edge to edge with crops can have up to 10 percent of its area planted with windbreak trees and still maintain the same yield. A Russian study, published in the *Handbook of Afforestation and Soil Melioration*, shows that the increase in production resulting from windbreaks can be 20 to 30 percent for grains, 50 to 75 percent for melon and orchard crops, and over 100 percent for sown grasses. These figures, however, come from large fields (410 feet x 984 feet to 1,312 feet x 1,968 feet, not exactly the size of many suburban yards), and they disguise the influence of the feeding roots of the trees that compose the windbreak. The rows closest to the shelterbelt suffer reduced yields. (See Fig. 5.6.)

All trees are lazy—they will feed at the most convenient buffet in town and will seek out the tastiest food. And since the roots of most trees are at least 1½ times wider than the canopy (up to 3 times wider in sandy soils), the shelterbelt must be a fair distance from the food-producing areas or you will have to compensate with enough extra water and nutrients to keep both the trees and the edible landscape happy.

A windbreak planted on the long side of a rectangular-shaped property may extend its roots under much of the landscape. Square parcels fare better. A good use of space is to place driveways or roads along the sheltered side of the windbreak, between

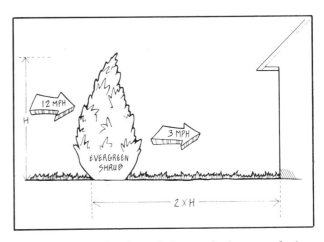

Figure 5.4 Shrubs slow wind near the house, reducing the chill factor.

the trees and the garden. The compaction of the soil will slow the growth of the tree's roots toward your garden. Whatever the geometry of your property, plan as much distance as possible between your shelterbelt and the vegetable and tree crops areas of your edible landscape.

If you cannot place the shelterbelt far from areas of intensive food production, make sure you use trees without greedy and invasive roots. Trees such as eucalyptus, willow, big-leaf maple, and poplar are known to be more aggressive and heavier feeders than pines, olives, cedars, and junipers. Check with local nurseries about tame-rooted shrubs and trees for your area.

If space is limited, a structural, non-living windbreak may be the best solution. Fences do not take much room or require food and water.

The Best Windbreaks Are Not Edible

It is important, whenever possible, to have one element serve several functions, but food and wind don't easily mix. Most wind-resistant trees are ornamental. The blossoms and fruit of most edibles are damaged by high winds. A few exceptions are carob, mulberry, olive, and nut trees.

Some less common trees and shrubs withstand wind and have edible fruits – American wild plum (*Prunus americana*), hollyleaf wild cherry (*Prunus illicifolia*), Russian olive (*Elaeagnus angustifolia*),

autumn olive (*Elaeagnus umbellata*), Carolina wild cherry (*Prunus caroliniana*), Siberian peashrub (*Caragana arborescens*), and hackberry (*Celtis occidentalis*). Their fruits are technically edible but more likely to be appreciated by wildlife than by people. Some of these marginally edible trees can be mixed with ornamental trees on the sheltered side of the windbreak. The large ornamental broadleaf trees and evergreens such as pine, cypress, and junipers are the best plants for the major elements of a windbreak.

Instant Windbreaks

Years, even decades, pass before some windbreak trees reach mature size. In that time, a lot of fat heating and cooling bills are paid, and many seasons of blossoms and seedlings could have used some protection. For an instant windbreak, try a fence. A 6-foot-high fence has a beneficial effect that extends 60 feet or more. A wooden slat fence with every other slat missing allows some of the wind to penetrate gently – making it preferable to a solid fence, which creates turbulence in its lee. Notice in Fig. 5.2 that there is also a zone of protection on the windy side two to five times the height of the windbreak. This zone of reduced wind also occurs on the windy side of a fence. This is a favorable microclimate for some of the seedling transplants that will grow to be a mature windbreak. The wind is not as strong there, and the seedlings can tolerate stronger winds as they grow higher.

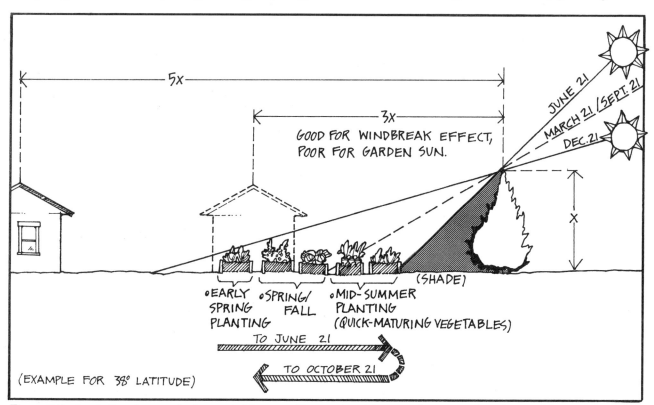

Figure 5.5 A windbreak may shade vegetable areas. Use a solar sighter to plan a rotation of vegetable sites that follow the seasonal movement of the sun. Keep the viewer close to the ground, at the level of the plants.

Use Vines First

To reduce energy costs now, plant vines, shrubs, and trees all at once. The vines quickly cover fences, trellises, walls, and windows and will be the first to affect heating and cooling costs. Once established, a vine is fairly easy to control (an advantage over many kinds of trees, which are difficult to prune when they are more than 15 feet in height).

Plant Several Species of Trees at the Same Time

One of the problems in choosing windbreak trees is that the fastest growing types have drawbacks. Eucalyptus or poplar may quickly grow to 20 feet, then, just as quickly, grow to be 40 feet or taller. The solution lies in planting two to four types of trees and shrubs with different growth rates then cutting out those that grow faster as the slower ones mature to the desired height. Notice in Fig. 5.7 that a second planting of *Myoporum lateum* has been added later on, farther out from the largest tree. Often, the lower branches of the taller trees wither and die. If the vacancy remains, wind can pass through the base of the windbreak at a speed greater than the original wind speed. A line of low shrubs on the windy side eliminates the problem.

Planting a Windbreak

The idea of a windbreak is unusual enough, but finding someone who knows how to plant one is even more unlikely. Remember, the sturdiest, tallest windbreak started with the smallest transplants. As a windbreak matures, the canopy be-

haves like a sail, grabbing more and more wind. In an attempt to get quick results, many people buy the largest container or balled plants available, but the taller the plant is, the more the roots have been damaged; without well-anchored roots, older windbreak trees have a tendency to blow over.

Trees as short as 3 feet in a 5-gallon container can be rootbound, with snarled masses of circling roots. Even if the roots are pruned and spread at the time of planting, some continue to grow in a circling pattern, failing to reach out and explore deeper soils. A pot-bound tree will not reveal its weakness until it is too late, toppling in high winds years after transplanting. Burlap-balled trees are less likely to have circling roots, but the taproot has been severed and may not re-grow to help anchor the tree.

Appendix 8 will help you locate a nursery that grows "tube seedling" trees. They are only 2 to 4 inches in diameter, but 12 to 24 inches deep; the trees are as tall as the tube is long. Buy only tube seedlings with undisturbed taproots, and be sure to plant them before the taproot comes through the bottom of the tube. After a day of planting hundreds of such trees, I can barely tell I did anything, looking at the planting from a short distance away. But the windbreak is off to a healthy, sturdy start.

To use tube-grown trees, plant a cluster of 6 to 12 at each of the chosen sites. After several years, the smallest, weakest trees can be clipped to the ground, leaving a few to continue. Once the fastest tree is about 4 to 5 feet tall, remove the others in each cluster.

To reap earlier savings on your heating and cooling bills, you will need to plant some fast-growing shrubs and trees. You can buy fast-growing shrubs and trees in containers because they will be removed or smothered before they get tall enough to

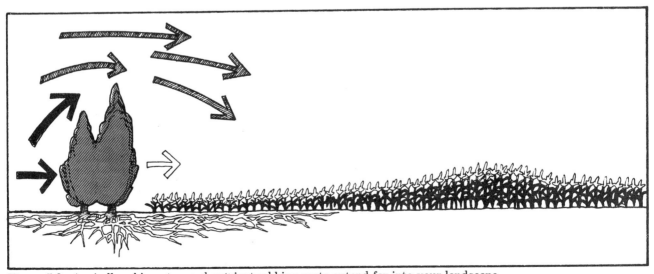

Figure 5.6 A windbreak's water- and nutrient-robbing roots extend far into your landscape.

blow over. Beware of rootbound plants, though. They may not even withstand winds in the second through tenth years, depending on the size of the top as compared to the size of the roots.

In Fig. 5.7, the 5-gallon *Prunus illicifolia* will quickly reach above the fence. The *Acacia verticillata* follows along as a secondary line of defense. The *Myoporum lateum* can be grown from a 1-gallon container plant. In the worst cases, I have seen 1-gallon plants outgrow larger, root-bound plants in a few years. The specific plants you use will vary, depending upon your climate and soil. Talk to your local soil conservation agent about the best species for your area.

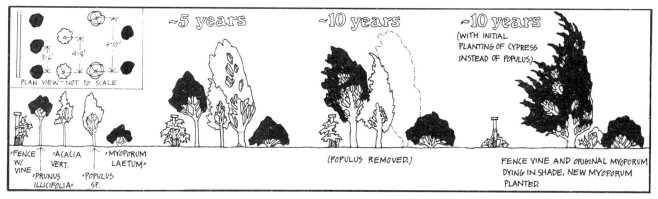

Figure 5.7 Planning for immediate and long-term wind protection. A good windbreak begins with two types of plants: fast-growing, short-lived varieties are eventually replaced by slow-growing, long-lived plants.

Chamberlin, Susan. **Hedges, Screens and Espaliers**. Tucson, AZ: HPBooks, 1983. The best book on the subject. Also the best step-by-step instructions on how to train espalier trees, with excellent color photos. Includes a mini-encyclopedia for each of the three topics. Good coverage of energy conserving design and muffling sound with plants.

Geisner, Rudolph. **The Climate Near the Ground**. Cambridge, MA: Harvard University Press, 1965. A classic textbook on microclimates. Highly technical, and expensive.

Kern, Barbara and Ken. **The Owner-Built Homestead.**. Charles Scribner's Sons, 1977. A classic for the homesteading movement. Very useful in considering ways to integrate energy, food, water, and waste systems for your home and yard. Though intended for rural settings, many of the examples can be adapted to the code restrictions and style of the suburbs. The most accurate information is contained in the chapters on site analysis, planning, and alternative construction techniques.

McPherson, Gregory. **Energy Conserving Site Design**. New York: American Conservation Association, 1984. A very technical, thorough presentation of case studies, site analysis, and master planning, with a historical review. For the professional only.

Moffat, Anne, and Schiler, Marc. **Landscape Design That Saves Energy**. New York: William Morrow, 1981. The best book on the subject, it is complete and offers plenty of data without feeling like a textbook. The analyses and design strategies are done by regional climate types, with good drawings and thorough lists of plant materials for each climate. An excellent resource.

U.S. Dept. of the Interior. **Plants, People and Environmental Quality**. Washington, DC: 1972. My favorite book of design criteria for making urban settings more livable with trees and shrubs that conserve energy, muffle sound, and filter soot and dust. For each application, the basic formulae and plants are listed. Where else can you find out how thick to plant a hedge of Rosa multiflora to stop a car moving at 30 miles an hour?

U.S.D.A. **Seeds of Woody Plants in the U.S.** Handbook No. 450. Washington, DC: Gov't. Printing Office, 1972. For the professional grower or serious hobbyist, the best manual on germinating seeds of ornamental and forest trees and shrubs.

SHAPING SUNLIGHT

Solar energy is a hot topic, and it should be – the sun fuels our edible landscapes and can heat our houses. But during the dog days of July and August, when the mere thought of solar heating makes you perspire, consider these ways to stay cool without higher air conditioning bills.

Cooling with Plants

Using vines, shrubs, and trees for cooling is a highly cost effective way to reduce your summer utility bills. Estimates show a one-half to two-thirds reduction in home cooling costs. The cooling benefits of shade trees are not be scoffed at – the air beneath a shade tree is often 10° to 20° cooler than the open air. By the second or third season the cost of the plants has been repaid in savings on your utility bills.

Vines for This Year

Planted early in the spring, the fastest growing annual vines can cover a trellis by August, providing some defense against the dog days of late summer. There are many ornamental annual vines to choose from: cup-and-saucer vine (*Cobaea scandens*), morning glory (*Ipomoea tricolor*), Japanese hop (*Humulus japonicus*), balsam apple and balsam pear (*Momordica balsamina, M. charantia*), moonflower (*Calonyction aculeatum*), cypress vine (*Quamoclit pennata*), cardinal climber (*Quamoclit sloteri*), and the black-eyed Susan vine (*Thunbergia alata*), to name a few. More are listed in Appendix 4.

Vines for shade provide a good chance to use edibles for more than one purpose. The tender vines can be used for shading the walls and windows of the house because the eave will protect them from frost. Following are some effective vining edibles:

Bitter melon

Cantaloupe

Cucumber

Climbing nasturtium
(edible leaves and flowers)

Luffa squash

Pole beans

Scarlet and 'Dutch White' runner beans
(annual in cold-winter areas)

Climbing tomatoes

Yard-long bean

Vining winter squash

Vines for the Future

Perennial vines begin to shade the house usefully within a few years. The edible choices for warm-winter areas include:

Chayote
(*Sechium edule*)

Evergreen grape
(*Rhoicissus capensis*)

Hyacinth bean
(*Dolichos lablab*)

Kiwi
(*Actinidia chinensis*)

Passion fruit
(*Passiflora caerulea*,
P. edulis.)

Scarlet and 'Dutch White' runner beans
(a perennial in mild-winter areas)

The cold-hardy vines include grape (*Vitis labrusca*, or *V. vinifera* west of the Rockies), hop (*Humulus lupulus*), kiwi (*Actinidia arguta*) and maypop (*Passiflora incense, P. incarnata*).

Vines that require a spray program for healthy growth and good yields may not suit you. For example, the sulfur spray used on grapes to control mildew is bad-smelling and may discolor house siding.

Trellises and Misted Shrubs

All vines that have tendrils (see Appendix 4) belong on a trellis that stands apart from the house. Otherwise, the tendrils will work their way into shingles and siding, requiring costly repairs. Leave room between the trellis and the house so you can shear the vine to control its growth. The space improves the vine's cooling influence, creating a natural chimney effect. Figure 5.8 shows the hot air between the trellis and the house exhausting out the top and the draft sucking cooler air in along the bottom of the trellis.

In addition to blocking sunlight, plants cool the immediate environment by transpiring water through their leaves. We can improve the effect with watering and misting. Air drawn through the vines by the chimney effect is cooled both by transpiration and by the evaporation of water on the leaves. Prune the foliage from the lower part of the vine for good air circulation. Plant shrubs a short distance from the trellis so that air can circulate freely, but make sure the shrubs are tall enough to shade the lower portion of the trellis and the wall.

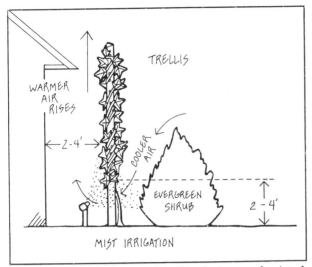

Figure 5.8 This system of trellised vines and misted shrubs uses evaporative cooling and convection currents to cool the house.

This vine-shrub-mist system works best in areas of low summer humidity. The south- and west-facing walls are the obvious first places to protect. But do not forget that east-facing windows admit considerable sunlight and heat before the eave of the house begins to cast a shadow, and should be protected in hot weather areas.

Hedges and Patios

Summer cooling can also be enhanced with carefully placed hedges. Two hedges planted in the shape of a large V, with the wide end toward the prevailing summer-afternoon breezes, will funnel a large volume of air and concentrate it at the narrow, open end of the V, increasing the wind's velocity and windchill factor as it passes through the narrow opening. (See Fig. 5.9.)

Some shrubs can provide fruit and channel gentle winds at the same time – Russian olive (*Elaeagnus angustifolia*), rose hips (*Rosa rugosa*), natal plum (*Carissa edulis, C. grandiflora*), carob (*Ceratonia siliqua*), hollyleaf cherry (*Prunus ilicifolia*), Catalina cherry (*Prunus lyonii*), strawberry guava (*Psidium littorale*), sugar bush (*Rhus ovata*), pineapple guava (*Feijoa sellowiana*), quince (*Cydonia oblonga*), pomegranate (*Punica granatum*), bamboo (*Bambusa* and *Phyllostachys* sp.) and jojoba (*Simmondsia chinensis*). Not all are for the windiest of places. Stay with the classic non-edible windbreak trees for the toughest winds.

Place a brick patio next to the small, open end of the V. When hosed down, the bricks soak up water and help cool the air as the moisture evaporates. Along with an arbor of vines overhead and mist-irrigated shrubs along the borders, your patio will

be a delightfully cool place to relax. The cooler environment around the patio's edge protects cooler-weather crops such as lettuce, spinach, kale, and peas, allowing you to harvest them longer than nearby unprotected plantings.

Trees and Vines for Southern Shade

South-facing walls need protection in the late summer and early fall when the sun's path begins to drop in the sky. Plant deciduous trees on the south side of the house in the area shown in Fig. 5.10, but note that trees planted within that area for summer cooling can cause too much winter shading. Though deciduous trees appear to allow plenty of winter light through their bare branches, in reality they block quite a bit of the sun. In many species, less than 50 percent of the available winter light actually gets through to warm your house. Figure 5.11 lists the percentage of winter shade for a number of deciduous trees. In most cases, the net effect of trees on the south side of houses with solar water or space heating is to *increase* the utility bills, not lower them.

Deciduous vines are helpful for cooling solar homes because they can be pruned back hard to admit the winter sunlight. This strategy is safest in mild-winter areas. In climates with very cold winters, pruning in the fall can cause freeze-damaged vines – it is best to wait until late winter or early spring to prune.

Summer pruning slightly retards the growth of plants, while winter pruning stimulates growth and branching. With a program of winter pruning,

Figure 5.9 The afternoon breeze is funneled past cool, moist bricks and shrubs before it enters the house.

your vines may become a thicket, providing too much shade from the bare winter branches. Try extensive summer pruning each year to keep the vines from growing too large.

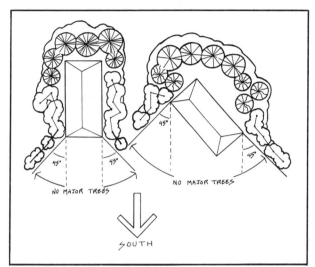

Figure 5.10 Trees planted along the south wall can give unwanted shade in winter. For the best effect, plant trees outside the area marked "no major trees."

Pruning for Winter Light and Summer Shade

Summer shade and winter sun are not incompatible, but to have both requires careful study and the removal of some lower branches. Figure 5.12 shows how to calculate the shade cast by existing trees during the heating season. Use graph paper, and draw everything to scale.

Pick the top of the highest window on the south side of your home as your point of reference for drawing the angles of the sun's altitude. Use the chart for your latitude in Appendix 2. (San Francisco, St. Louis, and Washington, DC all lie close to 38° latitude.) The area below the dotted lines indicates which branches to remove to let the sun strike the window and wall.

This method uses the figures for noon and works only for trees near the house. Early and late in the day, more distant objects can shade the house and garden, and you will have to "eyeball" their impact by standing in the landscape—it cannot easily be done on paper.

Chances are you will have to compromise between winter sun and summer shade. Notice how limbs that provide shade through October 21 begin to block the sun in mid-February, before the heating season is over. But cutting branches to admit sunlight till April 21 exposes the south wall to sunlight as early as August 21, when you still need the shade.

There are alternatives to making a scale drawing of your house and trees. You can use the solar devices described in "The Climate in Your Yard" to determine which limbs to remove.

Shady Results

Once your living shade is in place and growing, it is time to stretch out and enjoy some of the benefits of your edible landscape—cool mint tea, refreshing fruit and berries, chilled three-bean salad

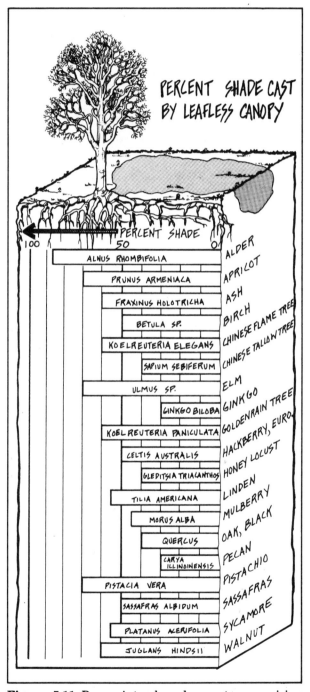

Figure 5.11 Bare winter branches cast a surprising amount of shade. For more winter sunlight, prune the canopy extensively in summer.

(made with beans gathered from the vines climbing up the walls), and the sweet fragrance of a citrus tree or honeysuckle vine as it shelters your home from the blistering heat.

Figure 5.12 Calculating which branches to remove for more winter sunlight. Draw everything to scale on graph paper and be sure to account for any slope in the landscape.

McPherson, Gregory. **Energy Conserving Site Design**. New York: American Conservation Association, 1984. A very technical, thorough presentation of case studies, site analysis, and master planning, with a historical review. For the professional only.

Moffat, Anne, and Schiler, Marc. **Landscape Design That Saves Energy**. New York: William Morrow, 1981. The best book on the subject, it is complete and offers plenty of data without feeling like a textbook. The analyses and design strategies are done by regional climate types, with good drawings and thorough lists of plant materials for each climate. An excellent resource.

Perkins, Harold O. **Espaliers and Vines for the Home Gardener**. Princeton, NJ: D. Van Nostrand, 1964. An older book with good detail on choosing and caring for vines and espalier plants. Not much detail on the specifics of training espalier fruit trees.

U.S. Dept. of the Interior. **Plants, People and Environmental Quality**. Washington, DC: 1972. My favorite book of design criteria for making urban settings more livable with trees and shrubs that conserve energy, muffle sound, and filter soot and dust. For each application, the basic formulae and plants are listed. Where else can you find out how thick to plant a hedge of *Rosa multiflora* to stop a car moving at 30 miles an hour?

Yanda, Bill, and Fisher, Rick. **The Food and Heat Producing Solar Greenhouse**. Rev. ed. Santa Fe: John Muir, 1980. The classic book for designing and building your own solar greenhouse, though it does not mention that solar greenhouses can cause moisture problems where winters are wet and humid; also, the recommended vent sizes are too small.

Chamberlin, Susan. **Hedges, Screens and Espaliers**. Tucson, AZ: HPBooks, 1983. The best book on the subject. Also the best step-by-step instructions on how to train espalier trees, with excellent color photos. Includes a mini-encyclopedia for each of the three topics. Good coverage of energy conserving design and muffling sound with plants.

Kern, Barbara and Ken. **The Owner-Built Homestead**. Charles Scribner's Sons, 1977. A classic for the homesteading movement. Very useful in considering ways to integrate energy, food, water, and waste systems for your home and yard. A major inspiration for me 12 years ago. Though intended for rural settings, many of the examples can be adapted to the code restrictions and style of the suburbs. The most accurate information is contained in the chapters on site analysis, planning, and alternative construction techniques.

SHAPING WATER

Water, the universal solvent, is a non-renewable resource. No new water is being made; what we have is simply recycled. Making wise use of the water cycle will improve the workings of your edible landscape.

Mining Water

Cities have convenient water. Where the pipes come from is often unknown; to the city dwellers, the source is irrelevant. But the sources and the quality of fresh water are dwindling. Tucson rose from the desert with no regard to its surroundings. Large deposits of water, accumulated long ago in rock deep beneath Tucson, are being pumped day and night to fill swimming pools, flush toilets and water lawns. These ancient pools of water cannot be replaced. They are as non-renewable as oil.

Other areas of the country are beginning to use more water than seasonal rains provide. The vast Ogalla aquifer, which lies beneath part of the wheat belt, is drying up. Yet, agriculture still manages to extract enough water to force ever greater yields. But food is water; and as the direct costs of irrigation escalate, the cost of food rises.

The single largest consumer of energy in California is the system of pumps that move water. A network of canals and aqueducts stretches over the entire state, requiring continual pumping. The lettuce shipped from California to New York City is a product of oil and water, and lots of both.

Personal, edible landscapes can be nurtured with a frugality unknown to agriculture. Society benefits from the net savings in energy and water, and the wise use of water protects the soil, conserves soil nutrients, and promotes abundant production.

Use Water Wisely

Rainfall on bare soil often puddles up. In clay soils, the puddling creates a thin crusty layer on top that cracks and turns rock-hard as it dries. Air enters the cracks, killing roots. The crust resists penetration by the next rain and irrigation. Getting water to quickly soak into soil is vital.

Slowing Water – Microscopically

A shallow layer of mulch helps to slow runoff and encourage soaking. The incorporation of organic matter into the soil surface also helps. The fiber acts as a sponge, quickly absorbing moisture. After the helpful bacteria in the soil have digested some of the organic matter, the water-holding capabilities of the soil are even greater. Humus, as mentioned earlier, is an end product of the decomposition of organic matter and has the ability to hold four times more water than clay. Humus helps clay soils resist cracking, and in sandy soils, holds onto the moisture, slowing the otherwise rapid drainage. High levels of organic matter and humus provide a bountiful harvest in part by storing more moisture in the soil, giving your edible landscape security from fluctuations in rainfall.

Slowing Water – Deep Storage

Your soil is a depository for water, and you can improve its storage capacity by slowing the passage of water on its way to nearby creeks and rivers. Roots must go in search of deep water, stored in soils 3 or more feet below the surface. The more friable a soil is, the easier it is for the tiny root hairs to grow. Cultivation is the common way to loosen hard, heavy soils, but deep soils cannot be easily cultivated to improve the soil structure.

Roots are among nature's "tools" for deep cultivation. Relentless implements of soil development, deep-rooted plants are essential to a healthy edible landscape. Dead roots add organic matter and humus to loosen soils, and act like a sponge to improve the storage of water deeper than we could ever dig. To improve your soil's moisture retention, plant and encourage deep-rooted plants, both edible and ornamental, in every area of your landscape.

Regulating Water's Power

Water is power, both subtle and grand. Nutrient release goes on at the molecular level. The residents of flooded Louisiana in 1983 and the victims of landslides of California in 1982 and 1983 can testify to water's harsher side. As the grand equalizer, water disperses its energy by meandering. The sinuous wanderings of a brook accommodate both the torrent and the placid shallows. A river protects itself from the ravages of momentum by dispersing stored energy at each turn. At one point in a river bend, the current cuts into the bank as in Fig. 5.13. The silt and gravel extracted soon settle downstream. Thus a gravel bar is formed, a new place for the current to carve into a bank. At all times, the river is consuming and rebuilding itself.

From an airplane, you can see these patterns. (Even the silty water running in your gutters has them.) Your driveways and sidewalks, however, may lack curves, and many suburban lots are graded with one simple slope, ignoring the safety of meander.

Sculpt Your Landscape for Meander

You can create land sculptures to help moderate the flow of water. Where drainage is needed, carve deep, narrow pools (called swales) lower than the

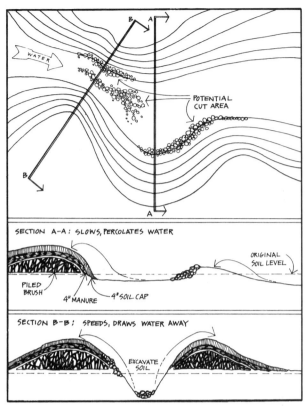

Figure 5.13 For a natural-looking creekbed, combine calm pools (A - A) with fast, deep channels (B - B). Protect potential cut areas with rocks.

water-logged areas. To encourage moisture to soak into dry soils, form broad, shallow waterways. Intense rains will run off into these shallow depressions to form temporary pools, and gradually the water will soak in and recharge the soil.

Where space is tight, you may have to mound the banks (called berms) of your newly sculpted creek, or riparian habitat, to help reduce flooding during heavy rains. A berm is also useful on lots with no drainage problems, to break the monotony of a flat landscape.

Recipe for Free Berms

Take a Large Helping of Brush and Prunings . . .

When the excavation of a waterway provides too little soil for a berm, substitute branches and whatever woody "waste" you have – brush, leaves, slash, straw, or scrap wood. Keep in mind that the brush berm settles as it decomposes. Mound the brush piles two or three times taller than the height of the berm you ultimately want.

Top with Soil and Manure . . .

Next, cap the brush mounds with a layer of manure and soil. You'll be planting directly into

this layer. The brush provides a slow release of nutrients, while the manure helps adjust the balance of carbon and nitrogen and speeds up the availability of nutrients. As the berm decomposes, adequate nutrients will be released for the plants.

Garnish with Riparian or Edible Plants . . .

Whether you are creating a creekside berm or simply a meandering mound to enhance your landscape, you'll need plants to protect it from erosion. Take a close look at local creek banks for ideas about the shape of waterways and the best plants to grow. Your local native plant society and soil conservation agents are also valuable resources. For a riparian habitat, use plants with underground runner roots or fibrous, shallow roots which have the ability to quickly self-root from broken twigs. Plant densely the first time to ensure cover for good soil retention. Also remember to use plants in the lowest part of a swale that will tolerate the extremes of flooding and dryness – plants such as willow, alder, blackberry, nettles, cottonwood, mint, cattail and horsetail.

For over 20 years, Lester Hawkins and Marshall Olbrich of Western Hills Rare Plant Nursery, in Occidental, California, have been sculpting berms and swales on four acres that were initially one simple slope. The berms began as clippings from clearing and pruning. The soil for the mounds was not trucked in, but came from the excavation of ponds. The sculpted curves of the berms and swales add to the dynamic visual appeal of this special place, and over the years, their plantings have evolved into one of the most exciting, flood- and drought-tolerant landscapes in California.

In 1982, their swales weathered, virtually intact, the most extreme storm in 125 years. More than 18 inches of rain fell in 20 hours. Grazed and farmed lands for miles around emerged from the same storm looking bombarded. The Western Hills Nursery was practically unscathed.

Planting the Berms

Riparian plants are easier than most to establish. First, fertilize and cultivate the sculpted area. To control the "weed" seeds in the tilled soil, simply lay newspaper three to five sheets thick over the entire area, making sure the edges are fully overlapped. Cover all newspaper with a 2- to 4-inch layer of loamy compost that is fairly free of seeds. Soak everything and allow to drain overnight.

To plant root and crown divisions, such as mints and comfrey, simply use an old kitchen paring knife to cut an X through the wet newspaper. Place the plant division or piece of root slightly below the cut and cover with compost. To transplant container plants, remove a portion of the newspaper.

For seeds, simply broadcast, rake in the seeds, tamp the soil, and water as needed. Nature does the rest.

Edible Berms

The berms that shape the flow of your meandering brook can look naturalized and yet be edible. There are many useful plants that thrive in the fluctuating environment of a swale. Figure 5.14 lists a variety.

Drywells

Downspouts unload large amounts of water to very small areas. To control the runoff, those green coils that are attached to the end of the downspout are often not too effective. They do not uncoil easily, and they seem to be able to leap beneath a passing lawn mower. In addition, they are not very attractive.

When a small yard does not allow the use of swales and berms, turbulence can be used to dissipate the energy of runoff water. Drywells reduce the power of downspout water through turbulence, and they encourage deep percolation of the rainwater into the soil. Drywells are very effective boxes built out of sight, underground. And you can build them yourself with scrap materials. Wooden boxes will rot over time, so for a more permanent solution, use mortared brick or cinder block or poured concrete.

The drywell allows the moderating effect of turbulence to occur within a small, confined area. As the water churns and foams within the box, the energy of motion is discharged. Some of the water soaks into the soil under the box; the remainder drains through an outlet pipe, at a less destructive velocity.

The grate (see Fig. 5.15) catches twigs, leaves and debris before they enter the box and is easily disguised by a few stones. The box must be large enough to accommodate occasional extreme rains. Figure 5.16 describes the formula for determining the size of the box.

Usually the limiting factor is the size of the hole you are willing to dig. The heavier the downpour, the bigger the box. The boxes constructed at the Farallones Institute Rural Center are three-foot cubes, and they functioned well during that same 18-inch rain mentioned earlier. Those boxes are in a very rocky, well-drained soil. A heavy clay soil would need a bigger box.

The outlet is placed at least halfway up from the bottom to allow as much water as possible to soak into the soil. If the drainage pipe travels a good distance, the water will reacquire momentum. To reduce that effect, avoid smooth-walled PVC pipe, and use flexible corrugated drainpipe. Drainage

EDIBLE PLANTS FOR BERMS

Common Name Botanical Name	Edible Portion	Tolerates Some Flooding
Arrowhead *Sagittaria latifolia*	Tuber	Yes
Blackberry *Rubus sp.*	Fruit	Yes
Cattails *Typha latifolia*	Pollen, "tail," root	Yes
Celery, wild *Apium graveolens*	Stem, leaf, seed	Yes
Chicory *Cichorium intybus*	Leaf, flower, root	Yes
Comfrey *Symphytum officinale*	Leaf, root	Yes
Fennel *Feoniculum vulgare*	Leaf, seed	No
French Sorrel *Rumex scutatus*	Leaf	Yes
Gooseberry *Ribes divaricatum*	Fruit	No
Gooseberry, wild *Ribes sp.*	Fruit	No
Horsetail *Equisetum arvense*	New shoots	Yes
Huckleberry *Vaccinium ovatum*	Fruit	No
Miner's lettuce *Montia perfoliata*	Leaf	No
Mints *Mentha sp.*	Leaf	Yes
Nasturtium *Tropaeolum majus*	Leaf, seed, flower	No
Nettle, stinging *Urtica dioca*	Leaf	Yes
New Zealand spinach *Tetragonia expansa*	Leaf	No
Nut grass *Cyperus esculentus*	Tuber	Yes
Oregon grape *Mahonia aquifolium*	Fruit	No
Raspberry *Rubus sp.*	Fruit	No
Strawberry, wild *Fragaria sp.*	Fruit	No
Thimbleberry *Rubus sp.*	Fruit	No
Violets *Viola odorata*	Leaf, flower	No
Watercress *Nasturtium officinale*	Leaf	Yes
Western chockeberry *Prunus caudatum*	Fruit	No
Wild ginger *Asarum candatum*	Root	No
Wild rose *Rosa californica or sp.*	Fruit	No

Figure 5.14

Figure 5.15 A drywell prevents erosion at a downspout. Use the formula in Fig. 5.16 to calculate the size of the box.

pipes that travel long distances down steep hills may require a series of drywells to reduce momentum and prevent erosion where the drainpipe discharges.

Wherever a drainpipe empties, your neighbor's property or yours, the soil needs further protection. A small cluster of rocks will help churn the stream of water. Establish water-loving plants with fibrous roots to help hold the soil together. Avoid aggressive plants such as mints, unless the end of the pipe is far from cherished plantings. Mint roots can travel great distances and become a maintenance nightmare.

Christopher Columbus may have discovered that the world is round, but Kansas is flat. It is futile to have a drainpipe in a drywell in a flat landscape—the trench required for it would be beyond reasonable effort. But the box itself will help. Just make it bigger to allow for more retention until the water soaks into the ground.

By good luck, my visual preference for curves matches the design guidelines for good water management. Our suburban and urban landscapes are saturated with harsh, straight lines. I prefer the grace and visual charm of a meander. My inclination is to use plants and landscaping to soften both

the concrete and emotional edges of "modern" construction, which also helps to temper water. Into every life a little rain must fall—so make good use of it.

The formula to determine the maximum cubic feet per hour (cfh) runoff from your roof is as follows:

Q = Aci(360)

Where Q = velocity in cubic feet per hour (cfh)

   A = area as a fraction of 1 acre (the area, in square feet, of the portion of the roof that feeds into each downspout, divided by 43,560)

   c = runoff coefficient (approximately .9 for a composite shingle roof)

   i = intensity, in inches per hour (from the 1-hour rainfall maps, Fig. 5.17) Pick the extreme number of inches of rain per hour that you want to be protected for.

   360 = seconds per hour

As an example, consider a 400-square-foot portion of a roof feeding one downspout in St. Louis, Missouri. Say I want to be safe from the 50-year extreme 1-hour rainfall. From the rainfall maps, I take the figure of 3 inches per hour. Using the formula, Q = .00918 × .9 × 3.0(360), or 8.92 cfh. To hold the extreme hourly rainfall for the 50-year storm, I would need a drywell that held approximately 9 cubic feet, or a box 2 feet by 2 feet by 2.25 feet.

Figure 5.16

Figure 5.17

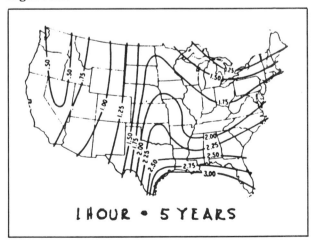

I HOUR • 5 YEARS

continued

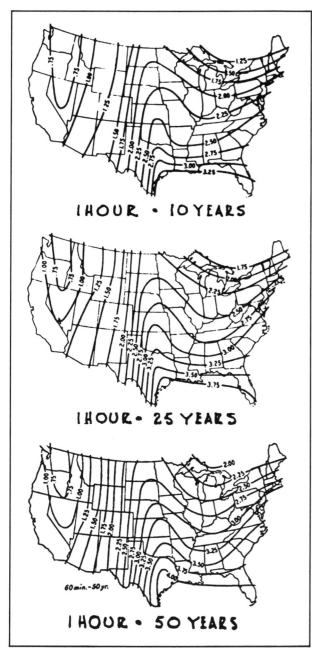

Figure 5.17 Choose a one-hour rainfall figure from these maps as "i" in Fig. 5.16.

Kern, Barbara and Ken. **The Owner-Built Homestead.** Charles Scribner's Sons, 1977. A classic for the homesteading movement. Very useful in considering ways to integrate energy, food, water, and waste systems for your home and yard. Though intended for rural settings, many of the examples can be adapted to the code restrictions and style of the suburbs. The most accurate information is contained in the chapters on site analysis, planning, and alternative construction techniques.

Moffat, Anne, and Schiler, Marc. **Landscape Design That Saves Energy.** New York: William Morrow, 1981. The best book on the subject, it is complete and offers plenty of data without feeling like a textbook. The analyses and design strategies are done by regional climate types, with good drawings and thorough lists of plant materials for each climate. An excellent resource.

Mollison, Bill, and Holmgren, David. **Permaculture One.** Stanley, Tasmania: Tagari Books, 1978. A good introduction to the Australian equivalent of sustainable/ holistic/integrated farms and gardens. The theories were an inspiration to me 7 years ago, but most of the examples are inappropriate for U.S. climates, property sizes, and lifestyles.

Mollison, Bill. **Permaculture Two.** Stanley, Tasmania: Tagari Books, 1981. Similar to its predecessor, with a big section appropriate only to gardeners who live where it rains less than 10 inches a year.

Reader's Digest. **Reader's Digest Illustrated Guide to Gardening.** Pleasantville, NY: Reader's Digest, 1978. A good overview of ornamental gardening, with a sprinkling of edibles. Nice line drawings similar to those in the Royal Horticultural Society's books. Some good step-by-step drawings.

Robinette, Gary. **Water Conservation in Landscape Design and Management.** New York: Van Nostrand, 1984. A thorough discussion of all the basics, with strategies that are not too high-tech or costly. A textbook-like review, but not too technical. Recommended reading.

Schwenk, Theodore. **Sensitive Chaos.** New York: Schocken Books, 1976. I love water, so I enjoyed this discussion of water's influence on germination and embryos, and the universe's subtle effects on water. Though I don't usually think in spiritual terms, Schwenk inspired me to contemplate the cosmic manifestations of the "universal solvent."

2 DESIGNING YOUR EDIBLE LANDSCAPE
Putting It All Together

SYNERGY

synergy *(sin'-er-je) n. 1. the simultaneous action of separate agencies which, together, have greater total effect than the sum of their individual effects ... 2. combined or cooperative action or force.*

It is possible to arrange the pieces of an edible landscape so that the whole has synergy. In my designs, the pieces not only work together, but they also do some of the gardening for me. Here are a few suggestions.

Integrate Home and Garden

Consider extending your house into the landscape with a solar greenhouse. A solar greenhouse can provide heating for your home, be a place to grow seedlings for the garden, and provide room to experiment with exotic plants. In climates where the winter air is very dry, solar greenhouses provide a wonderfully fragrant humidity. (In the wet winters of the Pacific Northwest, however, the high humidity of the greenhouse can be unhealthy and cause the walls of the house to mildew.) The details of solar greenhouse construction and cultivation are beyond the scope of this book; see the references at the end of this chapter.

The walls of your house or other buildings can serve as trellises. I have already talked about how much plants can do to cool and warm a house. Training plants on the walls can be good for both. Some of the benefits of the association are frost protection for tender vines, earlier growth in the spring, earlier flower and fruit ripening, and fewer rain-induced diseases.

Use the eaves of your house, as shown in Fig. 6.1, to protect tender plants that would not otherwise flourish in your climate. Fig. 6.2 shows some miniature, genetic dwarf apples trellised near a wall. For hundreds of years, training trees and shrubs close to a wall, in some form of espalier, has been used to protect sensitive plants out of their native habitat. Concrete water tanks can be used in much the same way, because the massive amount of water they contain tempers the air close to the tank.

Figure 6.1 The eaves of your house create a micro-climate that can shelter tender edibles.

Where water emerges from downspouts, consider water-loving plants. The roof delivers rain from a large area for use by a much smaller area, a useful magnification where summer rains are brief showers. Some of the edible plants that benefit include artichokes, asparagus, blackberries, blueberries, California bay trees, cardoons, cattails, cranberries, curly dock, elderberries, lotus, strawberries, water chestnuts, and wild gooseberries (*Ribes* sp.).

An arbor of vines can make a patio even more pleasant than usual. Two cautions: I do not recommend edibles for trellising directly over a patio because the falling fruit would stain the patio furniture and clothing. Also, avoid deciduous vines if you do not like raking up piles of leaves each fall.

Figure 6.2 Miniature 'Garden Delicious' apple trees are espaliered against a warm south wall under protective eaves.

If you have room for a windbreak, be sure to include some trees that can be cut for firewood—eucalyptus, acacia, black locust, oaks, hickory, mesquite, and osage orange have a high heat value. Consider trees and shrubs that attract bees and beneficial insects, those that are edible, or those that provide compostable materials.

A favorite integration of mine is to plant a variety of flowers, including some that are edible, some that provide blooms as well as improve the soil, and some that attract bees and beneficial insects. (See Fig. 4.8.)

Synergy and Original Thinking

Each edible landscape is unique and combines elements in new and productive ways. The best edible landscapes are products of original thinking. Perhaps our greatest limitation as designers is getting our minds to step beyond habits and to think differently. To get rid of conceptual blinders, try . . .

A Whack on the Side of the Head

Fantasy, eclectic thinking, brainstorming, the "Eureka-I-found-it" phenomenon, hypnosis, dreams: these are all labels for thinking differently. Creativity doesn't have to just happen—it can be learned. A useful tool for playing and working at thinking differently is a book by Roger von Oech, *A Whack on the Side of the Head* (published by Creative Think, P.O. Box 7354, Menlo Park, CA 94025). I highly recommend this book. According to von Oech, the ten causes of mental blocks are thinking that says:

- The right answer
- Follow the rules
- Avoid ambiguity
- Play is frivolous
- Don't be foolish
- That's not logical
- Be practical
- To err is wrong
- That's not my area
- I'm not creative

He goes on to review each mental block and to give pointers on how to break through to more creative ways of thinking. I've seen many practical examples of how new thoughts make better edible landscapes, so do practice "whacking the side of your head."

Thinking differently can also save you money. As an example, consider the solution I proposed for clients with a severe creekside erosion problem. When a small gully opened near their swimming pool, the clients were anxious to halt the erosion and heal the scar. A local landscaper gave an estimate of $1,300 for a typical reinforced concrete retaining wall. I was asked to consult on an alternative. I suggested arranging used tires up the side of the gully, like seats in an amphitheater, filling the hole of each tire with eroded soil and planting willow cuttings from an adjacent grove.

The clients were skeptical but spent a day collecting used tires and putting everything together. They thought things looked quite strange at the end of the day with all those twigs sticking out of the tires. However, within nine months they had a thicket of willows, and the tires were concealed. Their erosion problem is permanently solved, the swimming pool intact—for less than 2 percent of the cost of the proposed concrete wall.

Abraham, George and Katy. **Organic Gardening Under Glass**. Emmaus, PA: Rodale Press, 1975. The first book on the subject. Not up to date, but still a good general reference. For indoor use of beneficial insects, see William Jordan's *Windowsill Ecology*.

Alexander, Christopher; Ishikawa, Sara; and Silverstein, Murray. **A Pattern Language**. New York: Oxford University Press, 1977. This remarkable (and expensive) book is a must for designers, landscapers, and landscape architects. My favorite source of inspiration for composing more complex, creative landscape designs. It succinctly explains multi-purpose design (combining many patterns in the same space). If you are designing only your own landscape, ask your local library to get a copy.

Brookes, John. **The Garden Book**. New York: Crown Books, 1984. Portrays many garden styles in excellent color photos and color drawings, in which all plants are labelled. The best of the glossy overviews of landscape design.

Douglas, J. Sholto, and Hart, Richard. **Forest Farming**. London: Watkins Publishing, 1976. A source of inspiration for multi-story agriculture when I first became interested in alternatives to orchards. An excellent review of the principles of mixing tree crops and cattle. Unlike J. Russell Smith's *Tree Crops*, Douglas and Hart describe contemporary, working examples from around the world. Not relevant to small-scale, suburban settings.

Farallones Institute. **The Integral Urban House**. San Francisco: Sierra Club Books, 1979. A classic guide for developing a holistic home and garden in the suburbs or city. Covers solar heating better than vegetable culture, and is very weak on tree crops and perennial food plants. Good ideas on raising rabbits and chickens in small areas and integrating them with garden and kitchen.

Kern, Barbara and Ken. **The Owner-Built Homestead**. Charles Scribner's Sons, 1977. A classic for the homesteading movement. Very useful in considering ways to integrate energy, food, water, and waste systems for your home and yard. Though intended for rural settings, many of the examples can be adapted to the code restrictions and style of the suburbs. The most accurate information is contained in the chapters on site analysis, planning, and alternative construction techniques.

Leckie, Jim; Masters, Gil; Whitehouse, Harry; and Young, Lily. **More Homes and Garbage**. Rev. ed. San Francisco: Sierra Club Books, 1975. This updated classic on integrated, sustainable homes and gardens has much more on wind power, methane generation, and hydropower than does the Farallones Institute's *Integral Urban House*; but similarly, is very weak on perennial food plants and tree crops.

Tilth. **The Future is Abundant**. Arlington, WA: Tilth, 1982. An excellent reference for people interested in permaculture designs and theories, edible landscaping, and sustainable agriculture. A good collection of bibliographies, seed and plant sources, addresses of like-minded people, and short summaries of alternative gardening and farming techniques. The best feature is a 300-species index of edible and useful plants for the Pacific Northwest—every region needs an index like this one. Out of print.

2

CREATING YOUR DESIGN

Scale Drawings

The first step in designing a landscape is to make a scale drawing of your property. You will need paper with four squares to the inch, a pencil, an eraser, a tape measure, and time and patience. Begin by finding the longest, straightest side of your property. Measure the length and mark it along one edge of the graph paper. Use this as a reference point from which to measure distances at right angles to this property line. The grid on the graph paper can stand for intervals of feet per box. If your property will not fit, get a bigger piece of graph paper.

Be sure to locate buried utility lines. Most utility companies have a toll-free number to assist you in locating underground pipes and wires. Draw them into your sketch.

Make a permanent inked copy of your sketch and have it laminated. Lay tracing paper or clear plastic over the master drawing and sketch in possible major areas and projects. This is a good way to brainstorm how to put all the pieces together. You may have to do a separate, more detailed drawing of some of the projects, such as the location of the individual plants in a flower border.

When I present a set of plans, covered with bizarre symbols, most clients cannot really visualize what the landscape is going to look like. If drawings aren't your forte, you may want to use another tool to visualize your anticipated plan.

Clay Models

As you begin to get some solid ideas, try making a small model of your edible landscape. Use clay, twigs, and manufactured props. If you check out the variety of miniature items available from a hobby shop, you will be amazed at the selection of props you can use for modeling your edible landscape.

Photo Play

Another useful approach is to photograph the existing landscape and draw your edible landscape onto the photograph. Have large prints made, at least 8 by 10 inches. Again, sketch many possible solutions. At first, do not worry about the feasibility, practicality, or cost of your sketched landscapes. By beginning with a no-holds-barred approach to designing, you will often come up with plans that are both creative and practical. Draw plants onto the photos scaled to their mature, full size. You will note how quickly a landscape can become crowded. You may want to plant densely in the beginning to have a mature looking landscape

more quickly, but the plantings will soon require selective pruning and removal.

Previewing the Plants

The final step involves walking your yard: pacing the size of things, visualizing the design. Props can help – I use a long pole, see Figure 6.3, with marks every several feet or adjust my extending pole pruner to the desired height. Then I stand with the pole where a tree is to be planted and have the client view the height of the pole from several places within the landscape and from several windows. (See Fig. 6.3.) This is a good way to see what a hedge or windbreak may do to your favorite views.

Shrubs and smaller plants can be visualized by setting out container-grown plants. Purchase a few of each type of plant that you anticipate using. By grouping them close together, you can get an idea of the contrast and impact of the combinations of different foliages. Next, set the containers out at

Figure 6.3 The author, outstanding in a future landscape, holds a bamboo pole to help a client visualize how a proposed tree will affect the view.

the spacing you anticipated on your plan. Stand back and imagine the mature size and form of the plants. Move the containers around until you are happy with the arrangement, and try moving the plants to other locations. Lugging containers around is a good way to review your design before actually planting.

Remembering Good Design

Landscapes change over time, and new plants, desires, and lifestyle can lead you to alter your edible landscape. Just remember the design guidelines you used for the first plan – they will be helpful with your evolving landscape, too.

The following is a short summary and comparison of traditional landscape design and environmental design, the approach I favor:

In Traditional Landscape Design . . .

- Structures, not plants, dominate the landscape.

- The view and the ornamental form are more important than the function.

- A standardized formula is often applied.

- The finished product is thought to be fixed and permanent.

- The plan is a service provided by a designer/consultant, and is therefore less personalized and limits the growth of the client.

- The design is created with little or no regard for ecological dynamics; it tends to ignore local environmental resources and is costly.

Environmental Design . . .

- Softens archictecture by allowing plants to shape and dominate the landscape.

- Intends for the landscape to be lived in, chooses functional (including edible) aspects over purely ornamental form.

- Is personally designed by or with the owner.

- Is constantly evolving, suited to the changing needs of the owner.

- Furthers the personal growth of the owner.

- Is well-grounded in the local environment, is low-cost, encourages the utilization of renewable resources, and relies on ecological dynamics as a source of sustenance.

Alexander, Christopher; Ishikawa, Sara; and Silverstein, Murray. **A Pattern Language**. New York: Oxford University Press, 1977. This remarkable (and expensive) book is a must for designers, landscapers, and landscape architects. My favorite source of inspiration for composing more complex, creative landscape designs. It succinctly explains multi-purpose design (combining many patterns in the same space). If you are designing only your own landscape, ask your local library to get a copy.

Beckett, Kenneth; Carr, David; and Stevens, David. **The Contained Garden**. New York: Viking Press, 1982. Excellent examples of all types of potted and contained gardens, in perfect full color. Includes a thorough discussion of techniques and a good encyclopedia section, but covers few edible options.

Brookes, John. **A Place in the Country**. London: Thames and Hudson, 1984. Excellent color photographs mingle with blueprintlike drawings of home landscapes. For each landscape, there are details of construction and plant culture information. The title is a bit misleading—the landscapes are on the scale of an American suburban yard.

Brookes, John. **The Garden Book**. New York: Crown Books, 1984. Portrays many garden styles in excellent color photos and color drawings, in which all plants are labelled. The best of the glossy overviews of landscape design.

Clouston, Brian. **Landscape Design With Plants**. New York: Van Nostrand Reinhold, 1979. This hefty manual on the English approach to landscape design offers many photos of quality landscapes. One of the few books to give mathematical guidelines for the layout of flower borders, ground covers, shrubs, and trees.

Creasy, Rosalind. **The Complete Book of Edible Landscaping**. San Francisco: Sierra Club Books, 1982. The "other" edible landscaping book, by a good friend and collaborator. The plant encyclopedia section is an essential reference. The prerequisite, and perfect companion, to my book!

Creasy, Rosalind. **Earthly Delights**. San Francisco: Sierra Club Books, 1985. The newest release by the author of *The Complete Book of Edible Landscaping*. Covers a variety of gardens, from orchid collections to wildflower meadows, with examples of how to garden with an ecological perspective. There are three "edible" chapters: The Heirloom Vegetable Garden, The Gourmet Garden, and The Cottage Garden.

Damrosch, Barbara. **Theme Gardens**. New York: Workman Publishing, 1982. The helpful lists of plants appropriate for each theme make it a favorite for design inspiration. Not oriented toward edibles, but useful for choosing plants for visual pleasure.

Ferguson, Nicola. **Right Plant, Right Place**. New York: Summit Books, 1984. Next to the *New Western Garden Book*, this is the reference I turn to most frequently. The long lists of plants are organized by design criteria, such as plants for wet soil, red flowers, or fragrance. There is a small color photograph of every plant listed, and an index of botanical and common names. If you are designing a home landscape, this is a book to borrow; if you are a professional landscaper, this is one to buy.

Garland, Sarah. **The Herb Garden**. New York: Viking Penguin, 1984. My favorite book for ideas on using herbs in the landscape. Beautiful color photos cover the full range of styles, from classical knot gardens to wild, rambling plantings. Includes an excellent cultural encyclopedia that lists uses of the herbs.

Gessert, Kate. **The Beautiful Food Garden: The Encyclopedia of Attractive Food Plants**. New York: Van Nostrand, 1983. Primarily an encyclopedia of the "most attractive" edible annual vegetables and flowers, based on a limited, informal survey. Ignores the extent to which "most attractive" is based on personal taste. The chapter on bubble drawings and master planning strategies is one of the best descriptions in print of this important step in the design process. Review all the chapters on design before you begin your own. Out of print.

Harper, Pamela. **Perennials—How to Select, Grow and Enjoy**. Tucson, AZ: HPBooks, 1985. As with all HPBooks, this good, general review has lots of quality color photos.

Institute for Local Self-Reliance. **Gardening for Health**. Washington, DC: Institute for Local Self-Reliance, 1976. The source for the information in Fig. 4.3. An excellent chart ranks the most nutrient-productive vegetables by nutrients produced in a square foot each month. Also gives a nutritional analysis of three dozen vegetables.

Johnson, Hugh. **The Principles of Gardening**. New York: Simon and Schuster, 1979. A well-designed, colorful book with lots of visual inspiration and step-by-step details on installation. Not much about edibles, but excellent for overall landscape design. While some examples are of aristocratic English gardens, many of the designs can be duplicated by the industrious home gardener.

Kern, Barbara and Ken. **The Owner-Built Homestead**. New York: Charles Scribner's Sons, 1977. A classic for the homesteading movement. Very useful in considering ways to integrate energy, food, water, and waste systems for your home and yard. A major inspiration for me 12 years ago. Though intended for rural settings, many of the examples can be adapted to the code restrictions and style of the suburbs. The most accurate information is contained in the chapters on site analysis, planning, and alternative construction techniques.

Larkcom, Joy. **The Salad Garden**. New York: Viking Press, 1984. The best book on gardening with colorful, gourmet vegetables. Exquisite color photographs of gardens as well as a color close-up of each edible mentioned. A fair amount of space is given to edible weeds, edible flowers, and unusual leafy greens. Good cultural information. A book to buy.

Lathrop, Norma Jean. **Herbs—How to Select, Grow and Enjoy**. Tucson, AZ: HPBooks, 1981. Shows several herb farms and both formal and informal ways to design herbal plantings. A mini-encyclopedia gives a good general overview of the cultural needs of herbs. The recipe section includes instructions for herbal vinegars, beauty aids, and wreaths.

Lees-Milne, Alvilde, and Verey, Rosemary. **The Englishwoman's Garden**. London: Chatto and Windus, 1983. As this book shows, the role and accomplishments of women in landscape architecture are vastly underrated. The English landscapes shown are very classic, with an aristocratic overtone. The color plates are not as vibrant as the ones in Verey and Samuel's *The American Woman's Garden*. See a copy in your library.

MacCaskey, Michael. **Award Winning Small-Space Gardens**. San Francisco: Ortho Books, 1979. Much better quality of color photos than Llewellyn's *Little English Backyards*. Included with some of the examples are excellent construction details. An entire chapter is devoted to growing food on patios, decks, and porches—including container culture of herbs, vegetables, and genetic dwarf fruit trees. A must if you live in the city, or rent.

Miller, Michael. **Gardening in Small Spaces**. New York: G. P. Putnam's Sons, 1983. Lots of black-and-white and watercolor drawings of a wide range of tiny space gardens—balconies, steps, tiny yards, hanging baskets— with all plants identified. Best feature is that a design schematic of annual bedding plants for each of the four seasons is provided for each setting.

Reader's Digest. **Reader's Digest Illustrated Guide to Gardening**. Pleasantville, NY: Reader's Digest, 1978. A good overview of ornamental gardening, with a sprinkling of edibles. Nice line drawings similar to those in the Royal Horticultural Society's books. Some good step-by-step drawings.

Robinette, Gary. **Water Conservation in Landscape Design and Management**. New York: Van Nostrand, 1984. A thorough discussion of all the basics, with strategies that are not too high-tech or costly. A textbook-like review, but not too technical. Recommended reading.

Rose, Graham. **The Low-Maintenance Garden**. New York: Viking Press, 1983. This good book on an often-neglected subject includes a mini-encyclopedia, labor-saving designs, and tips on techniques.

Smith, Ken. **Western Home Landscaping**. Tucson, AZ: HPBooks, 1978. Like most American introductory landscaping books, the photos show conventional suburban examples. Includes more construction details than most American books.

Stevenson, Violet. **The Wild Garden**. New York: Viking Press, 1985. Excellent coverage of gardens that are more rough-and-tumble, though most still appear designed and cultivated. Covers heath, fern, herb, water, and rock gardens, and wildflower meadows and woodlands. Superb color.

Sunset. **New Western Garden Book**. Menlo Park, CA: Sunset Books, 1979, rev. ed. The reference I use most frequently. A must for every western gardener, landscaper, and edible landscaper.

Swanson, Faith. **Herb Garden Design**. Hanover, NH: University Press of New England, 1984. Black and white designs for dozens of herb gardens, by type or by function. Most designs are formal or very formal. Good ready-to-use "blueprints" for gardeners who don't want to create their own design.

Verey, Rosemary, and Samuels, Ellen. **The American Woman's Garden**. Boston, MA: New York Graphic Society, 1984. The important contributions that women have made to landscape architecture and horticulture are probably more neglected in the U.S. than in Europe. An inspiring display of 15 exceptional landscapes designed by American women, with better color plates than Lees-Milne and Verey's *The Englishwoman's Garden*.

von Oech, Roger. **A Whack on the Side of the Head**. Menlo Park, CA: Creative Think, 1983. My favorite guide to breaking through mental barriers in order to think differently and brainstorm effectively. Provides concrete lessons in how to perceive things innovatively, as do successful entrepreneurs. Roger has been a consultant to Silicon Valley computer companies, and writes a very entertaining book.

Wilkinson, Elizabeth, and Henderson, Marjorie, eds. **The House of Boughs**. Covelo, CA: Yolla Bolly Press, 1985. My favorite collection of visual inspirations for designing garden and landscape structures—from pathways and arbors to ponds and rock grottos. Unlike similar books from England, there is no tedious text about the history of some chalet or castle, and most examples are more applicable to the home landscape.

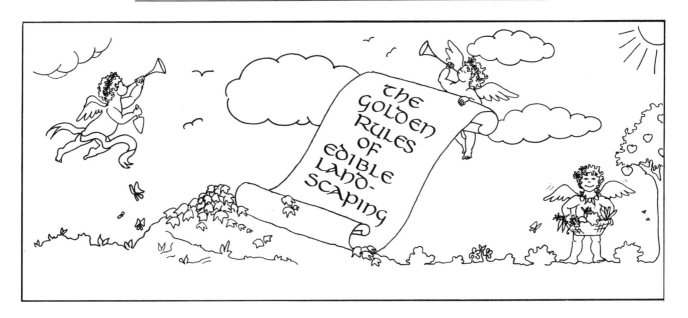

The Guidelines

These guidelines, my own golden rules, evolved over the past seven years as I wrestled with designs for edible landscapes that would easily fit into busy lives. Each rule contains a hidden R factor – the Reality coefficient. This factor lumps all of Murphy's Laws into one gigantic mathematical mess. Never underestimate the R factor in your garden, much less in your life.

As simple as these rules seem, some are consistently ignored. As with all rules, break them only if you are willing to face the consequences. But remember that breaking rules can lead to creative breakthroughs. So be flexible – try to follow the rules, but if you can't, have fun creating your own additions and refinements.

Enjoy your landscape – if it's just drudgery, you're doing something wrong. If your landscape becomes drudgery, why bother? Do something else instead that is pleasurable. You won't starve. Plan to make it easy to relax, recline and recreate in your edible landscape.

You have a lot to do besides landscaping – don't let your edible landscape take you over. We all have jobs, families, friends, and other leisure pastimes. Landscaping is great fun and therapy, but expect to let some areas of the edible landscape change or even die. As your life changes, modify your landscape to suit it.

Be lazy – let nature work for you. Learn how to use natural, biological processes to your advantage. Nature works 24 hours a day, and there are many ways to cooperate with nature to grow our food.

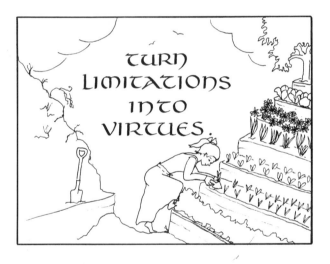

Turn limitations into virtues. Turn the restraints of your property inside-out and make your edible landscape pull together as a productive environment. Put plants in the right places to promote their best features.

Seek out the wisdom of your neighbors – someone else might just know more than you do. Most neighborhoods still have the living heritage of older, lifelong gardeners. They can give more good information about gardening in your locale than any book.

Your edible landscape is a community – a whole made up of individuals. The forest doesn't mourn the death of an individual tree. The role of a single plant is to serve the group as a whole. How the pieces, bugs, animals, and plants work together is the most important aspect of a healthy edible landscape. Respect the pieces, but work toward the betterment of the whole.

Time and money spent early means time and money saved later. An extra buck spent now for a lower maintenance landscape will save you many times that dollar each year for years to come.

Plan in advance—make your mistakes on paper, not in your landscape. Paper mistakes are less costly than landscaping mistakes. Sketch out several options and take the time to consider each. Review, re-think, get second opinions, and re-do the plan. It can be costly to be impatient.

Plan for the unexpected—nature will be, in all probability, unpredictable. The climate is getting more, not less, erratic. Plan to have options for several extremes of weather if you do not like to gamble with the food you are growing.

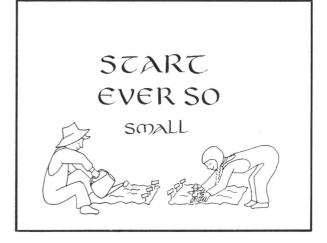

Start ever so small. A 100-square-foot vegetable bed is the *largest* area for a new gardener. Make this tiny plot picture perfect, then add on another 100 square feet each year until the Peter Principle is activated. That is, increase the area of the vegetable beds just short of the point where you can no longer master them.

Learn the multiple uses of plants to double the benefits of your landscape without doubling size or work. Many plants can serve more than one function. Some cool the house in the summer while ripening tasty fruits or nuts. Others have nutritious roots *and* leaves. Others kill pests *and* are edible. When possible, choose those plants that have multiple benefits.

Plant your vegetables no farther from the kitchen than you can throw the kitchen sink. There is a correlation between the distance to the kitchen and the demise of a vegetable bed. Almost literally, for every foot farther from the kitchen sink, the vegetables get forgotten a week sooner. The most distant vegetable beds return to weeds the soonest.

The Golden Rules were illustrated by Amie Hill.

GROWING VEGETABLES
No-Till Gardening: Less Work, Good Yields

Introduction

Nature abhors bare soil. She labors for centuries to build an inch of topsoil and is not about to waste any of it. Vulnerable to damage from excessive wind, sun, heat, and rain, bare soil can vanish in a fraction of the time required to build it. The few examples of bare soil formed by nature are landslides, fires, and the gravel bars of a river, which nature speedily covers and protects with so-called weeds. Where these healing plants appear, they are signs that something has gone amiss – soil has been disturbed and needs restoring.

Sunlight can heat bare soil enough to flamelessly burn the organic matter of the surface layer, diminishing or destroying its fertility. The heat of the sun can simply vaporize nitrogen near the soil's surface. In overheated soil, the beneficial bacteria and soil microorganisms die. Without their persistent work in digesting organic matter, there would be few nutrients available to plants. The sun can parch the soil, and once a soil gets too dry, phosphorus and potash, vital minerals for plant growth, become unavailable to the feeding roots. In warm areas such as the Southwest, Southeast, and parts of California, disturbed, bare soils force gardeners to fertilize the soil more heavily in order to get good yields. Though northern gardeners can bare and damage their soils too, the cooler weather tempers the loss.

Gardeners should do their best to avoid bare soil and imitate instead nature's model. Nature combines a mulch to cool and shield the soil, roots of weeds and other plants to conserve nutrients, plus a canopy to shelter the soil from wind and rain. If gardeners bare the soil by cultivating and tilling, they should turn to mulches such as leaves and straw to reduce the problems of soil erosion and overheating. The cooler temperatures under a mulch encourage an active soil life even in the hottest climates. And the mulch also helps to prevent erosion that reduces the nutrients available to the plant.

Gardeners should encourage live plants – including some of the cursed weeds – to cover the ground. The protective effects of mulch are enhanced by the layered canopy of foliage, and the roots of live plants act as a safety net below the soil, catching nutrients that would otherwise be leached away by rain or irrigation.

It's not necessary to till the soil in order to garden. Instead of digging, you can create a garden with surface layers of compost and mulches – less strenuous chores. Initially, the amount of time spent may equal the demands of a dug garden, but the effort is less. The methods outlined in this section take a bit more room than cultivated rows or intensive beds, but they are much easier. You have a wide range of methods to choose from. Pick those that suit your yard, physical fitness, and level of ambition. A garden does not have to be monopolized by one method of growing. Nature is diverse – gardening should be, too.

SHEET COMPOSTING FOR "WILD" AND "TAME" PLANTS

"What is a weed?
A plant whose virtues
have not yet been discovered."

Ralph Waldo Emerson

Wild and Woolly Vegetables

Wild edible weeds are food for the laziest and the most adventurous of gardeners. They take some getting used to – their flavors are often more powerful than those of common vegetables. But their strong flavors betray the superior nutritional value of "weedy" vegetables. (See Fig. 7.1.) I love strong, spicy vegetables, but not everybody does. If their texture or flavor is too unusual for your taste, try sneaking the wild edibles into your diet. When I have friends over who are unfamiliar with or squeamish about wild edibles, I dice the raw, leafy wild greens into small pieces and mix them with a larger portion of ordinary salad greens. That way, I can gently introduce these nutritionally power-packed vegetables to my friends without startling their taste buds. I also add the strongest flavored leaves and roots in small pieces to soups. Sometimes my guests are so bold as to pick out little pieces to sample individually. If they like the flavor, I encourage them to gradually increase the proportion of the "wild and woolly" vegetables with each meal.

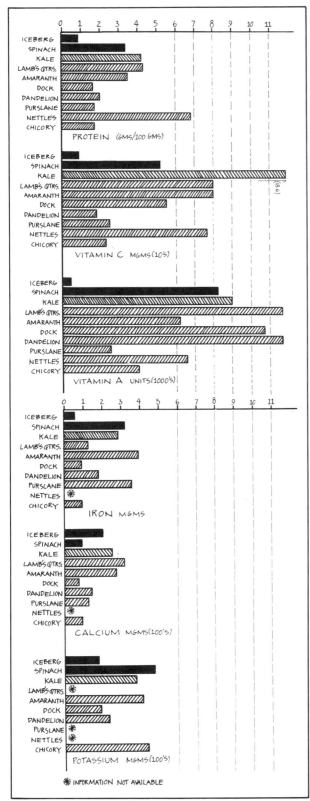

Figure 7.1 When it comes to nutrition, Iceberg lettuce is out to lunch. Many wild edibles are far more nutritious.

Some wild edibles are as tasty and succulent as any lettuce. My favorites are listed in Fig. 7.2. As a starting point for the beginning weed eater, I urge you to try at least one. I covet the patches of miner's lettuce that sprout each winter in secret places in the nearby woods. So sweet and succulent, they are superior to any head of Iceberg lettuce. Purslane, sometimes called pigweed, does not seem to mind the midsummer heat, and stays succulent longer into the summer than most other wild edibles. I have even gathered seeds of purslane so I could establish it in gardens where it did not already exist. For help identifying and preparing wild edibles, check the books listed at the end of this chapter and contact your local native plant society.

My Favorite No-Till Edibles
For leafy greens:

purslane	*(Portulaca oleracea)*
chickweed	*(Stellaria media)*
watercress	*(Nasturtium officinale)*
lamb's-quarters	*(Chenopodium alba)*
miner's lettuce	*(Montia perfoliata)*

For the fruit:

wild blackberries	*(Rubus* sp.*)*
thimbleberries	*(Rubus parviflorus)*
ground cherries	*(Physalis* sp.*)*
huckleberries	*(Vaccinium ovatum)*
wild strawberries	*(Fragaria* sp.*)*

For roots:

salsify	*(Tragopogon* sp.*)*

Figure 7.2

Sheet Composting and Wild Edibles

Once you become addicted to the superior flavor and nutrition of wild foods, you can naturalize your favorites in patches in your edible landscape. Wild edible patches do not fit many people's idea of pretty. The beauty in wild edibles is their taste, their nutritional superiority, and the ease with which they grow. If you like, hide these "weedy" patches behind a hedge or the garage.

The secret of naturalizing wild edibles is to establish your chosen plants in such a way that other plants cannot compete. The technique I favor for starting a wild patch combines sheet composting, which is like a short version of a typical compost pile, with a biodegradable weedkiller — newspaper and cardboard. Toxic herbicides are unnecessary.

The key to this system is to never disturb the soil. If you till or cultivate, especially the upper layers, you encourage formerly buried seeds to sprout. Well mulched, no-till gardens eliminate most weeding. Only the seeds in bird droppings and those blown in by the wind will sprout in your garden.

The Recipe

Start without tilling, right on top of whatever is there—grass or bare soil (see Fig. 7.3). First, apply a one-time application of organic fertilizers—slow release rock powders such as colloidal phosphate and granite dust—which nourish strong growth for years. If necessary, balance the pH with lime for acidic soils or sulfur for alkaline soils.

Next, add layers of raw materials (leaves, clippings, manure, sawdust, and so on), mixing the layers to achieve a carbon-to-nitrogen ratio of between 20 and 30 parts of carbon to 1 part nitrogen. Use the Carbon-to-Nitrogen Ratios in Appendix 5 for a guideline. This ratio can be used to judge a material's ability to decompose. The ideal ratio for healthy, rapid decomposition is 30:1. If the ratio is greater than 30 parts carbon, there is too much carbon and not enough nitrogen for rapid decomposition; such materials need a nitrogen-rich material such as manure to adjust the ratio. A material with a ratio below 30 has a high quantity of nitrogen and will give off nitrogen as a gas unless mixed with more woody materials. If you start on top of dense sod, the first layer should be manure because the fibrous mat of dead leaves and roots needs extra nitrogen in order to decompose.

Put down as many layers as you have the time or materials for. Six inches is the minimum depth to start with. The result is like a flat, miniature compost pile, which is why this method is called sheet composting. Don't forget that the initial application of sheet compost requires great amounts of materials. A cubic yard of bulky mulch will cover 100 square feet only 3 to 4 inches deep.

Some of the raw materials you use will be full of seeds. Left to sprout, these renegade seeds may out-compete the plants you are trying to establish. To smother them, put down a layer of newspaper or cardboard. This same biodegradable weedkiller helps to make sure that any noxious weeds that were in the raw materials don't survive. The newspaper and cardboard are temporary barriers. In a season or two, when they are no longer needed, they will have decomposed, and even added a small amount of organic matter and nutrients to the soil.

The more vigorous the lawn or native plants below your layered garden, the thicker the sheet compost and the paper layer must be. Three to five sheets of newspaper or one to three sheets of cardboard are usually sufficient, but you should experi-

ment with the thickness. Be sure to greatly overlap the edges to prevent vining, runner-rooted plants from twisting up through the layered sheets. Try soaking the newspaper briefly, or soak the cardboard for an hour or so—it makes the layering process easier.

The safest paper to use is the newsprint in a newspaper, because black and colored inks are made from organic pigments in order to save money. The colored inks used on glossy paper may contain toxic elements—such as lead, cadmium, and mercury—some of which can be absorbed by your plants. Avoid yellow and red inks, because they are potentially the most toxic. Ironically, few of the pages from the major gardening magazines are safe to use in your garden.

Nobody wants to look at a landscape littered with the Sunday paper, so be cosmetic. Cover the layer of paper with a "seed free" mulch. Compost prepared by the hot method, where temperatures of 140° to 160° F are generated throughout the pile, ordinarily will have very few viable seeds. Even so, if you make your own compost, avoid adding plants with mature seed heads and plants with vigorous running roots, such as periwinkle, crabgrass, and ivy.

To be lazy, skip compost. Each region of the country has a variety of seed-free materials. Look for leaf molds, wood chips, salt hay, sand, straw, sawdust, seaweed, and lawn clippings.

Domesticating Your Captive Edibles

Now you are ready to begin planting. The easiest way is to transplant seedlings from the wild. Take a kitchen knife and cut an X through the paper layer, which should be moist and easy to penetrate. Place a pocket of loamy compost on the X, and transplant into the pocket. These captured plants easily take root in their new home, even growing

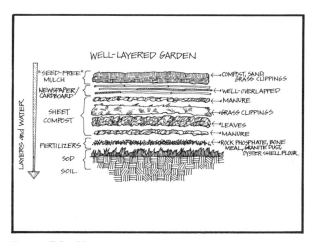

Figure 7.3 Sheet composting is a very easy way to improve soil without digging.

through pockets of raw materials—being "weeds," they can take the abuse. In fact, many wild edibles, among them lamb's-quarters, stinging nettle, amaranth, and chickweed, thrive on high nitrogen.

Of the sheet-composted, wild edible gardens I have started, no two turned out the same. I have used this technique for five years in nearly a dozen gardens, and each one was a delightful surprise.

If you would like to try out a lot of varieties quickly, start with seeds. Plan ahead, since the seeds of the wild edibles will mature in a different season than the one in which you will want to plant. Observe which wild edibles thrive in your local area in the harshest of conditions—those are the ones whose seed you will want to collect. Many wild seeds will keep for years or decades, so you need only collect each variety once in a great while. Blend the seeds collected from the wild and scatter them over the mulched surface. Don't worry about how many seeds to use: a jungle of plants will grow.

Water regularly until the seeds germinate. Once the seedlings have some leaves, start thinning—and do not forget to eat the thinnings! The youngest wild edibles are the sweetest and most succulent. Throughout the season, harvest as needed. This wild and woolly portion of your landscape will take care of itself.

Let some of the healthiest plants of each type go to seed every season. Apply compost to cover bare areas and mildly fertilize your wild and woolly food garden. Be sure to put the compost down before the seeds ripen so they can scatter themselves over the new mulch.

Protection from Invading Seeds and Roots

Wind-blown seeds are a major source of unwanted plants. When you choose a spot for your wild area, keep in mind that your house can act as a windbreak, and hedgerows can filter out seeds. Remember, too, that driveways and walks can bar invasive running roots from the garden. (See Figure 7.4.) A border of straw bales can act as a protective mulch, keeping out nearby plants. Break open the bales closest to the garden and spread the straw as a seasonal mulch. As the bales are used up, the wild edibles will expand to fill the area. (The soil under the bales will have been improved by the action of worms and soil bacteria.)

The same protective borders help contain the potentially rampant seeds of the wild edible garden. Some wild edibles are so persistent and invasive, however, that they may not be worth the risk of future maintenance nightmares. Examples are burdock (*Arctium lappa*), pigweed (*Amaranthus* sp.), French sorrel (*Rumex* sp.), plantain (*Plantago major*), and nettle (*Urtica dioica*).

Figure 7.4 Windbreaks help keep invasive seeds from blowing into or out of your self-seeding vegetable area.

Sheet Composting for "Tame" Plants

Sheet composting does not have to be reserved for the "weedy" or vegetable areas of your edible landscape. The method of soil preparation and development described can be used with the most colorful and common perennials—whether edible or not. Figure 7.5 in the color plates shows an ornamental flower border leading to my front door. I used the sheet compost technique to build and plant a raised area where the winter drainage is poor. The planting needed a lot of water the first summer, but as the roots of the ornamentals reach deeper into the native soil each season, they will need less summer irrigation.

Campbell, Stu. **Let it Rot**. Charlotte, VT: Garden Way Publishing, 1975. A very readable general review of composting dynamics and methods. The best book on the subject—a minor classic. Worth looking for in used book stores.

Clarke, Charlotte. **Edible and Useful Plants of California**. Los Angeles: University of California Press, 1977. I especially like this book because it covers edible weeds of urban and cultivated settings.

Fukuoka, Masanobu. **The One-Straw Revolution**. Emmaus, PA: Rodale Press, 1978. Reprinted NY: Bantam Books, 1985. The classic that inspired me to consider ways to garden without cultivation. Few of the techniques are relevant in U.S. gardens, since Fukuoka's main examples are citrus trees and rice. A wonderful discussion of the interplay between horticulture and spirituality.

Gibbons, Euell. **Stalking the Wild Asparagus**. Field Guide ed. New York: David McKay, 1970 A classic on identifying and preparing wild foods. Folksy text with good recipes.

Hatfield, Audrey. **How to Enjoy Your Weeds**. Sterling Publishing, 1971. Provides recipes and household uses for weeds. Though this guide is from England, most of the weeds it lists also grow throughout the U.S.

Institute for Local Self-Reliance. **Gardening for Health**. Washington, DC: Institute for Local Self-Reliance, 1976. The source for the information in Fig. 4.3. An excellent chart ranks the most nutrient-productive vegetables by nutrients produced in a square foot each month. Also gives a nutritional analysis of three dozen vegetables.

Jabs, Carolyn. **The Heirloom Gardener**. San Francisco: Sierra Club Books, 1984. The only quality book on this important subject. The losses from our edible plant gene pool are a biological tragedy; Jabs shows how each of us can help reverse the alarming trend. Includes interviews with collectors of heirloom varieties, how to secure seeds of heirlooms, and a thorough list of catalogs, exchanges, farms, museums, and books. Buy this book and put it to use.

Kirk, Donald R. **Wild Edible Plants of Western North America**. Happy Camp, CA: Naturegraph Publishers, 1975. A thorough reference. I especially like the table that indexes plants by their uses.

Larkcom, Joy. **The Salad Garden**. New York: Viking Press, 1984. The best book on gardening with colorful, gourmet vegetables. Exquisite color photographs of gardens as well as a color close-up of each edible mentioned. A fair amount of space is given to edible weeds, edible flowers, and unusual leafy greens. Good cultural information. A book to buy.

Minnich, Jerry. **Gardening for Maximum Nutrition**. Emmaus, PA: Rodale Press. 1983. One of the few books on this important aspect of vegetable gardening. Includes lists of the most nutritious fruit and vegetable varieties. Sample garden plans are included, though they may not match your climate or yard.

Mollison, Bill, and Holmgren, David. **Permaculture One**. Stanley, Tasmania: Tagari Books, 1978. A good introduction to the Australian equivalent of sustainable/holistic/integrated farms and gardens. The theories were an inspiration to me 7 years ago, but most of the examples are inappropriate for U.S. climates, property sizes, and lifestyles.

Mollison, Bill. **Permaculture Two**. Stanley, Tasmania: Tagari Books, 1981. Similar to its predecessor, with a big section appropriate only to gardeners who live where it rains less than 10 inches a year.

Robbins, W. W.; Bellue, Margaret; and Ball, Walter. **Weeds of California**. Sacramento: California State Dept. of Agriculture, 1970. My favorite source for the identification of native and naturalized weeds. Most of the weeds described occur throughout the U.S.

Stout, Ruth. **How to Have a Green Thumb Without an Aching Back**. New York: Simon and Schuster, 1955. A wise gardener describes her effortless gardening techniques in a delightful personal style. A classic on no-till gardening.

U.S.D.A. **Handbook of the Nutritional Contents of Foods**. New York: Dover Publications, 1975. The government's most complete listing of the nutritional content of foods most commonly eaten in America. Some edible weeds and a few unusual, exotic edibles are listed. Specific types, such as 'Red Delicious' and 'Arkansas Black' apples, are not compared.

SINK OR SWIM: SELF-SEEDING VEGETABLES

Always ready to test crazy, carefree methods for growing food, my friend Jamie Jobb and I have tried many ways to grow annual vegetables, flowers, and herbs, without fussy rows. We came to call the method I'm going to describe here the sink-or-swim approach. Correctly cared for, many annual vegetables can be grown as if they were perennials—they will make seeds, sow themselves, and reappear every year. With the sink-or-swim garden, you apply to familiar vegetables the sheet composting methods used in a wild and woolly garden.

Strength and Vigor

Knowing which plants will thrive and proliferate in sink-or-swim gardens can ease the burdens of the busy gardener. Avoid the modern vegetables that are pale descendants of their vigorous, wild ancestors and are dependent for survival on gardeners, farmers, and cultivation. Though hybrid vegetables can be extremely vigorous and useful in coping with specific disease and pest problems, they do not breed true. If your soil is infested with the spores of fusarium wilt, it is worth the work to grow, in a conventional way, hybrid tomatoes bred for resistance to fusarium wilt. But they don't belong in the sink-or-swim garden. Only the self-seeding pioneer plants do.

The Varieties

If the sheet compost and soil lack nitrogen, grow peas and beans. If your sheet compost is high in nitrogen, you should grow a larger percentage of broad-leafed greens which will rapidly convert the nitrogen surplus into abundant leafy food. The sheet mulched area is a disturbed environment much like a landslide is. The soil and organic matter will age and mellow over the coming years and be able to grow the full range of vegetables.

Vegetables that produce large fruits, such as squashes, melons, and tomatoes, may not do as well as leafy greens for a number of years—they need a fertile, aged soil to be fruitful. Root crops, with the exception of potatoes and Jerusalem artichokes, are also a gamble, since the newspaper layer is an obstruction for the first season. Jerusalem artichokes are so tough they establish themselves tenaciously in all types of soil: but plant them only where you can live with them forever; they are hard to eliminate and will spread. Potatoes do surprisingly well the first season, and their roots help improve the soil texture. Figure 7.6 lists plants that do well in a no-till garden.

Plants for No-Till Gardens	
Common Name	**Botanical Name**
Blackberry	*Rubus sp.*
Black nightshade	*Solanum nigrum*
Borage	*Borago officinalis*
Burdock	*Arctium minus*
Calendula	*Calendula officinalis*
Chickweed	*Stellaria media*
Chicory	*Cichorium intybus*
Corn salad	*Valerianella locusta*
Dandelion	*Taraxacum officinale*
Dill	*Anethum graveolens*
Dock	*Rumex sp.*
Fennel	*Foeniculum vulgare*
Ground cherry	*Physalis sp.*
Huckleberry	*Vaccinium ovatum*
Lamb's quarters	*Chenopodium alba*
Lemon balm	*Melissa officinalis*
Miner's lettuce	*Montia perfoliata*
Mustard	*Brassica sp.*
Nasturium	*Tropaeolum sp.*
Parsley	*Petroselinum crispum*
Pigweed	*Amaranthus retroflexus*
Plantain	*Plantago major*
Purslane	*Portulaca oleracea*
Salad burnet	*Sanguisorba officinalis*
Salsify	*Scorzonera hispanica*
Stinging nettle	*Urtica sp.*
Thimbleberry	*Rubus parviflorus*
Violets	*Viola odorata*
Wild strawberry	*Fragaria sp.*

Figure 7.6

Perennial Annuals

Once you establish your sink-or-swim planting, let the most vigorous plants flower, make seeds, and restart themselves. Beware, though, of heading vegetables such as cabbage, broccoli, and cauliflower. With lots of cross-pollination, they will begin to back-breed, that is, return to a more original leafy form. The strange variations can be fun, but if you want to maintain vegetables true to their original type, you must separate varieties in the same family from each other as well as from their wild relatives. Figure 7.7 gives the distances needed to prevent cross-pollination, as well as vegetables that do not cross-pollinate. In many gardens you will not be able to get enough distance. Then you either accept seasonal surprises, buy seed each year, or restrict yourself to one representative of each vegetable family. Also, make sure your neighbor's garden isn't cross-pollinating with yours.

PREVENTING CROSS-POLLINATION

Plant Family	Members of Family	Distance to Separate Varieties (in feet)
GOURD (*Cucurbitaceae*)	Winter and summer squashes, melons, cucumbers, pumpkins	1000+
BEET (*Chenopodiaceae*)	Beets, Swiss chard, and spinach	500-1000
CABBAGE (*Cruciferae*)	Cabbages, broccoli, cauliflower, kale, collards, Brussel sprouts, kohlrabi, radishes, daikon, and bok choy	1000+
PARSLEY (*Umbelliferae*)	Carrot, celery, celeriac, and parsley	200-1000
ONION (*Lillaceae*)	Onions, leeks, and garlic	100+
GRASSES (*Gramineae*)	Corn	1000+

Figure 7.7

The Recipe

Apply the same layers you would for a wild patch, but make sure the layer of newspaper or cardboard is as thin as possible since the roots of vegetables are somewhat weaker than those of wild plants. On tilled or bare soil, a thick layer of mulch can take the place of the newspaper layer.

For early salad greens, use transplants to get quick growth and a protective canopy. For annual transplants, cut a small hole out of the newspaper. This is considerably easier if the paper has been soaked beforehand. Use a neutral potting soil in the pocket to protect the tender roots of the transplant. When using transplants, it is especially important to thoroughly moisten all layers of the sheet compost so that moisture will not be drawn away from the transplants.

You can also plant perennial vegetable tubers, crowns, and root divisions. To establish perennials, cut an X in the paper layer, put in a piece of root or crown division, and cover with a handful of compost.

Tubers such as potatoes, Jerusalem artichokes, sweet potatoes, and taro can be placed below a hole cut in the newspaper or placed on top of all the layers with a handful of compost on top. After all the transplants, tubers, and roots are established, you can toss a variety of seeds over the entire area.

Test Plots

Here is an interesting way to test the ability of plants to mingle. Plant three or more types of vegetables (see Fig. 7.8) in an overlapping grid which lets you see how they grow alone and together. Be careful not to over-seed. Only a tablespoonful of small seeds, such as mustard, is enough for 100 square feet of garden when you blend different types of vegetables, something I learned the hard way.

I started the trial plot in the illustration during the California winter rains, and after the rains stopped in the spring, I did not water again. Though the plants were small because of over-seeding and drought, all I had to do was pick! The chicory lasted one season without any care. The kale provided salad greens for more than three months after the last spring rain. The French sorrel was there when I checked three years later. With its boundaries unprotected, the plot had long since been overrun by wild grasses, which pushed out the other plants. It is important to protect the perimeter from invasive seeds as described in the previous chapter. Overall, this unusual plot was easy to start, easy to harvest, and intriguing to watch as the different seasons brought changes.

Figure 7.8 The grid technique tests how well different edibles mingle and survive in a self-seeding plot. With clover seed cast over the entire plot, this grid tests 15 combinations in one season.

Don't Forget Clovers

In the sink-or-swim garden, there is a place for perennial clovers. They stabilize, if not increase, the nitrogen supply. Grown alone, they can add 100 to 200 pounds of nitrogen per acre to the soil each season. The low-growing sweet clovers compete very little with most of the vegetables. In my experience, Dutch white clover is a well-behaved perennial and quickly fills sunny patches without overwhelming the vegetables.

To establish clovers, wait until late spring when the soil has warmed up. When you buy clover seeds, buy the specific rhizobium bacteria inoculant for white clover. Moisten the seeds prior to dispersal and mix with the dry powdered inoculant. Another method is to dissolve the legume inoculant in water, and use a sprinkling can to water the soil with the mixture. Scatter several tablespoonfuls of Dutch white clover seeds per 100 square feet. To ensure good germination, apply some colloidal phosphate or superphosphate at the recommended rate. Keep the seeded area moist until the first set of true leaves shows.

Managing Slugs, Snails, and Diseases

Unfortunately, the rambling mix of plants in a sink-or-swim garden can provide an ideal habitat for bugs and diseases. Cabbages, broccoli, and cauliflower in a moist setting are often attacked by slugs or snails. I have found in California coastal gardens that an undercover of clover is a favorite hide-out for slugs. So is a straw mulch. By day the slugs and snails hide; by night they maraud among the succulent seedlings. For the cole (cabbage family) crops, bare soil may be easier to care for in the moist part of the season than a clover ground cover or a mulch. Without the clover cover crop, I had to pay a little more attention to fertilizing for a good crop of cabbages. Mulch can be applied after the plants are big enough to withstand slug attacks. Fall crops, planted during dry summer weather, are not as susceptible.

Just as currants and gooseberries are host plants for the blister rust that severely damages white pines, so, too, some edible weeds harbor potentially damaging diseases. Cucumber, muskmelon, and tomato mosaic viruses all infest and can be spread from the ground cherry (*Physalis* sp.). For domesticated relatives in the tomato family, the ground cherry may be a hazard. In a diverse garden ecology, diseases do not always get out of hand, but genetically weakened domesticated vegetables may be better off with some distance from a potential disease-carrying wild plant.

I hope that this method produces a productive and entertaining garden for you. Try a little playful experimentation. And as you toss your seeds into the mulched areas, yell out the special incantation my friend Jamie and I used: "Sink or swim, kids!"

Clarke, Charlotte. **Edible and Useful Plants of California**. Los Angeles: University of California Press, 1977. I especially like this book because it covers edible weeds of urban and cultivated settings.

Fukuoka, Masanobu. **The One-Straw Revolution**. Emmaus, PA: Rodale Press, 1978. Reprinted NY: Bantam Books, 1985. The classic that inspired me to consider ways to garden without cultivation. Few of the techniques are relevant in U.S. gardens, since Fukuoka's main examples are citrus trees and rice. A wonderful discussion of the interplay between horticulture and spirituality.

Gibbons, Euell. **Stalking the Wild Asparagus**. Field Guide ed. New York: David McKay, 1970 A classic on identifying and preparing wild foods. Folksy text with good recipes.

Hatfield, Audrey. **How to Enjoy Your Weeds**. Sterling Publishing, 1971. Provides recipes and household uses for weeds. Though this guide is from England, most of the weeds it lists also grow throughout the U.S.

Kirk, Donald R. **Wild Edible Plants of Western North America**. Happy Camp, CA: Naturegraph Publishers, 1975. A thorough reference. I especially like the table that indexes plants plants by their uses.

Mollison, Bill, and Holmgren, David. **Permaculture One**. Stanley, Tasmania: Tagari Books, 1978. A good introduction to the Australian equivalent of sustainable/holistic/integrated farms and gardens. The theories were an inspiration to me 7 years ago, but most of the examples are inappropriate for U.S. climates, property sizes, and lifestyles.

Mollison, Bill. **Permaculture Two**. Stanley, Tasmania: Tagari Books, 1981. Similar to its predecessor, with a big section appropriate only to gardeners who live where it rains less than 10 inches a year.

Robbins, W. W.; Bellue, Margaret; and Ball, Walter. **Weeds of California**. Sacramento: California State Dept. of Agriculture, 1970. My favorite source for the identification of native and naturalized weeds. Most of the weeds described occur throughout the U.S.

Stout, Ruth. **How to Have a Green Thumb Without an Aching Back**. New York: Simon and Schuster, 1955. A wise gardener describes her effortless gardening techniques in a delightful personal style. A classic on no-till gardening.

HAY BALE VEGETABLES: SOIL BUILDING FROM THE TOP DOWN

Hay bale gardening is inspired laziness, and makes the closest thing I know to an instant garden. Here, we really let nature take over. Simply put, hay bales become both the compost pile and the growing medium for vegetables. The bulk of the bale is reduced to plant food by a slow decomposition that feeds the hungry searching roots of the crop. In the end, you have loamy compost, the legacy of the bale, and a tasty crop.

Bale gardening was developed in Europe as an alternative to the use of chemicals in greenhouses. Instead of sterilizing the soil with steam or toxic methyl bromide, the whole greenhouse is swept clean after each crop and scrubbed with bleach or a mild fungicide. Then fresh bales of straw are brought in to grow the next crop on. Cycles of pests and diseases are broken and the used bales, mostly rotted, go to the fields as mulch or compost, adding valuable organic matter.

Hay bale culture is an experiment in composting dynamics. Most decomposing processes are not "hot," with disease-killing temperatures of 140° to 160° F. The forest floor, a rich litter of organic material, does not produce noticeable heat as it decomposes nor does it limit root growth. The limited amount of heat generated by a decomposing hay bale actually stimulates root growth. Roots that get too close to the heat in the center of the bale may die, but that only causes more feeder roots to branch out higher up on the root system.

A lot of bales are needed: an expensive proposition if it were not for unpredictable weather and hapless farmers and horse owners. The weather is always sneaking up on some unprotected hay pile, soaking it with rain and making some of the bales useless to the farmer. Almost every area has stables or farms that will give away or sell very cheaply soggy bales of straw or hay.

In a way, the older and wetter the hay is, the better, since more seeds will have sprouted. But the fresher and greener the bale, the more nourishing it will be for your plants. You pay more for oat and vetch hay or alfalfa, but they are worth more to you because their higher feed value translates to more nitrogen for your plants. (See Appendix 5.) They are not as easy to find — you may have to look more persistently or haggle more intensely, so improve your scrounging techniques and skills. Straw bales work well also, but you have to add nitrogen in some form to compensate for their higher carbon content.

The Bale Recipe

The idea of hay bale gardening is to save effort, but bales, especially wet ones, are very heavy. A wet bale can destroy your back more readily than digging does. Plan ahead — find dry bales to bring home during the summer. To move heavy bales, I roll them on and off my pickup truck on a 2-inch-by-6-inch ramp, with the help of a friend.

Add Gopher Protection . . .

If you have gophers, cover the area first with overlapped lengths of half-inch galvanized aviary netting. Whether you start with netting or not, place each bale with the end grain up; that is, leave the baling wire or twine exposed around the perimeter of the bale (see Fig. 7.9). Cluster the bales together three or four bales wide — this arrangement makes the vegetables easiest to reach from the outside edge. Grouping them also helps reduce watering by limiting excessive evaporation from the exposed perimeter. Use as many bales as you need for the length of your garden. If the bales are dry, soak them thoroughly and let them drain until very moist.

Figure 7.9 In a hay bale garden, decomposing bales improve the soil underneath while growing crops on top.

. . . fertilizer

To start the composting process in the bales, you must apply a high-nitrogen fertilizer to their tops (see Appendix 5). Use a thick layer of fresh chicken manure (12 to 50 pounds of chicken manure per bale, depending on how fresh it is). Options include 5 to 10 pounds of turkey manure, 10 to 20 pounds of rabbit manure, or 3½ pounds of blood meal mixed with 2 pounds of bone meal. To each of the above, add ¼ pound of sulfate of potash as a source of potassium. Do not hesitate to add your own urine — it's readily available (especially if you drink lots of coffee), high in nitrogen, and, if used fresh, not a carrier of dangerous disease. When using urine, be sure to add the 2 pounds of bone meal per bale and ¼ pound of sulfate of potash.

. . . compost

On top of the nitrogen layer add 6 to 8 inches of well-aged finished compost, a loamy soil, or a mixture of the two. Water the entire "layered cake" thoroughly and wait two to four weeks for the magic of composting to begin. This is not a race between roots and rotting. Give the decomposing layer a headstart. When the soil layer is warm, but not hot, it is time to plant.

. . . seedlings

Place seedlings or seeds into a pocket of new, neutral loamy soil. Water and mulch with fresh straw. Choose from the leafy vegetables in Fig. 7.6. These nitrogen-loving plants are the best for hay bale gardens, but don't hesitate to experiment with other possibilities. Although I have grown potatoes in hay bales and harvested perfect tubers, the yields were one-third that of an area the same size cultivated conventionally. Potatoes might work better in the second season, or cycle, of the hay bales.

. . . water often

You will need to water your bale-garden often. Initially, this is not a water-conserving technique. In fact, water consumption is higher than for any other method mentioned in this chapter. You are trading in a shovel for a sprinkler, at least for the first season or two.

You can help prevent evaporation from the exposed sides by growing winter squash vines nearby, especially on the south side (see Fig. 7.10). The large leaves are tall enough to shade the exposed straw, and they soften the hard-edge look of the bales.

. . . and "grow" a raised bed

After your first crop is harvested, pull back the straw mulch, transplant or seed a new crop directly into the soil layer, and replace the surface mulch. Water and harvest. After several seasons the bales "wear out," but you will find a well-textured soil underneath their loamy remains. The clay soil beneath some of my bales was so well-cultivated by worms, gophers, and bacteria that I could dig down almost a foot with my bare hands. Repeat the hay bale process another time in the same spot and you will develop a "raised bed" without a shovel or an aching back.

Figure 7.10 Squash vines shade a hay bale garden, reducing evaporation; they also help blend the bales into the landscape.

Stout, Ruth. **How to Have a Green Thumb Without an Aching Back**. New York: Simon and Schuster, 1955. A wise gardener describes her effortless gardening techniques in a delightful personal style. A classic on no-till gardening.

SURFACE CULTIVATION: GOOD YIELDS WITHOUT DIGGING

Surface cultivation is another approach to no-till gardening, but the name is confusing. There are two popular horticultural uses of the word cultivation – one refers to stirring the soil to prepare it for crops, the other to the care and tending of plants. Surface cultivation does not involve stirring the soil, but rather, tending plants without inverting the soil to maintain the natural stratification of soil life. To change crops, practitioners of surface cultivation use special tools to cut the plants just below the crown of the root system. The plants are removed with minimal disturbance to the soil. Instead of tilling, surface cultivators rely upon seasonal applications of compost, and the activities of roots, soil microbes, worms, and other soil life to develop good soil tilth.

English gardeners have practiced surface cultivation for at least 40 years, keeping records of the hours spent, materials used, and subsequent yields. Surface cultivation, while not leaving the soil completely undisturbed, has proven to be a practical, tempered way to ease the labor of gardening while maintaining decent yields.

The best definiton of surface cultivation comes from *Practical Organic Gardening* by Ben Easey:

The principles of organic surface cultivation are those of close imitation of nature by non-inversion of the soil; of economy of compost and organic matter by its employment as a surface mulch, where nature keeps her fertility promoting materials; of reduction of weed growth by ceasing to bring more and more seeds to the surface; and, by all these methods, of maintenance of a balance of air, moisture, biological life and plant foods.

(For a more detailed description, see *Intensive Gardening* by R. Dalziel O'Brien, Faber & Faber Ltd., London, 1956.) The most fundamental feature of this method is the mimicry of the dynamics of the forest. It avoids turning the soil. O'Brien's premise is that "every time the land is stirred, more humus is in fact burnt up." Since surface cultivation leaves the soil layers in place, it conserves plant nutrients and preserves the soil ecology.

Begin with Digging

Paradoxically, the English often begin surface cultivation with deep cultivation. This first stage is not exactly labor-saving. An area is cleared of its surface growth, then it is "bastard trenched." (I like to think the phrase comes from some Englishman, who, weary of the task, resorted to this explicative.) The gardener digs a trench two shovels deep, fills the bottom half with garbage or compost and manure – a time capsule dinner for the crop's roots – then replaces the soil. (See Fig. 7.11.)

Compost Is Crucial

The next step is to add a shallow layer of compost. This is much like the natural mulch of a forest floor. Easey's recommendation is to apply 2 to 4 inches of compost over the entire area (4 inches when the soil is especially clayey or sandy). This is ½ to 1 cubic yard of compost per 100 square feet. At 3 cubic yards of raw material per finished cubic yard of compost, that's definitely a heap of compost. Used as a surface mulch, compost must be applied each season. Easey's caution is to be heeded:

The supply of enough compost is the biggest snag, for surface cultivation will not work without it ... an autumn mulch of compost, two inches

Figure 7.11 Bastard-trenching improves the soil with buried kitchen scraps or compost. Unlike double-digging, this method inverts the soil layers.

thick ... and perhaps half this quantity ... in spring ... means over a cubic yard and a half ... for 18 square yards (162 square feet) of land—this on soil already of high organic matter.

Some folks, like myself, especially enjoy the magic and alchemy of making compost. But it can be a big job. One way to cut down on the quantity needed is to use the "natural herbicide" described in "Weeds as Food." Spreading one or two sheets of newspaper or cardboard before applying compost helps to smother sprouting weeds and reduces the amount of compost needed.

Surface cultivation is not labor-saving if you must haul in the raw materials needed to make the compost. I am reminded of a demonstration of sheet mulch gardening I did for a junior college class. Not having sufficient materials at hand, co-instructor Sarah Kidd and I hauled in three pickup loads of straw and manure for the 150-square-foot plot. Her only comment was, "I could've double-dug this in less time!" Alas, she was right.

Fortunately, urban and suburban areas are treasure troves of compost makings, with neighbors recklessly tossing their organic matter away. You can often arrange to have the lawn service crews, the "mower-blower" guys, haul their clippings and leaves to your place, saving them a dump fee. Watch out, though: many nasty chemicals are used by conventional gardeners. While a few of these chemicals will break down into harmless elements in a hot compost pile, others linger for years and decades. Before you accept a neighbor's clippings, make sure you know how their lawns are being cared for.

Unless your neighbors have poultry or livestock, they are not likely to provide manure for your compost pile, but no matter. O'Brien is a vegan, the type of vegetarian that avoids the use of all animal products. Her book describes the making of all-vegetable compost, a method that greatly simplifies gardening since the ingredients for compost can all be readily gathered or easily home-grown. (Recommendations for growing your own compost materials are in "Cover Crops and Green Manures – Grow Your Own Fertilizers.")

How do the plants receive enough nitrogen without tillage, fertilizers, or manure? O'Brien replies:

Our soil gets its nitrogen in the same way as the American prairie and the black earth soils of the Ukraine and Central Europe, chiefly from the free-living nitrogen-fixer Azotobacter croccoceum. It needs air and a certain balance of alkalinity, and it begins working in the compost heap. Our compost heaps include sufficient lime to keep the material alkaline, so that we gain by bacterial action about 25% more combined nitrogen than went in with the

plant residues, and when we spread the compost on the surface of the soil, the bacteria go on working.

By using compost made only from plants grown within the garden, O'Brien has truly patterned food production after nature's design. She uses one pile for rough or woody materials and another for succulent, fleshy greens. Fallow areas within the plot (where no vegetables are sown) are planted to vetch. The raw materials for the compost are weeds, vetch, and grass clippings from the pathways and perimeter of the garden. The weeds are gathered only when their growth threatens the crop. Vetch should be cut whenever the new foliage is 6 to 9 inches tall. Tender, young foliage is the highest in nitrogen and the quickest to decompose. Green grass clippings also compost readily. From years of experience, O'Brien has established how much area is needed to grow enough clippings for a plot under surface cultivation—for a 1-acre garden, 120 square yards of sod. That means devoting $\frac{1}{40}$ of a given area to sod for grass clippings. Throughout the season, cut the grass when it reaches $3\frac{1}{2}$ inches in height. If the rains aren't regular, irrigate to ensure lots of fresh, succulent growth.

Earthworms

Other natural activities come to the aid of a surface-cultivated garden, above all the labors of earthworms. From the definitive English soils manual, *Soil Conditions and Plant Growth:*

The outstanding action of the earthworm is to ingest soil particles along with the organic matter ... and excrete this calcium-saturated intimate mixture of organic matter and soil as a blackish-brown mold or loam. This mold, which in most soils is probably only produced by earthworms, is admirably suited for plant growth, having a very desirable air-water regime. On the lighter soils it has a considerably higher water-holding power than the soil itself, and on the heavier is more mellow and has a very favourable structure.

In my mulched gardens, the visible influence of worms upon the soil has been quite impressive. The friable nature of the soil and the distinctive aggregation of small soil crumbs cannot be duplicated by digging. The loamy structure feels different from any spaded soil. Whether or not worms actually enrich the soil is hotly debated, but the ability of worms to improve soil drainage and structure is widely accepted.

Surface Weeding

Surface cultivation demands weeding at specific times to ensure good yields (weeds are carefully composted to speed the cycling of nutrients). To make the weeding and the removal of spent crops easy, a hand tool called a Dutch hoe is used. You can see in Fig. 7.12 that it is designed for shallow hoeing. The intent is to scrape no more than 3½ to 4 inches below the soil's surface, cutting off the crowns of the root system. (A "Hula" hoe with a short handle can also be used.)

This approach is an elegant way to weed and improve soils at the same time. It removes only the portion of the root most likely to regenerate, leaving the bulk of the root system; the valuable organic matter decomposes in place. With the more deeply rooted plants—clovers, beets, dandelions, thistles—the deposited organic matter is deeper than cultivation could ever reach, and when it breaks down, it improves the structure and fertility of the subsoil. The slight stirring of the upper soil layer with the Dutch hoe brings few weed seeds up to germinate. In England, surface cultivators have very few weeds to hoe by the third year.

Surface cultivation attempts to duplicate and maintain the ecological interactions of nature's soils. O'Brien writes:

Nature ... maintains a corps of soil workers to deal with what falls on the surface when decay has already taken place above it—as when leaves fall and plants wither and die; and because this fallen vegetation is processed at surface level, it forms a humus which holds the plant nutrients where ... and when they are needed. The finer, shorter grasses and soft herbage which are nature's following crop are not in danger of becoming exhausted searching for their food at unfamiliar depths.

Yields for Surface Cultivation

It might seem that a surface-cultivated garden could not begin to match the production of a tilled and deeply fertilized one, but the dependable abundance of vegetables will surprise you. While O'Brien has used surface cultivation successfully in a commercial setting, she does not mention yields. Being a curious gardener, I wanted specific figures. I found them in Easey's book.

Easey starts off rather critically:

Figures, including crop yields, on surface cultivation are at the moment scarce, although this method has been well tried with much success in widely scattered parts of the world. Most of the existing records do not show comparative yields of crops grown on land similarly treated and cropped except insofar as surface cultivation is concerned.

But he goes on to summarize the findings of J. L. H. Chase in a seven-year trial comparing single-dug versus surface-cultivated plots. As Fig. 7.13 shows, the results are impressive, especially since surface cultivation eliminates tedious and tiring spading. Mr. Easey has found that the actual number of hours needed for surface versus tilled gardens (averaged over the years) was about the same, but the work was less strenuous with surface cultivation. Unfortunately, none of the proponents of the English method seem to have ever considered the "natural herbicide" of a newspaper layer, which would shift the hours of labor well in favor of the untilled gardens.

Take a close look at the total average figures for each year. There is a noticeable overall decline, becoming more pronounced in the fifth year. Mr. Easey also experienced such a decline in his no-till plots. His pragmatic solution ("rather than mere slavish imitation of nature") is to cultivate deeply every five or six years, boosting productivity, and then return to the surface cultivation.

As coincidence would have it, Masanobu Fukuoka's own son reached similar conclusions. Unlike his father, whose *One Straw Revolution* advocates no-till farming, he tills his rice fields once every five to seven years when the broadleaf weeds begin to be troublesome. His father's approach has been, literally, to avoid tillage at all costs. After returning from a speaking tour, he found more broadleaf weeds in one of his fields than he wanted. (It was a newly-acquired field that

Figure 7.12 The most effective hand tools for surface cultivation.

had been abandoned, unlike Fukuoka's weed-free fields that had been well-tended for 25 years without chemicals.) He killed the weeds in the new field with an herbicide, possibly contaminating the ground with dioxin. To me, that dramatizes the risks of gardening dogmatically. Dogma may be "am god" backwards, but I believe the best gardeners are those who embrace a range of options for a healthy edible landscape; such as occasional tillage to avoid dangerous chemicals.

Planting a New, No-Till Plot

A no-till plot starts with poorer soil texture, so do not try to grow too many plants at first. Also, choose those plants that most easily tolerate the lack of cultivation. Easey suggests potatoes, brassicas, and leafy greens as initial plantings for this method of cultivation. Potatoes are considered by many English gardeners to be excellent "cultivators" of soil. In my gardens, they have always noticeably improved clay soil.

The simplest way to plant potatoes is right on top of the compost. Cut a spud into pieces, each with three eyes. Place the pieces on top of the compost, cover them with 4 to 6 more inches of compost and a light cover of seed-free straw. As the potato "vines" grow, continue to add more straw until it is well over a foot deep. Harvest is simple—lift up the matted straw and pluck these "apples of the earth" with your bare hands.

While potatoes are helpful in developing your soil's structure, they are considered hungry feeders on the soil's nutrients, especially potash and nitrogen. To renew the nutrient content of your soil, add manure, or plant a soil-improving crop before and after each harvest of potatoes. I recommend planting legumes, including all types of garden beans and peas. Legumes add nitrogen to the soil—it is gathered by the beneficial bacteria that colonize their roots—and help renew the soil after a crop of potatoes.

A favorite of mine, also popular in England, is the fava bean or broad horsebean *(Vicia faba)*. Favas gather or "fix" up to 200 pounds of nitrogen per acre. After harvesting your potatoes, lime the soil, add some manure if you have it and a little potash (in the form of wood ash or bone meal), and sow the favas. In my climate, I can grow successive plantings of favas throughout the winter. They protect the soil from erosion and add nitrogen at the same time.

Soil-improving plants can be followed by any type of nitrogen-hungry plant, such as members of the brassica family. Brussels sprouts, for example, will appreciate the legacy of nutrients from a fava bean crop. To transplant Brussels sprout seedlings, cut off the fava tops near the ground (use the tops for making compost) and transplant the Brussels sprout seedlings right between the rows of the fava stubble. This technique has been used for

Figure 7.13 The average yields of a surface-cultivated garden were very close to the yields of a single-dug garden, in this study from England. Some surface-cultivated vegetables out-produced the single-dug vegetables.

decades as a profitable way to speed up cropping and to produce good yields in English market gardens.

No-Till Is Not for Everyone

For some, this approach will seem not so thoughtful as carefree, even abandoned. And this is not the method for those who really "want to be in touch with the earth." Some "dirt gardeners" feel they must work the soil or else they are not good gardeners. I like the novelty, the reduced effort, and the naturalness of the no-till garden. For the future to truly be abundant, I must have effort *and* relaxation. My no-till patches offer more play with less work, and yet plenty of vegetables.

Fukuoka, Masanobu. **The One-Straw Revolution**. Emmaus, PA: Rodale Press, 1978. Reprinted NY: Bantam Books, 1985. The classic that inspired me to consider ways to garden without cultivation. Few of the techniques are relevant in U.S. gardens, since Fukuoka's main examples are citrus trees and rice. A wonderful discussion of the interplay between horticulture and spirituality.

Stout, Ruth. **How to Have a Green Thumb Without an Aching Back**. New York: Simon and Schuster, 1955. A wise gardener describes her effortless gardening techniques in a delightful personal style. A classic on no-till gardening.

3

GROWING VEGETABLES
Tillage: A Little More Work, Greater Yields

SOD CULTURE: VEGETABLES IN THE LAWN

Early in my landscaping career, I saw lawns as banal greenery and, in the fertilizers and sprays applied to them, a wanton waste of fossil fuels. Over the years my disgust has waned. Although I still avoid installing lawns (because it is a tedious task), I have come to respect their place in suburbia, provided their size is limited. There is no effective substitute for a lawn for rough-and-tumble play. I have clients who find that 900 square feet of lawn is plenty for their kids to frolic on. For simple lounging, some of my clients' lawns are only 15 by 15 feet (225 square feet).

Sod culture is the term I use for methods of planting vegetables directly into a lawn or ground cover of clovers. The result is rows or otherwise-shaped beds of vegetables with clover or grass between them for paths. The advantages are:

- It is a fast, simple way to convert some lawn area to edibles.

- It retains some of the lawn aesthetic. With careful design, the lawn blends into the sod culture area.

- On steep slopes and in areas of high rainfall, it saves garden soil and nutrients that are usually lost to erosion.

- It allows rain to gently soak into the soil, as a reserve for plants. In spite of the moisture needs of the sod, this can be a water conserving technique for hilly areas. (However, some studies have shown that perennial sod under trees competes with the trees for water.)

- With less direct exposure of bare soil to the sun, wind, and rain, it helps to conserve valuable organic matter.

- It lowers the soil temperature, a benefit for the southern states where high summer temperatures can adversely affect seedling and plant growth.

Mowing the grass or clover strips between rows

maintains a good sod cover. The rows or beds require the usual garden weed control.

As with any horticultural technique, there are also limitations to sod culture.

- The yields are lower than with conventional gardening methods, perhaps by as much as 20 percent, because of the area in sod.

- Reduced soil temperature may be undesirable in northern and coastal gardens. Also, the soil will take longer to warm in the spring.

- A sod of pure grass stunts the growth of fruit and nut trees and reduces their yields. But the trees come into bearing earlier and the fruit has better color and ripens sooner.

- A sod cover may harbor pests such as cutworms, nematodes, June beetles, grubs, and Japanese beetles.

Mulching Your Lawn to Productivity

To begin sod culture, use the deep mulch technique described in "Sheet Composting for 'Wild' and 'Tame' Plants." Make sure you use a high-nitrogen layer directly on top of the existing grass. This will ensure that the thatch and sod rot in place. Since the nitrogen will be unavailable to other plants while the sod decomposes, use a slightly thicker layer of neutral compost or soil to help establish seedlings. Otherwise, the roots of the seedlings will soon run out of available nutrients, especially nitrogen, and be stunted. To be sure the lawn rots, pile the different layers of mulch quite deep, at least 8 to 12 inches.

Several considerations determine the width of the paths between beds. Large grass pathways integrate the garden with the rest of the lawn. The steeper your property or the rainier your climate, the wider the sod paths should be. If the grassy path is twice as wide as your lawn mower, it is a simple task to pass once in each direction, blowing the clippings as a mulch onto the beds on each side. This method works only with tall vegetables such as tomatoes, since lettuces and other small vegetables can be buried by the clippings. For small vegetables, use a mower with a rear bag. The rear-bag models also allow you to make narrower paths.

Tilled Beds Among the Sod

You can also establish vegetable beds in the lawn with a rotary tiller, but use a tiller sparingly. If the soil is too wet, has a high clay content, or is tilled repeatedly for years, the lower levels – slicked by the tines – develop a compacted "clay pan" zone that is resistant to the penetration of water and roots. A single use of a tiller when the soil is not too wet, however, causes no lasting problem.

Apply manure and other fertilizers on top of the lawn. If necessary, soak the area with a sprinkler and wait for the soil to dry enough to crumble in your hand. Then till in the amendments along with the sod. Sprinkle the area until it is moist, but not wet. Then relax, perhaps soaking your tiller-shaken body in a hot bath.

Allow the tilled beds to sit for two to six weeks, depending upon the warmth and moisture in the soil. During this time, soil microbes and bacteria will digest the green grass and thatch. The soil's nitrogen supply is temporarily tied up as protein in all the new bacteria needed for this decomposition. If you were to start transplanting during this period, the plants would not be able to quickly begin growing. And when transplants "just sit there," they will be slightly stunted and not produce optimal growth and yields. The warmer the weather, in a moist but not wet soil, the sooner the soil life will have digested much of the incorporated plant material.

Clover Culture

For an alternative to conventional grass that is just as good looking and more beneficial, grow clover in the paths. Perennial clovers, especially the well behaved low-growing Dutch white clover *(Trifolium repens)*, accumulate nitrogen around their roots (119 to 168 pounds per acre per year), have a lush green color, are easily mowed, spread well to become a dense cover, and have blossoms that attract bees.

However, clover has long been cursed by turf purists for some good reasons: clover leaves are easily bruised and leave a stubborn stain on clothing, and bees lured by blossoms don't always graciously share clover areas with people.

Using Clovers to Feed Corn

Corn planted in your clover-sod landscape can be partially nourished with nitrogen from nearby legumes. For nitrogen during the current growing season, it is best to use an inedible legume. Clovers are excellent options.

Consider Fig. 8.1. Double rows of corn with mulch beneath are separated by a ground cover of clover.

The mulch – produced by mowing the clover – provides some fertility, conserves moisture, and keeps the soil cooler, helping to maximize yields. The strips of clover are away from the majority of the young corn's feeding roots. As periodic mowing causes an increase in the nitrogen available in the soil, the corn roots spread into the clover area and use the nitrogen. (See "Grow Your Own Fertilizer – Cover Crops and Green Manures" for more details.)

Figure 8.1 Mowing legumes is an efficient way to increase nitrogen in the soil during the current growing season.

McLeod, Edwin. **Feed the Soil**. Graton, CA: Organic Agriculture Research Institute, 1982. A basic review of nitrogen-fixing plants and cover crops, with an encyclopedic reference. I dislike the opening dialog between rabbits and a worm, but I use the encyclopedia frequently.

DOUBLE-DIGGING:
A BALANCED REVIEW

The technique of double-digging is part of a larger method of gardening, which has a variety of popular names: raised bed, wide row, French intensive, biointensive and biodynamic French intensive. The last name is the most accurate since it encompasses the entire method. I will shorten it to BFI.

As a method, BFI was first articulated and practiced by Alan Chadwick. In the Farallones Institute *1979 Annual Report*, Michael Stusser describes the history of BFI:

BFI began when Alan Chadwick initiated the garden project on the Santa Cruz campus of the University of California in 1967. He presented a synthesis of several European horticultural and cultural traditions ... one is the example of the French Intensive ("culture maraîchère") system of production practiced by the market gardeners of Paris during the late 1800's. Another primary influence ... was Bio-dynamics, which stems from a series of talks given by Rudolf Steiner in 1924 ... At these lectures, the farmers were asked to investigate deeper influences, such as the character of the minerals in the soil and the influences of the cosmos, to gain a more holistic sense of their agricultural practices. The approach identified a reverence for some of the aspects of peasant life and wisdom ... asked that we acknowledge the vital or life force as something ultimate and self-sustaining ... [and view] humans as an instrument between heaven and earth, working to enhance and quicken biological dynamics. Alan himself created a special atmosphere within his gardens, an unmistakable vibrance and brilliance.

The most popular book on the subject is *How to Grow More Vegetables Than You Ever Thought Possible on Less Land Than You Can Imagine* by John Jeavons. His book is required reading if you are serious about double-digging and the BFI method.

Central to BFI is a mandate to nurture diverse ecosystems and amplify the forces of nature. Flowers, vegetables, fruit and nut trees, herbs, insects, animals, birds – all of nature – are encouraged to flourish within the BFI garden. The goal of BFI is a garden that can produce more and more of its own ecological needs, a sustainable edible landscape. BFI is the most methodically and persistently researched, practiced, and articulated style of hand-labor gardening, with a long history of experienced practitioners. (See the bibliography at the end of this chapter.)

While double-digging the soil is the most familiar aspect of BFI, there are other equally important cultural guidelines. Close plantings are favored because of the beneficial microclimate that is produced beneath the continuous cover of foliage. With all the leaves touching, the soil is cooler, healthier, more conserving of moisture and humus, and each plant grows more regular and robust. Once the soil is shaded by the canopy of the foliage, fewer weeds germinate. BFI uses much less water than conventional gardening (one-quarter or less of the water used by agricultural practices per pound of food produced). This water conservation occurs because of the combined effects of the deeply cultivated soil, the addition of compost, the "living mulch" of the crops' foliage, and the interplanting of deep- and shallow-rooted vegetables.

Nature's Models

There are natural models for the BFI method. Alan Chadwick often mentioned the observation by Greeks that plants proliferate on a landslide because of the loosened soil. The incorporation of air into the soil during a landslide allows for easier penetration by roots and a greater availability of moisture and nutrients. The rounded shape and the fractured soil of a landslide increases its surface area and is thought to allow for a healthier exchange of gases between the earth and atmosphere – the waste gases of soil life (carbon dioxide, sulfur dioxide, and others) being replaced by the growth-stimulating gases oxygen and nitrogen, among others.

Another example of naturally loose, fertile soils can be found in the gravel, silt, and sand deposited each season at a river bend. In both situations, the soil has been deposited with larger pieces at the bottom and finer particles closer to the surface.

Figure 8.2 Double-dug beds preserve the natural layering of soil particles, from small at the top to large at the bottom.

This stratification of particles encourages the upward capillary action of moisture from deeper supplies.

Double-digging is meant to duplicate landslides, sandbars, and other natural "cultivation" in order to stimulate growth and production. Figure 8.2 reveals the cross-section of a typical BFI bed, showing the gradation in the size of soil particles.

Learning to Double-Dig

BFI gardeners make beds 2½ to 5 feet wide, and of whatever length desired. Permanent paths separate the beds—cultivated soil is never walked on. The soil in the beds remains loose and friable, and its surface is noticeably raised due to the distinctive BFI type of cultivation. The BFI gardener loosens the soil as deeply as 24 inches without turning or churning it. With a spading shovel, the gardener removes the top 10 to 12 inches of soil, making an open trench across the width of the bed. Each spadeful of soil is heaved forward—as it hits the ground, it is aerated and texturized, though the natural layers are preserved. A spading fork is used to fracture the subsoil 10 to 12 inches deep in the trench. The gardener moves backward and creates a second trench across the bed, heaving forward the spadefuls of soil to fill the first trench. These steps are repeated the length of the bed. The critical detail, so hard to describe in words, is the avoidance of *inverting* the soil. Learning to spade the soil without disturbing its layers is best done in a hands-on workshop. (See Fig. 8.3 and Jeavons's book.)

The dense, close plantings of BFI gardening are another distinctive characteristic. In the beds, roots penetrate deeply. They do not have to spread to the side to find nutrients. With more roots going downward rather than sideways in pursuit of nutrients, vegetables can be planted closer together.

The spacing recommendations in Jeavons's book are much closer than most gardeners are used to, and *demand* deep cultivation. For broccoli, Jeavons recommends 15-inch spacing between plants and between rows. The usual recommendation is 18 inches apart in the row and 30 inches between rows.

BFI gardeners may plant a quick-growing vegetable such as lettuce with slower-maturing broccoli. The lettuce aids the broccoli by rapidly covering the soil with a protective (and tasty) canopy. By the time the lettuce is ready to harvest, the broccoli has grown large enough to provide its own living mulch.

Productive Points . . .

The BFI method produces many benefits for the gardener. Jeavons depicts them statistically in an often-quoted passage:

Our initial research seems to indicate that the method can produce an average of four times more vegetables per acre than . . . mechanized and chemical agricultural techniques. The method also appears to use ⅛ the water and ½ to zero the purchased nitrogen fertilizer and ¹⁄₁₀₀ the energy consumed by commerical agriculture, per pound of vegetable grown.

. . . and Counterpoints

A closer look at the origin of these figures will temper the claims. A footnote indicates that the energy figure is for the assumed condition of soil after five years of improvement, even though only three years of actual testing were done, and states that the figure does not include unproductive plots, which covered 10 percent of the area. So the full savings are not to be realized immediately, but only after a lot of hard work, unless you begin with a good soil. Virtually any method of hand labor

Figure 8.3

gardening uses far less energy (measured in calories expended) than machinery. People are, like ol' John Henry, more efficient at expending calories than machines (although not as speedy nor as persistent). Jeavons estimates that the energy inputs per unit of area in most hand gardening systems are similar, but the BFI yields are much higher per unit of labor. All things considered, the BFI method certainly uses considerably less energy than typical agriculture.

The BFI method is not the best approach for all vegetable areas, nor is it well-suited to every gardener's temperament and health. Those same Greeks who observed landslides also believed in moderation. Without proper training, BFI cultivation can be strenuous. As with any approach to edible landscaping, it is best to start small and master the method before trying more.

Spacing and Density

Jeavons recommends plantings at densities that do not apply to all soils. Give your soil a break. When you do not begin with a very good soil, start out with wider spacings between plants than recommended in Jeavons's book until your soil's fertility and structure have improved.

Pore Space and Tilth

Fertility is enhanced by the exchange of gases between the soil and the atmosphere. The channels for the movement of gases are called the soil's pore space. These form an extensive labyrinth of minute conduits. The "heavier" the soil, the less extensive are the passageways. Undisturbed soils slowly evolve a friable soil that is up to 50 percent pore space, through the action of worms, bacteria, fungi, and roots—processes that take decades and centuries.

Tillage attempts to speed up soil development. To show how rapidly the BFI method can improve the soil, Jeavons's presents figures from studies done at his Palo Alto, California, project that show that 8½ years of soil improvement were equivalent to as much as 500 years of natural soil development. Such remarkable figures are dependent upon a very conscientious and skilled application of "the method."

Pore space is very different from air pockets. Much of the tilth (crumbly structure) of a recently cultivated soil is from relatively large air spaces. These do not provide the same benevolent influences as a soil with good pore space. While water can just as easily drain downward, upward capillary action is impeded, root hairs are killed by the excessive air, and organic matter can be more easily oxidized.

Cultivation at the wrong time can actually set back the formation of natural pore space, with unhappy results for people who are new to the BFI method. In 1977, I helped train a crew for the development of a BFI garden. I tried to instruct the crew in the finer details of double-digging in lectures given indoors during the winter. Come spring the crew, well-intentioned but naive, proceeded to cultivate by the calendar. For months, they were proud of the well-formed, lofty raised beds, some over a foot higher than the nearby paths. But by the end of the summer, many of those beds had sunk lower than the paths! They were dismayed.

The very heavy clay soil had been worked when it was too wet. The action of the shovels had actually compressed the clay particles, and the loft of the bed had been artificially produced by air pockets, not pore space. Later, I was able to show them how clay soil looks, feels, and behaves when ready for cultivation. So much for the shortcomings of lectures and books.

Fortunately, when the soil is just moist enough for proper cultivation, it is also the easiest to work. Conversely, if you feel like you are working against the soil—it is sticking to your shovel and the clods aren't breaking easily—the soil is too wet. Take a break until the soil is drier and easier to work.

Effort

By its sheer weight and density, working the soil is the most strenuous part of the BFI method. Jeavons estimates that the initial preparation of a 100-square-foot bed will take 6 to 14 hours of labor. Two to 4 of these hours are spent double-digging. The remaining hours involve activities that would normally be done with just about any type of gardening—weeding, watering, shaping the beds, fertilizing, and planting. (Subsequent preparation is reduced to no more than 3 hours of double-digging and less than 4 hours of other activities.) If you are not used to this kind of labor, be careful. Double-digging, especially with the unfamiliar short-handled tools from England, can be exceedingly awkward and potentially harmful to some weekend gardeners.

You need not always start a garden with such labor. The various techniques reviewed in the previous chapter are useful forerunners to BFI gardening. Any one of them offers a less stressful and more expedient way to initially loosen the upper levels of heavy soils. Plan ahead: use the no-till techniques for one or more years where you expect to have a BFI bed in the future. Time and nature will do much of the work for you. Once you get around to double-digging, you will notice that a remarkable improvement in your soil's structure has already taken place.

When to Use the Method

... in the worst soils

The best application of BFI is in the worst-case situations. The heaviest clay soils require the most time and effort to transform, and the BFI method will produce the quickest results.

... when well-trained

Common sense and a practical understanding of body mechanics is required to protect your lower back. For more assurance of success with BFI, get training from someone who learned from a master. Alan Chadwick practiced and taught for years. His apprentices received a thorough theoretical and hands-on training, usually for two years or longer. To watch any of his apprentices prepare a bed is to witness sheer poetry of motion. The grace and economy of motion are truly inspiring. He taught people how to hold tools and utilize the leverage of the body. Every movement is patterned to economize movement, promote stamina, and counter strain.

Americans stoop too much. If you try to double-dig without keeping your back straight, you may hobble to work on Monday. Use your knees and legs and stay low without stooping whenever possible. Certainly, some of those early Greeks were ambitious; others just observed the landslide and did not try to make their own. And some knew how to keep their backs straight while working.

Many enthusiastic people received direct and second-hand training from Alan, and practitioners live in all parts of the country. The Alan Chadwick Society is a formal network of people inspired and trained by him. For information about training in your vicinity, you can write the Society at Green Gulch Farm, Star Route 1, Sausalito, CA 94965. (Be sure to include a stamped, self-addressed envelope and a small donation.) For a $15 membership, you will learn about new projects, the latest information, and current training possibilities.

For emotional and physical health, plan for a very small trial area the first season. Jeavons recommends experimenting with a 100-square-foot plot. I think that is the best size for a novice.

When Not to Double-Dig

... in sandy soils

The soils you naturally enjoy digging are most likely the ones that do not require double-digging. Sandy soils have decent drainage, and do not need extensive cultivation. Because of the greater pore space in sandy soils, the exchange of gases and the drainage of water happens more rapidly than in clay soils. Sandy soils have plenty of oxygen for good growth. In fact, enhancing the amount of oxygen in sandy soils can work against you. But I have seen gardeners shape towering mounds in sandy soils. Such sandy mounds can quickly dry out. It is possible to add the organic matter sandy soils so desperately need for nutrient and water retention without mounding the soil so high. It is more important to mark permanent pathways to avoid soil compaction in the planting areas. To take care of the lower level of nutrients in a sandy soil, use manure teas, green manures, and cover crops.

... in hot summer areas

The hotter the climate, the more you should consider whether or not raised beds are truly beneficial, especially with sandy soils. Sandy soils are likely to be low in nitrogen and organic matter; too much intensive digging may only exaggerate these problems. The hotter the summer climate, the faster organic matter is consumed. The more frequently you dig soils in hot summer weather, the more material you will need to add to compensate for oxidation. However, once the living mulch covers the bed, it will help to moderate high soil temperatures.

In a hot, dry summer climate, the soil in a raised bed may not only heat up too much but also be vulnerable to drying out—thus negating one of the benefits of BFI. If you want to try double-digging in places such as the South, plan to add clay soil (yes, some people add clay soil to hold onto water and nutrients!), to use more compost or organic matter initially, to use more water, and to use mulches early in the season to protect the soil and its moisture from the harsh sun and heat.

... in large backyards

There is less reason to use BFI beds or interplanting if you have a large backyard. A preoccupation with maximum yields per square foot is necessary only for ambitious gardeners with the smallest of yards. The lower yields produced by other methods of cultivation can easily be compensated for by simply planting an area that is two to four times larger, although more water and fertilizers will be needed. In many backyards, this will require only a small portion of the yard.

... with large crops

Fast-growing, high-value salad greens such as bibb lettuce, escarole, and endive are an excellent choice for a small BFI bed nearest the kitchen door, though even lettuce may not need deep cultivation if the soil is good. I have just enough patience with double-digging to use it for salad greens. But for crops like broccoli and corn it seems absurd to me.

Crops that are planted at large spacings require lots of effort. To prepare a BFI bed for a row of tomato plants (even using Jeavons's guidelines of 18 to 24 inches between plants) means *tons* of soil to be moved around. One zealous friend of mine triple-dug his beds and planted corn and many other vegetables in much closer intervals than Jeavons recommends. Even with lots of manure and additional compost, his corn plants were shorter with each passing season. The corn was revealing that he was taxing the limits of his soil and the method, trying to coax more than nature desired from a tiny area. If my friend had used the 15 to 18 inch spacing that Jeavons recommends, the corn would have been taller and the soil would not have been taxed as much. Of course, he would have had to dig a much larger area.

To get a better sense of the potential for root competition at dense spacings, consider a vining winter squash (see Fig. 8.4). Studies of a single winter squash plant show that, where the soil is relatively consistent and of good texture and where there are no pockets of localized nutrients, the diameter of the root system (at just 11 weeks old) will be 24 feet, the depth up to 3 feet! For vining winter squashes, Jeavons recommends 14 plants per 100 square feet on 30-inch spacings. The nutrients needed to sustain such a mass of roots are considerable. (The root zones of other vegetables are illustrated in Figs. 8.5 through 8.9.) You can trade off using more space in your landscape for not having to haul in lots of manure or to purchase additional amendments. The Hopi Indians were known to have planted hills of corn and squash many feet apart so as to conserve precious soil moisture and nutrients. They grew successful

Figure 8.4 The roots of a vining winter squash at 11 weeks.

Figure 8.5 The midsummer root development of Swiss chard.

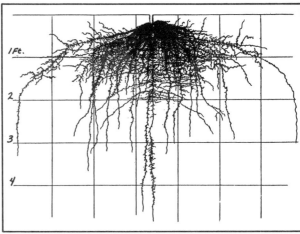

Figure 8.6 Cabbage roots, 75 days after transplanting.

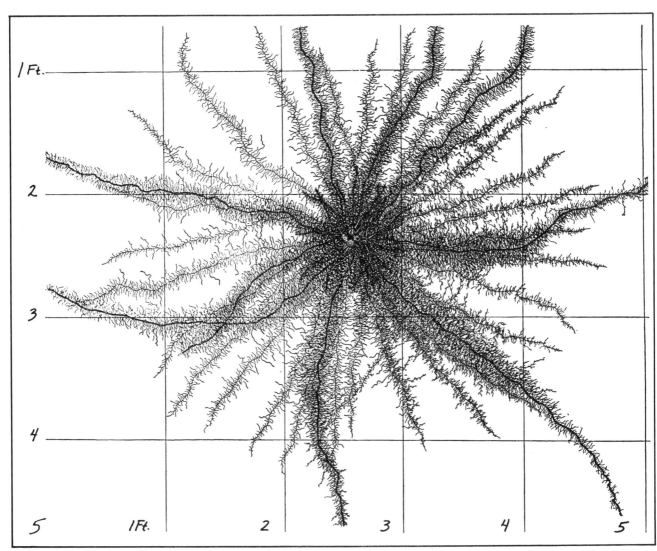

Figure 8.7 The roots of mature sweet corn in the first 12 inches of soil. Where the roots appear to end, they turn downward into deeper soil.

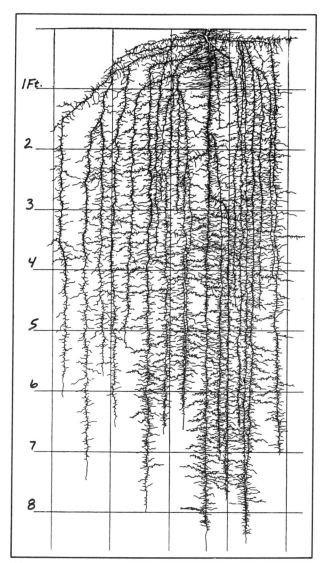

Figure 8.8 The root system of a mature kohlrabi.

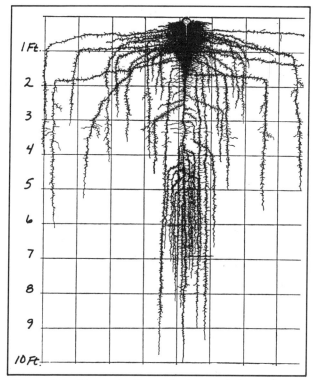

Figure 8.9 The roots of a garden beet at 3½ months.

crops without irrigation in a desert climate with limited natural rainfall. You will need to decide your own healthy compromise between space, water, and nutrients.

. . . when good air circulation is needed

Dense plantings may encourage specific diseases in certain climates. For example, in humid, rainy summer areas, tomatoes need all the air circulation they can get to avoid mildew and leaf blights. Rather than the dense plantings recommended by Jeavons, a better strategy would be to allow plenty of space between the foliage (reducing or eliminating the living mulch effect) by double-digging individual planting holes much farther apart than 18 inches. In some climates, you may want to leave several feet or more between the leaves of a mature tomato plant; this may mean the seedlings are placed as far apart as 4 feet. Also make sure to

prune off much of the lower foliage as soon as the plants begin to set fruit. This will help encourage air circulation beneath and around the plants. A straw mulch, instead of the foliage of the tomato plants, could easily protect the soil between plants from sun and erosion problems. Keep the mulch away from the base of each tomato plant to avoid stem rot. In hot, humid climates the mulch may encourage the spread of root rots in the soil, in which case more bare soil may be preferable.

. . . when you are not in shape

BFI digging is only for the strong and determined gardener. One should be in reasonably good physical condition. If you have a history of back problems, no-till may be just the ticket for you. Gardening should be part recreation, part relaxation, part exercise.

Lift without bending forward. Squat, holding the loaded fork or shovel close to the body, and rise, allowing the legs to provide all of the lift (see Figs. 8.10-8.12). Go for the distance, do not be afraid to rest when you feel tired, and gradually let the garden build your strength.

Once the soil is of good tilth, deep digging is not required every year. After a period of soil improvement, the bed can be maintained with a simple surface preparation and a seasonal application of compost. The Irish have even called established raised beds "lazy beds."

Figure 8.10 When double-digging, keep your back straight, your seat low, and grasp the shovel near the heavy end. The gardener is using a left-handed grip.

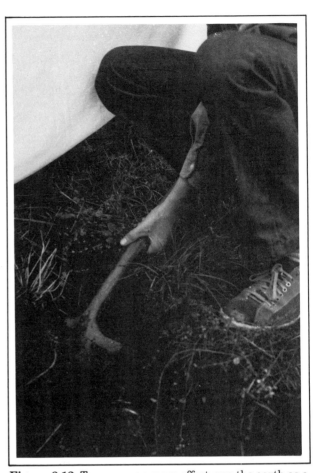

Figure 8.12. To save even more effort, use the earth as a fulcrum for the shovel.

Figure 8.11. To make the job easier, always use leverage – the gardener's arm is leveraged against one leg, the handle of the shovel against the other leg. A right-handed grip is shown.

Aquatias, A. **Intensive Culture of Vegetables, the French System**. Harrisville, NY: Solar Survival Press, 1913. A good historical and technical review of market gardens that surrounded most French cities in the early 1900s. Not very relevant today, but fascinating reading if you are interested in the roots of the bio-dynamic French intensive method.

Bio-Dynamic Farming and Gardening Association. **Bio-Dynamic Treatment of Fruit Trees, Berries and Shrubs**. Stroudsburg, PA: Bio-Dynamic Farming and Gardening Assoc., n.d. A short pamphlet on the techniques outlined by Rudolf Steiner and others. I have a hard time with some of the procedures described, such as wire-brushing the entire bark of fruit trees.

Campbell, Stu. **Let it Rot**. Charlotte, VT: Garden Way Publishing, 1975. A very readable general review of composting dynamics and methods. The best book on the subject—a minor classic. Worth looking for in used book stores.

Cuthbertson, Tom. **Alan Chadwick's Enchanted Garden**. New York: E. P. Dutton, 1978. The narrative, told from a rabbit's viewpoint, gets in the way. Currently the only book on this important horticulturist, but not worth buying. Rumor has it that a new book on Chadwick will be released soon.

Jeavons, John. **How to Grow More Vegetables**. Berkeley: Ten Speed Press, 1982. This bible of raised bed, bio-dynamic French intensive gardening should be on every gardener's bookshelf. Thorough and detailed, but some of the projections of crop yields seem too optimistic to me.

King, F.H. **Farmers of Forty Centuries**. Emmaus, PA: Rodale Press, 1911. A travelog through turn-of-the-century China when all farming was done by hand. A wonderful, though rambling, review of another culture's raised bed gardening methods.

Koepf, H.H. **Bio-Dynamic Agriculture**. Spring Valley, NY: Anthroposophic Press, 1976. A complete review of the spiritual basis for bio-dynamic farming. Requires real concentration and intense interest in the topic.

Leckie, Jim; Masters, Gil; Whitehouse, Harry; and Young, Lily. **More Other Homes and Garbage**. Rev. ed. San Francisco: Sierra Club Books, 1975. This updated classic on integrated, sustainable homes and gardens has much more on wind power, methane generation, and hydropower than does the Farallones Institute's *Integral Urban House;* but similarly, is very weak on perennial food plants and tree crops.

Levitan, Lois. **Improve Your Gardening With Backyard Research**. Emmaus, PA: Rodale Press, 1980. The only detailed book on the topic for the non-technical reader. For the serious and methodical gardener only.

National Gardening Association. **Gardening: The Complete Guide to Growing America's Favorite Fruits and Vegetables**. Boston: Addison-Wesley, 1986. An excellent guide to organic cultivation of the U.S.'s 40 favorite vegetables and fruits, and control of 40 common pests and diseases. Lots of color in this comprehensive 384-page reference. Buy it for your gardening bookshelf.

New Alchemy Institute. **Gardening for All Seasons**. Andover, MA: Brick House Publishing, 1983. An excellent book based on New Alchemy's thorough research and testing. Their integrated systems for food production and preservation are more current than those described in the Farallones Institute's *Integral Urban House*. Covers vegetable cultivation, greenhouse production, aquaculture, raising chickens, tree crops, recycling, and community gardens. Especially good for people living in colder winter climates of the U.S.

Organic Gardening Magazine, ed. **Getting the Most from Your Garden**. Emmaus, PA: Rodale Press, 1980. A poorly edited book that expands on Jeavons' *How to Grow More Vegetables*. It explains in detail how to adapt the French intensive method to a variety of climates, and gives much more information on cloches and coldframes. The inclusion of an index is a welcome improvement over Jeavons' book.

Seymour, John. **The Self-Sufficient Gardener**. Garden City, NY: Doubleday, 1980. A favorite that I turn to frequently. Includes information on wide-bed, deep-dug vegetable culture, steeped in the long history of English horticultural experience. Excellent color plates and drawings.

Sprague, H.B., ed. **Hunger Signs in Crops**. New York: David McKay, 1941. Good color plates detail the symptoms of nutritional deficiencies for major crops. Out of print; serious horticulturists should grab any copy they find in a used book store.

Steiner, Rudolph. **Agriculture**. Spring Valley, NY: Anthroposophic Press, 1924. Bio-dynamics explained, in the founder's own, esoteric, words.

Weaver, John. **Root Development of Field Crops**. New York: McGraw-Hill, 1926. Root maps by Weaver and associates, primarily of cereal grains, forage grasses, clovers, corn, sunflowers, and potatoes. Excellent drawings of what must have been very tedious excavations.

Weaver, John. **Root Development of Vegetable Crops**. New York: McGraw-Hill, 1927. The vegetable root zone charts pictured in this chapter are just a few from Weaver's book. Weaver spent most of his professional life excavating roots of vegetables, perennial prairie plants, trees, and shrubs. His books and articles are the largest single source of root zone maps in the world.

GROWING VEGETABLES
Growing Healthier Vegetables

Regardless of the way you garden, there are exciting ways to improve the growth and yields of any vegetable. Too often, gardeners feel that a good crop is the result of good luck. With new knowledge and technologies, however, you can *expect* high yields. Let's look at inoculants for stimulating the soil's biological activity, improved ways to start seedlings, and drip irrigation.

SOIL INOCULANTS

Tucked away in many retail nurseries are tiny packets containing a powdered culture of bacteria, an inoculant called rhizobium that colonizes the roots of leguminous plants and converts, or "fixes," nitrogen from the air. Without these bacteria, the legume cannot form the root nodules that are the the plant's nitrogen factory.

You may not need legume inoculants. Many soils have plenty of varieties of rhizobia which live on from year to year. Pull up some bean plants. If you can see small pinkish white nodules on the roots, the soil has the right type of rhizobium. If there are no nodules, or in the following circumstances, your soil will benefit from an application of inoculant.

Use inoculant:

- Where the topsoil has been removed. Exposed subsoils need to be transformed in order to be productive. Rhizobium bacteria are certain to be nonexistent or greatly reduced in such situations.

- When a soil has been fallow for a long time without any legumes in the ground cover. Rhizobia can lie dormant for several years, without an active association with a legume's roots. With time, however, dormant rhizobia die.

- In soils that have been heavily sprayed or fertilized with chemicals. Some synthetic fertilizers are caustic to the bacteria, and copper and mercury sprays are toxic.

- When planting a variety of legumes that have not been previously grown in your garden.

- Just to be safe. A packet of pea and bean inoculant costs less than $2.00 at my local nur-

sery, not much for a one-time application to help ensure healthy and productive beans and peas.

You must get the right inoculant to ensure success. The following chart shows the major species of rhizobia and the legumes they associate with. Most garden supply stores sell only a generic legume inoculant containing many species of rhizobia for a wide range of legumes. Most beans and peas are covered by the generic inoculants, but if you are planting clover, be sure you get the specific rhizobium needed.

If you are going to plant new and unusual varieties of leguminous plants, the species of rhizobium required for good nodulation may not be present in your soil. The Siberian peashrub *(Caragana arborescens)*, an exotic leguminous tree, is gaining in popularity for use in polycultural landscapes and windbreaks. When young Siberian peashrub trees were dug up at the New Alchemy Institute on Cape Cod, Massachusetts, there were no nodules on the roots. An inoculant of the correct species of rhizobium *(Caragana* Spec. #1) was secured (from Nitragin, 3101 West Custer Ave., Milwaukee, Wisconsin 53209) and added to the soil. Now the Siberian peashrub fixes nitrogen.

Just How Much Will Inoculants Increase the Yields of My Peas and Beans?

Plenty, especially if you plan to grow a type of bean or pea that has not been grown in your garden for years. A study done by the Rodale Research Center *(New Farm Magazine,* February, 1983) compared several fields of soybeans that were growing side-by-side: one field had no inoculants; the others were inoculated with two types of rhizobium inoculant. None of the fields had grown soybeans for ten years. The inoculant was similar to the powder you can purchase at the local retail nursery. The fields with inoculant had 67 percent greater yields than the untreated field.

Other Beneficial Bacteria for Vegetables

Azotobacter, another nitrogen-fixing bacteria, is free living and does not need association with roots as does rhizobium. Though azotobacter's nitrogen-fixing abilities are rather limited, it produced decent yield increases when used as a seed inoculant. Studies done in Russia and in the United States have consistently documented yield increases of 10 to 20 percent when compared to uninoculated soils. In isolated cases with specific crops, increases of up to 28 percent have been seen. The crops that have benefited from this bacteria are: corn, sunflowers, wheat, oats, rye, barley, sugar beets, potatoes, sorghum, cotton, cabbage, tomatoes, cucumbers, and flax. (All studies have recommended that azotobacter not be thought of as a substitute for fertilizers or for rhizobium.)

The beneficial effect of azotobacter seems to come from several sources in addition to its nitrogen-fixing capabilities. Among them:

- Azotobacter produces hormones that stimulate the length and number of young roots.
- Azotobacter appears to suppress certain viral, bacterial, and fungal diseases. (Some tests have produced mixed results, however.)

Azotobacter is available under the trade name "Soeco Seed Inoculant" from Soil Enterprise Corporation, P.O. Box 128, Stoneville, Mississippi 38776.

SEEDLINGS
THE SPEEDLING® WAY

Starting seeds is easy, right? Yes, but in horticulture there is always a new "correct" way to do things. Until recently, I had always reused the standard-size flats or six-packs left over from nursery purchases. The system served me well. Now, I have a new method that works even better: the Speedling System® and its TODD® planter flat. With this system, seedlings are less affected by transplant shock. It does not make the way you start seedlings obsolete, but it is well worth a trial.

The Root of the Difference

Figure 9.1 shows the differences between a TODD® planter flat and the six-packs commonly purchased in nurseries. The cells are narrower, deeper, and tapered – a shape that, combined with smooth styrofoam sides, allows for easy removal of the young transplant. In addition, the narrow cells allow many more plants per flat than a six-pack.

Figure 9.1 A cross-section of the TODD® planter. A hole at the bottom of each cell "air prunes" taproots, encouraging horizontal root growth. (Photograph by Speedling Inc., Sun City, FL 33586. All rights reserved.)

Notice the small hole at the bottom of each cell. This is the clue to the real advantage of the TODD® planter. The tapered sides of the cell guide the tiny taproot of the seedling toward the hole. When the root tries to grow out of the hole, its tip withers and dies. This may seem like a rude way to treat a young seedling, but there is a good reason. The death of the tip stimulates a greater development of the horizontal roots. More tiny root hairs develop, with a great surface area. The enhanced root system is less likely to experience transplant shock. The greater surface area and larger number of branched root hairs make for a seedling that quickly absorbs water and nutrients after transplanting.

The flats come in several sizes: 1-, 1½-, and 2-inch cells. Using a smaller cell means transplanting a small seedling sooner. I prefer the biggest size, except for lettuces, to get a larger transplant.

The Results

Last year I started a flat of 'Romanesco' broccoli in TODD® planter flats. The seedlings were a very healthy green and quick to grow to a transplantable size. The bed to receive the 'Romanesco' broccoli had been prepared several weeks in advance. Transplanting was quick and simple. The impressive part was soon to follow: the seedlings continued to grow as if nothing had happened! I was delighted to watch their rapid, healthy growth. Many plants went on to produce heads up to 14 inches wide. (See Fig. 1.2 in color plates.)

I think there is a much greater chance of transplant shock, reduced growth, and lower yields with six-packs than with TODD® flats. One reason is the shallower soil in a six-pack: the seedlings must be smaller if they are to be transplanted before getting too old and woody. And the six-pack produces a less fibrous horizontal root system.

Soil Mixes for TODD® Planter Flats

To work well, the TODD® flat needs a potting soil which retains moisture and is rich in phosphorus and potassium, the nutrients that promote healthy root growth.

To mix a 4-cubic-foot wheelbarrow load of the potting mix, use the following recipe:

- Mix equal parts of peat moss and medium or coarse vermiculite to get slightly less than 4 cubic feet.

- Add up to 20 percent compost.

To this mixture add the following amendments:

- 1½ lbs. bone meal (with a nitrogen-phosphorus-potassium ratio of 0-20-0)

- ½ lb. dolomite (for calcium and magnesium)

- ¼ lb. oyster shell flour (96% calcium)

- ½ lb. blood meal (14-0-0, use less if the compost is high in nitrogen)

- ¼ lb. gypsum (for calcium)

- ⅛ lb. kelp meal (1.5-.75-12, also for trace minerals and growth stimulants)

- ¾ lb. dried, granular molasses (.7-0-5, the sugar stimulates soil bacteria)

Mix the ingredients dry, then moisten before putting into the flats.

Do not use sand in the mix as it makes removing the seedlings more difficult. Perlite should be avoided—it tends to float to the top and does not absorb moisture. You can "cheat" on this recipe, as I have, by buying a rich, compost-based potting soil and adding vermiculite and compost.

It is essential that the TODD® flats are raised at least 2 inches off the bench or ground so that air is free to circulate and "air-prune" the roots. Two-by-fours make a handy prop.

Plant seeds in the usual way, taking care not to overwater the flats (which leaches out nutrients). Water with a gentle sprinkle until the first few drops drain out the bottom. A Haws oval watering rose is the best tool for this job. Adding a tablespoon of fish emulsion to each gallon of water at every other watering is usually helpful in providing nitrogen, the nutrient most important to young leaf growth and most likely to leach out.

To transplant, wait until the seedling is large enough to have an extensive root system. Test by tugging gently on the stem—the seedling will pop out of its cell for a root inspection. Thoroughly soaking the soil makes removal easier.

The cost of a TODD® planter is higher than other flats (each is $7 or more). However, a flat with 1-inch cells has 200 cells, the 1½-inch has 128 cells, and the 2-inch has 72 cells. With care, you should be able to get 20 to 30 uses from each TODD® planter flat. Use a 2 percent solution of bleach to sterilize the flats between seedings. Avoid boiling water, gasoline, and petroleum solvents, which will melt the styrofoam. I have found that the edges of the cells break if I garden in haste. To protect the styrofoam, I have glued a protective wooden edging to all sides (see Fig. 9.2). A 6-by-¼-inch redwood bender board makes a good edging. Use exterior panel, construction glue to attach the boards to the styrofoam. The top of the TODD® flat can be recessed for protection and the bottom still stays off the ground by at least 2 inches. The bender board is not heavy and the flats are still easy to cart around the garden.

On some TODD® flats, I have pre-nailed and glued four legs to the bender board before gluing it to the flat. This allows for excellent air circulation. On each leg, I apply a band of Tanglefoot™ to prevent hungry insects and slugs from climbing aboard.

I know gardeners who cut the flats into sections with a bread knife, making smaller transplanting jobs easier. With the smaller sections, the edges of the TODD® planter do not seem as prone to breaking.

Figure 9.2 A TODD® planter reinforced with bender board for durability.

Hartman, H.T., and Kester, D.E. **Plant Propagation**. 4th ed. Englewood Cliffs, NJ: Prentice-Hall, 1983. This bible of propagation covers all aspects, except for the latest in clonal tissue culture. Quite expensive—encourage your library to get a copy.

Johnston, Rob. **Growing Garden Seeds**. Albion, ME: Johnny's Selected Seeds, 1983. An excellent pamphlet that covers most of the basics of how to save your own seed. Includes distances required between varieties to prevent cross-pollination.

Reilly, Ann. **Park's Success With Seeds**. Greenwood, SC: George Park Seed Co., 1978. A good reference for starting ornamental seeds. A detailed encyclopedia comprises most of the book.

U.S.D.A. **Seeds of Woody Plants in the U.S.** Handbook No. 450. Washington, DC: Gov't. Printing Office, 1972. For the professional grower or serious hobbyist, the best manual on germinating seeds of ornamental and forest trees and shrubs.

Vandemark, J.S., and Courter, J.W. **Vegetable Gardening for Illinois**. Urbana-Champaign, IL: University of Illinois, 1978. A very good, inexpensive book for the beginning gardener and a useful reference for the experienced. Though planting dates are for Illinois, most apply throughout the Midwest. Especially helpful are drawings that show what each vegetable seedling looks like, a beginner's common question. I appreciate how this book does not mainline chemical solutions; the encyclopedia begins each vegetable listing with varieties that are disease-resistant.

DRIP IRRIGATION

Good gardeners do not leave watering to chance. Irrigation schemes were invented along with the development of agriculture. Over the millennia, watering methods have become more complex *and* more efficient.

The latest development, drip irrigation (sometimes called trickle irrigation) can swamp you with an alphabet soup of hardware—spaghetti tubing, goof plugs, tortuous path emitters, regulators, compression tees, self-flushing end caps. You may have to conquer "technophobia" to become familiar with it, but once you do, you will see it can be a liberating tool for managing your edible landscape. You can still water by hand for relaxation, but a drip system frees you for other gardening tasks you may enjoy more.

The common feature of all drip irrigation is the slow application of water to the root zone over a long period of time. Drip irrigation allows you to provide the right amount of water, in the right place at the right time. Rather than deep soaking on an occasional basis, drip irrigation maintains optimal soil moisture, never allowing the soil to get too dry or too wet. Free of periods of drought and water-logging, plants experience little shock and respond with consistent, regular growth. Drip irrigation is the most effective and easiest way I have found to water my edible landscape.

The Benefits

The advantages of drip irrigation can be summarized as follows:

Makes efficient use of water. Drip irrigation prevents losses due to wind-blown sprinkler spray, runoff, evaporation from puddling, soil surface evaporation, and deep percolation past the roots because of flooding—saving up to 60 percent of the water.

Increased yields, maybe. There have been some mixed results in university studies of yields; nevertheless, drip irrigation at least equals the production of furrow irrigation. In commercial applications, it has shown 10 to 30 percent increases in yields.

Fewer problems with saline water. Drip irrigation can be the most effective way to apply saline water without damaging crops: the high-frequency applications keep salts in dilute solution. And unlike sprinkler irrigation, there is no salt damage to the foliage. If a saline crust forms at the margins of the wetted area, an occasional flooding will flush the salts below the root zone.

Improved fertilization during the growing season. With the right kinds of hardware, it is easy to apply small amounts of liquid fertilizers. The ease of application also allows for more careful timing, and fertilizer does not leach away below the root zone.

Fewer weeds in dry climates. With widely spaced emitters, there is a wet circle around each emitter but dry soil between the circles. Only a fraction of the soil's surface is moist enough to sprout weed growth. When emitters are under the foliage of the plant, however, the shade augments weed growth.

Saves time and labor. The initial installation of a drip system can be time consuming, but thereafter, irrigation is only a twist-of-the-wrist away. Drip irrigation systems can be easily automated, reducing your watering time to zero.

Reduced disease problems. By eliminating water on the foliage in dry summer areas, drip irrigation reduces leaf diseases such as powdery mildew, leaf spot, anthracnose, shot hole fungus, fire blight, and scab.

Better water distribution on hills. Emitters designed to compensate for differences in water pressure due to elevation will prevent runoff while applying equal amounts of water to every plant. No more drought on the top of the hill and flooding at the bottom as with regular sprinklers.

Better soil structure. Heavy sprinkler irrigation can puddle clay soils, causing compaction. The slow, soaking action of drip emitters keeps the soil from getting too wet and compacted.

The Drawbacks

Initial costs are high. Even the simplest system is more costly than a hose with a sprinkler. The filters, pressure regulators, tubing, emitters, and other miscellanous parts take a big bite out of this month's paycheck, but the time it will save you quickly compensates for the expense. Automated systems are even more expensive, but virtually effortless once installed.

Clogging. Until recently, the clogging of emitters has been the Achilles heel of drip irrigation. Now there are self-flushing and self-cleaning emitters, but people still skimp on or skip filtration—resulting in costly and time-consuming replacement of the plugged emitters. A carefully designed and installed system, with the necessary filtration, is important.

Restricted root development. When too few emitters are used, the small amount of moist soil limits the extent of the feeding roots. With fewer roots, plants can experience slower growth, lower yields, and nutritional deficiencies. A properly designed system can avoid this pitfall.

Rodents can eat the tubing. Gophers, when the drip tubing is buried, and mice, when the tubing is above ground, have been known to eat holes in the tubing. I keep all emitters on top of the mulch and have had little damage from gophers (mice are not much of a problem in my area).

Green manures and cover crops are not always compatible. The drip tubing prevents tilling under cover crops as a green manure. It is practically impossible to remove once the cover crop has grown up around it. Also, drip-irrigated plantings have too much dry surface area to permit the seeding of cover crops.

It is difficult to weed around drip tubing. The small area of moist surface will have a lush crop of weeds. When the distribution lines are on the surface, it is tedious to weed around the tubing. The weeds can be controlled by mulching or by hanging the tubing on a trellis off the ground for easy weeding.

Drip Parts

There are four major components to a drip system—filter, pressure regulator, drip tubing, and emitters. (See Fig. 9.3.) There is a mind-boggling variety of brand names, parts, and prepackaged systems to choose from.

I do not recommend purchasing the prepackaged, "complete" kits or systems. They are usually not complete enough to do a good job in your situation. Often, the parts that come in kits are not standard sizes, and replacements and additions must be purchased through the mail. Thus, repairs and quick adjustments are not possible without a costly collection of spare parts. Some kits have standard fittings and parts, but each piece is more expensive because of the packaging.

The best approach is to survey the retail suppliers of drip irrigation hardware in your area. Choose a store whose staff can give you expert advice with each purchase and stay with that store. As your landscape changes and expands, they will be familiar with your situation and can help you adapt new parts.

After choosing a store, make a visit with some paper and a pencil to write down each part's name, model number, flow rate, and price. Ask for any free literature and layout or design guides to help with your planning. Do not try to design your first system while standing among a sea of confusing options. Do your planning at home, on paper. Then have the staff at the store review your plan and give suggestions. The major parts you will need to survey on your first visit are described below.

Filters

All drip systems must have good quality filters, regardless of the water source. A filter keeps silt and dirt from entering the system and clogging the emitters. Cleaning plugged emitters is a thankless and time-consuming task. Though municipal water is usually very clean, the filter is an important backup. Homes with their own wells usually have a filtration system, but another for the drip system is required. A good filter may seem expensive, but it is money well spent.

Filters come in a variety of screen or mesh sizes. The larger the number, such as 200 mesh, the finer the mesh and the smaller the particles that will be filtered. But the finer the mesh, the more the filter restics the flow of water. Each filter has a different flow rate, and the amount of water that will pass through a filter, in gallons per minute, is important to know when sizing your system. Ask for this figure and write it down. If the store personnel do not know, then you are at the wrong store. You will need a larger size filter if the water supply has a lot of sand, grit, or sediment.

Be sure to purchase a filter with a screen that can be easily flushed and replaced. This periodic maintenance is essential to keep your system trouble-free.

To protect the purity of your water supply, you should install an antisiphon valve. There is some risk to your family's health without this device. Every time the drip system shuts off it is possible that dirt and dissolved fertilizers can be sucked back into the drip hose and eventually be siphoned back into the main pipes of the house—and into your drinking water. The antisiphon valve prevents this. Install it on the main irrigation line just outside the house, before the filter, valves, or pressure regulator. Your local drip irrigation or plumbing supplier can describe the models available and the installation details. The one-time cost is a bit high—but it is worth the cost to know your family is drinking pure water.

Pressure Regulators

Drip systems, like people, need to be protected from blowing their fittings. Drip systems are very easy to assemble because most of the fittings simply snap or squeeze together, thus eliminating the mess and toxic fumes of the glues used to assemble plastic (PVC) pipe and the expense of PVC and metal. The drip fittings, however, cannot handle the same pressure as metal or PVC pipe. To protect the fittings and your investment, the pressure should always be kept below 25 psi (pounds per square inch). Municipal pressure is between 40 and 60 psi in most areas. If you suspect that the water pressure is abnormally high or low, borrow or rent a pressure gauge and take a reading at each hose bib. With a gravity-fed system it is necessary to measure the pressure at each hose bib for accurate sizing.

You will need a pressure regulator at the beginning of each separate system. There are types that have hose threads which screw directly onto an existing hose bib. And there are kinds that have pipe thread to be plumbed into any metal or plastic fittings. You must know how much water the regulator will allow through it. Make a note of the different model numbers along with each one's gpm (gallons per minute) for use when designing your system.

Drip Tubing

There are two types of tubing—the major supply lines, called tubing, or hose; and the smaller feeder line from the supply hose to an emitter, called spaghetti.

Drip hose comes in many sizes, but there is only one practical size to use: ½-inch (or O.580-inch inside diameter) hose. Anything smaller can deliver enough water to only the smallest of gardens. One-half-inch hose will pass 4 gpm (240 gph) at a pressure of 25 psi.

Spaghetti tubing comes in sizes of ¼- or ⅛-inch diameter. The size you will need depends upon the type of emitter that will be attached. Choose the best emitter first, then get the spaghetti tubing to match.

The flow rate of the spaghetti tubing is not critical, as long as the drip hose is supplying enough water. However, if you use lengths of spaghetti longer than 5 feet, the losses caused by the friction of the water passing through the tube will reduce the amount of water available to each emitter. It is better to lay your drip hose closer to each plant

Figure 9.3 The major components of a drip irrigation system. There are many more types of emitters than the five pictured here. Check with a local supplier for the latest and most effective hardware for your situation.

than to use long lengths of spaghetti tube.

Emitters

If you want to really experience confusion, survey the variety of emitters available. There are two basic types: compensating and non-compensating.

Non-compensating emitters have a simple orifice through which the water passes. While the hole is tiny, there is nothing to limit the water's flow at the lower and higher ranges of pressure. If the drip irrigation line changes elevation more than 15 feet, the emitters at the end and top of the line will pass less water than those at the beginning and low points, making it difficult to provide a consistent amount of water to each plant.

Pressure-compensating emitters are designed to adapt to pressure differences, regulating themselves to deliver the same amount of water regardless of elevation, pressure differences, and the length of the line. Of course, there are operating limits to the design of each emitter. Your local supplier can tell you the efficiency of compensation and the range of pressures at which the compensation is effective. These emitters are usually a little more costly than the non-compensating emitters, but worth the money. You can relax, assured that each plant is getting the amount of water it needs.

When you write down prices, make sure to note also the gph for each style of emitter. This figure is essential for designing your system and for determining how long it will take to fully irrigate each type of plant.

There are a variety of emitters that have advantages in special situations: in-line emitters, sometimes called tortuous path emitters, have a laminar flow and are not easily clogged; low-volume microsprinklers slowly water a large surface area; microspray heads have a fixed spray in a variety of patterns; bubble heads gently fill containers or planting basins; and many more. It is beyond the scope of this book to fully explain the pluses and minuses of each. Seek out your local retail store or an irrigation consultant for the details.

The details of sizing the emitters to your edible landscape and the layout of the system will depend on the kind of hardware you purchase and the local soil and climate. Installation of a drip system is almost as easy and fun as playing with Lincoln Logs™ or Legos™. Your local drip irrigation supplier will provide the required pointers to get you started. Some suppliers give lectures – if the ones in your area do not, encourage them to provide this service. If you don't have time for the project, hire a skilled landscaper – the cost will be higher, but the savings in time and water will soon compensate for it.

Out of Sight, Out of Mind . . . A Map for Future Reference

Whether you install your own system or not, once buried, it's hard to recall the precise location of all the hoses. Be sure to mark on the scale drawing of your landscape the location of all hose bibs and underground pipes, as well as the final drip irrigation design.

Maintenance for Reliability

Without periodic maintenance drip systems can malfunction. Flush the filter screen weekly to keep it clean. Once a month open the ends of the drip hose while the system is running to flush away any silt or dirt that may have accumulated. There are a number of options for capping the end of the hose, even a "flushing end cap" that automatically passes a small amount of water and any accumulated dirt each time the system turns on. On a periodic basis, walk through your landscape and check for clogged emitters. Plants showing signs of drought are one indicator. Also look for puddles and large wet areas caused by gopher and mouse damage to the drip lines. (Trapping may be required.) Then sit back and relax; the system waters for you.

Bressan, Tom, and Pearson, Mart. **Drip Irrigation, A User's Manual**. San Francisco: The Urban Farmer, 1982. This pamphlet provides the shortest, most coherent, and practical explanation of how to plan and size a drip system for your home landscape. Explains the basic components of a drip system and how to choose the right kind and number of emitters. Available from Harmony Farm Supply, P.O. Box 451, Graton, CA 95444.

INTERCROPPING

Intercropping, or mixing different crops in the same planting, is a way to produce healthier plants and greater yields. Intercropping can be achieved by:

- Layering shade- and sun-loving crops.

- Combining crops with complementary foliage— tall and short, wide and narrow.

- Interplanting deep- and shallow-rooted plants to minimize the competition for water and nutrients.

- Growing quick-maturing vegetables among slow-maturing vegetables.

Intercropping for Good Use of Sunlight

To keep the landscape as compact as possible, you can intercrop shade-tolerant plants with sun-loving plants. Though most vegetables seem to need full sun to prosper, there are exceptions. Leafy greens are good candidates for shady situations. Their leaves simply grow much bigger in order to absorb enough sunlight. You may need to grow your lettuce in full sun during early spring and late fall, but you can grow lettuce into the heat of summer by planting it beneath tall crops like corn and sunflowers. When you plant lettuce with young corn, it will receive plenty of early spring sunlight; as the season gets hotter, the lettuce will be shaded by the growing corn. Figure 9.3A shows other annual edibles that tolerate shade.

When designing your garden, keep in mind that shade-tolerant vegetables can be planted not only under taller, sun-loving plants but under trees, buildings, and fences as well. Also note that the deepest shade may be suitable only for miner's lettuce, spinach, and leaf lettuce.

One year, much to everyone's amusement, I grew Kentucky Wonder pole beans beneath a willow tree because all the area with full sun had already been planted. The leaves grew to be several times larger than normal and the pods half again as long. Though the yields must have been one-third to one-fourth that of a pole bean in full sun, I had more beans to eat than I had had the previous year, thanks to my planting new ground. The extra effort of tilling and planting was well worthwhile.

Use sun-loving plants to shelter the late-summer seedlings of winter crops. Angelina Flores uses the shade of a grapevine to shelter kale seedlings during the late summer (see Fig. 9.4). Once the grapevine loses its leaves, the kale has plenty of light for growth. Angelina harvests the kale before the vine leafs out in the spring.

SHADE-TOLERANT ANNUAL EDIBLES
Amaranth
Beans
Beets
Borage
Broccoli
Brussels sprouts
Cabbage
Calendula (flower only)
Cauliflower
Celery
Chard
Chervil
Cress
Cucumbers
Endive
Fava beans
Kale
Kohlrabi
Lamb's-quarters
Leaf lettuce
Leeks
Miner's lettuce
Nasturtiums
Nettles
Parsnips
Peas
Potatoes
Pumpkins
Purslane
Radishes
Salsify
Spinach
Squash
Rutabagas
Turnips

Figure 9.3A

Figure 9.4 A kale plant, near bloom, grows beneath a dormant grapevine. In summer and fall, the grapevine sheltered the kale from sun.

Intercropping for Good Use of Space

Vertical space is an ignored resource in many gardens. Tall plants can fit very closely to shorter ones, providing the vertical plants are on the north side, or, if carefully planned, on the east or west sides.

Oriental gardens provide the best examples of using vertical space. At the International Gardens in Seattle, trellises support squashes, beans, cucumbers, peas, melons, vining leafy greens, and tomatoes. Many of these tall plants do not bear close to the ground and soon lose their lower leaves, letting shade-tolerant vegetables grow nearby.

Vines are not the only tall vegetables for vertical gardening—sunflowers, corn, Jerusalem artichokes, and grain amaranth are tall plants that can shelter other vegetables. Cucumbers, started late in the season, can be trained up the stalks of early-planted sunflowers. Native Americans often grow squashes among rows of corn. The corn shelters the squash from excessive summer sun without severely reducing yields.

Even with lower growing vegetables there are differences of shape. Tall skinny plants such as leeks, garlic, salsify, celery, and onions can fit snugly next to lettuce, spinach, endive, and other leafy greens. Think of your edible landscape as having valuable air space. Plan to combine the tall and short, the skinny and fat for a more interesting and productive garden.

Intercropping Below Ground — The Shape of Roots

Roots may be out of sight, but don't put them out of mind. Since each vegetable has a distinctive root system—with a particular shape, exploring specific depths of the soil—you can reduce the competition for space, and maybe even for nutrients, by intercropping the right root systems. For example, you can mix carrots with shallow-rooted lettuces. Keep in mind that the upper levels of the soil provide a greater portion of a plant's water and nutrients, regardless of the depth of its root system. (For more detail, see "Deep-Rooted Myths.")

What we see above ground can be deceiving. As Fig. 9.5 reveals, beets have much less foliage than tomatoes, yet the beet's roots may forage as deep as 10 feet, and nearly as wide, while a tomato's fibrous root system is only 4½ feet deep and up to 6 feet wide.

The vegetables in Fig. 9.6 have a shallow root system, within the top 2 to 4 feet of soil.

Figure 9.5 The foliage above ground is not a good indicator of the shape or depth of the root system.

ROOTS TO 4 FEET DEEP		
Common Name	Depth (in feet)	Width, or Radius (in feet)
Basil	*	*
Beans (kidney)	3 to 4	2
Cauliflower	2 to 4	2 to 2.5
Garlic	2.5	1.5
Leek	1.5 to 2	1 to 2
Muskmelon	*	*
Onion	1.5 to 3	.5 to 1.5
Parsley	2 to 4	1.5
Pea	3	2
Pepper	3 to 4	1.5 to 3
Radish	2 to 3	1 to 2
Squash (summer)	*	*
Watermelon	*	*

Figure 9.6

Vegetables with roots that extend from 4 to 6 feet are listed in Fig. 9.7.

ROOTS TO 6 FEET DEEP		
Common Name	Depth (in feet)	Width, or radius (in feet)
Asparagus	4.5	10.5
Borage	*	*
Cabbage	4 to 5	3 to 3.5
Corn	5 to 6	1.5 to 4
Eggplant	4 to 7	4
Lettuce	4 to 6	.5 to 1.5
Okra	4 to 4.5	4 to 6
Pumpkin	6	13 to 19
Rutabaga	6	1 to 1.5
Spinach	4 to 6	1.5
Squash (winter)	6	13 to 19
Tomato	3 to 5	2.5 to 5.5
Turnip	5.5	2 to 2.5

Figure 9.7

Figure 9.8 lists vegetables that send their roots below the 6-foot level.

ROOTS DEEPER THAN 6 FEET		
Common Name	Depth (infeet)	Width, or Radius (in feet)
Beet	10	2 to 4
Carrot	6 to 7.5	1 to 2
Horseradish	10 to 14	2 to 3
Kohlrabi	7 to 8.5	2
Parsnip	6.5	4
Potato	*	*
Rhubarb	8	3 to 4
Swiss chard	6 to 7	3.5

Figure 9.8

*Data not specified in source (California Agricultural Experimental Station leaflet, *Suggestions on Irrigating Commercial Truck Crops*, L. D. Doneen and J. H. MacGillivary, 1946).

The data in Figs. 9.9 through 9.17 are from John E. Weaver, Professor of Plant Ecology at the University of Nebraska, who spent his entire professional life excavating plants to study the shape and formation of their roots. In *Root Development of Vegetable Crops* (McGraw-Hill, 1927), he disproved numerous assumptions and myths about root systems. Weaver's studies were done in good, deep soils where there are summer rains. If your soil has a clay pan or bedrock near the surface, his figures would not apply—instead, the root depth would be only to the obstruction and the width would be much greater than Weaver's.

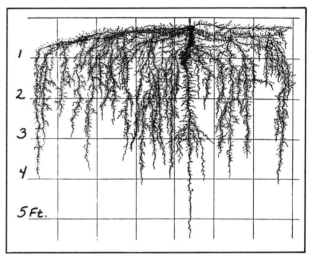

Figure 9.9 The root zone of a maturing lima bean plant. Its roots explored 200 cubic feet of soil.

Figure 9.10 The mature root system of an 'Improved Hollow Crown' parsnip in its second season of growth.

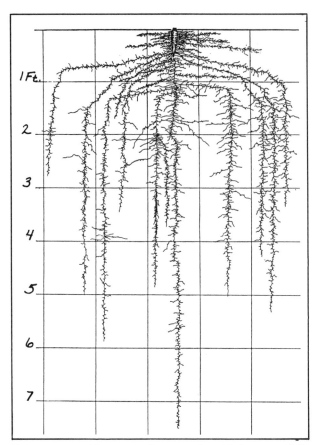

Figure 9.11 The roots of a carrot in mid-August, while still growing vigorously.

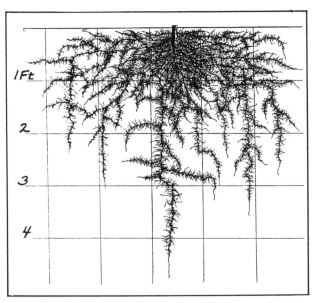

Figure 9.13 The root system of a cauliflower at the time of harvest.

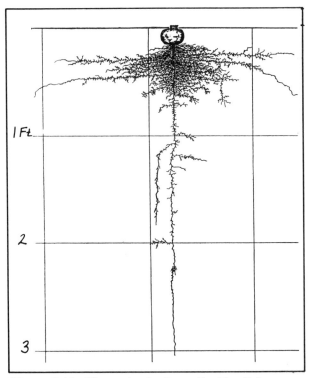

Figure 9.12 The roots of a 2-month-old radish.

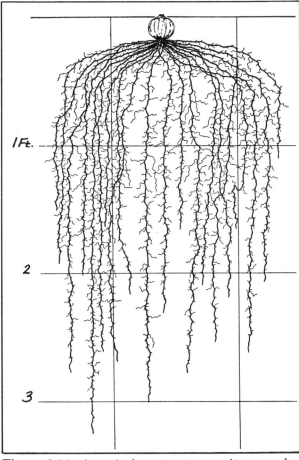

Figure 9.14 An onion's root system as it approaches maturity in late August.

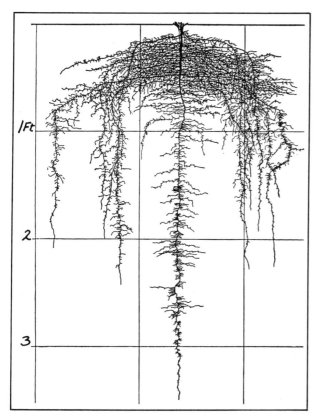

Figure 9.15 A spinach root system at 10 weeks.

Figure 9.16 The extent of a mature pepper plant's root system.

Intercropping Slow- and Fast-Growing Vegetables

Quick-maturing vegetables are good companions for vegetables that take their time to reach maturity. The quicker crop can help the slower crop by shading the soil from excessive heat, preventing erosion from rain or irrigation, and acting as a living mulch to conserve moisture and suppress weeds. At the very least, this alliance makes good use of space.

A classic example is the combination of cauliflower and lettuce. The two are planted at the same time, with the lettuce at intervals of 8 to 12 inches between the cauliflower seedlings at their usual 15- to 20-inch spacing. Since the cauliflower is a slow grower, the lettuce will be harvested before the foliage of the cauliflower fills in the area.

Another good example is the intercropping of leeks, needing 19 weeks to mature, with spinach, needing only 7 weeks to mature. This arrangement also makes excellent use of vertical space.

Figure 9.17 A lettuce plant's root system in mid-July when the flower stalk was 3 feet tall.

Figure 9.18 shows crops that mature in 9 weeks or less, depending on the season and your climate.

```
┌─────────────────────────────────────────────┐
│      FAST-GROWING INTERCROP PLANTS            │
│                                               │
│         Beets                                 │
│         Cauliflower (early varieties)         │
│         Kohlrabi                              │
│         Leaf lettuce                          │
│         Mustard greens                        │
│         Parsnips                              │
│         Radishes                              │
│         Spinach                               │
└─────────────────────────────────────────────┘
```

Figure 9.18

*Some varieties take more than nine weeks to mature; check the seed catalog or packet.

Some vegetables – such as chard, kale, okra, peas, summer squash, and certain beans – produce an early crop and then continue to bear over a long period of time, so they are not pulled out to make room for other maturing crops. Figure 9.19 lists vegetables that take more than 15 weeks (105 days) to mature.

```
┌─────────────────────────────────────────────┐
│      SLOW-GROWING "HOST" INTERCROPS           │
│                                               │
│         Cauliflower (late varieties)          │
│         Celery                                │
│         Garlic                                │
│         Leeks                                 │
│         Melons                                │
│         Onions                                │
│         Potatoes                              │
│         Pumpkins                              │
│         Salsify                               │
│         Summer squash                         │
│         Sweet potatoes                        │
│         Sunflowers                            │
└─────────────────────────────────────────────┘
```

Figure 9.19

Keep in mind that plants and the weather are fickle – these times are relative and will need to be adjusted to your climate and the season's eccentricities.

Colebrook, Binda. **Winter Gardening in the Maritime Northwest**. Everson, WA: Maritime Publications, 1984. The details of vegetable cultivation for northern California through Vancouver, B.C. are reviewed by an experienced farmer and gardener. Every region needs a guide like Colebrook's.

New Alchemy Institute. **Gardening for All Seasons**. Andover, MA: Brick House Publishing, 1983. An excellent book based on New Alchemy's thorough research and testing. Their integrated systems for food production and preservation are more current than those described in the Farallones Institute's *Integral Urban House*. Covers vegetable cultivation, greenhouse production, aquaculture, raising chickens, tree crops, recycling, and community gardens. Especially good for people living in colder winter climates of the U.S.

Philbrick, Helen, and Gregg, Richard. **Companion Plants and How to Use Them**. 8th ed. Old Greenwich, CT: Devin-Adair, 1976. One of the original sources of companion planting information. Contains some good information, but I find many of the folklore-based recommendations to be untrue or inappropriate.

Riotte, Louise. **Carrots Love Tomatoes**. Pownal, VT: Garden Way Publishing, 1984. The most popular book on companion planting. (Formerly *Companion Planting for Successful Gardening*.) Few scientific studies are cited. Riotte's recommendations overlap and sometimes contradict the Philbricks' in *Companion Plants and How to Use Them*.

Walker, J.C. **Diseases of Vegetable Crops**. New York: McGraw-Hill, 1952. A detailed, technical review for commercial growers.

Weaver, John. **Root Development of Field Crops**. New York: McGraw-Hill, 1926. Root maps by Weaver and associates, primarily of cereal grains, forage grasses, clovers, corn, sunflowers, and potatoes. Excellent drawings of what must have been very tedious excavations.

Weaver, John. **Root Development of Vegetable Crops**. New York: McGraw-Hill, 1927. The vegetable root zone charts pictured in this chapter are just a few from Weaver's book. Weaver spent most of his professional life excavating roots of vegetables, perennial prairie plants, trees, and shrubs. His books and articles are the largest single source of root zone maps in the world.

Figure 1.1 Ornamental kale is as tasty as the better-known green variety, and it adds a colorful highlight to a winter landscape. (Photograph by Rosalind Creasy.)

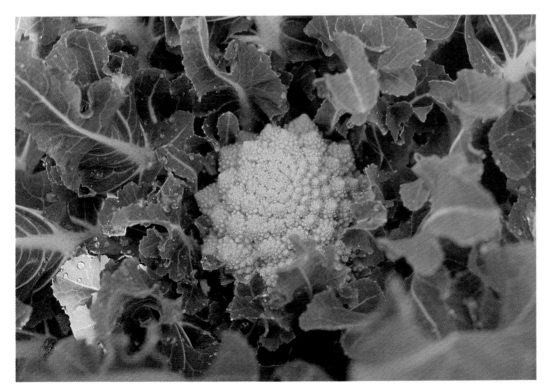

Figure 1.2 'Romanesco' broccoli, sometimes called 'Green Point,' should be planted in late summer in moderate winter areas, or in the early spring in cold winter areas. Be sure to give this spectacular plant a prominent place in your edible landscape.

Figure 1.3 Oriental persimmons are highlighted against a backdrop of early morning fog. Persimmon trees keep their colorful fruit long into winter, when bright colors are needed in an edible landscape.

Figure 1.4 For a blaze of spring blossom, the 'Garden Beauty' nectarine is hard to beat. The profuse bloom gives a preview of the copious crop soon to follow. While the newer miniature varieties have superior flavor, I often plant the 'Garden Beauty' for its unequaled floral display.

Figure 1.5 This colorful patio planting combines red and green chard, red-leaved lettuce, and a miniature 'Garden Prince' almond with ornamentals. It exhibits two important rules of edible landscaping: put the salad vegetables as close to the kitchen as possible, and start very small.

Figure 1.10 The Kelleys' landscape, viewed from their dining room. The rounded area at the end of each terrace is planted with seasonal flowers to add color and to soften the look of the wooden beds.

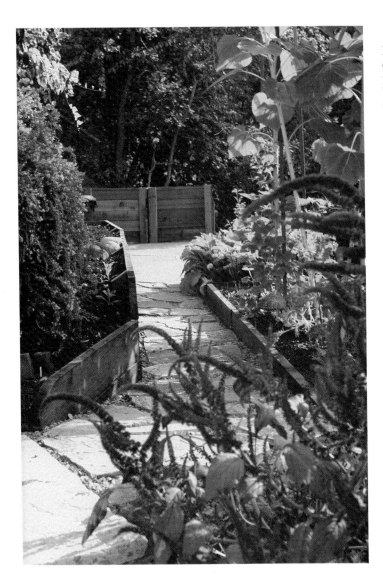

Figure 1.11 The Kelleys' kitchen door leads directly to the edible landscape and to the compost bins. To the left of the path is a narrow terrace of informally espaliered fruit trees. The colorful red plant in the foreground is red-leaved amaranth, or summer spinach (*Amaranthus* sp.).

Figure 1.12 Each of the three 100-square-foot vegetable terraces is planted intensively to get the most produce from a small area. The dense plantings are aided by fertile topsoil, compost, and by reflected light from the flagstones.

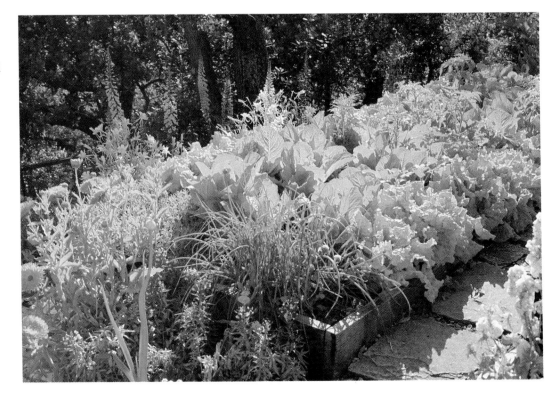

Figure 1.13 The informal wild border eases the transition from the geometric vegetable beds to the wilder areas surrounding the landscape. The herbaceous border includes medicinal herbs, edible flowers, and cut flowers, and provides pollen and nectar for beneficial insects.

Figure 1.14 Flagstones are set in packed gravel, without a plastic undersheet, for good percolation of winter rain. The stones' pleasing texture makes a safe, all-weather surface.

Figure 1.15 The edibles in this landscape bear earlier each spring and bear longer into winter than in nearby gardens, because the vegetable terraces are on a south-facing slope, and massive amounts of stone were used in walls and paths. The flagstones reflect extra light into the dense plantings, and the stones give off heat at night. The fieldstone wall was constructed without mortar to save money, to encourage drainage, and to give herbs and flowering plants a place to grow.

Figure 4.2 This edible landscape features redwood rounds and flagstones with Dutch white clover growing between them. The clover softens the hard look of wood and stone.

Figure 4.6 The Kelleys' edible landscape is compact and close to the kitchen. Size and proximity were carefully considered before construction, to make the design as labor-saving as possible.

Figure 4.9 One of the many "fruit salad" trees at the Floreses' apartments. A number of almond branches have been grafted to this peach tree. In the spring, the tree has a delightful mixture of pale pink and pure white flowers, all blooming at the same time.

Figure 7.5 These raised beds were built with the sheet composting method. Sheet composting improves the soil without tilling, and is effective for ornamentals as well as for edibles.

Figure 15.4 To soften the effect of an expanse of mulch, I plant colorful ground covers (both annuals and perennials) along the edge. The rambling ground cover (in this example, nasturtium with its edible flowers, leaves, and seed pods) also breaks the hard line created by the edge of the mulch.

Figure 16.12 This close-up of anise (*Pimpinella anisum*) shows the typical umbel flower buds that, once in bloom, provide large amounts of nectar to beneficial insects.

Figure 18.11 A mullein flower stalk blooms over many months and adds a wonderful accent to any flower border. Picked in early morning, mullein flowers (*Verbascum* sp.) are quite tasty. Keep them fresh in a vegetable crisper and add them to a lunch or dinner salad for a colorful highlight.

Figure 18.12 The blossoms of pineapple guava (*Feijoa sellowiana*) are my favorite edible flowers. The petals are soft and succulent, and their flavor is a harbinger of the delightful tropical fruit.

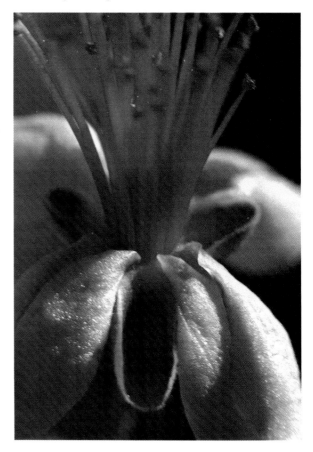

4 GROWING TREE CROPS
Choosing the Best Trees for Your Climate

I love the atmosphere that fruit and nut trees lend to a landscape. An old, well-weathered fruit tree is a testament to persistence and patience. An edible landscape without fruit trees seems raw and juvenile to me; mature trees are the climax of ecological momentum for a stable forest. As a symbol of wisdom, security, and permanence, the forest inspires me to pattern food production in its image.

In the book *Forest Farming*, J. Sholto Douglas and Robert A. de Hart present forests as special environments to be protected and nurtured:

The natural ecological climax for most parts of the world where more than one type of tree will grow is the mixed forest. This is the most productive and healthy form of land use and the one most beneficial to the soil and other factors . . . including man.

While all types of trees improve the environment – purifying the air, stabilizing and improving soil, slowing winds, and enhancing aesthetics – domesticated trees differ markedly from forest trees. The stability of a forest is owing largely to each tree's ability to be self-reliant. The hardy, long-lived trees of the forest protect themselves in strange and fascinating ways. Many forest trees produce chemicals that make the foliage poisonous and awful tasting. Alkaloids, glycosides, nerve poisons, stomach poisons, and tannins in the tree's foliage, wood, and fruit serve to repel pests, as well as man. Oaks, for example, contain high amounts of bitter, tannic acid. It takes hours of leaching to make a "sweet" acorn mush. Through centuries of breeding, the domesticated fruit and nut trees have gained flavor at the expense of their original chemical safeguards. They are very much dependent upon our care for good yields.

On an agricultural scale (based on USDA figures for California), tree crops take 7.6 percent more fuel and 60 percent more labor than vegetable crops. The work is periodic and somewhat involved. Still, though they are not as labor saving as some would assume, a limited number of well-chosen fruit and nut trees are a great asset to any edible landscape.

Since trees are vitually permanent additions to your edible landscape, take time to consider your options. A poor choice planted now may be nursed along for years in the futile hope that somehow the tree will improve. More than most elements in an edible landscape, fruit and nut trees should be what I call design intensive – most of the effort should be spent in study, planning, and design before planting. The desire to grow a favorite fruit or nut is often the main criteria for choosing a tree. You know what you like, but before you plant solely on the basis of flavor, consider carefully the information provided in the following chapters.

SPECIAL TREES FOR SPECIAL CLIMATES
Trees for Cold Winters

Fruit trees have different ranges of cold tolerance. Apples, sour cherries, and native American plums usually survive temperatures as low as -30° F. Slightly less cold hardy, safe to -20° F, are the sweet cherries, pears, and Japanese and European plums. Almonds, peaches, nectarines, and apricots are rated at -15° F. These general guidelines are good only for the wood of the tree – flower buds can be less tolerant of cold, especially when they are near to blooming. In a newsletter of high-altitude gardening, *Westcape*, editor Rick Hassett warns that "it's common knowledge in cold, *dry* climates that hardiness figures cannot be trusted because many plants seem to be hardier in drier areas than wetter ones. Thus, the great array of so-called tender ornamentals that thrive in Salt Lake City compare to cities at lower elevations but similar latitudes in the East." The age of the tree also makes a difference. Larry Geno, of Bear Creek Farms in the northeast corner of Washington State, has found that freshly planted trees are 10° to 15° less hardy than one-year-old trees, which are 5° to 10° less hardy than established trees.

Influencing Cold Hardiness

To promote hardiness, begin by maintaining good soil fertility. A balanced, fertile soil makes for a sturdier tree. But too much nitrogen, or nitrogen applied late in the growing season, can weaken a tree. The growth forced by fertilizers in late summer or early fall is more succulent and less likely to harden off properly, leaving the tree vulnerable to winter damage. Where there are no summer rains, too much irrigation late in the summer may have the same effect, forcing tender growth. Begin reducing the frequency of irrigation up to a month or more before your average first frost date to ensure an early transition into dormancy. Too little water, however, will stress the tree and make it prone to winter cold damage.

Summer pruning too late in the season also leaves a tree more vulnerable. Carefully reducing but not stopping irrigation after the last summer pruning helps the tree harden off properly. Severe winter pruning, especially in midwinter, also can be harmful; it leaves the tree more sensitive to hard freezes.

Dormant oil spray applied in the late fall at temperatures below 41° F will slow the hardening-off process, leaving the tree more sensitive to early hard freezes. In the coldest winter areas, wait for a warm day in the fall or until early spring to apply dormant oil sprays.

Low branches can create a cold pocket around the base of a tree. For every foot above the ground that branches are trimmed, you may gain as much as one degree of warmth. A few degrees can add up to critical protection during the coldest winter nights.

Don't forget about hardiness below ground. In cold, dry climates, the ground can freeze solid and prevent the rootstock from absorbing needed water. A tree's roots can actually dry up and die in frozen ground. The more deeply rooted the tree, the safer its roots are from winter desiccation. In cold, dry climates, mulching can be harmful: mulches encourage shallower root systems, leaving the roots more vulnerable.

Weather's Influence on Cold Hardiness

The way in which a fruit tree enters winter dormancy has a great influence on the tree's cold hardiness. Hardiness is greatly increased by a gradual transition from fall to midwinter. As the tree progresses into dormancy (hardens off), the flower buds are the first portion of the tree to develop winter hardiness. Then follow the twigs, branches, and trunk. Weather affects hardiness, as well. Late summer rains that encourage continued tip growth make the tree more susceptible to cold. A tree is not fully hardened off and dormant until early winter. Sudden cold snaps before December can damage one-year-old branch growth. After the tree has achieved full dormancy, a freak warm spell in late winter may cause flower and leaf buds to swell and the bark to split, leaving them vulnerable to hard freezes that follow. A high windchill factor can produce the same damage as very low temperatures, especially when combined with low humidity. In a marginal area, windbreaks can help fruit

trees to survive. (See "Shaping the Wind" for details on windbreaks.)

Hardy Varieties

For the safest guide to a tree's hardiness, obtain local information on the worst winters. Talk to gardeners who have witnessed record-breaking winters and who have recorded the survivors. A group with this kind of information is the North American Fruit Explorers, NAFEX (the address of their quarterly journal, *Pomona*, is listed in Appendix 10). After a record-breaking winter, amateur and commercial orchardists will write about which fruit trees survived and produced fruit. The following examples from *Pomona* are typical.

Randy Lee Brown lives in McDonald, Pennsylvania, where the temperature dropped to -20° F on two different days during the winter of 1981-82. He reported that the grapes with the least amount of winter kill were (in descending order): 'Concord,' 'McCambell,' 'Niagara,' 'Buffalo,' 'Delaware,' 'Candice,' and 'Lakemont.' At the Canadian/U.S. border, Eddy Dugas's orchard had low temperatures of -47° F in mid-February in 1979. (He lost 25 percent of his trees.) His most cold hardy varieties of apples to try were 'Alexander,' 'Carroll,' 'Labonte,' 'Red Melba,' 'Yellow Transparent,' 'Winter St. Lawrence,' 'Goodland,' and the Morden numbered selections. Of 23 types of peaches tried in Midland, Michigan, Caroline Grose has seen only the 'Polly' and 'Reliance' survive -20° to -30° F winters. (The Stark Brothers Nursery in Louisiana, Missouri, also experiences -20° F weather. Of the varieties they offer, the Stark 'Summer Pearl'™ Stark 'Encore'™, Stark 'Early White Giant'™, 'Starking Delicious'™, and Stark 'EarliGlo'™ peaches survived to bear abundantly. Other peaches that performed well were 'Belle of Georgia,' 'Reliance,' 'Envoy,' 'Biscoe,' and 'Cresthaven.' The Stark 'Crimson Gold' Nectarine™ also came through with flying colors.)

Trees for Milder Winters

Beware of the temptation to grow marginally safe varieties. It is especially strong for the tasty tropicals wherever winters are mild. For citrus, there is a range of frost and freeze tolerances. From hardiest to least hardy, it is: kumquat, limequats, 'Meyer' lemon, Mandarin orange, sour orange, sweet orange, tangelo, pummelo, grapefruit, lemon, 'Bearss' lime, 'Eureka' lemon, and 'Mexican,' or 'Key,' lime. The conservative limits of this range are 18° to 20° F for kumquats and 31° to 32° F for 'Mexican' limes. The type of rootstock used can influence cold hardiness. The trifoliate orange (used as a dwarfing rootstock, except for 'Meyer' lemon) and citrange rootstocks increase the hardiness of the variety grafted on them.

Major C. Collins, of Tifton, Georgia, another member of NAFEX, has a collection of 75 citrus varieties. He has documented some amazing figures in regard to cold hardiness. His 'Satsuma' orange shows little damage down to 15° F, the 'Meyer' lemons are safe at 20° F, and a kumquat survived the 1982 freeze that registered 9° F. Of his rare varieties there are some very cold-hardy types. Survivors of the same 1982 freeze included: 'Troyer' citrange (a cross of a navel orange and a cold-hardy citrus, *Poncirus trifoliata*), 'Thomasville' citrangequat (a cross of the cold-hardy citrus, sweet orange, and kumquat), 'Changsha' tangerine, and 'Taiwanica' (a cross of an unknown citrus with a sour orange).

Remember that guidelines for hardiness are imprecise. When planting varieties near their limits of hardiness, be sure to evaluate the microclimates around your home. A south facing wall with a large eave or a windbreak that blocks dry winter winds can make the difference between a fruitful tree and a damaged or dead tree.

Trees for Warm Winter Climates – The Chill Factor

Orchard trees need winter. Deciduous trees must spend time resting at certain temperatures in a state called dormancy before their flower and leaf buds open in the spring. Trees that do not get enough cold may fail to bloom and leaf out or may bloom poorly and erratically. Good spring blossom and leaf growth depends on a tree's exposure to a sufficiently long period of temperatures below 45° F (some researchers set slightly different temperatures). This period, measured in total number of accumulated hours, is called the chill factor or chilling requirement. In warm winter areas, the number of winter hours above 60° F offsets the total chilling effect. The number of hours above 60° F is subtracted from the number of hours below 45° F to determine the number of hours of chill received for a particular day. Note that neither the chilling hours nor the hours of warm temperature need be continuous.

Measuring the Amount of Chill

You needn't be constantly reading a thermometer to know your area's average chill. Use the map in Fig. 10.1, which is based on information gathered by the Dave Wilson Nursery of Hughson, California. For more detailed information, ask your local university cooperative extension agent, a retail nursery manager, or the staff of the United States Weather Bureau.

Chill requirements are not to be confused with winter hardiness. Many trees with low chill requirements will grow in cold areas. Nor are trees with high chill ratings more cold hardy. Hardiness is independent of the chill requirement.

Even though low-chill trees are more likely to flower early, the chill factor has no bearing on when a tree will ripen its fruit. Among the peaches that ripen in mid-July, the chill factors range from 300 to as high as 1,150 hours.

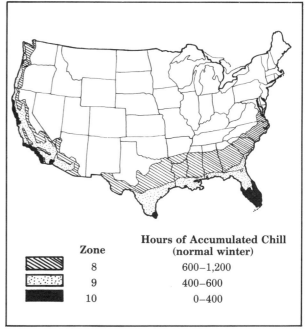

	Zone	Hours of Accumulated Chill (normal winter)
	8	600–1,200
	9	400–600
	10	0–400

Figure 10.1   The three main zones of low-chill winters.

Using Chill Requirements to Choose the Best Tree for Your Area

Knowing the hours of winter chill is vital to choosing fruit and nut trees, especially in warm winter areas – from the coastal areas of the Southeast, through the deep South, along the coastal regions of California, and on south-facing slopes in marginal zones. These are places where some trees would not receive enough winter chill for a healthy dormancy.

Be sure to take into account your property's microclimates, and check with local landscapers and nurserymen. Survey your neighborhood for bearing trees. According to the chill maps of my county, cherries will not bear in my neighborhood, but neighbors who live in frosty microclimates have bearing trees.

Plant only trees that have a chill requirement less than or close to the chilling they will receive in your area, making exceptions only for types of trees you see bearing nearby. By planting a number of fruit trees, each with a different chilling requirement, you can ensure your landscape and your harvest against erratic or extreme weather.

Figure 10.2 lists the range of chill requirements for many types of fruits and nuts. If your area's chill factor is low, see Fig. 10.3.

Figure 10.3

LOWEST CHILL REQUIREMENTS		
Fruit	Variety	Chill Requirement (hours)
ALMOND	'All-in-One'	300-400
	'Garden Prince'	300-400
	'Jordanolo'	300-400
	'Ne Plus'	400-500
APPLE	'Anna'	100-400
	'Beverly Hills'	200-300
	'Dorsett Golden'	100-400
	'Double Red Delicious'	>400
	'Ein Shemer'	200-400
	'Gordon'	200-400
	'Granny Smith'	600-700
	'Mutsu'	400-600
	'Ormsby'	>400
	'Pettingill'	300-500
	'Tropic Beauty'	300-400
	'Valmore'	300-400
	'Winter Banana'	200-600
	'Yellow Bellflower'	>400
APRICOT	'Earlygold'	>600
	'Gold Kist'	300-400
	'Golden Amber'	>400
	'Katy'	300-400
	'Newcastle'	>600
	'Royal'	400-500
ASIAN PEAR	'Ya Li,' 'Tsu Li'	350-600
JAPANESE PLUM	'Delight'	300-400
	'Howard's Miracle'	500
	'Mariposa'	300-400
	'Meredith'	*
	'Methely'	300-400
	'Santa Rosa'	300
	'Satsuma'	300-500
	'Sprite'	300-400
NECTARINE	'Desert Dawn'	250
	'Fantasia'	500-600
	'Garden Beauty'	350
	'Garden Delight'	350
	'Garden King'	350
	'Gold Mine'	200-400
	'Panamint'	200-400
	'Silver Lode'	*
	'Southern Belle'	300
	'Sunbonnet'	500
	'Sunred'	*

CHILL REQUIREMENTS	
Type of Fruit	Chill Requirement (in hours)
Almond	400-700
Apple*	400-1,800
Apricot*	350-1,000
Asian Pear (Chinese)	400-600
(Japanese)	300-750
Avocado	0
Blackberry	200-700
Blueberry (Florida)	0-200
Blueberry (northern)	700-1,200
Chestnut	400-750
Citrus	0
Crabapple	300-500
Currant	800-1,500
European pear	600-1,500
European plum	700-1,800
Fig	100-500
Filbert	800-1,600
Gooseberry	800-1,500
Grape	100-500
Japanese plum*	500-1,600
Kiwi*	400-800
Kiwi 'Tewi' (female)	0-200
Kiwi 'Vincent' (female)	0-200
Mulberry	400
Nectarine*	200-1,200
Peach*	200-1,200
Pecan	300-1,600
Persimmon	100-500
Pistachio	800-1,000
Plum-cot	400
Pomegranate	100-200
Quince	100-500
Raspberry*	100-1,800
Sour cherry	700-1,300
Strawberry	200-300
Sweet cherry (common varieties)	600-1,400
Walnut*	400-1,500
*Low-chill varieties are available.	

Figure 10.2

The varieties in Fig. 10.3 have among the lowest chill requirements of their type.

continued

Fruit	Variety	Chill Requirement (hours)
PEACH	'August Pride'	300
	'Australian Saucer'	300
	'Babcock'	450
	'Bonita'	450
	'Desertgold'	350
	'Earligrand'	250
	'Early Amber'	350
	'Fairtime'	650
	'Florabelle'	150
	'Flordaking'	450
	'Flordared'	100
	'Flordasun'	300
	'Flordawon'	150
	'Florida Prince'	150
	'Garden Gold'	350
	'Garden Sun'	350
	'Giant Babcock'	450
	'Gold Dust'	550
	'Honey Babe'	500
	'Midpride'	250-400
	'Peento'	350
	'Red Ceylon'	100
	'Redskin'	500
	'Redtop'	750
	'Redwing'	550
	'Rio Grande'	425
	'Rubidoux'	350
	'Sam Houston'	550
	'Shanghai'	300
	'Southern Flame'	400
	'Southern Rose'	300
	'Springtime'	500
	'Stark Gulf Queen'	150
	'Strawberry Cling'	650
	'Tejon'	350
	'Tropi-berta'	400-500
	'Ventura'	450
	'White Heath Cling'	550
PEAR	'Ambassador'	500-650
	'Placentia'	400-500
WALNUT	'Baldwin'	*
	'Cape's'	*
	'Comice'	400-600
	'Fan Stil'	*
	'Flordahome'	150
	'Hood'	*
	'Kieffer'	400-600
	'Monterey'	300-500
	'Orient'	400-600
	'Pineapple'	*
	'Sierra'	*

*Low chill, but no specific hours available.

Figure 10.3 Note: Chill data is approximate.

The Risks of Low-Chill Trees

In cold winter climates and where late spring frosts are likely, shy away from planting trees with low chill requirements unless they are naturally late bloomers. Early in the winter low-chill trees accumulate their chill requirement. From then on, the trees stay dormant because of the cold weather, not their need for more rest. A warm spell with temperatures above 40° F will prompt buds to begin opening and leave them vulnerable to cold and rain.

South-facing slopes with good air drainage are much warmer than higher and lower elevations, and are often called banana belts because they shelter cold-sensitive plants. But they are among the trickiest places to grow fruit and nut trees. During warm winters, trees with low chill requirements will bloom too early. Trees with high chill requirements may not get enough winter cold, even during normal winters. The safest course is to plant a variety of low-chill trees, each with a slightly different chill requirement. Each year, the blossoms on some trees will die, but others will flower and bear.

Cheating on Chill Requirements

Gardeners in the warmest areas can ensure that marginal trees get sufficient chill. First, plant your trees near the lowest spot on the property. The cool air that settles there will add some chilling hours to your winter. (Be careful, though; low areas are prone to drainage problems.) Planting on the north side of the house or carport, evergreen trees, or hills is another tactic. The winter sun is low in the sky, thereby providing extra shade which keeps the tree cooler. There is enough sunlight in summer to ripen certain fruits—to find out which ones, chart the height of the shade-maker on graph paper and use the solar charts in Appendix 2 to plot the angle of the sun from early spring through summer (using the process described in "The Climate in Your Yard"). Locate the tree so that it is shaded as late into spring as possible but has ripened its fruit before losing sunlight in the late summer. The best trees for this particular situation are the earliest ripening cherries, peaches, and nectarines. Fruits that ripen in late summer will not get enough sunshine for good flavor.

If you have a windbreak or hedge running along a slope perpendicular to the air drainage, you can plant in the cool air that "puddles" on the uphill side. If the planting falls on the north side of a windbreak, you get the bonus of shade cooling.

One last tactic is to paint the entire tree with a thin coat of white interior latex paint (diluted with water to make it easier to brush or spray onto the branches). The paint reflects the winter light, keeping the wood a bit cooler. Though this makes an interesting-looking tree, it is the least effective of the strategies described.

Choosing Fruit Trees for Hot Summer Areas

Summer sun and heat can be bad for some fruit and nut trees. Apples do not like high temperatures, especially in dry climates, and the skin of apples can be scorched by direct sunlight in hot weather. For example, late-maturing apples in California, which has an Indian summer weather pattern, are susceptible to sunburn. Varieties that do not sunburn in hot summer areas are 'Akane,' 'Red Delicious,' 'Golden Delicious,' 'Fuji,' 'Gala,' 'Apple Babe,' 'Mutsu,' 'Empire,' 'Garden Delicious,' 'Summerred,' and 'Anna.' Most apples do best where average summer temperatures are between 65° and 75° F.

Though persimmons can be grown in areas like Fresno, California, where there may be a dozen or more days above 105° F, the south and west sides of exposed fruits are sometimes blackened by the heat. The dark spots do not affect flavor, even though they may reduce commercial value.

Extremely high temperatures can make cherry trees produce doubled fruits (not a problem in the home garden); cause pit burn with 'Blenheim' apricots; and harm loquats, pears, Asian pears (especially 'Ishiiwase'), kiwis (the fruit burns in the deserts of Arizona), and English (Persian) walnuts. Temperatures above 100° F will darken, sunburn, or shrivel the meats of English walnuts. Summer pears, such as 'Bartlett,' can take temperatures slightly higher than apples. And contrary to popular belief, winter pears do fine in hot summer areas.

You can cheat a little by planting heat-sensitive trees along the east side of buildings or beside trees that give afternoon shade. With apples, the rootstock and style of pruning can make a big difference. The semi-dwarf MM 111 rootstock with a central leader program of pruning is best for preventing sunburn of fruits. Avoid open center trees and the more dwarfing rootstocks, such as M 26. (See "The Best Rootstocks for Your Soil" and "Central Leader Pruning.") The best approach, however, is to avoid planting "borderline" trees and to plant only heat-loving trees. Fruit and nut trees that thrive on high summer temperatures include almond, avocado, butternut, citrus, fig, hickory, jujube, nectarine, olive, passion fruit, peach, pecan, pineapple guava, pomegranate, sapote, and black walnut.

Chandler, William. **Deciduous Orchards**. 3rd ed. rev. Philadelphia: Lea & Febiger, 1957. For tree crops, one of four technical references that I consult most often. Worth searching for in used book stores.

Childers, Norman. **Modern Fruit Science**. 8th ed. New Brunswick, NJ: Horticultural Publications, 1978. Poor-quality illustrations greatly hamper this book. A good one to browse in the library; only serious tree crops enthusiasts need own it.

Davidson, John, and Reed, Clarence. **The Improved Nut trees of North America and How to Grow Them**. New York: Devin-Adair, 1968. Not as useful, up to date, or available as *Nut Tree Culture in North America* (Richard Jaynes, ed.).

Hedrick, U.P. **The Pears of New York**. Albany, NY: J.B. Lyon, 1921. Dozens of color plates of lovely hand-tinted etchings. A must for serious collectors of pear tree varieties. Many of the varieties described have been lost to cultivation. The 636-page book is available for $11 from Mrs. Rita Curtain, New York Agricultural Experimental Station, Geneva, NY 14456.

Jaynes, Richard, ed. **Nut Tree Culture in North America**. Hamden, CT: Northern Nut Growers Association, 1979. The most helpful and thorough book on the subject. (The Association publishes a quarterly journal with the latest news on nut growing.)

Nitschke, Robert. **Southmeadow Illustrated Catalog**. Birmingham, MI: Southmeadow Fruit Gardens, 1976. One of the best references for the shape, color, and taste of many antique, or heirloom, varieties of fruits (mostly apples). An excellent bargain.

Ray, Richard, and Walheim, Lance. **Citrus: How to Select, Grow and Enjoy**. Tucson, AZ: HPBooks, 1980. The best book on the subject for home edible landscapers. Another of HPBooks's colorful and concise reviews.

Riotte, Louise. **Nuts for the Food Gardener**. Charlotte, VT: Garden Way Publishing, 1975. A simple introduction to growing nut trees at home. Not very extensive, and covers mainly the common varieties.

Simmons, Alan. **Growing Unusual Fruit**. Walker and Company, 1972. An excellent review of many unusual and exotic fruiting plants. The plants and their cultural needs are described in detail.

Stebbins, Robert, and Walheim, Lance. **Western Fruits, Berries and Nuts**. Tucson, AZ: HPBooks, 1981. The best reference on these subjects, and the one I use the most. Complete with brilliant, condensed, easy-to-use charts. Excellent color photographs. HPBooks also publishes an equally excellent East Coast version, *How to Grow Fruits, Berries and Nuts in the Midwest and East*, by Theodore James, Jr., 1983.

Sunset. **New Western Garden Book**. Menlo Park, CA: Sunset Books, 1979, rev. ed. The reference I use most frequently. A must for every western gardener, landscaper, and edible landscaper.

Wickson, Edward. **California Fruits**. San Francisco: Pacific Rural Press, 1919. One of my favorite tree crops references, written prior to the use of many chemicals in orchard management. Details for adapting trees to local climatic and soil conditions make it especially valuable to California gardeners. Includes good pointers on pruning standard-size fruit trees. The rootstock information is outdated, but the virtues of many old varieties of fruit and nuts are described in detail. Many of the fruit varieties mentioned are still grown by members of North American Fruit Explorers.

4

FRUIT FOR ALL SEASONS

It is possible to eat something fresh off the tree all year long here in northern California. I prefer to eat directly from my edible landscape; canning and drying are tedious, energy-consuming processes. My fruit-eating season begins in mid-May with loquats and strawberries, stretches into fall with 'Arkansas Black' apples, 'Granny Smith' apples, quinces, figs, raspberries, and walnuts, and continues into midwinter with persimmons and chestnuts. Even after the first of the year, there are apples that still hang fresh and firm on the tree ('Winter Banana,' 'Alexander,' 'Pearmain,' 'Sweet Delicious,' 'Rhode Island Greening,' and 'Mulhall'), as well as citrus, avocados, and perhaps a few tenacious persimmons. From fall to spring, citrus varieties ripen at different times to fill out the year's cornucopia.

Many people are not thrilled to arrive home from work to find that today is the day all 200 pounds of the 'Gravenstein' apples are ready to be picked. That's why I favor dwarf varieties. Each tree gives a small crop, and more varieties can be planted in the same area than with standard-size trees, spreading the harvest over a longer period.

While the ripening dates in Fig. 10.4 are averages for Davis, California, the *relative sequence* of ripening applies in most climates and years.

Good Keepers

For climates with short growing seasons, design your landscape to have varieties of fruits that are good keepers. These need only be carefully wrapped in newspaper or packed in straw and stored in a cool, dry rootcellar or basement. Here are a few varieties that keep well.

Apple	'Hudson's Golden Gem,' 'Connell Red,' 'Fireside,' 'Sweet Delicious,' 'Yellow Newtown Pippin,' 'Winesap,' 'Hawaii,' 'Idared,' 'Jonamac,' 'Lodi,' 'Yellow Transparent,' 'Macoun,' 'Spartan,' 'Stayman Winesap,' 'Summerred,' 'Golden Russet,' 'Granny Smith,' 'Ashmead's Kernal,' 'Cox's Orange Pippin,' 'King,' 'Baldwin,' 'Rhode Island Greening,' and 'Spitzenburg'
Asian Pear	'Chojuro,' 'Okusankichi,' 'Shinko,' 'Nuitaka,' and 'Korean Giant'
Kiwi	All varieties
Pear	'Comice,' 'Moonglow,' 'Winter Nelis,' 'Kieffer,' and 'Monterey'

Figure 10.4

RIPENING DATES FOR FRUIT AND NUT VARIETIES
(averages for Davis, California)

Type/Cultivar	May	June	July	August	September	October	November
ALMOND							
'Nonpareil'				▓			
'Ne Plus Ultra'					▓		
'Garden Prince'					▓		
APPLE							
'Early Harvest'		▓					
'Red Astrachan'			▓				
'Lodi'			▓				
'Beverly Hills'				▓			
'Akane'				▓			
'Prima'				▓			
'Pettingill'					▓		
'Red Delicious'						▓	
'Golden Delicious'						▓	
'Winesap'						▓	
'Mutsu'						▓	
'Red Rome'						▓	
'Newtown Pippin'						▓	
'Granny Smith'							▓
APRICOT							
'Royal'		▓					
'Tilton'			▓				
'Golden Amber'			▓				

continued

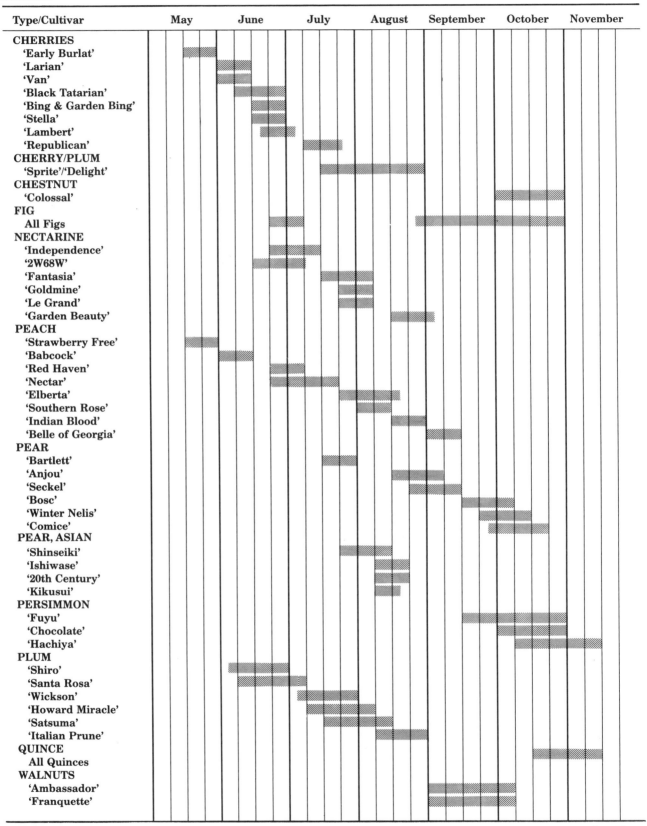

Type/Cultivar	May	June	July	August	September	October	November
CHERRIES							
'Early Burlat'							
'Larian'							
'Van'							
'Black Tatarian'							
'Bing & Garden Bing'							
'Stella'							
'Lambert'							
'Republican'							
CHERRY/PLUM							
'Sprite'/'Delight'							
CHESTNUT							
'Colossal'							
FIG							
All Figs							
NECTARINE							
'Independence'							
'2W68W'							
'Fantasia'							
'Goldmine'							
'Le Grand'							
'Garden Beauty'							
PEACH							
'Strawberry Free'							
'Babcock'							
'Red Haven'							
'Nectar'							
'Elberta'							
'Southern Rose'							
'Indian Blood'							
'Belle of Georgia'							
PEAR							
'Bartlett'							
'Anjou'							
'Seckel'							
'Bosc'							
'Winter Nelis'							
'Comice'							
PEAR, ASIAN							
'Shinseiki'							
'Ishiwase'							
'20th Century'							
'Kikusui'							
PERSIMMON							
'Fuyu'							
'Chocolate'							
'Hachiya'							
PLUM							
'Shiro'							
'Santa Rosa'							
'Wickson'							
'Howard Miracle'							
'Satsuma'							
'Italian Prune'							
QUINCE							
All Quinces							
WALNUTS							
'Ambassador'							
'Franquette'							

Figure 10.4 By choosing varieties that ripen at different times, you can spread your harvest over many months. (These dates are for Davis, CA and may vary considerably from area to area and year to year.)

Davidson, John, and Reed, Clarence. **The Improved Nut Trees of North America and How to Grow Them**. New York: Devin-Adair, 1968. Not as useful, up to date, or available as *Nut Tree Culture in North America* (Richard Jaynes, ed.).

Hedrick, U.P. **The Pears of New York**. Albany, NY: J. B. Lyon, 1921. Dozens of color plates of lovely hand-tinted etchings. A must for serious collectors of pear tree varieties. Many of the varieties described have been lost to cultivation. The 636-page book is available for $11 from Mrs. Rita Curtain, New York Agricultural Experimental Station, Geneva, NY 14456.

Jaynes, Richard, ed. **Nut Tree Culture in North America**. Hamden, CT: Northern Nut Growers Association, 1979. The most helpful and thorough book on the subject. (The Association publishes a quarterly journal with the latest news on nut growing.)

Kraft, Ken and Pat. **Grow Your Own Dwarf Fruit Trees**. New York: Walker Publishing, 1974. An early and simple review of the basics of dwarf fruit tree culture. Read a library copy.

Nitschke, Robert. **Southmeadow Illustrated Catalog**. Birmingham, MI: Southmeadow Fruit Gardens, 1976. One of the best references for the shape, color, and taste of many antique, or heirloom, varieties of fruits (mostly apples). An excellent bargain.

Ray, Richard, and Walheim, Lance. **Citrus: How to Select, Grow and Enjoy**. Tucson, AZ: HPBooks, 1980. The best book on the subject for home edible landscapers. Another of HPBooks's colorful and concise reviews.

Riotte, Louise. **Nuts for the Food Gardener**. Charlotte, VT: Garden Way Publishing, 1975. A simple introduction to growing nut trees at home. Not very extensive, and covers mainly the common varieties.

Simmons, Alan. **Growing Unusual Fruit**. Walker and Company, 1972. An excellent review of many unusual and exotic fruiting plants. The plants and their cultural needs are described in detail.

Stebbins, Robert, and Walheim, Lance. **Western Fruits, Berries and Nuts**. Tucson, AZ: HPBooks, 1981. The best reference on these subjects, and the one I use the most. Complete with brilliant, condensed, easy-to-use charts. Excellent color photographs. HPBooks also publishes an equally excellent East Coast version, *How to Grow Fruits, Berries and Nuts in the Midwest and East*, by Theodore James, Jr., 1983.

Sunset. **New Western Garden Book**. Menlo Park, CA: Sunset Books, 1979, rev. ed. The reference I use most frequently. A must for every western gardener, landscaper, and edible landscaper.

Wickson, Edward. **California Fruits**. San Francisco: Pacific Rural Press, 1919. One of my favorite tree crops references, written prior to the use of many chemicals in orchard management. Details for adapting trees to local climatic and soil conditions make it especially valuable to California gardeners. Includes good pointers on pruning standard-size fruit trees. The rootstock information is outdated, but the virtues of many old varieties of fruits and nuts are described in detail. Many of the fruit varieties mentioned are still grown by members of North American Fruit Explorers.

4

ENSURING GOOD POLLINATION

The flowers of most fruit trees need fertilization to produce fruit. Some trees are self-fruitful; that is, their flowers pollinate themselves or each other. Other trees are self-sterile; they need pollen from a different cultivar. For example, to bear fruit, a 'Bing' cherry must be pollinated by a 'Sam,' 'Van,' 'Larian,' 'Republican,' 'Black Tartarian,' 'Chinook,' or 'Early Burlat' cherry. Then there are ambivalent trees, known as partially self-fruitful; they set a much better crop with a pollinizer but can produce some fruit when planted alone. Bees and insects, and sometimes the wind—the agent for most nut trees—carry pollen from flower to flower and are known as pollinators.

Self-Fruitful Trees Save Space

In certain circumstances (for example, when space is at a premium) it is useful to plant only self-fruitful trees, such as those listed in Fig. 10.4-A.

SELF-FRUITFUL TREES

Apricot	Except for 'Earligold,' 'Goldrich,' 'Goldcot,' 'Rival,' and 'Perfection'
Avocado	
Banana	Able to form fruit without pollination, an ability called parthenocarpy
Cherry	Sour
Citrus	Parthenocarpic
Common figs	Different from 'Calimyrna,' which requires a male fig tree and a special wasp!
Heartnut	
Jujube	Chinese date
Loquat	
Macadamia nuts	
Nectarine	
Olive	
Peach	Except 'J. H. Hale,' 'Indian Free,' and 'Indian Blood Cling'
Persimmon	Parthenocarpic
Plum	European plum, except 'President'
Pomegranate	
Quince	
Walnut	English: 'Franquette,' 'Hartley,' 'Placentia,' and 'Spurgeon'

Figure 10.4-A

Trees Requiring Pollinizers

If you have plenty of room, you may plant self-unfruitful trees, setting out at least two cultivars of each type that require cross-pollination. Here are the trees that need partners.

TREES REQUIRING POLLINIZERS

Almond	
Apple	These trees will not pollinize other apples: 'Red Delicious,' 'Gravenstein,' 'King,' 'Mutsu' 'Northern Spy,' 'Winter Banana,' 'Ein Shemer,' 'Empire,' 'Jonagold,' 'McIntosh,' 'Stayman Winesap,' and 'Winesap'
Cherry	Sweet varieties
Chestnut	
Filbert	
Pear	
Plum	Japanese
Prune	

Figure 10.4-B

Self-Fruitful Exceptions to Trees Requiring Cross-Pollination

Among the fruit and nut trees that normally require a pollinizer, there are the following partially or fully self-fruitful cultivars.

CROSS-POLLINIZER EXCEPTIONS

Almond	'Garden Prince' and 'All-in-One'
Cherry	'Garden Bing' and 'Stella' (sweet)
Pear	'Bartlett,' 'Comice,' and 'Hardy' (only under very good conditions, such as in California)
Pecan	'Mohawk,' 'Mahan,' and others
Plum/Prune	'Burbank,' 'Delight,' 'Duarte' Japanese, 'Eldorado,' 'Elephant Heart,' 'Friar,' 'Kelsey,' 'Laroda,' 'Mariposa,' 'Nubiana,' 'Pipestone,' 'Queen Ann,' 'Redheart,' 'Santa Rosa, 'Satsuma,' 'Shiro,' 'Sprite,' 'Stark Giant Cherry Plum'™, 'Starking Delicious'™, 'Superior,' and 'Weeping Santa Rosa'
Walnut	'Placentia'

Figure 10.4-C

Choosing Pollinizers

The pollination charts in Figs. 10.5 and 10.6 (copyrighted by and used with permission from

Hilltop Orchards and Nurseries, Inc., Route 2, Hartford, MI 49057) are useful in choosing a pollinizer for the variety you wish to eat. Note that some combinations do not work together and that some varieties cannot pollinize themselves or any other variety (these are called pollen sterile).

To be on the safe side, three varieties each of the self-unfruitful types should be planted to ensure a good fruit set. All pollinizers should be within 50 feet of the variety to be pollinated, but the closer the better. For plums, almonds, and others that are difficult to pollinate, side-by-side planting is best.

If you do not have room for a pollinizer tree and your neighbors do not have a pollinizer tree, import pollen. Pick a large armful of flowering branches from a tree in the vicinity and put them in a bucket of water. Place the bucket beneath your tree or hang it from a ladder at the same height as the branches. This has worked for me when the pollinizer tree was too young to flower. Commercial orchardists use this technique to avoid growing a pollinizer that is not as marketable as the main

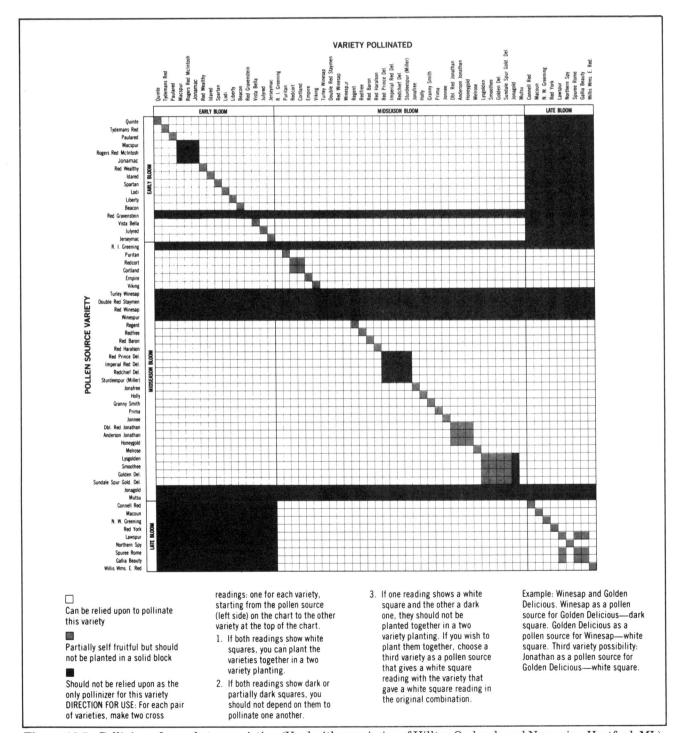

Figure 10.5 Pollinizers for apple tree varieties. (Used with permission of Hilltop Orchards and Nurseries, Hartford, MI.)

crop.

Another option is to graft a branch of the appropriate pollinizer onto the primary variety. Avoid grafting a slow-growing variety low on the tree, because the top will outgrow the graft and it will die.

Figure 10.6

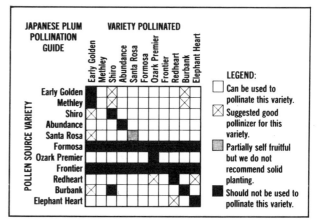

Figure 10.6 Pollinizers for sweet cherry, European plum, pear, and Japanese plum trees. (Used with permission of Hilltop Orchards and Nurseries, Hartford, MI.)

Chandler, William. **Deciduous Orchards**. 3rd ed. rev. Philadelphia: Lea & Febiger, 1957. For tree crops, one of four technical references that I consult most often. Worth searching for in used book stores.

Childers, Norman. **Modern Fruit Science**. 8th ed. New Brunswick, NJ: Horticultural Publications, 1978. Poor-quality illustrations greatly hamper this book. A good one to browse in the library; only serious tree crops enthusiasts need own it.

Davidson, John, and Reed, Clarence. **The Improved Nut trees of North America and How to Grow Them**. New York: Devin-Adair, 1968. Not as useful, up to date, or available as *Nut Tree Culture in North America*.

Hall-Beyer, Bart, and Richard, Jean. **Ecological Fruit Production in the North**. Quebec, Canada: Jean Richard, 1983. A must for fruit tree enthusiasts who live in Canada and in the coldest climates of the U.S.

Jaynes, Richard, ed. **Nut Tree Culture in North America**. Hamden, CT: Northern Nut Growers Association, 1979. The most helpful and thorough book on the subject. (The Association publishes a quarterly journal with the latest news on nut growing.)

continued

Kraft, Ken and Pat. **Grow Your Own Dwarf Fruit Trees**. New York: Walker Publishing, 1974. An early and simple review of the basics of dwarf fruit tree culture. Read a library copy.

Lovell, Harvey. **Honey Plants Manual**. Medina, OH: A.I. Root, 1966. The most comprehensive book on the subject, though out of print. A bible for beekeepers who want to help feed their hives.

Stebbins, Robert, and Walheim, Lance. **Western Fruits, Berries and Nuts**. Tucson, AZ: HPBooks, 1981. The best reference on these subjects, and the one I use the most. Complete with brilliant, condensed, easy-to-use charts. Excellent color photographs. HPBooks also publishes an equally excellent East Coast version, *How to Grow Fruits, Berries and Nuts in the Midwest and East*, by Theodore James, Jr., 1983.

Sunset. **New Western Garden Book**. Menlo Park, CA: Sunset Books, 1979, rev. ed. The reference I use most frequently. A must for every western gardener, landscaper, and edible landscaper.

DISEASE-RESISTANT TREES

No matter how dynamic your yard's ecology, some tree diseases are bound to show up. In your edible landscape, the best offense is a good defense. One defense is to practice the old adage, cleanliness is next to godliness (or, in this case, fruitfulness). A regular program of cleanup—burning fallen leaves, removing fruit before it rots, and spraying with a dormant oil in the fall—will help discourage pests and diseases. Another good defense is to select the naturally resistant trees from Fig. 10.7.

```
         DISEASE-RESISTANT
       EDIBLE TREES AND SHRUBS
```

Common Name	Botanical Name	Zone
Alpine strawberry	*Fragaria alpina semperflorens*	3-10
Beach plum	*Prunus maritima*	5-7
Blueberry	*Vaccinium spp.*	3-9
Carob	*Ceratonia siliqua*	9,10
Chayote	*Sechium edule*	8-10
Chestnut	*Castanea mollisima*	5-9
Elderberry	*Sambucus canadensis*	2-9
Fig	*Ficus carica*	8-10
Japanese bush plum	*Prunus japonica*	3-5
Jujube	*Zizyphus jujube*	.6-10
Kiwi	*Actinidia chinensis*	9,10
	A. arguta	6-10
Lemon guava	*Psidium littorale longipes*	10
Loquat	*Eriobotrya japonica*	8-10
Mulberry	*Morus nigra*	5-10
Nanking cherry	*Prunus tomentosa*	3-5
Natal plum	*Carissa grandiflora*	10
Olive	*Olea europaea*	9,10
Papaw	*Asimina triloba*	5-9
Pecan	*Carya illinoiensis*	5-9
Persimmon, American	*D. virginiana*	5-9
Persimmon, Oriental	*Diospyros kaki*	6-10
Pineapple guava	*Feijoa sellowiana*	9,10
Pine nut	*Pinus sp.*	3-10
Pistachio	*Pistacia vera*	7-9
Pomegranate	*Punica granatum*	9,10
Prickly pear	*Opuntia sp.*	5-10
Quince	*Cydonia oblongata*	5-9
Rose hips	*Rosa rugosa*	2-9
Salal	*Gaultheria Shallon*	6-9
Sapote	*Casimiroa edulis*	10
Strawberry guava	*Psidium littorale littorale*	10
Strawberry tree	*Arbutus unedo*	8,9
Walnut, black	*Juglans nigra*	3-9
Western sand cherry	*Prunus besseyi*	3-5

Figure 10.7

Use this list as a point of departure. While these plants are likely to escape the ravages of seasonal disease and pestilence, there may be special considerations in your area. Fortunately, there are dozens to hundreds of varieties of each type of fruit. For each disease that attacks a type of fruit tree, there is probably a variety that is resistant to the disease.

If you are unfamiliar with the tree diseases for your area, contact the local university cooperative extension service or local landscapers and nurseries to learn the major diseases for the types of fruit trees you hope to plant. With this information in hand, study Figs. 10.7 through 10.16 to find varieties with natural resistance to the diseases.

Chances are you will come up with varieties you have never tasted. It's often possible to sample antique or heritage fruits, if a collector lives near you and offers seasonal fruit tastings. The North American Fruit Explorers journal, *Pomona*, is a good place to find the names of enthusiasts of old-time fruit. If no such group exists near you, visit elderly gardeners who have old fruit trees, collect unusual types of fruit from them, and organize a tasting of your own. Also, there is a new business that sells antique apple samplers each fall: Applesource, Tom Vorbeck, Route One, Chapin, IL 62628. Applesource will mail a six-pack of apples that you choose from a list of 70 to 100 oldtime apple varieties.

There are many good-tasting varieties that are more disease-resistant than the varieties found in our supermarkets. Sometimes, though, you will have to make the tough decision between good-tasting fruit that is disease-prone and a care free tree that makes second-rate fruit. At least you will be conscious of the choice you are making, and can plan for disease-prevention maintenance.

Once you have sampled enough fruit to make a decision, it is time to find a source for the tree. Local retail nurseries may not be able to supply all the varieties you want. Check the mail-order nurseries in Appendix 8; while the varieties they carry are not listed, their areas of specialty are. Collect as many of their catalogs as possible, then wait for a rainy day when you'll have time to study them to find out which company supplies the varieties you have chosen. The colorful photos and tidbits of gardening information that you can glean from the catalogs will make your research far from boring. Also, *Pomona* lists people who sell grafted trees or scions (for grafting your own trees) of antique varieties. The best source for the new varieties of disease-resistant apple trees (see Fig. 10.15) is The New York State Fruit Testing Cooperative Association. To obtain a catalog, write to the Association, Geneva, NY 14456. Enclose a check for $5 to cover the cost of the catalog and the yearly membership fee.

Disease-Resistant Varieties

Figure 10.8

PEARS: FIRE BLIGHT
(Erwinia amylovora)

High to Moderate Resistance

'Comice'
'Dawn'
'Douglas'
'Duchess d'Angouleme'
'El Dorado'
'Fan-stil'
'Luscious'
'Mac'
'Magness'
'Maxine'
'Moonglow'
'Seckel'
'Starking Delicious'™
'Sugar'
'Sure Crop'
'Waite'
'Winter Nelis'

Moderately Susceptible

'Bartlett'
'Beierschmitt'
'Beurre Bosc'
'Beurre Hardy'
'Clapp Favorite'
'Gorham'
'Kieffer'
'Lee'
'Stewart Bartlett'

Very Susceptible

'Aurora'
'DeVoe'
'Forele'

Figure 10.9

APPLES: FIRE BLIGHT

High Resistance

'Alameda'
'Ben Davis'
'Caravel'
'Delcon'
'Delicious'
'Detroit Red'

'Empire'
'Fameuse'
'Golden Delicious'
'Grimes Golden'
'Grove'
'Haralson'
'Huidobro'
'Jonadel'
'July Delicious'
'Kidd's Orange Red'
'King David'
'Kinnard's Choice'
'Liberty'
'Maiden Blush'
'McIntosh'
'Melrose'
'Minjon'
'Ozark Gold'
'Paragon'
'Prima'
'Red Sharon'
'Red Westfield'
'Ruby'
'Smokehouse'
'Snow'
'Spartan'
'Spasserud'
'Spencer'
'Spigold'
'Stark LuraRed'™
'Starkrimson Red Delicious'™
'Starkspur Compact Red Delicious'™
'Starkspur Supreme Red Delicious'™
'Stark Supreme Staymared'™
'Starkspur UltraRed Delicious'™
'Stayman'
'Sweet Delicious'
'Virgina Beauty'
'Wellington'
'Wickson Crab'
'Williams Red'
'Winesap'
'Winter Sweet'
'Yellow Belleflower'

Somewhat Susceptible

'All Summer'
'Beacon'
'Caroline Hopkins'
'Cox's Orange Pippin'
'Dolgo Crab'
'Dorsett Golden'
'Early Harvest'
'Franklin'
'Gravenstein'

Figure 10.9 continued

'Jonagram'
'King Cole'
'Leonard Flatt'
'Macoun'
'Mammoth Black Twig'
'Maud'
'Milton'
'Mollie's Delicious'
'Monroe'
'Newtown Pippin'
'Pettingill'
'Quinte'
'Red Duchess'
'Redgold'
'Red June'
'Red Warrior'
'Rome Beauty'
'Roxbury Russet'
'Rusty Coat'
'Scockley'
'Summer Pearmain'
'Terry'
'Tompkins King'
'Virginia Crab'
'Webster'
'Whetstone'
'White Astrachan'
'Winter Pearmain'

Susceptible

'Beverly Hills'
'Cortland'
'Early McIntosh'
'Early Redbird'
'Fenton'
'Fyan'
'GoldenSweet'
'Greening'
'Holland'
'Horse Apple'
'Idared'
'Jonathan'
'King Luscious'
'Lakeland'
'Mantet'
'Monroe'
'Mutsu'
'New Holland'
'Orleans'
'Penland Red'
'Red June'
'Red Spitzenberg'
'Scarlet Baldwin'
'Summer Champion'
'Summer Rambo'

Figure 10.9 continued

Figure 10.9 continued

'Utter'
'Valmore'
'Wagener'
'Wayne'
'Wealthy'
'Whitney Crab'
'Yorking'

Highly Susceptible

'Barry'
'Buckley Giant'
'Earliblaze'
'Evans May'
'Greedale'
'Jonwin'
'Kendall'
'Lodi'
'Northern Spy'
'Oriole'
'Pink Pearl'
'Red Delight'
'Red Melba'
'Red Warrior'
'Summerred'
'Tydeman's Red'
'Wolf River'
'Yellow Transparent'

Figure 10.10

PEACHES: Peach Leaf Curl
(Taphrina deformans)

Good Resistance

'Amsden'
'Mayflower'
'Red Bird'
'Sunbeam'

Moderately Resistant

'Orange Cling'

Slightly Resistant

'Carmen'
'Elberta'
'Greensboro'
'J. H. Hale'
'Sneed'

The Western Washington Research and Extension Unit at Mt. Vernon, Washington has a breeding program for trees *resistant* to peach leaf curl. Recent introductions include:

'Q 1-8'
'Five Star Curlless' (the most resistant)
'Frost'
'Rosy Dawn'

Figure 10.11

PEACHES: BROWN ROT
(Monilinia laxa)

Very Resistant

'Elberta'
'Orange Cling'
'Red Bird'
'Sunbeam'

Good Resistance

'Carmen'
'Greensboro'
'Sneed'

Moderate Resistance

'Amsden'
'J.H. Hale'
'Mayflower'

Very Slight Resistance

'Peen-to'

Figure 10.12

PEACHES: GUMMOSIS
(Botryosphaeria)

High Resistance

'Harbrite'

Moderate Resistance

'Harken'
'Harmony'
'Pekin'
'Redskin'
'White English'

Susceptible

'Dixiland'
'Elberta'
'Glohaven'
'Indian Cling'
'Jones'
'Keystone'
'LaGold'
'LaPremier'
'Loring'
'Madison'
'Marqueen'
'Maygold'
'Monroe'
'October Cling'

Figure 10.12 continued

'Ranger'
'Redcap'
'Redglobe'
'Southland'
'Springcrest'
'Springgold'
'Suwanee'
'Triogem'
'Washington'
'Whynot'

Figure 10.13

PEACHES: BACTERIAL LEAF SPOT
(Xanthomonas pruni)

Resistant

'Belle of Georgia'
'Bicentennial'
'Biscoe'
'Candor'
'Clayton'
'Correll'
'Dixiland'
'Dixired'
'Earlired'
'Early Elberta'
'Ellerbe'
'Hamlet'
'Harbrite'
'Harken'
'Loring'
'Madison'
'Norman'
'Ranger'
'Redhaven'
'Com-Pact Redhaven'
'Sentinel'
'Winblo'

Figure 10.14

APPLES: SCAB
(Venturia inequalis)
POWDERY MILDEW
(Podosphaera leucotricha)

High Resistance to Both Scab and Mildew

'Brown Russet'
'Priscilla'
'Spartan'
'Stirling'
'Tohoku 4'
'Tydeman's Early'
'Tydeman's Red'
'Wolf River'

continued

Figure 10.14 continued

Highly Susceptible

'Burgundy'
'Idared'
'Jerseymac'
'Jonamac'
'Jonee'
'Julyred'
'Magnolia Rose'
'Melrose'

High Resistance to Scab Only

'Buckley Giant'
'Chehalis'
'Hudson's Golden Gem'
'Jefferies'
'Mother'
'Prima'
'Raritan'
'Red Baron'
'Sir Prize'
'Tompkins King'

High Resistance to Mildew Only

'Discovery'
'Early McIntosh'
'Holly'
'Macfree'
'Mutsu'
'Nova Easygro'
'Ozark Gold'
'Quinte'
'Stark Splendor'™

Apples Bred for Disease Resistance

After some 35 years of breeding, disease-resistant apples with good quality are finally becoming widely available. Figure 10.15 shows these selections and the diseases to which they are resistant.

Figure 10.15

DISEASE-RESISTANT APPLES

Variety	Apple Scab	Cedar Apple Rust	Fire Blight	Powdery Mildew
'Akane'	m	*	r	r
'Discovery'	r	*	*	r
'Florina'	vr	*	*	s
'Freedom'	vr	m	m	m
'Gavin'	vr	*	*	*
'Jonafree'	vr	*	*	*
'Liberty'	vr	vr	r	r
'Macfree'	vr	vs	r	r

continued

Fig. 10.15 continued

Variety	Apple Scab	Cedar Apple Rust	Fire Blight	Powdery Mildew
'Nova Easygro'	vr	vr	r	s
'Novamac'	vr	vr	r	*
'Priam'	vr	*	*	s
'Prima'	vr	vs	r	r
'Priscilla'	vr	vr	r	r
'Redfree'	vr	vr	r	r
'Sir Prize'	vr	s	vs	r
'Tydeman's Red'	r	*	*	r

vr – Very resistant. Occurrence of the disease virtually unknown.
r – Resistant. Rarely contracts the disease.
m – Moderately resistant. Better than most varieties.
s – Susceptible.
vs – Very susceptible.
* – Variety not tested for this disease.

Figure 10.16

WALNUTS: BLIGHT
(Xanthomonas campestris)

Fairly Tolerant

'Chandler'
'Eureka'
'Franquette'
'Hartley'
'Howard'
'Pedro'
'Tehama'
'Vina'

Susceptible

'Amigo'
'Chico'
'Ser'

Very Susceptible

'Ashley'
'Gustine'
'Marchetti'
'Payne'
'Sunland'

GROWING TREE CROPS
Roots, Soil, and Rootstocks

Your soil will be home to the tree's roots for decades to come. To keep a tree perennially happy and productive, it is important to make the right match between soil type and rootstock. Fortunately, there are fruit and nut tree rootstocks that tolerate a range of soil types—from sandy to clay, from acidic to alkaline. The outline of soil types in "Your Soil," the following description of how tree roots grow, and the rootstock charts should help you to make wise selections.

DEEP-ROOTED MYTHS

Gardeners, myself included, sometimes cherish mistaken ideas learned from older gardeners. For example, "The roots of trees spread only as wide underground as the branches spread aboveground." I've also been told many times, "A tree needs a deep soil because it grows a taproot. The taproot prevents the tree from blowing over." But respect for my older gardening friends didn't stop me from wondering. It seemed to me that reality was shrouded by deep-rooted assumptions. I sought studies of root excavations to check these commonly held "truths."

Rambling Roots

Much to my surprise, in studies almost 60 years old, I found that roots outreach branches. I had always mulched fruit trees to the dripline, believing the roots stopped there. As it turns out, the roots extend at least half again as far as the dripline and can even grow to three times the width of the branches (see Figs. 11.0 and 11.1).

The growth of roots is influenced by soil. Loamy and sandy soils, with their open texture, lower nutrient content, and drier nature, encourage roots to forage farther. Numerous studies of trees that grow in loamy soils found the roots to be 3 times wider than the branches. In heavy clay soils, which are usually more fertile than sandy soils, root growth spreads only 1½ times the dripline. The differences, however, may be small. A study from Russia, *The Root System of Fruit Plants*, calculated that the root area of fruit trees averaged 5 times that of the branches. This ratio remained the same throughout the life of the tree, regardless of the species, type of

rootstock, or soil type. The implications of the true root zone for gardeners are discussed in the section "Caring for Your Fruit and Nut Trees."

Sinking the Myth About Taproots

The next myth to crumble concerned fruit tree taproots. Numerous root excavations have shown that apples and pears, for example, have major horizontal roots from which large vertical roots (called sinkers) descend. Contrary to popular belief, fruit

Figure 11.0 The width, in meters, of four trees' roots compared to the width of their canopies (the dotted lines). From a Russian study.

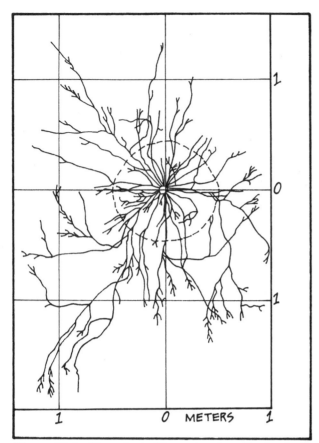

Figure 11.1 The extent of the root system of a standard-size pear tree compared to the width of its canopy (the dotted line). From a study by the East Malling Research Station, England.

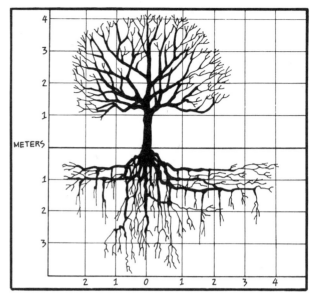

Figure 11.2 A 20-year-old standard-size apple tree (on Antonovka roots) studied in Russia.

Figure 11.3 A fruit tree's roots may be shallower than those of nearby vegetables. The findings of five different studies were combined here. Each study was done in ideal soil.

trees usually have at least several sinker roots, rather than a single taproot (see Fig. 11.2). The tripod-like combination of horizontal roots and deep sinker roots gives the tree stability. Figure 11.3 shows another surprise: a fruit tree's roots may be shallower than those of nearby vegetables.

When a tree is dug for transplanting, the digging machine cuts through many of the sinker roots. There is much debate as to whether the sinker roots regrow. Some people think that more of the horizontal feeding roots multiply rapidly, resulting in a shallower-rooted tree with few sinker roots. Others feel that the growth of new sinker roots is stimulated by the root pruning. My experience with bare-root trees is that not all the sinker roots regrow. Trees with true taproots—walnut, hickory, pecan, butternut, filbert, and heartnut—also have fibrous side roots, but commercial growers try to dig as much of the taproot as possible to ensure healthy growth.

Shaped by Their Environment

Roots respond to the environment. Listed below are some of their responses.

Some roots don't like to grow together. There is a natural aversion between the roots of the two apple trees in Fig. 11.4. In soils with low fertility, placing apple trees farther apart reduces competition for limited nutrients.

Roots avoid compacted soils. Figure 11.4 shows root growth inhibited by the compacted soil near the road. For the fullest root zone, don't plant trees near buildings, paths, roads, or other compacted soils.

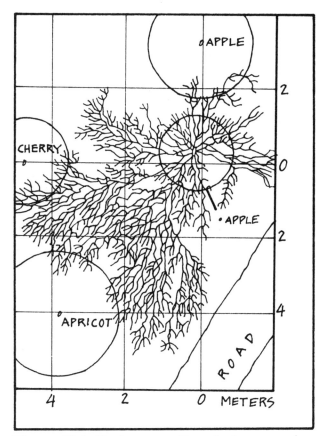

Figure 11.4 Twelve-year-old apple trees growing among other types of fruit trees. The canopy width is indicated by the solid circular line. Only one apple tree's roots are sketched.

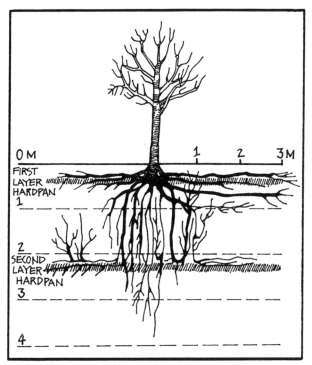

Figure 11.5 A Russian study of an apple tree growing in a soil with two hardpan layers.

Roots can't easily penetrate hardpan. A layer of very hard subsoil, sometimes natural and sometimes caused by tillage, is called hardpan. Hardpan acts as a barrier to roots. Figure 11.5 reveals a root's difficulties with hardpan. A few roots grew through fissures; other grew sideways or returned to the surface. If you have hardpan, try a drill or pickaxe to crack through this layer to looser soils below. If that is impractical, plant your trees much farther apart than usual because the roots will be forced to spread shallow and wide. A high water table will either form a similar hardpan or act like one—forcing the tree's roots horizontally. Watch to see if the trees need staking for protection from wind.

Hills change the pattern of roots. Figure 11.6 shows how roots grow slightly more uphill than downhill. Your mulch should be adjusted accordingly for trees on a slope. (The noticeable curve in the deeper roots is caused by an obstruction in the soil.)

Figure 11.6 A 16-year-old apricot tree growing on a terraced slope. From a Russian study.

4

THE BEST ROOTSTOCKS FOR YOUR SOIL

Tree roots are particular about the type of soil they grow in and the amount of water and nutrients they receive, but if you learn that your soil is suited only to plum roots, and you hate plums, don't despair. For decades, fruit tree growers have been grafting combinations of fruit trees on rootstocks that make it possible, for example, to grow peaches, nectarines, almonds, and apricots on a plum rootstock.

While your local retail nursery probably won't be able to provide all the combinations, you need only a little skill in grafting to produce a tree that fits both your soil and your taste buds. This is the kind of intimate relationship between plants and their environment that an owner-built edible landscape can achieve.

Choosing the best rootstock for your soil can mean the difference between a tree that limps along for years, requiring constant care (perhaps dying after an especially wet winter), and a tree that is an attractive and vigorous element in your landscape. Luckily, for every class of soil there are at least several types of trees that perform well. The charts that follow (Figs. 11.7 through 11.17) will help you determine the rootstocks that suit your soil. Take time to study them carefully. In addition, more and more mail order nurseries are providing detailed information about rootstocks and accurately listing the type used for each tree. Appendix 8 describes many of those nurseries.

How to Use the Rootstock Charts

If your local retail nursery knows about the best rootstocks for your area's soils and climate, use their recommendations and skip having to digest these fascinating, yet cumbersome, charts. Be sure to question the nursery people as to how they came to know about rootstocks and why they chose those they sell. I have found that many retail nurseries order trees according to fruit variety, without any consideration as to the virtues or limitations of the rootstock. Be firm but understanding in your questioning. If they are not well informed, have them buy this book and read these charts!

If you want to know more about rootstocks than your local nursery can tell you, begin by choosing the fruit or nut variety you want to eat. For this discussion I will use apples as an example.

Next choose the relative or approximate size of tree that you wish to grow, such as a dwarf apple tree. Turn to the appropriate chart, in this case, the "APPLE, Dwarf and Miniature" portion of Figure 11.8 on page 167.

Begin by scanning the categories of the chart, especially the columns under the "Resistance to:" section. Consider the most important limiting factors to rootstocks in your area. In my locale, too much water in the winter and subsequent crown rot is one of the most common problems. In Figure 11.8 one rootstock has not been evaluated (the *), another is rated medium (M 26), and the rest receive high ratings (good resistance to crown rot).

This Information Is Relative

When comparing the data within a chart and between charts, remember that the testing and evaluation were often done by different organizations, in different areas of the country or world. These charts provide a very relative index when comparing from rootstock to rootstock and especially when comparing between charts. Nonetheless, these charts are the only effective starting point. Experience is the best teacher, so time and experimentation will be your most helpful educators.

Next, read the comments for each potentially useful rootstock (disregarding the M 26 and Mark™ in this example). While reading the comments, keep an eye out for any other problems that might apply to your yard.

Now you will be faced with the ever difficult task of choosing the healthiest compromise: that is, the rootstock with the best features and the least number of limitations for your edible landscape design. You will have to weigh the pluses and minuses of each rootstock.

I generally use the M 9 rootstock, but the M 26 is another possible selection for my needs. In both cases, because they are not highly resistant to woolly apple aphid, I would consider using this rootstock as an interstem (where another, more vigorous rootstock is planted in the soil and this "rootstock" is a size-controlling piece in the trunk). By reading the comments, I see that if I choose to grow the M 9 rootstock, the tree must be staked for its entire life, suckers must be removed periodically, and I should watch for early signs of fire blight as well.

Also, I can refer to the top chart on page 167: "APPLE, Semi-Dwarf." The MM 111 and MM 106 are both rated medium or high in regard to woolly apple aphid. The MM 111 is rated higher in resistance to crown rot; therefore, I could use that rootstock and prune more heavily in the summer to control its size or use the MM 111 as the rooted base for an interstem of M 9 or M 26.

Once you've digested these charts, compare your potential choices with the experience of gardeners and growers nearby. Use the local voice-of-experience as a double check before ordering a tree. Good luck!

ALMOND, Standard (*Prunus amygdalus*)

Rootstock	Soil	Size (% of full-size)	Height (in feet)	Width (in feet)	Anchor-age	Oak Root Fungus	Crown Rot	Crown Gall	Bacterial Canker	Root-Knot Nematodes	Drought
								Resistance to:			
Almond seedling	sandy	100	30	30	exc.	S	very low	HS	S	S	R
Nemaguard (*P. persica*) seedling	sandy loam	85	24	24	very good	S	low	S	HS	R	T
Lovell (*P. persica*) seedling	sandy loam	90	25	25	very good	S	low	S	MR	S	T
Marianna 2624 (*P. cerasifera*) cutting	clay loam	70	20	20	good	MR	med. to high	MR	S	MR	S

COMMENTS:

Almond roots are not often used as a rootstock. More common are Nemaguard and Lovell, because of their resistance to root knot nematodes. Lovell is moderately tolerant of wet feet, and produces a bigger and more productive tree than Marianna. 'Nonpareil,' 'Milow,' 'Kapareil,' and some other varieties cannot be grafted to the Marianna 2624 rootstock. Marianna is used where oak root fungus is a problem and in heavy wet soils.

Figure 11.7

HR–highly resistant; MR–moderately resistant; R–resistant; T–tolerant; S–susceptible; MS–moderately susceptible; HS–highly susceptible; *–not tested, no data.

APPLE, Standard (*Malus pumila*)

Rootstock	Soil	Size (% of full-size)	Height (in feet)	Width (in feet)	Anchor-age	Crown Rot	Woolly Apple Aphid	Drought
							Resistance to:	
Seedling	sandy loam	100	28	18–28	exc.	high to low	med.	R
Robusta 5	clay loam	80	22	18–28	exc.	med.	high	S
Alnarp 2	clay loam	80	22	18–28	exc.	low	low	S
Antonovka	clay loam	90	25	18–28	exc.	med. to high	med.	*
M 13-A	clay loam	80	22–25	18–28	fair	high	high	S
Novole™	clay loam	100	28	18–28	exc.	high	med.	*

COMMENTS:

Seedling. A "generic" rootstock grown from the seeds of processed apples, commonly used for standard-sized apple trees. There is a fair amount of variation from tree to tree. Some nurseries select seeds from quality trees in order to ensure a good genetic background for the seedlings.

Robusta 5. The most important characteristic is its cold hardiness, though it is less cold hardy than Antonovka. The tree is short-lived, often ten years or less. Very resistant to fireblight and moderately resistant to powdery mildew.

Alnarp 2. A sturdy rootstock with limited cold hardiness, similar to the MM and EM series. It produces a wind resistant tree and some suckering. Very susceptible to fireblight and moderately susceptible to powdery mildew.

Antonovka. A very cold hardy rootstock. Susceptible to crown gall and fireblight.

M 13-A. More tolerant of poor drainage than any other apple rootstock. The tree is slow to come into bearing. Presently available only from the New York State Fruit Testing Cooperative Association, soon to be available through some mail order catalogs.

Novole™. Resistant to pine and meadow voles (mice). Induces somewhat earlier bearing than other vigorous rootstocks. Resistant to fireblight.

Figure 11.8

APPLE, Semi-Dwarf

Rootstock	Soil	Size (% of full-size)	Height (in feet)	Width (in feet)	Anchor-age	Resistance to: Crown Rot	Woolly Apple Aphid	Drought
MM 111	clay loam	75–85	20–24	16–20	good	high	med. to high	R
MM 106	sandy loam	60–75	14–21	14–18	good	poor	high, better than MM111	T
M 7-A	sandy and gravel loams	55–70	12–20	12–16	fair to good	low to medium	low	T

COMMENTS:

MM 111. Of all the semi-dwarf apple rootstocks, MM 111 produces the most upright and vigorous tree, with wide branch angles for strong attachment, but is the least precocious of the dwarf apple rootstocks. It has the best anchorage and the least amount of suckering. Prone to early defoliation, for a moderate amount of cold hardiness. Appears to tolerate wet soil slightly better than MM 106. Somewhat susceptible to fireblight and powdery mildew. Uses water more efficiently than standard rootstocks – good for sandy soils in hot climates. Susceptible to burr knot above ground.

MM 106. More precocious and heavier bearing than MM 111. Little suckering. Double the fireblight resistance of MM 111, susceptible to powdery mildew but resistant to latent viruses. Does not like wet roots and uses more water than a standard rootstock. Late to harden off, not very cold hardy (less hardy than MM 111). Tolerates high air and soil temperatures and high pH (alkaline soils). May induce delayed dormancy. Gets burr knots.

M 7-A. With a snow cover, fairly cold hardy. Precocious, not as heavy bearing as MM 106, and may need staking in the first several years. Suckers badly. Resistant to fireblight, moderately resistant to powdery mildew and susceptible to crown gall. Uses more water than a standard rootstock. Needs an ample supply of potassium. Gets burr knots.

Figure 11.8 continued

APPLE, Dwarf and Miniature

Rootstock	Soil	Size (% of full-size)	Height (in feet)	Width (in feet)	Anchor-age	Resistance to: Crown Rot	Woolly Apple Aphid	Drought
Dwarf:								
M 26	sandy and gravel loams	30–50	10–14	10–14	med.	med.	low	S
M 9	sandy and gravel loams	20–40	8–10	8-10	poor	high	low	T
Mark™	clay	30–45	8–12	8–12	good	*	low	*
Miniature:								
M 27	clay	20–30	5–8	2–8	poor	high	low	*

COMMENTS:

M 26. Has the best cold hardiness of all semi-dwarf and dwarf apple rootstocks. Needs staking the first 5 to 8 years. Precocious and heavy bearing. Limited suckering, less than M 7-A. Very susceptible to fireblight. Medium resistance to powdery mildew. Prone to forming burr knots above ground. Can form root galls at graft union. Some varieties ('Empire,' 'Delicious,' 'Mutsu,' 'Northern Spy,' and 'Vista Bella') have broken at the graft union. Due to early cropping, there is loss of the leader if not pruned or thinned properly.

M 9. Very precocious. Can be kept below 6 feet. Brittle wood and roots require that the tree be staked its entire life. Deeply planted trees do not root along the buried trunk, unlike other apple rootstocks. Needs a good, uniform soil and consistent moisture. Some suckering. Very susceptible to fireblight. Moderate resistance to powdery mildew. Not vigorous enough for commercial situations.

Mark™. This new rootstock will be available about 1987. It is precocious and heavy bearing, but does not require staking. Susceptible to fireblight.

M 27. Very precocious. Needs staking its entire life. Susceptible to fireblight. Suckering is very rare. Not very winter hardy – frequently killed by cold in the lower Midwest. Moderate resistance to powdery mildew. Unacceptable for commercial settings.

Figure 11.8 continued

APRICOT, Standard (*Prunus armeniaca*)

Rootstock	Soil	Size (% of full-size)	Height (in feet)	Width (in feet)	Anchor-age	Resistance to: Peach Tree Borer	Gophers and Mice	Oak Root Fungus	Crown Rot	Crown Gall	Bacterial Canker	Root-Knot Nematodes
Apricot seedling (standard size)	sandy loam	100	24	24	good	MR	H	S	low	MR	S	R
Marianna 2624 *P. cerasfera)* cutting	clay loam	70	20	20	good	*	*	MR	med. to high	MR	S	MR
Manchurian apricot seedling	sandy loam	100	24	24	good	*	H	*	*	R	*	R

COMMENTS:

Apricot Seedling. Not often used as a rootstock. More vigorous than plum roots, producing fairly hardy, long-lived trees. Adaptable to a wide range of soils except for heavy clay. Slightly resistant to chlorosis and alkaline soils. There are no compatible dwarfing rootstocks for apricots, except for 'Goldcot' on *Prunus bessyi*.

Marianna 2624. Tolerates all but the heaviest of soils. Roots are shallow for the first 3 or 4 years; avoid deep cultivation close to the trees. Good compatibility.

Manchurian. The Manchurian apricot, a very shrubby bush with small fruits, may add a measure of cold hardiness to the scion. Resistant to root knot and root lesion nematodes. Attracts and is susceptible to gophers. More resistant to crown gall than peach and plum rootstocks. More tolerant of lime than peach roots, but less tolerant than plum roots. Better compatibility with apricot scions than peach rootstocks and much longer lived.

Figure 11.9

HR–highly resistant; MR–moderately resistant; R–resistant; T–tolerant; S–susceptible; MS–moderately susceptible; HS–highly susceptible; *–not tested, no data.

AVOCADO, Standard (*Persea americana*)

Rootstock	Soil	Size (% of full-size)	Height (in feet)	Width (in feet)	Anchor-age	Resistance to: Root Rot	Drought
Seedling	sandy loam	100	20–50	20–50	good	S	S
Clonal Duke #7 and G-6	sandy	100	20–50	20–50	good	MR	S

COMMENTS:

Seedling. Sensitive to salt burn (brown edges on leaves). Yellow leaves indicates chlorosis (treat with iron chelates). Gets root rot easily in California.

Clonal Duke #7. Developed by Brokaw Nursery for more resistance to root rot. Vigorous, uniform growth, more cold tolerant than seedling Guatemalan strains. Sets a good crop.

Figure 11.10

CHERRY, Standard – Sweet Varieties *(Prunus avium, P. cerasus)*

Rootstock	Soil	Size (% of full-size)	Height (in feet)	Width (in feet)	Anchor-age	Peach Tree Borer	Gophers and Mice	Oak Root Fungus	Crown Rot	Crown Gall	Bacterial Canker	Root-Knot Nematodes	Verticillium Wilt
									Resistance to:				
Mazzard *(P. avium)* seedling	sandy loam & loam	100	35	30	exc.	MS	MR	MR	S	S	S	R	S
Mahaleb *(P. Mahaleb)* seedling	sandy loam	80	30	25	exc.	MS	HS	S	S	MR	R	MR	S
Colt	clay loam	60–75	25	20	good	*	*	*	H	MS	MR	*	*
Stockton Morello *(P. cerasus)* cuttings	clay loam	60–70	22	20	good	MR	MR	S	MR	MR	R	R	S
Vladimirasus *(P. cerasus)*	loam	30–40	10–14	8–10	poor	*	*	*	*	M	*	*	*

COMMENTS:

Mazzard. Produces a very large tree. Good for sweet and for tart cherries. Better compatibility with varieties than Mahaleb. Similar to Morello in water sensitivity. High transplant mortality rate in some regions. Susceptible to aphids. Shallow rooted – do not cultivate deeply around roots. Especially well anchored and the longest lived cherry rootstock. Prone to some zinc deficiency. Somewhat hardy. Slow to come into bearing. Gophers love all cherry rootstocks.

Mahaleb. The common rootstock for sour/tart cherries as well as sweet cherries. The best rootstock for sandy and gravely soil because it is more drought resistant and has the deepest roots. Does not like heavy, clay soils. More cold hardy and precocious than Mazzard. Less prone to zinc deficiencies. Tends to sucker. Very susceptible to crown and root rot.

Colt. Hardiness still uncertain, has been used in areas where winter temperatures drop to −20°F. Very precocious and heavy bearing. Compatible with most sweet and sour cherries. No suckering. Extremely drought sensitive. Best available rootstock for heavy soils. Drought susceptible.

Stockton Morello. Tolerant of wet soils. Earlier and heavier bearing. Hard to transplant. Resistant to bacterial gummosis. Suckers badly. Resistant to zinc deficiency. Not widely available.

Vladimir. Bears early, often in the second year. Not yet available commercially.

Figure 11.11

CITRUS *(Citrus sp., Poncirius sp.)*

Rootstock	Soil	Size (% of full-size)	Height (in feet)	Width (in feet)	Cold Hardiness	Crown Rot	Root-Knot Nematodes	Drought	Citrus Blight	Tristeza Virus
STANDARD										
Rough Lemon *(C. jambhiri)*	infertile coarse or sandy	100	25	35	low	low	S	T	S	T
Sweet Orange *(C. sinensis)*	loam	100	25	35	med.	very low	*	S	*	T
SEMI-DWARF										
Sour Orange *(C. anrantium)*	clay	80	20	28	high	high	S	T	*	VS
Trifoliate Orange *(Poncirius trifoliata)*	fertile clay	50	12	15	highest	med.	R	*	S	T
DWARF										
Flying Dragon *(P. trifoliata)*	fertile clay	25	6	5	high	*	*	*	*	*

COMMENTS:

Rough Lemon. More drought tolerant than Sour Orange. High yields and fruit matures earlier than other rootstocks, but juice quality is low. Susceptible to young tree decline (YTD). The least cold hardy, and the most susceptible to citrus blight.

Sweet Orange. The rootstock most susceptible to drought and root rot. Tolerant of YTD. Less cold hardy than sour orange.

Sour Orange. Produces the highest quality fruit and juice of excellent quality. Tolerant of YTD. The second most cold hardy rootstock. The best rootstock for grapefruit.

Trifoliate Orange. The rootstock of this deciduous tree makes a citrus variety go dormant earlier and be more cold hardy. Produces the most productive tree, but the fruits are smaller. Most resistant of crown rot. Intolerant of the virus exocortis viroid. Tolerant of YTD. Susceptible to blight, gummosis, and calcereous and saline soils. Very susceptible to citrus canker.

Flying Dragon. A new selection being tested at the University of California's South Coast Field Station. Nine-year-old orange trees on this rootstock are producing 1 to 1½ boxes per tree. True compatibility has not been confirmed; all trees grafted in 1972 show a strong union, though the rootstock overgrows the variety. Will be available in the near future.

Figure 11.12

HR–highly resistant; MR–moderately resistant; R–resistant; T–tolerant; S–susceptible; MS–moderately susceptible; HS–highly susceptible; *–not tested, no data.

PEACH AND NECTARINE, Standard (*Prunus persica*)

Rootstock	Soil	Size (% of full-size)	Height (in feet)	Width (in feet)	Anchor-age	Resistance to:						
						Peach Tree Borer	Gophers and Mice	Oak Root Fungus	Crown Rot	Crown Gall	Bacterial Canker	Root-Knot Nematodes
Halford seedling	sandy loam	100	20	18	good	HS	med.	HS	low	S	MR	S
Lovell seedling	sandy loam	100	20	18	good	HS	med.	HS	low	S	MR	S
Siberian C seedling	sandy loam	90	18	17	poor to good	*	med.	*	low	S	*	S
Nemaguard seedling	sandy or sandy loam	100	20	18	good	HS	med.	HS	low	S	HS	R
Amandier™ peach/almond cross	clay loam	100	20	18	good	*	*	*	high	*	*	*

(see also Myrobalan, for Plum)

COMMENTS:

Halford. Needs good drainage. Least likely to sucker. Do not use where peaches have been grown before. Similar to Lovell. Most nurseries get the seed from canneries; it may be infected.

Lovell. Potentially longer lived trees. Do not use where peaches have grown before. Higher disease resistance than other peach rootstocks. Some increased winter hardiness in the East, Midwest, and West. Highly recommended for the southern and eastern U.S. where short life of peach trees is a problem. Needs good drainage. Has good vigor.

Siberian C. A cold hardy rootstock. Encourages earlier defoliation and dormancy than other peach rootstocks, but prone to satisfy its chill requirement early and be susceptible to hard frosts in late spring after warm winter days. Suckers. Particularly unpredictable in heavier soils. A short-lived tree. More consistent fruiting and ripens the fruit several days earlier.

Nemaguard. The best rootstock for sandy soils because it is resistant to root knot nematodes. The least winter hardy of standard peach rootstocks. Used frequently in the West. Unless you fumigate, do not use where peaches have been grown before. Needs good drainage— gets root rot easily.

Amandier™. Developed in France. Compatible with all varieties of peaches and nectarines tested to date. Can be used to plant where peach roots have been used before. Can tolerate heavy, wet soils and calcareous conditions.

Figure 11.13

PEACH AND NECTARINE, Semi-Dwarf

Rootstock	Soil	Size (% of full-size)	Height (in feet)	Width (in feet)	Anchor-age	Resistance to:						
						Peach Tree Borer	Gophers and Mice	Oak Root Fungus	Crown Rot	Crown Gall	Bacterial Canker	Root-Knot Nematodes
St. Julian A *P. americana)* seedling	sandy loam	70–80	14	13	*	*	*	S	low	*	*	*
Citation (peach/plum cross) cuttings	sandy loam	70–75	14	13	good	*	*	*	high	S	*	MR

COMMENTS:

Damas™. A hybrid plum rootstock developed in France. Vigorous growth in the first several years. Good rootstock for heavy, wet, and alkaline soils. Fruit size is larger, matures earlier, and has better color.

St. Julian A. An older dwarfing rootstock from Europe. Not very appropriate since the development of the Citation rootstock.

Citation. Compatible with all peach, nectarine, plum, prune, and apricot varieties tested to date. Does not sucker. Reduces the canopy more than the height, by 30 to 40 percent, for better light penetration with less attention to pruning. (Watch for sunscald in canopy if overthinned.) Susceptible to crown gall. Well-anchored, does not need staking. Appears to be pest and disease resistant, except for some susceptibility to crown gall. Very tolerant of wet/heavy soils. Induces early defoliation, dormancy, and hardiness. Developed by Floyd Zaiger, Modesto, CA. Still being evaluated for commercial applications.

Figure 11.13

continued

PEACH AND NECTARINE, Dwarf

Rootstock	Soil	Size (% of full-size)	Height (in feet)	Width (in feet)	Anchor-age	Resistance to:						
						Peach Tree Borer	Gophers and Mice	Oak Root Fungus	Crown Rot	Crown Gall	Bacterial Canker	Root-Knot Nematodes
Western Sand Cherry (*P. besseyi*) seedling	loam	20–35	3–5	3–5	poor	*	*	*	high	*	S	*
Nanking Cherry (*P. tomentosa*) seedling	loam	15–25	2–4	2–3	poor	*	*	*	high	*	S	*

COMMENTS:

Western Sand Cherry. Tree fruits very early and heavily, but fruit quality is poor. Trees are short-lived, less than 10 years. Weak graft union and poor compatibility, needs staking its entire life. A hardy rootstock that suckers easily and profusely. Only for the experimental and ambitious gardener.

Nanking Cherry. A very dwarfing and precocious rootstock that produces a short-lived tree. Weak graft union and very poor compatibility with many varieties, but better than *Prunus besseyi*. Trees snap easily or blow over – they need staking their entire lives. Suckers easily and profusely. A hardy rootstock. Only for the experimental and ambitious gardener.

Figure 11.13

HR–highly resistant; MR–moderately resistant; R–resistant; T–tolerant; S–susceptible; MS–moderately susceptible; HS–highly susceptible; *–not tested, no data.

PEAR, Standard (*Pyrus* sp.)

Rootstock	Soil	Size (% of full-size)	Height (in feet)	Width (in feet)	Suckers	Oak Root Fungus	Crown Rot	Root-Knot Nematodes	Pear Root Aphid	Gophers and Mice	Fire blight
						Resistance to:					
Domestic French 'Bartlett' type (*P. communis*) seedling	clay loam	100	35	25	Yes	R	M	S	S	S	VS
Old Home (*P. communis*) cuttings	clay loam	100	35	25	Yes	R	M	*	S	S	R
Oriental (Harbin) Pear (*P. ussuriensis*) seedling	clay loam	100	35	25	No	MR	M	*	R	S	R
Oriental Pear (*P. betulafolia*) seedling	clay loam	120	40	25	No	*	Low	S	R	*	VR
Oriental Pear (*P. calleryana*) seedling	clay loam	100	35	25	No	MR	M	R	*	R	R

COMMENTS:

Domestic French. Suitable for European pears. Asian pears die out within 20 years. Has numerous, well-distributed roots. Tolerates a wide range of soils, except for the wettest. A tendency to sucker increases danger of fireblight. Good compatibility, rootstock overgrows scion wood, depending upon the scion variety.

Old Home. Numerous well-distributed roots. Tolerates a wide range of soils, except for the wettest. Used as an interstem on quince for varieties of pears that are not compatible with quince. Compatible with all pear varieties.

P. ussuriensis. Not recommended for the European varieties, suitable for Asian pears. Not as consistently vigorous as the European rootstocks. Needs a deep and fertile soil. Less tolerant of wet soils than European rootstocks. Not consistently compatible with Bartlett pear – Old Home is used as an interstem. The last of the Oriental rootstocks to come into bearing, but the hardiest and longest lived.

P. betulafolia. A very vigorous rootstock, 20 percent larger than standard pear rootstocks. Excellent for Asian pear varieties where winters are not too cold. Thrives in a wide range of soils and tolerates wet soil better than European rootstocks. More resistant to fire blight than European (*P. communis*) varieties. Tolerates dry soils better than *P. calleryana*. Fruit size is very large, but Anjou pears do not fruit well on this rootstock. Suckers.

P. calleryana. Makes vigorous, early bearing and productive trees, but the roots are slender and not well branched. Fruit is of good quality and size. Along with *P. betulafolia,* this is the most water- and clay-tolerant rootstock, but it does not tolerate drought as well as *P. betulafolia.* More sensitive to crown rot, winter injury, and kill than *P. betulafolia.* Not compatible with all varieties – Old Home is used as an interstem.

Figure 11.14

continued

PEAR, Dwarf

Rootstock	Soil	Size (% of full-size)	Height (in feet)	Width (in feet)	Suckers	Oak Root Fungus	Crown Rot	Root-Knot Nematodes	Pear Root Aphid	Gophers and Mice	Fire blight
								Resistance to:			
Quince (*Cydonia oblonga*)	loam	50	16	12	Yes	HS	R	R	R	R	S
Quince A	loam	50	16	12	Yes	*	R	R	R	*	S
Quince C	loam	30	11	8	Yes	*	R	R	R	*	S
OH X F 51	loam	30	11	8	*	*	*	R	S	*	HR
Hawthorn (*Crataegus* sp.)	loam	25	10	7	*	*	*	*	*	*	*

COMMENTS:

Rootstocks are for European pears only – at this time, there are no acceptable dwarfing rootstocks for Asian pears.

Quince. The most common commercially available dwarfing rootstocks for pears are quince rootstocks propagated from cuttings but not selected for particular virtues. Quince roots increase a pear tree's susceptibility to fireblight. Generally good to –15°F, not cold hardy. Some pear varieties are not compatible with quince. The following need an interstem of Old Home: 'Bartlett,' 'Bosc,' 'Seckel,' 'Winter Nelis,' 'Eldorado,' 'Clapp Favorite,' 'Forelle,' 'Farmingdale,' 'Beurre Hardy,' 'Bristol Cross,' 'Dr. Jules Guyot,' 'Doyenne d'Ete,' and 'William's Bon Chretien.'

Quince A. A named selection of dwarfing quince rootstock developed in England. Similar characteristics to the generic quince, but more consistent from tree to tree. Same incompatibility problems. Not cold hardy.

Quince C. Another named selection from England. This one is similar to Quince A except it is more dwarfing. Needs a good, fertile soil. Resistant to pear decline, crown gall, mildew, and root aphids. Bears fruit in 4 to 7 years. Not cold hardy.

OH X F51. A cross of Old Home and Farmingdale developed at Oregon State University, Corvallis. Selected to be more resistant to fireblight than quince roots and to be high yielding. As cold hardy as standard rootstocks. Very good water tolerance. One of the best dwarfing roots for pears. Another good rootstock from this series is OH X F333.

Hawthorn. For the experimental gardener, not used by commercial growers. Makes a smaller tree than either quince or OH X F 51. Needs an Old Home interstem due to incompatibility problems.

Figure 11.14

HR–highly resistant; MR–moderately resistant; R–resistant; T–tolerant; S–susceptible; MS–moderately susceptible; HS–highly susceptible; *–not tested, no data.

PERSIMMON, Standard (*Diospyros* sp.)

Rootstock	Soil	Size (% of full-size)	Height (in feet)	Width (in feet)	Root Rot	Root-Knot Nematodes	Crown Gall
						Resistance to:	
D. lotus	loam, clay loam	100	30	25	MS	S	MS
D. kaki	loam, clay loam	100	30	25	S	S	S
D. virginiana	loam, clay loam	100	40	25	T	S	MR

COMMENTS:

D. lotus. More susceptible to crown gall than *D. kaki*, incompatibility problems with non-astringent cultivars such as 'Fuyu,' and excessive fruit shedding is a problem with all cultivars. For these reasons, *D. kaki* is preferred over *D. lotus*. More cold-hardy and more uniform growth than *D. kaki*. In Japan, the preferred rootstock for sandy, dry, and alkaline soils.

D. kaki. The preferred rootstock for Oriental persimmons. Hardy from 10° to – 1°F. Produces very long taproots, and weak, brittle lateral roots – digging up bareroot stock is difficult. Tolerates wet soils better than *D. lotus,* but not as well as *D. virginiana*.

D. virginiana. The best rootstock for poorly drained or clay soils. It is more cold-hardy than the two Oriental rootstocks. Suckers freely. Tree size and vigor is more variable than with the other rootstocks. Hard to transplant.

Figure 11.15

PLUM AND PRUNE, Standard (*Prunus* sp.)

Rootstock	Soil	Size (% of full-size)	Height (in feet)	Width (in feet)	Anchorage	Peach Tree Borer	Gophers and Mice	Oak Root Fungus	Crown Rot	Crown Gall	Bacterial Canker	Root-Knot Nematodes
Myrobalan (*P. cerasifera*) seedling	clay loam	100	18	16	exc.	S	S	S	med.	HS	S	S
Myrobalan 29C	clay loam	100	18	16	fair	S	S	MS	med.	MR	S	R
Marianna 2624 (*P. cerasifera*) cuttings	clay loam	90	16	14	good	S	S	MR	med.	MR	HS	R
Lovell (*P. persica*) peach seedling	sandy loam	110	20	18	very good	HS	med.	S	low	S	MR	S
Nemaguard (*P. persica*) peach seedling	sandy loam	110	20	18	very good	HS	med.	S	low	S	S	R

COMMENTS:

Myrobalan. Tolerates all but the heaviest of clay soils. Good compatibility. More resistant to boron excess than peach or apricot rootstocks. Widely used where high winds require good anchorage.

Myrobalan 29C. Tolerates all but the heaviest of soils. Roots are shallow for the first 3 or 4 years. Good compatibility. Between Myrobalan and Marianna 2624 for resistance to oak root fungus. Usually more resistant to crown gall than Myrobalan. Less susceptible to bacterial canker than Marianna 2624.

Marianna 2624. Tolerates all but the heaviest of soils. Roots are shallow for the first 3 or 4 years – avoid deep cultivation close to the trees. Good compatibility. Trees are unaffected by prune brownline disease.

Lovell. Not generally used for plums or prunes, except where bacterial canker resistance is needed. Trees are potentially longer lived. Do not use where peaches have grown before. Some increased winter hardiness in the East, Midwest, and West. Needs good drainage. Prunes on this rootstock are subject to brownline disease.

Nemaguard. The best rootstock for sandy soils. It is resistant to drought and to root knot nematodes. Least winter hardy of standard peach rootstocks. Do not use where peaches have been grown before. Needs good drainage. Prunes and plums are usually grown on the first three listed rootstocks, but Nemaguard may be useful where better resistance to bacterial canker is needed. Prunes on this rootstock are subject to brownline disease.

Figure 11.16

PLUM AND PRUNE, Semi-Dwarf

Rootstock	Soil	Size (% of full-size)	Height (in feet)	Width (in feet)	Anchorage	Peach Tree Borer	Gophers and Mice	Oak Root Fungus	Crown Rot	Crown Gall	Bacterial Canker	Root-Knot Nematodes
St. Julian A (*P. americana*) cuttings	sandy loam	70–80	14	13	*	*	*	S	low	*	*	*
Citation (peach/plum cross) cuttings	sandy loam	70–75	14	13	good	*	*	*	low	S	*	MR

COMMENTS:

St. Julian A. An older dwarfing rootstock fron Europe. Not very appropriate since the development of the Citation rootstock.

Citation. Unlike most plum rootstocks, Citation does not sucker. Reduces the canopy more than the height, by 30 to 40 percent, for better light penetration with less attention to pruning. (Watch for sunscald of the trunk if canopy is overthinned.) Susceptible to crown gall. Well- anchored, does not need staking. Compatible to all peach, nectarine, plum, prune, and apricot varieties tested to date. Appears to be pest and disease resistant, except for susceptiblity to crown gall. Developed by Floyd Zaiger, Modesto, CA. Still being tested for commercial applications.

Figure 11.16 continued

continued

PLUM AND PRUNE, Dwarf

Rootstock	Soil	Size (% of full-size)	Height (in feet)	Width (in feet)	Anchor-age	Resistance to:						
						Peach Tree Borer	Gophers and Mice	Oak Root Fungus	Crown Rot	Crown Gall	Bacterial Canker	Root-Knot Nematodes
Western Sand Cherry (*P. besseyi*) seedling	loam	20–35	3–5	3–5	poor	*	*	*	high	*	S	*
Nanking Cherry (*P. tomentosa*) seedling	loam	15–25	2–4	2–3	poor	*	*	*	high	*	S	*
Pixie (*P. domestica*)	loam	30–40	6	5	good	*	M	*	low	*	MR	MR

COMMENTS:

Western Sand Cherry. The trees fruit very early and heavily, but live less than 8 years. Weak graft union and poor compatibility—needs staking its entire life. A hardy rootstock. Suckers easily and profusely. Only for the experimental and ambitious gardener.

Nanking Cherry. Very dwarfing and very precocious. Lives less than 10 years. Weak graft union and very poor compatibility, but better than *Prunus besseyi*. Tree snaps easily or blows over, needing staking its entire life. Suckers easily and profusely. A hardy rootstock. Only for the experimental and ambitious gardener.

Pixie. Compatible with all European-type plums tested so far, but not with peaches. Has a much smaller root than St. Julian A, but is well anchored. Precocious with heavy crops. Fruit is consistently smaller than that grown on St. Julian A, though the color is better and the fruit ripens 1 to 5 days earlier. Suckering is virtually nonexistent.

Figure 11.16

HR–highly resistant; MR–moderately resistant; R–resistant; T–tolerant; S–susceptible; MS–moderately susceptible; HS–highly susceptible; *–not tested, no data.

WALNUT, Standard *(Juglans* sp.)

Rootstock	Soil	Size (% of full-size)	Height (in feet)	Width (in feet)	Resistance to: Armillaria Root	Crown Rot	Crown Gall	Root-Knot Nematodes	Saline Conditions	Blackline Disease
Northern California Black Walnut *(J. hindsii)*	loam	100	70	50	S	low	HR	S	HR	VS
Paradox *(J. hindsii + J. regia)*	clay	110	80	60	MR	med. to high	S	S	MR	VS
Persian *(J. regia)* (English)	loam	90	60	60	S	low	S	S	S	HR

COMMENTS:
Even though the *J. hindsii* and Paradox rootstocks are immune to the devastating blackline disease, an English variety grafted onto them will be killed by blackline. English scions on Persian rootstocks do not get blackline, but their pollen may carry the virus, and they may possibly maintain the virus in the soil.

Figure 11.17

Chandler, William. **Deciduous Orchards**. 3rd ed. rev. Philadelphia: Lea & Febiger, 1957. For tree crops, one of four technical references that I consult most often. Worth searching for in used book stores.

Childers, Norman. **Modern Fruit Science**. 8th ed. New Brunswick, NJ: Horticultural Publications, 1978. Poor-quality illustrations greatly hamper this book. A good one to browse in the library; only serious tree crops enthusiasts need own it.

Davidson, John, and Reed, Clarence. **The Improved Nut Trees of North America and How to Grow Them**. New York: Devin-Adair, 1968. Not as useful, up to date, or available as *Nut Tree Culture in North America*.

Garner, R.J. **The Grafter's Handbook**. 4th ed. rev. London: Faber & Faber, 1979. The only book that provides a detailed review of all grafting techniques. For the most recent developments in grafting, see the latest edition of *Plant Propagation* by Hartman and Kester.

Hall-Beyer, Bart, and Richard, Jean. **Ecological Fruit Production in the North**. Quebec, Canada: Jean Richard, 1983. A must for fruit tree enthusiasts who live in Canada and in the coldest climates of the U.S.

Hartman, H.T., and Kester, D.E. **Plant Propagation**. 4th ed. Englewood Cliffs, NJ: Prentice-Hall, 1983. This bible of propagation covers all aspects, except for the latest in clonal tissue culture. Quite expensive—encourage your library to get a copy.

Jaynes, Richard, ed. **Nut Tree Culture in North America**. Hamden, CT: Northern Nut Growers Association, 1979. The most helpful and thorough book on the subject. (The Association publishes a quarterly journal with the latest news on nut growing.)

Kraft, Ken and Pat. **Grow Your Own Dwarf Fruit Trees**. New York: Walker Publishing, 1974. An early and simple review of the basics of dwarf fruit tree culture. Read a library copy.

Southwick, Lawrence. **Dwarf Fruit Trees for the Home Gardener**. Charlotte, VT: Garden Way Publishing, 1972. A very basic introduction for the home gardener. Thin on content.

Stebbins, Robert, and Walheim, Lance. **Western Fruits, Berries and Nuts**. Tucson, AZ: HPBooks, 1981. The best reference on these subjects, and the one I use the most. Complete with brilliant, condensed, easy-to-use charts. Excellent color photographs. HPBooks also publishes an equally excellent East Coast version, *How to Grow Fruits, Berries and Nuts in the Midwest and East*, by Theodore James, Jr., 1983.

Wright, David. **Fruit Trees and the Soil**. London: Faber and Faber, 1960. A short, succinct manual on the organic care of fruit trees. Presents the most understandable discussion I have read on the biochemistry of soil as it relates to organic home gardening. Demystifies soil fertility and how it influences fruit tree growth and production.

4 GROWING TREE CROPS

Trees of All Sizes

STANDARD, SEMI-DWARF, AND DWARF TREES

Trees are categorized by their mature sizes, from diminutive dwarfs to towering standards (see Fig. 12.1). Full-size, or standard, trees offer a wide range of heights and widths, as shown in Fig. 12.2.

There are several categories of mature tree sizes. The largest is the full-size, or standard, tree, ranging from 15-foot filbert trees to 40-foot apple trees and 60-foot walnut trees. Standard trees are usually grafted. Figure 12.2 lists the average height and width for an assortment of standard trees.

The texture and fertility of your soil will have a lot to do with the ultimate size of your trees. For example, walnut trees growing in the clay soil near my house rarely get above 30 feet, but a walnut tree planted in sandy loam 10 miles away is 50 feet tall—and some books list walnut trees as maturing at 70 feet tall.

Form . . .

Standard trees are wonderful elements in a landscape. They lend a sense of permanence that smaller trees cannot provide. A standard apple tree may live to be 125 years old, while a dwarf tree is over

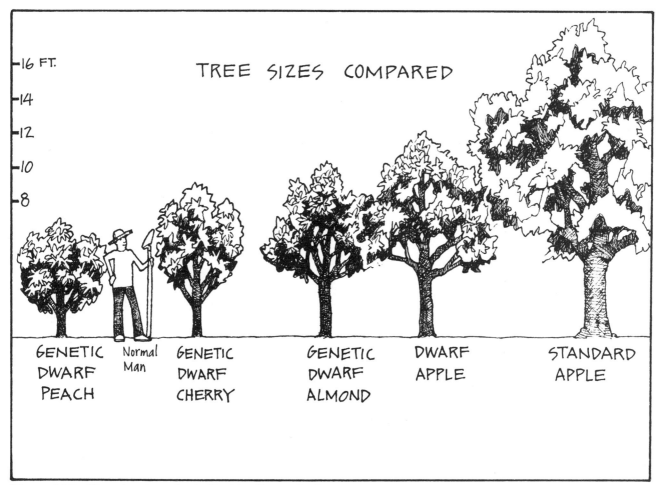

Figure 12.1 There is a tree size to fit virtually any landscape.

STANDARD TREES		
	Height	Width
Almond	35	30
Apple	40	40
Apricot	30	30
Avocado	35	40
Cherry	35	40
Chestnut	50	40
Fig	35	50
Filbert	20	20
Nectarine	25	25
Olive	40	30
Peach	25	25
Pear	40	25
Pecan	80	60
Persimmon	30	25
Pistachio	30	25
Plum	30	25
Pomegranate	12	15
Quince	20	20
Walnut	60	60

In feet, unpruned trees

Figure 12.2

the hill at age 35. The large limbs of an old fruit tree can even support a swing for children. Their shade is a welcome refuge during a hot summer afternoon and can help lower your home's cooling costs. Whenever possible, design for several, or more, large standard trees as dominant forms in the landscape.

It is important to remember that large trees are appropriate only for large properties. A mature chestnut tree in a small urban lot would overwhelm the design as well as shade the rest of the landscape. With a mature width of 40 feet, a chestnut tree needs perhaps another 30 to 40 feet of open space surrounding its foliage to accommodate a landscape design with a scale proportional to the size of the the tree.

. . . and Abundance

There is a mixed blessing from standard fruit and nut trees—copious production. Mature chestnut trees have yielded as many as 400 pounds of nuts a year! While the form of a large tree may be just the thing for your landscape design, do you really need the hundreds of pounds of fruit or nuts? Harvesting chestnuts is easy: they fall to the ground. Most fruits, however, are too ripe or rotten once they fall and must be harvested off the branches. Climbing around in a 30-foot tree with a heavy sack of fruit slung over your shoulder is not the safest or simplest of tasks.

Maintaining Standard Trees

Caring for a standard tree can involve another difficulty. Oriental and European chestnuts are rarely bothered by pestilence, but many of the more common fruit and nut trees require some type of spray program. Spray programs for pest and disease problems are almost out of the question on the tallest of trees; the average tank sprayer for home gardeners cannot spray above 15 feet, and sprayers that attach to garden hoses and trombone pump sprayers can reach only 20 to 25 feet.

Because of the spraying dilemmas, I usually plant ornamental trees as the largest forms in a landscape design. For food, there is a category of trees better suited to manageable production and care—semi-dwarf trees.

Semi-Dwarf Fruit and Nut Trees— High Yields, Less Work

Most common fruit stock can be grafted onto special rootstock that controls the size of the tree. The exceptions include pecan, hickory, macademia, pistachio, Asian pear, black walnut, English walnut, sour cherry, chestnut, fig, filbert, jujube, loquat, persimmon, and olive trees. A tree somewhat smaller than standard size is called a semi-dwarf. In popular terms, semi-dwarf trees range from 10 to 50 percent smaller than their standard equivalents. Semi-dwarf trees outproduce standard trees with regard to the amount of fruit in a given area: more trees can be planted in the area taken by a standard tree and each tree produces fruit more densely than standard trees.

Personally, I do not favor semi-dwarf trees. I use them only when the fruit variety is not available on a more dwarfing rootstock; when the rootstock is best suited to a given soil; when room is needed beneath the lower limbs for mowers, tractors, or plants; when solid anchorage for protection from high winds is required; or when more production per tree is desired than can be achieved with a smaller tree.

Dwarf Fruit and Nut Trees

Songwriter Randy Newman may think short people "got no business around here," but I think short fruit and nut trees are the greatest—for short *or* tall people. Dwarf trees bring all the work and the fun within easy reach—they grow only 6 to 12 feet high. Pruning, spraying, inspecting for the first signs of pests or diseases, and fruit thinning are time-consuming tasks that we do best with our feet planted firmly on the ground. Harvesting, or just snacking right off the tree, is more pleasurable without the hassle of ladders and pole pickers.

A dwarf tree does not have dwarf fruit. In fact, the amount of normal-size fruit produced by a dwarf tree, for a given area, is much greater than that produced by semi-dwarf or standard trees, a gain that is in part a result of how densely these trees can be planted.

The yield per tree is least on dwarf trees because of their small size, but the smaller harvest is a virtue in my eyes. Less fruit per tree but more trees in a given area means I can plant a smorgasbord. I can plant so that a different variety ripens virtually every week. That makes the fresh fruit season exciting and, in addition, reduces the need for canning. (See "Zones of Use, Multiple Use.")

Miniature Trees – Highest Yields, Least Effort

Last, but not least, the tiniest of trees – the miniature, or genetic dwarf. The dwarfing mechanism is in the tree, not in a rootstock. There are genetic dwarf trees that rarely grow taller than 6 feet, including varieties of peach, nectarine, cherry, apple, and almond (the last three will eventually grow a bit taller). In a separate category, there are dwarfing rootstocks for apple trees that shorten a scion so much that a grafted tree can be considered a miniature. An apple variety grafted onto the EM 27 rootstock will grow only to be 5 to 8 feet tall.

These trees may be short in stature, but they are not short on production. In fact, when yields per growing area are measured, they are the most prolific of all trees available. Imagine how easy it is to maintain and pick a tree that you can look down on for most of its life! These trees are so new and so special that I have devoted the next chapter to them.

Baker, Harry. **Fruit (The Simon & Schuster Step-by-Step Encyclopedia of Practical Gardening)**. New York: Simon & Schuster, 1980. One of my favorite recommendations for beginning and experienced gardeners who want a graphic review of the basics of fruit and nut culture. Based on the expertise of England's avid gardeners, yet usually appropriate to most U.S. climates. (Cold-region landscapers beware of Baker's temperate-winter bias).

Chandler, William. **Deciduous Orchards**. 3rd ed. rev. Philadelphia: Lea & Febiger, 1957. For tree crops, one of four technical references that I consult most often. Worth searching for in used book stores.

Childers, Norman. **Modern Fruit Science**. 8th ed. New Brunswick, NJ: Horticultural Publications, 1978. Poor-quality illustrations greatly hamper this book. A good one to browse in the library; only serious tree crops enthusiasts need own it.

Davidson, John, and Reed, Clarence. **The Improved Nut Trees of North America and How to Grow Them**. New York: Devin-Adair, 1968. Not as useful, up to date, or available as *Nut Tree Culture in North America* (Richard Jaynes, ed.).

Garner, R.J. **The Grafter's Handbook**. 4th ed. rev. London: Faber & Faber, 1979. The only book that provides a detailed review of all grafting techniques. For the most recent developments in grafting, see the latest edition of *Plant Propagation* by Hartman and Kester.

Griffith, Eugene and Mary. **Persimmons for Everyone**. Arcola, MO: North American Fruit Explorers, 1982. A down-home booklet that describes the history of persimmons and gives dozens of recipes. Every persimmon lover will want to borrow a copy of this out-of-print gem or urge NAFEX to reprint it.

Hall-Beyer, Bart, and Richard, Jean. **Ecological Fruit Production in the North**. Quebec, Canada: Jean Richard, 1983. A must for fruit tree enthusiasts who live in Canada and in the coldest climates of the U.S.

Hedrick, U. P. **The Pears of New York**. Albany, NY: J. B. Lyon, 1921. Dozens of color plates of lovely hand-tinted etchings. A must for serious collectors of pear tree varieties. Many of the varieties described have been lost to cultivation. The 636-page book is available for $11 from: Mrs. Rita Curtain, New York Agricultural Experimental Station, Geneva, NY 14456.

Hills, Lawrence D. **Grow Your Own Fruit and Vegetables**. Rev. ed. Thetford, England: Faber & Faber, 1979. An English manual with an organic bias that is better than most American books on organic gardening.

Jaynes, Richard, ed. **Nut Tree Culture in North America**. Hamden, CT: Northern Nut Growers Association, 1979. The most helpful and thorough book on the subject. (The Association publishes a quarterly journal with the latest news on nut growing.)

Kraft, Ken and Pat. **Grow Your Own Dwarf Fruit Trees**. New York: Walker Publishing, 1974. An early and simple review of the basics of dwarf fruit tree culture. Read a library copy.

New Alchemy Institute. **Gardening for All Seasons**. Andover, MA: Brick House Publishing, 1983. An excellent book based on New Alchemy's thorough research and testing. Their integrated systems for food production and preservation are more current than those described in the Farallones Institute's *Integral Urban House*. Covers vegetable cultivation, greenhouse production, aquaculture, raising chickens, tree crops, recycling, and community gardens. Especially good for people living in colder winter climates of the U.S.

Ray, Richard, and Walheim, Lance. **Citrus: How to Select, Grow and Enjoy**. Tucson, AZ: HPBooks, 1980. The best book on the subject for home edible landscapers. Another of HPBooks's colorful and concise reviews.

Smith, J. Russell. **Tree Crops**. Rev. ed. Old Greenwich, CT: Devin-Adair, 1977. Smith was the first to take a radical view of tree crops in agriculture, and was my original inspiration to experiment with polycultures of tree crops. His cultural examples are fascinating, but inappropriate for suburban settings, since they rely on animals to graze the fruits and nuts, and on people to eat the animals. Smith's idea that tree crops have deep taproots which give them a competitive advantage is in error.

Southwick, Lawrence. **Dwarf Fruit Trees for the Home Gardener**. Charlotte, VT: Garden Way Publishing, 1972. A very basic introduction for the home gardener. Thin on content.

Stebbins, Robert, and Walheim, Lance. **Western Fruits, Berries and Nuts**. Tucson, AZ: HPBooks, 1981. The best reference on these subjects, and the one I use the most. Complete with brilliant, condensed, easy-to-use charts. Excellent color photographs. HPBooks also publishes an equally excellent East Coast version, *How to Grow Fruits, Berries and Nuts in the Midwest and East*, by Theodore James, Jr., 1983.

Wickson, Edward. **California Fruits**. San Francisco: Pacific Rural Press, 1919. One of my favorite tree crops references, written prior to the use of many chemicals in orchard management. Details for adapting trees to local climatic and soil conditions make it especially valuable to California gardeners. Includes good pointers on pruning standard-size fruit trees. The rootstock information is outdated, but the virtues of many old varieties of fruits and nuts are described in detail. Many of the fruit varieties mentioned are still grown by members of North American Fruit Explorers.

GENETIC DWARF (MINIATURE) FRUIT AND NUT TREES

If you want a fruit or nut tree that is short and sweet, plant a genetic dwarf tree. A recent addition to the realm of tree crops, the genetic dwarf (or miniature) tree became available to home gardeners only 20 years ago. The more familiar semi-dwarf tree, by contrast, goes back to the early 1800s. However new, genetic dwarf trees are sold in a wide variety – almond, apple, apricot, cherry, nectarine, and peach. While there is only one miniature almond, there are over a dozen cultivars or varieties of miniature peaches and nectarines.

I will use the genetic dwarf, or miniature, peach and nectarine as examples, because these trees are the most readily purchased and the most productive, and they offer the largest selection of cultivars. I will also use the term preferred by the tree crops industry – miniature.

Distinctive

The miniature peach and nectarine are short, shrubby trees, rarely growing more than 6 feet tall and 6 to 10 feet wide. Figure 12.3 shows their distinctive size and shape. The dense canopy reminds me of the "schmoos" in Al Capp's comic strip of the mid-60s. Some call the trees mop-tops. The scientific phrase for this is brachytic dwarfism (quite a horticultural mouthful), which refers to the distance – the internode – between buds. The drastically shortened internodes account for the small size of the tree. As to the aesthetic appeal, you can decide for yourself; personally, I find the form attractive.

Figure 12.3 Miniature peach trees fill a raised bed planter, offering shade and privacy in summer.

Notice how close the buds are – two or more times as many buds grow in the same length of branch as on a standard-size tree (see Fig. 12.4). At least one leaf grows below each bud, which produces the characteristic thicket of foliage.

Figure 12.4 A miniature tree has two or more times as many buds as a standard-size tree in the same length of branch.

Why a Miniature Tree Is Small

The slow, compact growth of miniature trees is controlled by the tree's genes. A twig from a miniature tree, when rooted, exhibits the same compact growth of the parent tree. Rooting a twig from the top of a *grafted dwarf* peach, however, would produce a full-size tree. Generally, the pits of a miniature peach make trees with the same compact growth as the parent. (The fruit might be somewhat different because of the genetic variation caused by the pollination of the flower, but the compact size remains.)

Although miniature trees do not need a special rootstock for dwarfing, miniatures are, in fact, grafted. The wholesale grower grafts for ease of production and to have the best root for the soil. Remarkably, miniatures are grafted on standard-size rootstocks. Note how the roots are so much larger and more vigorous than the top (Fig. 12.5). The tree remains a miniature in spite of the vigor of the rootstock, because the genes in the scion wood control the tree's size.

Genetic dwarfing produces other surprises. Dick Fuget was not happy with the flavor of the peaches from his 'Garden Sun' miniature peach, so he grafted a scion of an 'Indian Blood' peach onto one of the

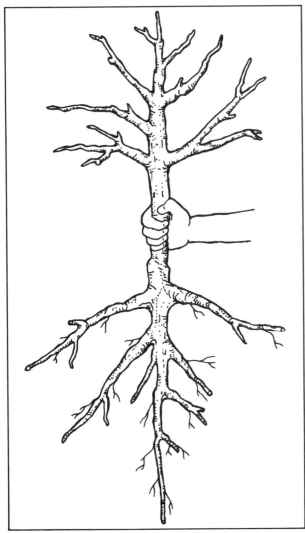

Figure 12.5 Compared to other tree sizes, a miniature tree's roots are proportionally much larger than its top.

branches of the miniature tree. The result is a vigorous full-size branch that is outgrowing the miniature tree and will soon overshadow it. The miniature tree did not act as a dwarfing stock for his scion; a miniature tree is made in the genes.

The History of Miniature Trees

Miniature fruit trees were discovered as natural mutations of seedling trees. In pursuit of a "naturally" dwarfed peach, millions of trees were grown in test plots to find the tiny fraction of seedlings with compact character. Then, breeders such as Floyd Zaiger and Fred Anderson (who recently died and whose work is now continued by Norman Bradford of LeGrand, California) hand-pollinated the seedlings with the pollen of top-quality varieties. It took years of breeding to blend the genes for good taste and color with the genes for miniature size.

The best trees went to trial plots all over the country for observation. The best from the trials were then propagated for retail sales. In all, it took twenty years for the first full cycle of breeding — from a natural seedling mutation to a reliable miniature tree for sale at your local nursery.

The Future

Miniature fruit trees are the wave of the future. At the 1980 North American Fruit Explorers conference at Stark Brothers Nursery, Paul Stark, Jr., stated that he sees the miniature trees as the predominant commercial tree in the near future. When the company responsible for introducing the nectarine as a major crop says something like that, I listen.

Robert Woolley, of Dave Wilson Nursery near Modesto, the wholesale grower of the largest variety and quantity of miniature trees in the United States, believes that commercial orchardists want a superior dwarfing rootstock for stone fruits — the Citation rootstock may be a candidate. (Superior dwarfing rootstocks are available for apples, most cultivars of pears, and cherries.) And he believes commercially economic genetic dwarf peaches and nectarines will be introduced in the next decade. Existing miniature peaches and nectarines, particularly the most recent introductions, have good flavor but lack the firmness needed for long-distance shipping, he says. For the home landscape, however, there is an ever-increasing variety of suitable miniature fruit and nut trees.

The Virtues of Miniatures

Early Bearing

Miniature peach trees bear fruit earlier than the standard peach. Flowering the year of planting is common. In fruit-tree talk, miniatures are known as "precocious."

High Yields

Miniatures produce an amazing density of bloom, which is just a preview of the fruit to come (see Fig. 1.4 in the color plates). The yields of miniature peach trees are being tested at the Kearney station of the University of California Cooperative Extension. The results are astounding. With trees 4 feet apart in the row, the yield per acre was a fantastic 13.4 tons in the first year. Standard peaches do not produce comparable yields until the fifth or sixth years (the average yield for *mature* standard peaches is 10 to 15 tons). In the sixth season after planting, the per-tree yield was 37 to 120 pounds per tree (or 168 tons per acre)!

The high yields are owing in part to the high number of trees per area and in part to their more efficient use of sunlight. The shorter internodes allow for a greater fruit density per volume of canopy. In the trials, the fruit averaged between 2.75 and 3 inches in diameter. The researchers state, "Clearly, the gene that dwarfs tree stature does not adversely affect fruit size." Though I find genetic peaches to be on the small end of the peach spectrum, the catalogs always list "full size" or "large." Another of life's relative terms.

Another advantage of the dwarfing effect is an abundance of flowers. While standard peach trees need yearly pruning to encourage flower bud formation, almost every bud on the new growth of miniature trees is a flower bud. Each spring the branches are laden with blooms. No pruning is required to stimulate flower and fruit production. To borrow an expression, "The future belongs to the efficient," and miniature trees ensure an efficient future.

Not Short on Flavor

If you tasted miniature nectarine and peach fruit a few years back and were dissatisfied, try some of the newer varieties; there have been rapid advances with breeding flavor into the fruit. The most recently introduced varieties have good to excellent flavor and varieties not yet released are even more flavorful. Soon, probably within the next five years, genetic dwarf peaches and nectarines will be comparable or superior to today's best commercial varieties.

While the taste of the first miniatures I grew was inferior to that of some standard peaches, there were advantages to the fruit. The skins of the fully ripened miniature peaches were very thin and practically pulled off the fruit as I picked it. In addition, the pits are proportionately small, so there is a good percentage of flesh in each fruit.

The flavor of other types of miniature fruit and nuts varies. The miniature 'Garden Prince' almond is as tasty and thin-shelled as any regular almond. The genetic apples resemble the standard commercial varieties, Red and Golden Delicious. I am not impressed. I think some of the "antique," or heirloom, varieties on the correct dwarfing rootstock give you much more flavor and texture than the miniature apples currently for sale. Miniature cherries have flavors comparable to those of commercial varieties.

Easy to Care For

With a mature height of 6 feet or less, miniatures are very easy to care for, and it takes them years to get that tall. Until then, it's actually stoop labor to harvest! Ladders are unnecessary for pruning and harvesting. The compact size makes it easy to keep an eye out for the first signs of pests and disease.

Spraying for pests and diseases is almost effortless, with little spray lost to the winds or blown back into your face. And much less solution is needed to thoroughly cover a tree. The small size brings the tree within the reach of people in wheelchairs and, in general, makes these trees very adaptable to many otherwise difficult situations.

Adaptable

In areas with moderate summers, such as in the Pacific Northwest, the lack of heat reduces the flavor and delays the ripening of peaches and nectarines. It is possible, however, to improve the fruit by training the tree as an informal espalier on a south-facing wall. If the wall is light in color, it will reflect additional sunlight and heat for better color and flavor, while speeding the maturity of the fruit. It is also helpful to use white gravel mulches below the tree to reflect light throughout the canopy. A miniature tree is easy to train and will not outgrow small areas.

Also, a low stone wall can enhance the ripening of fruit (see Fig. 12.6). Miniature trees need only a 4- to 5-foot wall. "Solarization" of this sort helps ensure good fruit in previously marginal areas. Elsewhere, it hastens ripening.

Where spring frosts and rain are a problem, the eaves of your home, especially if more than 2 feet wide, can protect a miniature tree's blossoms (see Fig. 6.1, page 83). You needn't worry about the shade cast by the eave; the sun reaches its highest point above the horizon on June 21, then begins a gradual descent. If you choose a variety that ripens in late summer, there will be plenty of sunlight to ripen the fruit.

Figure 12.6   A low wall of stone reflects heat and light, which helps fruit ripen in cool summer areas.

Diversity Without A Lot of Space

Planting a selection of early, middle, and late-season peaches is a great way to protect yourself from unpredictable weather. Spreading out the harvest with miniature trees means that each tree produces less fruit than a standard tree, but because different varieties ripen at different times, you have peaches at more times in the season, thereby reducing the need for canning. Because you can plant so many more trees in the same area as a single standard peach, the initial cost is greater; but the precocity and productivity of miniature trees quickly compensate for the initial higher cost. And the cost is coming down, thanks to a greater volume of sales, and may soon equal that of other dwarf fruit trees.

Easily Fenced

Planted densely, miniature trees are easy to fence against marauding pests—deer, rabbits, raccoons, squirrels, birds, and kids. Their height allows a lower, less costly fence. You can permanently leave bird netting over the entire fenced area.

Not Short on Life

An exciting virtue of these trees is their probable longevity compared to dwarf trees. With standard peaches, the expected commercial life is only 15 years. Dwarf peach and nectarine trees fare worse: grafted onto *Prunus tomentosa* or *P. besseyi* rootstock, they have a productive life of only 4 to 8 years. Figure 12.7 is Donald Harris of Novato, California, and his prize miniature peach. Mr. Harris bought the tree as a dwarf from the garden section of a local department store. For the first 7 years, he cared for it in a container. The photograph was taken after the tree had spent 7 years in the ground. Now, at 20 years, it's the oldest miniature peach I know of. Dave Wilson Nursery does not know of any older. The tree is vigorous and shows no signs of decline. Mr. Harris claims a yield of 300 fruits on this tree 4 feet high by 8 feet wide.

Figure 12.7 A 14-year-old miniature peach tree. Six years later, the tree is still healthy and fruitful.

On a visit to Long Island, New York, where the climate is much harsher than in Novato, I saw a 12-year-old miniature peach, Anderson's 'Bonanza' variety, that was still prolific, vigorous, and healthy.

Perhaps the reason miniatures appear to live longer than dwarfs is that the dwarf size of a miniature tree is not caused by the stress of a dwarfing rootstock. Or perhaps its root system, very large in relation to the canopy, allows for a better supply of nutrients. On this point, only mystery and theory rule—there is much to be studied.

Container Culture: The Portable Orchard

Miniature fruit trees can be grown in containers and still be fruitful, although growing trees in containers requires more work. Even though miniature trees are grafted onto standard roots, they will thrive in containers—if cared for by a fastidious and methodical gardener. Miniature trees planted in the ground always outproduce container plants, even those well cared for. To put a tree through the contortions of potted culture should be a last-resort strategy. Miniature trees are, for example, the only reasonable tree crops for decks, porches, and roof patios. The seasonal bloom alone will be a welcome addition to an urban container garden.

Use half a whiskey barrel with two or three holes drilled in the bottom, or a container of similar size, for miniature trees. A loose, well-drained mix is essential, high in organic matter and low in soil or clay, to hold the moisture without too much weight. Any of the commercial potting mixes that do not contain sand are fine. If you are mixing your own, use less than a fourth of very loamy soil, the rest compost and organic matter.

Since a half-barrel with moist soil can easily weigh 200 pounds, consider putting the container on a small wheeled platform at planting time. Then your miniature orchard will be somewhat portable; quite an advantage unless you are extremely strong or own a forklift.

It is best to water container plants daily, with just a bit of water to keep the soil moist but not wet. If the soil drys out too much, it will pull away from the walls of the container; the next time you water, the water ends up on the deck and not in the soil. Mulching the top during the growing season with aged compost will help keep the soil from pulling away from the container walls.

Because of the small soil volume, fertilize twice a month with a mild dilution of seaweed powder and fish emulsion. Watch for nutritional deficiencies and adjust the fertilization accordingly. The soil mix must be renewed every couple of years. While the tree is dormant and out of the container, wash away all soil, cut back any circling roots, and trim the fat thicker roots (leaving the fibrous, thinner roots to encourage new feeding roots), and replant with fresh potting soil.

Not a Loaded Deck

"Too heavy"—that is the first response most people have to rooftop orchards. Weight, however, is usually not a problem. As mentioned earlier, a half-barrel will weigh approximately 200 pounds when filled and watered. That is only .6 pound per square inch. I weigh 160 pounds. My weight on one foot is 3.3 pounds per square inch, so I put much more weight per square inch on the deck than a miniature tree in a half-barrel. Chances are, if you have a roof deck or porch, it was constructed well enough to hold many containers. Check the structural integrity of the roof or deck before you start, double-check the carrying capacity with a contractor; then enjoy creating a miniature, rooftop orchard—edible rooftops make cities even more livable.

Keep the soil mix light—don't use clay or sand. Use compost, peat moss, vermiculite, leaf mold, and sphagnum. It's a good idea to not cover every square inch of the deck with pots and to use pots with straight sides (the bigger "footprint" of the pot's bottom spreads the weight).

Winter Cold

Container trees can be stored during the winter in a dark place that stays between 20 and 45°F. Even when dormant, some moisture must remain in the soil, so check occasionally and water if needed. Keeping container trees indoors in the winter protects them from cold, and also can delay the bloom in the spring, if you choose.

Another advantage to container culture of miniature peach and nectarine trees is the control of peach leaf curl. Robert Norton, of the Northwest Washington Research and Extension Unit in Mt. Vernon, has studied a method of leaf curl control: moving miniature peach and nectarine trees out of the rain prior to the swelling of the flower and leaf buds. (Even six to ten applications of copper sulphate over the winter fails to give control where winters are very wet.) His results have been good—welcome news for the wet winter climates of western Washington, Oregon, and California.

Limitations of Miniature Trees

Miniature trees are not appropriate in some situations. To evaluate the usefulness of these trees for your edible landscape, consider the following points:

- The dense canopy requires pruning for good air circulation and proper ripening.

- You will need to stoop during the first 3 to 5 years to care for and harvest these trees.

- The fruits of some types are smaller than those from certain varieties of standard-size trees.

- The initial cost to plant a given area is higher than for any other category of fruit tree.

- Only the most recent, patented, and expensive peach introductions have good flavor. (Miniature almonds, nectarines, and cherries, however, have good flavor.)

- The life of some miniature varieties may be shorter than the standard size.

- Even when mature, miniature trees need protection from rabbits, deer, grazing animals, and, perhaps, children.

Special Care for Miniatures

Protect a new tree from the sun. Sunburned bark at the base of the trunk is the first place of entry for peach borers. Paint the trunk from just below the soil line up to the first several branches with any white latex paint (interior or exterior). Then be sure to get down on your knees occasionally to peek under the leaves to check for borer damage.

In the first season, remove all tiny, immature fruits to allow the roots to get established more easily. This is quite a test of willpower. Those who fudge do taste the fruit the first season, but their trees would be better off if the fruits were removed.

From the second year on, thin the young fruits to leave one every 3 to 4 inches along the branch. Wait until the fruit is as big as a jellybean; then you can be quite sure there will be no fruit drop after thinning. Thinning ensures the largest fruit possible. One of my clients failed to thin and had peaches as thick as grapes, too crowded to ripen well and too small to eat.

Not All Miniature Trees Are Equal

Figure 12.8 outlines some of the distinguishing virtues and limitations of the miniature trees. Keep abreast of the latest varieties through fruit tree catalogs and periodicals on gardening. There is bound to be a miniature tree in your future to help keep your home orchard short and sweet.

Figure 12.8

MINIATURE TREE VARIETIES

Cultivar	Height	Width	Self-fruitful, Y-yes, N-no	Fruits in year number	Can be grown in a container, Y-yes, N-no	Virtues	Limitations
ALMOND							
'Garden Prince'	10'	8'	Y	2	Y	Very prolific, thin shelled. Lovely, deep pink blossoms. Very good flavor.	Thin young nuts to get full-size nuts; protect blossoms from late frost and rain. Poorly sealed shells permit easy entry by navel orange worm. Fleshy husk rots easily.
APPLE							
'Garden Delicious'	8'	6'	Y	2	Y	Compact. Fruits well as an espalier. Good flavor, crisp.	Flavor similar to regular Delicious apples. Not as fruitful as some dwarfed spur-type apples. Often russeted, small fruit.
'Apple Babe'	8'	6'	N	2	Y	Tasty, summer apple. Russet free.	Needs another apple for a pollinizer.
CHERRY							
'Garden Bing'	7'	4'	Y	3	Y	Easy to protect from birds. Ornamental leaf. Narrow width is good for "edible hedges." Tastes like 'Bing' cherry, sweet.	Shy bearer. Roots need excellent drainage. Sometimes reverts to vigorous growth habit.
'North Star'	9'	6'	Y	3	N	Deep red fruit. Hardy.	Sour cherry, for pies.
NECTARINE							
'Garden Beauty'	6'	6'	Y	2	Y	Best color of blossom of all peach and nectarine trees—rich, deep red/pink. Low chill.	Roots need good drainage. Clingstone. Dense foliage reduces fruit color.
'Garden Delight'	6'	6'	Y	2	Y	Large fruit—three inches in diameter, with red blush. Low chill. Freestone.	Roots need good drainage. Dense foliage.
'Golden Prolific'	6'	6'	Y	2	Y	Very tasty. Prolific.	Clingstone. Roots need good drainage. High chill requirement. Dense foliage.
'Nectarina'	6'	6'	Y	2	Y	Ruffled, ornamental blossoms.	Medium chill. Roots need good drainage.
'Southern Belle'	6'	6'	Y	2	Y	Large fruit. Freestone. Very prolific. Low chill.	Blooms very early. Roots need good drainage.
'Sunbonnet'	6'	6'	Y	2	Y	Low chill. Prolific.	Clingstone. Not too sweet. Early bloom. Roots need good drainage.
'Nectar Babe'	6'	6'	N	2	Y	Tastiest miniature nectarine yet. Good red color. Prolific.	Needs another nectarine for pollinization. Roots need good drainage.
PEACH							
'Bonanza'	6'	6'	Y	2	Y	Highly aromatic. Large blossoms. Red blush on large fruit.	Roots need good drainage.
'Empress'	6'	6'	Y	2	Y	Highly colored, sweet fruit.	Roots need good drainage.
'Garden Gold'	6'	6'	Y	2	Y	Bears heavily. Red flesh near pit. Freestone.	Flavor not great. Roots need good drainage.

continued

Figure 12.8 continued

Cultivar	Height	Width	Self-fruitful, Y-yes, N-no	Fruits in year number	Can be grown in a container, Y-yes, N-no	Virtues	Limitations
'Golden Gem'	6'	6'	Y	2	Y	Firm texture. Good flavor and flower display.	Roots need good drainage.
'Golden Glory'	6'	6'	Y	2	Y	Large, juicy fruit. Good for cold climates.	High chill. Roots need good drainage.
'Garden Sun'	6'	6'	Y	2	Y	Freestone. Thin skinned.	Flavor not great. Roots need good drainage.
'Honey Babe'	6'	6'	Y	2	Y	Early harvest in hot regions. Does OK in cooler summer climates. High color. Freestone. May be best flavored. Prolific.	Roots need good drainage.
'Southern Flame'	6'	6'	Y	2	Y	Large fruit with good flavor and aroma.	Roots need good drainage.
'Southern Rose'	6'	6'	Y	2	Y	Low chill. Good eating peach.	Early bloom. Roots need good drainage.
'Southern Sweet'	6'	6'	Y	2	Y	Bears heavily.	Medium-size fruit. Roots need good drainage.

Figure 12.8 Miniature tree varieties.

Ray, Richard, and Walheim, Lance. **Citrus: How to Select, Grow and Enjoy**. Tucson, AZ: HPBooks, 1980. The best book on the subject for home edible landscapers. Another of HPBooks's colorful and concise reviews.

Stebbins, Robert, and Walheim, Lance. **Western Fruits, Berries and Nuts**. Tucson, AZ: HPBooks, 1981. The best reference on these subjects, and the one I use the most. Complete with brilliant, condensed, easy-to-use charts. Excellent color photographs. HPBooks also publishes an equally excellent East Coast version, *How to Grow Fruits, Berries and Nuts in the Midwest and East*, by Theodore James, Jr., 1983.

4

SPACING FRUIT AND NUT TREES

The simple way to determine how far apart to plant your trees is according to their mature width. Use the width listed in the nursery catalog you are ordering from, or use the recommendations in the rootstock charts and the list of standard tree heights and widths mentioned earlier in this section. For example, chestnut trees, which are listed as growing 40 feet wide, should be planted with their trunks 40 feet apart (if you can afford the space for more than one!).

If you are mixing tree types, total the widths listed for the two trees that will grow next to each other, then divide by two. This gives the planting distance between the two trunks. For example, a pruned, standard apple tree's spacing is listed as 28 feet, and a pruned, standard peach tree's spacing is listed at 18 feet. When planting one next to the other, space them 23 feet apart ($28+18\div2=23$).

Factors Affecting Spacing

Where space is at a premium, you need to consider the cultural care the trees will receive (including the pruning style you will be using), your yard's soil type, and the inherent growth characteristics of each variety of tree to be planted. The following list reviews the cultural conditions and methods, other than rootstocks, by which a tree's growth can be slowed or stimulated.

Figure 12.9

Limiting Tree Size	Stimulating Tree Size
Summer pruning with little or no winter pruning.	Heavy winter pruning, no summer pruning.
Prune back to two-year-old wood.	Prune only one-year-old wood.
Cut out vigorous limbs, shoots.	Cut out weak, spindly growth.
Train the tree to have a long distance from the ground to the first branches.	Train for a low-branching tree.
Encourage heavy, yearly yields.	Allow alternate, light crops.
Plant trees close together.	Plant trees farther apart.
Use a competitive ground cover.	Till the soil to eliminate any ground cover.
Limit the water and fertilizers.	Give plenty of water and fertilizers.
Prune to horizontal branches.	Prune to upright branches.
Plant in a heavy, clay soil.	Plant in a loamy, sandy soil.

Here are more ways to control or invigorate growth (the items that follow are not paired).

continued

Limiting Tree Size	Stimulating Tree Size
Score, girdle, or bark ring the limbs or trunk.	Use virus-free rootstocks.
Plant the graft union high above the soil.	Plant in a soil that has not grown the type of tree you are planting.
Prune the roots periodically.	Drain off excessive soil water.
Use a trellis to control growth.	Control pests and diseases.
Spread limbs down to a more horizontal position.	
Use spur-type varieties, having a closer spacing between leaf and blossom buds.	

Figure 12.9

By judicious pruning, watering, and fertilizing, you can check or stimulate a tree's growth at will. If, for example, space is short, you can summer prune, thereby keeping your trees smaller than usual.

Soil makes an important difference in the growth of trees, and the effect is often overlooked. I've seen a tree in a sandy loam grow two to three times faster than the same type in a heavy clay soil. Remember that the rootstock charts and nursery catalog recommendations are usually based on ideal soil conditions.

Variety Among Varieties

Among tree varieties, there is a considerable range in natural vigor. The following trees are varieties of apple trees on a standard rootstock that grow smaller than "normal."

- **10 Percent Smaller:** 'Regent,' 'Paulred,' 'Beacon,' 'Cortland,' 'Quinte,' 'Spartan,' 'Turley Winesap,' 'Tydeman's Red,' 'Granny Smith,' 'Newtown Pippin,' 'Prima,' 'Priscilla,' 'Akane,' 'Empire,' 'Hawaii,' 'Melrose,' 'Lodi,' 'Red Prince,' 'Red Queen,' and 'Summerred.'

- **20 Percent Smaller:** 'Red Haralson,' 'Idared,' 'Macoun,' 'Golden Delicious,' 'Imperial Red Delicious,' 'Jonee,' 'Smoothee,' 'Jonamac,' 'Jonagold,' 'Connell Red,' and 'Double Red Jonathan.'

- **25 Percent Smaller:** 'Miller Sturdeespur,' 'Spuree Rome,' 'Redchief,' 'Macspur,' 'Lawspur,' and 'Gallia Beauty.'

- **40 Percent Smaller:** 'Sundale Spur Golden,' 'Spur Winter Banana,' 'Gala,' and 'Discovery.'

Some apple trees are so vigorous that they grow *larger* than the "standard size" listed in the rootstock charts. Trees with extra vigor include

'Empire,' Rhode Island Greening,' 'Roger's Red McIntosh,' 'Mutsu,' 'Northern Spy,' 'Spigold,' 'Red Stayman,' 'Red York,' 'Gravenstein,' and 'Yellow Newtown.'

Keep these differences in mind as you choose a dwarf rootstock. An M 9 rootstock, for example, needs a spacing of 8 to 10 feet. If a 'Spur Winter Banana' were grafted onto this rootstock, the spacing could be just under five feet ($.6 \times 8' = 4.8'$) whereas an 'Empire' graft could be planted only 10 percent closer than the recommended spacing. However, 'Empire' apple trees planted in heavy soil, summer pruned, without supplemental summer watering, and trained to a central leader shape could be planted much closer—say 20 to 25 percent—than the recommended spacing.

Stebbins, Robert, and Walheim, Lance. **Western Fruits, Berries and Nuts**. Tucson, AZ: HPBooks, 1981. The best reference on these subjects, and the one I use the most. Complete with brilliant, condensed, easy-to-use charts. Excellent color photographs. HPBooks also publishes an equally excellent East Coast version, *How to Grow Fruits, Berries and Nuts in the Midwest and East*, by Theodore James, Jr., 1983.

Wickson, Edward. **California Fruits**. San Francisco: Pacific Rural Press, 1919. One of my favorite tree crops references, written prior to the use of many chemicals in orchard management. Details for adapting trees to local climatic and soil conditions make it especially valuable to California gardeners. Includes good pointers on pruning standard-size fruit trees. The rootstock information is outdated, but the virtues of many old varieties of fruits and nuts are described in detail. Many of the fruit varieties mentioned are still grown by members of North American Fruit Explorers.

Baker, Harry. **Fruit (The Simon & Schuster Step-by-Step Encyclopedia of Practical Gardening)**. New York: Simon & Schuster, 1980. One of my favorite recommendations for beginning and experienced gardeners who want a graphic review of the basics of fruit and nut culture. Based on the expertise of England's avid gardeners, yet usually appropriate to most U.S. climates. (Cold-region landscapers beware of Baker's temperate-winter bias).

Chandler, William. **Deciduous Orchards**. 3rd ed. rev. Philadelphia: Lea & Febiger, 1957. For tree crops, one of four technical references that I consult most often. Worth searching for in used book stores.

Childers, Norman. **Modern Fruit Science**. 8th ed. New Brunswick, NJ: Horticultural Publications, 1978. Poor-quality illustrations greatly hamper this book. A good one to browse in the library; only serious tree crops enthusiasts need own it.

Smith, J. Russell. **Tree Crops**. Rev. ed. Old Greenwich, CT: Devin-Adair, 1977. Smith was the first to take a radical view of tree crops in agriculture, and was my original inspiraton to experiment with polycultures of tree crops. His cultural examples are fascinating, but inappropriate for suburban settings, since they rely on animals to graze the fruits and nuts, and on people to eat the animals. Smith's idea that tree crops have deep taproots which give them a competitive advantage is in error.

GROWING TREE CROPS
Planting Trees

TO AMEND OR NOT TO AMEND

There are three types of amendments—those that improve soil fertility, those that improve soil drainage, and those that promote both. A time-honored recommendation has been to add many amendments—compost, well-aged horse manure, peat moss, composted sawdust, sand, even vermiculite—to the planting hole. Many authors and gardeners offer sure-fire results with their amendment techniques, but not many of those suggestions have been scientifically tested. Fortunately, some comparative research has been done. In several studies, from 1968 to present, trees planted without amendments fared better in terms of new shoot growth and the extension of the developing root system. One of the best-known studies was "Effects of Soil Amendments and Fertilizer Levels on the Establishment of Silver Maple," by Joseph Schultz and Carl Whitcomb. Because it contradicted the common guidelines for amendments, the report caused quite a stir, but a close look at this study will reveal that the sparing use of amendments is necessary in certain cases, mainly to improve fertility and drainage in clay soils. Let me explain why.

Amendments for Drainage

Heavy clay soils are especially difficult for certain fruit trees—almond, avocado, cherry, citrus, nectarine, peach, persimmon, and walnut. Compared to ideal soil, clay soils breathe more slowly (are less aerobic), drain more slowly, and waterlog more easily—all problems that stunt, or even kill, trees. Rather than forgo planting trees, most gardeners try to improve the drainage with amendments. With sandy soils, which have too much drainage and require frequent watering and fertilization, gardeners frequently add amendments that hold moisture and nutrients.

The Dangers of Amendments for Drainage

The amendments used in the Schultz and Whitcomb study were inert—peat moss; untreated, shredded pine bark; sand; and vermiculite. All were added to improve the soil's drainage, not its fertility. The inert amendments did not encourage

much growth. The maples with the greatest percentage of soil amendments (40 percent), especially pine bark, showed the least amount of new shoot growth. The nutritionally worthless amendments simply displaced nutrients that would have been in the native soil. Thus, the unamended trees produced more shoot growth.

A big difference between the texture of the amended soil in the planting hole and the uncultivated native soil provides a shock to the growing roots of plants. The radical transition from a loose planting mix to a heavier native soil produces what I call the "flowerpot effect"—young roots act as if they've hit the wall of a flowerpot when they reach the uncultivated soil. Often the roots stop in their tracks and begin to circle back into the planting hole. When working as a maintenance gardener, I often found mature plants that could easily be pulled from the ground, their roots a tangled, circling mess.

Unfortunately, the planting techniques used in the Whitcomb and Schultz study are typical for commercial landscaping and encourage the flowerpot effect:

Planting holes were dug 12 inches deep using a tractor mounted auger 24 inches in diameter. The soil at the existing site removed by the auger was placed in a five cubic foot cement mixer and combined with the proportionate volume of soil amendment. With check treatments, the existing soil was placed back into the planting hole with no amendments.

The action of an auger slicks the walls of the planting hole, smoothing the clay particles as if they were worked on a potter's wheel. The result resembles a clay pot in the ground. With a loose soil mix inside the augered hole, new roots will not venture into native soil. This can be partly corrected by fracturing the walls of the augered hole with a bar or pickax before refilling it. In the report, no mention is made of fracturing the slicked clay walls of the hole. Since a garden shovel can produce the same smooth-walled effect in moist, clay soil, I use a spading fork to dig the hole.

The heavier the soil, the *fewer* amendments used,

in order to avoid the flowerpot effect. Planting holes in sandy soils can accommodate more amendments than clay soils because new roots can easily make the transition from the planting hole to the uncultivated soil.

The Advantages of Amendments for Drainage

The first 6 to 12 inches of the root system is most sensitive to crown rot (*Phytophthora* sp.), also called root and collar rot. The symptoms of crown rot include sudden wilting of all leaves on the tree or on a major limb (at the same time, the leaves turn pale), death of the tree or a limb as fruit begins to size up and ripen, or the general decline of branches over several years. These symptoms are similar to those of other diseases, so for a more positive identification of crown rot, dig some soil away from the base of the tree, exposing the crown of the root system (where the major roots meet the trunk). Use a knife to scrape away a small strip of bark to reveal the tissue below. Trees infected with crown rot have brown discolored tissue where light green cambium wood should be.

Crown rot is especially harmful where high rainfall or heavy irrigation at the base of the tree is coupled with high soil temperatures and a heavy, poorly drained soil. Fruit trees particularly susceptible to crown rot are almond, avocado, cherry, citrus, nectarine, peach, persimmon, walnut, and some apples on dwarfing rootstocks.

Good drainage for the top 12 inches of the root system is essential to prevent this devastating disease. Though amended soil in the upper portion of the planting hole may help, planting on a raised mound will do a much better job of protecting your trees from crown rot.

A loose soil mix and a raised planting mound will dry out between rains or irrigations. To compensate during the first season, I use extra mulch or I water more frequently. After one year, most of the feeding roots will have grown beyond the mound and you will not need to water so frequently.

I conclude that when planting in a fairly well drained native soil, there is little justification for adding a lot of amendments for drainage. Any amendments added should be nutritious ones, such as aged compost, well-rotted manures, and decomposed straw. By avoiding inert amendments, you can both improve drainage and add nutrients for good growth.

Amendments for Fertility

Compost, aged manure, and rich topsoil are ideal amendments in sandy soil, adding both fertility and drainage. However, in heavy or clay soil, use fertilizers that don't add bulk such as phosphate, greensand, bone meal, wood ash, oyster shell flour, gypsum, kelp meal, blood meal, leather meal, and sulphate of potash. Phosphorus and potash, especially from non-chemical sources, don't leach more than several inches into soil. They must be incorporated deeply and widely to put them in direct contact with roots. Manures, blood meal, and leather meal can burn young roots and should be applied to the soil surface only in the second or third year. A heavy irrigation will leach the nitrogen into the root zone.

Too Many Amendments

Too many fertility amendments can actually *limit* the growth and production of the tree. If too much fertilizer is added to the planting hole, roots stay in amended soil and fail to explore native soil, and the tree requires much more care to be productive. Be sparing with all fertilizers: add only enough to give the young tree a boost in the first season. Since the roots of a tree extend as far as three times beyond the canopy of the tree, the root system should grow beyond the planting hole in the first year.

In Summary . . .

You SHOULD amend soil:

- When it is loose and sandy. In moderation, add high-fiber amendments that hold water and nutrients. Expect to apply additional nutrients and mulch each season, to a wider and wider area.

- When the crown of the root system needs the protection of extra drainage. Amend heavily only the raised planting area above the original soil level.

- When you are determined to grow a tree that hates heavy soil like yours. Plant high on a large raised planting area and expect to care for the tree as you would a container plant.

- When you want to localize the root system to dwarf the tree.

- When your soil is sandy and has nematodes. Add organic matter to discourage nematodes, which prefer sandy soil that is low in organic matter. (When planting a tree where the same type has grown before, when you know the soil has nematodes, and when other pathogenic organisms are present, try "solar fumigation." In summer, cover the area with clear or black plastic, weighting the edges with dirt. By summer's end, the heat-trapping plastic will have "cooked" the pests; then the plastic can be removed and the area safely planted.)

You SHOULD NOT amend soil:

- When it is heavy clay. Instead, choose root-stocks that tolerate poor drainage.

- When it is well-drained and fertile.

4

PREPARING THE HOLE, PLANTING THE TREE

Whether or not you amend the soil, careful timing is required when planting trees. Dig when the soil is mellow, just dry enough that a gentle whack on a lump of soil causes it to crumble. If you have to really work to break up the clods, the soil is too wet or too dry. Make the hole 18 to 24 inches deep and just a bit wider than the roots of the tree. Make separate piles for sod and weeds, topsoil, and subsoil. (See Fig. 13.1.) I prefer to dig a planting hole the summer before, since my garden's soil is often too wet in early spring. I completely prepare the planting hole in summer and cover it with mulch. Next spring, I need only a spading fork to open a pocket for the tree's bare roots.

Fracturing Walls

To loosen the native soil, I fracture the walls and bottom of the hole with a spading fork. In the bottom, insert the fork and rock it back and forth to slightly heave the soil. To prepare the walls, swing the fork's tines into the soil and twist. The fracturing makes it easier for roots to penetrate the native soil. Some gardeners recommend particular shapes for the hole to help prevent circling roots. I believe the shape of the planting hole doesn't matter if the walls and bottom are well-fractured.

Varmint Protection

If gophers or moles are a problem in your area, now is the time to line the hole with wire. I recommend aviary netting, which looks like chicken wire but comes in ½-inch mesh and has a heavier galvanized coating. The netting must extend 6 to 12 inches above the soil so that gophers can't sneak over the wire. Be forewarned that the aviary netting will probably rust away within two to five years. It is not permanent protection, but it gets the trees off to a safe start.

For more permanent protection of the upper portion of the root system, try broken glass. Use this approach only for perennials in *well-planned* landscapes that you do not expect to change. For safety's sake, soil with broken glass should never be tilled again. Wearing protective goggles and a dust mask, break bottles or jars inside a metal bucket or burlap sack. Be sure to crush the glass into pieces a quarter of an inch or smaller. The crushed glass is then mixed with the soil for the planting hole.

Crushed glass worked for me in a large planting where gophers were not too numerous to begin with, but it failed to protect a friend's artichokes. Perhaps the pieces were not small enough.

Refilling the Hole

Put the sod and weeds in a compost pile. If you

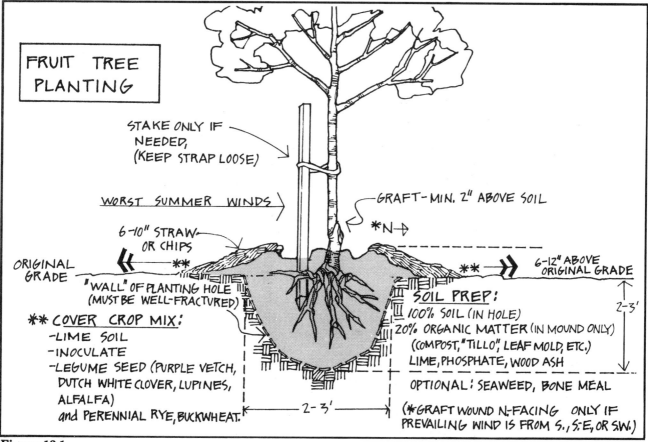

Figure 13.1

put them in the planting hole, an anaerobic condition can result that leads to the formation of methane gas, toxic to young roots. Return up to one-third of the excavated soil, mixed with small amounts of the mineral fertilizers – rock or colloidal phosphate, bone meal, oyster shell, and wood ash. I don't add compost or rotted manure until I reach the upper portion of the backfill. As mentioned in the previous chapter, the heavier the soil, the *fewer* organic matter amendments I use.

Mound for Protection

The conventional approach to planting calls for the tree to be planted at the same depth as it was grown, with the crown of the root system level with the existing soil level, and with a watering basin around the trunk. I believe this method encourages the proliferation of crown rot (*Phytophthora* sp.) which can damage or kill your new tree. The wetter your climate in spring or summer, the more vulnerable your tree. To discourage crown rot, mound soil 6 to 12 inches above the original soil surface over the entire area of the planting hole. The mound may settle as much as half its original height, but the crown of the root system will still be elevated for good drainage. The soil mixture for the mound should have a high percentage of amendments to encourage drainage. (The extra amendments will not cause a problem because most of the roots will grow down into the lower soil and not stay in the raised area.) The addition of compost, rotted horse manure, or leaf mold will help provide some of the additional volume needed to build the mound. Scrape some extra soil from nearby if more soil is required to make the mound.

When in doubt, mound higher. Too high is better than not high enough. Wood-sided planter boxes provide a good way to plant high without having to build up a wide area. The crown of the root system should be planted just below the surface of the raised soil (see Fig. 13.2). Since mounds dry out quickly, be sure to use mulch. The higher you mound soil, the deeper the water-conserving mulch should be.

The Fun Part – Planting the Tree

Bareroot trees, available only in early spring, are the cheapest and easiest to plant. They are superior to balled or container trees (which can be planted at any time of the year) because the root system is less damaged and distorted. I prefer to get the largest caliper (the trunk diameter 6 inches above the graft) unbranched tree available. This allows me to prune the whip (the single trunk, or leader) to the height I want and to force side branches where I want them. Branched trees often do not make as much new growth the first year as whips. Buying

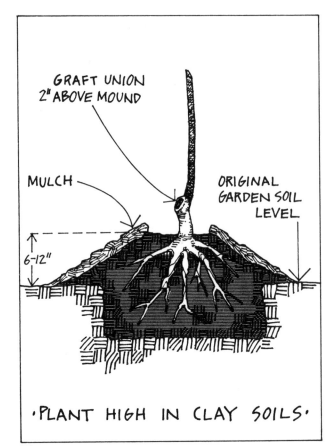

GRAFT UNION 2" ABOVE MOUND

MULCH

ORIGINAL GARDEN SOIL LEVEL

6-12"

·PLANT HIGH IN CLAY SOILS·

Figure 13.2

branched trees through the mail is risky because you don't know what the branch pattern will be like. If you are going to buy a branched tree, go to a local retail nursery and look at many trees and select the one with the branch pattern you desire.

The wholesale grower leaves a large portion of the root system behind, so don't trim the roots, except to prune off broken ones. Soak the roots in a bucket of water for 12 to 24 hours before planting, especially if you purchased a mail-order tree. If the nursery packed the tree in sawdust, rinse off any that remains.

Orienting the Graft

Before planting, be sure to consider the direction of the worst *summer* winds. Face the slightly curved portion of the graft into the wind, so that the circular cut at the graft faces away from the strongest winds (see Fig. 13.3). Recent research indicates that the orientation of the trunk may not have any particular effect on wind tolerance, but I think this precaution can't hurt. Some people recommend turning the cut to the north to shelter it from the scalding sun. Painting the trunk after

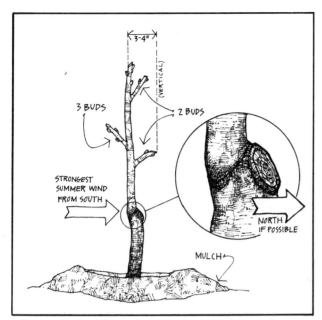

Figure 13.3 When planting a grafted tree, face the bowed area of the graft into the wind.

especially the weak-rooted M 9, M 7, and M 26 apple rootstocks, deeper than they were grown in the nursery row. While this may keep these trees from blowing over and prevent root suckers and limit burr knot problems, it should be done only in the sandiest, most well drained soils. For standard-size trees, some growers bury the graft so that the scion will root and the rootstock cannot easily send up "sucker" growth. In any case, avoid sinking the tree more than 4 inches deeper than it was grown in the nursery – planting deeper than that results in reduced growth.

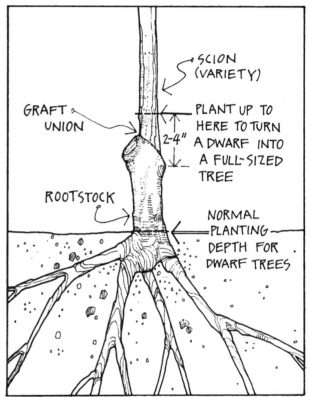

Figure 13.4 Trees with dwarfing rootstocks grow to full size if the graft is planted below the soil's surface.

planting, however, will protect the rootstock wound from sun, no matter how you orient it. In severe wind areas, plant the tree so that it leans as much as 6 inches *into* the strongest summmer winds.

After selecting the best orientation, use a spading fork to open a pocket in the mound. Place the tree so the top of the root system is just below the surface of the soil. (If you want a dwarf tree to grow to the size of a standard tree, place the graft below the surface of the soil. See Fig. 13.4 for details).

Water Thoroughly

Water the tree right after planting, using at least 5 gallons to settle the soil, and then tamp the soil with the heel of your shoe. Don't be afraid to really pack the soil – it is necessary to eliminate air pockets that will kill young root hairs. A watering basin in the shape of a doughnut, or moat, keeps water away from the base of the trunk and helps prevent crown rot, but should be used only at the time the tree is first planted. Afterwards, water the tree 18 inches or more from the trunk. I use a drip irrigation line around the base of the planting mound. The water spreads horizontally as well as vertically underground to water the new roots.

Not Too Deep

Some people advise planting dwarf rootstocks,

Staking a Tree

Stake trees only in particularly windy spots. The sturdiest trees are those that were not staked in their youth. Staking can make a tree taller and more wind vulnerable because of its thinner, weaker trunk and smaller root system. The trunk needs to bend with the wind in order to develop girth and toughness. (Weak-rooted trees like dwarf apples on M 9, M 26, and M 27 rootstocks, however, need staking their entire lives.)

Most bareroot trees do not need to be staked. If a bareroot tree is tall and spindly, cut it back close to the ground. Later, select the tallest and most vigorous shoot and prune the rest. Often the shoot grows nearly as tall as the unpruned tree would have. The pruned and unstaked tree develops a thicker trunk and better resistance to the wind.

Where winds are particularly strong, staking may be required for the first year or two. Here are some important guidelines.

- **Don't tie a tree tightly to a stake.** A tree must flex in the wind. A stake is meant just to prevent the tree from toppling.

- **The stake should be 6 to 12 inches from the trunk.** Tie the tree to the stake with a figure-8 loop around tree and stake. Use a length of old hose, or use the strips of tire tread sold as tree ties and a piece of wire on each end to fasten to the stake.

- **Tie low.** Each tree has a stiff lower portion and more limber wood higher up. To find the transition, grab the bottom of the trunk and shake the tree. The limber portion will show a different wavelength than the stiff portion. (With a container tree that has been staked all its life, the top often flops over when the stake is removed.) Put the tie 6 inches above the point where the trunk begins to flex the most.

Painting the Trunk

Now it's time to paint the trunk to prevent sunscald and borer damage. Trees grown for wholesale spend two or more years in crowded rows, perhaps only 12 to 24 inches apart. The foliage shades most of the trunk during that time, so the young bark is tender. When those trees are planted, the tender trunk often becomes sunscalded on the south or west sides. Once the tissue has been damaged, it may not callus over, and may attract borers; this is especially true of peach and nectarine trees.

To prevent sunscalding, coat the trunk with white interior or exterior latex paint diluted half-and-half with water. If white seems too harsh in your landscape, you can tint the paint a subtle pastel. Don't use oil-based paints, since they contain chemicals that can harm the bark. Paint the entire trunk to the second branch. Don't paint over buds that have begun to open. Pull the soil away from the base of the tree so you can paint an inch or so below the soil line—in case wind, water, or settling soil should expose that part of the trunk—and replace the soil after the paint dries. Painting below the soil line is very important because borers prefer entering damaged wood at the soil line and most sunscalding occurs at the base of the tree.

Details

In windy areas, young trees have a tendency to "walk around" in the planting hole, opening a funnel-shaped gap around the trunk in the top few inches of the soil, which prevents root hairs and roots from growing. The gap makes it difficult for the tree to develop good anchorage, especially when the rootstock or trees started as a cutting—as do Marianna 2624, Citation, quince rootstocks and trees, pomegranate trees, and fig trees. Check your trees for "walking" every few weeks after planting. Use your heel to repack the soil against the trunk. Adjust the tree tie, if necessary. Robert Woolley, of Dave Wilson Nursery, suggests heaping sand around the base of each tree. The sand works its way into the crevice automatically if the trunk walks around. (See Fig. 13.5.) His labor-saving trick also helps prevent crown rot and rodent damage.

Plastic tubes cut in a spiral along their length are often used to wrap the first several feet of the trunk. (See Appendix 8 for suppliers.) Aluminum screening is another inexpensive way to wrap the trunk. Both are good preventive measures against nibbling rabbits and mice. Be sure to bury several inches of the tube or wire to protect the base of the tree. Pea gravel around the top several inches of the root system and in a small pile above ground also discourages mice. Avoid crushed rock gravel—its sharp edges can cut a tree's bark. Another mouse deterrent is to keep the area around the trunk free of weeds, with no mulch directly against the trunk.

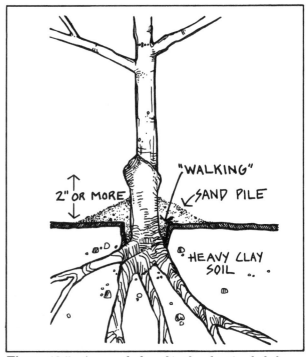

Figure 13.5 A mound of sand in the planting hole keeps the young tree from "walking around."

Keep a Map

Tag the tree with a permanent metal marker; fasten the label loosely, or the tree will girdle itself on the wire. After several years, switch to a longer wire, or fasten the label to a stake.

Make a scale drawing and mark the location of each tree, its name, rootstock, supplier, and date planted. I learned this lesson the hard way. After I planted dozens of trees, several months passed before I got around to making a map. By then, the sun had bleached the special "fade-resistant" ink on the plastic tree tags! I had to wait for each tree to come into bearing to double-check the name.

Baker, Harry. **Fruit (The Simon & Schuster Step-by-Step Encyclopedia of Practical Gardening)**. New York: Simon & Schuster, 1980. One of my favorite recommendations for beginning and experienced gardeners who want a graphic review of the basics of fruit and nut culture. Based on the expertise of England's avid gardeners, yet usually appropriate to most U.S. climates. (Cold-region landscapers beware of Baker's temperate-winter bias).

Chandler, William. **Deciduous Orchards**. 3rd ed. rev. Philadelphia: Lea & Febiger, 1957. For tree crops, one of four technical references that I consult most often. Worth searching for in used book stores.

Childers, Norman. **Modern Fruit Science**. 8th ed. New Brunswick, NJ: Horticultural Publications, 1978. Poor-quality illustrations greatly hamper this book. A good one to browse in the library; only serious tree crops enthusiasts need own it.

Hills, Lawrence D. **Grow Your Own Fruit and Vegetables**. Rev. ed. Thetford, England: Faber & Faber, 1979. An English manual with an organic bias that is better than most American books on organic gardening.

Stebbins, Robert, and Walheim, Lance. **Western Fruits, Berries and Nuts**. Tucson, AZ: HPBooks, 1981. The best reference on these subjects, and the one I use the most. Complete with brilliant, condensed, easy-to-use charts. Excellent color photographs. HPBooks also publishes an equally excellent East Coast version, *How to Grow Fruits, Berries and Nuts in the Midwest and East*, by Theodore James, Jr., 1983.

4 GROWING TREE CROPS
Pruning Fruit and Nut Trees

THE BASICS OF TREE GROWTH AND PRUNING

Gardeners tend to have extreme reactions to the task of pruning: they either hesitate and never prune, or they prune with carefree abandon. Happily, there is a wide range of pruning styles—from near neglect to highly meticulous espalier training—to suit almost any gardener. But no single style is best for all trees. While styles that demand skill, patience, and plenty of time can produce high yields, they may not be suited to the gardener's temperament or schedule. Styles that are less productive are usually simpler and less time consuming. This section details the benefits and limitations of several styles, so you can choose the best one for the tree's health and productivity as well as for your time and personality.

Over the years, teaching pruning, I have found that explaining how a tree fruits is more helpful for beginners than theoretical drawings, and it provides the insight needed to approach almost any fruit tree with confidence. Let's look at the basics of tree growth and how pruning takes advantage of and moderates the natural growth habits of trees. Finally, we'll examine several pruning techniques appropriate for most kinds of trees.

Terminal Buds

The terminal bud (sometimes called the apical bud), found at the tip of a branch, or shoot, is responsible for the lengthening of a branch. The more vertical the branch, the more growth its terminal bud stimulates, giving the branch a leggy look because of the long distances between each leaf. The terminal bud sends a hormone down the branch to discourage lower buds from growing into shoots. Leaving terminal buds uncut favors the extension of the branch and inhibits the formation and growth of side branches (laterals).

Dormant Buds

Below the terminal bud, on the current season's growth, each leaf has a small bud tucked between the stem and the branch. These are dormant buds—young and undeveloped. They remain dormant at the command of a hormone sent by the terminal bud. Dormant buds may produce either fruit or branches, and pruning can help the buds to "make up their minds." For example, cutting out the terminal bud causes some dormant buds to sprout into branch growth (because the stifling hormone from the top of the branch has been removed). Dormant buds need adequate sunlight to survive. If light levels are too low (below 30 percent of full sunlight), the bud withers (and is then called a trace bud). Trace buds leave tiny scars on barren portions of a limb and represent wasted opportunities.

Flower, or Fruit, Buds

Some dormant buds turn fruitful, prompted by their location, the position of their branch, hormones, and the storage of carbohydrates. They become robust, stubby buds, appearing to the experienced eye more fleshy, or fattened, than other buds, thanks to their having stored more carbohydrates than other buds. (See Figs. 14.1 and 14.2.) If the sunlight reaching the leaves attached to the flower bud is inadequate, the bud will wither and die. On an older branch, a new fruit bud rarely regrows where one has died.

Flower Buds Grow into Spurs

On certain types of trees, flower buds grow in

Figure 14.1 A young apple flower bud.

clusters called fruit spurs. Fruiting occurs for many years at these stubby, twig-like projections. Only one flower bud on a spur produces fruit each season. The other buds store up food to flower and fruit in subsequent years.

Spur-type trees include the apple, pear, Asian pear, cherry, plum, apricot, and almond. (The spurs on cherry, plum, and prune trees are the least pronounced—they are unbranched, with a whorl of many fat flower buds.) The life span of a fruiting spur varies from up to 20 years for apples, 5 years or more for cherry and pear trees, up to 5 years for almond and plum trees, and only 3 to 4 years for apricots.

Peach and nectarine trees fruit only on one-year-old branches with distinctive triple buds—two fat flower buds on either side of a leaf bud. These branches are often called hangers because they droop with the weight of the crop.

Figure 14.2 A peach flower bud. The buds of a nectarine tree look the same.

Beyond Buds: Branches for Strength . . .

A well-shaped tree has a full, but not crowded, canopy and branches strong enough to support the weight of each year's crop. The major limbs need sturdy attachments to the trunk. The wider the angle between trunk and branch, the smoother and therefore stronger the tissue where they join (see Fig. 14.3). Though a 90° angle has great strength, it tends to make an unproductive branch. Most of the dormant buds along a horizontal branch grow as a thicket of leafy, vertical shoots that fail to produce much fruit. Between these two extremes lies a healthy, fruitful compromise.

. . . and Fruit

Branches at an angle of 45° to 60° are the best behaved and most productive. In this range is the

welcome balance between strength and vigor. The terminal bud has limited influence: a reasonable amount of tip growth occurs, some dormant buds produce laterals, and an adequate number of dormant buds become flower buds.

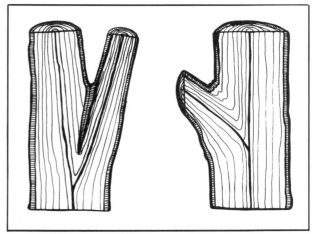

Figure 14.3 A narrow-angled fork forms a fissure that weakens its attachment to the trunk. A fork angle of 45° to 90° is much stronger.

How Limbs Prune Themselves

If you study an apple tree that has been spared from the clippers, you will notice two characteristics of the branches. Some reach toward the sky, straight and lean. Older branches weep low to the ground and are laden with small fruits. Vertical sprouts eventually bend down under their own weight and that of whatever fruit happens to form. Then an exciting thing happens. Just past the peak of the arch (see Figs. 14.4 and 14.5), many dormant buds turn into flower buds or short laterals with flower buds on the end. In zone A, more fruit spurs than branches form. And because the terminal bud loses influence in a downward position, the branch tip's rate of growth is greatly reduced.

Once fruit spurs form, the increasing weight of each season's crop soon bends the branch below horizontal, forming a weeping branch. Yields increase each year because more food from the leaves is stored in the spurs. In zone A, where most buds become fruit spurs, no new branches are formed to compete.

At the top of the arch, the buds grow into vigorous vertical limbs. The first bud to sprout quickly gains dominance over the others. It shoots upward more rapidly, getting long and leggy. With time it, too, arches down and becomes fruitful.

In a season, weeping branches grow only a few inches, while vertical shoots may gain more than 2 feet. In effect, the tree prunes itself to be more fruitful. Its shape, however, is considered unusual by some gardeners.

Figure 14.4 Section "A" is the most fruitful part of an arched limb.

Figure 14.5 A wild willow shows how the most vertical growth occurs near the peak of an arched limb.

Positioning Limbs for Fruiting

In edible landscapes, we shape fruit trees for good looks and for fruitfulness. Nature doesn't always cooperate when forming branches—sometimes you must redo them in a more fruitful position.

First, bend or tie fast-growing, vertical shoots to a 45° to 60° angle during the summer to mimic the weeping effect, or to open narrow forks to a wider angle for strong attachment. Don't worry about measuring the precise angle of the fork—use the simple "rule of finger." Slip your index finger into the fork. If you can see light below your finger—if it doesn't nestle snugly into the fork—spread the branch for strength and for fruit.

As with good comedy, the secret to spreading branches is in the timing—not too soon, not too late. Early in the season, new growth is too small. In late summer, new growth will be too stiff to bend easily. Near midsummer works best for my trees. In late spring, I walk leisurely from tree to tree, checking the new growth for size and limberness. Near midsummer (the date varies from year to year because of the weather) the new growth will be almost as thick as a pencil and a little bit stiff near the base. Then it's time for spreading branches.

Branch Spreaders

There are three ways to spread young branches. The first technique uses sticks made from pieces of lath ⅜ inch by 1½ inches or stakes 1 inch by 1 inch. Cut a V in both ends of the stick. Make the notch at least ¾ inch deep and the wide part of the V as wide as the stick. Make a supply of spreaders from 6 to 36 inches long. Cut a number of each length; then stack them together and notch the ends of the entire pile at once.

Place the spreaders between the trunk and narrow-angled branches to spread them to the desired angle. The spreaders slip unless they are wedged against a small branch or spur on both ends.

A spring-type clothespin makes another good branch spreader, and it stays put in the tree during high winds. Clip the clothespin to the stem, just above a fork. Position the other end above the shoot, forcing it down. (See Fig. 14.6.) Do the spreading before midsummer or the branches will be too stiff to train. The shoot will gradually turn upward, but its attachment will be strong, and the branch will fruit as if it were at a 45° to 60° angle.

My favorite method of spreading branches leaves my fruit trees full of toothpicks. (See Fig. 14.7.) I like to tell people they just grew there or that I'm growing instant hors d'oeuvres. I use toothpicks to spread supple, young shoots before midsummer. (Make sure to use round, hardwood toothpicks.) Insert one point in the shoot, 2 to 4 inches from the fork. If you press too hard, the toothpick will drill through the shoot and you will need to start over. Hold the toothpick in place with one hand; with the other hand, bend the shoot downward a little past the desired position. Insert the other point securely in the bark of the trunk. Release the shoot, and you're finished.

My first attempt at training branches with toothpicks resulted in only 3 failed tries out of 80.

The entire process took less than 30 minutes, and the young trees are proving to be heavy bearers. (There is a metal version of the toothpick spreader for older branches, a sturdy rod with naillike tips.) Use toothpicks or metal spreaders gently, since the sharp points make holes that can be a port of entry for disease.

These techniques are poorly suited to stiff, older branches. For them, use twine or rope to tie the limbs to stakes in the ground. Or for a more ornamental approach, try weighting stiff branches with ceramic or metal sculptures, planters, or birdfeeders.

Notching Reveals the Flow of Hormones and Carbohydrates

Any branch, regardless of its position on the tree, can be shaped or made more fruitful by notching, an age-old technique developed in Europe for intensive, espalier fruit culture. If you notch below dormant buds, many of them will grow into flower buds. The notch interrupts the flow of carbohydrates from the leaf to the rest of the tree. What the leaf produces then goes to nourish the bud, and the extra boost of carbohydrates predisposes it to be a flower bud. If you notch above dormant buds, many of the buds will sprout into shoots. The notch cuts off the stifling hormonal influence of the terminal bud, freeing the dormant bud to grow. (See Fig. 14.8.)

Figure 14.7 Toothpicks make fast, inexpensive branch spreaders.

Figure 14.6 Clothespins spread young branches to a stronger, more fruitful position.

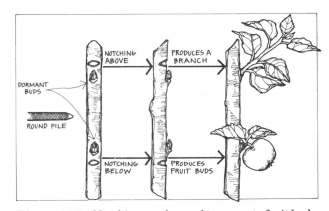

Figure 14.8 Notching can be used to promote fruit buds or branches.

You must be careful when notching. Make sure the cut is wide, but not deep, and that it arcs halfway around the branch close to the bud. You are making a scratch, not firewood—you need to go only as deep as the phloem and xylem, thin layers of cells which lie less than a millimeter below the surface of the bark. Emil Linquist, a lifelong fruit-tree enthusiast, has developed an effective technique. He uses a ⅛-inch round (rattail) file. With a single long stroke, the way one draws a bow on a fiddle, Emil scores a wide, shallow notch halfway around the shoot. A brush quickly cleans the file of clogging particles.

Timing is important. Emil recommends notching in late winter on last year's wood, before any leaves bud. However, in the spring, a callus of healing cells can easily leap a narrow notch and the effect will be lost. Therefore, make the notch as wide as possible, or wait until late spring or early summer, when notches made on the current season's growth take longer to heal over. The notch in Fig. 14.9 was made in late spring; by late summer, the young bud had become a flower bud.

Experiment to see what works best for you. Notch at different times, above and below buds, marking your trials with green plastic garden tape. Check later to see which notches worked, and look for any signs of disease (as with any pruning cut or wound). Used sparingly, notching is an easy way to shape a tree without using clippers.

Figure 14.9 The arrow points to the callus that has formed around a notch. The bud above the notch (at the base of the stem) is turning into a flower bud.

Basic Guidelines for Pruning

Before you choose a style of pruning, there are a number of considerations to take into account.

Here are the major ones.

All trees are not equal. Two 'Golden Delicious' apple trees growing side by side in different soils may have noticeably different growth and fruiting habits. And the growth of the 'Red Rome' is very different from that of the 'Golden Delicious.' The experienced pruner avoids forcing a single style on every tree, and, instead, combines a variety of techniques to suit the needs of each tree.

Prune for shape. Visualize the form you desire. Beauty is as important as productivity for fruit trees in an edible landscape. Make as few cuts as possible to achieve the effect you desire.

Pruning delays fruiting. Pruning early in the life of a tree, and removing substantial amounts of wood, delays the start of fruiting. Unpruned trees tend to bear a few seasons earlier than heavily pruned ones.

Dormant-season pruning promotes growth. Pruning deciduous trees when they are dormant encourages leafy, vegetative growth, not flower buds. Winter pruning causes new branches to form and stimulates the rapid extension of branch growth.

Summer pruning stunts growth. Removing foliage during the time of active photosynthesis reduces the tree's vigor and advances the formation of fruit buds on all sizes of trees. Summer pruning is an important part of caring for dwarf fruit trees. It also opens up the tree's canopy, letting in sunshine, which encourages fruit bud formation and keeps spurs healthy. However, summer pruning sometimes causes succulent new growth which is vulnerable to damage from winter freezes.

Pruning Rules of Thumb

There are also standard, age-old rules to remember, regardless of the pruning style you choose.

Remove dead and diseased wood. With any tree, the first order of business is the removal of dead and diseased wood. Pests and diseases enter damaged wood, then spread into the heart of the tree. Catch diseased wood early through periodic inspection. Prune it out, and to prevent the spread of spores and insects in your landscape, take it to a dump.

Remove crossing wood. The constant rubbing of two crossed branches leaves a raw, unhealed wound, another possible entry for pests and diseases. Remove one of the rubbing branches. Crossing branches that don't rub still crowd each other. Remove one and allow the other to receive more sunlight.

Remove weak wood. With standard-size trees,

pruning all but the most vigorous wood is important to a long-lived tree. Still, weak growth is not always bad. Within limits, leaving less-vigorous branches on dwarf trees is a technique preferred by some horticulturists, since it furthers the dwarfing effect.

Remove suckers. Some trees produce tall, spindly shoots that head straight to the sky and form scant fruit. These shoots are often called suckers, or water sprouts. Those that originate from the base of the tree are sprouts from the rootstock. Shoots higher up dominate and shade the lower portion of the tree. Cut out suckers in mid- to late summer to avoid stimulating additional spindly growth.

Avoid spreading disease. Pruning shears can pick up and spread certain diseases, among them fire blight *(Erwinia amylovora)*, bacterial canker *(Pseudomonas syringae)*, and viruses. To disinfect them, dip your shears in a 10 percent solution of laundry bleach or 100 percent alcohol after each cut. (It helps to oil the shears beforehand because the bleach corrodes the metal, especially aluminum. After you are done pruning and dipping, rub steel wool on all metal surfaces, sharpen the cutting edge, and oil all metal thoroughly.) As a cau-

tionary measure, you can spray a Bordeaux solution on large cuts; this will help prevent the entry of bacterial and fungal diseases, but not of viruses.

Where to Remove a Branch — Pruning Another Myth

Dr. Alex Shigo, a research pathologist for the USDA Forest Service in New Hampshire, studied the effect of various pruning cuts made on walnut trees 12 years earlier. He found that to have a fast-healing cut, it is vital to leave the branch collar intact (see Fig. 14.10). Within the branch collar lies a protective chemical zone. While the wound heals, the exposed wood is sealed by rot-resistant compounds in the zone, thus discouraging damage to the interior of the tree. Cuts made flush with the trunk remove portions of this protective zone, and the callus often fails to seal over the entire area exposed by the cut. Consequently, infection, spores, and water can work their way into the heartwood, weakening the entire tree. The proper cut leaves a slight stub.

Imagine a plumb line hanging from Point A. The angle formed from the bark ring to the plumb line should be transposed to the other side of the plumb line. This gives you the cut line (see line A-B). Cut

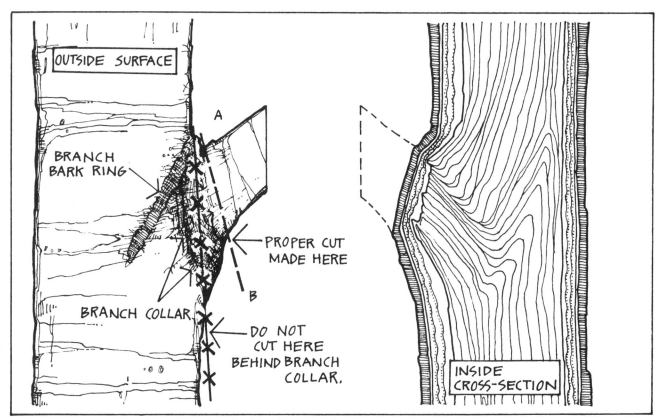

Figure 14.10 Prune at line A – B for a healthy, fast-callusing cut.

no farther from the branch collar than necessary; you don't want to leave unnecessary wood to rot and harbor pestilence.

The branch collar is more noticeable in some trees, such as oaks. The smaller the branch, the less noticeable the branch collar. When young wood is pruned with hand clippers, the well-placed cut appears flush, when in fact the tiny collar is still intact.

Figures 14.11 through 14.13 show how an untended oak "prunes" itself. In time, a dead limb breaks off at the branch collar area and the callus covers the wound completely. Inside the tree, the protective zone seals off the dead wood.

To Tar or Not to Tar

Gardeners are often convinced they must cover pruning cuts with a so-called wound dressing. Dr. Shigo studied pruning tars and found that the proper pruning cut was the most important way to promote rapid healing of pruning wounds. Tars are unnecessary on correctly made cuts and useless in protecting an improper cut. Shigo recommends painting the wound only for cosmetic reasons.

I've observed that wound dressings begin to crack and bubble after only one season, providing favorable conditions for the entry of small insects and decay spores. I much prefer to leave pruning cuts uncoated — and it's a welcome relief to do away with the sticky mess.

Though wound dressings are generally unnecessary, some commercial growers recommend Farwell's Tree-Doc™, sometimes called Seal and Heal, as a cover for tree grafts. Some grafts show better callusing with this compound. (It used to be called Red, Yellow, or Green Cap, depending on the color of the compound.) It is water soluble until it dries to a very elastic polymer.

Figure 14.11 While a dead oak limb slowly decays, protective chemicals inside the branch collar keep disease from entering the trunk.

Figure 14.12 A dead oak limb has fallen, but the callus has not yet healed over.

Figure 14.13 An oak tree's fully healed callus.

Baker, Harry. **Fruit (The Simon & Schuster Step-by-Step Encyclopedia of Practical Gardening)**. New York: Simon & Schuster, 1980. One of my favorite recommendations for beginning and experienced gardeners who want a graphic review of the basics of fruit and nut culture. Based on the expertise of England's avid gardeners, yet usually appropriate to most U.S. climates. (Cold-region landscapers beware of Baker's temperate-winter bias).

Chandler, William. **Deciduous Orchards**. 3rd ed. rev. Philadelphia: Lea & Febiger, 1957. For tree crops, one of four technical references that I consult most often. Worth searching for in used book stores.

Childers, Norman. **Modern Fruit Science**. 8th ed. New Brunswick, NJ: Horticultural Publications, 1978. Poor-quality illustrations greatly hamper this book. A good one to browse in the library; only serious tree crops enthusiasts need own it.

Jaynes, Richard, ed. **Nut Tree Culture in North America**. Hamden, CT: Northern Nut Growers Association, 1979. The most helpful and thorough book on the subject. (The Association publishes a quarterly journal with the latest news on nut growing.)

Stebbins, Robert, and MacCaskey, Michael. **Pruning: How To Guide for Gardeners**. Tucson, AZ: HPBooks, 1983. After Brickell's *Pruning*, this is a favorite of mine. Excellent for both ornamental and edible trees. The only pruning book that lists apple tree varieties by their fruiting type (spur, non-spur, spreading, and tip bearers). Gives specific recommendations for each type. Very detailed, and well-suited to U.S. climates.

Stebbins, Robert, and Walheim, Lance. **Western Fruits, Berries and Nuts**. Tucson, AZ: HPBooks, 1981. The best reference on these subjects, and the one I use the most. Complete with brilliant, condensed, easy-to-use charts. Excellent color photographs. HPBooks also publishes an equally excellent East Coast version, *How to Grow Fruits, Berries and Nuts in the Midwest and East*, by Theodore James, Jr., 1983.

THE NO-PRUNING STYLE

I have found that four pruning styles fit most situations. I'll begin with the least laborious and end with the most involved and productive style. There is much more to be said about them and about other styles than I have room for here. You can learn additional information from the books listed at the end of this section.

Not pruning is an often-overlooked approach. It can be productive – wild or abandoned trees often bear abundantly. Not pruning is for the busy or lazy gardener. It has one large drawback – unpruned trees lack classic ornamental looks.

Terminal-Bearing and Spur-Type Trees

In *The One-Straw Revolution*, Masanobu Fukuoka (famous for his method of farming without tillage or chemicals) simply states, "The trees will bear fruit every year and there is no need to prune." He is growing citrus, all of which are terminal-bearing trees. (Trees that bear terminally include quince, walnut, cane fruits, chestnut, persimmon, mulberry, fig, pomegranate, loquat, olive, and various subtropical fruits.) In general, the terminal-bearing fruits are the easiest to grow without pruning. Flowers usually form only on new growth, at the very end of a shoot. Thus, if adequate new growth occurs throughout the canopy each season, there is sufficient fruit. (Interestingly, terminal-bearing trees are good candidates for informal espalier training because new growth fruits even after severe pruning.)

Unpruned spur-type trees, such as apples and pears, produce less fruit of marketable quality than unpruned citrus. The important word here is *marketable*. Often, unpruned trees outproduce pruned trees in pounds of fruit, but the fruit is smaller and not as evenly colored as consumers desire. This is a problem for commercial growers, but not as great a hindrance for the home gardener, especially if the fruit will be made into cider.

Advantages and Disadvantages of Not Pruning

- **High yields.** Studies have shown that the yields of unpruned trees, in total pounds, are often higher than yields for pruned trees. Research by Utah State Agricultural Extension showed that during the first five years of production, the heaviest crops were on unpruned trees. (This sort of fruitfulness occurs only when the tree has sufficient water and soil fertility to sustain healthy growth.) Figure 14.14 shows similar results for trees studied in England.

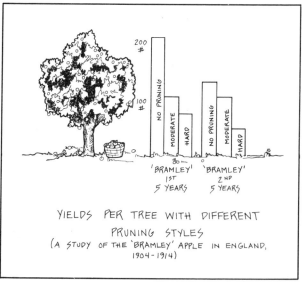

Figure 14.14 Unpruned trees often produce more total pounds of fruit than pruned trees.

- **Better flavor.** Since unpruned trees are not usually irrigated, their fruit is tastier than the fruit of well-watered trees; the juices have not been diluted with extra water.

- **Less work.** Enough said.

- **Less fruit near the ground, within reach.** The majority of an older unpruned tree canopy is fruitless. Of the mushroom-shaped thicket of foliage, only a fraction of the outer layer bears fruit. The dense shade of the interior withers fruit spurs. The older the tree, the higher and farther out of reach are its fruits.

- **Unevenly colored skin.** Because of the dense canopy, fruits lack an even blush. This is of no real concern to home gardeners, but it would be a problem for commercial growers.

- **Smaller fruit.** Usually, the fruits on unpruned trees are much smaller than those in the supermarket. If size is of any concern, it is important to thin the young fruits. Peaches and nectarines are particularly inclined to make tiny fruits unless pruned and thinned.

- **Alternate bearing.** Some trees, apples in particular, are prone to bearing heavy crops one year and light crops the next. Not pruning exaggerates this tendency – some trees bear no fruit on alternate years. Apple varieties with an alternate-bearing tendency include 'Yellow Transparent,' 'Golden Delicious,' 'Wealthy,' 'Baldwin,' 'Yellow Newtown,' 'Pippin,' and 'Black Twig.' Apples that bear more consistent crops are the

THE NO-PRUNING STYLE

'Gravenstein,' 'McIntosh,' 'Cortland,' 'Jonathan,' 'Mutsu,' 'Rome Beauty,' and 'Granny Smith.' Thinning young fruits during the heavy crop years helps unpruned trees bear fruit the next season and lessens the tendency for alternate bearing.

- **For use on the edges.** Because unpruned fruit trees are not ornamental in the traditional sense, they are best suited to less-visible areas, for example, the protected side of windbreaks and hedgerows.

- **Broken limbs.** The weight of the crop, each year farther from the trunk, can tear older limbs right off the tree. By making a few cuts at planting time, however, you can ensure that the main branches (known as the primary scaffold) have a strong attachment to the trunk. After this initial pruning for a strong primary scaffold, you can leave the tree unpruned.

Baker, Harry. **Fruit (The Simon & Schuster Step-by-Step Encylopedia of Practical Gardening)**. New York: Simon & Schuster, 1980. One of my favorite recommendations for beginning and experienced gardeners who want a graphic review of the basics of fruit and nut culture. Based on the expertise of England's avid gardeners, yet usually appropriate to most U.S. climates. (Cold-region landscapers beware of Baker's temperate-winter bias).

Chandler William. **Deciduous Orchards**. 3rd ed. rev. Philadelphia: Lea & Febiger, 1957. For tree crops, one of four technical references that I consult most often. Worth searching for in used book stores.

Childers, Norman. **Modern Fruit Science**. 8th ed. New Brunswick, NJ: Horticultural Publications, 1978. Poor-quality illustrations greatly hamper this book. A good one to browse in the library; only serious tree crops enthusiasts need own it.

Jaynes, Richard, ed. **Nut Tree Culture in North America**. Hamden, CT: Northern Nut Growers Association, 1979. The most helpful and thorough book on the subject. (The Association publishes a quarterly journal with the latest news on nut growing.)

OPEN CENTER PRUNING

At the cost of a little pruning, you can gain larger fruits and a stronger tree. Let's look at a style described in many pruning books, known as "open center" or "vase" pruning, where the trunk, or central leader, is cut out entirely when the tree is young to open up the center of the tree. Recommended for standard-size trees, open center pruning limits the tree's height while spreading the branches more to the side, allowing more light into the middle of the tree for improved yields. The open center method is especially useful with the stone fruit trees—almond, apricot, cherry, peach, plum, prune, and nectarine.

Pruning and Training the Open Center Tree

If the bareroot tree comes from the nursery as a single stem (or "whip"), simply cut it back to about 24 inches above the ground when you plant. Dormant buds below the cut will grow into vigorous branches. Before you make the cut, check for healthy buds below. Sometimes the buds have been damaged or removed by rough handling. In such cases, cut the whip above the first set of healthy buds. From the buds that open, three to five shoots are selected to be the primary scaffold. Remove unwanted branches by rubbing them off early in the summer or by pruning them late in the summer.

If the tree you purchased has branches, cut all branches back to two or three healthy buds—in some cases, the stubs will be only 3 or 4 inches long. Select wide-angled limbs to start an open-centered canopy.

For the next several years during winter pruning, keep only a few of the previous season's branches for the primary scaffold. Whenever possible, cut back to shoots that originate from the lower side of a branch (see Fig. 14.15). This promotes spreading. The goal is a pattern of branches opening away from the tree, as in Fig. 14.16. The tree should have more width than height, with a wide top and an open center, which allows more sunlight throughout the interior than in unpruned trees.

Fatal Flaw

Careless open center training encourages weak branch attachments, with the result that older trees split down the middle when laden with fruit. Though splitting can be prevented by propping branches, the work is tedious and the props are unattractive. Pay attention to the spacing of young primary branches. Often, the primary scaffold branches are too close together along the

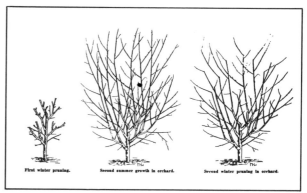

Figure 14.15 A peach tree with most branches cut back to an underside bud or branch. (Figures 14.15 through 14.19 are from *California Fruits* by Edward Wickson.)

Figure 14.16 The spreading main branches of an open center tree. All branches start from nearly the same height on the trunk.

length and around the circumference of the trunk. After a few seasons, they grow together (see Fig. 14.17), and the crowding causes the sort of weakness found in a narrow-angled fork.

Delayed Open Center Pruning

Delaying the pruning of the trunk makes open center trees sturdy and long lived (see Figs. 14.18 and 14.19). Notice that the central leader is unpruned for the first several years. At planting, you head back the tree to the same height (24 inches) as

Figure 14.17 With a plum or cherry tree, the open center style can create too many narrow-angled forks starting from the same point, which makes a weak primary scaffold.

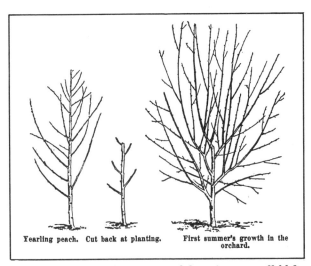

Yearling peach. Cut back at planting. First summer's growth in the orchard.

Figure 14.18 Early training of the primary scaffold for the delayed open center style.

you would for the usual open center method. Instead of removing all but three to five wide-angled branches, make sure to leave one sprout that grows up the middle. Sometimes you must tie a shoot to a stake to train it upward. Only one to three side branches are selected at first.

During the following winter, cut off half of the leader's growth from the previous season. More sprouts will appear. Select one or two. Make sure no branch is directly above, below, or across from another primary scaffold branch. Rub off or prune out any competing growth during the summer. During the next winter and summer, repeat the same reduction of the leader and selection of scaffold branches. Late in the third summer, remove the central leader for good, just above the highest primary scaffold branch.

This three-year program allows for the formation of primary scaffold branches that are well-spaced along a considerable length of the trunk and evenly distributed around its circumference. Note how the older tree in Fig. 14.19 fits Wickson's prescription:

A vastly stronger tree is secured by starting but four to five branches from the low trunk and letting them emerge from different sides of the stem [trunk], and at different levels . . . there is a succession of branchings, turned this way or that by the skillful pruner, occupying available air space, distributing the weight . . . and at the same time, knitting the fibers of the branch so that the weight of the fruit is well-sustained.

Figure 14.19 The sturdy trunk and primary scaffold of a mature delayed open center tree.

Figure 14.20 More than a century old, this pear tree's primary scaffold was trained in the delayed open center style.

Figure 14.20 shows a 90-year-old pear tree at the Farallones Institute Rural Center that was originally trained in the delayed open center fashion. This sturdy tree has produced more than 500 pounds of fruit in one year.

Living Guy Wires

There is another way to ensure the strength of an open center tree: using a support that gets stronger with age. Two young limbs tied together across the middle of the tree can form a living guy wire. In Europe, the method is called pleaching.

During midsummer, take two supple sprouts from opposite branches and twist them together. Scoring the bark on each sprout and matching the wounds will speed their union. Tie the twisted branches together near their terminal buds. After several seasons, the sprouts will grow together as if grafted. Once they have, remove the tie. Pleached branches get stronger with age. Figures 14.21 and 14.22 show some of these living guy wires on 50-year-old apple trees near my home.

Continuing Care for Open Center Trees

Maintenance of an open center tree includes removing vertical sprouts that crowd the center (best done in late summer), thinning older branches

for high levels of sunlight throughout the canopy (also in late summer), selecting for branches that grow outward (best done in winter), and cutting back older horizontal branches so the tree doesn't get too wide (in winter if side shoots are desired, in summer if growth is to be controlled). As the tree matures, remove an occasional older branch in the canopy with winter pruning. This forces vigorous growth to renew spur formation and to ensure strong, healthy branches. For impressive form, long life, and a productive shade tree, the delayed open center method is hard to beat.

Figure 14.21 Open center apple trees gain support from "pleached" branches.

Figure 14.22 Young branches are twisted together to form a living guy wire.

Baker, Harry. **Fruit (The Simon & Schuster Step-by-Step Encyclopedia of Practical Gardening)**. New York: Simon & Schuster, 1980. One of my favorite recommendations for beginning and experienced gardeners who want a graphic review of the basics of fruit and nut culture. Based on the expertise of England's avid gardeners, yet usually appropriate to most U.S. climates. (Cold-region landscapers beware of Baker's temperate-winter bias).

Brickell, Christopher. **Pruning (The Simon & Schuster Step-by-Step Encyclopedia of Practical Gardening)**. New York: Simon & Schuster, 1979. Another good volume in a great series. My second-favorite review of pruning. Now out of print, buy and cherish any copy you find.

Chandler, William. **Deciduous Orchards**. 3rd ed. rev. Philadelphia: Lea & Febiger, 1957. For tree crops, one of four technical references that I consult most often. Worth searching for in used book stores.

Childers, Norman. **Modern Fruit Science**. 8th ed. New Brunswick, NJ: Horticultural Publications, 1978. Poor-quality illustrations greatly hamper this book. A good one to browse in the library; only serious tree crops enthusiasts need own it.

Jaynes, Richard, ed. **Nut Tree Culture in North America**. Hamden, CT: Northern Nut Growers Association, 1979. The most helpful and thorough book on the subject. (The Association publishes a quarterly journal with the latest news on nut growing.)

Stebbins, Robert, and MacCaskey, Michael. **Pruning: How To Guide for Gardeners**. Tucson, AZ: HPBooks, 1983. After Brickell's *Pruning*, this is a favorite of mine. Excellent for both ornamental and edible trees. The only pruning book that lists apple tree varieties by their fruiting type (spur, non-spur, spreading, and tip bearers). Gives specific recommendations for each type. Very detailed, and well-suited to U.S. climates.

Wickson, Edward. **California Vegetables**. San Francisco: Pacific Rural Press, 1913. An interesting record of typical vegetable culture prior to the proliferation of chemicals. Some of the time-proven techniques may seem strange, such as adding salt as a fertilizer to beds of asparagus. Good reading for California gardeners; many aspects apply to other parts of the U.S., as well.

CENTRAL LEADER PRUNING

The distinctive characteristic of a central leader tree (referred to as a dwarf pyramid tree in England) is the trunk (the central leader). The leader is never completely removed, and all of the main branches radiate from it. Each main branch is trained to a 45° to 60° angle of attachment for good growth and excellent fruiting. The overall shape is similar to a Christmas tree. This form of training improves color and flavor, eliminates the need for ladders, makes efficient use of land, and increases yields. I believe the central leader shape is the most useful for fruit trees in small edible landscapes. The trees provide greater yields with less work – not a bad combination.

Sized for Comfort

The central leader method requires a dwarf tree. A standard tree with an uncut central leader soon grows far beyond convenient reach. The height should be limited to 14 feet. (See the charts on dwarfing rootstocks in "The Best Rootstocks for Your Soil.")

The Overall Goal

Keep in mind the image of a Christmas tree. The cone shape lets sunlight reach the low branches. The branches should grow from the central leader in tiers, with three to five branches spaced around the trunk in each tier. The tiers are spaced 18 to 36 inches apart (figures vary among practitioners, rootstocks, and scions). The gaps between tiers form light wells. As more tiers form, adequate sunlight still penetrates most of the canopy to maintain healthy fruit spurs. If you were to view a central leader tree from above, you would see that none of the limbs in a tier overlaps, ensuring even distribution of light. While in older open center trees as much as 30 percent of the lower canopy is unfruitful because of low light levels (see Fig. 14.23), only 2 to 5 percent of a central leader tree is dark to the point of fruitlessness.

Shaping the Central Leader Tree

Four major pruning and shaping techniques form central leader trees:

- **Constructive training**
- **Spreading branches to 45°**
- **Partial pruning of the central leader**
- **Summer pruning**

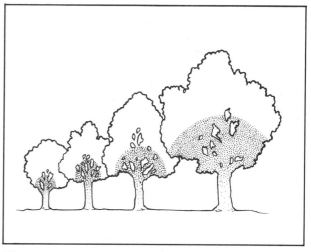

Figure 14.23 Interior shade causes fruit spurs to die. From left to right: (1) A dwarf tree trained in central leader style – less than 5 percent of its canopy is unfruitful; (2) a semi-dwarf tree in central leader style – 5 to 10 percent unfruitful; (3) a semi-dwarf tree in open center style – up to 15 percent unfruitful; and (4) a standard tree in open center style – up to 30 percent unfruitful.

Constructive Training

The central leader system requires a few carefully placed cuts after planting (even though, as mentioned earlier, pruning a young tree delays fruiting). The drawback of slightly delaying the production of fruit with a single "hard" pruning at the time of planting is far outweighed by its constructive influence. If you use a bareroot whip, cut it back to a height of 24 inches. Cutting shorter than 24 inches has advantages – it forces more dormant buds to form shoots, produces more vigorous growth in shoots, and causes the lowest branch to be closer to the ground.

If you can purchase a well-branched tree, with the branches in the appropriate places, you can skip the first winter's pruning. You may want to cut back a small part of the leader, making sure its highest bud remains the highest on the tree.

You may benefit from leaving branches close to the ground. Most pruning books suggest having the first limbs 2 to 3 feet above the ground, but this guideline originated in commercial orchards, where there must be plenty of room to drive a tractor beneath the tree. In a home setting, branches for the first few years of a tree's life can be as low as 12 to 18 inches off the ground if a lawnmower is to be used beneath the tree, and lower still if you use mulch beneath the tree. Allowing branches close to the ground gives you more fruit earlier in the life of the tree. In a few years, when fruit weights low branches to the ground, remove them with late-summer pruning. By then, branches higher up will be producing plenty of fruit.

Spreading Branches to a Fruitful Position

Not all new branches cooperate by growing at the ideal 45° to 60° angle. You must spread narrow-forked branches, as described earlier. (If by chance a shoot should grow at a 90° angle, simply use string to pull the branch upward.)

Reducing the Leader's Dominance

The width of a central leader tree is moderated by the bud at the tip of the leader. (To some extent, the weight of the crop, by lowering the terminal buds of each branch, also limits their extension.) The leader is left with the highest terminal bud on the tree. Any side branch that outgrows the leader must be spread in summer, pruned back to a small branch growing outward, or pruned to a dormant bud on the outside or underside of the shoot.

To encourage branching at intervals along the leader, you cut back half of the leader's growth from the previous season. The highest sprout is allowed or trained to grow vertically as the new leader. If the first shoot below the cut doesn't begin to grow vertically, tie a long stick to the leader, leaving several feet of the stick above the terminal bud, and tie the wayward shoot to the stick until it straightens up.

Summer Pruning

Almost everyone who attends my pruning workshops has followed the old adage, Prune fruit trees in the winter only. With summer pruning, people fear endless oozing, disease problems, and even the death of the tree. In fact, summer pruning is both helpful and safe. Indeed, apricot trees in central California and peach trees in the southeastern United States are best pruned in the summer.

Winter pruning stimulates growth; summer pruning stunts growth. From the second through fifth years, central leader training gradually moves from winter pruning to predominately summer pruning.

Summer pruning is especially helpful for renovating overgrown trees and for thinning large branches. You can remove large branches without stimulating the usual thicket of sprouts, often called suckers, or water sprouts. Pruning wounds begin to callus over while the tree is still in leaf, and wounds are less likely to sprout the next season during the strong flush of spring growth. Large cuts made in the winter are more likely to sprout vigorously. Thinning the canopy to admit sunlight helps color and ripen your crop and is best done in summer.

Summer pruning also helps spread your work over more of the year, reducing the panic of trying to squeeze in all the pruning just before spring budding.

Summer Pruning Without Tools

Pinching is an easy way to shape the canopy and promote the formation of fruit buds. Much of it can be done with tools that are always close at hand—fingernails.

In early summer, when new growth is 12 inches long and still supple, pinch out as much as half the growth (see Fig. 14.24). The next several buds below will sprout. In the latter part of the summer, pinch (or clip, if the wood is too stiff) the stem behind the original pinch. Make a third and final cut, a month or so before leaf fall, removing all of the stem except the last three true leaves (don't count the little cluster of small leaves at the base of stem). The dormant buds become fruit spurs. If you skip the last cut and wait until early spring pruning to cut back to three or four buds, the first bud usually sprouts as a branch and the others remain fruit buds. You encourage fruiting and foliage at the same time.

It takes practice to learn how late in the summer to pinch for the most fruitful influence on buds. Try different cuts and tag them with dates. Once you have a rough timetable for pinching, don't forget that the weather is different each summer—the rate of growth will vary from year to year. One recent summer, my area was so cool and foggy that the time for pinching was six to eight weeks later than in the previous year.

Where frosts come early and hard, be careful not to prune or pinch too late. Late pruning forces growth, and the first hard freeze can damage or kill a tender shoot.

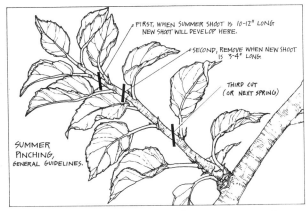

Figure 14.24 A sequence of summer pruning or pinching encourages more fruit buds at the base of first year growth.

Baker, Harry. **Fruit (The Simon & Schuster Step-by-Step Encyclopedia of Practical Gardening)**. New York: Simon & Schuster, 1980. One of my favorite recommendations for beginning and experienced gardeners who want a graphic review of the basics of fruit and nut culture. Based on the expertise of England's avid gardeners, yet usually appropriate to most U.S. climates. (Cold-region landscapers beware of Baker's temperate-winter bias).

Brickell, Christopher. **Pruning (The Simon & Schuster Step-by-Step Encyclopedia of Practical Gardening)**. New York: Simon & Schuster, 1979. Another good volume in a great series. My second-favorite review of pruning. Now out of print, buy and cherish any copy you find.

Chandler, William. **Deciduous Orchards**. 3rd ed. rev. Philadelphia: Lea & Febiger, 1957. For tree crops, one of four technical references that I consult most often. Worth searching for in used book stores.

Childers, Norman. **Modern Fruit Science**. 8th ed. New Brunswick, NJ: Horticultural Publications, 1978. Poor-quality illustrations greatly hamper this book. A good one to browse in the library; only serious tree crops enthusiasts need own it.

Jaynes, Richard, ed. **Nut Tree Culture in North America**. Hamden, CT: Northern Nut Growers Association, 1979. The most helpful and thorough book on the subject. (The Association publishes a quarterly journal with the latest news on nut growing.)

Stebbins, Robert, and MacCaskey Michael. **Pruning: How To Guide for Gardeners**. Tucson, AZ: HPBooks, 1983. After Brickell's *Pruning*, this is a favorite of mine. Excellent for both ornamental and edible trees. The only pruning book that lists apple tree varieties by their fruiting type (spur, non-spur, spreading, and tip bearers). Gives specific recommendations for each type. Very detailed, and well-suited to U.S. climates.

4

SPECIAL EFFECTS: ESPALIER, OBLIQUE CORDON, AND MINIATURE TREES

The Espalier Method

An espalier is any tree trained flat against a lattice, trellis, wall, or fence. (Summer pruning originated with and is indispensable to this style of training.) The espalier method is the most architectural and productive form of fruit tree culture available. In a formal setting, it is hard to find a more impressive or pleasing element than the cultured symmetry of an espaliered apple or pear tree laden with fruit.

Espaliers take many forms. The best known are the candelabralike forms called the double U cordon and the double and triple horizontal cordon. (In England, these are now generally referred to as espalier.) Other forms include the fan, oblique cordon, vase, four-winged pyramid, and vertical cordon. (See Figs. 14.25 through 14.27.)

Most forms of espalier, especially the double U cordon and the horizontal cordon, violate the natural dynamics of fruit formation. Notice how all branches are either perfectly horizontal or perfectly vertical. Since neither position is naturally conducive to fruiting, careful training and constant effort are needed to encourage fruit spurs. It is especially difficult to make espaliered peach and nectarine trees, since neither form spurs. They need renewal pruning each year for good yields, making espaliered training *very* difficult.

The skill and time required to ensure good fruiting are costly. Espaliers were developed by skilled, fulltime horticulturists who managed the palatial estates of European aristocrats. Most of us can't

Figure 14.26 An oblique cordon espalier.

Figure 14.27 A horizontal palmette, or cordon, espalier.

Figure 14.25 A palmette verrier espalier.

afford a fulltime gardener; besides, having someone else prune takes away the fun and pleasure. I recommend limiting the use of espalier to a single tree or to no more than a few trees. Work with this method for a few seasons before planting other trees.

The Oblique Cordon

If you want to experiment, start with an oblique cordon. Since 45° is a perfect angle for a branch, grow the whole tree at that angle. Gardeners in Great Britain have done it for hundreds of years, growing a single trunk covered from top to bottom with clusters of fruit spurs. Of all the shapes of espalier, this is the most practical and least time consuming. Nonetheless, it still requires more effort than the central leader form. It makes the most sense for small urban lots or for container-grown trees.

For apples, use one of the most dwarfing rootstocks, such as M 9 or M 27. These two rootstocks produce trees that are precocious and productive (see "The Best Rootstocks for Your Soil" for their limitations). They require staking or trellising for the life of the tree, a perfect match for oblique cordon training. Miniature trees, spur-type or compact apple cultivars on standard apple rootstocks, and pear cultivars on dwarfing quince rootstocks are well-adapted to espalier.

Trellising Oblique Cordon Trees

A trellis is important. The simplest is a series of horizontal wires between posts, as seen in most vineyards. For more than a few trees, however, you may need a sturdier trellis. The best trellis systems I have seen are constructed with a special high-tensile fence wire. The galvanized wire has a life expectancy of 35 years in humid areas and is able to support a 1,200-pound load per strand at the recommended tension of 250 pounds. It adjusts the tension as the temperature changes and can carry an increasing weight of fruit over the years. Instructions for trellis systems are given in *How to Build Orchard and Vineyard Trellises*. (For a copy, send $6 plus local sales tax, payable to: Kiwi Fence, RD 2, Box 51A, Waynesburg, PA 15370).

Planting and Pruning the Oblique Cordon

Oblique cordons are planted at a 45° angle. I use a template made from a rectangular piece of plywood marked with a 45° line through one corner. When planting, make sure that the curved part of the graft union is on top, since this is the strongest orientation for the graft.

If you plant a whip, cut off half the leader, making sure a bud remains near its top. This stimulates many dormant buds to form shoot growth. Throughout the summer, make sure none of these shoots grows higher than the terminal bud on the leader. Pinch back competing growth to an outside bud. Near the end of summer, tip back each side shoot to leave only three or four true leaves above the cluster of small basal leaves. As with the care of central leader trees, you encourage formation of fruit buds.

The English prefer to plant a tree that has side branches; it is called a feathered maiden. All side branches are cut back to three or four buds. In the first year, little or no summer pruning is done, which allows plenty of leaves to feed the tree and its root system. Don't let any shoots grow higher than the terminal bud on the leader. During the

following winter, cut all lateral growth back to two or four buds. All but the single bud closest to the winter cut will probably "hold" as flower buds. In the next season, pinch the vegetative shoots to promote flower bud formation. Pinch in mid- to late summer, and end by pruning to the last three or four real leaves.

Each summer the leader will curve upright. Periodically, tie it back to the 45° angle, using for support a 1-inch-square stake tied to the trunk of the tree, extending 2 to 4 feet beyond the tip of the leader. (Each season, as the leader grows, the stake can be moved upward.) *Some* vertical growth helps with extension of the leader; but before the new growth begins to stiffen, tie down the leader. You encourage a healthy mix of leafy shoot growth and flower buds. Tie the lower portion of the trunk directly to a trellis wire. Each season, be sure to check for girdling.

The controlled tip growth of the leader combined with the attention to spur formation produces a single trunk laden with fruit spurs. With the oblique cordon method, you soon have an ornamental hedge or wall of fruit.

Shaping Miniature Peach and Nectarine Trees

Since the growth of miniature peach and nectarine trees is naturally packed with flower buds, pruning to influence flower bud formation is not required. However, the trees' dense, leafy canopies heavily shade the ripening fruit. The trees need pruning to let in sunlight. Really open up the middle of the canopy, but be careful when pruning older trees — open up the canopy early in the season so the exposed wood does not sunburn.

Miniatures can be pruned in any fashion. The wide, open center style of pruning, potentially so damaging to standard trees, works fine. Open center miniature trees need propping only when bearing the heaviest crops. Usually, the robust branches carry fruit without the need for propping. And in cold-winter climates, they resist the weight of ice and snow without help.

The milder your summer weather, the more open the canopy should be. In the cool, coastal California summers, a somewhat espaliered shape is needed. By cutting the branches to a thin, fan shape, with the width facing due south, the fruit gets excellent exposure. In fact, the tree can be shaped like a solar collector. Angle the fan to face directly into the sun, August through September. (Figure 14.28 is an example for 38° latitude.) Such fine-tuned pruning and shaping is one of the pleasures of an edible landscape. Orchards managed by machine can never duplicate such nurturing.

Figure 14.28 A radical shape exposes ripening fruit to the most sunlight.

Practice Makes Perfect

The secret to pruning is practice. Try several styles, and watch the trees carefully; over time, the trees will reveal more and more about their own chemistry. Soon, you will be in a productive partnership with the tree, each leaving an impression on the other.

Baker, Harry. **Fruit (The Simon & Schuster Step-by-Step Encyclopedia of Practical Gardening)**. New York: Simon & Schuster, 1980. One of my favorite recommendations for beginning and experienced gardeners who want a graphic review of the basics of fruit and nut culture. Based on the expertise of England's avid gardeners, yet usually appropriate to most U.S. climates. (Cold-region landscapers beware of Baker's temperate-winter bias).

Brickell, Christopher. **Pruning (The Simon & Schuster Step-by-Step Encyclopedia of Practical Gardening)**. New York: Simon & Schuster, 1979. Another good volume in a great series. My second-favorite review of pruning. Now out of print, buy and cherish any copy you find.

Chandler, William. **Deciduous Orchards**. 3rd ed. rev. Philadelphia: Lea & Febiger, 1957. For tree crops, one of four technical references that I consult most often. Worth searching for in used book stores.

Childers, Norman. **Modern Fruit Science**. 8th ed. New Brunswick, NJ: Horticultural Publications, 1978. Poor-quality illustrations greatly hamper this book. A good one to browse in the library; only serious tree crops enthusiasts need own it.

Kiwi Fence Systems. **How to Build Orchard and Vineyard Trellises**. Waynesburg, PA: Kiwi Fence Systems, 1982. An excellent booklet on how to build extremely sturdy high-tension trellises.

Perkins, Harold O. **Espaliers and Vines for the Home Gardener**. Princeton, NJ: D. Van Nostrand, 1964. An older book with good detail on choosing and caring for vines and espalier plants. Not much detail on the specifics of training espalier fruit trees.

Stebbins, Robert, and MacCaskey, Michael. **Pruning: How To Guide for Gardeners**. Tucson, AZ: HPBooks, 1983. After Brickell's *Pruning*, this is a favorite of mine. Excellent for both ornamental and edible trees. The only pruning book that lists apple tree varieties by their fruiting type (spur, non-spur, spreading, and tip bearers). Gives specific recommendations for each type. Very detailed, and well-suited to U.S. climates.

GROWING TREE CROPS
Caring for Your Fruit and Nut Trees

DRIP IRRIGATION, MULCHING, AND FROST PROTECTION

Water and Yields

Water management is the most critical element of tree crop care, especially for yields. Water affects fruit in two ways: by conducting the soil's nutrients into the tree and fruit, and as the major component of the fruit itself. (Of course, too much water pumps up the size of fruit at the expense of flavor, a common problem with commercial fruit.) While some nutrients reach the plant no matter what the moisture content of the soil, the optimum—not too wet, not too dry—provides the greatest amount of nutrients.

When a soil is saturated with water, the exchange of gases between soil and atmosphere is greatly reduced or eliminated. Deprived of air, the soil provides fewer nutrients to the tree; in addition, waterlogged roots can suffocate or rot. While the deeper levels of soil supply small amounts of nutrients and moisture, they lack oxygen and are relatively inhospitable—their supplies are drawn on for sheer survival, providing a measure of security against drought.

The upper, more aerobic levels of the soil are the most important for production. In studies of alfalfa, peaches, and almonds (see Fig. 15.1), the first 2 feet provided as much as 62 percent of the moisture needed for good production. Sixty to 80 percent of the moisture for growth came from the top 4 feet of the soil. Each of these crops has a root system far deeper than 4 feet; yet most of the moisture they absorbed is from the upper horizons of the soil.

The secret to good yields is ensuring an optimal supply of moisture to the tree from pollination to fruit maturity. The local apple growers who can afford to irrigate get at least three times the yields of their neighbors, and larger, more attractive fruit. Regular watering also produces the healthy growth that leads to good fruiting the coming season. I prefer drip irrigation, since it avoids the alternating periods of waterlogging and dryness common to most watering systems.

Drip Irrigation for Trees

I'm currently using a drip system in my edible landscape which has the following virtues: it is simple to install and simple to adapt to any pattern of planted trees, water is evenly distributed around the perimeter of the tree's drip line, cultivation around the system is easy, the emitters do not clog, and the system easily adapts to the tree's expanding circumference. (I use the same system on edible and ornamental shrubs and on larger herb plants such as rosemary, marjoram, lavender, and angelica.)

The in-line tubing has a built-in emitter (see Fig. 15.2), which contains a tiny maze (the complex or tortuous path for which the emitter is named). The complex path helps equalize the pressure along the length of the tubing, but it is not as equalizing as the best of the pressure-compensating emitters. The emitter's main virtue is its ability to resist clogging. Particles and sediment are "dumped out" at the corners of each turn along the path. The final orifice is quite large, allowing whatever was not already filtered out to pass freely. I once installed this system for 80 trees that were watered from a dirty creek. I left instructions to clean the two filters on a regular basis. When I returned six weeks later, I found the maintenance had not been done. Both filters were two-thirds full of sand and sediment. When I opened the end of each drip line, the water flushed brown for 30 to 45 seconds. Yet not a single emitter was clogged! Since that time, I have used the same emitter where the water is loaded with iron sediment—there is a brown stain at each orifice but still no clogging after two seasons of use.

To install the system, run a line of solid drip irrigation hose past each tree. Use a compression Tee in the solid hose line to run the in-line emitter tubing to each tree. Compression fittings require no glue or hose clamps—you just cut the tube and insert the fitting—it seals itself and seals better, in fact, as the pressure rises.

Attach in-line tubing to the Tee and around each tree at the edge of the drip line. I purchased tubing with emitters at 12-inch intervals because my trees are in rather sandy soil. On clay soil, the emitters need be only 24 to 36 inches apart, depending on the soil and how long you water. The loop puts a doughnut of moisture around the tree in the zone of new feeder roots.

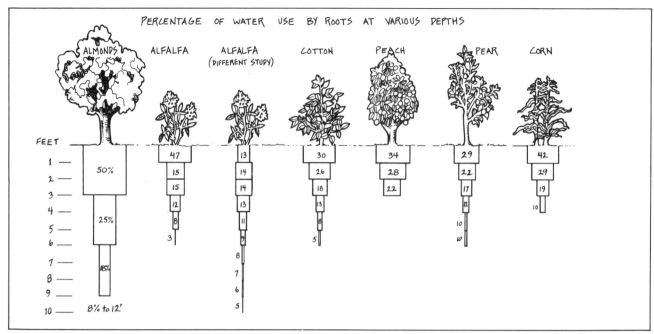

Figure 15.1 Most of the water that affects yields of perennial crops comes from the top 2 to 3 feet of soil, regardless of the depth of the roots.

Dripper Core

Figure 15.2 The interior of a complex, or tortuous path, emitter resists clogging and helps equalize pressure.

Bury the solid hose in the ground between the mulched plants and lay the in-line emitter tubing on the mulch the first year. That makes it possible, though somewhat tedious, to move the lines for cultivation and weeding. After the second year, if you use permanent mulch and gophers are a problem, keep the in-line tubing on top. If gophers aren't a problem, cover the in-line tubing with mulch for a more aesthetic look.

As the trees get older, add new lengths of in-line tubing to the loop to keep the water at the edge of the root system, thereby encouraging a wide and extensive root system, particularly helpful in windy areas where the tree needs a solid foothold. Again, use compression fittings. Even if you have only a few fruit or nut trees or ornamental shrubs, this drip system is a valuable addition anywhere rains are sporadic.

Mulching to Conserve Moisture

After learning about the true extent of roots, I took another look at the mulch around my favorite old pear tree (see "The Best Rootstocks for Your Soil"), with its 25-foot-wide canopy. I knew how great an effort it took just to mulch the area beneath the drip line, and the prospect of mulching more than twice that area, to cover the root zone extending half again as wide as the branches (a circle 37½ feet in diameter), dampened my enthusiasm. I began to consider ways to reduce the effort. Since this pear is more than 80 years old, I wondered if the feeding roots near the trunk were useful or abundant. Root hairs form only on newer roots. Having dug up older trees, I knew that their main roots had a barklike covering. My suspicion was that older roots have few root hairs near the trunk.

A study from England provided some guidance. It showed that 10-year-old apple trees had less than 10 percent of their feeding roots in a circle 4½ feet from the trunk. Leaving a bare circle near the trunk would still mean a lot of ground to mulch. With my favorite pear tree, beginning 4½ feet out from the trunk and extending to 37½ feet, I would use only 18 percent less mulch—not much of a savings.

I finally reasoned that mulching only from the drip line out to the calculated width of the roots would probably cover the majority of the feeding roots (see Fig. 15.3). A 6-foot wide doughnut of mulch beginning at the dripline and extending outward would use nearly 40 percent less mulch than covering the entire root zone. This seemed a healthy compromise between the needs of the tree and the amount of time, effort, and mulch I wanted to invest. (Even though this tree fruited for decades without mulch, the method has greatly improved its growth and yields.)

Young trees have proportionally more feeding roots near the trunk than older trees. Since active, vigorous root growth is important when establishing new trees, mulch closer to the trunk. As the tree grows, strike the sort of balance I did between mulch and root system on the old pear tree.

There are two important points to remember: mulch absorbs some irrigation water, and mulch makes for a shallower-rooted tree. Be sure to dig into the soil the first several times you irrigate to check how deeply and how wide the water soaks.

Adjust the time you irrigate accordingly. You want deep roots to anchor the tree for protection from winds. Roots are lazy—they will feed at the closest banquet. Applications of mulch (and fertilizers) tend to keep the roots localized. You may need to mulch in a wider circle if you have a windy location, since the wider the root system, the better the tree is anchored.

I use a decorative mulch of shredded bark or wood chips beneath my trees. To soften the edges and mask the doughnut shape, I use bedding plants such as foxgloves, marigolds, and alyssum, or edible ornamentals such as nasturtiums, calendulas, pansies, and pinks, which help to integrate the mulched area into the landscape (see Fig. 15.4 in color plates). The same mulching system can also provide nutrients for your trees. Read "Perennial Mulch for Fertility" in the next chapter.

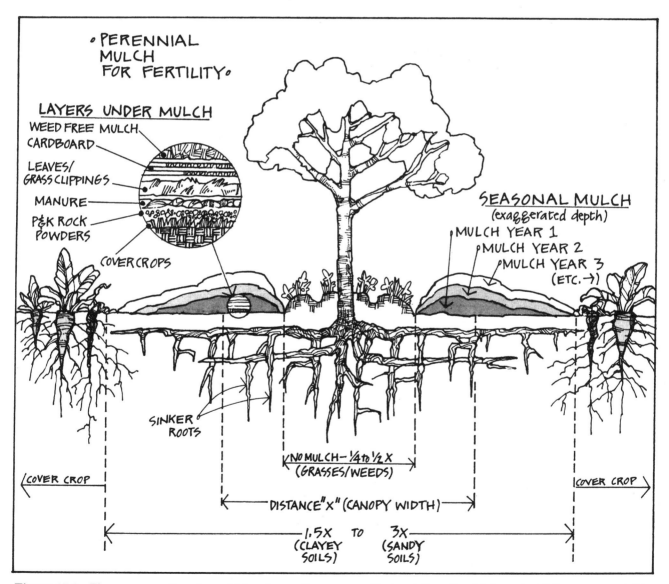

Figure 15.3 The sequence of yearly mulching. Leave the area near the trunk free of mulch to protect it from crown rot. You can use the sheet composting method described in "Sheet Composting for 'Wild' and 'Tame' Plants."

Frost Protection for Trees

The best protection is prevention. If a particular type of tree needs shelter from frost in your neighborhood and you don't care for the work of covering it, plant a different type of tree. The best bets are those trees that leaf out the latest—generally speaking, terminal and co-terminal bearing trees. These trees do not blossom until some leaf growth has begun, and they tend to leaf out later than other deciduous fruit and nut trees. (See Fig. 15.6.) There are noticeable differences among the common stone fruits. The order of blossoming, from earliest to latest, is almonds, apricots, Japanese plums, nectarines, freestone peaches, cling peaches, European plums, prunes, and cherries. Within the same fruit type, some varieties bloom earlier than others. Usually, the lower the chilling requirement, the earlier the bloom. (See "Special Trees for Special Climates.")

As a strategy for frost protection, there are ways to delay a tree's blooming. If you plant trees on the north side of buildings, sheds, and walls, the cooler, darker conditions extend the dormancy period slightly. However, choose varieties that ripen early in the season so the shade cast by the structure in the late summer and early fall doesn't interfere with ripening.

To protect blossoms and early leaves from frost, use misters or sprinklers placed near the tree and left on during cold nights. They will help in two ways: the high humidity keeps the air around the tree 1 to 2 degrees warmer, and if ice forms on flowers and leaves, it will remain at 32° F even when the air temperature gets much lower. Mist the air under and near the tree, but don't sprinkle the tree directly. Turn on the sprinklers or misters before the temperature reaches freezing, and keep them on throughout the night, applying up to a half gallon per hour per tree.

There is a last-ditch (and unattractive) strategy for frost protection—throwing sheets over threatened trees. This is practical only with small trees and shrubs. Keeping an electric bulb lighted under the sheet helps during an extra-cold snap. With young citrus trees, which have tender wood, it helps to wrap the trunk below the foliage with newspaper, fiberglass insulation, or a burlap sack.

TERMINAL BEARING EDIBLES

Avocado

Blackberry

Chestnut

Citrus

Elderberry

Fig*

Filbert

Grape

Jujube

Kiwi

Mulberry

Olive

Pecan

Persimmon

Pineapple guava

Pomegranate

Quince*

Raspberry

Strawberry

Walnut

*Terminal and co-terminal bearing.

Figure 15.6

Hall-Beyer, Bart, and Richard, Jean. **Ecological Fruit Production in the North**. Quebec, Canada: Jean Richard, 1983. A must for fruit tree enthusiasts who live in Canada and in the coldest climates of the U.S.

Hills, Lawrence D. **Grow Your Own Fruit and Vegetables**. Rev. ed. Thetford, England: Faber & Faber, 1979. An English manual with an organic bias that is better than most American books on organic gardening.

FERTILIZING TREE CROPS

The basis for a productive tree is the health of the first 2 to 4 feet of soil—the most aerobic and fertile zone. The ideal, aerobic soil is loose or loamy, with tiny pores that allow beneficial oxygen to enter and toxic gases (such as the carbon dioxide given off by roots) to escape. The longer it takes for soil to inhale and exhale, the slower the exchange of nutrients, and the lower the tree's production. The deeper the roots, no matter how loamy the soil, the longer it takes them to expel toxic gases and breathe in life-giving oxygen. While a tree's deeper roots are an anchor in winds and insurance against drought, good production relies on nutrients available to roots in the first 2 to 4 feet of soil.

Do You Really Need to Fertilize?

To see if your soil already has adequate fertility, check the growth of your trees against the list in Fig. 15.7. (This chart draws on the experience of West Coast gardeners and orchardists. Check with your local experts and adjust the figures accordingly.) If your trees show the amount of new growth listed for "Home Garden—Seasonal Growth," there is no reason to add nitrogen fertilizers. As an example, for apples in the western states, a home gardener can assume healthy growth and adequate yields if the seasonal growth is 10 inches or more. With that amount of new growth each year, there is sufficient nitrogen in the soil. Adding nitrogen may increase the yields but isn't necessary if you are happy with the current harvest. Keep in mind that adding too much nitrogen forces leafy growth at the expense of fruiting and makes the tree more susceptible to pest and disease problems.

Treat Tree Roots Like Vegetable Roots

If you need to fertilize, treat the roots as if they are as shallow as those of most vegetables. Beware of tilling under fertilizers—you can damage a tree's feeding roots. Till no deeper than 6 to 8 inches in the fall to avoid excessive damage to the root system.

Fertilizers

If seasonal feeding is needed to help increase the growth and yields of your trees, use the rates in Fig. 15.8 as a guideline. Three different rates are shown because experts are not in agreement and soil varies from place to place. If new growth is less than indicated in the "growth" column, start with the lowest fertilizer rates and adjust only after observing a year of growth.

Use the numbers in Fig. 15.9 to convert pounds of actual nitrogen to the total pounds of the fertilizers you plan to use.

SEASONAL GROWTH INDICATING ADEQUATE NITROGEN		
Tree Crop (standard-size)	Home[1] (in inches)	Orchard[2] (in inches)
Almond	8 to 15	36
Apple	6 to 10	12 to 18
Apricot	10	12 to 18
Cherry	*	18 to 24
Citrus	*	12 to 18
Fig	6	12
Filbert	*	6 to 8
Grape	36	24 to 48
Nectarine	6 to 12	24
Peach	6 to 12	24
Pear	12 to 18	24
Persimmon	12	*
Plum, Japanese	12	48 to 72
Plum, European	12	18
Plum, prune	12	18
Quince	*	12
Walnut	*	18

*no data available

[1] Brooks, Reed. *Western Fruit Gardening*. Berkeley: U.C. Berkeley Press, 1953.

[2] John Smith, former U.C. Cooperative Extension agent, Sonoma County, CA. Figures are averages for Sonoma County.

Figure 15.7

To find the true cost of a fertilizer, compare the cost of the element desired, not the cost per pound of the raw material. Currently, in northern California, bone meal is $37.70 per 100 pounds, and colloidal phosphate is $13.96 per 100 pounds. Considering the difference in available phosphorus (12 percent versus 2 percent), the actual cost is $3.16 per pound for bone meal and $7.00 per pound for colloidal phosphate. The price of a sack of colloidal phosphate is one-third that of bone meal, but the real cost is more than double that for phosphorus in the first year.

I prefer not to dig the soil around a tree each year as I might in the vegetable garden, so when I want leafy growth in a particular season I use fertilizers that leach readily. The natural sources of nitrogen—manures, blood meal, leather meal, fish emulsion, and cottonseed meal—are nearly as soluble as the chemical ones. The difference is that a pound of chemical nitrogen has far more actual nitrogen than a pound of manure.

NITROGEN REQUIREMENTS OF FRUIT AND NUT TREES

Crop	Sufficient Growth (inches per year)	Pounds of Nitrogen Needed for Sufficient Growth			Poultry Manure (pounds)	Steer Manure (pounds)
		A	B	C		
Almond	8 to 12	2	–	2.5	90	180
Apple	6 to 10	1	.6	1	40	90
Apricot	10	1.5	–	1.28	45	90
Avocado	2 to 4	1.5	–	1.05	30	100
Cherry	6 to 12	1	.1	.8	30	70
Citrus	4 to 6	4	–	1.5	40	100
Fig	6	–	–	.4	25	70
Grape	24 to 48	–	–	.21	5	15
Peach/nectarine	6 to 12	2	.8	1.12	40	80
Pear	12 to 18	.5	.3	.96	40	80
Plum/prune	10 to 16	1	.3	.8	30	70
Walnut	12 to 16	10	–	2.4	80	150

Rates are for standard-size trees and vines. For trees less than 5 years old, use ¼ to ½ these amounts; give dwarf trees an amount proportional to their size. Poultry and steer manure rates are for column C only.

A – from *Western Fruit Gardening*
B – from *Fertilizers and Crop Production*
C – from U.C. Cooperative Extension

Figure 15.8

CONVERTING NITROGEN TO ORGANIC AMENDMENTS

Fertilizer	Percentage Nitrogen	Percentage Phosphorous	Percentage Potassium	Pounds of Material to Equal 1 Pound Actual Nitrogen
"Barnyard" manure	.5 to 1.5	.4 to 1	.4 to 1	70 to 200
Bat guano	1 to 12	2.5 to 16	0	1 to 8
Blood meal	12 to 14	0	0	7 to 8
Bone meal	2	20	0	50
Chicken manure	1.1 to 4	.8 to 3	.5 to 2	25 to 99
Colloidal phosphate	0	18	0	–
Cottonseed meal	6 to 9	2 to 3	1 to 2	11 to 16.5
Fish emulsion	5	1	1	20
Fish meal	10	6	0	10
Hoof and horn meal	10 to 15	1.5 to 2	0	6 to 10
Horse manure	.7	.3	.6	150
Granite dust	0	0	3 to 5	–
Greensand	0	1.6 to 2	5	–
Kelp meal, Pacific	1	0	10	100
Phosphate rock	0	33	0	–
Poultry manure	5 to 10	5 to 10	2 to 10	10 to 20
Rabbit manure	2.4	1.4	.6	41
Steer manure	.7	.3	.4	150
Sulphate of potash	0	0	50	–
Wood ash	0	1 to 2	4 to 10	–

Figure 15.9 Most tree crops require less nitrogen for good yields than vegetable crops.

Compared to other plants, trees use little nitrogen; far less than leafy greens, for example. Figure 15.10 shows the amount of nitrogen used by a number of crops.

THE NITROGEN NEEDS OF
TREE CROPS & VEGETABLES

Crop	Nitrogen Required (pounds per acre) Annual	Perennial
Soybeans	325	
Celery	280	
Cabbage, potatoes	270	
Beets	255	
Corn	250	
Cantaloupes	220	
Almonds		200
Tomatoes	180	
Snap beans	175	
Sweet potatoes	155	
Grapes		125
Apples		120
Peaches		95
Lettuce	95	
Prunes		90
Pears		85
Squash	85	
Broccoli	80	

Figure 15.10

Phosphorus and Potassium (Potash) for Fruit

The major nutrients needed for good bloom and fruit production are phosphorus and potassium (potash). Most soils in the United States have plenty of total phosphorus and potash, but may have an inadequate supply of these elements in available, or soluble, form.

Sadly, most of the organic amendment sources of phosphorus and potash are not readily soluble. But even in soluble form, phosphorus and potassium do not leach any significant distance in soil. Clay particles bind potash and phosphorus quickly and tightly, limiting their utility for tree roots when applied to the surface. (An advantage to the binding is that a single application does not leach out of the root zone and is slowly released, over many years.)

Phosphorus deficiency is indicated by dull and bronze-colored foliage in the late summer. Stone fruits may have a brighter, more intense color and ripen earlier. Phosphorus-deficient citrus have poor-quality fruit and puffed-up skins. Correct a deficiency by applying 1 pound of elemental phosphorus (for example, 20 pounds of bone meal equals 1 pound of elemental phosphorus) per inch of trunk diameter. Work it into the soil in a doughnut shape, starting at the drip line and extending 1 or 2 feet outward.

Potash deficiencies usually show up only on almonds (small, cupped leaves and poor growth), prunes and European plums (scorched leaves and dieback of the new shoots), and olives (yellowish leaves and dieback of shoots). Almonds and olives are the only trees that respond to applications of potash—and only to a large amount, 7½ to 14½ pounds of actual potash per mature tree.

Notice in Fig. 15.9 that animal manures supply quite a good amount of phosphorus and potash. The only additional requirement would be to increase the organic matter content of the soil. Two other common sources of phosphorus are bone meal and colloidal phosphate (a powdered form of rock phosphate). Bone meal releases much more phosphorus in the first season than colloidal phosphate (as much as 12 percent for the former and 2 percent for the latter). For potash, the three most common sources are wood ashes, rock powders, and kelp. The first is the cheapest since it's free. Of the others, greensand is the most cost effective. (Based on current rates, greensand is $2.83 per pound of actual potash and kelp is $5.50 per pound.) It takes soil bacteria a while to make the nutrient available. With kelp, you get a lot more than potash. Kelp provides a wide range of trace minerals and tiny amounts of beneficial growth hormones. A lesser-known source of potash, sulphate of potash, is cheaper (only $0.56 per pound) and more effective than other sources. "Sulphate of potash" sounds like a chemical fertilizer, and indeed some forms of sulphate of potash are chemically derived by treating rock powders with sulfuric acid. But Great Salt Lake Minerals and Chemicals Company, which sells to fertilizer, farm, and feed stores, produces an organic form that is soluble and concentrated (50 percent potash by weight and 50 percent soluble). That company extracts the sulphate of potash by settling and dehydration from the Great Salt Lake. The resulting fertilizer is "legal" under the State of California legislation defining certified organic amendments.

Phosphorus and potash must be added each season when they are deficient, which is costly and time consuming. The long-term solution is to build up the organic matter content of the soil, liberating an adequate amount of the naturally occurring supply. Use cover crops and green manures (see "Grow Your Own Fertilizers—Cover Crops and Green Manures") as well as mulch.

Perennial Mulch for Fertility

For trees that need amendments for good fruiting, it is helpful to apply the amendments to the soil's surface each year then cover with a thick mulch. The mulch keeps the soil moist and somewhat cooler in the summer, which helps keep the soil life active and thriving, making nutrients available to the feeding roots. While worms and other soil life cycle nutrients deeper down, they are not as influential as fertilizers. At the same time, fertilizers increase the population and stimulate the activity of worms and soil microorganisms.

The mulch must be applied consistently every year. Since a perennial mulch encourages roots to grow near the surface, to stop mulching is potentially harmful – shallow roots become vulnerable to drought, heat, and lack of nutrients. (However, a well-mulched and shallow-rooted tree is susceptible to freeze damage in cold winter areas.) Each year the decomposing mulch adds nutrients and tilth to the soil. In the long run, a loamy layer develops on top of the original soil. The deeper the mulch, the faster the homemade soil develops. Think of mulch as a flat compost pile. Without the effort of composting, you can recycle garden and kitchen scraps beneath your trees, but remember to add sources of nitrogen sparingly. Also, if you are using kitchen scraps, cover them with a thick layer of straw or leaves to keep out flies and to prevent odors. If the scraps attract dogs or rodents, stop mulching with them.

As mentioned in the previous chapter, the mulched areas can be made of decorative shredded bark or wood chips and planted with ornamental bedding plants or edible ornamentals (see Figs. 15.4 and 15.5 in color plates). Keep mulch away from the trunk to help the soil dry quickly and forestall crown rot, and to discourage mice from chewing on the trunk. Where it rains heavily in the summer, consider planting a ground cover of clovers and grasses or ornamental bedding plants in the area directly around the trunk. The plants will wick surplus water out of the soil around the crown of the root system. Trim foliage 6 to 12 inches away from the trunk to discourage mice.

Each year add a new layer to the old mulch and increase the diameter of the doughnut. First, I dust the old mulch with a thin layer of well-aged manure, colloidal phosphate, oyster shell flour (my soil is acidic), and sulphate of potash. There are other possibilities – greensand, granite dust, or bone meal (the high-priced spread, used only for special trees).

Annual renewal of the mulch helps build the soil. As the mulch rots, the feeder roots grow into the fertile zone. Failure to renew the mulch will leave these new roots vulnerable to drought and heat. If you use weed-free mulch and pull the occasional weed, maintenance gets easier over the years.

There are some drawbacks to deep mulch, including:

- Mulch can hide the presence of gophers and moles and is a good habitat for other rodents.

- Fallen leaves and fruit are harder to remove from the mulched area. The leaves may harbor spores that will reinoculate the trees with diseases such as apple scab, peach leaf curl, rusts, and bacterial blights. The fruit can be a haven for the overwintering of insect pests.

- Soil temperatures under the mulch are lower in the spring, which may delay flowering – a problem in regions with short growing seasons – and retard the biological activity needed for good nutrient availability.

Despite the disadvantages, however, mulching helps build the fertility and tilth of the soil over the years – from the top down.

Cover Crops for Perennial Fertility

Beyond the mulched area, I suggest establishing a cover crop of several types of ground covers. The cover crop can be mowed to resemble, or blend into, a lawn. (See "Growing Your Own Fertilizers – Cover Crops and Green Manures.") The roots of the cover crop gradually improve the soil by penetration, rotting, and the accumulation of nutrients in their tissues. While nitrogen is important, trees don't need as much as vegetables. Too many legumes in the cover crop may lead to weak, leggy growth and less fruit.

Keep in mind that plants with taproots are as important as nitrogen-fixing legumes. Taprooted plants can improve soil to a greater depth than tillage can. Some send roots to ten feet deep and beyond. They add organic matter, via the decay of roots, to very deep levels for use by the tree roots. This deeply placed organic matter also improves the absorption of water and nutrients, since the tiny channels left behind by the decayed roots help improve the soil's drainage. Figure 15.11 lists some beneficial, taprooted plants that can be seeded as part of a cover crop.

Check the list of seed suppliers in Appendix 8 for sources of bulk seed. Prepare the soil as you would for a typical vegetable seedbed. Broadcast seed at slightly less than the recommended rate since you're mixing several types of seed. Water until germinated, and continue to irrigate as you would a low-maintenance perennial area. A periodic mowing will help hinder invasive grasses and promote the growth of the legumes as well as making a lawnlike view.

If a cover crop is growing when the tree is first planted, it will improve the the soil for years before the tree's roots invade. This type of soil improvement is very slow and gradual, but virtually effortless for the gardener.

Unlike people, trees cannot move very far to gather food. But like people, a well-fed tree is healthy and productive. A well-fed fruit or nut tree will continue to help feed your family for decades. If you give your trees the same respect and care you give yourself, you will have a healthy, perennial edible landscape.

```
┌─────────────────────────────────────────────────┐
│         COVER CROPS WITH DEEP TAPROOTS          │
│                                                 │
│  Beets                    Chicory               │
│    (Beta vulgaris)          (Cichorium intybus) │
│  Collards                 Kale                  │
│    (Brassica oleracea)      (Brassica oleracea) │
│  Parsley                  Parsnips              │
│    (Petroselinum sativa)    (Pastinaca sp.)     │
│  Salsify                  Angelica*             │
│    (Tragopogon              (Angelica pornfolia)│
│     archangelica)         Dill*                 │
│  Comfrey*                   (Anethum officinale)│
│    (Symphytum             Hollyhock             │
│     officinale)             (Althea rosea)      │
│  Fennel*                  Dock*                 │
│    (Foeniculum vulgare)     (Rumex sp.)         │
│  Lupines                  Burdock*              │
│    (Lupinus sp.)            (Arctium minus)     │
│  Dandelion*               Cow parsnip*          │
│    (Taraxacum vulgare)      (Pastinaca sativa)  │
│  Wild carrot*             Mallow                │
│    (Daucus carota)          (Malva sp.)         │
│  Black mustard            Wild radish           │
│    (Brassica negra)         (Raphanus sativus)  │
│                                                 │
│  *particularly invasive and sometimes hard to   │
│   eradicate.                                    │
└─────────────────────────────────────────────────┘
```

Figure 15.11

Baker, Harry. **Fruit (The Simon & Schuster Step-by-Step Encyclopedia of Practical Gardening)**. New York: Simon & Schuster, 1980. One of my favorite recommendations for beginning and experienced gardeners who want a graphic review of the basics of fruit and nut culture. Based on the expertise of England's avid gardeners, yet usually appropriate to most U.S. climates. (Cold-region landscapers beware of Baker's temperate-winter bias).

Brooks, Reid. **Western Fruit Gardening**. Berkeley: U.C. Berkeley Press, 1953. A book that still makes a lot of sense, though not biased toward organic methods. It provides reasonable guidelines well-suited to home gardeners, not commercial growers. The source of the data in Fig. 15.7, for how much tree growth indicates sufficient nitrogen.

California Fertilizer Association. **Western Fertilizer Handbook**. Danville, IL: The Interstate Printers & Publishers, 1980. My favorite handbook for calculating fertilizer rates, converting chemical rates to organic amendments, and reviewing basic soil chemistry.

Chandler, William. **Deciduous Orchards**. 3rd ed. rev. Philadelphia: Lea & Febiger, 1957. For tree crops, one of four technical references that I consult most often. Worth searching for in used book stores.

Childers, Norman. **Modern Fruit Science**. 8th ed. New Brunswick, NJ: Horticultural Publications, 1978. Poor-quality illustrations greatly hamper this book. A good one to browse in the library; only serious tree crops enthusiasts need own it.

Hills, Lawrence D. **Grow Your Own Fruit and Vegetables**. Rev. ed. Thetford, England: Faber & Faber, 1979. An English manual with an organic bias that is better than most American books on organic gardening.

Jaynes, Richard, ed. **Nut Tree Culture in North America**. Hamden, CT: Northern Nut Growers Association, 1979. The most helpful and thorough book on the subject. (The Association publishes a quarterly journal with the latest news on nut growing.)

Wright, David. **Fruit Trees and the Soil**. London: Faber and Faber, 1960. A short, succinct manual on the organic care of fruit trees. Presents the most understandable discussion I have read on the biochemistry of soil as it relates to organic home gardening. Demystifies soil fertility and how it influences fruit tree growth and production.

4

BIOLOGICAL BALANCE WITH INSECTS
Companion Planting: Sometimes Fact, Sometimes Fiction

COMPANION PLANTING: SOMETIMES FACT, SOMETIMES FICTION

Organic gardeners advocate companion planting—the association of different plants to create greater productivity. The goal is clear, but the mechanisms are not. Companion planting achieves success in many ways, some still poorly understood. Among species with proven benefits, there are companion plants that:

- Are detrimental to their neighbors ("anticompanions" that act as weed suppressants)

- Attract good insects

- Repel bad insects

- Improve the soil

- Assist nearby plants through compatible growth and life cycles

In this chapter and the following one, I will discuss the first three points. The fourth point is covered in detail in Part 7, and the last point is explained in "Intercropping."

Soil Mates, Not Soul Mates

The long list of companion plants in gardening books contain many dubious recommendations. Often plants that are said to "like" each other merely prefer similar growing conditions. For example, consider the recommendation, "lamb's-quarters . . . should be allowed to grow in the garden in moderate amounts, especially in corn." (*Companion Planting for Successful Gardening* by Louise Riotte). When lamb's-quarters (*Chenopdium album*) grows in a garden, I know that the soil is fertile, high in nitrogen, loose, full of humus, and cultivated. Corn favors these same conditions. In my area, lamb's-quarters always appears in plantings of corn (especially corn fertilized with cow or horse manure). This does not mean, however, that lamb's-quarters and corn are good companions. Although they thrive in the same kind of soil, they may actually compete for nutrients and water.

Some plants that make good companions simply have compatible life cycles. Intercropping—growing two or more plants together whose forms and growth habits are mutually beneficial—relies on the efficient and noncompetitive use of the landscape's environment and resources. Some examples are planting shade lovers under taller plants, fast-maturing vegetables between slow-maturing ones, and heavy-feeding plants with soil-improving plants (see "Intercropping" for more detail).

Plants as Antagonists—Anticompanions

Some plants exude chemicals that either promote their own growth or discourage the growth of others, an antagonism known as allelopathy. Allelopathic chemicals can repress or stunt the growth of nearby plants, and even, in some cases, prevent the germination of seedlings. (While this detrimental effect is well-documented, very little has been discovered about chemicals made by one plant that promote the growth of another.) The chemicals are washed off the foliage or exuded from the roots in tiny amounts; therefore, the more plants, the greater the effect. In most cases, the allelopathic influence happens on a grand scale and is primarily a dynamic of plant communities, also referred to as populations and stands. Because the chemicals are made in small quantities, heavy rains and irrigation can dilute or eliminate their effect. Also, the effects are more noticeable in soils low in organic matter and less noticeable in the rich soils commonly found in edible landscapes.

Allelopathy

Some common garden plants are allelopathic. Sunflowers and potatoes are said to stunt each other's growth. In fact, sunflowers (*Helianthus annuus*) produce chemicals that act as growth inhibitors to a number of plants, not just potatoes. We also know that there is a difference in allelopathic effect from one variety of sunflower to another. However, no study has been done of the influence of sunflowers on crop plants. Another example is the black walnut (*Juglans nigra*). It stunts, or even kills, tomatoes, blackberry, alfalfa, asparagus, chrysanthemum, dock, potatoes, cereal grains, pine trees, and apple trees. Yet Russian olive shrubs, black raspberries, ferns, goldenrod, asters, mints, violets, wild grape, clovers, buckwheat, peach trees, pear trees, plum trees, and Kentucky bluegrass grow fairly well beneath or near black walnut trees. Other allelopathic crop plants include wheat, oats, rye, asparagus, corn, cowpeas, cucumbers, and tomatoes. Again, the effect varies from variety to variety. A study of the world collection of 538 cucumber varieties (see *Science* 185:370-372) found one that suppressed the growth of millet and white mustard by 87 percent, yet only 25 varieties inhibited growth by 25 percent or more.

Crop plants can also be inhibited by non-edible plants. Tomato plants are stunted by mesquite (*Prosopis glandulosa torreyana*), greasewood (*Sarcobatus vermiculatus*), creosote bush (*Larrea tridentata*), and white bur sage (*Ambrosia dumosa*). Other non-crop allelophathic plants include marigolds (*Tagetes* sp.), wild black mustard (*Brassica nigra*), sweet white clover (*Melilotus alba*), several salvias (*Salvia leucophylla, S. mellifera, S. apiana*), some species of sagebrush (*Artemisia californica, A. cana, A. arbuscula, A. frigida, A. nova,* and *A. tridentata*), eucalyptus trees, the hollyleaf cherry (*Prunus ilicifolia*), the Catalina cherry (*Prunus lyonii*), hedge bindweed (*Convolvulus sepium*), and sycamore trees (*Platanus occidentalis*). Current studies are looking at pigweed (*Amaranthus retroflexus*), lamb's-quarters (*Chenopodium album*), plaintain (*Plantago* sp.), corn spurry (*Spergula arvensis*), and wild radish (*Raphanus sativus*).

Researchers are just beginning to study how allelopathy can be used to the advantage of vegetable crops. Presently the focus is on using allelopathic cover crops in rotation with crop plants. One study found that growing barley, oats, rye, sorghum, Sudan grass, and wheat for a season and turning under the plants reduced weed growth in the next season's crop by 75 percent. However, the response of the crop varies. Yields were greater with cucumbers, peas, and snap peas, but lettuce, radish, and tomato yields were reduced. There is not much sense in using plants to suppress weeds if the crop's yields are decreased.

Koepf, H.H. **Bio-Dynamic Agriculture**. Spring Valley, NY: Anthroposophic Press, 1976. A complete review of the spiritual basis for bio-dynamic farming. Requires real concentration and intense interest in the topic.

Organic Gardening Magazine, ed. **Getting the Most from Your Garden**. Emmaus, PA: Rodale Press, 1980. A poorly edited book that expands on Jeavons' *How to Grow More Vegetables*. It explains in detail how to adapt the French intensive method to a variety of climates, and gives much more information on cloches and coldframes. The inclusion of an index is a welcome improvement over Jeavons' book.

Philbrick, Helen, and Gregg, Richard. **Companion Plants and How to Use Them**. 8th ed. Old Greenwich, CT: Devin-Adair, 1976. One of the original sources of companion planting information. Contains some good information, but I find many of the folklore-based recommendations to be untrue or inappropriate.

Philbrick, Helen and John. **The Bug Book**. Charlotte, VT: Garden Way Publishing, 1974. A good, no-nonsense book on safe, organic methods for pest control. Well worth purchasing.

Riotte, Louise. **Carrots Love Tomatoes**. Pownal, VT: Garden Way Publishing, 1984. The most popular book on companion planting. (Formerly *Companion Planting for Successful Gardening*.) Few scientific studies are cited. Riotte's recommendations overlap and sometimes contradict the Philbricks' in *Companion Plants and How to Use Them*.

Rodale Press. **The Encyclopedia of Organic Gardening**. Emmaus, PA: Rodale Press, 1978. *The* bible for organic gardeners. Sometimes too wordy, sometimes too lean; still, a must for every edible landscaper's library.

COMPANION PLANTS
THAT REPEL PESTS

Pest control and companion planting are often spoken of in the same breath. Since I am always interested in saving time, when I first started gardening, I faithfully used the standard companion plants recommended for pest control. But my experience did not always corroborate the recommendations. The shoofly plant *(Nicandra physalodes)* was recommended as toxic to whiteflies. The shoofly plant I grew was covered all season with white flies; however, the tomato plant next to it stayed free of whiteflies. Well, maybe it's the result that counts. Instead of finding that tansy kept ants away, I actually found a potted tansy plant with a prospering colony inside! And it was ironic, at best, to see butterflies land on the blossoms of marigolds then continue on to another plant in my landscape to lay the eggs that soon became caterpillars. So much for the idea that marigolds repel certain pests.

The Traditional Guidelines:
Faith or Fact?

For me, a frustrating aspect of traditional companion lists is their almost total failure to give sources for the recommendations. What works for someone else may not work for me. With climates as different as the upper elevations of the Rocky Mountains and the humid swamps of Georgia, the arid deserts of California and the moist summers of New England, it is absurd to state that X plant protects from Y insect and that certain plants should be grown together. In the past decade, growing tomatoes in the coastal California climate, I have seen a total of perhaps five tomato hornworms. Yet a single tomato plant in my dad's garden in St. Louis may have that many.

Sometimes the traditional lists ignore basic ecology. Basil is suggested as an ally of tomatoes because "it repels flies and mosquitoes." No mention as to which of the 87,000 species of flies are repelled, nor that most flies, except for the pepper maggot, do not harm tomatoes. More important, some flies are beneficial insects. The 1,400 species of tachinid flies are parasites of other insects, including caterpillars such as the tomato fruitworm. (Of course, I'm still waiting to see a tomato carried away or devoured by a mosquito.)

Other recommendations are downright foolish. I would have to be desperate to consider planting horseradish "in rows between the potatoes [to] protect against the potato bug and blister beetle," as recommended in *Organic Gardening*. Harvesting the potatoes would mean breaking off pieces of the horseradish roots, with each piece giving rise to a new horseradish plant. After a few seasons of digging intercropped potatoes, my former potato patch would be a wall-to-wall horseradish patch.

For eight years, I have looked for "hard data" to double-check and substantiate the traditional companion planting guidelines. I found a mixed bag of results: less than half of the studies confirmed the recommendations; the majority seemed to indicate that faith, not fact, may have been an important aspect of many specific recommendations and that new research is needed.

The marigold, the well-known companion plant which has even been called "the workhorse of the pest deterrents," has not yet been found to effectively control insects above ground. (Some varieties suppress soil nematodes.) Instead, studies of marigolds show that they sometimes attract more pests to the garden or stunt the growth and yields of neighboring plants with allelopathic chemicals.

Figure 16.1 summarizes studies that used control plantings to double-check the recommendations of traditional companion planting lists. In only a few cases did researchers find that the guidelines worked.

Plantings That Do Reduce Pests

Many plant combinations *are* effective at reducing pests. Newer studies refer to these combinations as intercropping rather than companion planting, but when used in regard to pest control, the two terms are synonymous. I use "companion planting" when referring to the traditional guidelines and "intercropping" to distinguish the new scientific recommendations. (For information on intercropping in relation to compatible root zones and growth, see "Intercropping" in "Growing Healthier Vegetables.") As indicated in Fig. 16.2, which lists the results of intercropping studies, the most striking point is that many of the traditional companion planting recommendations do not appear. Please note that the location of each study is listed so you can compare your climate. Keep in mind that this list is just a steppingstone for trial studies in your unique microclimate and ecology. Successful intercropping or companion planting for pest management is very specific to the local environment. When the Florida study of amaranth and corn by Miguel Altieri was repeated in another climate (Berkeley, California) the results did not match the Florida experiment, and there was no significant reduction of pests.

The Double-Edged Sword of
Beneficial Plants

Some beneficial plants have secondary effects that outweigh their good features. At certain times in the season, I see black aphids literally stuck to the stems of flowering tobacco *(Nicotiana* sp.) I once thought having aphids clinging to an ornamental plant protected my vegetables from them. Then one evening at dusk, I spotted a hawk, or sphinx, moth – the adult stage of the feared tomato hornworm! – feeding on the nectar of the blossoms. Tomato hornworms are much more destructive than a few aphids, so I dropped flowering tobacco as a pest-control plant. There are plenty of other options for controlling aphids.

Brussels Sprouts and Deterring the Imported Cabbage Butterfly

As an extreme example of the differences between companion planting lore and the latest reseach, consider "brussels sprouts/weedy ground cover" in Fig. 16.2. This study found that bare, brown soil below a brussels sprout plant makes the plant very visible to the cabbage butterfly. Anything that keeps the background green helps make the brussels sprout plants less visible. The researchers even used brown and green burlap sacks, and found that the green sacks acted as a pest control, reducing the number of cabbage worms on the plants. As I'm fond of saying, this means even Astroturf™ could be used as a pest control! The traditional lists of companion plants mention nine different plants to repel cabbage moths, yet all you may need is a piece of green cloth or Astroturf.™

Fewer Pests Don't Always Mean No Sprays

It is important to note that a reduction in pests as a result of companion planting or intercropping does not mean that you can, in all cases, avoid spraying or that the yields are greatly improved. All of these studies found fewer pests, but for the most part, they failed to determine if the reduction was enough to eliminate sprays altogether. The few studies that considered spraying concluded it was needed to reduce the damage to economically acceptable levels. (As home gardeners, we can tolerate more cosmetic and actual damage than a farmer would.) In many cases, the yields of the main crop were slightly less than that of a monocrop in an equivalent area. Where the intercrop was another cash crop, it often yielded far less than it did as a monocrop. However, the two crops yielded a greater total than if the field were planted solely to either crop.

When to Use Intercropping or Companion Planting for Pest Control

- **When you want to experiment.** Start with the examples from the intercropping chart (Fig. 16.2) that were tested in a climate similar to yours. Do a control experiment – plant one area with a crop and one companion and an equivalent area with just the crop. Be sure to isolate the two plots by as much space as you can. By watching the growth and weighing the production, you get an accurate indication of the companion's performance.

- **When space is at a premium** and you are forced to plant everything close together.

- **For aesthetic reasons.** Some intercropping schemes may not work, but the visual interplay between plants can be striking. Whether or not marigolds protect or even stunt the growth of other plants, I like to set some out among the vegetables for a quick splash of midsummer color. Other companions that add a colorful highlight are chives, borage, and rosemary.

When Not to Use Intercropping or Companion Planting for Pest Control

- **When there is plenty of space,** there is no need to make dense plantings of the vegetable and its companion. The companion plant can be some distance away from the vegetable and still reduce pests, and the vegetables will probably produce greater yields when given more room.

- **When you know or suspect an allelopathic influence.** Keep an eye out for stunted growth and poor yields by the vegetable plants closest to a suspected allelopathic plant (see previous chapter). I particularly like to use silver grey foliage to highlight and complement dark green foliage. So the traditional recommendation of planting wormwood *(Artemisia absinthium)* with cabbages would suit my aesthetic tastes, but I know the chances are that the allelopathic compounds leached from the wormwood will stunt the growth of the cabbages.

- **When the intercrop or companion competes for sun, water, or nutrients.** In many cases, a companion plant keeps away bad bugs and yet reduces yields because of competition. Fast-growing, aggressive plants such as mints, catnip, tansy, horseradish, and tomatoes can actually outgrow and smother the main crop.

- **When the intercrop or companion and the main crop attract the same pests.** Flea beetles love nasturtiums and cabbages, yet these two are recommended as companions. Nasturtiums in my garden seem to be a favorite residence for aphids, yet they are recommended as repellents for aphids. Eggplants are said to prefer the company of peppers, tomatoes supposedly "love" peppers, and potatoes reputedly thrive next to peppers; yet all these plants are the favorite food of the Colorado potato beetle. Similarly, peas are supposed to "like" beans in spite of their shared attractiveness to the bean leaf beetle. When you try traditional companion plants, watch out for the duds.

- **Where funguses, mildews, and rots are prevalent** because of poor air circulation. In hot, humid summer climates your vegetables need all the air circulation they can get. If you are experimenting with intercropping or companion plantings, allow plenty of space between the plants or rows.

Figure 16.1

COMPANION PLANTING RESEARCH SUMMARIES
Scientists Test Traditional Guidelines

Marigolds

Although the wild Tagetes minuta, *'Stinking Roger,' has been used successfully as a fly repellent on livestock, the National Garden Bureau writes that "horticultural marigolds (*T. erecta *and* T. patula*) don't repel insects; in fact, they are attacked by or shelter the usual garden varieties of bugs, beetles and caterpillars."*

One of [the] southern U.S. researchers was Dr. David Rickard, who, while working for the North Carolina Department of Agriculture, found that some cultivars of both T. erecta *and* T. patula *were effective in nematode control. But the more highly bred the marigold, says Rickard, the less well it seemed to work; and the closer to the wild it was — for example, an odorous nonhybrid—the more it exhibited what has been called "the Tagetes effect," with* T. patula *cultivars such as 'Tangerine,' 'Petite Gold,' 'Petite Harmony,' and 'Goldie' the best, with 'Tangerine' the most effective. George W. Park Seed Co. offers a special, nematode-resistant marigold seed blend dubbed 'Park's Nemagold.' The [active] compounds "affect mainly the marigold and anything a couple of inches away from it," says Potter, and the National Garden Bureau of the U. S. notes that "no benefit has been shown to result from the plantings of occasional marigolds among other garden plants.[1]*

Potatoes with catnip, coriander, nasturtium, and tansy

Interplantings with potatoes resulted in the following reductions of Colorado potato beetle infestations[2]:

- catnip – 71% reduction
- coriander – 41% reduction
- nasturtium – 56% reduction
- tansy – 76% reduction

Peppers with catnip and nasturtium

Interplantings with peppers showed these reductions of green peach aphid infestations[2]:

- catnip – 91% reduction
- nasturtium – 43% reduction

Broccoli with catnip and tansy

Imported cabbageworm larval populations were increased on broccoli intercropped with catnip and tansy.[2]

Cabbages, potatoes, roses, and snap beans

- Cabbages with geraniums, marigolds, wormwood, tansy, tomatoes, and catnip – no effective influence.
- Potatoes with marigolds, horseradish, snap peas, and garlic – no effective influence.
- Roses with chives, garlic, nasturtiums, basil, and parsley – no effective influence.
- Snap beans significantly reduced Colorado bean beetle and leafhoppers on potatoes – but yields were lower.

Nasturtiums actually attract the crucifer flea beetle.

Marigolds and wormwood significantly reduce flea beetle populations [on cabbages], but the competitive, or allelopathic, effect of these companions seriously reduced both cabbage yield and quality.

[In] recent studies at the University of California [with] cabbages and snap beans ... grown with anise, basil, thyme, marigolds, catnip, summer savory and sage as companions ... the total yield of cabbages was lowered ... In snap bean trials, the control plot without companions had fewer whiteflies than the plots with basil, catnip and nasturtiums.

Agriculture Canada's experimental station in Nova Scotia interplanted every two rows of cabbages with three rows of tomatoes, compared this planting with a cabbage monoculture and found that the solid block of cabbages had 42 percent more insect damage than the interplanted block.

A lowered count of diamond-back moths and flea beetles has also been reported by other researchers in trials where tomatoes or tobacco were interplanted among cabbages.

A group of scientists at Cornell University ... has shown that cabbage butterflies ... prefer interplanted, dispersed cabbages rather than those in a solid block.[3]

Radishes with cucumbers, snap beans with potatoes, thyme with cabbage, and catnip with eggplant

The companionate combinations used in our tests showed no measurable or visible indication of offering protection from insect damage.[4]

Beans with French marigold, calendula, petunia, summer savory, Dalmatian pyrethrum, apple-of-Peru, and nasturtium

Significantly fewer Mexican bean beetles occurred on beans bordered by French marigold ... However, this effect was overshadowed by the alleopathic response of French marigold to beans [the bean yields were lower in the companion plot].

Companionate planting described in this study does not appear to be a useful strategy for insect pests of P. vulgaris *[snap beans] in home gardens.[5]*

Collards with santolina, rosemary, lavender, catnip, onion, marigold, rue, thyme, southernwood, chives, shallots, peppermint, wormwood, tansy, sage, and garlic

Companion herbs did not repel P. rapae [imported cabbage worm] but instead significantly encouraged colonization of the insect ... P. rapae laid significantly more eggs on collards hidden between sage than ... other companion plants.[6]

Cabbage with marigold, nasturtium, pennyroyal, peppermint, sage, and thyme

Our data indicate that companionate planting did not result in a decrease in insect damage. In fact...some companionate plants may be attractive [to the imported cabbage worm] resulting in higher damage to cabbage.[7]

continued

Figure 16.1 continued

Pepper, cabbage, and potato with coriander, marigold, nasturtium, onion, oregano, and tansy

In looking at the varied results obtained from these trials, we may conclude that (1) effects were seen in some of the treatments and (2) the effects are not seen over a very long distance. It is hoped that a more intensive planting design will help in determining the effectiveness of herbal interplanting and sprays. As of this writing, it cannot be said that such methods of pest control are or are not effective.[8]

Pepper and Squash with catnip and tansy

Pepper plants planted with either catnip or tansy had considerably less aphids than did the control plots. However, pepper plants interplanted with catnip or tansy were obviously stressed due to overcrowding.

Both catnip and tansy interplanted plots had fewer squash bugs than the control plots. Considerable crowding was seen in the interplant plots, the squash plants being much smaller.[9]

Potatoes and tansy

These results do not show any benefit from using sprays of tansy . . . in a Colorado potato beetle management program.[10]

'Wisconsin Golden Acre' cabbage with a living mulch of annual ryegrass and Dutch white clover

All treatments had significantly fewer flea beetles than the bare ground check.

The living mulches of ryegrass or clover . . . also reduced cabbage yields. Mulch of clover green chop also reduced flea beetle numbers without reducing cabbage yields.[11]

Peppers, squash, and broccoli with tansy and catnip

The interplants tansy and catnip were most effective in reducing aphid numbers [on pepper plants], but also competed vigorously with the pepper plants.

Interplanted squash plants [with catnip and tansy] were noticeably smaller and slower in development and flowering.

All of the interplant treatments [of broccoli with catnip and tansy] seemed to have an attractive rather than a repellent effect on the cabbageworm butterflies.[12]

Cabbage and beans with anise, marigold, nasturtium, catnip, summer savory, and basil

Anise as a companion plant significantly reduced the numbers of imported cabbageworm eggs deposited on nearby cabbages.

[Marigold slightly reduced the amount of injury to cabbage heads.] All companion plants were associated with reduced weights of cabbage heads.

On beans, significantly higher whitefly levels occurred . . . in plots planted with basil and catnip . . . and nasturtium.

Although several species of companion plants reduced imported cabbageworm numbers by modest levels, such reductions did not necessarily result in diminished worm damage to cabbage. Any beneficial effects of companion plants were negated by substantial reductions in cabbage yields.[13]

Potatoes and peppers with catnip and tansy

Colorado potato beetle population on potato plants was reduced 60–100% when interplanted with tansy and 58–83% when interplanted with catnip, while green peach aphid (Myzus persicae) populations on peppers were reduced 82% when interplanted with catnip and 59% when interplanted with tansy.

While this study was limited in scope, the results confirm the validity of the concept of interplantings with tansy for the control of the Colorado potato beetle . . . or the use of tansy oil.[14]

Tomatoes and beans with marigold and chrysanthemum

Test results showed no crops to have their insect populations drastically reduced by the companion planting . . . Importantly, tomato and bean yields were significantly higher without companion plants of marigold and chrysanthemum . . . presumably because the companion plants competed with the crop plants for light, moisture, and nutrients. Garlic . . . had no significant effect on yield.[15]

Potatoes with fava beans

Fava beans were significantly lower in all the intercropping treatments [companion plantings]. Both intercropping [companion] systems depressed total potato yield.[16]

Carrots with stinging nettles

Carrot fields bordered by hedges with stinging nettles had higher numbers of carrot flies. The researchers concluded:

The herb layer [stinging nettles] provides important shelter for [carrot] flies.[17]

Beans with squash and corn

Researchers tested this polyculture as a way to reduce the egg masses of the European corn borer by increasing the number of predaceous ground beetles, and found:

Intercropping [with beans and squash] may act to decrease the predation rate and abundance of certain predators or parasites . . . because of the higher plant density.[18]

Cucumbers, corn and broccoli

Per-plant yields were significantly greater in monocultures than in polycultures.[19]

Cauliflower with borders of mustard and radish

In a test for protection from cabbage loopers and flea beetles,

[Insect infestations] actually increased in plots with mustard/radish borders.[20]

Carrots with French marigolds

As protection from carrot fly,

Mixed cropping with the French marigold, Tagetes patula, was ineffective.[21]

[1] Harrowsmith eds. 1984. Nematode nemesis. *Harrowsmith* 8(53): 125–126.

[2] Matthews, D. 1981. *The Effectiveness of Selected Insect Repellant Crops.* Rodale Report #81/28.

[3] Bennett, J., and Forsyth, A. 1984. Horticultural hocus-pocus? *Harrowsmith* 9(55): 83–87.

[4] Gesell, S. G.; Precheur, R. J.; and Hepler, R. W. 1975. *Companionate Plantings–Do They Work?* Brooklyn Botanic Gardens Handbook #77, 1975.

[5] Latheef, M. A., and Irwin, R. D. 1980. Effects of companionate planting on snap bean insects, *Epilachnia varivestia* and *Heliothis zea. Environ. Entomol.* 9(2): 195–198.

[6] Latheef, M. A., and Ortiz, J. H. 1983. The influence of companion herbs on egg distribution of the imported cabbageworm, *Pieris rapae (Lepidoptera: Pieridae),* on collard plants. *Canadian Entomol.* (115): 1,031–1,038.

[7] Latheef, M. A., and Ortiz, J. H. 1979. The effect of companionate planting on lepidopteran pests of cabbage. *Canadian Entomol.* 111(7): 863–864.

continued

continued

[8]Matthews; Edwards; Ganser; and Weinsteiger. 1981. *The Effectiveness of Selected Insect Repellant Crops*. Rodale Report #80/8.

[9]Matthews, D. 1982. *The Effects of Interplanting with Catnip and Tansy on Insect Pest Populations on Potatoes, Peppers and Squash*. Rodale Report #81/3.

[10]Matthews, D., and Schearer, W. 1984. *Tansy: A Potential Repellent for the Colorado Potato Beetle*. Rodale Report #84/6 .

[11]Matthews, D.; Orr, C.; and Bacon, S. 1984. *Summary of 1982 and 1983 Flea Beetle Research*. Rodale Report #84/5 .

[12]Matthews, D.; Michalak, P.; and MacRae, R. 1984. Effect of traditional insect-repellent plants on insect numbers in a mixed planting system. *Environmentally Sound Agriculture*, Praeger Publishing.

[13]Koehler; Barclay; and Kretchun. 1983. Companion plants. *Calif. Ag.*, 13–15.

[14]Panasiuk, O. 1984 Response of Colorado potato beetles to volatile components of tansy, *Tanacetum vulgare*. *J. Chem. Ecol.* 10(9).

[15]Cantelo, W. W., and Webb, R. 1983. An examination of selected companion plant combinations, and how such systems might operate. *Proc. Wash. Acad. Sci. 73(3): 100–106* .

[16]Lamberts, M. 1980 *Intercropping with Potatoes*. Thesis. U. C. Davis, CA .

[17]Wainhouse, D., and Coaker, T. H. 1981. The distribution of carrot fly (*Psila rosae*) in relation to the flora of field boundaries. *Pests, Pathogens and Vegetation* 263–272 .

[18]Risch, S.; Wrubel, R.; and Andow, D. 1982. Foraging by a predaceous beetle, *Coleomegilla maculata (Coleoptera: Coccinellidae)*, in a polyculture: Effects of plant density and diversity. *Entomol. Soc. Am.* 11(4): 949–950 .

[19]Bach, C., and Hruska, A. J. 1981. Effects of plant density on the growth, reproduction and survivorship of cucumbers in monocultures and polycultures. *J. Appl. Ecol.* 18:929–943 .

[20]Van Dusen, D. 1985. Weeds – future partners on the farm? *Cultivar* 3(1): 1–3 .

[21]Uvah, I. and Coaker, T. H. 1984. Effect of mixed cropping on some insect pests of carrots and onions. *Entomol. Exper. & Appl.* 36:159–167

Figure 16.1

Figure 16.2

INTERCROPPING FOR PEST REDUCTION Successful Scientific Trials				
Crop	**Intercrop**	**Pest(s) Reduced**	**Mechan-ism**	**Site**
Apple	*Phacelia* sp., *Eryngium* sp.	San Jose scale, aphids[1]	W	Russia
	Weedy ground cover	Tent caterpillar and codling moth[2]	W	Canada
Barley	Alfalfa, red clover	Aphids[47]	P	Czechoslovakia
Bean	Goosegrass *(Eleusine indica)*, red sprangletop *(Leptochioa filliformis)*	Leafhoppers[29]	C	Tropics
Brassicas	Candytuft *(Iberis amara)*, shepherds purse *(Capsella bursapastoris)*, wormseed-mustard *(Erysimum cheiranthoides)*	Flea beetles[59]	C	New York
	Similar-sized crops	Rootfly, cabbage butterfly and moth[61]	C, P	England
Brussels sprouts	Weedy ground cover	Imported cabbage butterfly[4]	P	England
	French beans, grasses	Aphids[39]	I	England
	White clover	Cabbage root fly, aphids, white cabbage butterfly[45]	V	England
	Clover	Aphids[36]	I	England

continued

Figure 16.2 continued

Crop	Intercrop	Pest(s) Reduced	Mechan-ism	Site
Cabbage	Tomato	Diamondback moth[44]	*	Tropics
	Hawthorn *(Crataegus* sp.)	Diamondback moth[6]	AP	**
	Red and white clover	Cabbage aphids, imported cabbage butterfly[7]	I, P	England
	Clover	Cabbage root fly[28]	P	Ireland
	Green ground cover	Imported cabbage butterfly[38]	V	**
Carrots	Onions	Carrot fly[61,55]	C	England, Africa
Cauliflower	Corn spurry *(Spergula arvensis)*	Cabbage looper, flea beetles, aphids[64]	P	California
	Lamb's-quarters	Imported cabbage butterfly[64]	P	California
	White or red clover	Cabbage aphids, imported cabbage butterfly[43]	I, P	England
Collards	Tomato, ragweed *(Ambrosia artemisiifolia)*	Flea beetle[8]	C	New York
	Pigweed *(Amaranthus retroflexus),* lambs-quarters *(Chenopodium album), Xanthium stramonium*	Green peach aphid[9]	P	Ohio
	Weedy ground cover	Cabbage aphid[33]	W	California
	Weedy ground cover with wild mustards	Flea beetle[33]	P	California
	Tomato, tobacco	Flea beetle[21]	C	New York
	Weedy ground cover	Flea beetle, cabbage butterfly[42]	*	New York
	Weedy ground cover	Flea beetles[63]	V	New York
Corn	Wild parsnip *(Pastinaca sativa),* wild mustard *(Brassica kaber),* chickweed *(Stellaria media),* Shepherds purse *(Capsella bursa-pastoris),* and lady's thumb smartweed *(Polygonum persicaria)*	Black cutworm[51]	W	Illinois
	Pigweed *(Amaranthus hybridus)*	Fall armyworm[52]	W	Florida
	Giant ragweed	European corn borer[10]	AP	Canada
	Sweet potatoes	Leaf beetles[11]	W	Tropics
	Beans	Leafhoppers, leaf beetle, fall armyworm[12]	I, P	Tropics
	Beans, weeds	Fall armyworm[27]	P	Tropics
	Pigweed *(Amaranthus* sp.), Mexican Tea *(Chenopodium ambrosiodes),* goldenrod *(Solidago altissima),* beggertick *(Bidens pilosa)*	Fall armyworm[30]	P	Florida
	Soybean	Corn earworm[31]	P	Florida
	Peanuts	Corn borer[40]	V	**
	Clover	Corn borer[46]	I	England
Cow pea	Sorghum	Leaf beetle[13]	C	**
Cucumber	Corn, broccoli	Striped cucumber beetle[14]	I	Michigan
Crucifers	Wild mustards	Cabbageworms[15]	W	**
Fruit trees	Rye, wheat, sorghum used as mulch	European red mite[32]	P	Michigan
	Alder *(Alnus* sp.), bramble	Red spider mites[34,35]	P	England
Grapes	Wild blackberry *(Rubus* sp.)	Grape leafhopper[24]	AW	**
	Johnson grass *(Sorghum halepense)*	Pacific mite[25]	P	**
	Sudan grass, Johnson grass	Willamette mite[3]	P	California
Kale	Kale, closely planted	Aphids[58]	V	England
Mung beans	Weedy ground cover	Beanfly[16]	I	**
Oats	New Zealand white clover	Fruit fly[53]	I	England
Onions	Carrots	Thrips[66]	V	Africa
Peach	Ragweed *(Ambrosia artemisiifolia)*	Oriental fruit moth[17]	AW	Virginia
	Strawberry	Oriental fruit moth[18]	P	**
	Ragweed, smartweed *(Polygonum* sp.), lamb's quarters *(Chenopodium* sp.), goldenrod *(Solidago* sp.)	Oriental fruit moth[48]	*	**

continued

PLANTS THAT REPEL PESTS   ⑤

Figure 16.2 continued

Crop	Intercrop	Pest(s) Reduced	Mechanism	Site
Radish	Broccoli	Green peach aphid[54]	W	Washington
Soybean	Corn, weed cover	Corn earworm[50]	W	Georgia
	Sicklepod *(Cassia obtusifolia)*	Velvet bean caterpillar, green stink bug[29]	*	Georgia
	Desmodium sp., *Croton* sp., *Cassia* sp.	Corn earworm[31]	W	Georgia
	Barley, wheat	Monitored only predators of soybean pests[57]	P	Virginia
	Rye	Seedcorn maggot[60]	I	Ohio
Squash	Corn	Cucumber beetle[19]	I	Tropics
	Corn, cow pea	Western flower thrips[26]	P	California
Sugar beet	Manure	Pests preyed upon by predatory ground beetles[62]	P	Ireland
	Broccoli	Green peach aphid[54]	W	Washington
Sweet potato	Morning glory *(Ipomoea asarifolia)*	Argus tortoise beetle[20]	AW	**
Tamarack trees	White spruce and shrubs	Sawflies[56]	C	Canada
Tomato	Cabbage	Flea beetles[21]	C	**
	Cabbage	Diamondback moth[22]	C	Tropics
Turnip	Dutch white clover	Cabbage root maggot[41]	C	Pennsylvania
Vegetables, misc.	Wild carrot *(Daucus carota)*	Japanese beetle[23]	W	**
Walnut	Weedy ground cover	Walnut aphid[49]	AW	California

AP – alternative host plant for pest(s)
AW – alternative host plant for parasitic wasps
C – masking by chemical repellent
I – physical interference (e.g., a tall plant blocks wind-borne and flying insects)

P – increase in predators
V – visual masking
W – increase in parasitic wasps
*See original paper for discussion of mechanism.
**Temperate-climate study. See original paper for specific sites.

[1] Telenga, N. A. 1958. Biological method of pest control in crops and forest plants in the USSR. *Rep. of Soviet Delegation, 9th Int. Conf. on Quarantine and Plant Protection, Moscow,* 1–15.

[2] Leius, K. 1967. Influence of wildflowers on parasitism of tent caterpillar and codling moth. *Canadian Entomol.* 99:444–446.

[3] Altieri, M. A.; Schoonhoven, A.; and Doll, J. D. 1977. The ecological role of weeds in insect pest management systems: A review illustrated with bean *(Phaseolus vulgaris)* cropping systems. *PANS* 23:185–206.

[4a] Smith, J. G. 1976. Influence of crop background on natural enemies of aphids on brussels sprouts. *Ann. Appl. Biol.* 83:15–29.

[4b] Smith, J. G. 1976. Influence of crop background on aphids and other phytophagous insects on brussels sprouts. *Ann. Appl. Biol.* 83:1–13.

[5] Theuinissen, J., and den Ouden, H. 1980. Effects of intercropping with *Spergula arvensis* on pests of brussels sprouts. *Entomol. Experiment. & Applic.* 27:260–268.

[6] van Emden, H. F. 1962. Observations on the effects of flowers on the activity of parasitic Hymenoptera. *Entomol. Monthly* 98:225–236.

[7] Dempster, J. P. 1969. Some effects of weed control on the numbers of the small cabbage white *(Pieris rapae)* on brussels sprouts. *J. Appl. Ecol.* 6(2): 339–405.

[8] Tahvenainen, J. C., and Root, R. B. 1972. The influence of vegetational diversity on the population ecology of a specialized herbivore *Phyllotreta cruciferae* (Coleoptera: Chrysomelidae). *Oecologia* 10:321–346.

[9] Horn, D. J. 1981. Effect of weedy backgrounds on colonization of collards by green peach aphid, *Myzus persicae,* and its major predators. *Environ. Entomol.* 10:285–289.

[10] Syme, P. D. 1975. The effects of flowers on the longevity and fecundity of two native parasites of the European pine shoot moth in Ontario. *Environ. Entomol.* 4:337–340.

[11] Risch, S. 1979. A comparison, by sweep sampling, of the insect fauna from corn and sweet potato monocultures and dicultures in Costa Rica. *Oecologia* 42:195–211.

[12] Altieri, M. A.; Francis, C. A.; Schoonhoven, A.; and Doll, J. 1978. Insect prevalence in bean *(Phaseolus vulgaris)* and maize (Zea mays) polycultural systems. *Field Crops Res.* 1:33-49.

[13] Litsinger, J. A., and Moody, K. 1976. Integrated pest management in multiple cropping systems. *Multiple Cropping.* Madison: Amer. Soc. of Agron. (Spec. Pub. No. 27): 293–316.

[14] Bach, C. E. 1980. Effects of plant density and diversity on the population dynamics of a specialist herbivore, the striped cucumber beetle, *Acalymma vittatta. Ecology* 61:1515–1530.

[15] National Academy of Sciences. 1969. Principles of Plant and Animal Control. *Insect Pest Manag. & Control* 3:100–164.

[16] Litsinger, J. A., and Moody, K. 1967. Integrated pest management in multiple cropping systems. *Multiple Cropping.* Madison: Amer. Soc. of Agron. (Spec. Pub. No. 27): 293–316.

[17] Bobb, M. L. 1939. Parasites of the oriental fruit moth in Virginia. *J. Econ. Entomol.* 32:605–607.

[18] Marcovitch, S. 1935. Experimental evidence on the value of strip cropping as a method for the natural control of injurious insects, with special reference to plant lice. *J. Econ. Entomol.* 28:62–70.

[19] Risch, S. J. 1980. The population dynamics of several herbivorous beetles in tropical agoecosystems: The effect of intercropping corn, beans and squash in Costa Rica. *J. Appl. Ecol.* 17:593–612.

[20] Carroll, C. R. 1978. Beetles, parasitoids and tropical morning glories: A study in host discrimination. *Ecol. Entomol.* 3:79–86.

[21] Tahvanainen, J. C., and Rooth, R. B. 1972. The influence of vegetational diversity on the population ecology of a specialized herbivore *Phyllotreta cruciferae* (Coleoptera: Chrysomelidae). *Oecologia* 10:321–346.

Figure 16.2 continued

22 Raros, R. S. 1973. Prospects and problems of integrated pest control in multiple cropping. *IRRI Saturday Seminar* Proc., Los Banos, Philipp., 1–20.

23 King, J. L., and Holloway, J. K. 1930. *Tiphia popilliavora*, a parasite of the Japanese beetle. *USDA Circ.* (145): 1–11.

24 Doutt, R. L., and Nakata, J. 1973. The *Rubas* sp. leafhopper and its egg parasitoid: An endemic biotic system useful in grape pest management. *Environ. Entomol.* 2:381–386.

25 Flaherty, D. 1969. Ecosystem trophic complexity and Willamette mite *Eotetranychus willametei (Acarina: Tetranychidae)* densities. *Ecology* 50:911–916.

26 Letourneau, D. K., and Altieri, M. A. 1983. Abundance patterns of a predator, *Orius tristicolor (Hemiptera: Anthocoridae)*, and its prey, *Frankliniella occidentalis (Thysanoptera: Thripidae)*: Habitat attraction in polycultures versus monocultures. *Environ. Entomol.* 12:1464–1469.

27 Altieri, M. A. 1980. Diversification of corn agroecosystems as a means of regulating fall armyworm populations. *Florida Entomol.* 63:450–456.

28 Ryan, J.; Ryan, M. F.; and McNaeidhe, F. 1980. The effect of interrow plant cover on populations of the cabbage root fly, *Delia brassicae. J. Appl. Ecol.* 17:31–40.

29 Altieri, M. A. 1981. Weeds may augment biological control of insects. *Calif. Ag.* (May-June); 22–24.

30 Altieri, M. A., and Whitcomb, W. H. 1980. Weed manipulation for insect pest management in corn. *Environ. Manag.* 4:483–489.

31 Altieri, M. A.; Lewis, J. W.; Nordlund, D. A.; Gueldner, R. C.; and Todd, J. W. 1981. Chemical interactions between plants and *Trichogramma* sp. wasps in Georgia soybean fields. *Protection Ecol.* 3:259–263.

32 Putnam, A. R. 1983. Allelopathy: A breakthrough in weed control? *Fruit Grower* (June): 10.

33 Gliessman, S. and Altieri, M. A. 1982. Polyculture cropping has advantages. *Calif. Ag.* (July): 15–16.

34 Solomon, M. G. 1975. The colonization of an apple orchard by predators of the fruit tree red spider mite. *Ann. Appl. Biol.* 80:119–122.

35 Solomon, M. G. 1982. Phytophagous mites and their predators in apple orchards. *Ann. Appl. Biol.* 101:201–203.

36 O'Donnell, M. S., and Coaker, T. H. 1975. Potential of intracrop diversity for the control of brassica pests. *Proc. 8th Brit. Insectic. Fungic. Conf.*, 101–105.

37 Smith, J. G. 1976. Influence of crop background on aphids and other phytophagous insects on brussels sprouts. *Ann. Appl. Biol.* 83:1–14.

38 Southwood, T. R. 1962. Migration of terrestrial arthropods in relation to habitat. *Biol. Review* 37:171–214.

39 Tukahirwa, E. M., and Coaker, T. H. 1982. Effect of mixed cropping on some insect pests of brassicas; reduced *Brevicoryne brassicae* infestations and influences on epigeal predators and the disturbance of oviposition behavior in *Delia brassicae. Entomol. Exper. & Applic.* 32:129–140.

40 Litsinger, J. A., and Moody, K. 1976. Integrated pest management in multiple cropping systems. *Multiple Cropping.* Madison: Amer. Soc. of Agron. (Spec. Pub. No. 27): 293.

41 Matthews, D. L.; Orr, C.; and Bacon, S. 1984. Summary of 1982 and 1983 cabbage root maggot research. *Rodale Res. Rep.* (RRC/EN-84/4).

42 Pimentel, D. 1961. Species diversity and insect population outbreaks. *Ann. Entomol. Soc. Am.* 54:76.

43 Dempster, J. P., and Coaker, T. H. 1974. Diversification of crop ecosystems as a means of controlling pests. *Biology in Pest and Disease Control.* New York: Wiley & Sons, 106.

44 Buranday, R. P., and Raros, R. S. 1975. Effects of cabbage-tomato intercropping on the incidence and oviposition of the diamondback moth, *Plutella xylostella. Philipp. Entomol.* 2:369.

45 O'Donnell, M. S., and Coaker, T. H. 1975. Potential of intracrop diversity for the control of brassica pests. *Proc. 8th Brit. Insect. Fung. Conf.* 1:101.

46 Perrin, R. M. 1977. Pest management in multiple cropping systems. *Agro-Ecosystems* 3:93–118.

47 Stary, P. 1978. Seasonal relations between lucerne, red clover, wheat and barley agro-ecosystems through the aphids and parasitoids *(Homoptera, Aphididae; Hymenoptera, Aphidiidae). Acta Entomol. Bohemoelovaca* 75:296–311.

48 Clausen, C. P. 1936. *Ann. Entomol. Soc. Am.* 29:201–223.

49 Sluss, R. R. 1967. *Ecology* 48:41–58.

50 Altieri, M. A., and Todd, J. W. 1981. Some influences of vegetational diversity on insect communities of Georgia soybean fields. *Protection Ecol.* 3:333–338.

51 Foster, M. A., and Ruesink, W. G. 1984. Influence of flowering weeds associated with reduced tillage in corn on a black cutworm *(Lepidoptera: Noctuidae)* parasitoid, *Meteorus rubens. Environ. Entomol.* 13:664–668.

52 Tingle, F. C.; Ashley, T. R.; and Mitchell, E. R. 1978. Parasites of *Spodoptera exigua, S. eridania* and *Herpetogramma bipunctalis* collected from *Amaranthus hybridus* in field corn. *Entomophaga* 23(4): 343–347.

53 Adesiyun, A. A. 1979. Effects of intercrop on frit fly, *Oscinella frit*, oviposition and larval survival on oats. *Ent. Exper. & Applic.* 26:208–218.

54 Tamaki, G.; Annis, B.; and Weiss, M. 1981. Response of natural enemies to the green peach aphid in different plant cultures. *Environ. Entomol.* 10:375–378.

55 Uvah, I. I., and Coaker, T. H. 1984. Effect of mixed cropping on some insect pests of carrots and onions. *Entomol. Exper. & Appl.* 36:159–167.

56 Monteith, L. G. 1960. Influence of plants other than the food plants of their host on host-finding by tachinid parasites. *Canadian Entomol.* 42(9): 41–652.

57 Ferguson, H. J.; McPherson, R. M.; and Allen, W. A. 1984. Effect of four soybean cropping systems on the abundance of foliage-inhabiting insect predators. *Environ. Entomol.* 13:1105-1112.

58 Brook, J. 1973. The effect of plant spacing on the number of aphids trapped over cocksfoot and kale crops. *Ann. Appl. Biol.* 74: 279–285.

59 Feeny, P.; Paauwe, K. L.; and Demong, N. J. 1970. Flea beetles and mustard oils: Host plants specificity of *Phyllotreta cruciferae* and *P. striolata* adults *(Coleoptera: Chrysomelidae). Ann. Entomol. Soc. Am.* 63(3): 832–841.

60 Hammond, R. B. 1984. Effects of rye cover crop management of seedcorn maggot *(Diptera: Anthomyiidae)* populations in soybeans. *Environ. Entomol.* 13:1302–1305.

61 Pears, P. M. 1984. Intercropping/companion planting for vegetable pest control. *Henry Doubleday Res. Newsl.* 95:20–21.

62 Purvis, G., and Curry, J. P. 1984. The influence of weeds and farmyard manure on the activity of *Carabidae* and other ground-dwelling arthropods in a sugar beet crop. *J. Appl. Ecol.* 21:271–283.

63 Cromartie, W. J. 1975. The effect of stand size and vegetational background on the colonization of cruciferous plants by herbivorous insects. *J. Appl. Ecol.* 12:517–532.

64 Van Dusen, D. 1985. Weeds – future partners on the farm? *Cultivar* 3(1): 1–3.

NATURE'S BALANCE: GOOD BUGS AND BAD BUGS

Among the nooks and crannies of our gardens, there's a silent, relentless war in progress. Without the unsung heroes of this war, the predatory and parasitic insects, we would be over our heads in a mass of bugs. It's been estimated that in one year a single adult aphid, left unchecked by nature's ecological controls, would bury the earth a mile deep in new aphids!

Biological Balance Begins with Diversity

I believe in the underlying premise of organic, or biological, horticulture: diversity furthers health. The more variety a landscape has, the more sustainable it can be. The insects we call "pests" live in dynamic interplay with the surrounding environment. Insects cannot be eliminated entirely, nor should we want to eradicate them. Even pests are essential to the scheme of things, for without pests, the predatory and parasitic insects would not be able to reproduce. Nature doesn't eradicate insects, but maintains, instead, a kind of balance between the opposing sides.

Since pest problems are community related, a single insect does not always mean a problem, nor does it require a program of "control." A classic case is aphids. When my clients spot a couple of "the dread aphids," they call on me to bring forth every weapon at my disposal for eradication. Much to their surprise, my first suggestion is to wait and watch. In my experience, aphids are not a problem until they reach certain numbers. Sometimes the population never gets to what I would consider a threatening level. On many occasions, I could point out to the client a number of bloated and empty aphid bodies called mummies. These are a result of parasitizing by the larvae of a tiny wasp of the family Chalcidoidea (see Fig. 16.3). Parasitized aphids indicate to me a healthy balance between the aphid and parasitic wasps. Almost any spray, whether botanical or synthetic, would greatly reduce the population of the parasitic wasps.

Good Insects – Predators and Parasites

Insects have devised many ways to eat other insects. There are predators, those that eat insects; and parasites, or parasitoids, those that deposit an egg within the insect (or host) from which a larva emerges to devour the host's innards.

Predators don't waste time – they attack and devour. As consumers of insects, parasites take much longer. For example, after a braconid wasp lays eggs inside a tomato hornworm, it takes many days for the larvae to mature. If the larvae were to eat too fast, they would run out of food before they became adults. The parasitoids are very useful in your edible landscape as persistent search-and-destroy teams, always at work looking for pesty invaders.

As adults, female parasitoids need a high-energy fuel as they fly from place to place looking for hosts. They eat nectar, pollen, sap, and the honeydew of insects. The parasitic insects can be encouraged by providing the concentrated energy they need – primarily by growing plants that offer lots of pollen and nectar. Happily, many predators also need an abundant supply of pollen and nectar to fuel their searching activities.

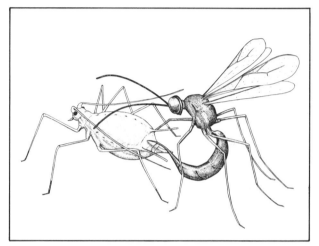

Figure 16.3 A beneficial parasitic wasp inserts an egg into an aphid.

Recognizing Adults and Larvae

It is important to be able to identify both adult and larva stages of predatory insects. When I first started looking at insects, some looked so ugly that I assumed they must be bad. Many of the people in the workshops I lead start out with the same mistaken assumption. Here's a cautionary example: the ladybug larva (see Fig. 16.4) is a warty, spiny, sluglike creature often assumed to be a pest by uninformed gardeners. But the larva does nearly as much damage to real pests as the adult and ought to be encouraged in your landscape.

Another example is the snakefly (*Apulla* sp.) pictured in Fig. 16.7. With its long, skinny neck and large, imposing head, the adult snakefly looks like a miniature dinosaur, but it is a helpful predator, stalking smaller bugs. Or take the green lacewing. The adult stage is a beautiful, delicate-winged insect. The undeniably ugly alligator-shaped larva has prominent needlelike jaws and a voracious appetite for insects.

Among the predators you ought to know and cultivate are ladybug beetles, predatory mites, big-eyed bugs, damsel bugs, minute pirate bugs, crabid beetles, robber flies, and green lacewings. They will help maintain a healthy ecological balance in your edible landscape.

Figure 16.4 The larval stage of the ladybug (3) and (4) is so ugly that people often assume it is a pest. Other stages are (1) eggs; (2) close-up of an egg; (5) larva about to shed its skin; and (6) larva shedding skin. (7), (8), and (9) are different species of adult ladybugs.

General and Specific Eaters

Some beneficial insects have very specific diets, while others will eat much that crosses their path.

General Predators and Parasites

Syrphid flies (Syrphidae family)	Prey upon aphids, leafhoppers, and mealybugs. (See Fig. 16.5.)
Predatory mites (Phytoseiidae family)	Prey on all types of mites.
Lacewings (Chrysopidae family)	Prey upon aphids, mealybugs, scale, whiteflies, mites, other lacewings, and the eggs of mites, thrips, and other insects.
Chalcid wasps (Chalcidoidea superfamily)	Parasites of aphids, scale, whiteflies, (Chalcidoidea and mealybugs.
Spiders (Arachnida order)	Prey on anything that gets stuck in their webs.
Tachinid flies (Tachinidae family)	Parasites of many grasshoppers, beetles, sawflies, caterpillars, and true bugs.
Trichogramma wasps (Trichogrammatidae family)	Parasites of the eggs of moths and butterflies.
Bee flies (Bombyliidae family)	Predators of locust eggs, parasites of the larvae of flies, wasps, bees, beetles, and ants.
Humpback flies (Phoridae family)	Predators of termites, bees, ants, crickets, caterpillars, and ladybug beetles.
Praying mantids (Manteodea family)	Eats any insect it catches, including beneficial ones.

Dragonflies (Odnata order)	Eat small flying insects, including midges and mosquitoes.
Soldier beetles (Cantharidae family)	Feed on cutworms, gypsy moth larvae, cankerworms, snails, and slugs. (See Fig. 16.6.)
Snakeflies (Raphidiidae and Inocelliidae families)	Eat small and weak insects. (See Fig. 16.7.)

Other general predators include tachinids, ichneumonids, minute pirate bugs, big-eyed bugs, assassin bugs, collops beetles, damsel bugs, earwigs (the endemic earwig, not the European earwig, which eats our young seedlings and plants), ants (yes, again, in certain situations; other times, they "farm" aphids!), lygus bugs, and anthicid beetles.

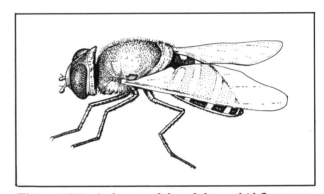

Figure 16.5 A closeup of the adult syrphid fly, resembles a bee.

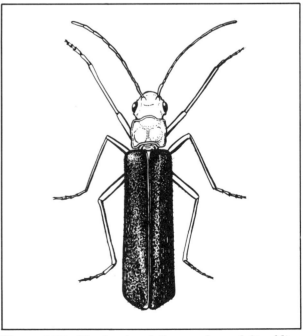

Figure 16.6 The head and thorax of an adult soldier beetle are orange, and the wings are black.

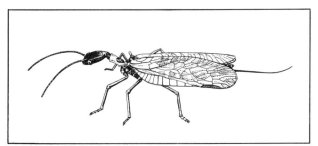

Figure 16.7 The menacing adult snakefly is often mistaken for a pest.

Specific Predators and Parasites

Ladybird beetles or ladybugs
(Coccinellidae family)

Hippodamia convergens	Eats aphids.
Adalia bipunctata	Eats aphids.
Cryptolaemus montrouziere	Eats mealybugs.
Chilocorus orbis	Eats armored scales.
Stethorus punctum	Eats mites.

Braconid wasps
(Braconidae family)

Apanteles sp.	Parasitizes caterpillars.
Aphidius sp.	Parasitizes aphids.

Fly Parasites
(Pteronalids family)

Tachinaephagus zealandicus	Parasitizes fly larvae and pupae.
Spalangia endius	Same.
Muscicifurax raptor	Same.

Thick-headed flies
(Conopidae family)

Thick-headed flies	Parasites of bees and ants.
Marsh flies	Predators and parasites of slugs and snails.

Mealybug predator
(Coccinellidae family)

Cryptolaemus montrouzieri	Eats mealybugs above ground.

Whitefly predator
(Aphelinidae family)

Encarsia formosa	Parasitizes whitefly pupae.

Predatory mites
(Phytoseiidae family)

Phytoseiulus perimilis	Eats other harmful mites.
Metaseiulus occidentalis	Same.
Amblyseius californicus	Same.

Parasitic chalcids
(Eulophidae family)

Aphelinus sp.	Parasites of aphids.
Aphytis sp.	Parasites of red scale.

Gypsy moth parasite
(Eupelmidae family)

Anastatus sp.	Parasites of the gyspy moth egg.

Black scale parasite
(Encyrtidae family)

Metaphycus helvolus	Parasites of adult black scale.

Cottony cushion scale parasite
(Cryptochaetidae family)

Cryptocheta iceryae	Parasitizes cottony cushion scale.

Grain moth parasite
(Ptermalidae family)

Habrocytus sp.	Larval parasites of the grain moth.

Ground Beetles
(Carabidae family)

Carabus sp.	Eats slugs and snails.
Scaphinotus sp.	Eats snails.

Biological Balance Means "Good" Diversity

A healthy ecosystem develops only when you carefully choose the plants in your edible landscape. There is good diversity, diversity that makes little difference, and bad diversity. For example, you wouldn't put in plants that attract aphids and others that help control aphids. Some weeds (such as plantain – *Plantago sp.*) improve the soil, yet these same weeds may attract pests (aphids) that can damage your apple trees by providing a favorite food and a winter habitat for rosy apple aphids. Polyculture – growing many types of plants in the same landscape – makes for diversity and tends to protect crops if you carefully select the plants.

Plants to Regulate Insect Pests

Landscaping plants can help regulate pests in a variety of ways, including:

- **Masking the crop plant from pests.** (Masking, of course, depends on proximity of the companion or intercrop.)

- **Producing olfactory inhibitors,** odors that confuse and deter pests. (Since the odors are subtle, this works only in intensive intercropping.)

- **Acting as trap plants** by providing an alluring food that entices pests away from crops.

- **Serving as nurse plants,** breeding grounds for beneficial insects.

- **Serving as insectary plants** that produce the food beneficial insects need as they search for and destroy pests.

- **Providing an alternative host/habitat,** usually in the form of a shelterbelt or hedgerow, where beneficial insects live and reproduce during the "off" season.

Plants that offer masking or produce olfactory inhibitors are listed in Fig. 16.2, Intercropping for Pest Control.

Using Trap Plants to Regulate Pests

Using plants to reduce pest problems requires you to know what mechanisms are at work and to accept the risk that things may not go as planned. Consider the use of nasturtiums in the landscape. They are listed in traditional companion planting charts as repelling aphids on broccoli and other cabbage family members; yet I have often noticed high populations of aphids on nasturtiums—they are among the first plants to be infested in spring. The nasturtium appears to me, in this case, to be a favorite host, acting as a trap plant, not as a repellent. Nasturtiums also have a possible role as nurse plants for the beneficial predators of aphids.

Whatever the truth, nasturtiums sound good on paper, and they work in certain situations; but there is a risk that the aphids they feed will migrate to nearby crops. Sometimes a colony of wingless aphids gets so crowded that it gives birth to winged young that ride the breeze to look for greener pastures.

Trap plants are a double-edged sword. They are not so delectable that they literally trap the pests for the whole season; but they can also act as nurseries for beneficial insects.

Using Nurse Plants to Regulate Pests

Even a crop plant can act as a nurse plant for beneficial insects. One spring at the Farallones Institute Rural Center, I followed a colony of aphids from crop to crop. It started on the fava beans as the pods filled out. The top 6 inches of many plants were covered with a black mass of aphids. Four types of beneficial insects soon showed up—ladybird beetles and their larvae, soldier beetles (see Fig. 16.6), parasitic wasps, and syrphid fly larvae (the adult syrphid fly is pictured in Fig. 16.5 and its larva is on the stem in Fig. 16.8). After many weeks, the aphids moved en masse to snow pea plants that were beyond the peak of production. The fava bean plants produced an abundant crop. The beneficial insects and their progeny soon found the new location of the aphids.

There are a number of ornamental and uncommon plants that support high populations of pests without any significant problem. As an example, I have seen oleander shrubs blackened by scale and aphids without any sign that the oleander suffered, nor did I see any aphid problems in the adjoining landscape. (As a drought-resistant evergreen plant, an oleander is a good candidate for a nurse plant in the perimeter hedgerow or windbreak.)

Sow thistle (*Sonchus* sp.) is a common "weed" in

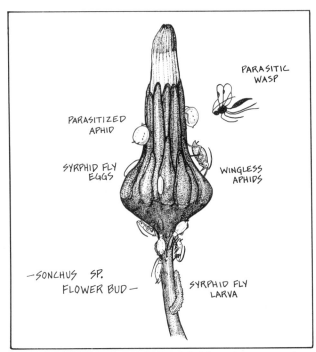

Figure 16.8 Two types of beneficial insects are preying on the aphids. The two spherical aphids on the bud have already been parasitized by wasps, and a syrphid fly larva munches a path through the herd of aphids on the stem.

most landscapes around my county. It is one of the first places each spring that I spot beneficial insects eating and parasitizing aphids. Since the plant is easily controlled, I always leave some sow thistle to grow through the winter to act as an early spring nurse plant.

Another possible nurse plant for out-of-the-way places is stinging nettle *(Urtica dioica).* (Beware, nettle can become a very tenacious weed. A good design strategy is to plant it in a moist soil at the base of a slope or hill, making sure there is a zone of very dry soil between the nettles and the rest of your landscape.) This moisture-loving perennial is best known for leaving a fiery sting on the legs of wandering hikers, but it is also a hardy herbaceous plant that harbors no important pest or pathogen of common vegetables. One particular aphid feeds on stinging nettle, but not on food crops. A study done in England found that eleven types of predators and parasites fed upon the nettle aphids. The populations of the predators and parasites increased in late April and early May, prior to the increase of pests in the nearby fields, building a reserve of beneficial insects. While the results were not conclusive, it appears that cutting the nettles at the right time would force some of the beneficial insects (for example, ladybird beetles) onto the crop.

Studies are underway in this country with corn spurry *(Spergula arvensis)* as a nurse plant for syrphid (hover) flies. This well-behaved weed does not compete with the main crop, it is easy to eliminate, it helps develop a loose soil structure, and it can be mowed and fed to cattle. Corn spurry harbors innocuous aphids that the hover flies feed on. Once the population of hover flies increases, it can then move out into the landscape in pursuit of aphids that colonize food crops.

To be on the safe side, use the plants that you know are preferred by pests around the perimeters of your landscape. Intercropping is risky. Be prepared to step in with a botanical spray if you think the pests are migrating to nearby crops, or simply cut the infested plants and add to a fresh, hot compost pile.

Borror, Donald, and White, Richard. **A Field Guide to the Insects**. Boston: Houghton & Mifflin, 1970. My favorite insect reference since the bug-collecting days of my youth.

Carr, Anna. **Color Handbook of Garden Insects**. Emmaus, PA: Rodale Press, 1979. An excellent color reference, with brief suggestions for pest management. Best for Eastern and Midwestern gardeners—gives poor coverage of insects of the Western U.S.

Metcalf, C.L. **Destructive and Useful Insects**. New York: McGraw-Hill, 1962. An early review of good bugs and pests. Your library may have a copy.

Philbrick, Helen, and Gregg, Richard. **Companion Plants and How to Use Them**. 8th ed. Old Greenwich, CT: Devin-Adair, 1976. One of the original sources of companion planting information. Contains some good information, but I find many of the folklore-based recommendations to be untrue or inappropriate.

Philbrick, Helen and John. **The Bug Book**. Charlotte, VT: Garden Way Publishing, 1974. A good, no-nonsense book on safe, organic methods for pest control. Well worth purchasing.

Riotte, Louise. **Carrots Love Tomatoes**. Pownal, VT: Garden Way Publishing, 1984. The most popular book on companion planting. (Formerly *Companion Planting for Successful Gardening*.) Few scientific studies are cited. Riotte's recommendations overlap and sometimes contradict the Philbricks' in *Companion Plants and How to Use Them*.

Rodale Press. **The Encyclopedia of Organic Gardening**. Emmaus, PA: Rodale Press, 1978. *The* bible for organic gardeners. Sometimes too wordy, sometimes too lean; still, a must for every edible landscaper's library.

ATTRACTING GOOD BUGS

You can lure beneficial insects to your place without using pests as bait, by growing flowers that fuel the search-and-destroy missions of good insects. Insectary plants can serve more than just the function of pest control; some are edible, some colorful, and some fragrant.

Designing to Include Insectary Plants

While we may be able to somewhat shape the insect ecology of our yards by the types of flowering plants we grow, keep in mind that there is very little research on the subject, and I run the risk of starting new myths by mentioning specific plants and specific insects. When designing your edible landscape to attract good insects, remember that:

- The following examples are steppingstones for study, experimentation, and observation, and they may not work in your climate or ecology.

- You will need to carefully observe the relationship of all kinds of flowers and insects in your area to come up with local possibilities not mentioned here. Make as many trials as possible over many years to determine what works in your area.

- This is great backyard research—watching insects can be exciting and entertaining. Close study of insects' habits tends to make the observer more appreciative, and often cures a fear of insects.

- Insect behavior changes from year to year and from place to place.

- The use of flowers to regulate pests is not a cure-all—you will probably need to intervene to control any number of pests each year.

Types of Flowers That Attract Beneficial Insects

Most beneficial insects need a high-protein, high-sugar food, and most parasitic insects and predators have short mouthparts that cannot reach far into a flower for nectar and pollen. Small flowers, their pollen and nectar within reach, are preferred by many beneficial insects. Two major categories of flowers fit their needs—the sunflower and parsley families.

Umbellifers

Parsley belongs to the Umbelliferae family (recently renamed the Apiaceae family), plants distinguished by many tiny flowers arranged in clusters, with the clusters arranged in an umbel, an umbrella shape (see Fig. 16.12 in color plates).

Vegetables in this family include carrots, parsnips, parsley, celery, celeriac, and Florence fennel. The common herbs – dill, cumin, anise, coriander, and caraway – belong to this family. Some uncommon herbs in the Umbelliferae family include: gotu kola, lovage, angelica, chervil, and skirret. Some wild or native umbellifers include poison hemlock (*Conium maculatum*); water hemlock (*Ciculta douglasii*); Queen Anne's lace, or wild carrot (*Daucus carota*); toothpick weed (*Amni visaga*); and cow parsnip (*Pastinaca sativa*).

As a group, umbellifer flowers produce large amounts of nectar for short periods of time. Each flower quickly fades, but the entire cluster blooms for some time (although for a shorter period than many plants in the sunflower family). Most of these plants produce thousands of seeds each year and are quite invasive if not tended to.

Composites

The members of the sunflower family (recently renamed the Asteraceae family) are classified as composites and have many tiny flowers arranged together in one large cluster or composition. Artichoke, lettuce, endive, salsify, chicory, edible chrysanthemum, cardoon, sunflower, dandelion, and Jerusalem artichoke belong to this family. The herbs that belong to this family include: yarrows, artemisias, elecampane, feverfew, costmary, and tansy. There are hundreds of varieties of ornamental plants in this family, among them marigolds, zinnias, thistles, asters, calendulas, and gazanias.

While the flowers of a Compositae have less nectar than those of Umbelliferae, the flower heads mature over a longer time, prolonging the flow of nectar. I like to think of the sunflower family as providing the "background music" for attracting beneficial insects. The parsley family provides the "percussion" for emphasis at times during the year.

Flowers at the Right Times

From midsummer until early fall, a landscape with any variety at all has plenty of sources of nectar and pollen available. The difficult time is early spring. Aphids awake from winter quite early and function well at temperatures as low as 45° F or less. It takes some searching and experimenting to find insectary plants that bloom early enough to overlap with the early spring aphid "bloom." In my area, there are very few umbellifers and not many composites in bloom before May. The best umbellifer for early bloom, in the coastal hills around my house, is the cow parsnip *(Pastinaca sativa)*. This poisonous plant has a glorious pure white umbel and is the first of the umbellifers to attract quantities of parasitic wasps. Sometimes the temperatures are so cool while the cow parsnip is blooming that the parasitic wasps are not active, even though the aphids are breeding faster than rabbits. Each year beneficial insects arrive at different times, but there is usually something on the cow parsnip flowers that eats or parasitizes aphids.

Some members of the composite family that bloom around my house in early spring are gazanias, African trailing daisies, and calendulas, but I have not seen many bugs gathering on these flowers, certainly far fewer than on a cow parsnip flower head. I planted thousands of square feet of African trailing daisies when I was a landscaper and never noticed many insects visiting the blossoms.

Other Flowers for Insectary Plantings

The umbellifers and composites do not have a corner on the insectary market; Fig. 16.9 lists other plants that may work in your edible landscape. As you experiment with these insectary plant candidates, please keep in mind the limitations and cautions given at the beginning of the chapter.

Figure 16.9

POTENTIAL INSECTARY PLANTS

Common Name/ Botanical Name	Beneficial Insects Attracted
Alfalfa (*Medicago sativa*)	Minute pirate bugs, big-eyed bugs, damsel bugs, assassin bugs, ladybugs, parasitic wasps[2]
Angelica (*Angelica* sp.)	Ladybugs; lacewings; potter, mud-dauber, and sand wasps[5]
Baby blue eyes (*Nemophila inignis*)	Syrphid flies[4]
Buckwheat (*Fagopyrum esculentum*)	Syrphid flies[4]
California buckwheat (*Eriogonum* sp.)	Potter, mud-dauber, and sand wasps; tachina, chloropid, and syrphid flies; minute pirate bugs[1]
California coffeeberry (*Rhamnus californica*)	Tachinid and syrphid flies; ladybugs; mud-dauber, sand, ichneumon, and braconid wasps; lacewings[1]
Camphorweed (*Heterotheca subaxillaris*)	Stink bugs, assassin bugs, ground beetles, spiders[3]
Candytuft (*Iberis umbellata*)	Syrphid flies[4]
Carrot (*Daucus carota*)	Minute pirate bugs, big-eyed bugs, assassin bugs; lacewings; parasitic, potter, and predaceous wasps[2]
Coriander (*Coriandrum sativum*)	Tachinid flies[5]
Coyote brush (*Baccharis pilularis*)	Syrphid, chloropid, and tachina flies; braconid, ichneumon, potter, mud-dauber, sand, and chalcid wasps[1]

Common Name/ Botanical Name	Beneficial Insects Attracted
Evening primroses (*Oenthera laciniata* and *O. biennis*)	Ground beetles[3]
Evergreen euonymus (*Euonymus japonica*)	Lacewings; chloropid, tachinid, and syrphid flies; chalcid, braconid, mud-dauber, sand, and ichneumon wasps; ladybugs[1]
Fennel* (*Foeniculum vulgare*)	Potter, braconid, mud-dauber, and sand wasps; syrphid and tachinid flies[1]
Goldenrod (*Solidago altissima*)	Predaceous beetles, big-eyed bugs, ladybugs, spiders, parasitic wasps, long-legged flies, assassin bugs[3]
Ivy (*Hedera* sp.)	Flower and tachinid flies; braconid, potter, mud-dauber, sand, hornet, and yellow jacket wasps[5]
Meadow foam (*Limnanthes douglasii*)	Syrphid flies[4]
Mediterranean umble (*Bupleurum fruticosum*)	Tachinid flies; sand, mud-dauber and potter wasps[1]
Mexican tea (*Chenopodium ambrosioides*)	Stink bugs, ladybugs, assassin bugs, big-eyed bugs[3]
Morning glory, perennial ornamental (*Convolvulus minor*)	Syrphid flies, ladybugs[4]
Oleander (*Nerium oleander*)	Minute pirate bugs, big-eyed bugs, assassin bugs, ladybugs, soft-winged flower beetles, lacewings, syrphid flies, parasitic wasps[2]
Pigweed* (*Amaranthus* sp.)	Ground beetles[3]
Ragweed (*Ambrosia artemisiifolia*)	Ladybugs, assassin bugs, spiders[3]
Rue (*Ruta graveolens*)	Ichneumon and potter wasps[1]
Saltbush (*Atriplex* sp.)	Potter, sand, and mud-dauber wasps[1]
Silver lace vine (*Polygonum aubertii*)	Tachinid and syrphid flies[1]
Snowberry (*Symphoricarpos* sp.)	Flower and tachinid flies[5]
Soapbark tree (*Quillaja saponaria*)	Syrphid and chloropid flies; lacewings; ladybugs; ichneumon, chalcid and braconid wasps[1]
Tree of heaven* (*Ailanthus altissima*)	Syrphid and chloropid flies; braconid, ichneumon, and potter wasps; lacewings[1]
White clover (*Trifolium repens*)	Parasitic wasps of aphids, scales, and whiteflies[5]
White sweet clover (*Melilotus alba*)	Tachinid flies; mud-dauber, sand, hornet, and yellow jacket wasps[5]
White mustard (*Brassica hirta*)	Braconid and ichneumon wasps[5]
Wild lettuce (*Lactuca canadensis*)	Soldier beetles, lacewings, earwigs, syrphid flies[3]
Yarrow (*Achillea* sp.)	Ladybugs; parasitic wasps of aphids, scales, and whiteflies[5]

*Warning: invasive plant

continued

Figure 16.9 continued

[1]Bugg, Robert. *Perennial Insectary Plants*. List. Winters, CA: International Tree Crops Institute, 1980.
[2]Crepps, William, and Ehler, L. E. *Influence of Specific Non-Crop Vegetation on the Insect Fauna of Small-Scale Agroecosystems*. (n.p., n.d.)
[3]Altieri, Miguel, and Whitcomb, Willard. *Manipulation of Insect Populations Through Seasonal Disturbance of Weed Communities*. Agricultural Experiment Station Journal Series No. 1283. Gainsville, FL: Dept. of Entomology, Univ. of Florida, 1979.
[4]Hills, Lawrence; Director, Henry Doubleday Research Assoc., Bocking, England. Letter, 1983; and reprints from *Soil and Health* Newsletter, 1979.
[5]Tilth. *The Future is Abundant*. Arlington, Wa: Tilth, 1982.
(end of figure)

The results of your experiments may be as varied as the scientific data. In England, plots of fava beans that were intercropped with meadow foam had only 1.6% blackfly infestation, compared to 37% infestation in the control plot without meadow foam. But for carrot, alfalfa, and oleander, other research found that "Non-crop vegetation planted close to vegetable plants did little to reduce naturally occurring pest infestations. A number of natural enemies inhabited the insectary plants, but in most instances this did not lead to an increase in their densities on crop plants . . . An increase in the floral diversity within an agroecosystem will not necessarily ensure decreased pest densities or problems."

Organic Gardening Magazine, ed. **Getting the Most from Your Garden**. Emmaus, PA: Rodale Press, 1980. A poorly edited book that expands on Jeavons' *How to Grow More Vegetables*. It explains in detail how to adapt the French intensive method to a variety of climates, and gives much more information on cloches and coldframes. The inclusion of an index is a welcome improvement over Jeavons' book.

Philbrick, Helen, and Gregg, Richard. **Companion Plants and How to Use Them**. 8th ed. Old Greenwich, CT: Devin-Adair, 1976. One of the original sources of companion planting information. Contains some good information, but I find many of the folklore-based recommendations to be untrue or inappropriate.

Philbrick, Helen and John. **The Bug Book**. Charlotte, VT: Garden Way Publishing, 1974. A good, no-nonsense book on safe, organic methods for pest control. Well worth purchasing.

Riotte, Louise. **Carrots Love Tomatoes**. Pownal, VT: Garden Way Publishing, 1984. The most popular book on companion planting. (Formerly *Companion Planting for Successful Gardening*.) Few scientific studies are cited. Riotte's recommendations overlap and sometimes contradict the Philbricks' in *Companion Plants and How to Use Them*.

Rodale Press. **The Encyclopedia of Organic Gardening**. Emmaus, PA: Rodale Press, 1978. *The* bible for organic gardeners. Sometimes too wordy, sometimes too lean; still, a must for every edible landscaper's library.

INTEGRATED PEST MANAGEMENT

Spraying chemicals to control insects has always seemed to me to resemble antiguerilla warfare – an all-out assault using brute strength against an elusive and insidious enemy. In fact, pests are never totally eliminated by any type of assault; they adapt, multiply, and develop more creative and diabolical ways to besiege our crops. "Control" seems to come only with continuous assault and ever-increasing armaments. It is a vicious cycle of assault followed by counterattack.

A different sort of "control" is possible: coexistence. Integrated pest management (IPM) is a fancy phrase for an approach to bug control that respects the environment; it works with the ecology of plants and bugs and relies on the educated skill of the gardener. The IPM approach tries to maintain a healthy balance between good bugs and bad. If the balance should shift, and pests begin to threaten a satisfactory harvest, then and only then are other techniques brought to bear – techniques that are the least complex, least costly, and least upsetting to the environment, and which may include the limited use of chemical poisons. IPM walks the zone between human intervention and the checks and balances of a natural ecology.

The IPM Guidelines

Throughout the guidelines that follow, I will use the ubiquitous aphid as an example. At the end of the chapter (see Fig. 16.10) are suggestions for biological controls for many other pests. The purpose of the following guidelines is to show that the more you understand the pests in your landscape, the less you will need this book – or any book – to tell you how to control them. You'll be able to formulate your own IPM strategy.

Begin with a healthy soil.

A soil with good tilth and the full range of balanced nutrients usually has the least amount of insect and disease problems. Simply adding plenty of fertilizers does not necessarily help – for example, too much nitrogen can promote insect and disease problems.

Observe the plants and insects that inhabit your edible landscape and learn about their place in the surrounding environment.

This is the fun part of pest control – getting to know your enemies, your allies, and the nature of the plants you want to protect. Reading gardening books helps, but there's no substitute for getting outside, growing plants, watching the insects that colonize or visit them, and learning where the insects come from. You will notice that aphids often show up first on a few weeds surrounding the vegetables, that snow pea plants don't often get infested with aphids until they are past their peak of production, that ladybug beetles are not the first beneficial bugs to attack aphids in the early spring, that aphids are awfully difficult to rinse off the leaves of Dwarf Siberian Curled Kale, that many aphids don't have wings to fly to other plants. Your observations are the start of an IPM program.

Get to know the major pests of your area – learn how they look, live, reproduce, what kind of damage they inflict, and how much tolerance different plants have to them.

Many pests are specific to a particular type of plant and will not move from one plant to another. Aphids come in all colors and types. The black aphids that inhabit fava bean plants do not bother apple tree leaves. If survival is threatened, a single female aphid gives birth to live young without the need of mating. Many crops support high populations of aphids without too much reduction in yield. In my landscape, mustard greens are rarely bothered by aphids, whereas brussels sprouts seem to be a preferred place of residence. Though they may not be responsible for much direct damage, aphids are vectors (a transmitting organism) for a number of diseases and plant viruses.

Monitor the populations of pests throughout the season.

Get down on your knees – observe, count, and catch those insects. Don't attack until you are sure there is a problem; give beneficial insects, changes in the weather, and other natural agents of balance a chance to work.

Pheromone traps provide an accurate and convenient way to monitor many pests of tree crops. A pheromone is a chemical substance produced by insects and animals that stimulates certain behavior of other members of the same species. The traps (working on the principle that insects rely on the odor of the opposite sex to aid them in finding mates) are baited with the female odor of a particular insect and will indicate when the male pests, and by extension, the females, first arrive on the scene. Pheromone traps come in all kinds and shapes, but each has a very sticky coating and a capsule of the liquid scent of the female. For each pest there is a different trap, and many state agricultural extension services publish handbooks explaining how to use the traps as monitoring devices. By counting the trapped males, you can estimate when to spray to control adults, recently laid eggs, or newly hatched larvae. A single pheromone trap does not act as a control, even though it takes a lot of eligible males out of circulation. And the traps are too expensive to use in numbers great enough for control.

Learn the weaknesses of the major pests. At what point in their life cycle are they killed most easily? Find out what your local ecology does to keep the major pests in check.

Some insects are best controlled at only one stage of their life cycle: egg, larva, pupa, or adult. Others are vulnerable at several stages. Adult scale is best controlled by a dormant oil spray in the winter. Soft-bodied pests, such as aphids, are vulnerable during most of their life cycle to innocuous controls such as diatomaceous earth, soapy water, garlic juice, and ashes. However, none of these is effective against aphid eggs.

In my area, a number of predatory and parasitic insects attack aphids—each at a different time in the season. First to show up are soldier beetles (pictured in Fig. 16.6). They are followed by ladybird beetles, then syrphid fly larvae, and finally tiny wasps that parasitize the aphids (see Fig. 16.3).

When the weather is hot and dry, aphids are seldom a problem, but frequent overhead watering extends the aphid season into the hot summer months.

Starting with a good defense, develop an integrated plan to moderate pest populations before they get out of hand.

The first step in defending your landscape is to plant varieties resistant to your area's major pests. I plant more mustard greens than brussels sprouts, partly because aphids don't bother the spicy mustard greens (but mostly, because I prefer tons of mustard greens to even a pound of brussels sprouts). Figure 16.11 lists some vegetables with pest resistance.

When it's time to act, use the most effective strategy to attack the pest at its most vulnerable stage.

Observe carefully and wait until absolutely necessary to act. Time is the best teacher. Years of gardening will sharpen your instincts about when to wait and when to act. When it's time for action, first use the techniques that least harm the beneficial insects and the environment. Sometimes a quick pinch of the fingers is all that is needed to stop a blossoming aphid colony in its tracks. I often use pruning clippers for pest control. I clip leaves with dense "herds" of aphids and add them to the compost pile. Though the larvae of some beneficial insects also end up in the compost, most of the adults escape unharmed.

When spraying, people usually forget to think of the innocent bystanders, many of them good insects. The mildest of insecticidal sprays can easily kill predatory insects because they are just as sensitive, or even more so, to the sprays as aphids are. Clipping and pinching are far less damaging than any type of spray—even plain water—because fewer beneficial insects are disturbed or destroyed.

If you spray, some aphids survive. They are more likely to repopulate your plants than are the beneficials, especially the parasitic wasps. At temperatures as low as 55° F, aphids can bear two or more young a day. Below 59° F, the parasitic braconid wasp virtually stops laying eggs. At low temperatures, there is practically no way for the parasitic wasps to catch up with a booming aphid population. At higher temperatures, the wasps easily repopulate fast enough to control the aphids, but it takes time.

When heavy applications of toxic sprays kill bad *and* good insects, a vicious cycle can begin. By creating an environment devoid of natural enemies, the reemerging pests bounce back quickly, requiring yet another, more powerful, spray. Many beneficial insects, including ground beetles and some ladybird beetles, have only one life cycle (or generation) each year; once killed, they are gone for the year. A cycle of insecticidal spraying can develop with *both* chemical and botanical, or organic, sprays. This self-perpetuating cycle is an important reason for holding back on sprays until absolutely necessary. In my toolshed is a bottle of Safer's Insecticidal Soap™ and some diatomaceous earth in case I need a last resort.

Change your plan according to how the pests respond.

Any control program that is based on the calendar or a product label's recommendations is probably a waste of time and money. Preventive sprays, based on the assumption that pests always show up, are the most foolish of all. When and if insects show up is dependent on climate, not the calendar.

If you can accept the amount of damage an insect makes, refrain from attacking. Often, bad insects fail to become pests. I've mentioned that certain fava bean plants in my landscape often have the top 6 to 8 inches covered with aphids. By observation and restraint, I learned that the aphids often move on or disappear with no lasting effect on the yield of the favas.

However, some pests should not be totally ignored. With pests such as the codling moth, tomato hornworm, tent caterpillar, and carrot rust fly, the pupa or egg stage takes place on the plant or in the soil below. If left totally unchecked, these pests may return in greater numbers each year. You cannot eliminate these pests, but with seasonal control, you can prevent a general buildup.

Be prepared for the unexpected. Have a backup plan.

Late each spring, the apple tree near my office window is likely to have an outbreak of rosy apple aphids. I attempt to prevent this infestation by placing a band of Tanglefoot™, a sticky goo, around the trunk several feet off the ground. (Put Tanglefoot™ directly on the bark of only those trees that are at least four years old. For younger trees, you must first tie a protective layer of plastic to the trunk, then smear the Tanglefoot™ on the plastic.) Knowing that aphids are not very good fliers and that they often are transported into trees by ants, I use the Tanglefoot™ band to stop the ants, and therefore the aphids.

In spite of the Tanglefoot™, some years aphids attack the new growth in great numbers. This past year was particularly bad for apple aphids, so I used a spray of Safer's Insecticidal Soap™. While spraying, I hit at least six parasitic wasps, but I continued, trying to prevent the twisted growth characteristic of apple aphid damage. IPM often involves such painful compromises.

Work to improve the environment of your landscape so that it will augment the strategies you are using.

Design your edible landscape to attract as many beneficial insects as possible. My vegetable beds are bordered by perennial flower beds that include many of the potentially useful insectary plants.

Sanitation can be a great help in preventing a buildup of pests. All diseased plants should be either disposed of or placed into the middle of a very hot compost pile. All fruits and nuts that fall to the ground and begin to rot should receive the same treatment. Some diseases of fruit trees, such as scab, brown rot, shot hole fungus, powdery mildew, and peach leaf curl, winter over on the dead leaves lying beneath the tree. Spring rains spread the spores of these diseases back up into the trees in increasing quantities over the years. Rake up the leaves of diseased plants in the fall and compost or dispose of them. Dried fruits or nuts left hanging on a tree harbor pests and diseases and should be treated in the same way as the fallen leaves.

Some pests of vegetables proliferate in untilled soil; examples are symphylans (or garden centipede), tomato hornworms, codling moths, striped cucumber beetles, cutworms, earwigs, slugs, snails, grubs, Japanese beetles, june bugs, and wireworms (larval stage of the click beetle). Tillage can disrupt the life cycle of these pests. The no-till method is not as appropriate as tilling when these pests are prevalent.

Diversify the ecosystem.

Diversity can help to provide stability in natural ecosystems. As mentioned earlier, however, diversity can be good *and* bad. Study the possible impact of new plants before planting. Design your edible landscape to have a manageable amount of productive diversity. You can add and subtract from your yard's variety each year to experiment with new blends of diversity. Be sure to carefully watch the interactions that develop after introducing each new plant.

IPM in Brief

The examples in Fig. 16.10 reveal the variety of responses possible when dealing with pests. For almost every pest there are several or more alternatives. Choose the least troublesome option first, for you and for the environment. New strategies for dealing with pests are being researched and discovered every month. The best journal about the latest in biological controls is *Common Sense Pest Control Quarterly* from BIRC, P.O. Box 7414, Berkeley, CA 94707.

In summary: observe; wait and see; when in doubt, don't. And above all, be gentle. Promote diversity—use companion plantings judiciously; don't try to eliminate all plants that are preferred by the pesty bugs, and cultivate flowering plants that attract beneficial insects.

Figure 16.10

NECESSARY BIO-SELECTOR™ FOR INSECT PEST CONTROL

Deterrent Actions				Traps		Common Insect Pests	Biologicals		Minerals, oils				Beneficials		Botanicals			
Variety selection	Planting date	Crop rotation	Trapping crops	Pheromone traps	Catch traps		BT-B. Thuringiensis	Other pathogens	Dormant oil	Safer's soap	Miscible oil	DE-Diatom. Earth	Parasites	Predators	Ryania	Rotenone	Pyrethrins	Nicotine
						Alfalfa Caterpillar	★						★	★				
						Alfalfa Looper	★						★	★				
★			★		★	Aphids [1]				★				★			★	★
						Asparagus Beetle							★		★	★		
						Bagworm	★											
★		★				Cabbage Butterfly [10]	★						★					
★		★				Cabbage Looper [2]	★							★	★	★		
					★	Cockroaches						★			★	★		
				★	★	Codling Moth [3]	★	★	★		★		★	★	★		★	
★	★	★	★	★	★	Corn Earworm [4]			★		★		★	★	★		★	
★		★				Diamondback Moth [6]	★											
★	★	★				European Corn Borer [9]							★		★	★	★	
						Fall Webworm	★											
						Flea Beetles [7]					★					★	★	★
						Fleas					★					★	★	
★						Grasshoppers		★						★				
						Green Cloverworm	★											
				★	★	Gypsy Moth	★							★			★	
						Hornworm	★						★	★				
				★	★	Housefly							★	★		★	★	★
	★		★			Japanese Beetle [11]		★								★	★	
					★	Leafhopper [8]				★		★						
				★		Leafroller	★						★	★			★	
						Mealybug			★	★	★			★				
★	★		★			Mexican Bean Beetle [12]							★			★	★	
★						Mites			★	★	★			★		★	★	★
						Oriental Fruit Moth				★			★	★	★		★	
						Pear Psylla			★	★	★			★				
						Scale [13]			★	★	★			★				
★	★	★	★			Spotted Cucum. Beetle [5]										★	★	★
						Spruce Budworm	★										★	
	★					Stinkbugs					★					★	★	
★	★	★	★			Striped Cucum. Beetle [5]										★	★	★
						Tent Caterpillar	★										★	
						Thrips [14]				★				★			★	
				★		Tobacco Budworm	★						★	★	★		★	
		★		★		Tomato Fruitworm	★						★	★	★		★	
						Tussock Moth	★										★	
						Velvetbean Caterpillar	★											
					★	Whitefly [15]				★	★						★	★

continued

ADDITIONAL STRATEGIES FOR PEST CONTROL

(from "Biological Control of Insect Pests," Altieri et al. *American Horticulture*, 1982, 61 (2):28-35.)

[1] **Aphids.** Use sticky yellow traps. Foil mulch acts as a repellent. Botanical insecticides include coiine, and a spray of garlic and onion juice. Predators include ladybugs, lacewings, soldier beetles, earwigs (for apple aphids), and syrphids.

[2] **Cabbage looper.** Cultivate the soil early in the spring to disrupt pupae. Hand pick. Predators include the encyrtid parasite and paper wasps. Another botanical control is the pathogenic polyhedral virus.

[3] **Codling moth.** Tie burlap and cardboard strips around the trunk to trap pupating larvae. Predators include *Trichogramma* wasps and brachonid larval parasites. Another pathogen includes the granulosis virus.

[4] **Corn earworm.** Apply oil to the silks 3 to 7 days after they appear. Predators include the *Trichogramma* egg parasite. Use a water extract of pigweed (*Amaranthus* sp.) to attract the egg parasites.

[5] **Cucumber beetles.** Controls include lime spray and road dust. Early spring cultivation disrupts eggs and adults. Radishes act as an early trap plant.

[6] **Diamondback moth.** Intercropping with tomatoes and/or southernwood (*Artemsia abrotanum*) will reduce the problem. A predator is the ichneumonid wasp.

[7] **Flea beetles.** Rotate crops. Try an intercrop of lettuce-radish-kohlrabi-radish-lettuce. Till under the foliage and stems each fall to disrupt the pupae cycle.

[8] **Leafhopper.** Weed out alternate host plants. Blackberry borders for grapes, and grassy weeds around beans, provide a habitat for the predators of leafhoppers. Botanical sprays include nicotine sulphate.

[9] **European corn borer.** Till under all foliage and stalks to disrupt the pest cycle. Rotate with soybeans, red clover, and alfalfa. Predators include the tachnid parasite, brachonid wasp, and protozoan parasite.

[10] **Cabbage butterfly.** Hand pick caterpillars. A predator is the brachonid wasp.

[11] **Japanese beetle.** Pathogens include the bacterial milky spore. Sticky yellow traps, if baited with a pheromone, help trap adults. Jimson weed (*Datura stramonium*) is an effective intercrop (*warning: datura is very poisonous*). Trap crops include soybean, African marigold, evening primrose, and woodbine. Predators include parasitic wasps, moles, skunks, and birds.

[12] **Mexican bean beetle.** Till under infested crops and destroy egg masses. Intercrop with potatoes.

[13] **Scale.** Control ants with Tanglefoot™ on the trunks of trees. Predators include parasitic wasps, aphid lions, syrphid fly larvae, and ladybugs.

[14] **Thrips.** Keep plants well-watered. A light oil spray is effective.

[15] **White fly.** Use sticky yellow traps. The juvenile hormone Kinosprene stops their cycle. Use French marigolds and nasturtiums as an intercrop. The main predator is the eulophid wasp (*Encarsia formosa*).

Figure 16.10

Figure 16.11

PEST-RESISTANT
VEGETABLE VARIETIES

Crop	Insect	Resistant Varieties
Bean	Mexican bean beetle	'Wade'[1]
		'Black Valentine'[2]
		'Idaho Refugee'[2]
		'Logan'[2]
		'Super Green'[2]
	Melon fly	'Kentucky Wonder'[1]
	Pod borer	'Wild Lima Bean'[1]
	Potato leafhopper	'Redkloud'[2]
		'Fordhook'[2]
	Seedcorn maggot	'Charlevoix'[2]
		'Red Kidney'[2]
		'Royal Red'[2]
		'Viva'[2]
		'Spartan'[2]
		'Arrow'[2]
Cabbage	Cabbage maggot	'Early Jersey'[1]
	Cabbage root maggot	'Red Dutch'[1]
Corn	Corn earworm	'Dixie 18'[3]
		'Calumet'[3]
Cucumber	Cucumber beetle	'Stono'[3]
		'Fletcher'[3]
		'Niagra'[3]
Muskmelon	Cucumber beetle	'Hearts of Gold'[3]
		'Gold Cup 55'[1]
	Melon aphid	'Smith's Perfect'[3]
		'Cuban Castillian'[3]
		'Rocky Dew'[3]
		'Homegarden'[3]
		'Texas Resistant #1'[3]
Onion	Onion thrip	'Sweet Spanish'[1]
	Onion maggot	'Hishiko'[2]
		'Nebuka'[2]
		'Welsh Onion'[2]
Pea	Pea aphid	'Champion of England'[2]
		'Laurier'[2]
		'Melting Sugar'[2]
		'Prince of Wales'[4]
Potato	Colorado potato beetle	'Sequoia'[3]
	Flea beetle	'Sequoia'[2]
	Green peach aphid	'De Sota'[2]
		'British Queen'[2]
		'Early Pinkeye'[2]
		'Houma'[2]
		'Irish Daisy'[2]
		'La Salle'[2]
Pumpkin	Squash vine borer	'Green Striped Cushaw'[1]
		'Dickson'[1]
		'Large Sweet Cheese'[1]
		'Sweet Potato'[1]
		'Kentucky Field'[1]
Spinach	Aphid	'Manchuria'[1]

Crop	Insect	Resistant Varieties
Squash	Cucumber beetle	'Royal Acorn'[1]
		'Early Golden Bush Scallop'[1]
		'White Bush Scallop'[1]
		'Summer Crookneck'[1]
		'Early Prolific Straightneck'[1]
		'Butternut'[1]
	Squash bug	'Royal Acorn'[1]
		'Butternut'[1]
		'Table Queen'[3]
		'Sweet Cheese'[3]
		'Early Golden Bush Scallop'[3]
		'Early Summer Crookneck'[3]
		'Early Prolific Straightneck'[3]
		'Improved Green Hubbard'[3]
	Squash vine borer	'Butternut'[1]
Sweet potato	Southern potato wireworm	'Centennial'[2]
		'Jewel'[2]
		'Nemagold'[2]
		'Resisto'[5]
		'Regal'[5]
	Grubs	'Resisto'[5]
		'Regal'[5]
	Sweet potato flea beetle	'Centenniel'[2]
		'Jewel'[2]
		'Nemagold'[2]
		'Porto Rico'[2]
		'Travis'[2]
	Sweet potato weevil	'Del Valle'[2]
		'Picadita'[2]
Tomato	Spider mites	'Kewalo'[2]
	Tobacco flea beetle	'Oxneart'[2]
		'Pearson A'[2]
Turnip	Root maggot	'Petrosky'[1]

[1]Nath, Dr. Prem. *Breeding Vegetable Crops for Resistance to Insect Pests*. Rome: FAO.

[2]Hallman, Guy. "Doing Your Part for Pest Resistance." *The New Farm*, Vol. 4, No. 3 March/April, 1982.

[3]Painter, Reginald. *Insect Resistance in Crop Plants*. University Press of Kansas, 1951.

[4]Entomology Society of Ontario. *1936 Annual Report*. Vol. 67, pp. 40–45.

[5]Brusko, Mike. "Plants Pests Don't Like." *The New Farm*, Vol. 6, No. 4, May/June, 1984.

Jordan, William, Jr. **Windowsill Ecology**. Emmaus, PA: Rodale Press, 1977. The most detailed of the non-technical references on the use of beneficial insects in greenhouses, atriums, and homes.

Philbrick, Helen and John. **The Bug Book**. Charlotte, VT: Garden Way Publishing, 1974. A good, no-nonsense book on safe, organic methods for pest control. Well worth purchasing.

SOIL IS HEALTH – IMPROVING SOILS, FREE FERTILIZERS

Feeding the Soil

FEEDING THE SOIL

Organic gardening treats the soil as a living organism. Chemical gardeners act as if the soil is just a medium for chemical solutions – it could just as easily be Styrofoam pellets. The basic idea of organic gardening is that you feed the soil and its diverse population of beneficial creatures – from amoebas and bacteria to worms – then the soil feeds your plants. Well-fed soil is healthy, productive soil.

Sir Albert Howard, the founding father of organic gardening and farming, stated it clearly in *An Agricultural Testament:* "There must always be a perfect balance between the processes of growth and decay. The consequences of this condition are a living soil, abundant crops of good quality, and livestock which possess the bloom of health."

Plenty of Humus

Humus, the decomposed, nearly stable remains of organic matter, is responsible for the transformation of nutrients from mineral form into the soluble form that plants require. Without renewal, humus is soon consumed, and without it an edible landscape would wither and die. Humus is essential.

Two important ways to turn plants into organic matter and then into humus are cover crops and green manures. Each has an important role in feeding the soil of an edible landscape. Before we look at how to promote the renewal of humus, let's consider what the major nutrients do for the growth of plants and how you can stop "importing" nutrients by growing your own fertilizers.

Macronutrients for Healthy Soil

On every sack of fertilizer there is an esoteric series of numbers such as 0-10-10, 20-10-10, or 20-0-0. Those numbers represent percentages of the three most important nutrients, or macronutrients – nitrogen, phosphorus, and potassium. A sack marked 20-10-5 has 20 percent N (nitrogen), 10 percent P (phosphorus, or phosphate), and 5 percent K (potassium, or potash). Another macronutrient is calcium (Ca). Knowing the roles these four elements play in your soil's fertility will help you grow healthy plants.

Nitrogen

Nitrogen is part of all protein and all living cells. It contributes to gardening by:

- Increasing leaf area, which boosts photosynthesis.

- Making leaves more succulent.

- Giving a rich, dark green color to foliage.

- Promoting above-ground growth.

- Governing and assisting in the utilization of potassium, phosphorus, and some minerals.

Too much nitrogen may adversely affect plants by:

- Delaying the ripening and maturation of fruit and seed.

- Weakening stems, making the plant more vulnerable to wind.

- Reducing the quality of grains and some fruits.

- Increasing a plant's susceptibility to disease and pest infestations.

Nitrogen is easily lost in gaseous or soluble form, but it is the easiest organic fertilizer to find – there is a fresh supply in every stable, corral, coop, or hutch.

Phosphorus

For good gardening, phosphorus must be available in adequate supply. From my favorite American book on soils, we learn:

With the possible exception of nitrogen, no other element has been as critical in the growth of plants in the field as has phosphorus. A lack of this element is doubly serious since it may prevent other nutrients from being acquired by plants. (H. O. Buckman and N. C. Brady, *The Nature and Properties of Soils.*)

Phosphorus is responsible for:

- Promoting balanced, healthy growth.
- Ensuring and speeding crop maturity.
- Encouraging strong root growth.
- Assisting flower, fruit, and seed formation.
- Adding tone and vigor for resistance to disease.

While most soils have abundant reserves of phosphorus, the amount of soluble (that is, available) phosphate in a soil is usually a very small percentage of the phosphorus present. Clay particles grab soluble phosphate and bind it tightly, making the phosphate unavailable.

Most soils are slow to convert phosphate into soluble form.

At any one time, perhaps 80-90% of the soil phosphorus is in "very slowly available" forms. Most of the remainder is in the slowly available [intermediate stage] form since perhaps less than one percent would be expected to be readily available. (H. O. Buckman and N. C. Brady, *The Nature and Properties of Soil.*)

The release of 1 percent or less for absorption by roots is quite a bottleneck in soil fertility.

Phosphorus is released naturally by the action of microorganisms, by high levels of humus and organic matter, and in soils with a pH of 6.0 to 7.0. As an organic gardener, you can influence these three mechanisims of release. You may never obtain the commercial yields generated by large doses of chemical phosphorus, but you can come close, and the environment will be better off.

Potassium

Potassium, or potash for short, is the third macronutrient listed on every fertilizer sack. It is responsible for:

- The general tone and vigor of the plant, making the plant more resistant to disease.
- Promoting root development, especially important for healthy tuber and root crop development.
- Balancing the ripening influences of phosphorus and tempering the ill effects of too much nitrogen.
- Assisting in the formation and movement of sugars.
- Making healthy kernels and good yields in grain crops.

Potash is even more prevalent than phosphorus in the soils of the United States, but only 1 to 2 percent of the potash is soluble and ready for the roots to absorb. From 1 to 10 percent of the total amount is in a transitory state between mineral and soluble. As with phosphorus, potash availability is dependent upon the amount of humus in the soil.

Calcium

Calcium (Ca) is a common nutrient—few soils are deficient in calcium. Though lime (calcium carbonate) is often used to adjust a soil's pH, lime's effect on pH is not to be confused with calcium's role in soil and plant ecology. Calcium helps plant growth by:

- Contributing to the growth of new cells and especially of cell walls.
- Counteracting the toxic effects of oxalic acid in cells.
- Promoting healthy, disease-resistant stems and stalks.
- Promoting the growth of soil bacteria.
- Permitting efficient nitrogen fixation in legumes.
- Increasing the availability of phosphorus, potassium, and magnesium.
- Counteracting the buildup of saline soil conditions.

Though buying store-bought sacks of fertilizer is easy and you get a measured quantity of macronutrients to add to your landscape, the natural sources of these nutrients, in the long run, are much better "fare" for your soil.

McLeod, Edwin. **Feed the Soil**. Graton, CA: Organic Agriculture Research Institute, 1982. A basic review of nitrogen-fixing plants and cover crops, with an encyclopedic reference. I dislike the opening dialog between rabbits and a worm, but I use the encyclopedia frequently.

Pieters, Adrian. **Green Manuring**. New York: John Wiley and Sons, 1927. The best and most comprehensive book on the subject, with lots of scientific studies. Required reading for serious students of green manuring. Out of print—look for it at university agricultural libraries.

U.S.D.A. **Soils & Men: Yearbook of Agriculture 1938**. Washington, DC: U.S. Dept. of Agriculture, 1938. This rare volume was written before chemical fertilizers had an iron grip on commercial agriculture and when farmers still grew most of their own fertilizers. An excellent review of soil preserving and soil building techniques. Includes William Albrecht's best paper on nitrogen fixing and green manures, *Loss of Soil Organic Matter and Its Restoration*.

NATURE'S NUTRIENTS AND DYNAMIC ACCUMULATORS

Legumes – Nature's Source of Nitrogen

You can raise some of your own nitrogen by growing leguminous plants, mainly members of the bean and pea family. Legumes gather nitrogen gas from the air through the nodules of beneficial bacteria on their roots. For me, the idea of growing my own nitrogen has always been appealing, but it turns out to be deceiving. To make good use of legumes, we need to understand exactly how the nitrogen is made and used by the plant.

The Life of a Legume

Many of the "pioneer" plants, those benevolent colonizers of disturbed, damaged, or infertile soils, are legumes. During the growing season, the nitrogen gathered by a legume's roots is banked in a temporary "savings account" in the stems and leaves of the entire plant. When the plant flowers, the demand for nitrogen overwhelms the roots, and the plant draws on its nitrogen savings account to make seed pods. Researchers have found that just before flowering as much as 60 percent of a legume's nitrogen is in the leaves, only half of it from root nodules. (See Fig. 17.1.) After seed pods are formed, a mere 8 percent remains in the leaves,

while 70 percent of the plant's total nitrogen has accumulated in the seeds. The roots and remaining nodules, after the seeds have matured, have even less nitrogen than the leaves – as little as 3 to 6 percent of the total accumulated by the plant. In short, legumes offer little nitrogen in a form other plants might use – they hoard it for the next generation.

A Myth: Beans Feed Corn

Many gardening books recommend planting corn and beans together so that the nitrogen-loving corn will prosper by the association. The thinking behind this axiom is "... the roots of legumes ... take large amounts of nitrogen out of the air and make it available to the roots of other plants" (*Encyclopedia of Organic Gardening*, Rodale Press, 1978).

True, legumes improve the soil by adding nitrogen to it, but very little if any of the nitrogen gathered by a bean plant is going to be shared with the corn plant in the current season. The nitrogen accumulated by the bean's roots goes to its seeds. There are almost no studies to show an improved yield in corn grown with beans. I have found studies showing greater yields when a legume is intercropped with a grass (corn is in the grass family), but all are from tropical regions and not applicable

Figure 17.1 A legume offers the most nitrogen before it blooms. After the beans or seeds have been harvested, only a small amount of nitrogen remains for other plants.

to the United States. There are, however, numerous studies that substantiate the well-known and traditional practice of planting legumes in rotation with grains, corn, and cereal grains. (For details, see "A Five-Year Plan for Soil Improvement.")

Nitrogen for the Current Season

To get useful nitrogen from a legume during the current growing season, the nitrogen-fixing nodules must separate from the roots of the legume. Once released from their symbiotic association with the bean's roots, the nodules decompose and release their valuable nutrients.

Stress makes roots shed nodules. When bean plants die, the nodules separate (but too late to be of benefit to that season's corn). Drought, shading, and defoliation cause shedding, but such conditions stunt the corn. An animal grazing on a legume stimulates the shedding of nodules, but I don't know of any grazing animals that eat beans and not corn.

The amount of nitrogen gathered by a legume in one season per acre ranges from 40 pounds to as high as 250 pounds, depending on the legume. The numbers in Fig. 17.2 are not accurate to the pound (results vary considerably from soil to soil and from climate to climate), but the relative ranking holds true.

Nitrogen Gathered by Legumes		
Legume: Common Name Botanical Name	Pounds per Acre	Vegetables with Equal or Less Need for Nitrogen
Field beans *Pisum arvensis*	40	
Peanuts *Arachis hypogae*	40	
Hairy vetch *Vicia villosa*	80	Broccoli
Dutch white clover *Trifolium repens*	100	
Soybeans *Glycine max*	100	Asparagus, lettuce, squash, and broccoli
Alsike clover *Trifolium hybridum*	140	
Red Clover *Trifolium pratense*	140	
Sweet white clover *Melilotus alba*	160	Sweet potatoes and all the above
Alfalfa *Medicago sativa*	250	Corn, beans, tomatoes, cantaloupes, and all the above

Figure 17.2 Only the most productive nitrogen-fixing legumes can supply the quantities of nitrogen that the "hungriest" vegetables require.

No legume grows well in all climates. Figure 17.3 lists the best legumes for climates around the country. For more accurate information, consult your local cooperative extension agent, the soil conservation office, local landscapers, and farmers.

Dynamic Accumulators

One of my goals as a contemporary organic gardener is to try to be self-sufficient with fertilizers. For the old-timers, cycling nutrients within a farm was a fact of life. Of course, some cheated by exhausting the soil and moving on. But the good farmers used dynamic accumulators, or plants that amass a greater than usual amount of a particular nutrient in their foliage.

Are there plants that accumulate an element in higher concentrations than other plants, even on soils deficient in that element? Or do the accumulators in Fig. 17.4 simply grow where there are especially high concentrations of the element they supposedly concentrate? This question is hotly debated, and it is a favorite of mine. The answer probably falls somewhere in the middle, embracing two types of plants. The first type is plants that accumulate a mineral even in soils low or deficient in that particular mineral. We've already considered one example, for nitrogen – the legume family. The presence of legumes is often a clue that the soil is low in nitrogen, but this applies only to natural conditions. Legumes also grow in nitrogen-rich soil, as you can prove by growing beans in your garden.

Most of the plants in Fig. 17.4 are of the second type, which thrive in soils with high concentrations of certain minerals, or send their roots down to layers where the nutrients are in abundance. The concentration of minerals in their tissues is related more to the soil than to their powers as accumulators. These plants tolerate conditions in the soil that might be toxic to other plants.

While it won't help a gardener, it is interesting to note that Dr. R. R. Brooks of Massey University in New Zealand has been using plants to prospect for nickel ore without leaving his lab. He writes:

It has long been known that the mineral content of plants reflects the mineral content of the substrate on which they grow. For example, plants growing over rocks high in nickel often contain higher than normal concentrations of nickel in their tissues. A few plants which grow over nickel-containing rocks contain exceedingly high concentrations. Such plants are called hyperaccumulators of nickel... it is reasonable to assume that if one discovers a plant which is a hyperaccumulator of nickel, it [is] growing over rocks high in nickel content. (Missouri Botanical Garden Bulletin, Jan. 1978)

A similar approach has been used to locate copper and selenium deposits. (The ornate way that scientists describe this research is "geobotany and biogeochemistry in mineral exploration"!)

Accumulator plants can correct soil nutrient problems. For example, a zinc deficiency of corn in Florida was corrected by allowing zinc-accumulating "weeds" to flourish during years when the field was fallow. After these accumulators were tilled into the soil, the corn crop grew without signs of deficiency. Use Fig. 17.4 to design your soil-building program. Grow accumulator plants in or around your landscape to gather nutrients for use in the edible areas.

Phosphate Accumulators

Legumes accumulate phosphorus and help release it from the soil. For example, when alfalfa is left in the field, there is a slow improvement in the soil's supply of available phosphorus. Using alfalfa, or any of the legumes, as a cover crop or green manure is a way to enhance the cycling of phosphorus within your backyard. (Details are explained in the next chapter.) Two other important accumulators are buckwheat and mustards. All three not only dissolve and absorb the mineralized forms of phosphorus, but actually exhibit a "subsequent excretion [out of the roots] of appreciable amounts of the phosphorus [absorbed]." ("Root Interactions of Plants," W. F. Loehwing, *The Botanical Review*, 1977.) Mustard is a good-soil improving crop for the cooler part of the season, while buckwheat is an excellent soil builder for the summer. Mustards have deeper roots and a more taprootlike structure. They are useful in improving the drainage and tilth of deeper, clay soils. Buckwheat has a more fibrous and somewhat shallower root system. The large quantities of fiber deposited in the soil by buckwheat roots help to loosen a clay soil and improve the moisture and nutrient retention of a sandy soil. All three of these plants — alfalfa, mustard, buckwheat — deserve an important

GREEN MANURE PLANTS		Legume	Soil Preference	Lime Requirements (Low, Medium or High)	Adapted to Soils of Low Fertility	Relative Longevity of Seed	Seeding Rate (lbs. per acre)	Seeding Rate (lbs. per 1000 sq. ft.)	Depth to Cover Seed	N.E. and N.C. States	Southern and S.E. States	Gulf Coast and Florida	Northwestern States	Southwestern States	When to Sow	When to Turn Under	Comments
Alfalfa		Yes	Dry Loams	L		Long	15	1	½	•			•		Spring 2nd Year at 1st Blossom	Spring or Early Fall	Fixes nitrogen in soil. Deep roots bring trace elements to surface.
Barley		No	Loams	L		Long	100	2½	¾	•			•	•	Spring / Fall	Summer / Spring	Not good on sandy or acid soils. Sow spring varieties in north, winter varieties in milder climates.
Beans	Mung	Yes	Widely Adaptable	L	•	Short	70	2	1		•	•		•	Spring or Summer	Summer or Fall	} Warm weather crops. Do not sow until ground is warm and weather is settled.
	Soy	Yes	Loams	M		Short	90	2½	1½	•	•	•	•	•	Spring or Summer	Summer or Fall	
	Velvet	Yes	Loams	L		Short	120	4	2			•			Spring or Summer	Summer or Fall	
Beggar Weed		Yes	Sandy Loams	L	•		15	½	½			•			Spring or Early Summer	Summer or Fall	Seeding rate is for scarified seed. Treble the amount if unhulled seed is used.
Brome Grass, Field		No	Widely Adaptable	L		Long	30	1	½	•					Fall / Spring	Spring / Fall	Good winter cover. Easy to establish. Hardier than rye. More heat tolerant.
Buckwheat		No	Widely Adaptable	L	•		50	1½	¾	•		•			Late Spring and Summer	Summer or Fall	Quick growing. Plant only after ground is warm.
Bur Clover		Yes	Heavy Loams	M		Long	30	1	½	•	•	•		•	Fall	Spring	Not winter hardy north. One of the best winter crops where mild winters prevail.
Chess or Cheat Grass		No	Loams	L		Long	40	1	¾				•		Fall	Spring	
Clover	Alsike	Yes	Heavy Loams	M		Long	8	¼	½	•		•	•		Spring / Fall	Fall / Spring	Less sensitive to soil acidity and poorly drained soils than most clovers.
	Crimson	Yes	Loams	M	•	Medium	30	1	½	•	•	•	•	•	Fall / Spring	Spring / Fall	Not winter hardy north. A good winter annual from New Jersey southward.
	Subterranean	Yes	Loams	M		Medium	30	1	½	•	•	•		•	Fall	Spring	
Corn		No	Widely Adaptable	L		Medium	90	2½	1	•	•	•	•	•	Spring or Summer	Summer or Fall	Do not sow until ground is warm.
Cow-Pea		Yes	Sandy Loams	L	•	Short	90	2½	1½	•	•		•		Late Spring or Early Summer	Summer or Fall	Withstands drought and moderate shade well. Do not sow until weather is warm and settled.
Crotalaria		Yes	Light Loams	L	•	Long	15	½	¾	•	•	•			Spring or Summer	Summer or Fall	Does well on acid soils. Resistant to root knot nematode. Sow scarified seed.
Fenugreek		Yes	Loams	L		Long	35	1	½				•		Fall	Spring	
Guar		Yes	Widely Adaptable	L	•	Long	40	1½	1				•		Spring or Early Summer	Summer or Fall	Thrives on warm soils. Do not plant too early.
Indigo, Hairy		Yes	Sandy Loams	L	•	Short	10	½	½	•	•		•		Spring or Early Summer	Summer or Fall	
Kale, Scotch		No	Widely Adaptable	H	•	Long	14	¼	½	•	•	•	•	•	Summer or Fall	Spring	Can be eaten after serving as winter cover. In Northern areas interplant with winter rye for protection. Except in deep south, plant in summer for good growth before frost.
Lespedeza	Common	Yes	Loams	L	•	Short	25	1	½	•					Early Spring	Summer or Fall	} Easy to establish on hard, badly eroded soils. } Good on acid soils of low fertility.
	Korean	Yes	Loams	L	•	Short	25	1	½	•					Early Spring	Summer or Fall	
	Sericea	Yes	Loams	L	•	Medium	25	1	½			•			Early Spring	Summer or Fall	
Lupine	Blue	Yes	Sandy Loams	L		Short	100	2½	1		•				Spring / Fall	Summer / Spring	Less popular than the yellow lupine and blue lupine. } Good on sour and acid soils.
	White	Yes	Sandy Loams	L		Short	120	2½	1	•	•				Spring / Fall	Summer / Spring	
	Yellow	Yes	Sandy Loams	L		Short	80	2	1	•	•				Spring / Fall	Summer / Spring	
Millet		No	Sandy Loams	L		Long	30	1	½	•					Late Spring or Summer	Summer or Fall	Sow only after ground is warm, a week or ten days after normal corn planting time. Fast growing.
Mustard, White		No	Loams				8	¼	¼	•					Spring	Summer	

Areas For Which Best Adapted

continued

Figure 17.3 Choose the cover crop plants best suited to your yard's soil and climate from this chart of options.

Figure 17.3 continued

| GREEN MANURE PLANTS | | | | | | | | | | | | | | | Areas For Which Best Adapted | | |
Common Name		Legume	Soil Preference	Lime Requirements (Low, Medium or High)	Adapted to Soils of Low Fertility	Relative Longevity of Seed	Seeding Rate (lbs. per acre)	Seeding Rate (lbs. per 1000 sq. ft.)	Depth to Cover Seed	N.E. and N.C. States	Southern and S.E. States	Gulf Coast and Florida	Northwestern States	Southwestern States	When to Sow	When to Turn Under	Comments
Oats		No	Widely Adaptable	L		Long	100	2½	1	●	●	●	●	●	Spring Fall	Summer or Fall Spring	Winter oats (sown in fall) are suitable only where mild winters prevail.
Pea	Field	Yes	Heavy Loams	M		Short	90	2½	1½	●	●	●	●		Early Spring Fall	Summer Spring	Sow in fall only where winters are mild. Distinctly a cool weather crop.
	Rough	Yes	Sandy Loams	L	●	Medium	60	1½	1					●	Fall	Spring	
	Tangier	Yes		M		Medium	80	2½	1	●				●	Spring	Summer	
Rape		No	Loams	L			8	¼	¼	●			●		Spring or Summer	Summer or Fall	
Rescue Grass		No	Widely Adaptable	L		Long	35	1	¾		●		●				Adapted to mild winters and humid climates.
Rye, Spring		No	Widely Adaptable	L		Long	90	2	¾	●	●				Spring	Summer	
Rye, Winter		No	Widely Adaptable	L		Long	90	2	¾	●	●				Fall	Spring	One of the most important winter cover crops. Can be sown late.
Rye-Grass, Italian		No	Widely Adaptable	L		Long	35	1	¾	●	●	●	●	●	Fall Spring	Spring Summer	An important winter cover crop where winters are mild. In severe climates sow in spring or summer.
Sesbania		Yes	Widely Adaptable	L	●	Long	25	1	¾		●	●		●	Spring or Summer	Summer or Fall	Quick grower. Is better adapted to wet soils and will grow at higher altitudes than crotalaria.
Sorghum		No	Light Loams			Long	90	2½	¾	●	●			●	Late Spring or Summer	Summer or Fall	Do not sow until ground is warm and weather is settled. More drought resistant than corn.
Sudan Grass		No	Widely Adaptable	L		Long	35	1	¾	●	●	●	●	●	Late Spring or Summer	Summer or Fall	Rapid grower. Do not sow until ground is warm and weather is settled.
Sunflower		No	Widely Adaptable	L			20	¾	¾	●	●	●	●	●	Spring or Summer	Summer or Fall	Intolerant of acid soils.
Sweet-Clover	Common White	Yes	Heavy Loams	H		Long	15	½	½	●	●		●	●			Quite winter hardy. Best results are from fall sowing.
	Annual (Hubam)	Yes	Loams	H		Long	15	½	½	●			●				A true annual. Best results from spring sowings.
	Yellow	Yes	Loams	H		Long	15	½	½	●	●		●	●			Stands dry conditions better than common white sweet clover.
	Yellow Annual	Yes	Loams	H		Long	15	½	½	●	●	●	●	●			Most useful south of the cotton belt as winter cover. North not winter hardy. Makes short summer growth.
Vetch	Common	Yes	Widely Adaptable	L		Medium	60	1½	¾	●	●	●	●	●	Spring Fall	Fall Spring	Not winter hardy where severe cold is experienced. Needs reasonably fertile soil.
	Hairy	Yes	Widely Adaptable	L	●	Long	60	1½	¾	●	●	●	●	●	Spring Fall	Fall Spring	The most winter hardy vetch. Best sown in fall mixed with winter rye or winter wheat.
	Hungarian	Yes	Heavy Loams	L		Long	60	1½	¾	●	●		●	●	Spring Fall	Fall Spring	Next to hairy vetch the most winter hardy of the vetches. Not winter hardy where winters are fairly fertile soil.
	Purple	Yes	Loams	L		Long	60	1½	¾	●	●	●	●	●	Spring Fall	Fall Spring	Least hardy of the vetches. Suited for winter cover in mild climates only.
	Woolly Pod	Yes	Widely Adaptable	L		Long	60	1½	¾	●	●	●	●	●	Spring Fall	Fall Spring	
Wheat, Winter		No	Loams	L		Long	100	2½	¾	●			●		Fall	Spring	

Used by permission. From: *Improving Garden Soil with Green Manure* by Richard Alther and Richard (Dick) Raymond, published by Garden Way Publishing. This and other gardening books may be purchased from Storey Communications, P.O. Box 105, Pownal, VT 05261.

role in the design and maintenance of your edible landscape.

Potassium Accumulators

Dynamic accumulators can increase your landscape's supply of potash, an element as difficult to liberate from its mineral state in the soil as phosphorus. Once a plant has freed an element from its mineral form and used it to grow, you can recycle the element for the growth of other plants in a number of ways—composting, mulching, cover cropping, and green manuring. An interesting example of a potash accumulator is the bracken fern (see Fig. 17.4), used as a source of potash for washing in the early 1900s in England. (Many current detergents are potassium based.) "During the summer the leaves were collected green, dried and then burned and the resulting ash ... was then moistened and moulded into balls, which were used in washing; but the cheapness of soda has now killed this industry." (*The Story of the Bracken Fern*, H. C. Long.) Alan Chadwick, the father of biodynamic French intensive gardening, had his students collect green bracken ferns each spring which were then composted for root crops. He was probably practicing English folklore, and with good reason: green bracken ferns average 25 percent potash and can contain as much as 55 percent. From weed to asset!

Calcium Accumulators

Oak leaves are dynamic accumulators of calcium. It's fascinating that there can be high levels of calcium in the leaves even when the soil has barely detectable or very low levels of available calcium. Alan Chadwick appreciated the value of oak leaves—he taught his students to line the bottom of seed flats with oak leaves and broken eggshells as sources of calcium. A better way to make calcium available to plants is to mix oak leaves with a nitrogen fertilizer, compost them, and use the finished compost in the seed flats or in your edible landscape.

Fig. 17.4

DYNAMIC ACCUMULATORS

Name	Botanical Name	Sodium	Iodine	Flourine	Boron	Silica	Sulfur	Nitrogen	Magnesium	Calcium	Potassium	Phosphorus	Manganese	Iron	Copper	Cobalt
Alfalfa	*Medicago sativa*							X						X		
Arrowroot										X						
Bladderwrack			X						X					X		
Borage	*Borago officinalis*					X					X					
Bracken, eastern	*Pteridium aquifolium*										X	X	X	X	X	X
Bridal bower												X				
Broom drops									X							
Buckwheat	*Fagopyrum esculentums*											X				
Burdock	*Arctium minus*													X		
Calamus							X				X	X				
Caragreen		X					X			X						
Caraway	*Carum carvi*											X				
Carrot leaves	*Daucus carota*								X		X					
Cattail	*Typha latifolia*						X									
Century											X					
Chamomile, corn	*Anthemis arvensis*									X	X					
Chamomile, German	*Chamomilla recutita*									X	X	X				
Chickweed	*Stellaria media*										X	X	X			
Chicory	*Cichorium intybus*									X	X					
Chives	*Allium sp.*	X									X					
Cleavers	*Galium aparine*	X									X					
Clovers	*Trifolium sp.*							X			X					
Clover, hop	*Medicago lupulina*							X			X					
Clover, rabbit foot								X			X					
Clover, red	*Trifolium protense*							X			X					
Clover, white	*Trifolium repens*							X			X					
Coltsfoot							X		X	X	X			X	X	
Comfrey	*Symphytum officinale*					X			X	X	X	X		X		
Dandelion	*Taraxacum vulgare*	X				X			X	X	X	X		X	X	
Devil's bit	*Veratrum californicum*		X						X					X		
Docks	*Rumex sp.*									X	X	X		X		
Dock, broad leaved	*Rumex obtusifolias*									X	X	X		X		
Dulse		X	X							X	X			X		
Eyebright	*Anagallis arvensis*						X				X					
Fat hen	*Atriplex hastata*									X				X		
Fennel	*Foeniculum vulgare*	X					X				X					
Flax, seed	*Linum usitatissimum*										X					
Garlic	*Allium sativum*			X			X					X				
Groundsel	*Senecio vulgaris*													X		
Horsetails	*Equisetum sp.*					X			X	X				X		X
Horsetail, field	*Equisetum arvense*					X			X	X				X		X
Horsetail, marsh						X			X	X				X		X
Iceland moss			X													
Irish moss														X		
Kelp		X	X				X		X	X				X		
Lamb's quarters	*Chenopodium album*							X		X	X	X	X			
Lemon Balm	*Melissa officinalis*											X				
Licorice root, leaves								X				X				
Lupine	*Lupinus sp.*							X				X				
Marigold, flowers	*Tagetes sp.*											X				
Meadow sweet	*Astilbe sp.*	X					X		X	X		X		X		

continued

continued

DYNAMIC ACCUMULATORS

Name	Botanical Name	Sodium	Iodine	Flourine	Boron	Silica	Sulfur	Nitrogen	Magnesium	Calcium	Potassium	Phosphorus	Manganese	Iron	Copper	Cobalt
Mistletoe									X							
Mullein, common	Verbascum sp.						X		X		X			X		
Mustards	Brassica sp.						X					X				
Nettles, stinging	Urtica urens	X					X	X		X	X			X	X	
Oak, bark	Quercus sp.									X						
Oat Straw						X										
Parsley									X	X	X			X		
Peppermint	Mentha piperita								X	X						
Pigweed, red root	Amaranthus retroflexus									X	X	X		X		
Plantains	Plantago sp.						X	X		X	X			X	X	
Primrose	Oenothera biennis								X							
Purslane	Portulaca oleracea									X		X		X		
Rest harrow		X					X		X	X				X		
Salad burnet	Poterium sanguisorba													X		
Sanicle											X					
Sarsparilla			X													
Savory	Satureja sp.													X		
Scarlet Pimpernel	Anagallis arvensis									X						
Shepherd's purse	Capsella bursa-pastoris	X					X			X						
Silverweed										X	X				X	
Skunk cabbage	Navarretia squarrosa								X							
Sorrel, garden	Rumex sp.	X								X		X				
Sorrel, sheep	Rumex acetosella	X								X		X				
Sow thistle	Sonchus arvensis									X	X			X		
Spurges	Euphorbia sp.					X										
Strawberry, leaves	Fragaria sp.													X		
Tansy	Tanacetum vulgare										X					
Thistle, Canada	Cirsium arvense													X		
Thistle, creeping	Sonchus arvensis									X	X			X		
Thistle, nodding	Carduus nutans													X		
Thistle, Russian	Salsola pestifer													X		
Toadflax	Linaria vulgaris									X	X			X		
Tobacco, stems/stalk	Nicotiana sp.							X								
Valerian	Valeriana officinalis						X									
Vetches	Vicia sp.							X			X	X			X	X
Watercress	Nasturtium officinale	X		X			X		X	X	X	X		X		
Waywort		X					X			X						
Willow, bark	Salix sp.									X						
Willow, black	Salix sp.	X														
Wintergreen	Gaultheria procumbens									X						
Yarrow	Achilea millefolium							X			X	X			X	

The above data are from the following sources:

Cocannouer, Joseph. *Weeds: Guardians of the Soil.* New York: Devin-Adair, 1950.
Easey, Ben. *Practical Organic Gardening.* London: Faber & Faber, 1955.
Gibbons, Euell. *Stalking the Healthful Herbs.* New York: McKay Publishing, 1966.
Hill, Stuart. *Weeds as Indicators of Soil Conditions.* MacDonald Journal, June 1977.
Pfeiffer, Ehrenfried. *Weeds and What They Tell.* Springfield, IL: BioDynamic Farming and Gardening, n.d.
Rateaver, Gargyla and Gylver. *The Organic Method Primer.* Pauma Valley, CA: B. and G. Rateaver, 1973.

Additional citations in numerous scientific journals were graciously provided by Ron Whitehurst, horticultural author and consultant.

Figure 17.4

Hills, Lawrence. **Comfrey.** New York: Universe Books, 1976. The definitive book on this important, though tenacious, herb.

McLeod, Edwin. **Feed the Soil**. Graton, CA: Organic Agriculture Research Institute, 1982. A basic review of nitrogen-fixing plants and cover crops, with an encyclopedic reference. I dislike the opening dialog between rabbits and a worm, but I use the encyclopedia frequently.

Rateaver, Bargyla and Gylver. **The Organic Method Primer**. Pauma Valley, CA: Bargyla and Gylver Rateaver, 1973. The first good reference for patterning organic gardening after nature's dynamics. A true classic of organic gardening, though some of the sources remain obscure. Out of print; look for a used copy.

Turner, Newman. **Fertility Pastures**. 2nd ed. rev. Pauma Valley, CA: Bargyla and Gylver Rateaver, 1975. My favorite book on plants as indicators of soil fertility and plants as soil improvers in cover crops and herbal leys. Written for dairy farmers, but much of the information relates to edible landscaping, as well.

U.S.D.A. **Soils & Men: Yearbook of Agriculture 1938**. Washington, DC: U.S. Dept. of Agriculture, 1938. This rare volume was written before chemical fertilizers had an iron grip on commercial agriculture and when farmers still grew most of their own fertilizers. An excellent review of soil preserving and soil building techniques. Includes William Albrecht's best paper on nitrogen fixing and green manures, *Loss of Soil Organic Matter and Its Restoration*.

Walters, Charles, Jr., and Fenzau, C.J. **an Acres U.S.A. Primer**. Raytown, MO: Acres, U.S.A., 1979. A long-winded but interesting survey of a genre of organic farming found throughout the Midwest. Though some of their conclusions are hard to accept, these farmers get good results and yields.

GROW YOUR OWN FERTILIZERS: COVER CROPS AND GREEN MANURES

The practice of growing dynamic accumulators and letting them be is called cover cropping. Turning the accumulator into the soil is green manuring. Cover crops and green manures improve the soil by:

- **Greatly increasing the organic matter content of the soil.**

- **Increasing the availability of nutrients and decreasing leaching.**

  The roots of cover crops and green manures are a safety net catching nutrients that otherwise leach away. (In older books, another term for cover crops is catch crop.) In addition, the thousands of foraging root hairs liberate nutrients from mineral form and assimilate them.

- **Improving the soil's tilth.**

  Green manures and cover crops decompose, forming humus, which acts like a glue, binding together particles of soil in a way that opens pore spaces. The crumbly, granular texture so typical of a loamy soil that is full of worms results in part from humus.

  Soil structure is also improved by the action of the roots. As roots grow and die each day, tiny channels are left for the exchange of gases, the percolation of water, and the movement of worms and bacteria. This accounts in part for the spongy, soft texture of an unspoiled forest soil.

- **Reducing "weeds."**

  A dense cover crop helps choke out undesirable plants. Tall, bulky cover crops, such as fava or bell beans, vetch, and Sudan grass, produce so much foliage and shade that plants germinating after the cover crop wither and die. Even rye and oats, which grow only 6 to 8 inches tall before being tilled under as a green manure, can smother unwanted "weeds." Tillage also helps destroy "weeds" that have already sprouted. (Be careful, however, to seed or transplant soon after green manuring, because tilling brings "weed" seeds to the surface to germinate.

- **Reducing soil pests.**

  The roots of a cover crop and the decomposing foliage of green manures such as Mexican marigold *(Tagetes minuta)*, ornamental marigolds (to a lesser degree), and the crotolaria legumes exude chemicals which help suppress soil nematodes. Avoid cover crops and green manures similar to the intended crop: they may harbor pests. A cover crop of mustards can allow the cabbage root maggot to flourish, which would endanger a following crop of cabbage. Likewise, avoid grasses for green manures if you plan to grow grains.

- **Enhancing the soil's biological activity.**

  The shade of cover crops and green manures moderates the extremes of heat and moisture that bare soil suffers. Soil life is healthier. Green manures also provide raw food for soil life.

Establishing A Cover Crop or Green Manure

Whether you plan to grow a cover crop or green manure, start with a seedbed. While I have tossed seed into wild grass, the resulting germination and growth were very poor. You'll get better results with a rotary tiller, some time, muscle, and a soil that is neither too dry or too wet.

Choose a cover crop or green manure seed from Fig. 17.3 that prospers in your soil and climate and is suited to the coming season. Mix at least one type of legume with several herbal or herbaceous plants, and add a grass if none grows on the site.

Some plants are a little wild and woolly for an ornamental landscape—for example, vetch, Sudan grass, sorghum, and kale. Others look like a verdant lawn during the first portion of the season—rye grass, oats, clovers, millet, and barley are examples. Some cover crops make an impressive floral display. During the midsummer heat, a swath of buckwheat with its pure white flowers in full bloom is a spectacular sight. (And buckwheat attracts beneficial insects, an extra bonus for your landscape.) One of my favorite spring blossoms is the potent red of crimson clover. In a cover crop, crimson clover provides a colorful highlight as other early spring flowers fade. Its dramatic display lures the eye away from more mundane cover crops; it is a visual camouflage. Other cover crops with nice floral displays include bird's-foot trefoil, yellow and rose clovers, crotalaria, lupines, mustards, sesbania, and sunflower.

Except with the leguminous plants, all you need to do is work the soil to form a seedbed, rake in the seed, apply a light mulch, and water. If you have a new house surrounded by exposed subsoil, you will be better off adding soil amendments (fertilizers and organic matter) and topsoil to improve the raw subsoil. Even though some cover crops do quite well in harsh conditions, it is worth the expense and effort to provide a better soil horizon at the start. Improving subsoils solely with cover crops and green manures takes years.

The Needs of Young Legumes

While legumes are, in nature, colonizers of disturbed soils, they need certain conditions to sprout and flourish. For initial growth, they require a minimum level of available phosphate. Colloidal phosphate provides only 2 percent of its weight as phosphate in the first season, and only 18 percent over many years. The chemical forms of phosphate offer more available phosphorus the first season. Superphosphate is 20 percent soluble phosphorus and triple superphosphate has 46 percent of the desired element. Being very soluble and concentrated, they ensure the sprouting legumes a healthy start. Their judicious use makes sense in sites with poor soil. Like any synthetic fertilizer, however, superphosphates can do harm. For one thing, the higher concentration makes superphosphate easier to misuse. Also, beneficial, decomposing fungi and beneficial bacteria are reduced with repeated applications. And even though the soil "locks up" a lot of superphosphate, leached phosphorus from commercial applications has polluted streams and rivers, something that will not happen with the slow-release action of rock powders.) There's no harm, however, in using a small amount for the initial growth of legumes. A single application of super- or triple superphosphate should not be considered debilitating.

Legumes tolerate a slightly acidic soil (pH 4.8 to 6.3). If your soil supports good, healthy blueberry or camellia bushes, the pH is too acidic. To adjust the pH, lime (calcium carbonate) will be needed. Besides adjusting the pH, lime increases the growth of young leguminous plants and makes phosphates more available.

Crop-yield data available also support the conclusion that the liming of more acid soils (with a pH below 6.5) over a period of time renders the phosphorus of the soil more available to plants . . . the fixation of nitrogen from the atmosphere by legumes is more effective where high levels of calcium are present in available form. The root nodule bacteria of alfalfa and sweetclover do not persist well in a soil when its pH is below 6.5. (U.S.D.A. 1938 Yearbook.)

Legumes and Inoculants

If you sow legumes, be prepared to use rhizobial inoculant, a powder containing the strain of nitrogen-fixing bacteria that forms root nodules on your legumes. If your site has wild or "weedy" legumes, the proper bacteria may already be present. Look for bur clover *(Medicago hispida)*, lupines *(Lupinus*

sp.), and beggarweed *(Desmodium purpureum)*, among others. To be safe, buy the right inoculant when you buy seed and follow the directions on the packet. For more detail on specific inoculants and when to use them, see "Soil Inoculants."

Green Manures – An Investment in Your Soil's Fertility

There are many times during the season, and at different stages of plant growth, when you can till under a cover crop. Each time has virtues and drawbacks, and choosing a time is much like picking a savings plan. You can invest wisely or squander your capital, but no single plan is "the best" – for protection, use a number of plans, each for a specific situation.

Short-Term Investments, Rapid Return

Succulent young plant tissue has the highest amount of readily available nutrients. For a quick return on your investment, grow dynamic accumulators until just before they bloom, then turn them under as a green manure. They will release nutrients quickly for the crop that follows. However, you must wait three to four weeks before planting, while the soil digests the green manure. If you plant earlier, your crop will get less nitrogen, since much of the nitrogen will be tied up in the bodies of microorganisms. Once they digest the manure, large numbers die and decompose, releasing nitrogen for the crop.

Long-Term Investments, Slow Payback

Dry, dead plant material does not have as much nitrogen as green foliage, and the nitrogen is firmly bound up in a form that does not easily decompose. This can be a liablity or an asset – depending on your investment strategy. If you need plenty of nitrogen in the next few months, do not till under dead cover crops. The soil's bacteria will be so busy trying to digest what you tilled under that little, if any, nitrogen would reach your crops.

As a long-term deposit, however, tilling dead plants under is an ideal way to keep organic matter and nitrogen in the soil. In fact, nature uses this investment scheme often – the forest is littered with the branches and trunks of these "long-term accounts." The slow decay and the billions of bacteria tying up nitrogen in their bodies ensure that this precious element does not leach or vaporize.

Timing

As with trading stock on Wall Street, timing is everything. To maximize gains, you must turn under the accumulator at the right time. The cooler the soil, the longer decomposition takes. Midspring warmth signals the beginning of the green manuring season. The hottest part of the summer is a "down market," too hot for healthy decomposition. The cooling soils of early fall are again ready for green manuring.

While the standard guideline calls for waiting three to four weeks after green manuring before seeding or transplanting, the wait is much, much longer if you tilled in brown, or mature, plants. The warmer the soil, the sooner you can plant. You will have to green manure for a number of seasons to discover the timing that works best with your climate, soil, and accumulators; but patience pays dividends.

Depositing Your Green Capital

With tall and bulky green manure plants such as fava beans, vetch, mustards, kale, Sudan grass, and sunflowers, a rotary tiller is difficult to use. Bastard trenching (see "Surface Cultivation") is the best way to proceed. First, cut the plants above ground and chop up the stems and foliage with a machete. Then open up a trench, fill it half full with chopped plants, and cover with the soil taken from the next trench.

If you prefer tilling, grow the accumulators only 6 to 12 inches tall. A tiller can easily chop and till under short green manures. By immediately seeding a new green manure and tilling again when it reaches the same height, you can greatly speed up the improvement of your soil. You can grow a rapid succession of green manures throughout the summer. Choose plants that thrive in summer heat — buckwheat, rye grass, crotolaria, millet, sesbania, sorghum, Sudan grass, and sunflower. During the drought of the late 1970s in northern California, I put my clients' flower beds into a winter and fall green manuring program. After two years, clients were calling to say thanks for the wonderful improvement in the soil — though nature had done most of the work.

Hills, Lawrence. **Comfrey**. New York: Universe Books, 1976. The definitive book on this important, though tenacious, herb.

McLeod, Edwin. **Feed the Soil**. Graton, CA: Organic Agriculture Research Institute, 1982. A basic review of nitrogen-fixing plants and cover crops, with an encyclopedic reference. I dislike the opening dialog between rabbits and a worm, but I use the encyclopedia frequently.

Pieters, Adrian. **Green Manuring**. New York: John Wiley and Sons, 1927. The best and most comprehensive book on the subject, with lots of scientific studies. Required reading for serious students of green manuring. Out of print—look for it at university agricultural libraries.

Raymond, R., and Altha, R. **Improving Garden Soil With Green Manures**. Charlotte, VT: Garden Way Publishing, 1979. A brief, excellent review of cover crops and green manures. Contains a very good table that outlines the virtues and limitations of many plants (reproduced in Figure 17.3).

Turner, Newman. **Fertility Pastures**. 2nd ed. rev. Pauma Valley, CA: Bargyla and Gylver Rateaver, 1975. My favorite book on plants as indicators of soil fertility and plants as soil improvers in cover crops and herbal leys. Written for dairy farmers, but much of the information relates to edible landscaping, as well.

U.S.D.A. **Soils & Men: Yearbook of Agriculture 1938**. Washington, DC: U.S. Dept. of Agriculture, 1938. This rare volume was written before chemical fertilizers had an iron grip on commercial agriculture and when farmers still grew most of their own fertilizers. An excellent review of soil preserving and soil building techniques. Includes William Albrecht's best paper on nitrogen fixing and green manures, *Loss of Soil Organic Matter and Its Restoration*.

Walters, Charles, Jr., and Fenzau, C.J. **An Acres U.S.A. Primer**. Raytown, MO: Acres, U.S.A., 1979. A long-winded but interesting survey of a genre of organic farming found throughout the Midwest. Though some of their conclusions are hard to accept, these farmers get good results and yields.

Albrecht, Dr. William. **The Albrecht Papers**. Raytown, MO: Acres USA, 1975. Albrecht was a pioneer in the science of cover crops and green manures. Though somewhat tedious, the only collection of his writings.

A FIVE-YEAR PLAN
FOR SOIL IMPROVEMENT

Chances are, when you start your edible landscape, you will not cultivate, fertilize, and plant the entire area in the first season, so consider a plan of soil developmment for both immediate and long-term effects. Figure 17.5 shows progressive soil development, and Fig. 17.6 shows what it might look like in a yard. Much depends on your landscape and its design, but these rules of thumb apply to any setting.

Double-Dug Salad Beds

I usually recommend that a client begin with 100 to 200 square feet of double-dug vegetable beds, placed as close to the kitchen door as possible. Plant the beds with herbs and salad greens as they are the most frequently used and the most costly to buy. The effort required to dig the beds is rapidly repaid with abundant produce and a sense of satisfaction. (See "Double-Digging—A Balanced Review.")

Rotating Your Capital Accounts

Each salad bed can grow its own fertility, with a long-term "banking" plan that rotates "accounts" of green manures, cover crops, and vegetables. Figure 17.7 outlines a 7-year program of rotation for vegetable beds. The chart is derived from the hundreds of years of crop rotation in Europe and more recent experience of truck farmers in the United States. There are many different versions of crop rotations. In Europe, some farmers practice 27-year rotation schemes. Whatever the rotation scheme, all the plans rely on the periodic use of legumes, both edible and non-edible soil improvers, and a respect for the soil's need to rest from time to time, to recover from cropping and to rebuild fertility.

While crop rotation means more area set aside to beds, I find a lot of satisfaction in growing all the fertilizers and amendments for my vegetable beds in my own backyard. You can ignore rotation schemes if you plan to "import" manures and fertilizers each season or if you have an ambitious program of composting.

The sequence of rotation and the number of beds in Fig. 17.7 should be adjusted to your site, soil, and climate. Rotations can even be done within one large bed. Where the illustration shows a grass/legume fallow, choose from Fig. 17.3 a mixture of grasses and legumes that grows well in your area. For clover, you can substitute any low-growing legume suited to your climate and soil. Instead of

Figure 17.5 A 5-year plan for gradual development of soil and of an edible landscape.

Figure 17.6 An example of how your 5-year plan might look.

tilling in the cover crop, you could just as easily sheet compost. (See "Sheet Composting for 'Wild' and 'Tame' Plants.") By using the rotation illustration and the cover crop chart as steppingstones for your experiments and by using different rotation plans in different beds, you will arrive at a plan that fits your site, needs, and time.

Ornamental Green Manures and Cover Crops

At the same time you plant the beds, I recommend planting an area near or around the beds with a cover to be green manured when it is 6 to 10 inches tall. If this area is visible from the house, plant a rich green cover with finely textured foliage, such as grasses, oats, millet, barley, and clovers (especially Dutch white clover). Grasses germinate and grow so quickly that they make an ideal cover within view of the house for repeated green manuring. They soon hide the bare soil left by green manuring. Devote as much space to green manures as you plan to use later for fresh, daily vegetables. When you dig new beds, you'll thank the green manures. The digging is easier and the

soil more fertile.

If you have enough time or energy the first season, establish a cover crop in those areas that you will not be able to plant for several years. Or, seed those areas in the second or third years. If they are visible from the house, use ornamental and herbal dynamic accumulators. Good choices include borage, corn, chamomile, chicory, crimson clover, lupines, marigolds, mullein, primroses, savory, and yarrows. If an area will eventually be heavily cultivated, do not use plants that propagate easily from their roots, such as comfrey, tansy, sorrel, and horsetails. Also, avoid plants that make lots of seed—borage, caraway, dandelion, mallow, and mustards are a few. However, if the area is to be planted with trees or shrubs and covered with a sheet compost that includes a layer of newspaper or cardboard, the accumulators that produce abundant seed are not much of a problem. It is possible to establish a cover crop area that resembles a flower border. While your neighbors admire the flowers, your soil is steadily improving. (There are also perennial, ornamental shrubs that fix nitrogen—see "Finishing Touches: Perennial Legumes, Edible Flowers, and Mulches.")

SEVEN-STEP ROTATION FOR FERTILITY

SECTION:

SCHEME:

A
- GRASS/LEGUME FALLOW.
  (OATS, RYE, BUCKWHEAT, VETCH, CLOVER, FAVA/BELL BEANS, etc.)
- CUT/MOW SEVERAL TIMES FOR COMPOST MATERIAL.

B
- GRASS/LEGUME FALLOW.
  (OATS, RYE, BUCKWHEAT, VETCH, CLOVER, FAVA/BELL BEANS, etc.)
- CUT/MOW SEVERAL TIMES FOR COMPOST MATERIAL.

C
- TILL IN FALLOW (SPRING), PLANT VEGETABLES.
- FALL APPLICATION OF MANURE.
- FALLOW THRU WINTER—(WARM WINTER AREAS, PLANT COVER CROP.)

D
- TILL IN FALLOW/COVER CROP (SPRING).
- PLANT VEGETABLES (SPRING-SUMMER.)
- LATE SUMMER, PLANT GRASSES.

E
- BROADCAST CLOVER SEED.
- CUT GRASSES (SPRING) BEFOR SEED HEADS FORM. SOW MORE CLOVER.
- GROW CLOVER THROUGH SUMMER.

F
- TILL IN CLOVER (SPRING), PLANT VEGETABLES.
- LATE SUMMER, PLANT WINTER LEGUME COVER CROP.

G
- EARLY SPRING, TILL IN LEGUME, PLANT VEGETABLES.
- LATE SUMMER, RE-SEED GRASS/LEGUME MIX. (START ROTATION CYCLE AGAIN AT "A".)

Figure 17.7 This 7-year sequence of soil management can be applied to any vegetable bed, no matter what shape. Rotation schemes like this one can eliminate the need for compost and manures.

Wildflower "Meadows" Around Fruit Trees

I plant trees in the first year or two, seeding the area beyond the mulch with many deeply rooted "cultivators" whose roots grow 4 feet or deeper. For California, my favorites are chicory (*Cichorium intybus*), purple hairy vetch (*Vicia villosa*), Dutch white clover (*Trifolium repens*), dock (*Rumex* sp.), mustards (*Brassica nigra*), and plantain (*Plantago major*). The area around the fruit trees resembles a miniature wildflower meadow. Other accumulators that add to the wildflower look (whether their roots go 4 feet deep is not known) include birds-*foot trefoil (Lotus* sp.), wild carrot (*Daucus carota*), cornflower (*Centaurea cyanus*), goldenrod (*Solidago* sp.), eyebright (*Anagallis arvensis*), filaree (*Erodium* sp.), horehound (*Marrubium vulgare*), lemon balm (*Melissa officinalis*), lupine (*Lupinus* sp.), mullein (*Verbascum* sp.), salad burnet (*Poterium sanguisorba*), speedwell (*Veronica* sp.), and yarrow (*Achillea* sp.).

Sometimes it's necessary to make a seedbed. Other times, I can simply toss out the seed, and plenty will sprout and thrive. I don't usually plant grasses, as the soil has an abundance of dormant seed; but in barren subsoils, add grass seed such as annual rye or oats for another zone of soil-improving roots.

With each new season, I expand the ring of mulch around each tree, covering the soil-improving plants. They rot in place, with results much like green manuring, but without the effort of digging.

Discreet Compost Bins

If you compost, the first season is the time to build compost bins. For composting kitchen scraps, the bins must have lids and solid walls and be located near the kitchen (in a discreet location where odors will not enter the house). Put the bins near a water spigot and where there is room to drive up with a load of manure or straw. Flowering, fragrant shrubs around three sides help camouflage the bins and their odor. I have used honeysuckle vines and shrubs, jasmine, and citrus (which love the surplus nitrogen and water that leach from the bins).

Permanent Nutrition – Ornamental Plants for Compost and Mulch Materials

Finally, establish an area where you can harvest nutrient-rich foliage for years to come to use in composting and mulching. I call such areas herbal leys, a phrase used in England to refer to pastures that have been planted to a complex mixture of herbs, grasses, and legumes. The English have found increased health in their cattle and improved soil tilth and fertility after years of growing an herbal ley. (Of course, you are probably not raising cattle.) Herbal leys look much like an ornamental wildflower meadow. Some, however, are utilitarian patches hidden from view.

Establish herbal leys in the third to fifth years – you will probably be too busy with other areas of your landscape until then. Herbal leys are your insurance policy for home-grown fertility and an ecologically sustainable edible landscape.

Sow the dynamic accumulators that look good. Many wildflowers are in the legume family – be sure to use them. Examples of leguminous wildflowers include thermopsis (*Thermopsi gracilis*); perennial sweet pea (*Lathyrus latifolius*); lupines (*Lupinus* sp.); locoweed (*Astragalus* sp. – watch out, this one spreads!); wild licorice (*Glycyrrhiza lepidota*); pignut (*Hoffmanseggia densiflora*); bur clover (*Medicago hispida*, it spreads also and is painful to bare feet); alfalfa (*Medicago sativa*); white sweet clover (*Melilotus alba*); yellow sweet clover (*Melilotus officinalis*); honey mesquite (*Prosopis chilensis*, a shrub/tree); Colorado river hemp (*Sesbania macrocarpa*); true clovers (*Trifolium* sp.); vetches (*Vicia* sp.); trefoils (*Lotus* sp.); crotolaria (*Crotolaria* sp.); lablab (*Dolichos lablab*); sainfoin (*Onobrychis sativa*), lespedeza (*Lespedeza* sp.), sesbania (*Sesbania* sp.), tepary bean (*Phaseolus acutifolius*), and velvet bean (*Stizolobium deeringianum*).

Comfrey, the King of Accumulators

Another plant for homegrown fertility is comfrey (*Symphytum officinale)*, an herb I call "design intensive." Plan carefully, because it persists once it becomes established. Put it where you want it, because you can't remove it. Still, comfrey is a fantastic plant for productivity and tolerates harsh environments.

Comfrey produces an abundance of coarse, fuzzy leaves that can reach 4 feet in height and a flower stalk that grows 4 to 6 feet high with small, deep blue flowers. There is also a more colorful variety with rich, red flowers *(Symphytum rubra)*. Comfrey does not produce viable seed; it spreads by expansion of the root crown. We gardeners spread comfrey by tiny root cuttings or by dividing the crown. Remarkably small pieces of root will sprout and grow to be a robust plant. (Also, the plant is sometimes spread underground by the feeding habits of gophers.)

As a source of organic matter, comfrey is in a league all its own. Studies at the University of California at Davis have found that comfrey outproduces alfalfa in tons of foliage cut from a field in one season. The average yields are 15 to 20 tons per acre; the world's record is 100 tons!

Comfrey leaves are loaded with nutrients. They accumulate silica, nitrogen, calcium, potassium, and iron. Comfrey leaves can be used as an herbal tea, an herbal poultice, a salad green (in small amounts), and as feed for animals. The roots can be steamed as a vegetable. (Recent studies, still greatly disputed, show that animals which were fed more than 4 percent of their daily diet in dried comfrey leaf developed liver problems and cancer of the liver over a long period of time.)

Silica tied up in foliage is very helpful in growing certain vegetables. Studies in Germany have shown that incorporating comfrey in the soil helps reduce the incidence of rusts in potatoes. Open a trench for the potatoes, fill the bottom third with comfrey leaves, cover with soil, and plant the potato "seed." Make sure you cut the comfrey leaves 2 to 3 inches above the soil, for if any piece of the root crown gets into your potato trench, a new comfrey plant is there to stay.

There is so much nitrogen in comfrey leaves that no additional manure is required to make compost, but making compost from comfrey foliage alone produces a slimy mess. Alternate layers of dry fibrous stalks or straw with the comfrey to maintain aerobic conditions and to absorb moisture.

The calcium content is so high that comfrey is used as a supplemental feed for chickens to make the eggshells stronger. Again, do not feed the chickens (or yourself) more than 4 percent of the daily diet in dried comfrey leaf—if you use fresh leaves, the percentage can be greater.

Comfrey for Permanent Fertility

Once you have worked in your edible landscape for three to five years, consider where to establish a bed or row of comfrey. Some good places are: the center strip down the middle of those driveways that have two concrete strips for tires (in this case, use for compost only, not food); at the base of a dry, unirrigated hill or slope; in the yard of neighbors you hate; as a fire-retardant swath if your property borders a wild grass area; or encircling a dog pen or chicken coop. Comfrey flourishes in raw manures—it absorbs surplus nitrogen and generates extra foliage. Comfrey makes a great border for animal pens: nitrogen that might otherwise leach away is recycled into the foliage. Comfrey will survive where there are no summer rains, but the more water, the more foliage.

If you harvest the foliage frequently, you can use a lawn mower with a bag attachment. Otherwise, use a scythe or a motorized weed cutter. I use the fresh foliage as a mulch, tucked discreetly among perennial herbs and flowers where it can decompose unseen. I also layer comfrey leaves beneath a decorative mulch and above the cardboard or newspaper layer in sheet compost. However you use comfrey leaves, you nurture the fertility of your edible landscape with the resources of your own yard—a measure of ecological sustainability.

Albrecht, Dr. William. **The Albrecht Papers**. Raytown, MO: Acres USA, 1975. Albrecht was a pioneer in the science of cover crops and green manures. Though somewhat tedious, the only collection of his writings.

Hills, Lawrence. **Comfrey.** New York: Universe Books, 1976. The definitive book on this important, though tenacious, herb.

McLeod, Edwin. **Feed the Soil**. Graton, CA: Organic Agriculture Research Institute, 1982. A basic review of nitrogen-fixing plants and cover crops, with an encyclopedic reference. I dislike the opening dialog between rabbits and a worm, but I use the encyclopedia frequently.

Pieters, Adrian. **Green Manuring**. New York: John Wiley and Sons, 1927. The best and most comprehensive book on the subject, with lots of scientific studies. Required reading for serious students of green manuring. Out of print—look for it at university agricultural libraries.

Raymond, R., and Altha, R. **Improving Garden Soil With Green Manures**. Charlotte, VT: Garden Way Publishing, 1979. A brief, excellent review of cover crops and green manures. Contains a very good table that outlines the virtues and limitations of many plants (reproduced in Figure 17.3).

Russell, E.W. **Soil Conditions and Plant Growth.** 10th ed. New York: Longman, 1974. The only book I know of that combines a very scientific review of soil chemistry with an emphasis on organic methods. Extensive footnotes and citations from international literature. Often refers to the important research on organic farming by the Rothamsted Agricultural Station in England. Superior book for frequent referral by designers, students of organic methods, and researchers.

Turner, Newman. **Fertility Pastures**. 2nd ed. rev. Pauma Valley, CA: Bargyla and Gylver Rateaver, 1975. My favorite book on plants as indicators of soil fertility and plants as soil improvers in cover crops and herbal leys. Written for dairy farmers, but much of the information relates to edible landscaping, as well.

U.S.D.A. **Soils & Men: Yearbook of Agriculture 1938**. Washington, DC: U.S. Dept. of Agriculture, 1938. This rare volume was written before chemical fertilizers had an iron grip on commercial agriculture and when farmers still grew most of their own fertilizers. An excellent review of soil preserving and soil building techniques. Includes William Albrecht's best paper on nitrogen fixing and green manures, *Loss of Soil Organic Matter and Its Restoration*.

7 MIXING TREES, LAWNS, FLOWERS, HERBS, VINES, AND VEGETABLES

As you increase the complexity and diversity of your landscape, the more dynamic and synergistic it will become, until at times it will seem as if parts of the landscape have a life of their own and are caring for themselves. But a productive community of plants is not achieved by haphazard design. The more diversity you introduce into your landscape, the more carefully you must juxtapose all the elements. Here are some practical considerations for creating harmony among trees, lawns, herbs, flowers, vines, and vegetables.

COMPETITION FOR SUN, WATER, AND FERTILIZER

Shade

When the diversity of your landscape increases, conflicts arise as a result of competition for sunlight, incompatible water and fertilizer requirements, and because some plants attract pests. As the shrubs and trees of a landscape mature, especially in small yards, shade casts its dark influence. While most edible plants need 4 to 6 hours of direct sunlight to thrive, there is quite a selection that will grow in shade.

The plants in Fig. 18.1 are suggestions for experimentation. Do not be afraid to try out the same plant in full sun and in several degrees of shade. I have seen pineapple guavas on the east side of a building, persimmons on the north side of a grove of redwood trees, and rosemary growing with only two hours of direct sunlight—yields were low and the growth a bit leggy, but they provided tasty food. Keep in mind that every climate has its own quality of sunlight. Full sun in a foggy, coastal zone is similar to shade in an Arizona summer. In one place, the plant will be sickly in the partial shade; in another, it may be spindly, but healthy. It's true that the deeper the shade, the lower the yields. Still, shady areas are rarely devoted to food production, so when you use them for edibles, you increase your net harvest.

Figure 18.1

Edible Plants That Grow in Half Shade

Alpine strawberry
(Fragaria alpina)

Bee balm (leaves for tea)
(Monarda didyma)

Cranberry, bush
(Viburnum trilobum)

Day lily (flowers, tuber)
(Hemerocallis fulva)

Huckleberry
*(Vaccinium ovatum,
V. membranaceum,
V. parvifolium)*

Peppermint (leaf, tea)
(Mentha piperita)

Oregon grape
*(Mahonia nervosa,
M. aquifolium)*

Salmonberry
(Rubus spectabilis)

Sorrel, French (leaf)
(Rumex scutatus)

Strawberry tree
(Arbutus unedo)

Thimbleberry
(Rubus parviflorus)

American persimmon
(Diospyros virginiana)

Comfrey (leaf, root)
(Symphytum officinale)

Currant
*(Ribes aurem, R. cereum,
R. lacustre, R. nigrun,
R. sanguineum)*

Elderberry
*(Sambucus caerulea.
S. canadensis, S. racemosa)*

Papaw
(Asimina triloba)

Mallow (leaves)
(Malva parviflora, M. sp.)

Rhubarb (stem)
(Rheum rhabarbarum)

Sassafras
(Sassafras albidum)

Spearmint (leaf, tea)
(Mentha spicata)

Tea (leaf, tea)
(Camellia sinensis)

Wood betony (leaf, tea)
(Stachys officinalis)

Edible Plants That Grow in Full Shade

Guava, Chilean
(Ugni molinae)

Salal
(Gaultheria shallon)

Split-leaf Philodendron
(Monstera deliciosa)

Sweet violet (flowers)
(Viola odorata)

Wild ginger (root)
(Asarum caudatum)

Primrose (flowers)
(Primula vulgaris)

Sorrel, redwood
(leaf, spice)
(Oxalis oregana)

Stinging nettle (leaf)
(Urtica dioica)

Woodruff, sweet
(leaf, wine flavor)
(Asperula odorata)

Plants That Grow in Limited Shade in Hot, Sunny Climates, or in Full Sun in Cool, Hazy Climates

American plum
(Prunus americana)

Black cherry
(Prunus seratonia)

Black mulberry
(Morus nigra)

Buffalo berry
(Shepherdia canadensis)

Black raspberry
(Rubus occidentalis)

Blackberry
*(Rubus laciniatus,
R. procerus, R. ursinus)*

Cattail (all but leaves)
(Typha latifolia)

Chokecherry
(Prunus virginiana)

continued

Chives (leaves, flowers) *(Allium Schoenoprasum)*	Dandelion (leaf, flowers) *(Taraxacum officinale)*
Cornelian cherry *(Cornus mas)*	Gooseberry *(Ribes divaricatum)*
Fennel (leaves, flowers) *(Foeniculum vulgare)*	Guomi *(Elaeagnus multiflora)*
Guava, pineapple *(Feijoa sellowiana)*	Hawthorn *(Crataegus Douglasii)*
Hazelnut *(Corylus americana, C. cornuta, C. heterophylla)*	Kiwi *(Actinidia chinensis)*
Jerusalem artichoke (tubers) *(Helianthus tuberosus)*	Lowbush blueberry *(Vaccinium angustifolium)* Plantain (leaves) *(Plantago major, P. lanceolata)*
Lemon balm (leaves for tea) *(Melissa officinalis)*	Sage (leaf, spice) *(Salvia officinalis)*
Oriental persimmon *(Diospyros kaki)*	Serviceberry *(Amelanchier alnifolia, A. canadensis, A. laevis)*
Rosemary (leaf, spice) *(Rosmarinus officinalis)*	Sour cherry *(Prunus Cerasus)*
Sage, pineapple (leaf, tea) *(Salvia elegans)*	Tarragon (leaf, spice) *(Artemisia Dracunculus)*
Silverberry *(Elaeagnus commutata)*	Viola (flowers) *(Viola cornuta, V. cucullata)*
Sweet cicely (leaf) *(Myrrhis odorata)*	Wild strawberry *(Fragaria chiloensis, F. virginiana)*
Thyme (leaf, spice) *(Thymus vulgaris)*	

Figure 18.1

Water and Fertilizer

Often an aesthetically pleasing design is counter to the cultural needs of plants. For example, the dark green foliage of a ground-hugging mint contrasts pleasingly with the silver-grey, variegated foliage of purple sage, but the sage can suffer and even die from the association. The water needed to keep the mint happy would probably cause the sage's roots to rot. There are usually options, however. Creeping thyme, gazanias, green carpet, and bird's-foot trefoils have the same sort of drought resistance and drainage requirements as sage and the dark green foliage and low profile of mint.

For plants with unusual needs, consider isolation. I try to place drought-loving herbs in groups. I prepare the soil with lots of sand or crushed rock (¼ inch or smaller) for the drainage that so many herbs need. I fertilize with phosphate and potash, using almost no nitrogen, and water at a minimum with a drip irrigation that is independent from the line for the vegetables. I have found that the flavor of herbs grown in sandy, rocky, dry soil is superior to that of herbs grown in a fertile, loamy soil with plenty of water.

For plants with divergent needs, consider separation. The most neglected case for separation is

that of lawns and fruit and nut trees. A good-looking lawn requires water and nitrogen in amounts not needed by, and perhaps harmful to, many fruit and nut trees and edible shrubs (see Fig. 18.2.) And since a tree's roots are much wider than its canopy, plenty of space is needed between trees and lawns (see "Caring for Your Fruit and Nut Trees"). Although I do not recommend mixing trees and lawns, there are times when a landscape requires it or a homeowner prefers it. If you must mix them, be sure to carefully choose the trees.

TREES THAT PREFER NOT TO BE PLANTED IN A LAWN
(when grown on their own root)

Cherry	Pomegranate
Almond	Apricot
Fig	Nectarine
Peach	Persimmon
Walnut	Apple
Chestnut	Olive

Figure 18.2

Some edible trees and shrubs tolerate the water and fertilizer that a lawn needs. Citrus trees require plenty of water and nitrogen for good growth. However, citrus need a more acidic soil than turf does. In Fig. 18.3, each citrus tree has a cultivated circle that allows special amendments for pH and fertilizers. Frequent irrigation of the lawn may actually help reduce spider mites, a common pest of citrus in hot, dry climates. The humidity generated by lawn sprinklers is harmful to the spider mites. (Still, too much water near citrus trees can lead to root rot and other diseases.) Figure 18.4 lists edible plants that can be used judiciously in or near lawns. (See also "Sod Culture: Vegetables in the Lawn.")

If your lot is so small that you must mix edible plants with a lawn, then take precautions. Plant the edibles farther apart than recommended and prune foliage with an open style, to allow for good air circulation. (As they say in the Pacific Northwest, "Prune so you can throw a dog through the tree!") Lay a wide ring of weed-free gravel around the base of each plant (the wider, the better) to ensure proper drainage at the crown of the root system.

Grasses as Ground Covers

All grasses—the type used for lawns and the wild native grasses used in the popular new "prairie meadow" landscapes—limit the growth of trees.

With a pure stand of any kind of grass, the competition with the trees for water and nutrients, the thatch (which blocks the free exchange of gases between the soil and the atmosphere), and the slight allelopathic effect of some grasses act to stunt the growth of fruit trees.

In England, it is common to plant pure stands of wild grasses called swards to slow the growth of vigorous, standard-size fruit trees. A sward causes the trees to remain shorter, bear less, require additional irrigation (in some climates) for good yields, and make smaller fruit. On the positive side, trees in a sward bear earlier in their life, have better-colored fruit, and ripen their crop sooner than trees in bare dirt. (In wet spots, the grasses can help to transpire excess moisture, lessening the chances of crown or collar rot.) For a ground cover beneath fruit trees, however, I advise keeping the proportion of grasses to a minimum.

If you want a living ground cover beneath your trees, use plants that are compatible with the watering and fertilizing schedule of the trees, those able to withstand foot traffic, and those that are low-growing. Some choices include perennial clovers, bird's-foot trefoils, orchard grass (if kept mown and mixed with other herbs and weeds), plantains (except beneath apple trees), burnet, chicory, prostrate yarrows, bur clover, fescues, and other native or drought-resistant grasses.

The cover you use may have an effect on yields. In a study of colonial bentgrass, red fescue, creeping bentgrass, two varieties of Dutch white clover, Kentucky bluegrass, Chewing's fescue, and the variety of wild white clover ('Kent') grown as a cover beneath corn and cabbage, all but the last three covers reduced yields.

Sprinklers and Trees

Figure 18.5 shows a common mistake made by novice edible landscapers – fruit trees randomly placed in a lawn, with sprinklers irrigating the lawn as well as the tree's trunk and foliage. These trees are in peril from crown rot disease (*Phytophthora* sp.) that so easily can girdle and kill fruit and nut trees. Frequent watering on a trunk can also promote armillaria root rot, clitocybe root rot, white root rot, and black root rot. And sprinkling a tree's foliage can promote diseases such as brown rot, fire blight, rust, scab, peach leaf curl, mildew, and mold. In areas with summer rain, it's enough to battle the diseases nature promotes without causing more yourself. In the arid West, it is a shame to see pear trees afflicted with an uncommon disease such as fire blight because of overhead irrigation. The apple trees in the foreground and the pear tree in the background in Fig. 18.5 get sprayed more than once a week. In the dry climate

of Davis, California, fire blight is rare, but these trees suffer from it.

I have seen plenty of exceptions to this guideline. Many times a tree, even when burdened with pest and disease problems, bears well for many years. But caution works in your favor, so try to avoid sprinkling trees and shrubs.

Figure 18.3 Unlike many trees, citrus trees can be planted in a lawn, flourishing with the high amounts of water and nitrogen that the lawn requires.

TREES AND OTHER EDIBLE PLANTS THAT MAY GROW WELL IN OR NEAR LAWNS

Mint	Strawberry
Cane fruit	Blueberry
Jujube	Cranberry
Bamboo	Pineapple guava
Salal	Elderberry
Gooseberry	Rhubarb
Artichoke	Loquat
Currant	Mulberry
Kiwi	Passion fruit

Figure 18.4

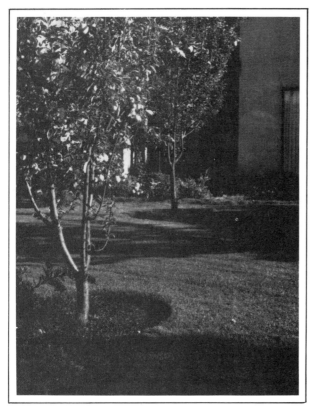

Figure 18.5 Planting fruit trees in lawns that are watered with overhead sprinklers can aggravate tree diseases.

mildew when their foliage stays moist too long. Wide spaces between rows of cane fruits promote good air circulation and drying. Drip irrigation also helps—it keeps the foliage dry.

Isolating the cane fruits lets you manage diseases and pruning more easily. Summer cane fruits produce their largest crops on two-year-old canes (except for everbearing and autumn-fruiting varieties). Most gardening books recommend that each fall you cut out the canes that bore the previous summer, a tedious and time-consuming task. If you have enough room, there is a simpler way. Plant twice as many rows of cane fruits as you need. Each fall, cut to the ground all the canes in every other row. These rows will fruit in two years. The uncut rows fruit the next spring or summer. In the fall, cut to the ground all the canes that fruited. Each fall and winter, your berry patch will look half empty (see Fig. 18.6). Each summer, half of your rows will fruit, while the other half gets ready to fruit the next year.

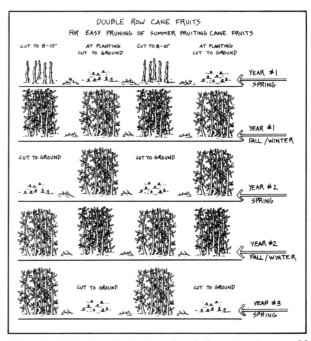

Figure 18.6 Avoid the hassle of thinning 2-year-old raspberry canes—plant 2 rows and prune them in alternate years.

Trees, Lawns, and Fertilizer

Nitrogen promotes the vigorous, dark green growth desirable for lawns and trees. Especially in trees, however, too much nitrogen leads to leggy, weak, succulent growth that invites bugs and disease. (See "Caring for Your Fruit and Nut Trees.") Aphids love plants overfertilized with nitrogen. Aphids are not sucking insects; they simply pierce a plant to reach the sapstream, where the plant's own pressure system fills them up. Nitrogen enters the plant in solution, and the higher the nitrogen content in the soil, the greater the volume and pressure of the sap. Too much nitrogen produces a banquet for aphids. The same is true for organic sources of concentrated nitrogen such as manures and blood, cottonseed, and leather meal. Be judicious with nitrogen fertilizers around fruit and nut trees.

Cane Fruits

Cane fruits, such as blackberries, raspberries, loganberries, and olallieberries, need plenty of water and fertilizer, but they are prone to rust and

Stebbins, Robert, and Walheim, Lance. **Western Fruits, Berries and Nuts**. Tucson, AZ: HPBooks, 1981. The best reference on these subjects, and the one I use the most. Complete with brilliant, condensed, easy-to-use charts. Excellent color photographs. HPBooks also publishes an equally excellent East Coast version, *How to Grow Fruits, Berries and Nuts in the Midwest and East*, by Theodore James, Jr., 1983.

DIVERSITY, PESTS, AND DISEASES

In spite of all the blessings that diversity brings to your edible landscape, it also has its hazards. Some plants—called host plants—harbor pests and diseases. While a host plant may not succumb to its own infestations, it can infect other, more vulnerable edible plants. Figure 18.7 lists a number of suspect wild and cultivated plants. If you know that a pest or disease on the list is a problem in your area, avoid using the host plants. Your neighbors may grow them, but you have a measure of protection from your relative isolation. If you must grow an ornamental that is listed as a host plant, watch for the first signs of its pests or diseases on other plants. (And when you see them, don't automatically reach for a poison spray; read "Integrated Pest Management" first.)

Growing these plants in your edible landscape does not guarantee that your food plants will be infected or attacked. As an example, consider the last listing—German chamomile. One summer at the Farallones Institute Rural Center a bed of chamomile grew only 20 feet from a bed of strawberries. Commercial growers of strawberries do not allow chamomile to grow that close because it harbors the lygus bug, which causes a dimple or puckering in the berry (called cat-facing); and while the fruit and plant are not harmed, the cat-facing is considered cosmetically unacceptable. At Farallones, very few of the fruits had cat-faces.

You need only to consider reducing the diversity of plants in your landscape if your area has a high incidence of the pests and diseases mentioned. For example, I always rake up or mulch over dead leaves, since apple scab is a problem in my area. And I always try to limit the number of wild umbellifers near my vegetables, to reduce the chances of infestations of carrot maggots. However, I don't bother to eradicate chickweed and mallow near the vegetables, because my landscape is never troubled with cucumber mosaic virus. To reiterate the intent of the section entitled "Biological Balance," a diverse community of plants must be carefully planned and must exclude problem plants for your area.

Insects That Spread Diseases

Some insects can be agents for disease—such insects are called vectors. Some pests, such as aphids on peppers, may not cause a direct problem. The green peach aphid, however, is a vector of the potato virus, which can harm the pepper plant and reduce its yields. Figure 18.8 lists a number of vectors for diseases of edible plants.

Don't reflexively reach for insecticides (even "organic" sprays) at the sight of the first insect. Pull out the plants that look infected, see if a problem develops, and spray only as a last resort.

Figure 18.7

HOST PLANTS FOR DISEASES		
Host Plant	Disease/Pest	Endangered Edible
Perennial wild plants	Aster yellows	Carrot, lettuce
Lilac, cherry, pear, poplar, rose, forsythia	Bacterial blights	Beans, lima beans
Catnip, chickweed, jimsonweed, mallow, nightshade, pokeweed, wild lettuce, chickweed seed	Cucumber mosaic virus	Cucurbits, celery, lettuce
Wild umbellifers (carrot, celery, etc.)	Celery mosaic virus	Celery
Seed of wild brassicas	Downy mildew	Brassicas
Perennial wild plants	Watermelon mosaic virus	Cucurbits
Clovers, vetches, alfalfa	Viruses	Peas
Wild solanums	Tobacco etch virus	Peppers
Alfalfa	Alfalfa mosaic virus	Peppers
Southern grasses	Leaf spot	Corn
Johnson grass	Maize dwarf mosaic	Corn
Johnson grass	Maize chlorotic mosaic	Corn
Wild grasses, oats, wheat, barley, rye, stinkgrass, foxtail, panicum	Wheat streak mosaic	Corn
Wild and ornamental plants	Spotted wilt	Tomatoes
Dead leaves on ground	Scab	Apples, pears
Pyracantha	Fire blight	Apples, pears
Cedar trees, hawthorn	Cedar apple rust	Apples
Dandelion, clover	Blossom-end rot	Apples, pears
Plantain	Aphids	Apples
White oak, oak tree roots	Armillaria, clitocybe, and white root rots	Many fruit and nut trees
Dead leaves on ground	Cherry leaf spot	Cherries
Lamb's-quarters, pigweed, nightshade, ground cherry	Verticillum wilt	Stone fruits, vegetables

continued

continued

Host Plant	Disease/Pest	Endangered Edible
Peppers, eggplants, horse nettle, chokecherries	X-disease	Peaches, cherries
Wild umbellifers (carrot, cow parsnip, fool's parsley	Carrot maggot	Carrots
German chamomile	Lygus bugs	Strawberries

Figure 18.7

DISEASE VECTORS		
Vector	Disease	Endangered Edible
Insects	Angular leaf spot	Beans
Insects	Choanephora wet rot	Cucurbits
Insects	Cercospora leaf spot	Beets
Leafhoppers	Aster yellows	Carrots, lettuce
Green peach aphids, aphids, cucumber beetles	Cucumber mosaic virus	Cucurbits, lettuce, tomatoes, celery
Green peach aphids, aphids	Celery mosaic virus	Celery
Green peach aphids, aphids	Watermelon mosaic virus	Cucurbits, legumes
Cucumber beetles	Squash mosiac virus	Cucurbits
Cucumber beetles	Bacterial wilt	Cucurbits
Aphids	Viruses	Peas
Green peach aphid, potato aphid	Tobacco etch virus	Peppers
Green peach aphid, aphids	Potato virus	Peppers
Green peach aphid	Alfalfa mosaic virus	Peppers
Aphids	Blight	Spinach
Flea beetles	Stewart's bacterial wilt	Corn
Insects	Smut	Corn
Aphids	Maize dwarf mosaic	Corn
Leafhoppers	Maize chlorotic mosaic	Corn
Toxin from wheat curl mite	Kernel red streak	Corn
Leafhoppers	X-disease	Peaches, cherries
Nematodes (in soil)	Stem pitting	Stone fruits
Leafhoppers (bluegreen sharpshooter)	Pierce's disease	Grapes

Figure 18.8 While a pest may not eat too much of a vegetable, it may infect the crop with diseases.

Abraham, George and Katy. **Organic Gardening Under Glass**. Emmaus, PA: Rodale Press, 1975. The first book on the subject. Not up to date, but still a good general reference. For indoor use of beneficial insects, see William Jordan's *Windowsill Ecology*.

Garland, Sarah. **The Herb Garden**. New York: Viking Penguin, 1984. My favorite book for ideas on using herbs in the landscape. Beautiful color photos cover the full range of styles, from classical knot gardens to wild, rambling plantings. Includes an excellent cultural encyclopedia that lists uses of the herbs.

Hedrick, U.P., Editor. **Sturtevent's Edible Plants of the World**. New York: Dover Publications, 1972. The most extensive listing of the edible characteristics of thousands of unusual and obscure plants. For unfamiliar plants, use this book with caution; many references are based on old citations and were not personally tested by the author. Many cold-sensitive, tropical plants are included.

Hylton, William. **The Rodale Herb Book**. Emmaus, PA: Rodale Press, 1974. This 650-page book is the most exhaustive on the subject. Contains a complete encyclopedia of the care and uses of 150 herbs. As with all Rodale books, the emphasis is on how-to.

Spoerke, David, Jr. **Herbal Medications**. Santa Barbara, CA: Woodbridge Press, 1980. The only book I know of that gives the active chemical, medicinal ingredients of herbs. Provides scientific confirmation of folk remedies, adding credibility to the medicinal use of herbs.

FINISHING TOUCHES:
PERENNIAL LEGUMES,
EDIBLE FLOWERS, AND MULCHES

Perennial Legumes

The previous section discussed leguminous annuals that can be composted or tilled under to improve your soil. There are *perennial* leguminous trees, shrubs, and herbaceous plants as well. While the techniques described in "Grow Your Own Fertilizers—Cover Crops and Green Manures" provide much faster results, the perennial legumes will, over time, help fertilize your landscape. For example, the lupines (genus *Lupinus*) are nitrogen-fixing plants that grow well in almost every environment in America. The colorful Giant Russell Lupine, though short-lived and susceptible to mildew where the air circulation is poor, provides nitrogen and phosphorus to neighboring plants. The native varieties are relatively easy to grow and are fairly free of pests and diseases.

Because nitrogen-fixing shrubs are generally shorter lived than many shade trees and fruit and nut trees, they can be grown as soil-improving fillers between slower growing trees. Properly spaced, they begin to wither and die as the other trees fill out. Figure 18.9 includes some common and unusual shrubs and trees in the legume family.

LEGUME FAMILY SHRUBS AND TREES

Common Name	Botanical Name	Height (in feet)
Wattle	*Acacia verticillate*	10 to 15
Desert holly	*Hymenelytra*	1 to 3
Quail bush	*Atriplex lentiformis*	3 to 10
Siberian peashrub (edible)	*Caragana arborescens*	20
Sennas	*Cassia* sp.	3 to 10
Redbud	*Cercis occidentalis*	10 to 18
Flame pea	*Chorizema cordatum*	3
Coral tree	*Erythrina* sp.	15 to 30
Golden chain tree	*Laburnum anagyroides*	10 to 30
Mesquite	*Prosopis chilensis*	20
Japanese pagoda	*Sophora japonica*	20 to 30

Figure 18.9

Some members of the legume family have never been observed to have the distinctive root nodules that fix nitrogen—examples include Honey locust (*Gleditsia* sp.), Carob (*Certonia siliqua*), and Wisteria (*Wisteria* sp.). Though they easily grow in your landscape, they are not adding to the nitrogen supply of the soil.

There are non-leguminous plants that also have beneficial, nitrogen-fixing bacteria living in association with their roots. They, too, improve the soil. In this category, we find many of the common shrubs for hedges and wild borders. (See Fig. 18.10.)

NON-LEGUMINOUS, NITROGEN-FIXING SHRUBS AND TREES

Common Name	Botanical Name	Height (in feet)
Alders	*Alnus* sp.	30 to 50
Beefwood	*Casuarinus* sp.	20 to 60
New Jersey tea	*Ceanothus americanus*	3
Mountain whitethorn	*Ceanothus cordulatus*	2 to 5
Mountain mahogany	*Cercocarpus montanus*	9 to 20
Russian olive	*Elaeagnus angustifolia*	20
Silverberry	*Elaeagnus commutata*	12
Cherry eleagnus	*Elaeagnus multiflora*	6 to 12
Silverberry	*Elaeagnus pungus*	6 to 15
Autumn olive	*Elaeagnus umbellata*	15

Figure 18.10

Even if you never uproot these plants to make room for fruit trees, your property will benefit from the continual soil improvement. The more you mix nitrogen-fixing plants into perennial plantings, the healthier your landscape will be.

Edible Flowers

As described in "Zones of Use, Multiple Use," my favorite way to get multiple uses from a landscape is to include plants with edible flowers. These unusual edibles are the highlight of my salads, especially in winter (see Fig. 18.11 and 18.12 in color plates). Figure 18.13 lists many edible flowers, but please heed the following cautions:

If you have hay fever, consider skipping edible flowers. The risk of a reaction to the pollen is too great. Use the flowers as decorations to be removed before eating.

This information has *not* been tested on a national basis. Day lily flowers and tubers are listed in virtually every book about wild edibles; yet some students of wild edibles became very sick from sampling day lily tubers during a field trip for a class at the University of Michigan. In one year, some 50 to 60 cases of sickness from day lilies were reported in the northern Midwest (with one report from Long Island, New York). The reason for the toxic response is still in question, but some botanists think it may be because localized subspecies of day lily have developed a toxic compound.

The first time you sample an edible flower, taste only a small piece. Wait at least several hours before sampling more. Sample minute amounts, taste before swallowing, and don't experiment by yourself. Treat the adventure like wild mushroom sampling—potentially fatal. Some people have allergic reactions to the unusual compounds in flowers, so be cautious, not frivolous.

If it tastes bitter, too spicy, weird, or caustic, spit it out. Not all the flowers on this list taste the same everywhere. Soil, climate, and varietal differences will affect the flavor.

Do not eat unknown flowers. If it is not listed here, or if you don't reconize the flower by name, do not take the risk.

If any other part of the plant is poisonous, do not eat the flowers. In an enthusiastic attempt to be innovative, even though the sweet pea is not found on any of the edible flower lists and is in fact a toxic plant, one "haute cuisine" restaurant served sweet pea flowers.

Figure 18.13

EDIBLE FLOWERS
a list to use with caution

Common Name	Botanical Name
Apple blossom	*Malus* sp.
Bee balm	*Monarda didyma*
Borage	*Borago officinalis*
Calendula	*Calendula officinalis*
Carnation and pinks	*Dianthus* sp.
Cattail	*Typha latifolia*
Chamomile	*Matricaria chamomilla* or *Anthemis nobilis*
Chickweed	*Stellaria media*
Chicory	*Cichorium intybus*
Chives	*Allium* sp.
Chrysanthemum	*Chrysanthemum* sp.
Clover, red	*Trifolium pratense*
Comfrey	*Symphytum officinale*
Daisy	*Bellis perennis*
Dandelion	*Taraxacum officinale*
Day lily	*Hemerocallis fulva*
Dill	*Anethum graveolens*
Elder	*Sambucus canadensis*
Fennel	*Foeniculum vulgare*
Geranium	*Geranium* sp.
Gladiolus	*Gladiolus* sp.
Goldenrod	*Solidago* sp.
Hawthorn	*Crataegus* sp.
Hibiscus	*Hibiscus rosa-sinensis*
Hollyhock	*Althea rosea*
Honeysuckle	*Lonicera* sp.
Hyssop	*Hyssopus officinalis*
Jasmine	*Jasminum* sp.
Johnny-jump-up	*Viola tricolor*
Lavender	*Lavandula officinalis*
Lemon balm	*Melissa officinalis*
Lemon blossom	*Citrus limon*

continued

Common Name	Botanical Name
Lemon verbena	*Aloysia triphyllia*
Lilac	*Syringa vulgaris*
Mallow	*Malva neglecta*
Marjoram	*Origanum majorana*
Mullein	*Verbascum* sp.
Mustard	*Brassica* sp.
Nasturtium	*Tropaeolum* sp.
Orange blossom	*Citrus sinensis*
Oregano	*Origanum vulgare*
Pansy	*Viola* sp.
Passion flower	*Passiflora caerulea*
Pelargonium	*Pelargonium* sp.
Petunia	*Petunia hybrida*
Plum blossom	*Prunus* sp.
Poppy	*Papaver* sp.
Primrose	*Primula vulgaris*
Rose	*Rosa* sp.
Rosemary	*Rosmarinus officinalis*
Sage	*Salvia* sp.
Saint-John's-wort	*Hypericum* sp.
Squash blossom	*Cucurbita* sp.
Thistle	*Cirsium* sp.
Thyme	*Thymus* sp.
Tulip	*Tulipa* sp.
Violet	*Viola* sp.
Woodruff	*Asperula odorata*
Yucca	*Yucca* sp.

Figure 18.13

The Final Touch: A Mulch for All Reasons

You've probably noticed that I abhor bare soil. As described in "Caring for Your Fruit and Nut Trees," I rely heavily on mulches to conserve moisture and to help fertilize the soil. Also, I mulch vegetables and new plantings. While an attractive layer of mulch is the finishing touch for both ornamental and edible areas of your landscape, Fig. 18.14 lists some practical considerations.

To Mulch . . .	. . . or Not to Mulch
Conserves moisture.	In poorly drained soil, you want to encourage evaporation.
Keeps down weeds.	A ground cover helps dry out poorly drained soils.
Keeps the soil cooler in the heat of the summer.	Early vegetables may need a bare soil, which warms faster in the spring.
Prevents the erosion of valuable topsoil.	Why would anyone want to encourage erosion?
Conserves nitrogen, by preventing the sun from heating the soil's surface.	Mulch high in carbon robs some nitrogen from the surface; and if tilled in, from the soil.
Protects roots from hard winter freezes.	Bare soil outside the canopy helps prevent spring frost damage better than mulching.

Figure 18.14

Garland, Sarah. **The Herb Garden**. New York: Viking Penguin, 1984. My favorite book for ideas on using herbs in the landscape. Beautiful color photos cover the full range of styles, from classical knot gardens to wild, rambling plantings. Includes an excellent cultural encyclopedia that lists uses of the herbs.

Hylton, William. **The Rodale Herb Book**. Emmaus, PA: Rodale Press, 1974. This 650-page book is the most exhaustive on the subject. Contains a complete encyclopedia of the care and uses of 150 herbs. As with all Rodale books, the emphasis is on how-to.

Larkcom, Joy. **The Salad Garden**. New York: Viking Press, 1984. The best book on gardening with colorful, gourmet vegetables. Exquisite color photographs of gardens as well as a color close-up of each edible mentioned. A fair amount of space is given to edible weeds, edible flowers, and unusual leafy greens. Good cultural information. A book to buy.

Stamets, Paul, and Chilton, J. S. **The Mushroom Cultivator**. Olympia, WA: Agarikon Press, 1983. The best reference on growing exotic mushrooms. Includes extensive details on how to grow shiitake mushrooms on oak logs in your backyard and how to grow some types of mushrooms in the woodchip mulch of garden pathways.

Swanson, Faith. **Herb Garden Design**. Hanover, NH: University Press of New England, 1984. Black and white designs for dozens of herb gardens, by type or by function. Most designs are formal or very formal. Good ready-to-use "blueprints" for gardeners who don't want to create their own design.

THE GOLDEN HITS
OF EDIBLE LANDSCAPING

The best fun in growing an edible landscape is putting the produce to good use – so let's eat, in style! The following edibles are my personal favorites because they are relatively easy to grow, they have unique, superlative flavor, and they are versatile in recipes. The suggestions on how to use the plants in your landscape and in your kitchen are intended as jumping-off points; no doubt, you will find many more uses for these special plants.

In regard to the recipes, it seems that most styles of cooking become fads at one time or another. A revival of regional American cuisine is all the rage now in "gastronomical" circles. But no style is more authentic and more lasting than a cuisine that originates with your family, based on the fresh foods that grow best in your own garden. I encourage you to experiment, to find a style that suits your family's tastes *and* the plants that thrive in your landscape.

Credit for the "effort scale" of edible plants goes to Rosalind Creasy, who used the scale in *The Complete Book of Edible Landscaping*. The scale is a relative – and subjective – ranking that combines a plant's required care, the difficulty or ease of harvest, and the effort needed to prepare the produce. The lowest-effort plants are ranked #1. Persimmons, pineapple guavas, Chilean guavas, figs, loquats, and mulberries are in this category: they are disease-resistant and their fruit can be eaten right off the tree. On the other hand, to have a good looking, worm-free apple using organic methods is one of the most time consuming challenges of fruit culture – and would rate a #5, at the top of the effort scale. (If you were to grow a disease-resistant variety and didn't mind a few wormy apples, then the effort would be a #3 or a #4.) Other edibles deserving a #5 are: cabbage, free of insect holes; black walnuts, without walnut husk flies; peaches, without peach leaf curl in cool-summer areas; carrots, during the season of carrot rot maggot; blanched endive; and espalier apple and pear trees. You may rank the following plants differently than I have, according to your own tastes and gardening methods; my numbers are intended as guidelines.

MENU

Ornamental kale
'Romanesco'
Rosemary
Asian pear
Chayote
Chinese chestnut
Fava bean
Corn salad
Kiwi
Persimmon
Garlic
Quince
'Pink Pearl' apple

Ornamental kale

ORNAMENTAL KALE

(*Brassica oleracea, B. campestris*)

Effort: 2

Zones: All zones. Best where it can be grown throughout the winter.

Soil: Prefers a fertile soil.

Planting: Late summer plantings taste best, after frost brings out the sweet flavor. In the coldest winter areas, plant in early spring.

Watering: Standard amount and frequency for vegetables.

Fertilizing: Needs average fertility. Too much organic matter may cause the plants to lean as they mature.

Harvesting: Pick single leaves from the lower portion of the head throughout the growing season.

Height: 8 to 12 inches

Width: 12 to 16 inches

Shape: A flattened, cabbagelike head

Foliage: Colors range from pink and red to blue, green, and white.

Flower: When the plant bolts, or goes to flower, it has the same yellow flowers as most members of the cabbage family.

Landscape Uses: Ornamental kale gives perhaps the most dramatic display of fall and winter color of any annual edible. Transplant it among the fading color of late summer bedding plants in showcase settings – near the front door or along a walkway. Excellent in clay pots for porches, decks, and window ledges. One of the best combinations of color, flavor, and nutrition available.

ENSALADA DE FLORES

Edible flowers and ornamental kale are a delightful way to enliven a salad, especially in winter when salads tend to get the green blahs. Begin by ringing a salad bowl or plates with leaves of ornamental kale. Mix pieces of the kale with your favorite salad greens (I prefer bib, red leaf, and red romaine lettuces), and toss with flower petals. Garnish with different colored rings of petals, a layer of mixed petals, or whole blossoms arranged like a bouquet. In cold-winter areas, you may want to cultivate your favorite "salad" flowers and ornamental kale in a greenhouse, to ensure a winter supply of blossoms and nutrition.

Here are my favorite edible flowers for each season, and how I like to use them.

Flower	Season	Uses	Colors
Borage	Sp, W	A top garnish	blue
Calendula	Sp, W	Mix throughout	yellows and oranges
Chicory	S	Mix throughout	blue
Chives	S	Mix throughout, for a spicy accent	purple
Daylily	S	Arrange like a bouquet on top	most colors
Dill	S	Make a little "forest" of whole sprigs	yellow
Fennel	S	Same as dill	yellow
Gladiolus	S	Cluster 2 or 3 whole blossoms on top	most colors
Honeysuckle	S	Ring bowl with a garland, for fragrance	cream and yellow
Lavender	Sp, W	A floral arrangement on top; remove before eating	lavender
Mullein	S	Mix throughout	yellow
Mustard	Sp	Sprinkle on top	yellow
Nasturtium	Sp, W	Mix petals throughout, garnish top with rings of whole blossoms	red, orange, yellow
Orange blossoms	Sp, W	A top garnish, for fragrance	white
Rose	S	Mix petals throughout, garnish top with 1 or 2 whole roses	most colors
Rosemary	Sp	Sprinkle on top (flowers are tedious to pick)	blue
Squash blossoms	S	Arrange on top like a bouquet	yellow
Violet	Sp	Arrange in clusters like a bouquet	white, blue, pink

Chives

The perfect complement to a floral salad is a fresh herbal dressing, such as . . .

PESTO VINAIGRETTE

Combine the following ingredients in a blender or shaker bottle:

¼ C Balsamic vinegar
1   Tbs. freshly squeezed lemon juice
½ C olive oil
1   Tbs. Dijon mustard
3   cloves garlic, pressed
1   Tbs. minced parsley
2   Tbs. minced basil
salt and freshly ground pepper to taste
¼ C grated Parmesan cheese, if desired

Borage

BLUE CHEESE DRESSING WITH GARLIC

1   C mayonnaise
1   clove garlic, pressed
2   Tbs. lemon juice
1   C sour cream
½ C bleu cheese, crumbled
salt to taste

Whisk all ingredients together and let stand at least 1 hour to let the flavors blend.

'ROMANESCO'
(*Brassica* sp.)

Effort:	3
Zones:	All zones
Soil:	Prefers a rich soil. Too much organic matter will cause the plants to lean as the heavy heads mature.
Planting:	In areas where broccoli can be grown through the winter, plant in the late summer to early fall. In all other areas, plant in early spring.
Watering:	Standard for vegetables
Fertilizing:	Responds to a top dressing of manure halfway through the growing season.
Harvesting:	Wait until the heads are large and a rich, yellow-green color. Harvest the entire head at once.
Height:	18 to 36 inches
Width:	24 to 36 inches
Shape:	The huge, peaked head and whorled flowerlets make it perhaps the most striking vegetable in existence.
Foliage:	Blue-green leaves, typical of broccoli or cauliflower.
Flower:	If left to flower, the pale yellow-green head produces the small yellow flowers of the cabbage family.
Landscape Uses:	This gorgeous vegetable deserves to be viewed by all. Place a few in a prominent place – along the path to the front door, outside the living room window, by the mail box. Try mixing with ornamental kale for a winter ornamental vegetable border. The lower leaves fall and make the stalk look messy – fill in around the base with annual bedding plants such as calendulas, primroses, violas, and sweet alyssum. The blue tone of the foliage is more striking when planted next to plants with rich green, glossy leaves or silver-grey foliage.

'ROMANESCO' WITH HOLLANDAISE

Serves 4

½   C melted butter
1½ Tbs. garlic vinegar (or lemon juice)
3   egg yolks
1   Tbs. boiling water
3   Tbs. water
1   large head 'Romanesco'

Rinse and steam the head of 'Romanesco' til just slightly crunchy. Drain the water from the steamer, replace the cover, and set aside.

Arrange on the stovetop:

- Double boiler with water nearly boiling in lower pan
- Saucepan with melted butter
- Saucepan with boiling water
- Measuring cup with vinegar or lemon juice
- Glass of water

(*Important:* From start to finish, you must constantly whisk the cooking sauce. Use a whisk to whip in each ingredient. If at any time the eggs begin to congeal on the side of the pan, remove it immediately and lower the heat under the water.)

Place the egg yolks in the top pan of the double boiler, whisking constantly. Add the boiling water.

When the yolks begin to fluff up, drizzle in the melted butter in several small portions. Whisk thoroughly during and after each addition.

After all the butter has been added, slowly pour in the vinegar or lemon juice. Keep whisking!

If the sauce is too thick, thin it with water or a little lemon juice. Whisk to a fluffy consistency, and serve immediately.

Serving

Cover a platter with ornamental kale leaves, arrange the steamed 'Romanesco' on top, and surround it with steamed baby potatoes and carrots. Serve the Hollandaise sauce on the side.

ROSEMARY
(*Rosmarinus officinale*)

Effort:	1
Zones:	All zones
Soil:	Prefers a rocky soil with low fertility. Leaves turn yellow and plant gets woody with less foliage if grown in too fertile a soil.
Planting:	Prefers to grow in hot, dry weather.
Watering:	Keep water to a minimum for the best flavor. Very drought resistant.
Fertilizing:	Use rock powders for phosphorus and potash, but no nitrogen fertilizers.
Harvesting:	Pinch sprigs of new growth as needed. Rosemary can be shaped with pinching.
Height:	2 to 6 feet
Width:	3 to 6 feet
Shape:	If left unpruned, it becomes spindly or sometimes columnar. It is easily pruned to a hedge or Christmas tree shape. (Another variety of rosemary, *R. o. prostratus,* is commonly used as a ground cover, but it does not have as good a flavor as the upright rosemary.)
Foliage:	Rich, dark green
Flower:	Royal and pale blue. Some varieties have white and pink flowers.
Landscape Uses:	One of the most useful plants for an edible landscape. I use it extensively as a backdrop for silver foliage plants and for plants with bright red and blue flowers; as an easily shaped, petite hedge; as an accent plant for winter and early spring color; and as a foundation planting to accent the vertical lines of a building or an arbor.

GRILLED CHICKEN WITH ROSEMARY

Serves 4

4 chicken breasts, with or without bones
olive oil
fresh rosemary

Several days in advance:

Harvest 16 to 32 sprigs of rosemary, cutting only the young, supple growth.

Rinse the sprigs, pat dry, and place in a tall, narrow jar. Cover with extra virgin olive oil and seal.

To Prepare:

Remove all fat and skin from the chicken breasts. Press 2 or 3 sprigs of oil-soaked rosemary into both sides of each breast.

Sandwich the chicken and rosemary between a pair of hinged grills. (The grills are turned as a unit, which keeps the tender chicken from sticking and tearing.)

Grill over mesquite charcoal or apple wood coals, Each time you turn the chicken, baste with the rosemary oil.

Serve on a bed of a wild and brown rice, with a flower salad and poached Asian pears.

ASIAN PEAR

(Pyrus pyrifolia, P. ussuriensis)

Effort:	3
Zones:	5 through 9
Soil:	Prefers a rich, deep soil. Can tolerate clay soils better than most fruit trees.
Planting:	Blooms at the same time as early European pear trees – plant where there are no late spring frosts. The fruit ripens mid- to late September.
Watering:	Keep the soil moist, but not wet, with a regular schedule of irrigation or drip irrigation.
Fertilizing:	Asian pears are vigorous trees and may need some nitrogen fertilizer. Use the rates recommended for pear trees in "Fertilizing Tree Crops."
Harvesting:	It's hard to tell when to harvest the fruit because Asian pears are very juicy and tasty when firm. Try the fruit every week beginning in mid-August. Some varieties keep well on the tree when ripe; others store well if picked slightly green. I wait to pick until the stem separates easily when the fruit is gently lifted.
Height:	30 to 40 feet
Width:	20 to 30 feet
Shape:	A pyramidal shape similar to the common European pear tree.
Foliage:	The new leaves of some varieties

have a distinctive tinge of purple or rose. The rich green summer foliage turns to bright gold in fall, particularly at higher elevations.

Flower:	The white blossoms are the same as those of the European pear.
Landscape Uses:	An excellent accent tree, especially when planted in the background where it can be viewed from the house. Large enough to be a shade tree. Until an adequate dwarfing rootsock is found, Asian pear trees are not easily espaliered.

The unique Asian pear is one of my favorite summer delights. The round fruit is as crisp as a watermelon, as juicy as a ripe peach, and has none of the graininess of a regular, European pear. I have to eat many pounds of Asian pears right off the tree before I think about other ways to use them.

In cooking, Asian pears offer an exciting advantage over European pears: they keep some of their crispness when lightly poached or baked.

Asian pears come in a wide range of flavors, from sweet and juicy varieties that lack flavor, to kinds with a complex aroma and taste reminiscent of allspice.

ASIAN PEAR CHUTNEY

12	lbs. Asian pears, peeled, cored, and sliced into 8ths
8	limes, thinly sliced (with the rind)

–with–

2	lbs. raisins or currants
2	lbs. onions, thinly sliced
6	large garlic cloves, pressed
4	tsp. ground ginger

–or–

2	Tbs. grated fresh ginger
4	tsp. allspice
1	tsp. cloves
2	tsp. cayenne
4	lbs. brown sugar
2	qts. apple cider vinegar

Place all ingredients in a large stainless steel pot and bring to a boil. Reduce heat and simmer and skim for 2 hours, til the flavors are well blended. Stir occasionally, being careful not to break the fruit.

Immediately hot-pack into sterile, hot jars, sealing with hot canning lids. After cooling, refrigerate any jars that did not seal well.

(Courtesy of Myra Portwood, owner of The Bakery, Sebastopol, CA. Her delectable almond croissants helped fuel this book project.)

ASIAN PEAR SALAD

Serves 4 to 6

Make your favorite vinaigrette dressing, or use the following:

½   tsp. Italian herbal salt
⅛   tsp. freshly ground black pepper
¼   C garlic vinegar (or another herbal vinegar)
½   tsp. Dijon white wine mustard
¾   C virgin olive oil

Blend or shake well, and set aside.
In a large salad bowl, combine:

2   lemon cucumbers, sliced or cubed
4   tomatoes, sliced
1   small jicama, peeled and thinly sliced
1   yellow bell pepper, thinly sliced (remove seeds)
4   to 5 medium Asian Pears, cored, de-stemmed, and sliced

Chill for several hours, toss with vinaigrette to taste, and serve with a sprig of spearmint.

ASIAN PEARS POACHED IN RED WINE

Serves 2 to 3

4   large Asian pears
Cabernet Sauvignon or your favorite red wine
2   sticks whole cinnamon
4   to 7 whole cloves
2   to 3 tsp. grated lemon peel
sugar
cream

Cut the pears in half, and core and peel them, leaving the stem on one half of each pear.

Put the pears in a saucepan, and cover with wine. Add seasonings, and sugar to taste, taking care not to overpower the dryness of the wine.

Simmer for 25 to 30 minutes, stirring occasionally. Chill overnight.

Drain and reserve the wine sauce. Serve the pears with a pool of lightly whipped cream, and garnish with a sprig of peppermint. The wine sauce can be re-used to poach more pears; it also makes a delicious addition to pear butter and applesauce.

CHAYOTE

(*Sechium edule*)

Effort: 1

Zones: 9 and 10; and zone 8, in sheltered places.

Soil: Needs excellent drainage and good fertility.

Planting: Requires a long growing season. Tubers will rot in areas of heavy winter rain, and will freeze in cold winter climates.

Watering: Needs copious quantities of water on a regular basis.

Fertilizing: Needs large amounts of nitrogen to sustain its vigorous growth. Mulch with manures.

Harvesting: Harvest the first 4 to 6 inches of the succulent vine tips throughout the growing season. Harvest firm, dark green fruits in late summer and early fall. Tubers can be dug after harvesting the fruits, but leave some behind to sprout new vines the coming spring.

Height: 50 to 80 feet

Width: The vines will grow as wide as you let them, if the vertical shoots are cut back. Vines will travel great lengths along a fence, if that is their only support.

Shape: A sprawling vine that takes the shape of its support.

Foliage: Rich green

Flower: Inconspicuous

Landscape Uses: The dense summer vines quickly cover trees, fences, trellises, and arbors, and can be used to disguise unattractive structures.

CHAYOTE PARMIGIANA

Unlike eggplant, chayote does not get mushy when cooked, nor does it absorb much oil. The finished entre has a richer flavor, more texture, and less oil than the typical eggplant Parmigiana. For a lower oil content, bake the breaded chayote instead of frying it.

Serves 4 to 6

1½   qts. spaghetti sauce
4   large chayotes
4   eggs, beaten
4   to 6 C coarse cornmeal
½   tsp. Italian herbal salt
2   tsp. freshly ground black pepper
olive oil
1   to 2 C grated Romano or Parmesan cheese
1   C walnut pieces

1 or 2 days before serving:

Make 1 to 1½ quarts of your favorite spaghetti sauce. To save time, I start with Paul Newman's Own "industrial strength" sauce, to which I add plenty of fresh rosemary, oregano, thyme, and mushrooms. (The profits from Newman's products benefit organizations such as Save the Children Foundation.)

To Prepare:

Preheat oven to 375° F.

Wash the chayotes, and slice them lengthwise, ⅜ inch thick.

Steam the slices for a few minutes, until they just begin to lose their crispness. Dry on paper towels.

Combine the cornmeal and seasonings. Dip the chayote slices in the beaten egg, and then into the corneal mixture. Fry in olive oil until golden brown, and drain on paper towels.

In a large covered casserole, alternate layers of sauce, chayote slices, walnuts pieces, and grated cheese. Top with a thick layer of sauce and plenty of grated cheese.

Bake covered for 20 to 25 minutes. Remove the cover and bake 5 to 10 more minutes, until the cheese is brown.

CHAYOTE PICKLES

Slice the chayotes ¼ inch thick, or cut them into long, thin strips. Pack the slices tightly into sterilized canning jars.

To calculate the amount of pickling liquid you will need, fill the jars with enough cold water to completely cover the chayote slices, then pour out the water into a measuring cup.

For *each cup* of water, add:

¾	C apple cider vinegar
2	Tbs. honey
1	Tbs. pickling spice
½	tsp. salt

Bring to a boil and pour into the jars, making sure to completely cover all the chayote. Seal with sterile lids.

Let the chayote pickle for two days before serving. Once a jar is opened, the pickles will keep for two weeks or so, refrigerated.

CHINESE CHESTNUT
(*Mollissima* sp.)

Effort:	1
Zones:	5 through 9
Soil:	Requires a deep, fertile soil.
Planting:	An excellent tree to plant where late frosts are a problem. Chestnuts bloom so late that the blossoms are rarely damaged by frost. The nuts mature in early fall.
Watering:	Chestnut trees are drought-resistant. Water monthly to establish young trees; mature trees need no watering even when there are no summer rains.
Fertilizing:	No fertilizer is required if grown in a rich soil.
Harvesting:	The mature nuts fall to the ground inside a protective burr. Step on the edge of a burr to pop out the nut(s).
Height:	60 to 80 feet
Width:	40 to 80 feet
Shape:	A well-proportioned, mushroom-shaped canopy. Needs no pruning for a perfect form.
Foliage:	The rich green leaves have a wavy or serrated edge. Their fall color is a deep yellow-ocher color.
Flower:	Inconspicuous
Landscape Uses:	The Chinese chestnut is one of the most disease- and pest-resistant trees. Excellent as a shade tree and dominant accent tree for large yards. Needs to be far from the house and in proper scale with the rest of the landscape.

In fall, my fancy turns to thoughts of chestnuts. Gathering them from among the fallen yellow-ochre leaves in crisp blue-and-gold light is a yearly treat. I love chestnuts freshly roasted on my woodburning stove, and have to eat many pounds before I move on to more complicated recipes.

ROASTED CHESTNUTS WITH GARLIC BUTTER

With a sharp, pointed knife, make a slit through each nutshell. (The "experts" quarrel: some make a single slit halfway around the nut, some make an X across one end, and some carve an X in the dome-shaped side.)

Bake the slitted nuts in a 350° F oven, roast on top of a woodstove, or cook in a heavy skillet, stirring frequently, for 20 to 30 minutes.

Cool and shell the nuts. Gently squeeze each warm kernel to crack the brown paperlike membrane, then peel it off (it can be bitter).

In a heavy skillet, melt plenty of butter and add the pressed garlic. I use as many as two heads of garlic for 2 to 3 pounds of chestnuts.

Add the peeled chestnuts and sauté until the garlic is cooked and the chestnuts have soaked up most of the butter. Serve warm – and indulge!

CHESTNUT SOUP

To your favorite chicken soup recipe, add one cup of roasted garlic chestnuts for every two cups of soup.

Serve hot with warm bread, and chilled sliced persimmons for dessert.

CHESTNUT SOUFFLÉ

Serves 4 to 6

Pre-heat oven to 350° F. Make a collar for a 6-cup soufflé dish. Butter and flour the dish and collar.

3 Tbs. butter
4 Tbs. flour
1 C cream
6 egg yolks
1 C chestnut puree
2 tsp. honey
¼ tsp. vanilla
½ tsp. cinnamon
dash of nutmeg
dash of cloves
1 Tbs. Gran Marnier
6 egg whites, at room temperature
⅛ tsp. cream of tartar
dash of salt

Slit the unshelled chestnuts and steam them for 40 to 50 minutes. Remove the shells and the papery brown inner husk. (Or, slit and bake them for 10 minutes, turning a couple of times. Then remove the husks and the inner peels, and steam the chestnuts for 20 to 30 minutes or until soft.)

Mash or puree the cooked chestnuts. If they are too dry to puree, thin them with just enough cream so the puree holds together in a thick paste.

Melt the butter, stir in the flour, then whisk in the cream a little at a time to make a smooth sauce.

Remove from heat, and whisk in the egg yolks, one at a time, then the chestnut puree, honey, and flavorings.

In a separate bowl, add the cream of tartar and a dash of salt to the egg whites, and whisk them until they form stiff, moist peaks. (If you use a copper bowl, omit the cream of tartar.)

Stir about ½ C of the beaten egg whites into the chestnut sauce, then slowly fold in the remaining egg whites.

Gently pour the mixture into the soufflé dish, and bake for 35 to 40 minutes.

Remove the collar, dust the top of the baked soufflé with cinnamon and powdered sugar, and serve immediately with slices of fresh tangerines or oranges.

FAVA BEAN
(Vicia faba)

Effort:	1
Zones:	All zones
Soil:	Grows well in (and improves) poor soils; flourishes in fertile soils.
Planting:	In moderate winter areas, plant fava beans early in the fall as a cover crop. Elsewhere, they must be planted early in the spring, or summer heat will prevent pollination of the flowers.
Watering:	Water only to germinate the seed and then let winter rains do all the work for you. If you plant them in spring, water fava beans as you would most vegetables.
Fertilizing:	Fava beans fix nitrogen, and need no fertilizer. Use an inoculant if pink root nodules are not present. (See "Soil Inoculants.")
Harvesting:	Harvest the beans when the pods have filled out, but before they begin to turn brown.

Height:	3 to 6 feet
Width:	8 to 16 feet
Shape:	Favas are tall and spindly; single plants flop over without a support. It is best to plant them in small groves.
Foliage:	Rounded, blue-green leaves
Flower:	The fragrant white blossoms resemble those of sweetpeas.
Landscape Uses:	Not a beautiful plant by classic ornamental standards, but I like the color of the foliage and especially enjoy the fragrance of the flowers. This plant does so much good for the landscape that it should be used despite its farmlike look. Plant favas farther from the house and turn them under as a green manure before many pods form, to avoid the uglier late-season foliage. If you plan to harvest the green beans, pick them as early as possible.

I think favas are the best steamed beans there are—they are "meatier" and more succulent than the best peas. I usually make an entire meal of this dish. The shucking is tedious, so I do it while watching a M*A*S*H re-run.

FAVA BEANS WITH ARTICHOKE HEARTS

Serves 4

4	large artichokes
5	to 6 lbs. fava beans, whole
⅛	to ¼ lb. butter
1	to 2 heads of garlic, peeled and pressed

salt

Rinse the artichokes, and slice off the top third of each. Place upside down in a steamer or pressure cooker, and steam til a knife can be easily inserted into the heart. (Home-grown 'chokes take much less time to cook than store-bought 'chokes.)

Drain and set aside. When cool, remove the leaves and eat their bases, or discard them.

Clean the "hairs" away and cut the hearts into large slices.

Shuck the beans from their pods, and steam them for a few minutes, until you can "pop" a cool one from its skin by pressing one end between two fingers. (The thick skin contains all the bean's bitterness; without it, favas are sweet and tender.) Cool and "pop" all the favas. (This is easier than trying to peel them raw!)

In a skillet, saute the garlic, artichoke hearts, and salt in butter until the garlic is browned.

Add the beans and stir-fry until they are coated with garlic butter. Serve and eat with gusto!

CORN SALAD
(*Valerianella locusta*)

Effort:	1 (Reseeds so easily that it almost becomes a pest.)
Zones:	All zones
Soil:	Likes most soils of a neutral pH, and thrives in a fertile soil.
Planting:	Can be grown through the winter in many climates. A good plant for coldframe culture in the coldest of climates. Plant in mid- to late summer in moderate winter areas, and elsewhere, plant in early spring. Corn salad does not like heat.
Watering:	Standard for vegetables
Fertilizing:	Treat corn salad as you would a lettuce crop.
Harvesting:	Pick individual leaves or wait 2 to 3 months to harvest the entire head.
Height:	4 to 8 inches
Width:	6 to 12 inches
Shape:	A nice rosette of rounded, spinach-like leaves that grow somewhat flat like a bib lettuce.
Foliage:	Rich green
Flower:	Harvest before it flowers.
Landscape Uses:	Corn salad is a good edible ground cover and filler plant in a flower border. Let a few go to seed where they do not show too much, for next year's crop. The foliage is pretty enough to use by itself in an annual bed; a dark brown mulch really sets off the dark green color.

Years before nouvelle cuisine got excited about corn salad (or maché, as the gourmet restaurants call it) my friends and I were growing the trouble-free salad green. It has a lovely texture that falls between bib lettuce and spinach. I love to mix large quantities of the dark green leaves into my salads. Like spinach, the leaves grow very close to the ground and require careful washing.

CORN-SALAD SALAD

Serves 3 to 4

Use your favorite vinaigrette dressing, or the following:

2	Tbs. oil
2	Tbs. herbal vinegar
2	Tbs. water
2	tsp. honey

paprika and minced hot peppers, to taste

Combine in a blender or shaker bottle, and set aside.

1½	C hominy style corn, rinsed and drained
1	large tomato, chopped
½	C green onions or scallions, chopped
3	Tbs. cilantro or parsley, minced
1½	C feta cheese, crumbled
3	to 4 C corn salad greens, washed and patted dry

Toss the salad ingredients (except the greens) with the marinade, and chill at least one hour, stirring occasionally.

Arrange the corn salad greens on salad plates, and center spoonfuls of the marinated mixture on top of them.

KIWI
(*Actinidia chinensis, A. arguta*)

Effort:	2
Zones:	9 and 10 (*Actinidia chinensis*) 6 through 10 (*A. arguta*)
Soil:	Needs a rich, fertile, well-drained soil.
Planting:	Blooms early – plant out of danger of frosts.
Watering:	Needs frequent irrigation.
Fertilizing:	Needs regular fertilization.
Harvesting:	Pick fruits when vine-ripe.
Height:	To 40 feet
Width:	20 to 40 feet if trained sideways on a trellis
Shape:	An unpruned kiwi vine is sprawling, with cascading shoots.

Foliage:	Dark green, somewhat shiny leaves with a distinctive golden brown, fuzzy underside.
Flower:	The blossoms are large and creamy with crepe-paper-like petals.
Landscape Uses:	An excellent deciduous vine for energy-conserving uses. The dramatic color of the leaves' undersides makes kiwi vines a nice arbor plant. They are easily trained to frame windows.

KIWICOLADAS

Serves 2 to 4

Place in a blender:

¼	C Bacardi 151 Dark Rum
¾	C coconut/white grape juice blend*
2	to 3 large ripe kiwis, peeled
2	Tbs. kiwi jam**, or honey
1	C small pieces of ice

and blend til smooth and creamy.

Serve in tall glasses garnished with sprigs of mint and slices of kiwi.

*If you can't get a coconut/white grape juice blend, such as Knudsen's Coconut Nectar™, then make your own blend to taste. An equally delicious drink can be created by eliminating the coconut milk and substituting apple juice for the white grape juice.

**Available from Kozlowski's Farms, 5566 Gravenstein Hwy. No., Forestville, CA 95436. Write for their free mail-order catalog of jams and other fruit delicacies.

ORIENTAL PERSIMMON
(*Diospyros kaki*)

Effort:	1
Zones:	6 through 10
Soil:	Handles a wide range of soils, but needs good drainage around the crown of the roots.
Planting:	Because they bloom so late, the blossoms are rarely bothered by late frosts. Fall frosts deepen the color of the fruit.
Watering:	Though regular watering increases yields, persimmon trees are quite drought-resistant; established trees can go through an entire summer with no rain or irrigation.
Fertilizing:	No fertilizers are needed.

Harvesting:	Pick in late fall or early winter, when fruits are very soft, slightly translucent, and deep red-orange. Or, pick firm fruits with full color and ripen them on a kitchen shelf.
Height:	20 to 35 feet
Width:	20 to 35 feet
Shape:	Forms a perfect umbrella or mushroom-shaped shaped canopy without any pruning.
Foliage:	The glossy, dark green leaves are among the most attractive of the ornamental, edible plants.
Flowers:	Inconspicuous green
Landscape Uses:	I use this pest- and disease-resistant tree all the time in designs because it is so well-behaved and dramatic. The glossy, dark green leaves make a lovely backdrop for silver-grey shrubs and for blue and red flowering shrubs and vines. The fall color is a spectacular blaze of yellows, oranges, and reds. After the leaves drop, the waxy red fruits hang like ornaments late into winter. Persimmon trees are easily trained in an informal espalier against a wall or along a fence. Easy to care for and so colorful – a perfect tree for the edible landscape.

There are two basic types of persimmons: the astringent varieties, of which the pointed-bottomed 'Hachiya' is most common; and the smaller, non-astringent varieties, such as the round-bottomed 'Fuyu.' If you dislike the mushy texture of a fully ripe 'Hachiya,' or dislike the long wait until they ripen in late fall, try the non-astringent 'Fuyu.' It can be eaten earlier in the season while still firm.

Persimmons can be frozen, whole or pureed. If using an astringent variety, be sure to pick fully ripe fruits. To use whole frozen persimmons, thaw, peel, and puree 3 to 4 persimmons for each cup of pulp required.

Note: These recipes use fully ripe astringent-type persimmons.

PERSIMMON ICE CREAM

For a 4-qt. ice cream freezer – serves 6 to 8.

Whip with a wide whisk:

6	C cream
2	C milk
2	C sugar

6	eggs
⅛	tsp. nutmeg, freshly ground
2	tsp. cinnamon, freshly ground

Simmer the mixture in a double boiler, stirring constantly at 150°F for 30 minutes or until the back of the spoon is thickly coated.

Add:

4	tsp. vanilla extract
3	tsp. lemon peel, finely grated

and chill the mixture for at least four hours.

In a blender, puree:

10	cups persimmon pulp

Add the puree to the chilled cream mixture and pour it into the churn canister. Churn for 10 to 20 minutes, until the mixture stiffens, then freeze the canister for 2 to 4 hours. At serving time, garnish with raspberries.

PERSIMMON PUDDING

Serves 4 to 6
Preheat oven to 350°F.

Sift together:

1½	C flour
¼	tsp. salt
¾	tsp. double-acting baking powder
½	tsp. baking soda
¼	tsp. nutmeg, freshly grated
½	tsp. cinnamon, freshly ground

In a separate bowl, combine:

2½	C persimmon puree
½	C sugar
¾	C milk
2	eggs, slightly beaten
	grated peel of half a lemon
½	tsp. vanilla extract
2	Tbs. butter, melted

Stir the dry ingredients into the persimmon mixture until well blended.

Pour the batter into a greased 9 × 12 inch baking dish. Bake at 350°F for 45 minutes or until the pudding is firm on top but still very moist inside.

Serve hot or cold with whipped cream, vanilla bean ice cream, hot lemon sauce, or hot rum sauce.

DRIED PERSIMMONS

Peel 'Hachiya' persimmons (or another astringent variety) that are nearly ripe but still firm. (Don't use fully ripe fruit for these methods: in my first attempt to "line-dry" persimmons, I ended up with persimmon "jam" on my floor and walls!)

Using a needle, string the persimmons on stout

thread, leaving plenty of space between each fruit. (Some people leave the stem, calyx, and last inch of peel on the fruit, and tie the stem to a string.) Hang them in a warm, dry area, such as over a hot water heater or stove.

When dry, cut the persimmons into thick slabs. To remove any remaining moisture, lay them on a stainless steel screen (or another non-corrosive surface) in a warm, dry place for two or three more days. (You can also finish drying them in an oven at the lowest temperature with the door propped open.)

Wrap the dried pieces individually or pack them into jars. (If you are drying the persimmons in an electric or solar food drier, do not sulfur them – they become astrigent. Slice them into thick pieces and dry as you would pears or apricots.)

DRIED PERSIMMONS WITH CURRIED PECAN CREAM CHEESE

Mix thoroughly:

8	oz. cream cheese, softened
½	tsp. curry powder
4	Tbs. pecan pieces, minced

Cover and chill. Serve with slices of dried persimmon and fresh lemon.

PERSIMMON PECAN APPETIZERS

Sandwich a whole pecan nutmeat between thick slices of dried persimmon. This simple treat is perhaps the tastiest appetizer or snack I've ever eaten (of course, I *love* persimmons).

GARLIC
(*Allium sativum*)

Effort:	2
Zones:	All zones
Soil:	Requires a fertile, loose soil with plenty of organic matter. Does best in a pH of 6 to 7.
Planting:	Plant in the spring where springs are long and temperatures moderate; or plant in late October, in zone 10. Prefers moist, cool weather. Garlic bolts, or flowers, when hot weather arrives.
Watering:	Needs a consistently moist soil, until just before you harvest it. Mulch heavily to conserve moisture and suppress weeds. When the tops begin to brown, reduce the water. Once the tops of the plants are half brown, stop watering and let the crop dry out in place.
Fertilizing:	Use lots of manure and organic matter to prepare the soil. Top dress the crop with manure halfway through the season.
Harvesting:	Harvest when the soil is completely dry and the tops totally dead. Continue drying the cleaned heads after harvesting. Store in a cool, dry place or peel the cloves and preserve them in olive oil.
Height:	12 to 18 inches
Width:	4 to 6 inches
Shape:	Narrow, vertical leaves like those of an iris. The tips arch outward.
Foliage:	Blue-green
Flower:	White
Landscape Uses:	Garlic plants have a striking vertical line with a graceful curve during the first half of the season, but the browning leaves look disheveled while the crop is maturing and drying. Surround them with plants whose foliage will be tall enough to mask the brown leaves of the garlic. You can leave some to flower in the middle of a flower border; the round, white allium flower is somewhat attractive. Plant them in blocks to make weeding and watering easy.

CORNISH GAME HENS STUFFED WITH GARLIC AND SUMMER SAVORY

Serves 3
Preheat oven to 375°F.

3   cornish game hens, cleaned, washed and dried
1   C wild rice, washed and drained
1   tsp. salt
20 cloves red garlic, peeled
2   stalks celery, chopped

Saute the garlic, celery, and rice in a skillet with a dash of olive oil, until the garlic is just slightly cooked. If the rice gets too dry, add a little water.

Remove from heat and add:

1½ Tbs. fresh summer savory, minced
3   Tbs. fresh parsley, minced
Italian herbal salt, and pepper, to taste

Stuff each bird ¾ full and close the cavity with toothpicks or skewers. Arrange in a casserole with new potatoes, baby carrots, boiling onions, and sprigs of summer savory. Baste the top with olive oil or melted butter, and cover.

Bake for 1 to 1½ hours, removing the cover during the last 15 to 25 minutes to brown the birds. Baste occasionally with the juices in the bottom of the casserole.

Serve the birds and vegetables on a bed of wild rice and long grain brown rice. Sprinkle with paprika and garnish with sprigs of summer savory. Serve with a fresh garden salad, fresh Asian pears with lemon juice, and lightly steamed golden beets.

HOT AND SWEET BAKED GARLIC

Baked garlic is a wonderful side dish for any meal. The garlic turns quite sweet and mild when baked. At one dinner, I served the dish (without the chili oil) and even a 4-year-old ate a whole garlic head!

Serves 5 to 6
Preheat oven to 375°F.

Remove the outer skins from 10 to 12 large, firm heads of red garlic, leaving the cluster of cloves intact (don't peel the cloves). Slice off the top ⅓ of each head, saving any cloves that fall off for other garlic recipes.

Arrange the heads in an 8 × 14 inch covered casserole.

In a quart jar or blender, mix:

¾   C extra virgin olive oil
¾   C water
¼   C tamari or soy sauce
2   Tbs. hot chili oil (from an Oriental market)
paprika

Pour the mixture over the garlic in the casserole. Cover and bake for 25 to 30 minutes.

Remove from the oven, cool for 5 minutes, sprinkle with paprika, and serve warm. This is great finger food, though a little messy.

QUINCE
(*Cydonia oblonga*)

Effort:	3
Zones:	5 through 9
Soil:	Tolerates heavy, dry soils better than most edible tree crops.
Planting:	A very late blooming shrub that almost always escapes late spring frosts.
Watering:	Though quince trees can grow through completely dry summers without irrigation, regular watering greatly improves yields.
Fertilizing:	Rarely needs fertilizers.
Harvesting:	Pick quinces while they are still firm, in late fall before the first frost.
Height:	15 to 20 feet
Width:	10 to 20 feet
Shape:	Unpruned quince trees have a round, mushroom-shaped canopy.
Foliage:	Light to dark green leaves
Flower:	Pale pink flowers near the ends of the branches
Landscape Uses:	The quince tree is another well-behaved and pest-free edible. It isn't dramatic, but makes a useful background shrub or tree, and mixes well with drought-resistant herbs. The canopy can be trained in an arbor shape or in an informal espalier.

Few people know what to do with quinces, except to make jelly, but how much quince jelly can one household eat? Mrs. Flores' recipe for quinces with tomatoes and garlic (see page 64) is one of my favorite ways to use the uncommon fruit. Other creative recipes can be found in cookbooks featuring Armenian, Middle Eastern, and Italian cuisine. The recipe that follows makes a wonderful dessert. Baked quinces have a strong, tart, applelike aroma and flavor, and are much firmer than a baked apple.

BAKED QUINCES FLAMBÉ

Serves 4

4   large, firm quinces
nuts and dried fruit
honey
cinnamon and nutmeg, freshly ground
powdered ginger
1   C Bacardi 151 rum

Scrub and rinse the quinces. Cut them in half and remove the cores.

Stuff each half with your favorite mixture of nuts and dried fruit. Drizzle with honey, and dust with the spices.

Place the quinces in a glass casserole with an inch of water. Cover and bake at 350°F for 40 to 50 minutes, or until fork-tender.

Warm a cup of rum in a saucepan over low heat. (*Warning: 151 rum is highly flammable – follow the instructions on the label. Do not pour rum into the pan while the burner is on, and do not pour rum while a match is lit.*)

Dim the lights, quickly pour the warm rum over the baked quinces, and light it with a match. Serve with whipped cream or ice cream.

'PINK PEARL' APPLE

Effort:	4 to 5 (Though not as easy to care for as other edibles listed in this chapter, the delectable pink fruit and the deep pink blossoms make the 'Pink Pearl' well worth the effort.)
Zones:	3 to 9
Soil:	Prefers a deep, fertile soil. Don't plant in low, wet spots.
Planting:	Plant where late spring frosts and rains are not too prevalent.
Watering:	Use a typical fruit tree watering schedule.
Fertilizing:	Does not need much nitrogen (see Fig. 15.8).
Harvesting:	Pick when the pink color of the flesh shows through the light green skin. The stem should easily separate from the spur when the fruit is gently lifted.
Height/ Width:	See Fig. 11.8.
Shape:	Standard-size trees have a mushroom-shaped canopy; dwarfed trees are pyramid shaped.
Foliage:	Typical apple-green leaves
Flower:	'Pink Pearl' blossoms are the pinkest of all apple varieties; the color resembles that of crabapple blossoms.
Landscape Uses:	Locate where the dramatic spring blossoms can be seen from the house. Use dwarf trees in the taller portion of a border planting (with a footpath for pruning and harvesting). Cluster 3 to 5 trees together for a grove effect. Because of falling fruit, not suitable for paved path and patio plantings. A good choice for espalier training.

The 'Pink Pearl' is a delightful apple, fresh or cooked. In addition to the remarkable pink color of the flesh, it offers a complex sweet flavor with a little tartness and a crisp texture. The flavor alone is ample reason to grow the 'Pink Pearl.' Cooking transforms the fruit into a glowing pink that astonishes the uninitiated. The recipe that follows has received more rave reviews for color and flavor than any other recipe in this chapter.

'PINK PEARL' APPLE TART

Serves 8 to 12
Pre-heat oven to 350° F.

Almond Pastry Crust

1¼   C unbleached white flour
¼   lb. ground roasted almonds
4   oz. unsalted butter
¼   C brown sugar
1   large egg yolk
⅛   tsp. ground cloves
½   tsp. ground cinnamon
pinch of nutmeg
1   tsp. vanilla
zest of one organic lemon, minced

Combine all the ingredients at once, and mix until a dough forms. Press it into a ball, wrap in plastic and chill for 30 minutes to an hour.

Roll the dough out to about ⅛ inch thick and press into a 12-inch tart pan.

Pre-bake the crust for 20 minutes at 350° F or until golden brown. Set aside to cool.

Filling

10   to 12 'Pink Pearl' apples, sliced in half and cored – do not peel!
butter
brown sugar
cinnamon

nutmeg
cloves
¼   C toasted almonds, coarsely chopped
raspberry jam
1   tsp. vanilla
apple leaves

Slice enough apples to make one layer in the tart crust – slice them about ⅛ inch thick.

Place the slices on a buttered baking sheet; and sprinkle with sugar and cinnamon. Bake at 350° F until just tender. Remove from oven and set aside.

Cut the rest of the apples into cubes, and saute them with sugar, nutmeg, cinnamon, and cloves to taste. When soft, remove from heat and add vanilla.

In a blender or processor, puree about ⅓ of the applesauce until smooth. Stir the puree into the chunky applesauce.

Assembling the Tart

Paint the tart shell with raspberry jam, and sprinkle it with most of the roasted almonds.

Spread the applesauce evenly over the shell, and top it with the baked apple slices, arranged in concentric circles.

Paint the finished tart with rasberry jam and garnish with the remaining almonds and apple leaves.

(Special thanks to Doug Gosling, pastry chef supreme, who created this remarkable dessert.)

Climate Zones

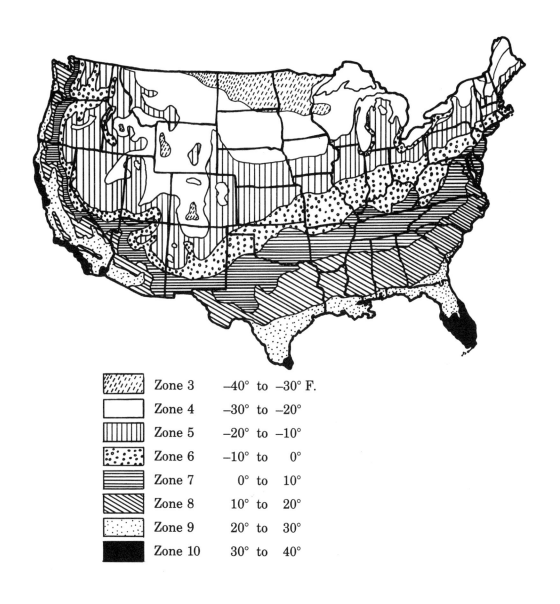

	Zone 3	−40° to −30° F.
	Zone 4	−30° to −20°
	Zone 5	−20° to −10°
	Zone 6	−10° to 0°
	Zone 7	0° to 10°
	Zone 8	10° to 20°
	Zone 9	20° to 30°
	Zone 10	30° to 40°

1

Solar Charts

SUN MOVEMENT CHARTS

SUN CHART
32°N LATITUDE

SUN CHART
36°N LATITUDE

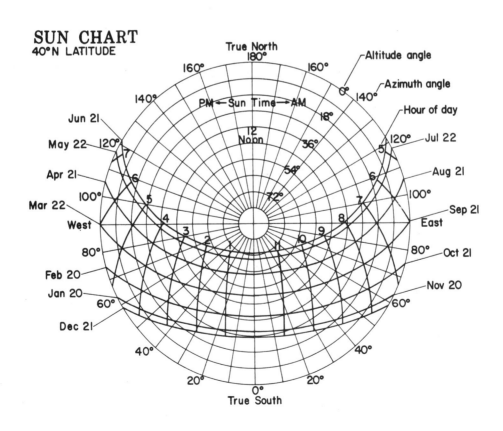

SUN CHART
40°N LATITUDE

2
APPENDIX

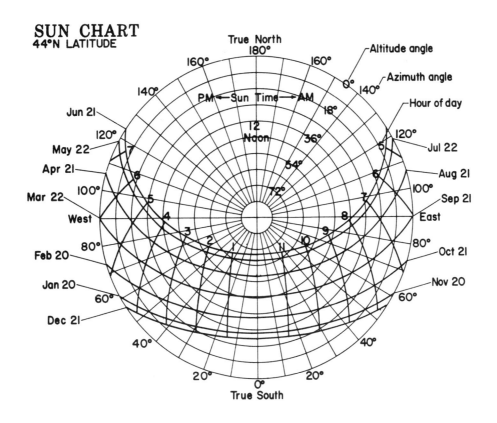

SUN CHART
44°N LATITUDE

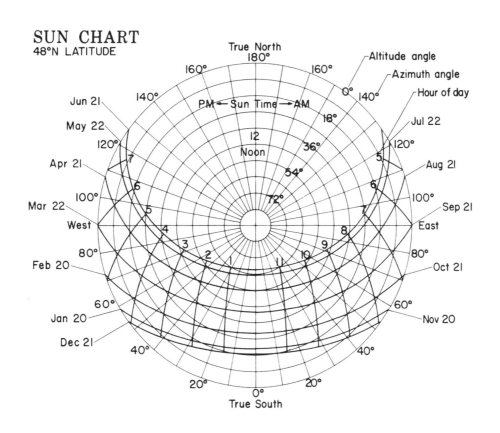

SUN CHART
48°N LATITUDE

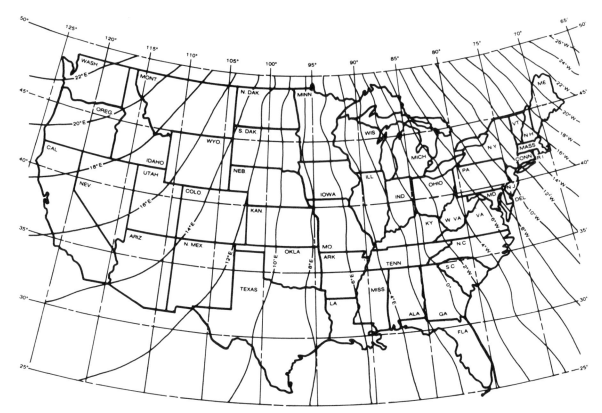

Isogonic Chart shows magnetic deviations for continential U.S.

Site Analysis Survey

A SITE CHECKLIST

This is the checklist I use to jog my memory when analyzing a client's site. It is a good summary of many of the points covered in the section "Understanding Your Property." Perhaps the most important part of the checklist are the points discussed under #7, "Personal Considerations." Spend some extra time thinking over these points. The edible landscape you are planning is for your enjoyment and should be as carefully tailored to your desires as possible.

Your Site Analysis Checklist

1. SITE

   a. Parcel number

   b. Latitude

   c. Utilities, location of:

      1) gas line

      2) water line

      3) electric line

   d. Easements, legal limitations as per title or deed

   e. Existing buildings, size and location

2. EXISTING VEGETATION – record for trees, shrubs, herbs, and grasses

   a. Soil indicators

   b. Water indicators

c. Potential uses:

   1) fuel

   2) edible

   3) compostable

   4) insectary plants

   5) others

3. CLIMATE INFORMATION

   a. Evapo-transpiration

      1) rainfall, yearly and monthly averages

      2) humidity, yearly and monthly averages

      3) wind, prevailing and monthly average

      4) temperature, monthly maximum, minimum, and average

   b. Frost — average and extreme first and last dates

   c. Spring bloom sequence

   d. Leaf fall sequence

   e. Insolation, number of sunny and cloudy days

   f. Heating and cooling degree days (for solar applications)

4. PHYSICAL CHARACTERISTICS

   a. Elevation

   b. Slope

      1) erosion potential

      2) air drainage

c. Water table's distance from surface

d. Pollution sources and impacts

5. SOIL SURVEY

a. Clay, sand, and silt content

b. Structure

c. Organic matter content

d. pH

e. Nutrients – nitrogen, phosphorous, potassium, and trace minerals.

6. ECOLOGY

a. People impacts – foot traffic, views from and to neighbors, and sounds

b. Animals – gophers, deer, moles, and other varmints

c. Pests

d. Diseases

7. PERSONAL CONSIDERATIONS

a. Aesthetic priorities – favorite colors, plants, and fragrances

b. Allergies

c. Fear of insects – especially wasps and bees

d. Leisure time for maintanence

e. Budget for installation and maintenance

f. Diet and taste favorites

g. Privacy from sound and sight

3

Deciduous and Evergreen Vines

DECIDUOUS VINES

Common Name/ Botanical Name	Height (in feet)	Climbing Method	Flower Color	Fragrant	Edible Fruit
American bittersweet (*Celastrus scadens*)	10–20	twining	white	no	no
Blueberry climber (*Ampelopsis brevipedunculata*)	10–20	tendrils	inc.	no	no
Chayote (*Sechium edulis*)	30–80	tendrils	inc.	no	yes
Clematis (*Clematis jackmanii*)	10+	twining	pink-red and purple	no	no
Clematis, anemone (*C. montana*)	20+	twining	pink	no	no
Clematis, downey (*C. macropetala*)	6–30	twining	lavender	no	no
Coral vine (*Antigonon leptopus*)	50–100	tendrils	rose, pink	no	no
Cup-and-saucer vine (*Cobaea scadens*)	10–40	tendrils	purple	no	no
Dutchman's pipe (*Aristolochia durior*)	20–30	twining	brownish	no	no
Gourds, ornamental (*Cucurbita* sp.)	10–40	tendrils	yellow-white	no	no
Grape, mustang (*Vitis mustangensis*)	60–150	tendrils	inc.	no	yes
Hyacinth bean (*Dolichos lablab*)	15-25	twining	white, purple	no	no
Hydrangea, climbing (*H. anomala*)	30-80	clinging	white	no	no
Ivy, Boston (*Parthenocissus quinquefolia*)	20+	clinging	inc.	no	no
Japanese hop (*Humulus japonicus*)	20–35	twining	yellow	no	no
Kiwi vine (*Actinidia chinesis*)	10–20	twining	cream	yes	yes
Luffa vine (*Luffa cylindrica*)	20–40	tendrils	yellow	no	yes
Moonflower vine (*Ipomoea alba*)	25–50	tendrils	white	yes	no
Morning glory (*Ipomoea* sp.)	20–40	tendrils	blue	no	no
Nasturtium, trailing (*Tropaeolum majus*)	10–15	trailing	various	no	no
Scarlet runner bean (*Phaseolus coccineus*)	10–20	twining	red, white	no	yes
Silver lace vine (*Polygonum aubertii*)	20+	twining	pale	no	no

Deciduous Vines, continued

Deciduous vines, continued

Common Name/ Botanical Name	Height (in feet)	Climbing Method	Flower Color	Fragrant	Edible Fruit
Sweet pea (*Lathyrus oloratus*)	6+	tendrils	various	yes	no
Trumpet creeper, common (*Campsis radicans*)	40+	clinging	orange	no	no
Virginia creeper (*Parthenocissus quinquefolia*)	50+	clinging	inc.	no	no
Wisteria, Chinese (*Wisteria sinensis*)	30+	twining	violet	yes	no

inc.   —inconspicuous flowers
twining –spirals around slender posts, rope, wire, or itself. Doesn't easily wrap around large posts.
clinging–suction cup discs, hooks, or small roots attach to crevices and flat surfaces. Vines can damage walls or roofs.
tendrils –delicate curling projections wrap around anything they encounter.
arching –long, sprawling shoots arch over unless tied to a vertical support.
trailing –long, sprawling shoots trail along the ground unless tied to a support.

EVERGREEN VINES

Common Name/ Botanical Name	Height (in feet)	Climbing Method	Flower Color	Fragrant	Edible Fruit
Asparagus, ornamental (*A. setaceus*)	10–20	twining	white	no	no
Bougainvillea (*B. spectabilis*)	15–25	twining	various	no	no
Bower vine (*Pandorea jasminoides*)	20–30	twining	pink	no	no
Camellia (*C. sasanqua*)	10–20	arching	various	yes	no
Carolina jessamine (*Gelsemium sempervirens*)	20–35	twining	yellow	yes	no
Clematis, evergreen (*C. armandii*)	15–25	tendrils	white	yes	no
Cross vine (*Bignonia capreolata*)	50–60	clinging	orange	no	no
Euonymus (*E. fortunei*)	15–25	clinging	inc.	no	no
Evergreen grape (*Rhoicissus capensis*)	30–50	tendrils	inc.	no	yes
Fig, creeping (*Ficus pumila*)	20–60	clinging	inc.	no	no
Fiveleaf akebia (*A. quinata*)	15–20	twining	purple	no	no
Flame vine (*Pyrostegia ignea*)	25–40	clinging	orange-red	no	no
Guinea gold vine (*Hibbertia volubilis*)	15–30	twining	yellow	no	no
Honeysuckle, giant Burmese (*Lonicera hildebrandiana*)	40–80	twining	yellow	yes	no

Evergreen Vines, continued

4
APPENDIX

Evergreen vines, continued

Common Name/ Botanical Name	Height (in feet)	Climbing Method	Flower Color	Fragrant	Edible Fruit
Honeysuckle, Japanese (*Lonicera japonica*)	15–30	twining	orange, yellow, cream	yes	no
Honeysuckle, trumpet (*Lonicera sempevirens*)	15–20	twining	coral	yes	no
Ivy, English (*Hedera helix*)	50–90	clinging	pale yellow	no	no
Jasmine, common white (*Jasminum officinale*)	20–30	arching	white	yes	no
Lilac vine (*Hardenbergia comptoniana*)	10–15	twining	violet	no	no
Madeira vine (*Anredera cordifolia*)	20–30	tendrils	white	yes	no
Marmalade bush (*Streptosolen jamesoni*)	8–10	arching	orange	no	no
Mexican flame vine (*Senecio confusus*)	20–25	twining	orange-red	no	no
Orchid vine (*Stigmaphyllon ciliatum*)	10–20	twining	gold-yellow	no	no
Passion fruit (*Passiflora edulis*)	20–35	tendrils	white	no	yes
Passion flower, blue crown (*Passiflora caerulea*)	20–35	tendrils	various	no	no
Philodendron (*Philodendron* sp.)	varies	clinging	green	no	no
Plumbago (*P. auriculata*)	8–12	trailing	blue	no	no
Potato vine (*Solanum jasminoides*)	10–30	twining	white	no	no
Rosa de montana (*Antigonon leptopus*)	20–40	tendrils	pink	no	no
Scarlet kadsura (*K. japonica*)	10–20	twining	white	no	no
Sky flower (*Thunbergia grandiflora*)	30–50	twining	blue	no	no
Star jasmine (*Trachelospermum jasminoides*)	10–20	twining	white	yes	no
Trumpet vine (*Campsis radicans*)	50–60	clinging	orange	no	no
Trumpet vine, vanilla (*Distictis laxiflora*)	20–35	tendrils	purple	no	no
Trumpet vine, violet (*Clytostoma callistegioides*)	30–60	tendrils	violet	no	no
Trumpet vine, yellow (*Doxantha unguis-cati*)	25–40	clinging	yellow	no	no
White bladder flower (*Araujia sericifera*)	20–30	twining	white	no	no
Wire vine (*Muehlenbeckia complexa*)	15–25	twining	inc.	no	no
Xylosma (*X. congestum*)	4–6	arching	inc.	no	no

inc. —inconspicuous flowers
twining —spirals around slender posts, rope, wire, or itself. Doesn't easily wrap around large posts.
clinging—suction cup discs, hooks, or small roots attach to crevices and flat surfaces. Vines can damage walls or roofs.
tendrils—delicate curling projections wrap around anything they encounter.
arching —long, sprawling shoots arch over unless tied to a vertical support.
trailing —long, sprawling shoots trail along the ground unless tied to a support.

4

Carbon-to-Nitrogen Ratios and the N-P-K of Compostable Materials

NITROGEN CONTENT AND CARBON-TO-NITROGEN RATIOS
for Waste Materials

Material	Nitrogen (% of Total Weight)	Ratio of Carbon to Nitrogen (C:N)
Activated sludge	5–6	6:1
Alfalfa	2.4–3	16–20:1
Blood	10–14	3:1
Bone meal	*	3.5:1
Bread	2.10	*
Buttercup	2.2	23:1
Cabbage	3.6	12:1
Carrot, whole	1.6	27:1
Clover, red	1.8	27:1
Cocksfoot	2.55	19:1
Cottonseed meal	*	5:1
Fern	1.15	43:1
Fish scrap	6.5–10	5.1:1
Garbage, green	3	18:1
Garbage, raw	2.15	25:1
Kentucky bluegrass	2.4	19:1
Lawn clippings, young	4	12:1
Lettuce	3.7	*
Manure, farmyard (avg.)	2.15	14:1
Manure, chicken	3.2	7:1
Manure, cow	1.7	18:1
Manure, horse	2.3	25:1
Manure, human	5.5–6.5	6–10:1
Manure, pig	3.75	*
Manure, poultry	6.3	15:1
Manure, sheep	3.75	*
Manure, steer	1.35	25.3:1
Meat scraps	5.1	*
Milorganite™	*	5.4:1
Mustard	1.5	26:1

Material	Nitrogen (% of Total Weight)	Ratio of Carbon to Nitrogen (C:N)
Newspaper	.05	812:1
Oat straw	1.05	48:1
Onion	2.65	15:1
Peanut hull meal	*	11:1
Pepper	2.6	15:1
Pigweed (*Amaranthus* sp.)	3.6	11:1
Potato tops	1.5	25:1
Purslane	4.5	8:1
Ragwort	2.15	21:1
Sawdust, raw	.11	511:1
Sawdust, rotted	.25	208:1
Seaweed	1.9	19:1
Sewage, fresh	*	11:1
Slaughterhouse wastes	7–10	2:1
Soybean meal	*	5:1
Timothy grass	.85	58:1
Tobacco	3	13:1
Tomato	3.3	12:1
Turnip tops	2.3	19:1
Turnip, whole	1	44:1
Urine	15–18	.8:1
Vegetables, non-legum.	2.54	11–19:1
Wheat flour	1.7	*
Wheat straw	.3	128:1
Wood, white fir	.06	767:1

*no data

Leckie, J.; Masters G.; Whitehouse H.; and Young L. *Other Homes and Garbage*. San Francisco: Sierra Club Books, 1975.

Farallones Institute. *The Integral Urban House*. San Francisco: Sierra Club Books, 1979.

Gotaas, H. *Composting*. Geneva: World Health Organization, 1956.

Material	Nitrogen (%)	Phosphoric Acid (%)	Potash (%)	Material	Nitrogen (%)	Phosphoric Acid (%)	Potash (%)
Alfalfa hay	2.45	0.50	2.10	Incinerator ash	0.24	5.15	2.33
Apple (fruit)	0.05	0.02	0.10	Kentucky bluegrass (green)	0.66	0.19	0.71
Apple (leaves)	1.00	0.15	0.35	Kentucky bluegrass (hay)	1.20	0.40	1.55
Apple pomace	0.20	0.02	0.15	King crab (dried and ground)	10.00	0.26	0.06
Apple skins (ash)	—	3.08	11.74	King crab (fresh)	2.0–2.5	—	—
Banana skins (ash)	—	3.25	41.76	Leather (acidulated)	7.0–8.0	—	—
Banana stalk (ash)	—	2.34	49.40	Leather (ground)	10.0–12.0	—	—
Barley (grain)	1.75	0.75	0.50	Leather, scrap (ash)	—	2.16	0.35
Bat guano	1.0–12.0	2.5–16.0	—	Lemon culls, California	0.15	0.06	0.26
Beet roots	0.25	0.10	0.50	Lemon skins (ash)	—	6.30	31.00
Bone (ground, burned)	—	34.70	—	Lobster refuse	4.50	3.50	—
Brewer's grains (wet)	0.90	0.50	0.05	Lobster shells	4.60	3.52	—
Brigham tea (ash)	—	—	5.94	Milk	0.50	0.30	0.18
Cantaloupe rinds (ash)	—	9.77	12.21	Mussels	0.90	0.12	0.13
Castor-bean pomace	5.0–6.0	2.0–2.5	1.0–1.25	Molasses residue in manufacturing of alcohol	0.70	—	5.32
Cattail reed and stems of water lily	2.02	0.81	3.43	Oak leaves	0.80	0.35	0.15
Cattail seed	0.98	0.39	1.71	Oats, grain	2.00	0.80	0.60
Coal ash (anthracite)	—	0.1–0.15	0.1–0.15	Olive pomace	1.15	0.78	1.26
Coal ash (bituminous)	—	0.4–0.5	0.4–0.5	Olive refuse	1.22	0.18	0.32
Cocoa-shell dust	1.04	1.49	2.71	Orange culls	0.20	0.13	0.21
Coffee grounds	2.08	0.32	0.28	Orange skins (ash)	—	2.90	27.00
Coffee grounds (dried)	1.99	0.36	0.67	Pea pods (ash)	—	1.79	9.00
Common crab	1.95	3.60	0.20	Peanuts, seeds or kernels	3.60	0.70	0.45
Corncobs (ground, charred)	—	—	2.01	Peanut shells	0.80	0.15	0.50
Corncob (ash)	—	—	50.00	Peanut shells (ash)	—	1.23	6.45
Corn (grain)	1.65	0.65	0.40	Pigeon manure (fresh)	4.19	2.24	1.41
Corn (green forage)	0.30	0.13	0.33	Pigweed, rough	0.60	0.16	—
Cottonseed	3.15	1.25	1.15	Pine needles	0.46	0.12	0.03
Cottonseed-hull (ash)	—	7.0–10.0	15.0–30.0	Potatoes, tubers	0.35	0.15	0.50
Cowpeas (green forage)	0.45	0.12	0.45	Potatoes, leaves and stalks	0.60	0.15	0.45
Cowpeas (seed)	3.10	1.00	1.20	Potato skins, raw (ash)	—	5.18	27.50
Crab grass (green)	0.66	0.19	0.71	Prune refuse	0.18	0.07	0.31
Cucumber skins (ash)	—	11.28	27.20	Pumpkin, flesh	0.16	0.07	0.26
Dog manure	1.97	9.95	0.30	Pumpkin seeds	0.87	0.50	0.45
Dried jellyfish	4.60	—	—	Rabbit-brush ashes	—	—	13.04
Dried mussel mud	0.72	0.35	—	Ragweed, great	0.76	0.26	—
Duck manure (fresh)	1.12	1.44	0.49	Red clover, hay	2.10	0.50	2.00
Eggs	2.25	0.40	0.15	Redtop hay	1.20	0.35	1.00
Eggshells (burned)	—	0.43	0.29	Residuum from raw sugar	1.14	8.33	—
Eggshells	1.19	0.38	0.14	Rockweed	1.90	0.25	3.68
Feathers	15.30	—	—	Roses, flower	0.30	0.10	0.40
Field bean (seed)	4.00	1.20	1.30	Rhubarb, stems	0.10	0.04	0.35
Field bean (shells)	1.70	0.30	0.35	Rock and mussel deposits from sea	0.22	0.09	1.78
Fire-pit ashes from smokehouses	—	—	4.96	Salt-marsh hay	1.10	0.25	0.75
Fish scrap (red snapper and grouper)	7.76	13.00	0.38	Salt mud	0.40	—	—
Fish scrap (fresh)	2.0–7.5	1.5–6.0	—	Sardine scrap	7.97	7.11	—
Freshwater mud	1.37	0.26	0.22	Seaweed (Atlantic City, N.J.)	1.68	0.75	4.93
Garbage rubbish (New York City)	3.4–3.7	0.1–1.47	2.25–4.25	Sewage sludge from filter beds	0.74	0.33	0.24
Greasewood ashes	—	—	12.61	Shoddy and felt	4.0–12.0	—	—
Garden beans (beans and pods)	0.25	0.08	0.30	Shrimp heads (dried)	7.82	4.20	—
Gluten feed	4.0–5.0	—	—	Shrimp waste	2.87	9.95	—
Greensand	—	1.6–2.0	5.00	Siftings from oyster-shell mound	0.36	10.38	0.09
Grapes, fruit	0.15	0.07	0.30	Silkworm cocoons	9.42	1.82	1.08
Grapefruit skins (ash)	—	3.58	30.60	Soot from chimney flues	0.5–11.0	1.05	0.35
Hair	12.0–16.0	—	—	Spanish moss	0.60	0.10	0.55
Harbor mud	0.99	0.77	0.05	Starfish	1.80	0.20	0.25
Hoof meal and horn dust	10.0–15.0	1.5–2.0	—	String bean strings and stems (ash)	—	4.99	18.03

5

APPENDIX

Liquid Measure Conversions

VOLUME AND LIQUID MEASURE

2 Pints = 1 Quart

3 tsp. = 1 Tbsp.

4 Quarts × 4 = 1 Gallon

1 Tbsp. = 3 tsp. = ½ oz.

9.39 Gallons × 9.39 = 1 Bushel

2 Tbsp. = 1 Fluid oz.

8 Fluid ounces × 8 = 1 Cup

2 Cups = 1 Pint

1 pt. / 100 Gal. = 1 tsp./Gal.

6

Sizing Materials for Landscaping

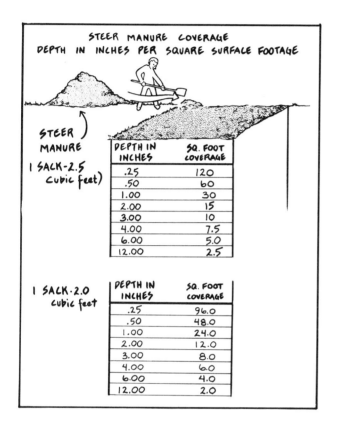

STEER MANURE COVERAGE
DEPTH IN INCHES PER SQUARE SURFACE FOOTAGE

STEER MANURE

1 SACK-2.5 cubic feet)

DEPTH IN INCHES	SQ. FOOT COVERAGE
.25	120
.50	60
1.00	30
2.00	15
3.00	10
4.00	7.5
6.00	5.0
12.00	2.5

1 SACK-2.0 cubic feet

DEPTH IN INCHES	SQ. FOOT COVERAGE
.25	96.0
.50	48.0
1.00	24.0
2.00	12.0
3.00	8.0
4.00	6.0
6.00	4.0
12.00	2.0

TOPSOIL COVERAGE
IN SQUARE FEET PER CUBIC YARD

TOP SOIL

DEPTH IN INCHES	SQ. FOOT COVERAGE
1/4	1296
1/2	648
1	324
2	162
4	81
6	54
8	40
10	33
12	27

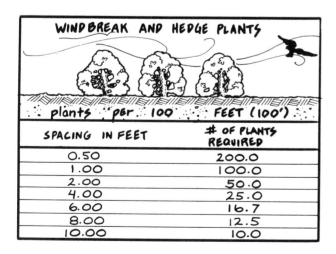

WINDBREAK AND HEDGE PLANTS

plants per 100 FEET (100')

SPACING IN FEET	# OF PLANTS REQUIRED
0.50	200.0
1.00	100.0
2.00	50.0
4.00	25.0
6.00	16.7
8.00	12.5
10.00	10.0

STRAW COVERAGE PER BALE: DEPTH IN INCHES PER SQUARE SURFACE FOOTAGE

STRAW

DEPTH IN INCHES	SQ. FOOT COVERAGE
1.00	200
2.00	100
4.00	50
8.00	25
12.00	16.6

COVERAGE: BRICK FLAT WORK

SIDE EXPOSED NO MORTAR JOINT	SQ. FT. (a×b) PER 1000 BRICKS	BRICK PER SQ. FEET
FLAT (4"×8")	222	4.5

PLANTS REQUIRED PER 100 SQ. FEET: VARIOUS SPACINGS

SPACING BETWEEN PLANTS	PLANTS PER 100 SQ. FT.	SPACING BETWEEN PLANTS	PLANTS PER 100 SQ. FT.
4"	900	24"	25
8"	225	30"	16
12"	100	48"	6.25
16"	56	60"	4.51

OF FLATS REQUIRED TO PLANT 100 SQ. FEET

SPACING BETWEEN PLANTS	# OF PLANTS PER FLAT 64	100
4"	14.06	9.00
8"	3.51	2.25
12"	1.56	1.00
16"	.87	.56
24"	.39	.25
30"	.25	.16

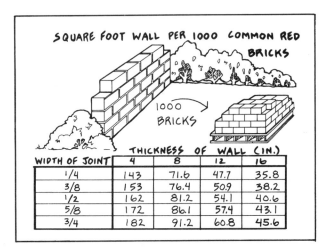

SQUARE FOOT WALL PER 1000 COMMON RED BRICKS

1000 BRICKS

WIDTH OF JOINT	THICKNESS OF WALL (IN.) 4	8	12	16
1/4	143	71.6	47.7	35.8
3/8	153	76.4	50.9	38.2
1/2	162	81.2	54.1	40.6
5/8	172	86.1	57.4	43.1
3/4	182	91.2	60.8	45.6

SOILS - * ANGLES OF REPOSE DRY TO MOIST

20°-35° SAND   20°-40° LOAM   30°-50° GRAVEL

* THE SLOPE AT WHICH A GIVEN MATERIAL WILL MAINTAIN WITHOUT SLIDING.

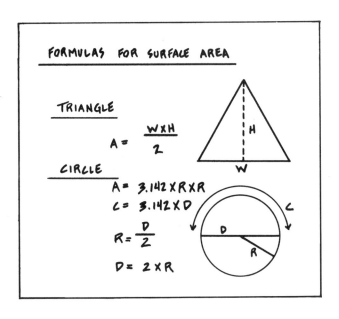

FORMULAS FOR SURFACE AREA

TRIANGLE

$$A = \frac{W \times H}{2}$$

CIRCLE

$$A = 3.142 \times R \times R$$

$$C = 3.142 \times D$$

$$R = \frac{D}{2}$$

$$D = 2 \times R$$

Mail-Order Suppliers of Plants, Seeds, and Gardening Tools

MAIL-ORDER SUPPLIERS OF PLANTS, SEEDS, AND GARDENING TOOLS

Plants and Seeds

Abundant Life Seed Foundation
P.O. Box 772
Port Townsend, WA 98368

Sells only seed, for trees, shrubs, wildflowers, flowers, herbs, vegetables; and books. A non-profit corporation interested in native and naturalized plants of the North Pacific Rim and the preservation of the natural environment.

Adams County Nursery, Inc.
P.O. Box 108
Aspers, PA 17304

These fruit tree specialists carry a number of older varieties of apples on various dwarfing rootstocks, as well as some older types of pears, cherries, plums, peaches, and nectarines.

Adams' Rootstock & Nursery, Inc.
P.O. Box 444
Schoolcraft, MI 49087

Offers all the common commercial rootstocks, standard and dwarfing, for conventional fruit trees.

Agway, Inc.
R.D. 4, Zeager Rd.
Elizabethtown, PA 17022

Standard varieties of vegetable seeds.

J. S. Akin
P.O. Box 6
Sibley, LA 71073

A small, backyard nursery, but one of the few to offer grafted mayhaw, raisin tree, chinquapin, papaw, hardy citrus, Eleagnus multiflora, low-chill apples, and other rare edible trees and vines. Their supply – mostly seedlings – is quite variable.

Alexander's Blueberry Nurseries
376 Wareham St.
Middleboro, MA 02346

One of the most extensive offerings of blueberry cultivars.

Alpine Valley Gardens
2627 Calistoga Rd.
Santa Rosa, CA 95404

Hundreds of varieties of daylilies.

Alston Seed Growers
Littleton, NC 27850

Seeds for rare, non-hybrid corn varieties.

Amberg's Nursery, Inc.
3164 Whitney Rd.
Stanley, NY 14561

Unusual and antique varieties of apples on many types of dwarfing roots.

Applesource
Rte. One
Chapin, IL 62628

A unique service. They mail-order fresh fruit of dozens of varieties of antique apples. A fantastic way to sample rare varieties before buying trees.

Appleton Forestry
1369 Tilton Rd.
Sebastopol, CA 95472

Carries a variety of tube-grown tree seedlings for windbreaks and reforestation.

Al Bacharach, Inc.
Lake Oswego, OR 97034

A wholesale supplier of common fruit tree varieties, including Asian and red pears.

The Banana Tree
715 Northampton St.
Easton, PA 18042

Tropical seeds, bulbs, and plants, including more than 40 varieties of bananas. A catalog is 40 cents.

Barney's Ginseng Patch
Rte. 2
Montgomery City, MO 63361

A small operation that sells seeds and starter roots for the cultivation of one form of ginseng.

Bear Creek Farms
P.O. Box 248
Northport, WA 99157

An excellent listing of hardy fruits, nuts, shrubs and grafted trees for home gardeners and commercial farmers. Features standard-size trees for longevity and form. They also carry shrubs and trees for hedgerows, windbreaks, and wildlife habitat. Has one of the best selections of grafted nut tree varieties, and claims to have "the largest selection of antique and hardy apples in the world." An informative and thorough catalog. Highly recommended.

Becker's
R.R. #1, Trout Creek
Ontario P0H 2L0 Canada

Sells seed potato "eyes" of 21 varieties, including heirloom varieties. Has red, blue, white, and yellow skinned varieties and white and yellow fleshed types. Ships once a year to U.S. customers who order by April 15th.

Beaverlodge Nursery Ltd.
P.O. Box 127
Beaverlodge, Alberta Canada T0H 0C0

Features cold-hardy ornamental and edible trees and shrubs. One of the few places where you can buy bareroot seedlings of named varieties of Saskatoons (Amelanchier sp.).

Bishop Seeds Ltd.
Box 338
Belleville, Ontario K8N 5A5

Seed for vegetables, flowers, cover crops, and grains.

Boston Mountain Nurseries
Rte. 2
Mountainburg, AR 72946

Good selection of cane fruits.

Bountiful Gardens
5798 Ridgewood Road
Willits, CA 95490

Interesting varieties of organically grown vegetable and herb seeds, including some heirlooms. They also carry biological controls and supplies, and help support John Jeavons' research work.

Breck's
U.S. Reservation Center
6523 No. Galena Rd.
Peoria, IL 61632
 Bulbs from Holland.

Bueno Food Products
P.O. Box 293
Albuquerque, NM 87103
 One of the few sources of Hopi blue corn seed.

Burgess Seed and Plant Co.
905 Four Seasons Rd.
Bloomington, IL 61701
 Conventional flower and vegetable seed, and trees.

W. Atlee Burpee Co.
Warminster, PA 18974
 Relatively uninteresting, typical vegetable seed varieties;
 however, they do list open-pollinated varieties.

D. V. Burrell Seed Growers Co.
Rocky Ford, CO 81067
 Standard varieties of flower, herb, and vegetable seeds for the
 commercial grower. Family owned and featuring melon
 varieties.

Butterbrooke Farm
78 Barry Rd.
Oxford, CT 06483-1598
 This very friendly co-op offers untreated seeds and open-
 pollinated varieties. Offers "personal 24 hour service."

C & O Nursery
P.O. Box 116
Wenatchee, WA 98801
 Their retail catalog lists mostly ordinary tree crop varieties,
 but has a decent selection of spur-type apple trees. They also
 sell wholesale.

California Nursery Co.
P.O. Box 2278
Fremont, CA 94536
 A good cross-section of fruit and nut trees as well as bamboo,
 vines, and citrus. One of the few places where you can get the
 'Pink Pearl' apple tree.

California Rare Fruit Growers, Inc.
The Fullerton Arboretum
California State University
Fullerton, CA 92634
 Holds a yearly plant sale of exotic and tropical edibles in
 containers. No mail order.

Callahan Seeds
6045 Foley Ln.
Central Point, OR 97502
 A large listing of seed for forest trees and some shrubs. Most
 are for revegetation and forestry, a limited amount are native
 edibles. Supply varies from year to year. They also do custom
 seed collecting.

Callender Nursery Co.
and Feijoa Growers of California
P.O. Box 2326
Chico, CA 95927
 Carries two of the best commercial varieties of pineapple
 guava from New Zealand. Plants are grown and shipped in
 large plastic tube containers.

Carlton Plants
P.O. Box 398
Dayton, OR 97114
 A wholesale and retail supplier of bareroot tree crops who
 carries mostly typical commercial varieties. Offers pear trees
 on quality dwarf rootstocks, red pear varieties, cherry
 varieties on the dwarfing Colt rootstock, and a good selection of
 Asian pear trees.

Carroll Gardens
Box 310
Westminster, MD 21157

Native wildflowers, ferns, herbs, roses, bulbs, vines, shrubs,
 and trees.

Casa Yerba
Star Rte. 2, Box 21
Days Creek, OR 97429
 A family business offering organically grown herb plants and
 an extensive collection of herb seeds.

Chestnut Hill Nursery
Rte. 3, Box 477
Alachua, FL 32615
 Their sole offering is the 'Dunstan' chestnut, a cross between a
 blight-resistant American chestnut tree and an Oriental
 chestnut, which was then backcrossed to the American chestnut. The tree is resistant to chestnut blight and has the virtues
 of both parents. Grafted trees only.

Columbia Basin Nursery
P.O. Box 458
Quincy, WA 98848
 A wholesale supplier of most popular apple varieties and other
 common fruits grown in commercial Washington orchards.
 Their catalog explains their amazing research with high-
 density apple orchards: standard trees on 4-foot centers with
 an "M" wall training technique and the lowest branches only a
 few inches off the ground.

Comstock, Ferre & Co.
263 Main St.
Withersfield, CT 06109
 Old and new varieties of vegetable, flower, and herb seeds.

Converse Nursery
Amherst, NH 03031
 A collector of antique apple varieties who offers quite a few
 each year. The supply is variable.

L. E. Cooke Co.
26333 Rd. 140
Visalia, CA 93277
 A wholesale supplier of fruit trees, flowering trees, grapes,
 shrubs, berries, and small fruits.

The Cook's Garden
Box 65050
Londonberry, VT 05148
 Offers more than 20 varieties of lettuce seed. Describes other
 salad greens and explains which are suited to coldframe and
 greenhouse culture.

CORNS
c/o Carl and Karen Barnes
Rte. 1, Box 32
Turpin, OK 73950
 An organization interested in the production and preservation
 of the genetic diversity of open-pollinated corn varieties. They
 have seed for approximately 80 varieties.

C. A. Cruickshan Ltd.
1015 Mount Pleasant Rd.
Toronto, Ont. M4P 2M1
 A supplier of Dutch Van Tuhergen bulbs, garden supplies, and
 books.

Culver Pecan Nursery
Farmersville, CA 93223
 Pecan tree varieties.

Cumberland Valley Nurseries, Inc.
P.O. Box 430
McMinnville, TN 37110
 One of the largest listings of peach trees, including low-chill
 and antique varieties. Some nectarines, pecans, and plums, as
 well.

William Dam Seeds Ltd.
P.O. Box 8400
Dundas, Ontario
Canada L9H 6M1
 A better selection of vegetable seeds than the conventional
 seed companies, including more cold-tolerant varieties.

DeGiorgi Co., Inc.
P.O. Box 413
Council Bluffs, IA 51502

Very unusual varieties of vegetable and flower seeds, with an extensive listing of flowers.

Dominion Seed House
Georgetown, Ontario L7G 4A2

An informative catalog for Canadian gardeners only – no catalogs are mailed to the U.S. Lists many seeds that Burpee and Harris Seeds no longer ship to Canada.

Earl Douglass Chestnuts
Red Creek, NY 13143

Douglass has developed his own cross between an American and an Oriental chestnut. Some cankers form, but they don't spread. Sells only seed and seedlings.

Eastville Plantation
P.O. Box 337
Bogart, GA 30622

One of the best selections of fruit and nut trees and grapevines for warm winter areas and the deep South. Features many low-chill varieties, including the 'Florida' series of peaches – the lowest chill peach trees in existence.

Endangered Species
12571 Red Hill
Tustin, CA 92680

An amazing selection of bamboo varieties, and exotic, tropical ornamentals. They ship container plants only.

Environmental Seed Producers, Inc.
P.O. Box 5904
El Monte, CA 91734

A wholesale source of wildflower seed. They sell pre-mixed "meadow" blends and single varieties by the pound. Ask for their informative card deck on the cultural needs of each wildflower they carry.

Epicure Seeds Ltd.
P.O. Box 450
Brewster, NY 10509

Seeds for international varieties of vegetables and herbs; also books, garden supplies, fertilizers, and pesticides.

Exotica Seed Company
8033 Sunset Blvd., Suite 125
West Hollywood, CA 90046

A good listing of rare tropical and semi-tropical seeds. They do a lot of their own collecting. A catalog costs $2.

Ed Fackler
Rte. 1, Box 104
New Salisbury, IN 47161

An active member of NAFEX who sells scion and bud wood of many unusual and antique varieties of fruit trees, especially apples.

Fall City Herb Farm
32804 Iss. Fall City Rd.
Fall City, WA 98024

Two hundred varieties of herb plants. Direct sales only, no mail order.

Dr. Yoo Farm
P.O. Box 290
College Park, Maryland 20740

An extensive listing of Oriental vegetable seeds. The largest selection of mushroom spawn – 13 varieties – for culturing Oriental mushrooms in a sawdust medium.

Farmer Seed and Nursery
Faribault, MN 55021

A supplier of mostly typical varieties of vegetable seed. They do carry bareroot tree crops for cold, northern climates and the 'Fireside' apple.

Fiddyment Pistachios
5010 Fiddyment Rd.
Roseville, CA 95678

Supplying only budded seedlings and seeds for pistachio trees.

Henry Field Seed & Nursery Co.
Shendandoah, IA 51602

A conventional catalog and mostly ordinary varieties of vegetable seeds.

Fiore Enterprises, Inc.
P.O. Box 67
Prairie View, IL 60069

Carries some wild edible shrubs and trees – mostly ornamentals. Ships burlap balled trees.

Forest Farm
990 Tetherow Rd.
Williams, OR 97544

Lists wild plants, American native plants, windbreak trees, nitrogen-fixing trees and shrubs, honey plants, and plants for birds and wildlife. They ship tube-grown plants with soil.

Fowler Nurseries, Inc.
525 Fowler Rd.
Newcastle, CA 95658

Their "Homestead and Family Orchard" catalog has a good general listing. One of the best sources for a large variety of Asian pear trees, miniature fruit trees, and persimmon trees. Their wholesale catalog has some of the best color photographs available of red and Asian pears.

Fox Hill Farm
444 W. Michigan Ave., Box 7
Parma, MI 49269

An herb farm with an extensive selection of live plants. They hold the "Oh Boy, Basil!" festival each summer.

Friends of the Trees
P.O. Box 1064
Tonasket, WA 98855

An extensive offering of seeds for trees, vines, and shrubs for reforestation, wildlife habitat, erosion control, and bee forage. They produce a newsletter for those interested in the hardy kiwi (Actinidia arguta), and will be offering seedlings and grafted vines.

Frosty Hollow Nursery
P.O. Box 53
Langley, WA 98260

Plants and designs for a sustainable future – forest trees and shrubs, and some nut tree seedlings.

Full Moon
P.O. Box 6138
Olympia, WA 98502

Sell kits and spores for growing a variety of your own edible mushrooms, and ships fresh shiitake mushrooms.

Garden Magic Co.
P.O. Box 6570
Zephyr Cove, NV 89449

Flower and vegetable seeds, and garden supplies.

Gardenimport, Inc.
P.O. Box 760
Thornbill, Ont. L3T 4A5

Imported bulbs, seeds and rare plants from all over the world; seeds from the Suttons Seed Co. collection, especially ones suited for northern climates. They also offer tools and books.

Gilberg Horticultural Services
Rte. 1, Box 1116B
Glencoe, MO 63038

A good listing of over 50 herbs and perennials. Live plants only; no mail-order sales.

Gleckler's Seedsmen
Metamora, OH 43540

Unusual seed specialties and very interesting varieties. They feature the 'Peron' tomato with 2 1/2 times the vitamin C of most tomatoes.

Good Seed Co.
P.O. Box 702
Tonasket, WA 98855

Open-pollinated seeds for northern gardens; untreated seeds and very fine varieties – many heirlooms. Good cultural information, and short essays on garden subjects. A fine catalog.

Greenmantle Nursery
3010 Ettersburg Rd.
Garberville, CA 95440

The very tasteful catalog ($2) features antique trees, especially apples developed by Albert Etter. They carry Etters' "most acclaimed apple," the 'Pink Pearl'. They also have a good selection of old-fashioned roses.

Grimo Nut Nursery
R.R. 3, Lakeshore Rd.
Niagara-on-the-Lake, Ontario L0S 1J0

A good selection of seedlings and grafted nut tree varieties; and apricots, mulberries, and American persimmons for colder climates.

Grootendorst Nurseries
Lakeside, MI 49116

A good source for small quantities of dwarfing apple rootstock. They are the propagators for Southmeadow Fruit Gardens.

Gurney's Seed & Nursery Co.
Yankton, SD 57079

Quite a selection of vegetable and flower seeds, trees, and gardening supplies. Many unusual and harder to find selections such as blue potatoes, 'Anoka' apples, white tomatoes, 'Walla Walla" onions, and many more.

Halcyon Gardens, Inc.
P.O. Box 124
Gibsonia, PA 15044

A good selection of herb plants and seeds for mail order.

Halifax Seed Co. Ltd.
Box 8026, Station A
Halifax, Nova Scotia B3K 5L8

Features short-season vegetable seed and supplies for greenhouse gardening.

Harris Seeds
P.O. Box 432
Gresham, OR 97030

Standard varieties of flower and herb seeds, particularly hybrids.

Hartman's Plantation, Inc.
Earleten, FL 32631

Blueberry plants.

The Heirloom Garden Project
Roger Kline
Dept. of Vegetable Crops
157 Plant Science Bldg.
Cornell University
Ithaca, NY 14853-0327

Features a collection of seeds of vegetables that were popular in the Northeast in the 1900s. They sell an informative booklet with or without seed collections. Send a SASE for a price listing.

Heirloom Gardens
P.O. Box 138
Guerneville, CA 95446

Culinary, historic, and rare seeds.

Herb Gathering, Inc.
5742 Kenwood
Kansas City, MO 64110

European herb and vegetable seeds.

The Business of Herbs
P.O. Box 559
Mackson, VA 22727

An excellent bi-monthly newsletter about herbs. More than just folksy, it covers the science and business of raising and selling herbs. All major herb growers and seed suppliers have advertisements in it. Best for serious herb collectors and commercial growers. A subscription is $18 per year.

Herbs 'n Honey
P.O. Box 124
Monmouth, OR 97361

More than "600 varieties of culinary, fragrance, and tea herb plants." Their herb chart/catalog is $4.95.

Hidden Springs Nursery
Rte. 14, Box 159
Cookeville, TN 38501

Features "edible landscaping, tree crops, and herbs." Their good selection of plants includes medlar, *Elaeagnus multiflora*, and other unusual varieties.

Horticultural Enterprises
P.O. Box 810082
Dallas, TX 75381-0082

The second-largest selection of pepper seeds in the country.

J. L. Hudson, Seedsman
Box 1058
Redwood City, CA 94064

Lists a huge variety of seeds for common and unusual vegetables, trees, flowers, and shrubs; does not list hybrids. Catalog costs $1.

Ed Hume
Box 1450
Kent, WA 98032

Specializes in seeds for vegetables and flowers suited to short seasons.

A. H. Hummert Seed Co.
2746 Chouteau Ave.
St. Louis, MO 63103

Seeds for annuals, perennials; cacti and succulents; bulbs, herbs, vegetables, and extensive flower varieties; and fertilizers, chemicals, and related supplies.

Hurov's Tropical Seeds
P.O. Box 1596
Chula Vista, CA 92012

A very extensive listing of seeds for tropical indoor and outdoor, ornamental and medicinal plants.

Island Seed Co.
P.O. Box 4278, Station A
Victoria, B.C. V8X 3X8

Hybrid and open-pollinated varieties of vegetable and flower seeds, with an extensive flower listing. Recipes included.

Jacklin Seed Co.
West 5300 Jacklin Ave.
Post Falls, ID 83854-9499

Sell seeds for wildflower meadows.

Johnny's Selected Seeds
Albion, ME 04910

THE place to get carrot seeds; great brassica and hot-season seeds. Their seeds are generally untreated; they offer hybrids and non-hybrids, and very good varieties that are reliable and germinate well. Their catalog has great cultural information, and lists gardening supplies and books.

Robert S. Judd, Jr.
Arborist
163 Clapboard Ridge Rd.
Danbury, CT 06810

Judd, who took over Baum's Nursery, features antique dwarf apple trees.

J. W. Jung Seed Co.
Randolph, WI 53957

Seeds for flowers, vegetables, and herbs; bareroot ornamental and fruit trees, and berries; garden supplies, fertilizers, and pesticides.

Kester's Wild Game Nurseries, Inc.
Box V
Omro, WI 54963

A large selection of seeds and tubers of wild edibles that make good wildlife forage. Many are edible for people, as well.

Kitazawa Seed Co.
356 W. Taylor St.
San Jose, CA 95110

A good selection of Oriental vegetable seeds.

La Fayette Home Nursery, Inc.
La Fayette, IL 61449

"Environmental native plant specialists," featuring seedlings and bareroot stock of native, wild edibles.

Lago Marsino Seeds, Inc.
5116 Folsom Blvd.
Sacramento, CA 95819

Dependable old varieties and new hybrids of flowers and vegetables, including some especially nice varieties.

Lamb Nurseries
E. 101 Sharp Ave.
Spokane, WA 99202

An extensive listing of hardy perennials and rock garden plants, including some wild edibles.

Larner Seeds
Box 60143
Palo Alto, CA 94306

Seeds for native plants of California and New England.

Las Pilitas Nursery
Star Rte. Box 23X
Santa Margarita, CA 93453

Specialists in protecting, preserving, and propagating California natives; 220 species of plants in pots, and seeds of 60 species.

Lawyer Nursery
Rte. 2, Box 95
Plains, MT 59859

The most extensive listing of small, bareroot seedlings for windbreaks, hedgerows, and wildlife habitat; and native edibles. Reasonable prices.

Le Jardin du Gourmet
West Danville, VT 05873

Vegetable and flower seeds and bulbs from Europe and Africa, but little information is given about them. They offer small, 20-cent seed packets for people who don't plant large areas and don't want to store leftover seeds. Also, gourmet foods and books. A catalog costs 50 cents.

Le Marche Seeds International
Box 566
Dixon, CA 95620

Seeds from Europe and Asia, and American heirloom varieties. Great lettuce, radicchio, and pepper varieties. Good cultural information and recipes. A favorite source of gourmet vegetables for many comercial truck farmers, because of the high germination rates.

Living Tree Centre
P.O. Box 797
Bolinas, CA 94924

Heirloom apples and a few organically grown vegetable seeds. Their catalog is $3.50.

Henry Leuthardt Nurseries, Inc.
P.O. Box 666
East Moriches, NY 11940

The only place where you can buy already formed espalier apple trees, bareroot. They also have a good selection of fruit tree varieties.

Lewis & White Fairacre Nursery
Rte. 1, Box 1068
Prosser, WA 99350

Specializes in grapevines for wine and juice, bareroot. For any variety, the minimum order is 25.

Lindenberg Seeds Ltd.
803 Princess Ave.
Brandon, Manitoba R7A 0P5

Seeds for standard perennials, bulbs, and flowers.

Living Off the Land
P.O. Box 2131
Melbourne, FL 32902

These people publish a newsletter and seed list emphasizing tropical and semi-tropical edibles. They also have seed for a number of unusual tree crops.

Lowden's Better Plants and Seeds
Box 7010
Ancaster, Ontario L9G 2C0

Specialists in tomato seeds and raspberry plants, particularly varieties suited to northern climates.

Makielski Berry Farm and Nursery
7130 Platt Rd.
Ypsilanti, MI 48197

Features cane fruits, including three varieties of purple raspberries.

May Nursery Co.
P.O. Box 1312
Yakima, WA 98907

A good selection of common fruit trees, with more cherry varieties than most catalogs. Also lists a cold-hardy miniature peach. Commercial and retail prices.

Earl May Seed & Nursery Co.
Shendandoah, IA 51603

Offers conventional vegetable and flower seeds, berries, fruit trees, bulbs, shrubs and vines.

Mayo Nurseries
8393 Klippel Rd.
Lyons, NY 14489

Lists a regular cross-section of common fruit tree varieties, and blueberries.

Michael McConkey
Edible Landscape Nursery
Afton, VA 22920

A good source for some rare types and varieties of fruiting trees, shrubs, and vines. One of the few places where you can get selections of hardy kiwi. Michael is one of the premier collectors of unusual fruiting plants. The prices are a bit high, but well worth it; support this nursery.

Meadowbrook Herbs & Things, Inc.
Whispering Pines Rd.
Wyoming, RI 02898

An extensive listing of herb seeds, along with dried herbs, herbal cosmetics, syrups, and other household goods.

Mellingers, Inc.
2310 W. South Range
North Lima, OH 44452

Mostly a tool catalog, but very reasonable prices on vegetable seeds by the ounce and pound.

Midwest Wildflowers
P.O. Box 64
Rockton, IL 61072

An extensive selection of wildflower seed in packet quantities only.

J. E. Miller Nurseries, Inc.
Canandaigua, NY 14424

A good list of antique apple varieties. They sell multiple-grafted apple ("modern" and antique versions) and pear trees. They also carry the yellow-fruited 'Fallgold' raspberry.

Moore Water Gardens
Port Stanley, Ontario N0L 2A0

Carries many types of aquatic edibles, but the emphasis is on ornamental value. A large selection of water lilies and tubers.

Moses Lake Conservation District Nursery
Rte. 3, Box 415
Moses Lake, WA 98837

Bareroot and potted trees for windbreaks and wildlife habitat.

Mountain Seed & Nursery
P.O. Box 9107
Moscow, ID 83843

Features seeds for short summer areas. Carries selections of "super early" tomatoes from the University of Idaho.

Musser Forests
P.O. Box 340-M
Indiana, PA 15701-0340

Bareroot seedlings of hundreds of types of trees and shrubs for ornamental, windbreak, and wildlife habitat uses.

Mushroom People
Box 158
Inverness, CA 94937

Spores and equipment for growing edible mushrooms. An informative catalog.

Native Seeds – SEARCH
3950 W. New York Dr.
Tucson, AZ 85745

A co-op for non-hybrid, open pollinated native seedstock from the greater Southwest. Many drought-tolerant varieties.

The Naturalists
P.O. Box 435
Yorktown Heights, NY 10598

Featuring seeds for culinary, tea, and medicinal herbs.

Nelson's Pine Patch
4301 Lynwood Dr.
Chula Vista, CA 92010

Many pines and native plants, as well as an excellent selection of tropical and semi-tropical fruiting vines and trees. Offers the cold-hardy kiwi and 7 varieties of the Chinese kiwi.

New York State Fruit Testing
Cooperative Association, Inc.
Geneva, NY 14456

A good place to get antique tree crop varieties, and a great place to get unnamed selections to test from University breeding programs. Support this group – $5 covers a year's membership and catalog.

Nichols Garden Nursery
1190 No. Pacific Hwy.
Albany, OR 97321

This family business is geared to market gardeners, offering seeds for unusual new and old varieties. A great deal of cultural and other information; and garden supplies, herbal teas, potpourri blends, oils. Their seed quality is not always reliable.

Northern Groves Hardy Bamboo
1507 S.E. Alder
Portland, OR 97214

Rare and common varieties of bamboo, for edible, structural, and ornamental uses.

Nourse Farms, Inc.
Box 485
RFD South Deerfield, MA 01373

An extensive selection of bareroot, virus-free strawberry varieties. Also, cane fruits, asparagus, and evergreen tree seedlings.

L.L. Olds Seed Co.
Box 7790
Madison, WI 53707-7790

An old seed house offering heirloom and new varieties of vegetable and flower seeds.

Orange Heights Pecan Nursery
Hawthorne, FL 32640

Specializes in pecan tree varieties.

Oriental Seed Catalog
Sunrise Enterprises
P.O. Box 10058
Elmwood, CT 06110

One of the largest selections of Oriental vegetable seeds. In English and Japanese.

Richard Owen Nursery
2300 East Lincoln St.
Bloomington, IL 61701

Unusual varieties of ornamental and fruit trees.

Pacific Tree Farms
4301 Lynnwood Dr.
Chula Vista, CA 92010

This excellent list, by experts on tropical food plants, is the most extensive on tropical and semi-tropical edibles. Varieties include 11 avocados, 7 white sapotes, 80 citrus (including some rare forms), 5 macadamias, hardy kiwi and 9 bananas. They also list some pines and ornamentals. All plants are shipped in containers with soil.

Palouse Seed Co.
P.O. Box 866
Tekoa, WA 99033

Featuring tube-grown native edibles, trees, and shrubs. Reasonable prices.

Park Seed Co.
Hwy. 254 North
Greenwood, SC 29647

A standard selection of vegetable and flower seeds, many hybrids.

Parrott's Walnut Nursery
Newberg, OR 97132

Walnut tree varieties.

Pataky's Nut Grove Nursery
Mansfield, OH 44901

Varieties of nut trees.

Patrick's Vineyard, Orchard, Nursery,
and Farm Market
Pomegranate Blvd.
Tyty, GA 31795

A good selection of fruit and nut trees, grapevines, cane fruits, and berries for the deep South. Also a good selection of grafted pecan trees and named varieties of figs. Offers the papaw tree.

The Theodore Payne Foundation.
10459 Tuxford St.
Sun Valley, CA 91352

This non-profit organization for the preservation of California native plants sells many varieties of wildflower seeds by mail. They have a 22-acre nursery for retail sales of container plants (no mail order).

Peaceful Valley Farm Supply
11173 Peaceful Valley Rd.
Nevada City, CA 95959

A catalog mostly of tools and organic pest controls. They offer a wide selection of tree crops each winter.

Pecoff Brothers Nursery and Seed, Inc.
Rte. 5, Box 215 R
Escondido, CA 92025

Seeds and a hydro-seeding service for establishing native wildflowers, erosion controlling ground covers and shrubs, and for revegetating disturbed land.

The Pepper Gal
Dorothy Van Vieck
10535 119th Ave.
Largo, FL 33543

The largest selection anywhere of sweet and hot pepper varieties (seeds only). The supply of this small home business varies each season.

Pine Tree Garden Seeds
New Gloucester, ME 04260

Their vegetable, flower, and herb seeds are untreated and surprisingly inexpensive. Hybrids and old varieties.

Plants of the Southwest
1812 Second St.
Santa Fe, NM 87501

Ancient and modern vegetable seeds for the arid Southwest, including Papago and Hopi blue corn seed. Also, many types of wildflowers for arid conditions.

Porter & Son, Seedsmen
P.O. Box 104
Stephenville, TX 76401

Specializing in tomato, watermelon, and cantaloupe seed; also, garden and lawn fertilizers, insecticides, and supplies.

Preservation Apple Tree Co.
P.O. Box 279
Mt. Gretna, PA 17064

Offers 20 varieties of antique apple trees.

Raintree Nursery
391 Butts Rd.
Morton, WA 98356

Edible landscape plants for the Pacific Northwest. One of the most educational catalogs in the U.S. An extensive listing of antique varieties and newest releases suited to the Pacific Northwest.

Steve Ray's Bamboo Gardens
909 - 79th Place South
Birmingham, AL 35206

A good selection of timber and cane bamboos, at reasonable prices. Sells clumps of bareroot rhizomes.

Rayner Bros., Inc.
P.O. Box 1617
Salisbury, MD 21801

One of the largest selections of strawberry varieties. Bareroot sales only.

The Redwood City Seed Co.
P.O. Box 361
Redwood City, CA 94064

This great catalog has an extensive list of rare edible and ornamental plant seeds. Perhaps the slowest service in the trade; order months ahead of time. A catalog costs 50 cents.

Otto Richter and Sons, Ltd.
Box 26
Goodwood, Ontario L0C 1A0

An extensive collection of herb seed varieties, including some harder to find types.

Clyde Robin Seed Co., Inc.
P.O. Box 2855
Castro Valley, CA 94546

Carries an extensive selection of wildflower seed, at bulk rates. Poor germination has been a common complaint among growers. A catalog costs $1.

Robinson's Oakville Nursery
29730 Harvest Dr.
Albany, OR 97321

Offers only blueberry varieties. A quality poster/chart describing the varieties is available for $2.

Roses of Yesterday and Today
802 Brown's Valley Rd.
Watsonville, CA 95076

A great selection of antique varieties of roses, the ones with good disease resistance and fantastic fragrance. A catalog costs $1.

Rural Advancement Fund
P.O. Box 1029
Pittsboro, NC 27312

Dedicated to stopping the erosion of the gene pool of edible plants and the decline of family farming. They do not sell seed, but for $2 will mail an attractive list of all suppliers of heirloom and ancient seed. Support this organization – send a donation and ask to receive their newsletter.

S & S Seeds
910 Alphonse
Santa Barbara, CA 93103

Sells wildflower seeds by the pound in pre-mixed combinations or by the species. One of the few places where you can buy *Lotus* sp. legumes.

Saginaw Valley Nut Nursery
Birch Run, MI 48415

Various nut tree varieties.

Sanctuary Seeds
2388 W. Fourth
Vancouver, B.C. V6K 1P1

Favors older varieties of Canadian seeds; all are open-pollinated non-hybrids. Lists seeds for vegetables, flowers, and medicinals; also spices, dried fruits and nuts, grains, vitamins, and botanicals.

Saratoga Horticultural Foundation
15185 Murphy Ave.
San Martin, CA 95046

Breeds, selects, and sells special cultivars of native and Mediterranean plants for the California climate. Wholesale and direct sales only, no mail order.

F. W. Schumacher Co.
36 Spring Hill Rd.
Sandwich, MA 02563-1023

A wide variety of seeds by the ounce and pound for forest trees, windbreak trees and shrubs, and some edible trees and shrubs. Reasonable prices.

C. D. Schwartze Garden & Nursery
2302 Tacoma Rd.
Puyallup, WA 98371

A short list of fairly typical apple trees on the M 26 dwarfing rootstock.

Seed Center, Ltd.
Box 3867, Station D
Edmonton, Alberta T5L 4K1

Seeds and plants hardy to the northern provinces of Canada.

Seed Savers Exchange
R.R. 2
Princeton, MO 64673

The network of seed collectors for heirloom varieties of vegetables and tree crops. For a yearly subscription of $8, you get the *Yearbook*, which includes a seed saving guide, questions and answers on backyard seed breeding, and an antique plant finders service.

Seeds Blum
Idaho City State
Boise, ID 83707

This personable family's folksy catalog is full of all sorts of information and witty illustrations, and lots of unusual varieties of heirloom seeds. Their potato seed collection will soon be the largest available by mail-order in the U.S. Support these hard-working, dedicated people.

Sharp Bros. Seed Co.
Healy, KS

Open-pollinated and hybrid seeds for grain, corn, wheat, soybean, and grass.

Shepherd's Garden Seeds
7389 W. Zayante Rd.
Felton, CA 95018

Fine European seeds for "gourmet" varieties. Lists recipes and books. Expensive, but good quality.

R. H. Shumway Seedsman, Inc.
P.O. Box 777
Rockford, IL 61105

Standard varieties of vegetable seeds.

Siberia Seeds
Box 3000
Olds, Alberta T0M 1P0

Another source of seeds suited to short season, northern climates. For a catalog, send 50 cents and a SASE.

Sierra Gold Nurseries
5320 Garden Hwy.
Yuba City, CA 95991-9499

Fruit tree specialists, wholesale only, of fairly typical tree crop varieties. They do have a good selection of spur-type apple trees.

Keith Somers Trees Ltd.
10 Tillson Ave.
Tillsonburg, Ontario N4G 2Z6

Sells in Canada only. Grafted fruit trees for cold, Canadian climates, as well as bareroot seedlings of windbreak trees, natives, and ornamental trees.

Sonoma Antique Apple Nursery
4395 Westside Rd.
Healdsburg, CA 95448

More than 60 varieties of organically grown, antique apple trees and numerous other fruit tree varieties. A good place to buy the 'Pink Pearl' apple and several good cider apples. Support these good people who are doing good work.

Dan Sorensen's Hardy Kiwis
R.D. 2, Box 2028E
Russell, PA 16345

Sells only named varieties of the cold-hardy kiwi.

Southern Exposure Seed Exchange
P.O. Box 158
North Garden, VA 22959

This family-owned business offers seeds for modern and old varieties of vegetables and flowers; almost all are open-pollinated. They will exchange heirloom varieties. Their catalog has good cultural notes, and also lists books and supplies. They carry the best heirloom seeds for southern conditions.

Southmeadow Fruit Gardens
Lakeside, MI 49116

Still the largest selection of antique fruit tree varieties, from one of the oldest such nurseries. Dozens of selections of all the common fruit types, and the largest selection of named gooseberries (12 varieties) in the country. Their *Southmeadow Illustrated Catalog* is the most detailed and readily available description of hundreds of antique fruits. The catalog (with black and white photos only) is $8. There is also a free, several page list of the varieties that are available each season.

St. Lawrence Nurseries
R.D. 2
Potsdam, NY 13676

An excellent offering of fruit tree varieties for northern climates. Includes more than 100 apple varieties, edible honeysuckle, three named varieties of elderberry, edible mountain ash, and other unusual fruiting plants.

Stark Bro's Nurseries
Louisiana, MO 63353

A well-known catalog of fruit and nut tree varieties. Some unusual varieties and many typical ones.

Steele Plant Co.
Gleason, TN 38229

Specializing in potatoes and sweet potatoes.

Stock Seed Farms, Inc.
R.R. 1, Box 112
Murdock, NE 68407

Offers prairie wildflower seeds – annuals, biennials, and perennials.

Stokes Seeds, Inc.
737 Main St., Box 548
Buffalo, NY 14240

A good selection of European vegetable seeds and an especially good offering of flower seeds. Excellent growing tips and a full description of each variety. They offer one of the best selections of cabbage varieties.

SunSweet Fruit & Bulb Nursery
P.O. Box Z
Sumner, GA 31789

Bareroot fruit and nut trees and ornamental bulbs for the deep South. A good selection of fig varieties.

Sunrise Enterprizes
P. O. Box 10058
Elmwood, CT 06110-0058

Seeds for Oriental vegetables and herbs. One of the few places where you can get taro tubers and ginger roots.

Talbot Nursery
R.R. 3
Linton, IN 47441

Sells bareroot American persimmon trees, and Chinese chestnut, walnut, and hardy pecan trees.

Tater Mater Seeds
R.R. 2
Wathena, KS 66090

An amazing selection of seeds for unusual (and strange) tomato varieties. A small operation with an irregular supply.

Taylor's Herb Gardens, Inc.
1535 Lone Oak Rd.
Vista, CA 92083

An excellent selection of live herb plants shipped in sturdy cardboard boxes. Some hard to find varieties. A catalog costs $1, and is worth it.

Territorial Seed Co.
P.O. Box 27
Lorane, OR 97451

Specialists in varieties suitable to maritime climates, primarily for the home gardener. Seeds are generally untreated. The catalog has great cultural information.

The Theodore Payne Foundation
for Wildflowers and Native Plants, Inc.
10459 Tuxford St.
Sun Valley, CA 93152

A non-profit corporation specializing in wildflowers, trees and shrubs – seeds and live plants.

Thompson and Morgan Seedsmen
P.O. Box 100
Farmingdale, NJ 077278

Seeds for an extensive variety of rare flowers and vegetables; also trees and shrubs. Non-organic. Prices are on the high side, but they do carry some seeds not available elsewhere.

Tillinghast Seed Co.
P.O. Box 738
LaConner, WA 98257

Seeds of vegetables, and bulbs and plants of ornamentals – many well-suited to coastal climates of the Pacific Northwest.

Tolowa Nursery
360 Stephen Way
Williams, OR 97544

Selected tree crops for the Pacific Northwest.

Tomato Growers Supply Company
P.O. Box 2237
Fort Meyers, FL 33902

Lists seeds for more than 100 varieties of tomatoes, mostly hybrids. Also carries supplies, books, and pest controls for tomato culture.

Tsang and Ma
1306 Old County Rd.
Belmont, CA 94002

A good selection of Oriental seed varieties and kitchen supplies.

Twilley Seed Co.
P.O. Box 65
Trevose, PA 19047

Except for a fairly extensive selection of corn varieties, mostly seeds for common hybrid vegetables and ornamental annual varieties.

The Urban Farmer, Inc.
P.O. Box 444
Convent Station, NJ 07961

Unusual vegetable seeds from Europe, the Orient, and heirloom varieties.

Valley Nursery
P.O. Box 4845
Helena, MT 59604

"Home of Chinook country hardy plants." Mostly hardy shrubs and trees for reforestation, windbreaks, and ornamental landscaping. Lists some edibles.

Van Bourgendien
P.O. Box A
Babylon, NY 11702

Dutch and domestic bulbs; herbs, ferns, wildflowers, fruit trees, berries, and gardening accessories.

Van Ness Water Gardens
2650 No. Euclid Ave.
Upland, CA 91786

Plants and accessories for water gardens. Many selections of water lilies, and some edible plants, including water chestnuts.

Van Well Nursery
P.O. Box 1339
Wenatchee, WA 98801

Wholesale and retail of bareroot fruit trees and berries, mostly common commercial varieties. They do offer the compact 'Elberta' and 'Red Haven' semi-miniature peach trees.

Vans Pines, Inc.
West Olive, MI 49460

A cheap source of seedling trees for windbreaks and ornamental use, and some nut trees. Wholesale only; stock is sold bareroot by the 100s or 1,000s.

Vermont Bean Seed Co.
Way's Lane
Manchester Center, VT 05255

A wide variety of vegetable seeds from around the world, especially beans, peas and corn – both new hybrids and heirlooms. Also sells flowers and gardening supplies, and an endive forcing kit.

Vesey's Seeds Ltd.
York
Prince Edward Island C0A 1P0

Vegetable and flower seeds for short growing seasons.

Vita Green Farms
217 Escondido Ave.
Vista, CA 92083

Organic seeds for old-fashioned varieties of herbs and vegetables; and books.

Waynesboro Nurseries, Inc.
Waynesboro, VA 22980

Bareroot fruit and nut trees. Mostly ordinary varieties, but a decent selection of peach trees.

Well Sweep Herb Farm
317 Mt. Bethel Rd.
Port Murray, NJ 07865

An extensive selection of 2 or 3 inch potted herb plants: close to 60 varieties of thyme, 10 culinary sages, 25 lavendars, and much more.

Wildlife Nurseries
P.O. Box 2724
Oshkosh, WI 54903-2724

Seeds for wildlife forage plants. Some edible water and bog plants and wild grasses.

Willhite Seed Co.
P.O. Box 23
Poolville, TX 76076

Standard vegetable varieties, but one of the world's largest melon seed growers – their catalog lists 76 melon varieties! All seeds are treated with Thiram.

Willow Drive Nursery Inc.
Rte. 1, Box 348 5-NW
Ephrata, WA 98823

A wholesale source of bareroot seedling and dwarfing rootstocks for fruit trees.

Leslie H. Wilmoth Nursery
Rte. 2, Box 469
Elizabethtown, KY 427018

An amazing selection of grafted, named variety nut trees, including dozens of walnut varieties. Also apple, peach, pear, apricot, and cherry trees.

Wilton's Organic Seed Potatoes
Box 28
Aspen, CO

The only organic, high-altitude seed potatoes in the country. Seed is certified as well.

Wolf River Nurseries
Rte. 67
Buskirk, NY 12028

An ordinary selection of bareroot fruit trees.

Yerba Buena Nursery
19500 Skyline Blvd.
Woodside, CA 94062

Container plants of California natives. They sell retail and wholesale at their nursery, and ship UPS, depending on the size of plants.

Gardening Tools

Bailey's
P.O. Box 550
Laytonville, CA 95454

This supplier for the professional logger and tree trimmer carries a good cross-section of of pruning and chainsaw equipment.

Ben Meadows
P.O. Box 2781
Eugene, OR 97402

The largest selection of tools for the professional forester, lumberman, surveyor, tree trimmer, and conservationist. An amazing top-notch variety, including weather stations, chainsaw equipment, first aid kits, and pruning tools. Write to ask the price of their catalog.

Brookstone Co.
Vose Farm Rd.
Peterborough, NH 03458

Carries quality garden tools and some gadgets. Well-known for their specialty tools and woodworking tools.

Gardener's Eden
P.O. Box 7307
San Francisco, CA 94120

Offers more fancy garden fixtures and decorations than actual tools. Some of the tools are not as practical as their prices would warrant. Published by the Williams-Sonoma gourmet-food people.

Gardener's Supply Co.
133 Elm St.
Winooski, VT 05301

A comprehensive list of practical and sturdy quality tools for serious gardeners. Their seasonal catalogs feature row tunnel materials and cloches in the spring; watering aids and weeding devices in the summer; harvesting, processing, and composting tools in the fall; and practical gift items in the winter.

Green River Tools, Inc.
P.O. Box 1919
Brattleboro, VT 05301

An excellent source of quality tools. I especially like the Jupiter system of hand cultivators and weeders for small-scale truck farms or for large family gardens. Hand-forged digging tools, top-quality pruning shears, and many useful accessories.

Harmony Farm Supply
P.O. Box 451
Graton, CA 95444

Offers a complete line of drip irrigation supplies, organic soil amendments, and biological insecticides. Also carries hand-forged tools, cover crop seed, bulk vegetable seed, and, each winter, a selection of bareroot fruit and nut trees. The owners are a certified entomologist and an irrigation design specialist who are active in California Certified Organic Farmers. Write for a catalog.

David Kay Garden and Gift Catalogue
4509 Taylor Lane
Cleveland, OH 44128

The emphasis is on ornamental novelties, toys, and gift items. Perhaps the best place to order cute gifts for part-time gardeners.

Joshua Roth, Ltd.
P.O. Box 496
Santa Rosa, CA 95402

Features imported Japanese bonsai tools, knives, sickles, and pruning saws.

Kama Imports, Ltd.
P.O. Box 612
Central City, KY 42330-0612

Imports 11 types of Japanese hand sickles, and also carries a wide assortment of Japanese garden tools.

Kinsman Co.
River Rd.
Point Pleasant, PA 18950

Features imported hand-forged tools, cold frames, shredders, and other mechanical gardening aids and hand tools.

A. M. Leonard, Inc.
P.O. Box 816
Piqua, OH 45356

One of the best sources of tools used in professional greenhouses, nurseries, tree-trimming businesses, and landscaping. Reasonable prices. Every serious gardener should have their comprehensive catalog.

Mellinger's
2310 W. South Range
North Lima, OH 44452-9731

Standard tools and gadgets for the home gardener. They offer a little bit of everything – English hand-forged tools, netting, chemical poisons, and several seedling systems. Their catalog lists a page of botanical insecticides, including Mormon cricket spore; they also offer some unusual vegetable and flower seeds.

Necessary Trading Co.
New Castle, VA 24127

A wide range of tools, seeds, soil amendments, biological controls, and books for organic gardeners and farmers. An excellent resource.

Walt F. Nicke
P.O. Box 667G
Hudson, NY 12534

A large selection of garden tools, gadgets, and garden hardware. One of the oldest mail-order garden tool companies. Less emphasis on fashionable gourmet tools and more on the standard workhorses of the U.S. and Europe, at reasonable prices.

Geo. W. Park Seed Co.
Greenwood, SC 29647

Carries a standard selection of tools and gadgets. Does not offer top quality, hand-forged tools.

Peaceful Valley Farm Supply
11173 Peaceful Valley Rd.
Nevada City, CA 95959

A complete selection of garden tools, English hand-forged spading tools, irrigation supplies, organic fertilizers, biological controls, beneficial insects, and cover crop seed. Dedicated to promoting organic gardening.

The Plow and Hearth
560 Main St.
Madison, VA 22727

A mixture of decent tools and novelty items, including a good selection of gourmet birdfeeders and birdhouses.

Ringer Research
6860 Flying Cloud Dr.
Eden Prairie, MN 55344

Tools to improve lawns, and soil amendments, compost activators, and vegetable seeders. They also carry soap sprays and biological controls for grubs, caterpillars, and mosquitoes.

Smith and Hawken
25 Corte Madera
Mill Valley, CA 94941

Premier quality tools in the European tradition. The first to import hand-forged tools from England. Unequaled in selection and service, they offer the full spectrum of hand tools, axes, Japanese tools, pruning devices, plus highly crafted garden furniture. Very few gadgets and accessories.

White Flower Farm
Litchfield, CT 06759-0050

In addition to perennial plants, they also carry several lines of garden furniture, including teak, and white molded resin.

Producers and Suppliers of Biological Pest Control Agents

PRODUCERS AND SUPPLIERS OF BIOLOGICAL PEST CONTROL AGENTS

Producers

Abbot Laboratories
14th and Sheridan Rds.
North Chicago, IL 60064
Dipel™ (formulation of *Bacillus thuringiensis*) and DeVine, for control of milkweed vine.

AgBioChem
3 Fleetwood Ct.
Orinda, CA 94563
Galltrol-A™, for prevention of crown gall.

Albany International
P.O. Box 1907
Albany, NY 12201
Many pheromone products, e.g., a trap for *Heliothis zea* and *H. virenscens*, and Nomate PDW™, a mating confusant for the artichoke plume moth.

BBS Products
1603 - 63rd St.
Emeryville, CA 94608
Buzz-Inn Fly Traps™.

Ben Meadows Co.
3589 Broad St.
Atlanta, GA 30366
Rattlesnake-proof boots and leggings.

Bend Research Inc.
64550 Research Rd.
Bend, OR 97701
Pheromone products with the trademark Biolure™.

Biochem Products
P.O. Box 264
Montchanin, DE 19710
Bactimos™ for control of mosquitoes and blackflies.

Chem Samp Co.
P.O. Box 20305
Columbus, OH 43220
Many pheromone products.

Colorado Insectary
P.O. Box 3266
Durango, CO 81301
Nosema locustae for grasshopper control.

Detjen Corp.
P.O. Box 150
Clinton Corners, NY 12514
Insectocutor Fly Traps™ (electrical).

Environmental Technologies Inc.
1030 W. Ellsworth Ave.
Denver, CO 80223
Hopper Stopper™ for grasshopper control.

Fairfax Biological Labs, Inc.
Clinton Corners, NY 12514
Doom™, for control of the Japanese beetle.

General Marketing Ltd.
Japanese Beetle Prevention Services
1022 Wilson Blvd., Ste. 2616
Arlington, VA 22209
Milky spore disease for control of the Japanese beetle.

Hercon Division
Health Chem Corporation
1107 Broadway
New York, NY 10010
Pheromone traps and dispensers such as Boll Weevil Scout™, and Disrupt™ for the pink bollworm.

Herculite Products Inc.
1107 Broadway
New York, NY 10010
Many pheromone dispenser systems.

High as a Kite
691 Bridgeway Rd.
Sausalito, CA 94965
or
The Kite Factory
P.O. Box 9081
Seattle, WA 98109
Kites in the shape of predatory birds, for bird control.

Laport Insectaries Inc.
2220 North Hwy. US 287
Fort Collins, CO 80524
Locucide™ bait for grasshopper control.

Lethelin Products
15 MacQuesten Parkway So.
Mount Vernon, NY 10550
Magi-Kil Ant Traps™.

Nichols Net and Twine Co.
R.R. 3, Bend Rd.
East St. Louis, IL 62201
Nets and net-making materials for bird barriers.

Omnidata International
P.O. Box 3489
Logan, UT 84321
Miniature, battery-operated microcomputers that predict periodic biological development of plants and insects.

Reuter Laboratories
2400 James Madison Hwy.
Haymarket, VA 22069
Nosema locustae for grasshopper control.

Safer Agro Chem
13910 Lyons Valley
Jamul, CA 92035
Insecticidal soaps, including Safer's Insecticidal Flea Soap™.

Sandoz Inc.
Crop Protection Division
480 Camino Del Rio South
San Diego, CA 92108
Thuricide™, for control of blackflies and mosquitoes; Certan™, for the wax moth; and Elcar™, for corn earworm (*Heliothis zea* and *H. virescens*).

Seabright Enterprises Ltd.
Harlan St.
Emeryville, CA 94608
  Stickem Special™ to capture or repel insects, or as a barrier to ants and slugs.

Stauffer Chemical Co.
Westport, CT 06880
  Pro-Drone™ for control of fire ants.

Summit Chemical Co.
117 W. 24th St.
Baltimore, MD 21218
  Luretape™, traps, and pheromone for gypsy moth control.

Upjohn Co.
9700-50-1
Kalamazoo, MI 49001
  Sok-BT™ for control of northern jointvetch.

USDA Forest Service
Rocky Mt. Forest Range Expt. Station
240 W. Prospect St.
Ft. Collins, CO 80526
  Collapsible quail trap (write for "A Collapsible Quail Trap," Research Note RM-400).

U.S. Diversified Industries
21 Charles St.
Westport, CT 06880
  Repel'M Gypsy Moth Egg Mass Remover™ and Gypsy Moth Caterpillar Tape™.

Zoecon Corporation
975 California Ave.
Palo Alto, CA 94394
  Many pheromone attractant traps and kits, including Mirex-5E™ for control of leafminer in chrysanthemums; Altosid™, for mosquitoes, and Precor™, for fleas.

Suppliers of Beneficial Organisms

Beneficial Organisms	Target Pests	Suppliers (numbers refer to list below)
Decollate snail	Snails (*Helix aspersa*)	2, 17, 18, 24, 39, 40, 44
Fly predator	Flies	38, 45
Green lacewing	Aphids, mites, thrips, insect eggs	8, 10, 14, 23, 24, 26, 30, 33, 35, 38, 40, 44, 46
Lady beetle	Aphids and other insects	5, 8, 10, 19, 20, 22, 23, 24, 26, 28, 29, 33, 35, 37, 38, 40, 44, 46
Mealybug predator	Citrus, *itrophilus* long-tailed and other mealybugs	2, 10, 18, 23, 24, 26, 30, 33, 35, 38, 40, 44
Praying mantis	Many insects	8, 22, 28, 29, 31, 32, 33, 37, 40, 46
Predatory mites	Spider mites, Pacific mite and others	1, 2, 7, 10, 12, 16, 23, 24, 33, 34, 40, 41, 43, 44
Predatory nematodes	Soil larvae and grubs	13, 36, 40
Egg parasitoid	*Lepidopterous* sp. eggs	6, 8, 9, 10, 11, 14, 18, 19, 21, 22, 23, 24, 27, 29, 33, 34, 40, 41, 42, 43, 44
Fly parasitoids	Flies	3, 4, 8, 10, 14, 18, 24, 26, 33, 35, 38, 40, 44, 45, 46
Greenhouse white-fly parasitoid	*Trialeurodes vaporariorum* and others	1, 7, 10, 16, 24, 30, 33, 38, 40, 41, 42, 43, 44, 46, 47
Mexican bean beetle parasitoid	*Epilachna varivestis*	25, 30
Navel orangeworm parasitoid	*Paramyelois transitella*	14, 40, 44
Scale parasitoids	Red and black scale	2, 10, 17, 18, 24, 38, 40, 44

Suppliers

1. Applied Bionomics
    Agriculture Canada Research Station
    8801 East Saanich Rd.
    Sidney, B.C., Canada V8L 1H1

2. Associates Insectary
    P.O. Box 969
    Santa Paula, CA 93060

3. Beneficial Biosystems
    1603-F 63rd St.
    Emeryville, CA 94608

4. Beneficial Insectary
    245 Oak Run Rd.
    Oak Run, CA 96069

5. Beneficial Insects Co.
    P.O. Box 323
    Brownsville, CA 95919

6. Beneficial Insects Ltd.
    P.O. Box 154
    Banta, CA 95304

7. Better Yield Insects
    13310 Riverside Dr. East
    Tecumseh, Ontario, Canada

8. Bio Control Co.
    P.O. Box 247
    Cedar Ridge, CA 95924

9. Biogenesis, Inc.
   P.O. Box 36
   Mathis, TX 78368

10. Bio Insect Control
    1710 So. Broadway
    Plainview, TX 79072

11. Bio Insect Control
    P.O. Box 9134
    Alexandria, VA 22304

12. Biotactics, Inc.
    7765 Lakeside Dr.
    Riverside, CA 92509

13. B. R. Supply Co.
    P.O. Box 845
    Exeter, CA 93221

14. California Green Lacewings
    P.O. Box 2495
    Merced, CA 95340

15. Colorado Insectary
    P.O. Box 3266
    Durango, CO 81301

16. Elk Lake Garden Centre
    5450 Patricia Bay Hwy.
    Victoria, B.C., Canada V8Y 1T1

17. Fillmore Insectary
    533-C Sespe Ave.
    Fillmore, CA 93015

18. Foothill Agricultural Research, Inc.
    510 W. Chase Dr.
    Corona, CA 91720

19. Fossil Flower
    463 Woodbine Ave.
    Toronto, Ontario, Canada M4E 2H5

20. Fountain's Sierra Bug Co.
    P.O. Box 114
    Rough and Ready, CA 95975

21. Gothard Inc.
    P.O. Box 370
    Canutillo, TX 79835

22. Gurney Seed and Nursery Co.
    Yankton, SD 57079

23. Harmony Farm Supply
    P.O. Box 451
    Graton, CA 95444

24. Integrated Pest Management
    305 Agostino Rd.
    San Gabriel, CA 91776

25. John W. Kennedy Consultants
    608 Washington Blvd., Ste. 406
    Laurel, MD 20707

26. King's Natural Pest Control
    224 Yost Ave.
    Spring City, PA 19475

27. Kunafin Trichogramma Insectaries
    Rte. 1, P.O. Box 39
    Quemado, TX 78877

28. Lakeland Nurseries Sales, Inc.
    340 Poplar St.
    Hanover, PA 17331

29. Mellinger's Nursery
    2310 W. South Range Rd.
    North Lima, OH 44452

30. Metro Pest Management Consultants
    P.O. Box 1029
    Arvada, CO 80001

31. Mincemoyer's Nursery
    R.D. 7, P.O. Box 379
    Jackson, NJ 08527

32. Nationwide Seed and Supply
    P.O. Box 91073
    Louisville, KY 40291

33. Natural Pest Controls
    9397 Premier Way
    Sacramento, CA 95826

34. Nature's Control
    2518 Stewart Ave.
    Medford, OR 97501

35. Necessary Trading Co.
    328 Main St.
    New Castle, VA 24127

36. The Nematode Farm
    2617 San Pablo Ave.
    Berkeley, CA 94702

37. Organic Control, Inc.
    5132 Venice Blvd.
    Los Angeles, CA 90019

38. Organic Pest Control Naturally
    19920 Forest Park Dr., NE
    Seattle, WA 98155

39. Pacific Agricultural Labs, Inc.
    P.O. Box 439
    San Luis Rey, CA 92068

40. Peaceful Valley Farm Supply
    11173 Peaceful Valley Rd.
    Nevada City, CA 95959

41. Pest Management Group
    545 West 8th Ave.
    Vancouver, B.C., Canada V5Z 1C6

42. Professional Ecological Services
    555 Hillside
    Victoria, B.C., Canada V8T 1Y8

43. Resh Greenhouses and Hydroponic Garden Center
    12626 Bridgeport Rd.
    Richmond, B.C., Canada V6V 1J5

44. Rincon Vitova Insectaries
    P.O. Box 95
    Oak View, CA 93022

45. Spalding Laboratories
    760 Printz Rd.
    Arroyo Grande, CA 93420

46. Unique Nursery
    5504 Sperry Dr.
    Citrus Heights, CA 95610

47. Whitefly Control Co.
    P.O. Box 986
    Milpitas, CA 95035

9

"Edible" Organizations and Periodicals

"EDIBLE" ORGANIZATIONS AND PERIODICALS

Abundant Life Seed Foundation
P.O. Box 772
Port Townsend, WA 98368

An excellent source of open-pollinated and heirloom seeds. And in the catalog is a good newsletter on saving seeds, genetic diversity, and sustainable agriculture and gardening.

Acres U.S.A.
Charles Walters, Jr.
P.O. Box 9547
Kansas City, MO 64133

Publisher of one of the oldest publications for organic farmers; most of the examples are from the American grain belt. Some articles and editorials are a bit too paranoid for my tastes.

agAccess
P.O. Box 2008
Davis, CA 95617

The best source in the country for books in print related to horticulture. Write for a sample of its fantastic quarterly publication, which lists a variety of new books—from the most technical to the basic—on every topic from tropical agriculture to computer-assisted design. There is also a rare book search service and a list of readers' out-of-print wants. A must for all serious horticulturists.

Agroecology Program
Department of Environmental Studies
University of California
Santa Cruz, CA 95064

Perhaps the best program available for students wishing to study sustainable agriculture. The course work and field study is oriented to a fully integrated study of ecology. The field work takes place at the Farm and Garden Project site, a site picked by Alan Chadwick when he was working on the university campus.

American Bamboo Society
1101 San Leon Ct.
Solana Beach, CA 92075

The society publishes a newsletter about bamboo as an ornamental and edible plant.

American Community Gardening Association
P.O. Box 8645
Ann Arbor, MI 48107

If you don't have the space at home to landscape or garden, contact these people for information about local community gardens or how to start your own.

American Horticultural Society
Mount Vernon, VA 22121

The society publishes a colorful magazine on all aspects of horticulture, with an emphasis on ornamentals and botanical collections.

Amity Foundation
P.O. Box 11048
Eugene, OR 97440

Does good research work and practical applications for aquaculture, organic gardening, and coldframes and greenhouses.

Aprovecho Institute
80574 Hazelton Rd.
Cottage Grove, OR 97424

A good appropriate technology organization. Best at Lorena stoves, but developing a comprehensive training and demonstration site in Oregon.

Avant Gardener
Horticultural Data Processers
P.O. Box 489
New York, NY 10028

An excellent review—via short abstracts—of new ideas, trends, and research in all aspects of horticulture. Oriented to the non-technical reader.

Beltsville Agricultural Research Center
Beltsville, MD 20705

This is heaven for those, like me, who love to thoroughly research all aspects of food production and use. Twenty floors of paper and helpful librarians!

Bio-Dynamic Farming & Gardening Association
P.O. Box 253
Wyoming, RI 02898

Publishes a journal about trends, research, and working farms—all related to the strict application of biodynamics.

Brooklyn Botanic Garden
1000 Washington Ave.
Brooklyn, NY 11225

Great gardens to visit. Publishes a series of helpful, introductory booklets. They also do workshops at the garden.

The Business of Herbs
P.O. Box 559
Madison, VA 22727

This is required reading for serious growers and sellers of herbs. The emphasis is on aspects of the trade and how to sell to and educate the buyer of dried herbs.

California Agrarian Action Project
P.O. Box 464
Davis, CA 95646

A network and "lobby" for changing government policy to support organic farmers and the availability of certified organic produce.

California Agriculture
Agricultural Experiment Station
University of California
Berkeley, CA 94720

Free to California residents. A good periodical to keep up with the latest published work of the UC system of agriculture and horticulture. Technically oriented.

California Certified Organic Farmers
1920 Maciel Ave.
Santa Cruz, CA 95062

If you want to be a certified organic grower in California, this is the organization for you. Anyone interested in helping to make the public aware of the benefits of organic produce should contact this group of dedicated people.

California Rare Fruit Growers
The Fullerton Arboretum
California State University
Fullerton, CA 92634

The best quarterly journal on this half of the continent for people interested in learning about tropical and semi-tropical edibles and in sharing seeds and plants of such.

Camp Joy
131 Camp Joy Rd.
Boulder Creek, CA 95006

One of the oldest gardens begun under the influence of Alan Chadwick. They still do occasional seminars, lectures, and apprenticeship programs.

The Chadwick Society
Green Gulch Farm
Star Rte. 1
Sausalito, CA 94965

This is the national network for practitioners and students of the biodynamic/French intensive method as taught by Alan Chadwick. They have the largest collection of Chadwick's writings, tapes of lectures, and memorabilia. They offer a membership with periodic newsletters.

Cheyenne Community Solar Greenhouse
3714 Whitney Rd.
Cheyenne, WY 82001

Perhaps the best model of a community greenhouse gardening program in the country.

City Farmer
801–318 Homer St.
Vancouver, B.C. V6B 2V3 Canada

For Canadian urban gardeners. Similar to the former Integral Urban House in Berkeley, CA.

Community Environmental Council
930 Miramonte Dr.
Santa Barbara, CA 93109

A great program geared toward developing a plan for environmentally sound food and energy systems for the greater Santa Barbara area. They do a variety of educational programs and have an internship program.

Cornell University Cooperative Extension—New York City
15 E. 26th St., 5th Floor
New York, NY 10010

The cooperative extension program for New York City, with an emphasis on community gardens.

The Cultivar
Agroecology Program
College Eight
University of California at Santa Cruz
Santa Cruz, CA 95064

One of the best journals for the unscientific to keep up with the latest research on sustainable agricultural and gardening methods. These people are doing some of the most important research in the country. Required reading.

Ecology Action of the Midpeninsula
Bio-Intensive Mini-Farming Program
2225 El Camino Real
Palo Alto, CA 94306

Still one of the most dedicated groups for promoting the biodynamic/French intensive method of gardening and nutritionally oriented gardening.

Elfin Permaculture
P.O. Box 202
Orange, MA 01364

The group that networks East Coast permaculture organizations. They offer and sponsor a variety of educational courses and do occasional permaculture design courses.

Emma Prusch Farm
647 S. King Road
San Jose, CA 95116

A restored heritage farm, offering a wide range of seminars and lectures on edible landscaping, gardening, and ornamental horticulture.

Farallones Institute
15290 Coleman Valley Rd.
Occidental, CA 95465

Formerly a leader in the development of renewable energy systems, organic gardening, and edible landscaping. Write for a listing of the current program(s). (The Integral Urban House is no longer a public facility, the Institute's work originates solely from the Rural Center site.)

Fruition
The Plan
P.O. Box 872
Santa Cruz, CA 95061

Promoting the planting of publicly accessible fruit and nut trees. Also, an emphasis on harvesting free food from public lands for a raw vegetable, fruit, and nut diet.

Goddard College School in Social Ecology
Plainfield, VT 05667

One of the oldest institutions applying art, science, and humanities to renewable energy issues and biological agriculture and gardening.

The Goodfruit Grower
1005 Tieton Dr.
Yakima, WA 98902

This commercial tree crops magazine comes from the heart of the Washington State apple growers' district. While the approach is entirely chemical, I subscribe because it has the best up-to-date information on high-density orchard techniques (the wave of the future).

Graham Center Seed Directory
Frank Porter Graham Center
Rte. 3, Box 95
Wadesboro, NC 28170

Fantastic network for information about genetic diversity, heirloom seeds and plants, and what is happening in national politics relative to sustainable agriculture.

Harrowsmith
The Creamery
Charlotte, VT 05445

Formerly published only in Canada, there is now an American edition. The in-depth articles, filled with the best photography possible, are outstanding. While each issue does not have a lot of articles on food production, the content and variety are fantastic. Subscribe to this one. (The Canadian version, which is great for all northern U.S. gardeners, is from Camden House Publishing Ltd., 7 Queen Victoria Rd., Camden East, Ontario, Canada K0K 1J0.)

Healthy Harvest: A Directory of Sustainable Agriculture and Horticulture Organization.
Susan Sanzone, ed.
Potomac Valley Press
Washington, DC, 1985.

A book published that is just like this appendix—only much more extensive and more up-to-date.

Henry Doubleday Research Association
Convent Lane
Bocking, Braintree, Essex, England

One of the best organizations in the world promoting and researching the details of organic gardening and farming. Excellent newsletter.

The Herbalist
The Herb Society of America
300 Massachusetts Ave.
Boston, MA 02115

The official newsletter of the national herb society. Each issue features one or more specific herb plants in detail. A good periodical for the generalist.

The Herb Quarterly
Newfane, VT 05345

An excellent periodical for the general reader.

Herb Society of America
300 Massachusetts Ave.
Boston, MA 02115

Excellent newsletter on an important topic.

Home Orchard Society
c/o Winnifred Fisher
24640 Wallen
Estacada, OR 97023

One of the better regional organizations for people who wish to preserve antique varieties of fruit trees and experiment with intensive home-orcharding.

Horticulture
755 Boylston St.
Boston, MA 02116

One of the most professional and colorful horticultural monthly magazines in America. More and more articles on edibles with each issue.

HortIdeas
Rt. 1
Gravel Switch, KY 40328

Perhaps the single most important periodical in my library. There is no faster way to keep up with the deluge of new horticultural information than by subscribing to this monthly. It abstracts the most fascinating articles from dozens and dozens of technical, trade, and lay publications. This publication gives you perhaps the best value for your money of any horticultural publication in print. More technically and scientifically oriented than *Avant Gardener*. Highly recommended.

IFOAM Bulletin
International Federation of Organic Agriculture Movements
Rodale Research Center
R.D. 1, Box 323
Kutztown, PA 19530

The journal for the International Federation of Organic Agriculture Movements. A good international network.

Institute for Local Self-Reliance
2425 18th St., NW
Washington, DC 20009

Excellent source for information about the nutritional aspects of food and gardening. Although they no longer do any "hands-on" garden projects, the institute does good work with governmental policy lobbying.

International Association for Education, Development and Distribution of Lesser Known Food Plants and Trees
P.O. Box 599
Lynwood, CA 90262

With a site in Mexico's Baja region, this group is doing very practical work with the locals. Paul Jackson is the director and an amazing source of botanical and gardening information.

International Dwarf Fruit Tree Association
Department of Horticulture
Michigan State University
East Lansing, MI 48824

This organization's quarterly and annual reports are perhaps the most important sources of information on the latest in dwarf fruit tree culture.

International Society of Arboriculture
Box 71
Urbana, IL 61801

The quarterly journal published by this association is the best way to keep abreast of the latest research in ornamental tree culture and maintenance.

International Tree Crops Institute USA, Inc.
Rte. 1
Black Lick Rd.
Gravel Switch, KY 40328

This is the American office of a worldwide group dedicated to the use of tree crops in farming (agroforestry). They have published a quarterly journal on occasion.

The Land Institute
Rte. 3
Salina, KS 67401

This group is single handedly developing a perennial gra.
the American grain belt. One of the most dedicated and serio.
groups in America, researching sustainable agriculture for its bioregion. Join this group and receive the quarterly newsletter, which outlines current research and political issues facing agriculture.

The Landscape Center
Miami-Dade Community College
11011 SW 104th St.
Miami, FL 33176

The only group in America that offers landscaping information in the manner of the owner-builder centers. It offers a range of workshops and lectures for owner-built landscapes: edible landscaping, energy-conserving landscaping, ornamental landscape design, freshwater-pond management, and organic gardening.

Living Off the Land
P.O. Box 2131
Melbourne, FL 32902

The newsletter put out by this informal network is the best source of information on tropical and semi-tropical food plants in the eastern half of the country.

Living Tree Center
P.O. Box 797
Bolinas, CA 94924

Publishes an informative catalog/newsletter oriented to saving and proliferating heritage tree crops. Also sells a wide range of antique apple tree varieties.

Longbranch Environmental Center
Rte. 2, Box 132
Leicester, NC 28748

A local organization promoting an environmentally sane way of living with nature and natural farming and gardening. Hosts a variety of workshops, including edible landscaping seminars.

Maine Organic Farmers and Gardeners Association
P.O. Box 188
Hallowell, ME 04347

Perhaps the best regional organization for promoting, watchdogging, and certifying organic farmers.

Maritime Permaculture Institute
P.O. Box 7611
Olympia, WA 98507

A good local, active, and long-lived group for the Pacific Northwest. Active in all aspects of permaculture—including mushroom cultivation, chestnut orcharding, and weeder geese management.

Merritt College
c/o Horticulture Department
12500 Campus Dr.
Oakland, CA 94619

Has integrated edible landscaping workshops and lectures into its horticulture program. Has a house and site developed much like the former Farallones Institute Integral Urban House.

Middle Atlantic Workers on Organic Farms (MAWOOF)
1601 Lakeside Ave., No. 607
Richmond, VA 23228

A regional network for organic farmers.

Missouri Botanical Gardens
P.O. Box 299
St. Louis, MO 63166–0299

One of the best botanical gardens in America. They are developing a four-million dollar demonstration project for edible landscaping, vegetable gardening, and owner-built residential ornamental landscaping. The educational department also hosts workshops in all the above topics.

The Mother Earth News
Eco-Village
105 Stoney Mountain Rd.
Hendersonville, NC 28739

The grand old dame of the back-to-the-land movement. Its magazine has been greatly improved from the days of the too-cute-to-be-useful articles. Much more emphasis on practical skills and realistic projects.

National Council for Therapy and Rehabilitation through Horticulture
9041 Comprint Ct., No. 103
Gaithersburg, MD 20877

Besides the purely therapeutic aspects of horticulture, many of the projects networked via this organization involve food production as an important aspect.

National Gardening Association
180 Flynn Ave.
Burlington, VT 05401

With its new format and gorgeous fullcolor on almost every page, this is one of my favorite monthly magazines. The articles are thorough, comprehensive, and well researched. The photography is exceptionally fine, illustrating many difficult details, such as beneficial and harmful insects. Required reading for all home gardeners and edible landscapers. Highly recommended.

Native Seeds/SEARCH
3950 W. New York Dr.
Tucson, AZ 85745

Besides selling heirloom seeds, this group's quarterly newsletter is an excellent way to be up-to-date on saving genetic diversity and heirloom seeds.

New Alchemy Institute
237 Hatchville Rd.
East Falmouth, MA 02536

One of the grandparent organizations of the alternative energy and appropriate technology movement. Still going strong after more than a decade of dedicated work. Hosts a variety of workshops—including edible landscaping, aquaculture, and organic greenhouse management. The demonstration site is the most diverse, well maintained, and informative in America. Become a member of this group and receive its excellent and informative quarterly newsletter. Top-notch organization.

New York State Fruit Testing Cooperative Association
Geneva, NY 14456

The annual catalog of tree crop varieties is also a nice little informative newsletter about diversity.

North American Fruit Explorers
c/o Mary Kurle
10 S. 055 Madison St.
Hindsdale, IL 60521
Madison, KY 42431

My favorite tree crop organization. All edible landscapers should have a subscription to the *Pomona*, a quarterly newsletter. The subscription rate ($8 per year) is the best deal in horticulture. This is also the oldest continuous network in America of fruit tree enthusiasts. I learn more about trees from this journal than I do anywhere else.

Northern California Fruit Growers Society
Box 27073 West Portal Sta.
San Francisco, CA 94116

A local chapter of the national rare fruit growers organization. Start a local chapter in your area.

Northern Nut Growers
4518 Holston Hills Rd.
Knoxville, TN 37914

The quarterly newsletter and annual are the best sources available on the latest in nut tree culture.

Organic Gardening Apprenticeship Program
33 E. Minor St.
Emmaus, PA 18049

Helps people find places to apprentice in organic gardening methods.

People, Food & Land Foundation
34756 Weymiller Rd.
Tollhouse, CA 93667

The best newly developing appropriate technology training and demonstration project. With a special emphasis on native foods and drought resistant food plants and growing techniques, these people are doing some of the most important work in the country. They offer a variety of workshops on edible landscaping, the culture and use of herbs, gourmet native food cookery, and alternative power systems. Their *Sun Mt. Research Center Bulletin* will keep you informed of all events. Their annual report is very educational, and worth a membership alone.

Permaculture Institute and Stanley/Tagari Publications
Box 96
Stanley, Tasmania, Australia 7331

The official international hub of the permaculture network. Writing to this institute is the best way to contact Bill Mollison, the "founder" of permaculture, and find out about his worldwide training programs.

Permaculture Institute of North America
6488 So. Maxwelton Rd.
Clinton, WA 98236

The official national network for permaculture enthusiasts. This central organization publishes an excellent quarterly newsletter that networks all regional permaculture groups, lists all training programs, coordinates the "certification" program, and has many informative articles. Many local and national workshops are sponsored by PINA, write for a complete listing—tell them Robert sent you. A group well worth supporting.

Pomona
c/o Mary Kurle
10 S. 055 Madison St.
Hinsdale, IL 60521

My favorite periodical on the topic of fruit and nut trees—their care, cultural tricks of the trade, and rare and new varieties. This is the best network in the country for people who want to exchange varieties of all kinds of fruit and nuts. One of the best values for your money in horticulture today.

RAIN Magazine/Rain Community Resource Center
2270 NW Irving
Portland, OR 97210

A valuable newsletter for keeping up with the latest trends in appropriate technology. The emphasis on food-production techniques has been mostly replaced by food-policy-related issues. The most recent focus is on the current fascination with computers as tools, data banks, local area networks, and all forms of networking.

Regenerative Agriculture Association
222 Main St.
Emmaus, PA 18049

Robert Rodale's most recently founded organization to effect both local and international food systems—to assist in the evolution toward regional, ecological self-reliance and less hunger.

Rodale Research Center
Box 323, R.D. 1
Kutztown, PA 19530

Where the Rodale "empire" does its most practical and scientific research. A fantastic example of what creative research can be done outside of the university land-grant (chemically biased) system. Serious edible landscapers should have copies of all their research reports on file.

Rodale's Organic Gardening
33 East Minor
Emmaus, PA 18049

This is still the most popular monthly for organic gardeners. With a new layout and editorial policy, there is more information on ornamentals and less on food crops. The magazine is much more realistic and not folksy-to-a-fault, like its older form. Still worth reading each month.

The Rural Education Center, Inc.
Stoneyfield Farm
Wilton, NH 03086

Networks people interested in organic gardening, sustainable farming, and edible landscaping in the New England area. Has offered workshops and lectures in the past, write for the current schedule.

Seed Banks Serving People, 1982
Meals for Millions
Box 42622
Tucson, AZ 85733

This is a very effective national and global organization. Dedicated to promoting food self-reliance, heirloom varieties, and stopping hunger in its tracks. The profits from Paul Newman's gourmet food products go to this helpful organization so that our consumption can help those less fortunate.

Seed Savers Exchange
R.R. 2
Princeton, MO 64673

This group's yearly is the bible on heirloom and antique seeds—the most effective way to share rare and endangered seed with others. Everyone should join and support this organization.

Southern Exposure Seed Exchange
P.O. Box 158
North Garden, VA 22959

Dedicated to preserving the seed diversity of the hot-and-humid American south.

Southern Organic Apprenticeship Program
Box 45
Utopia, TX 78884
(512) 966-3724

Their name says it all.

Steering Committee for Sustainable Agriculture
P.O. Box 1394
Davis, CA 95617

The sponsors of the annual Ecological Farming Conference each year near San Francisco, with over 500 participants. It also sponsors a series of on-the-farm tours of quality organic farms.

Tilth
4649 Sunnyside No.
Seattle, WA 98103

One of the oldest networks for regional interest in organic gardening, edible landscaping, sustainable agriculture, and permaculture. It has offered an extensive variety of courses in the past, write for current listings.

Tree People
12601 No. Mulholland Dr.
Los Angeles, CA 90210

The most impressive urban tree planting organization in America. These people coordinated the planting of more than one million smog-tolerant trees in the Los Angeles area in the year prior to the Olympics. They also offer a range of workshops on ornamental horticulture and edible landscaping. Write for the current listing of programs.

Urban Farm Institute Apprenticeship Program
7214 Blair Rd. NW
Washington, DC 20012

A new organization that trains apprentices in the context of an actual landscape business. After training some of the students have a chance to become partners in the business.

Volunteers in Technical Assistance (VITA)
3706 Rhode Island Ave.
Mount Ranier, MD 20822

One of the best appropriate technology organizations in the country. Has literature on everything from agricultural methods to mechanical devices.

Western Fruit Grower
Meister Publishing Company
37841 Euclid Ave.
Willoughby, OH 44094

While exclusively oriented to chemical orcharding, I read this monthly magazine to keep up on the latest on pruning, disease identification, and new varieties of fruits and nuts.

Whole Earth Review, formerly the *CoEvolution Quarterly*
P.O. Box 428
Sausalito, CA 94966

While the current emphasis is on computers, technology, and political issues, the magazine is still a good place to find out about the latest books on gardening and edible landscaping.

The Windstar Foundation
P.O. Box 286
Snowmass, CO 91654

The best group researching and demonstrating gardening techniques for high altitudes and short season areas. It offers workshops and apprenticeships that focus on greenhouse and coldframe cultivation.

Worldwatch Institute
1776 Massachusetts Ave. NW
Washington, DC 20036

This group's forte is articulating and educating people about important national and global environmental issues. Its series of reports is required reading for the serious environmentalist.

A

Acacia, for windbreak and firewood, 84
Acacia verticillata (Wattle)
 as nitrogen-fixing perennial, 291
 for windbreak, 71
Acarol, toxicity of, 20
Accent plants, design role, 42
Accumulator plants, 266–70
Achillea millefolium. See Yarrow
Acid soil
 lime for, 39
 plant indicators, 35, 36–38
Acres U.S.A. Primer, An (Walters, Jr. and Fenzau)
 on indicator plants, 35
 on weed management, 39
Actinidia chinensis; A. arguta. See Kiwi
Actinomycetes, soil depth and, 31
Aeration, for lawns, 10
African marigold. *See* Marigold
African trailing daisy, as poor insectary plant, 252
Agricultural extension services. *See* Extension services
Agricultural Testament, An (Howard), 261
Agrimony, as soil indicator, 36
Agropyron repens (Quack grass), as soil indicator, 36
Ailanthus altissima (Tree of heaven), as insectary plant, 252
Air, as soil component, 29, 30, 31
Air circulation
 dense plantings may inhibit, 121
 intercropping and, 134, 239
 for TODD® flats, 128
Akebia, fiveleaf (*Akebia quinata*), for shade, Appendix 4
Alan Chadwick Society, 118
Alder. *See Alnus* sp.
Aldrin, toxicity of, 20
Alexander, Christopher, 47, 50, 57, 61
Alfalfa (*Medicago sativa*)
 for bale gardening, 105
 as cover crop or green manure, 267
 disease, alfalfa mosaic virus, 287
 as disease host, 287
 as dynamic accumulator, 269
 as insectary plant, 252, 253
 intercropping success, with barley, 241
 as leguminous wildflower, 280
 as nitrogen source, 266, Appendix 5
 pests
  IPM for, 258
  as disease vectors, 288
 soil pH and, 274
 water use and root depth, 226
Alfalfa caterpillars, IPM for, 258
Alfalfa loopers, IPM for, 258
Alfalfa mosaic virus

 host plants for, 287
 insect vectors of, 288
Algae, soil depth and, 31
Alkaline soil
 plant indicators, 36–38
 sulfur for, 39
Allelopathy, 235–36, 238
Allergies, edible flowers and, 291, 292
Allium cepa var. *viviprium* (Egyptian top-set onion), 58, 59
Allium sativum. See Garlic
Allium schoenoprasum. See Chives
Allium sp. *See* Chives; Garlic; Onion
Almond (*Prunus amygdalus*)
 'All-in-One'
  chill requirement, 142
  as self-fruitful, 151
 average seasonal growth, 229
 chill requirement, 142
 choosing, by rootstock, 166
 clay soil problem, 193
 cold hardiness, 139
 diseases
  bacterial canker, 166
  crown gall, 166
  crown rot, 166, 194
  oak root fungus, 166
  rootstocks resistant to, 166
 drought-tolerant rootstocks, 166
 in Flores garden, 63, 64
 frost tolerance, 228
 'Garden Prince'
  chill requirement, 142
  flavor, 185
  in Malcolm-Neeb garden, 2
  pros and cons, 188
  ripening dates, 147
  as self-fruitful, 151
 genetic dwarf, 181, 183
  flavor, 185, flavor, 187
  pros and cons, 188
  size, 179
 grafted with peach, 64
 grafted with plum, 63, 64
 as hot-summer tolerant, 144
 low-chill varieties, 142
 'Ne Plus Ultra'
  chill requirement, 142
  ripening dates, 147
 nematode-resistant rootstocks, 166
 nitrogen requirements, 230, 231
 pest resistance, by rootstock, 166
 planting locations
  for pollination, 152
  separate from lawns, 284
 pollinizers required by, 151
 potassium/potash deficiency signs, 231
 pruning, open center style for, 213
 ripening dates, by variety, 147
 rootstocks, matching to soil types, 166
 self-fruitful cultivars, 151
 as spur-type tree, 204
 standard
  height and width, 180
  matching to soil types, 166
 water use and root depth,

 226
 yields, 53
Alnus sp. (Alder)
 intercropping with fruit trees, 242
 as nitrogen-fixing, 291
 rhombifolia
  for erosion prevention, 78
  winter shade cast by, 75
Aloysia triphyllia (Lemon verbena)
 as edible flower, 292
 in Flores garden, 64
Alpine strawberry. *See Fragaria* sp.
Althea rosea (Hollyhock)
 as edible flower, 292
 as fruit tree cover crop, 233
Altieri, Miguel, intercropping study, 237
Alyssum
 under fruit trees, 227
 in Malcolm-Neeb garden, 2
Amaranthus sp. (Amaranth; Pigweed)
 grain amaranth, 134
 hybridus (Pigweed), intercropping with corn, 242
 as insectary plant, 252
 intercropping, 133, 134
  with corn, 237, 242
 as invasive, 98
 as multi-purpose edible, 59
 nitrogen content and C:N ratio, Appendix 5
 as nitrogen-lover, 98
 nutritional value, 96
 as shade tolerant, 133
 retroflexus (Pigweed; Prostrate pigweed; Red root pigweed)
  as dynamic accumulator, 270
  as indicator plant, 35, 37
  intercropping with collards, 242
 water extract, to attract predators, 259
Ambivalent fruit trees, 151
Ambrosia artemisiifolia (Ragweed)
 as insectary plant, 252
 intercropping successes, 242
Amelanchier sp. (Serviceberry), shade tolerance, 284
Amendments. *See* Soil amendments
American bittersweet (-*Celastrus scadens*), for shade, Appendix 4
American persimmon. *See* Persimmon
American wild plum (*Prunus americana*)
 as edible windbreak, 69
 shade tolerance, 283
Amni visage (Toothpick weed), as insectary plant, 251
Ampelopsis brevipedunculata (Blueberry climber), for shade, Appendix 4
Anagallis arvensis (Eyebright; Scarlet Pimpernel)
 as dynamic accumulator, 269, 270
 as fruit tree cover crop, 280
 as soil indicator, 37
Anderson, Fred, 184
Andropogon virginicus L.

 (Broom sedge), reducing, 39
Anemones, ease of care, 54
Anethum graveolens. See Dill
Angelica (*Angelica* sp.)
 as fruit tree cover crop, 233
 as insectary plant, 251, 252
 as multi-purpose edible, 59
Angles of repose, Appendix 7
Angular leaf spot, insect vectors of, 288
Animal feed, multi-purpose plants for, 59
Anise (*Pimpinella anisum*)
 companion planting studies, 239, 240
 as insectary plant, 16, 251
 as multi-purpose edible, 59
Annuals
 indicator plant unsuitability, 35
 multi-purpose, 58, 59–60
Anredera cordifolia (Madeira vine), for shade, Appendix 4
Anthemis arvensis (Corn chamomile), as dynamic accumulator, 269
Anthemis cotula (Mayweed), as soil indicator, 37
Anthemis noblis (Chamomile), as edible flower, 292. *See also* Chamomile
Anthicid beetles, as beneficial predators, 246
Anthracnose
 drip irrigation reduces, 129
 London plane sycamore prone to, 44
Anticompanions, 235
Antigonon leptopus (Coral vine), as deciduous, Appendix 4
Antigonon leptopus (Rosa de montana), as evergreen, Appendix 4
Antisiphon valve, 130, 131
Ants
 as beneficial predators, 246
 predators and parasites of, 246, 247
 tansy and, 237
Aphid lions, for scale, 259
Aphid wasps, design to attract, 5
Aphids
 on apple, 166, 167, 247, 257
 beneficial insects against, 5, 12, 245–47, 252
  attracting, 248, 251–52, 287
 beneficial plant problem, 237–38
 as disease vectors, 288
 on fava beans, 248
 on fruit trees, nitrogen excess and, 286
 green peach (*Myzus persicae*)
  companion planting, with peppers, 239, 240
  as disease vectors, 287, 288
  intercropping successes, 242, 243
 potato varieties resistant to, 260
 intercropping for, 241, 242, 243
 as IPM example, 255–59
 on kale, close planting for,

 242
 nasturtiums and, 238, 248
 pear rootstock resistance, 173–74
 on peppers, companion planting studies, 239, 240
 pest control myth, 245
 positive view of, 19–20
 spinach variety resistant to, 260
 on walnut, weedy ground cover deters, 243
Apiaceae. *See* Umbelliferae
Apical (terminal) buds, 203
Apium graveolens (Wild celery), for berms, 79
Appetizer recipes
 Dried Persimmons with Curried Pecan Cream Cheese, 306
 Persimmon Pecan Appetizers, 306
Apple (*Malus* sp.)
 See also Fruit and nut trees
 'Akane'
  as disease resistant, 159
  ripening dates, 147
  size, 191
  as sunburn resistant, 144
 'Alexander'
  as cold hardy, 140
  holds well on tree, 147
  as keeper, 65
 alternate-bearing varieties, 211
 'Anna,' climate considerations, 142, 144
 'Anoka'
  as Linquist favorite, 65
  for flavor, 2
 antique, sources of, 155
 'Apple Babe,' pros and cons, 144, 188
 average seasonal growth, 229
 'Baldwin'
  as alternate-bearing, 211
  as good keeper, 147
 'Beacon'
  fire blight susceptibility, 156
  pollinizers for, 152
  size, 191
 'Beverly Hills'
  chill requirement, 142
  fire blight susceptibility, 156
 ripening dates, 147
 blossoms as edible, 292
 chill requirements, 142
 choosing, by rootstock, 166–67
 for cider, Linquist's favorites, 65
 cold hardy, 139, 140
 'Connell Red'
  as keeper, 65, 147
  pollinizers for, 152
  size, 191
 consistent-bearing varieties, 211–12
 'Cortland'
  as consistent bearer, 212
  fire blight susceptibility, 156
  pollinizers for, 152
  size, 191
 'Discovery'
  as disease resistant, 159
  size, 191
 disease-resistant root-

stocks, 166–67
disease-resistant varieties, 156–57, 158–59
mail-order source, 155
diseases
crown rot, 166–67, 194
fire blight, 156–57, 159, 285, 286
host plants to avoid, 287
powdery mildew, 158–59
scab, 158–59, 287
'Dorsett Golden'
chill requirement, 142
fire blight susceptibility, 156
'Double Red Jonathan'
pollinizers for, 152
size, 191
drought-tolerant rootstocks, 166–67
dwarf
life span, 179–80
size, 179
yields, 53
dwarfing rootstocks
climate and, 144
diseases and, 167, 194
drought tolerance, 167
for espalier, 222
matching to soil types, 167
pest resistance, 167
size reduction with, 181
staking needed for, 199
'Early Harvest'
fire blight susceptibility, 156
ripening dates, 147
'Early McIntosh,' disease resistance, 156, 159
effort rankings, 295
'Ein Shemer'
chill requirement, 142
pollinizer required by, 151
'Empire'
as fire blight resistant, 156
as sunburn resistant, 144
spollinizer for, 151, 152
size, 191, 192
espalier training, 222, 295
fire-blight-resistant varieties, listed, 156–57
'Fireside,' as keeper, 65, 147
flavor considerations, 185
in Flores garden, 64
'Gala'
size, 191
as sunburn resistant, 144
'Gallia Beauty'
pollinizers for, 152
size, 191
'Garden Delicious'
espaliered against wall, 83, 84
pros and cons, 144, 188
genetic dwarf, 181, 183
for espalier, 222
flavor, 185
pros and cons, 188
'Golden Delicious'
as alternate-bearing, 211
as fire blight resistant, 156
pollinizers for, 152
ripening dates, 147
size, 191
as sunburn resistant, 144
good keepers, 147
'Granny Smith'
chill requirement, 142
as consistent bearer, 212
as good keeper, 147
for flavor, 2
pollinizers for, 152
ripening dates, 147
size, 191
'Gravenstein'
as consistent bearer, 212
fire blight susceptibility, 156
pollinizer required by, 151
size, 192
'Hawaii'
as good keeper, 147
size, 191
'Holly'
disease resistance, 159
pollinizers for, 152

as hot-weather-damage susceptible, 144
'Hudson's Golden Gem'
disease resistance, 159
as keeper, 65, 147
'Idared'
disease susceptibility, 156, 159
as keeper, 147
pollinizers for, 152
size, 191
'Imperial Red Delicious'
pollinizers for, 152
size, 191
intercropping success, 241
'Jerseymac'
disease susceptibility, 159
pollinizers for, 152
'Jonafree'
as disease resistant, 159
pollinizers for, 152
'Jonagold'
pollinizers for, 151, 152
size, 191
'Jonamac'
disease susceptibility, 159
as keeper, 147
pollinizers for, 152
size, 191
'Jonathan'
as consistent bearer, 212
fire blight susceptibility, 156
'Jonee'
disease susceptibility, 159
size, 191
pollinizers for, 152
'Julyred'
disease susceptibility, 159
pollinizers for, 152
keepers, 65
'King'
as keeper, 147
pollinizer required by, 151
'Lawspur'
pollinizers for, 152
size, 191
'Liberty'
as disease resistant, 156, 159
pollinizers for, 152
life spans, 179–80
Linquist work with, 65–66
'Lodi'
fire blight susceptibility, 156
as keeper, 147
pollinizers for, 152
ripening dates, 147
size, 191
low-chill varieties, 142
'Macoun'
fire blight susceptibility, 156
as keeper, 147
pollinizers for, 152
size, 191
'Macspur'
pollinizers for, 152
size, 191
'McIntosh'
as consistent bearer, 212
as fire blight resistant, 156
pollinizer required by, 151
'Melrose'
disease susceptibility, 156, 159
pollinizers for, 152
size, 191
miniature rootstocks, characteristics, 167
mulching, 226
'Mulhall,' as keeper, 65, 147
'Mutsu'
chill requirement, 142
as consistent bearer, 212
disease resistance, 156, 159
pollinizers for, 151, 152
ripening dates, 147
size, 192
as sunburn resistant, 144
'Newtown Pippin'
fire blight susceptibility, 156

ripening dates, 147
size, 191
nitrogen requirements, 230, 231
'Northern Spy'
fire blight susceptibility, 156
pollinizers for, 151, 152
size, 192
oldtime varieties, sources of, 155
'Ozark Gold,' disease resistance, 156, 159
'Paulared'
pollinizers for, 152
size, 191
'Pearmain,' as keeper, 65, 147
pest control
intercropping successes, 241
rosy apple aphids and, 247, 257
with resistant roostocks, 166–67
weather monitoring for, 25
'Pettingill'
chill requirement, 142
ripening dates, 147
'Pink Pearl,' 308–9
Apple Tart (recipe), 308–9
cultural guidelines, 308
fire blight susceptibility, 156
planting locations, 47, 191–92, 284
pollination chart, 152
preventing hot-weather damage in, 144
'Prima'
disease resistance, 156, 159
pollinizers for, 152
ripening dates, 147
size, 191
'Priscilla'
disease resistance, 158, 159
size, 191
pruning
espalier method, 222
for hot-weather-damage prevention, 144
no-pruning style, 211
'Quinte'
disease resistance, 159
pollinizers for, 152
size, 191
'Red Baron'
disease resistance, 159
pollinizers for, 152
'Red Delicious'
pollinizer required by, 151
ripening dates, 147
as sunburn resistant, 144
'Red Haralson'
pollinizers for, 152
size, 191
'Red York'
pollinizers for, 152
size, 192
'Regent'
pollinizers for, 152
size, 191
'Rhode Island Greening'
as keeper, 147
pollinizers for, 152
size, 192
ripening dates, by variety, 147
'Roger's Red McIntosh'
pollinizers for, 152
size, 192
'Rome Beauty'
as consistent bearer, 212
fire blight susceptibility, 156, 157
rootstocks
see also dwarfing rootstocks; semi-dwarf rootstocks
disease susceptibility, 166–67, 194
for espalier, 222
hot-weather damage and, 144
matching to soil types, 166–67

miniatures from, 181
size variations, 192
root zones, 161, 162
self-pruning by, 204
semi-dwarf rootstocks
characteristics, 167
as sunburn tolerant, 144
yields, 53
'Smoothee'
pollinizers for, 152
size, 191
spacing, 191–92
'Spartan'
disease resistance, 156, 158
as keeper, 147
pollinizers for, 152
size, 191
'Spigold'
as fire blight resistant, 156
size, 192
'Spuree Rome'
pollinizers for, 152
size, 191
as spur-type tree, 204
'Spur Winter Banana'
size, 191
spacing, 192
standard rootstocks
characteristics, 166, 191–92
life span, 179–80
root zone, 162
size variations, 179, 180, 191–92
yields, 53
'Stayman Winesap'
as keeper, 147
pollinizer required by, 151
'Summerred'
fire blight susceptibility, 156
as keeper, 147
size, 191
as sunburn resistant, 144
sunburn, preventing, 144
'Sundale Spur Golden Delicious'
pollinizers for, 152
size, 191
'Sweet Delicious'
commercial problems, 65–66
as fire blight resistant, 156
as keeper, 65, 147
as Linquist favorite, 65, 66
thinning, with no-pruning method, 212
'Turley Winesap'
pollinizers for, 152
size, 191
'Tydeman's Red'
disease resistance, 156, 158, 159
pollinizers for, 152
size, 191
water core in, 65–66
'Wealthy'
as alternate-bearing, 211
fire blight susceptibility, 157
'Winesap'
as fire blight resistant, 156
as keeper, 147
pollinizer required by, 151
ripening dates, 147
'Winter Banana'
chill requirement, 142
as keeper, 65, 147
pollinizer required by, 151
'Wolf River'
disease resistance, 158
Linquist on, 65
'Yellow Bellflower'
chill requirement, 142
as fire blight resistant, 156
'Yellow Newtown'
as alternate-bearing, 211
size, 192
'Yellow Newtown Pippin,' as keeper, 147
'Yellow Transparent'
as alternate-bearing, 211
as cold hardy, 140
fire blight susceptibility,

156
as keeper, 147
yields, 53
Apple-of-Peru, companion planting studies, 239
Applesource, 155
Apricot (Prunus armeniaca)
See also Fruit and nut trees
average seasonal growth, 229
chill requirement, 142
choosing, by rootstock, 168
cold hardiness, 139
disease-resistant rootstocks, 168
dwarf, yields, 53
'Earligold'
chill requirement, 142
pollinizer requirement, 151
in Flores garden, 63, 64
frost tolerance, 228
'Golden Amber'
chill requirement, 142
ripening dates, 147
grafted on plum, 63
low-chill varieties, 142
nitrogen requirements, 230
pest-resistant rootstock, 168
planting locations, 45, 284
pruning, 213, 218
rootstocks, matching to soil types, 168
'Royal'
chill requirement, 142
ripening dates, 147
self-fruitful varieties, 151
semi-dwarf, yields, 53
as spur-type tree, 204
standard rootstocks
characteristics, 168
height and width, 180
yields, 53
winter shade cast by, 75
yields, 53
Apulla sp. See Snakeflies
Arachis hypogae (Peanuts)
intercropping success, 242
nitrogen gathered by, 266
Araujia sericifera (White bladder flower), for shade, Appendix 4
Arbors, 1
in Mexican-American gardens, 63
patio caution about, 83
Arbutus unedo (Strawberry tree)
as disease resistant, 155
ease of care, 44, 45
as shade tolerant, 283
Arctium lappa (Burdock), as invasive, 98
Arctium minus (Burdock)
as dynamic accumulator, 269
as fruit tree cover crop, 233
for no-till gardens, 101
Argus tortoise beetle, intercropping success, 243
Aristolochia durior (Dutchman's pipe), for shade, Appendix 4
Armillaria root rot
in fruit trees, from overwatering, 285
host plants for, 287
walnut rootstock resistance, 177
Armored scales, predators of, 247
Arrowhead (Sagitarria latifolia), for berms, 79
Arrowroot, as dynamic accumulator, 269
Artemisia abrotanum (Southernwood)
companion planting studies, 239
for pest control, 259
Artemisia absinthium (Wormwood), as allelopathic, 238, 239
Artemisia biennis (Biennial wormwood, as soil indicator, 38
Artemisia dracunculus (Tarragon), shade tolerance, 284

Artemisia maritima, as soil indicator, 36
Artemisia sp., as insectary plants, 251
Artemesia vulgaris (Mugwort), as soil indicator, 37
Artichoke
　for color, 1
　for downspout outlets, 83
　as insectary plant, 251
　as lawn tolerant, 285
Asarum caudatum (Wild ginger)
　for berms, 79
　as shade tolerant, 283
Asclepius syriaca (Milkweed), as soil indicator, 37
Ash (*Fraxinus holotricha*), winter shade cast by, 75
Ashes, for pest control, 256
Asian pear; Pear apple (*Pyrus pyrifolia; P. ussuriensis*), **299–300**
　chill requirements, 142
　cultural guidelines, 299
　designing with, 1, 299
　effort ranking, 299
　good keepers, 147
　'Hosui,' described, 2
　as hot-weather-damage susceptible, 144
　low-chill varieties, 142
　as nondwarfable, 180
　recipes using, **299–300**
　ripening dates, by variety, 148
　as spur-type tree, 204
Asian Pear Chutney (recipe), **299**
Asian Pears Poached in Red Wine (recipe), **300**
　as shade tolerant, 283
Asimina triloba. *See* Papaw
Asparagus
　for downspout outlets, 83
　root zones, 135
Asparagus, ornamental (*Asparagus setaceus*), for shade, Appendix 4
Asparagus beetles, IPM for, 258
Asperula odorata (Sweet woodruff; Woodruff)
　as edible flower, 292
　as shade tolerant, 283
Assassin bugs, as beneficial, 246
　plants to attract, 252
Association, as design element, 42
Aster
　ease of care, 54
　as insectary plant, 251
　soil indicators, 36
Asteraceae, beneficial insects lured by, 251, 252
Aster yellows
　host plants for, 287
　insect vectors of, 288
Astilbe sp. (Meadow sweet)
　as dynamic accumulator, 269
　as soil indicator, 37
Astragalus (Locoweed), as leguminous wildflower, 280
Astroturf™ as pest control, 238
Asymmetry, as design element, 42
Atriplex hastata (Fat hen)
　as dynamic accumulator, 269
　as soil indicator, 36
Atriplex lentiformis, as nitrogen-fixing perennial, 291
Atriplex sp. (Saltbush), as insectary plant, 252
Autumn olive (*Elaeagnus umbellata*)
　as nitrogen-fixing, 291
　as windbreak, 69
Aviary wire, for deterring rodents, 45, 197
Avocado (*Persea americana*)
　chill requirement, 142
　choosing, by rootstock, 168
　clay soil problem, 193

disease resistance, 168, 194
　as hot-summer tolerant, 144
　Massida's cultivation of, 63
　nitrogen requirements, 230
　ripening dates, northern California, 147
　rootstocks, characteristics, 168, 180
　as self-fruitful, 151
Azimuth chart, using, 26
Azotobacter
　beneficial effects from, 108, 126
　honeydew used by, 19
　as seed inoculant, 125–26
　source of, 126

B

Baby blue eyes (*Nemophila inignis*), as insectary plant, 252
Baccharis pilularis (Coyote bush), as insectary plant, 252
Bacteria
　inoculants, 125–26
　soil depth and, 31
Bacterial blights, host plants for, 287
Bacterial canker (*Pseudomonas syringae*)
　pruning caution, 208
　rootstocks resistant to
　　almond, 166
　　apricot, 168
　　chery, 169
　　peach/nectarine, 171–72
　　plum/prune, 175–76
Bacterial leaf spot (*Xanthomonas prunii*), peaches resistant to, 158
Bacterial wilt, insect vectors of, 288
Bagworms (*Thyridopteryx ephemeraeformis*), 44, 258
Baked Quinces Flambé (recipe), **308**
Balance, as design element, 42
Bale gardening, 105–6
Balsam apple; Balsam pear (*Momordica balsamina; M. charantia*), for quick shade, 73
Bamboo (*Bambusa* sp.)
　for cooling hedg, 74
　as lawn tolerant, 285
Bamboo (*Phyllostachys* sp.), for cooling hedge, 74
Banana, 64, 151
Banks. *See* Berms
Banks, C.J.
Bark, as fruit tree mulch, 232
Barley
　azotobacter inoculant for, 126
　as cover crop or green manure, 267, 273, 278
　as disease host, 287
　intercropping success, 241, 243
Basil
　companion planting studies, 239, 240
　lemon, for flavor, 2
　planning area for, 53
　root zones, 135
　tomatoes and, 237
Baskets, plant sources for, 39
Bastard trenching, 107
　for green manuring, 275
Bat guano, nutrient percentages, 230
Bay, California, for downspout outlets, 83
Beach plum (*Prunus maritima*)
　as disease-resistant, 155
　as low-effort edible, 45
Bean, hyacinth (*Dolichos lablab*), for shade, 73, Appendix 4
Beanfly, intercropping success, 242
Bean leaf beetle, companion planting myth, 239
Beans

aphids increased yield of, 20
companion planting, 239, 240, 265–66
　as cover crop or green manure, 267
diseases
　host plants to avoid, 287
　insect vectors, 288
growing on trellises, 134
inoculants for, 125, 126
intercropping, 133, 241, 242
Kentucky Wonder pole, as shade tolerant, 133
kidney, root zones, 135
lima
　disease host plants, 287
　root zones, 134, 135
marigolds as allelopathic to, 239
mung, as cover crop or green manure, 267
as nitrogen fixer, 110
for no-till gardens, 101
peas and, as myth, 239
pests
　companion planting studies, 239, 240
　disease vectors, 288
　intercropping successes, 241
　grassy weeds to control, 259
　varieties resistant to, 260
planting before potatoes, 110
scarlet runner (*Phaseolus coccineus*), for shade, Appendix 4
snap
　nitrogen requirements, 231
　companion planting studies, 239
　surface cultivation vs. single-dug yields, 110
　for quick shade, 73
　as shade tolerant, 133
　surface cultivation vs. single-dug yields, 110
Beans, bell, as cover crop, 273
Beans, fava. *See* Fava beans
Beans, field (*Pisum arvensis*), nitrogen gathered by, 266
Beans, soy. *See* Soybeans
Beans, velvet. *See* Velvet beans
Bedding plants, under fruit trees, 227, 232
Bedrock, 30, 31
Beds
　BFI, 115, 116
　from hay bale gardening, 106
　preparing, time requirements, 55
　size considerations, 46
Bee balm (*Monarda didyma*)
　as edible flower, 292
　as multi-purpose edible, 59
　as shade tolerant, 283
Bee flies, as beneficial predators, 246
Beefwood (*Casuarinus* sp.), as nitrogen-fixing, 291
Bees
　attracting, 5–6, 58, 59, 114
　parasites of, 246, 247
　as pollinators, 114
Beet family (Chenopodiaceae), preventing cross-pollination among, 102
Beetles, predators and parasites of, 246
Beets (*Beta vulgaris*)
　diseases, insect vectors, 288
　in Flores garden, 64
　as fruit tree cover crop, 233
　intercropping, 64, 133
　nitrogen requirements, 231
　preventing cross-pollination in, 102
　as quick-maturing, 138
　root zones, 134, 135
　as shade tolerant, 133
　sugar, azotobacter inoculant

for, 126
　surface cultivation vs. single-dug yields, 110
Beggar-tick (*Bidens pilosa*), intercropping with corn, 242
Beggarweed (*Desmodium purpureum*)
　as cover crop or green manure, 267
　as nitrogen-fixing bacteria sign, 274
Bell beans, as cover crop, 273
Bellflower (*Campanula* sp.), as soil indicator, 36
Bellis perennis (Daisy; English daisy)
　as edible flower, 292
　as soil indicator, 36
Beneficial insects, 245–53
　See also specific insects
　companion plant locations, 47
　designing for, 5–6
　flies as, 237
　plant choices for attracting, 39, 59, 84, 247–53
　spraying destroys, 256
　at Village Homes, 12
Beneficial plants, 237–43
Ben Meadows Company, 24, 25
Berms, 78–79
Bermuda grass, control expensive, 46
Berries, yields, 53. *See also* specific kinds
Berry, Wendell, on kindly use, 15
Beta vulgaris. *See* Beets
Betula sp. (Birch), winter shade by, 75
Beverage recipe, Kiwicoladas, **304**
BFI. *See* Biodynamic French intensive gardening
Bidens pilosa (Beggar-tick), intercropping with corn, 242
Big-eyed bugs, 246, 252
Bignonia capreolata (Cross vine), for shade, Appendix 4
Bindweed (*Convolvulus* sp.), as soil indicator, 36
Biodynamic French intensive gardening (BFI), 15–16, 115–21
　crop choice for, 118–19, 121
　cultural guidelines, 115, 116, 121
　energy conservation with, 116–17
　history of, 115
　interplanting in, 116
　maintenance considerations, 121
　nature's models for, 115–16
　space between plantings in, 115, 116
　time and effort required for, 55, 117
　training required for, 117, 118
　when not to use, 118–19, 121
　when to use, 118
　yields per area with, 51
Biointensive gardening. *See* Biodynamic French intensive gardening
Biological husbandry, concept of, 15–16
Biological magnification, 19
Biological zones, compared, 13
Biomass, environment and, 12, 13
Birch (*Betula* sp.), winter shade by, 75
Bird's-foot trefoil (*Lotus* sp.)
　as cover crop, 273
　under fruit trees, 280, 285
　for downspout outlets, 83
　for herbal lawns, 10
　as leguminous wildflower, 280
Birds

for, 126
　surface cultivation vs. single-dug yields, 110
　fencing out, genetic dwarf trees, 186
　as Japanese beetle predators, 259
　planning for sacrifice to, 52
Bitter melon, for quick shade, 73
Bittersweet, American (*Celastrus scadens*), for shade, Appendix 4
Black aphids, beneficial plant problem, 237–38
Blackberry (*Rubus* sp.)
　for berms, 79
　chill requirement, 142
　cultural hints, 286
　for downspout outlets, 83
　for erosion prevention, 78
　intercropping with grapes, 242, 259
　for no-till gardens, 101
　shade tolerance, 283
　wild, as favorite no-till fruit, 96
　yields, 53
Black cherry (*Prunus seratonia*), shade tolerance, 283
Black cutworms, in corn, 242
Black-eyed Susan vine (*Thunbergia alata*), for quick shade, 73
Blackflies, insectary plant study, 253
Black henbane (*Hyscyamus niger*), as soil indicator, 37
Blackline disease, walnut rootstock resistance, 177
Black locust (*Robinia pseudoacacia*), as multi-purpose plant, 59, 84
Black medic. *See Medicago lupulina*
Black mulberry. *See* Mulberry
Black mustard. *See* Mustard
Black nightshade (*Solanum nigrum*), for no-till gardens, 101
Black plastic mulch, for solar fumigation, 194
Black raspberry (*Rubus occidentalis*), shade tolerance, 283
Black scale, parasites of, 247
Black walnut. *See* Walnut
Black willow (*Salix* sp.), as soil indicator, 38
Bladderwrack, as dynamic accumulator, 269
Blight
　insect vectors of, 288
　on walnut, 159
Blister rust, 103
Blood, nitrogen content and C:N ratio, Appendix 5
Blood meal
　for fruit trees, 194, 229, 230
　for hay bale garden, 105
　for lawns, 10
　nutrient percentages, 230
　in potting mix, 127
Bloom sequence, data gathering on, 27, 63
Blossom-end rot, host plants for, 287
Blueberry (*Vaccinium*)
　chill requirements, 142
　as disease-resistant, 155
　for downspout outlets, 83
　ease of care, 45
　as lawn tolerant, 285
　lowbush (*Vaccinium angustifolium*), shade tolerance, 284
Blueberry climber (*Ampelopsis brevipedunculata*), for shade, Appendix 4
Blue Cheese Dressing with Garlic (recipe), **297**
Bluegrass, Kentucky, nitrogen content and C:N ratio, Appendix 5
Bok choy, preventing cross-pollination in, 102
Bone meal
　cost factors, 229
　for fruit trees, 197, 198, 232
　for hay bale garden, 105

nutrient content, 230, Appendix 5
as phosphorus source, 231
as potassium/potash source, after potato harvest, 110
in potting mix, 127
in sheet composting, 97
Borage (*Borago officinalis*)
as cover crop, 278
as dynamic accumulator, 269
as edible flower, 292, 296
intercropping with, 133
for color, 238
as multi-purpose edible, 59
for no-till gardens, 101, 102
in recipe, **296**
root zones, 135
as shade tolerant, 133
Bordeaux solution, on pruning cuts, 208
Borders
comfrey for, 281
corn salad for, 303
cover crops as, 278
Borers, fruit tree, 200. *See also* Peach tree borer
Boron, accumulator plant, 270
Boston ivy (*Parthenocissus quinquefolia*), for shade, Appendix 4
Botanical insecticides, 19, 20
in IPM, 256, 258, 259
Botryosphaeria (Gummosis), 158
Bougainvillea (*Bougainvillea spectabilis*), for shade, Appendix 4
Bower vine (*Pandorea jasminoides*), for shade, Appendix 4
Brachytic dwarfism, 183
Bracken, eastern (*Pteridium aquifolium*)
as dynamic accumulator, 269
as soil indicator, 36
Braconid wasps, 247
breeding and temperature, 256
pests controlled by, 259
plants to attract, 5, 252
Bradford, Norman, 184
Brady, N.C., 261, 262
Brambles, intercropping with fruit trees, 242
Brassica hapus. See Rape
Brassica oleracea. See Collards; Kale
Brassicas
See also Broccoli; Brussels sprouts; Cabbage; Cauliflower; Collards; Kale; Mustards
diseases, host plants to avoid, 287
intercropping successes, 241
for no-till gardens, 110
planting nitrogen fixer before, 110
Brassica sp., 'Romanesco, **297–98**. *See also* Brassicas; Mustards
Bread, nitrogen content and C:N ratio, Appendix 5
Bricks
amount needed, for flat work or walls, Appendix 7
for cooling, 74
Bridal bower, as dynamic accumulator, 269
Broad-leaved dock (*Rumex obtusifolius*), as dynamic accumulator, 269
Broccoli
See also Brassicas; 'Romanesco'
BFI unsuited to, 119
companion planting studies, 239, 240
intercropping with, 133, 242, 243
nitrogen requirements, 231
in no-till gardens, slug or snail problems, 103
pests, cabbageworms, 240
pests, imported cab-

bageworm, companion planting studies, 239
planting with lettuce, in BFI, 116
preventing cross-pollination in, 102
self-seeding caution, 101
as shade tolerant, 133
Brome grass, field, as cover crop or green manure, 267
Brooks, Dr. R.R., 266
Broom drops, as dynamic accumulator, 269
Broom sedge (*Andropogon virginicus L.*), reducing, 39
Brown rot (*Monilinia laxa*), in fruit trees
from overwatering, 285
peach varieties resistant to, 158
sanitation and, 257
Brown, Randy Lee, 140
Brussels sprouts
green ground cover for, 238, 241
intercropping with, 133, 241
pests control successes, 238, 241
planting after fava beans, 110
preventing cross-pollination in, 102
as shade tolerant, 133
Bryophyta sp. (Mosses), as soil indicator, 37
Buckeye, California, leaf drop role, 21
Buckman, H.O., 261, 262
Buckwheat
as cover crop or green manure, 267, 273, 275
as insectary plant, 273
Buckwheat (*Fagopyrum esculentum*)
as dynamic accumulator, 269
as insectary plant, 252
Buckwheat, California (*Eriogonum* sp.), as insectary plant, 252
Buffalo berry (*Shepherdia canadensis*), shade tolerance, 283
Building. See Construction
Bupleurum fruticosum (Mediterranean umble), as insectary plant, 252
Bur clover (*Medicago hispida*)
as cover crop or green manure, 267
under fruit trees, 285
as leguminous wildflower, 280
as nitrogen-fixing bacteria sign, 274
Burdock (*Arctium minus*)
as dynamic accumulator, 269
as fruit tree cover crop, 233
for no-till gardens, 101
Burdock (*Arctium lappa*), as invasive, 98
Burnet. See Salad burnet
Buttercup (*Ranunculus acris*; *R. repens*)
as compost material, nitrogen content and C:N ratio, Appendix 5
as soil indicator, 36
Butterflies
marigolds and, 237
parasites of, 246
Butternut squash
as hot-summer tolerant, 144
root system, 161
Buying drip equipment, 130–32
Buying fruit and nut trees, 155, 198
Buying windbreak trees or shrubs, 70–71

C

Cabbage
See also Brassicas
azotobacter inoculant for,

126
companion planting studies, 238, 239, 240
as compost material, nitrogen content and C:N ratio, Appendix 5
effort ranking, 295
ground covers with, 285
intercropping with, 133, 242, 243
mulching, research on, 240
nasturtiums and, 238, 248
nitrogen requirements, 231
in no-till gardens, slug or snail problems, 103
pest-resistant varieties, 260
pests, aphids, 242, 248
pests, cabbage butterflies, 239
pests, cabbage maggots, 260
pests, cabbage root flies, 242
pests, cabbage root maggots, 260
pests, diamondback moths, 239, 242
pests, flea beetles, 239, 240
pests, imported cabbage butterflies, 242
pests, imported cabbageworms, 240
preventing cross-pollination in, 102
root zones, 135
self-seeding caution, 101
as shade tolerant, 133
surface cultivation vs. single-dug yields, 110
yields, 239, 240
Cabbage aphids. See Aphids
Cabbage butterflies
companion planting studies, 239
intercropping successes, 241, 242
IPM for, 258, 259
Cabbage family (Cruciferae), preventing cross-pollination among, 102
Cabbage loopers
on cauliflower, 240, 242
IPM for, 258, 259
Cabbage maggots, 260
Cabbage moths, 241
Cabbage root flies, 242
Cabbage root maggots, 260
Cabbageworms, 240, 242
imported, 239, 240
Calamus, as dynamic accumulator, 269
Calcium
accumulator plants, 268, 269–70
comfrey as source of, 281
role of, 262
Calendula (*Calendula officinalis*)
companion planting studies, 239
dead-heading time required, 54
as edible flower, 292, 296
under fruit trees, 227
as insectary plant, 251, 252
for intercropping, 133
as multi-purpose plant, 58
for no-till gardens, 101
in recipe, **296**
as shade tolerant, 133
California bay, for downspout outlets, 83
California buckeye. See Buckeye, California
California buckwheat (*Eriogonum* sp.), as insectary plant, 252
California coffeeberry (*Rhamnus californica*), as insectary plant, 252
Calonyction aculeatum (Moonflower), for quick shade, 73
Camellia (*Camellia sasanqua*), for shade, Appendix 4
Camellia sinensis (Tea), as shade tolerant, 283
Camium amplexicaule (Hen-

bit), as soil indicator, 37
Campanula sp. (Bellflower), as soil indicator, 36
Camphorweed (*Heterotheca subaxillaris*), as insectary plant, 252
Campion (*Lychnis alba*), as soil indicator, 36
Campsis radicans (Trumpet creeper), as deciduous, Appendix 4
Campsis radicans (Trumpet vine), as evergreen, Appendix 4
Canada thistle (*Cirsium arvense*)
as dynamic accumulator, 270
as soil indicator, 38
Candytuft (*Iberis* sp.)
as insectary plant, 252
intercropping with brassicas, 241
Cane fruits
cultural guidelines, 286
as lawn tolerant, 285
pruning, 286
Cankerworms, predators of, 246
Canning, reducing need for
with dwarf trees, 181
with genetic dwarf fruit trees, 185–86
by seasonal fruit eating, 147
Cantaloupe
nitrogen requirements, 231
for quick shade, 73
Capsella bursa-pastoris. See Shepherd's purse
Captan, 2
Caragana arborescens (Siberian peashrub)
as multi-purpose plant, 59, 60
as nitrogen-fixing perennial, 291
as windbreak, 69
Caragreen, as dynamic accumulator, 269
Caraway (*Carum carvi*)
cover crop problems, 278
as dynamic accumulator, 269
as insectary plant, 251
as multi-purpose edible, 59
Carbon-to-nitrogen ratios, for sheet composting, 97
Cardaria draba (Field peppergrass), as soil indicator, 37
Cardboard, as weed-killer, 96, 97, 102, 108
Cardinal climber (*Quamoclit sloteri*), for quick shade, 73
Cardoon
for downspout outlets, 83
as insectary plant, 251
Carduus nutans (Nodding thistle)
as dynamic accumulator, 270
as soil indicator, 38
Carissa edulis; *C. grandiflora*. See Natal plum
Carnation. See *Dianthus* sp.
Carob (*Ceratonia siliqua*)
for cooling hedge, 74
as disease resistant, 155
ease of care, 44, 45
as edible windbreak, 69
Carolina jessamine (*Gelsemium sempervirens*), for shade, Appendix 4
Carolina wild cherry (*Prunus caroliniana*), as windbreak, 69
Carpet, as path mulch, 45, 47
Carpetweed (*Mollugo verticillata*), as soil indicator, 36
Carrot (*Daucus carota*)
companion planting studies, 240
as compost material, 269, Appendix 5
diseases
host plants to avoid, 287, 288

insect vectors, 288
as dynamic accumulator, 269
effort ranking, 295
as insectary plant, 251, 252, 253
intercropping with, 134, 242
pests
carrot flies, 240, 242
carrot maggots, 288
carrot rust flies, 256–57
preventing cross-pollination in, 102
root zones, 134, 135, 136
wild
as disease host, 287, 288
as fruit tree cover crop, 233, 280
as insectary plant, 251
intercropping with vegetables, 243
Japanese beetle repelled by, 243
as soil indicator, 36
Carrot flies, 240, 242
Carrot maggots, host plants for, 288
Carrot rust flies, 256–57
Carum carvi (Caraway), as dynamic accumulator, 269
Carya illinoiensis. See Pecan
Casimiroa edulis. See Sapote
as disease resistant, 155
as hot-summer tolerant, 144
as low-effort perennial, 45
Cassia obtusifolia (Sicklepod), intercropping with soybeans, 243
Cassia sp. (Sennas)
intercropping with soybeans, 243
as nitrogen-fixing perennial, 291
Castanea mollissima. See Chestnut
Casuarinus sp. (Beefwood), as nitrogen-fixing, 291
Catalina cherry (*Prunus lyonii*), for cooling hedge, 74
Catchfly, night-flowering (*Silene noctiflora*), as soil indicator, 36
Caterpillars
marigolds and, 237
positive role of, 21
predators and parasites of, 5, 16, 246, 247
Cat-facing, in strawberries, 287
Catnip
companion planting studies, 239, 240
as disease host, 287
as intercrop competition, 238
Cattail (*Typha latifolia*)
for berms, 79
for downspout outlets, 83
as dynamic accumulator, 269
edible portion, 79, 292
for erosion control, 11, 78
shade tolerance, 283
as soil indicator, 35, 36
Cauliflower
See also Brassicas
companion planting studies, 240
early, as quick-maturing, 138
intercropping with, 133, 137, 242
late, as slow-maturing, 138
in no-till gardens, slug or snail problems, 103
pests, intercropping successes, 240, 242
preventing cross-pollination in, 102
root zones, 134, 135, 136
self-seeding caution, 101
as shade tolerant, 133
surface cultivation vs. single-dug yields, 110
Ceanothus americanus (New Jersey tea), as nitrogen-fixing, 291

Ceanothus cordulatus (Mountain whitethorn), as nitrogen-fixing, 291
Cedar
  as disease host, 287
  windbreak suitability, 69
Cedar apple rust
  apple varieties resistant to, 159
  host plants for, 287
Celandine, as soil indicator, 36
Celastrus scadens (American bittersweet), for shade, Appendix 4
Celeriac
  as insectary plant, 251
  preventing cross-pollination in, 102
Celery
  diseases
    host plants to avoid, 287
    insect vectors, 288
  as insectary plant, 251
  intercropping with, 133, 134
  nitrogen requirements, 231
  preventing cross-pollination in, 102
  as shade tolerant, 133
  as slow-maturing, 138
  wild (*Apium graveolens*), for berms, 79
Celery mosaic virus, 287, 288
Celtis australis (European hackberry), winter shade cast by, 75
Celtis occidentalis (Hackberry), as windbreak, 69
Celtuce, as multi-purpose edible, 59
Cement paths, 47
Centaurea cyanus (Cornflower), as fruit tree cover crop, 280
Centaurea nigra (Knapweed), as soil indicator, 37
Central leader pruning, 217–18
Century, as dynamic accumulator, 269
Ceratonia siliqua. See Carob
Cercis occidentalis (Redbud), as nitrogen-fixing perennial, 291
Cercocarpus montanus (Mountain mahogany), as nitrogen-fixing, 291
Cercospora leaf spot, insect vectors of, 288
Chadwick, Alan
  BFI and, 115
  on soil air, 31
Chalcid wasps, 246, 247
  plants to attract, 252
Chamomile
  Anthemis nobilis, as edible flower, 292
  corn (*Anthemis arvensis*)
    as dynamic accumulator, 269
    as soil indicator, 36
    as cover crop, 278
    in Flores garden, 64
  German (*Chamomilla recutita*)
    as disease host, 287, 288
    as dynamic accumulator, 269
    as soil indicator, 36
    for herbal lawns, 10
  Matricaria chamomilla, as edible flower, 292
  as sitting bench, 1
  as edible flower, 292
Chard
  for intercropping, 133
  red, designing with, 1, 2
  as shade tolerant, 133
  Swiss, preventing cross-pollination in, 102
Chase, J.L.H., 109, 110
Chayote (*Sechium edule*), 300–301
  cultural guidelines, 300
  as disease resistant, 155
  ease of care, 45, 300
  as eggplant or zucchini substitute, 59
  as multi-purpose edible, 58, 59

recipes using, 300–301
  for shade, 73, Appendix 4
Chayote Parmigiana (recipe), 300–301
Chayote Pickles (recipe), 301
Chemical fertilizers, inoculants and, 125
Chenopodiaceae (Beet family), preventing cross-pollination among, 102
Chenopodium album. See Lamb's-quarters
Chenopodium ambrosioides (Mexican tea)
  intercropping with corn, 242
  as insectary plant, 252
Cherimoya, Massida's greenhouse-grown, 63
Cherry, black (*Prunus seratonia*), shade tolerance, 283
Cherry, Carolina wild (*Prunus caroliniana*), as windbreak, 69
Cherry, Catalina (*Prunus lyonii*), for cooling hedge, 74
Cherry, cornelian (*Cornus mas*), shade tolerance, 284
Cherry, ground. See Ground cherry
Cherry, hollyleaf (*Prunus ilicifolia*)
  for cooling hedge, 74
  as multi-use plant, 58
  wild
    for cooling hedge, 74
    as edible windbreak, 69, 71
Cherry, Nanking (*Prunus tomentosa*)
  as disease resistant, 155
  as low-effort perennial, 45
Cherry, sour (*Prunus cerasus*)
  chill requirement, 142
  as cold hardy, 139
  as nondwarfable, 180
  root zone, 161
  as self-fruitful, 151
  shade tolerance, 284
Cherry, Surinam, Massida's greenhouse-grown, 63
Cherry, sweet (*Prunus avium*; *Prunus cerasus* rootstocks)
  average seasonal growth, 229
  'Bing'
    pollination for, 151, 153
    ripening dates, 148
  chill requirements, 142
  choosing, by rootstock, 169
  clay soil problem, 193
  cold hardiness, 139
  designing with, 1
  as disease host, 287
  disease-resistant rootstocks, 169
  diseases
    bacterial canker, 169
    crown gall, 169
    crown rot, 169, 194
    host plants to avoid, 287, 288
    insect vectors, 288
    oak root fungus, 169
    verticillium wilt, 169
  double fruits on, from hot weather, 144
  dwarf, yields, 53
  'Early Burlat'
    as pollinizer, 151
    ripening dates, 148
    in Flores garden, 64
  frost tolerance, 228
  'Garden Bing'
    pros and cons, 188
    ripening dates, 148
    as self-fruitful, 151
  genetic dwarf, 181, 183
    pros and cons, 185, 187, 188
    size, 179
  hot weather problems, 144
  'Lambert'
    pollinizers for, 153
    ripening dates, 148
  'Larian'
    as pollinizer, 151

ripening dates, 148
  nitrogen requirements, 230
  pest-resistant rootstocks, 169
  planting locations, separate from lawns, 284
  pollination requirements, 151, 153
  pruning, open center style for, 213
  'Republican'
    as pollinizer, 151
    ripening dates, 148
  rootstocks, matching to soil types, 169
  'Sam,' pollination, 151, 153
  self-fruitful cultivars, 151
  as spur-type plant, 204
  standard, characteristics, 53, 169, 180
  'Stella'
    as pollinizer, 153
    ripening dates, 148
    as self-fruitful, 151
  'Van'
    pollination, 151, 153
    ripening dates, 148
    yields, 53
Cherry, Western sand (*Prunus besseyi*)
  as disease resistant, 155
  as low-effort perennial, 45
Cherry, wild, for erosion control, 11
Cherry eleagnus (*Elaeagnus multiflora*), as nitrogen-fixing, 291
Cherry leaf spot, hosts for, 287
Cherry plum
  ripening dates, 148
  'Stark Giant,' as self-fruitful, 151
Chervil
  as insectary plant, 251
  for intercropping, 133
  as shade tolerant, 133
Chess or cheat grass, as cover crop or green manure, 267
Chestnut (*Castanea mollissima*; *Castanea* sp.)
  alternative to growing, 51
  chill requirement, 142
  Chinese (*Mollissima* sp.), 301–2
    recipes using, 301–2
  designing with, 1, 301
  as disease resistant, 155
  ease of care, 45, 180, 301
  as nondwarfable, 180
  planting locations, separate from lawns, 284
  pollinizer required by, 151
  recipes using, 301–2
  ripening dates, northern California, 147
  size, 180
  spacing, 191
  yields, 53, 180
Chestnuts, Roasted, with Garlic Butter (recipe), 301
Chestnut Soufflé (recipe), 302
Chestnut Soup (recipe), 302
Chicken, Grilled, with Rosemary (recipe), 298–99
Chicken manure
  for hay bale garden, 105
  nutrient content, 230, Appendix 5
Chicken raising, 57, 59
Chicken wire, aviary netting vs., for fruit trees, 197
Chickweed (*Stellaria media*)
  as disease host, 287
  as dynamic accumulator, 269
  as edible flower, 292
  gathering, as growing alternative, 51
  intercropping with corn, 242
  as nitrogen-lover, 98
  for no-till gardens, 96, 101
  as soil indicator, 36, 38, 98
Chicory (*Cichorium intybus*)
  as cover crop, 278
  as dynamic accumulator, 269
  as edible flower, 292, 296

as fruit tree cover crop, 233, 280, 285
  as insectary plant, 251
  as multi-purpose edible, 59
  for no-till gardens, 101, 102
  nutritional value, 96
  'Radicchio,' for color, 1
  as soil improver, 59
  as soil indicator, 36
Chilean guava (*Ugni molinae*)
  effort ranking, 295
  as shade tolerant, 283
Chilean potato farmers, 16
Chill factor
  fruit tree choice and, 141–44
  wind speed and, 67
Chill requirements, 141–43
  cheating on, 143–44
  winter hardiness vs., 141
Chinese chestnut. See Chestnut
Chinese date. See Jujube
Chinese flame tree (*Koelreuteria elegans*), winter shade by, 75
Chinese tallow tree (*Sapium sebiferum*), winter shade by, 75
Chives (*Allium* sp.)
  Allium schoenoprasum, shade tolerance, 284
  companion planting studies, 239
  designing with, 2, 238
  as dynamic accumulator, 269
  as edible flower, 292, 296
  in Flores garden, 64
  as multi-purpose plant, 58, 59
  as onion substitute, 58
  in recipe, 296
Chlordane, toxicity of, 20
Chloropid flies, plants to attract, 252
Choanephora wet rot, insect vectors of, 288
Chokecherry; Western chokeberry (*Prunus virginiana*)
  for berms, 79
  as disease host, 288
  shade tolerance, 283
Choosing cover crops or green manures, 267–68
Choosing fruit and nut trees
  chill factor and, 141–44
  for climate, 139–44
  for disease resistance, 155–59
  for hot-summer areas, 144
  by rootstock, 165–77
  by size, 179–81
Choosing plants
  for BFI, 118–19, 121
  intercropping, 133–38
Chorizema cordatum (Flame pea), as nitrogen-fixing perennial, 291
Chrysanthemum (*Chrysanthemum* sp.)
  C. leucanthemum (Ox eye daisy), as soil indicator, 36
  companion planting studies, 240
  edible, as insectary plant, 251
  as edible flower, 292
Chutney, Asian Pear (recipe), 299
Cicuta douglasii (Water hemlock), as insectary plant, 251
Cicuta maculata (Spotted water hemlock), as soil indicator, 38
Cinquefoil, silvery (*Potentilla argentea*), as soil indicator, 36
Cirsium arvense (Canada thistle), as dynamic accumulator, 270
  as soil indicator, 38
Cirsium sp. (Thistle), as edible flower, 292
'Citation' rootstocks
  anchorage promotion, 200

future of, 184
Citrangequat, 141
Citrange rootstock, cold hardiness and, 140–41
Citrus (*Citrus* sp.; *Poncirus* sp., rootstock)
  average seasonal growth, 229
  chill requirement, 142
  choosing, by rootstock, 170
  clay soil problem, 193
  crosses, 141
  disease-resistant rootstocks, 170
  diseases, 170, 194
  drought-tolerant rootstocks, 170
  fertilizing, 230, 231
  frost protection for, 228
  frost tolerance, 140–41, 170
  as hot-summer tolerant, 144
  as parthenocarpic, 151
  pest-resistant rootstocks, 170
  phosphorus deficiency signs, 231
  planting locations
    around compost bins, 280
    in lawns, 284, 285
  pruning, no-pruning style, 211
  ripening dates, northern California, 147
  rootstocks, characteristics, 170
    cold hardiness, 140–41, 170
  as self-fruitful, 151
Citrus blight, 170
Citrus limon (Lemon blossom), as edible flower, 292
Citrus sinensis (Orange blossom), as edible flower, 292
Clay, in subsoil, 31. See also Clay soil
Clay models, 87
Clay soil, 30
  double-digging recommended for, 118
  fruit trees in, soil amendment debate, 194–95
  humus for, 30
  increasing water-holding capacity, 77
  plant indicators, 35, 36–38
  pore space vs. air pockets in, 117
  potatoes improve, 110
  tilling caution, 114
Claytonia perfoliata. See Miner's lettuce
Cleavers (*Galium aparine*), as dynamic accumulator, 269
Clematis (*Clematis* sp.), deciduous and evergreen vines, Appendix 4
Clements, Fredrick, 35
Click beetles, tillage and, 257
Climate, 23–28
  BFI contraindications, 118
  choosing tree crops for, 139–44
  companion plant success and, 237
  fruit and nut plantings and, 52
  genetic dwarf fruit trees and, 185
  intercropping success and, 237
  mulching and, 292
  sun quality and, 283
  zones, Appendix 1
Clitocybe root rot
  in fruit trees, from overwatering, 285
  host plants for, 287
Clod-Buster™, for lawns, 1
Clover (*Trifolium* sp.)
  See also Clover, bur; Clover hop; Clover, sweet
  alsike (*T. hybridum*)
    as cover crop or green manure, 266
    nitrogen gathered by, 266

as cover crop, 273
  disadvantages, 10
  under fruit trees, 285
crimson
  as cover crop, 273, 278
  as green manure, 267
  disadvantages, 10, 114
  as disease host, 287
Dutch white (*T. repens*)
  advantages of, 114
  as fruit tree cover crop, 280
  as green manure, 278
  with turnip, 243
  as living mulch with cabbage, 240
  nitrogen gathered by, 266
  for no-till garden, 102–3
  in tree plantings, 10
  as dynamic accumulator, 269
  for erosion control, 11
  as green manure, 273, 278
  growing in paths, 47, 114
  growing vegetables in, 113–14
  for herbal lawns, 10
  intercropping successes, 241, 242, 243
  as leguminous wildflower, 280
  New Zealand white, intercropping with oats, 242
  as nitrogen source, 102
  for no-till garden, 102–3
rabbit foot
  as dynamic accumulator, 269
  as soil indicator, 36
red (*T. pratense*)
  as dynamic accumulator, 269
  as edible flower, 292
  intercropping successes, 241, 242
  nitrogen content, 266, Appendix 5
  as soil indicator, 36
rose, as cover crop, 273
  slugs hide in, 103
  for sod culture, 113, 114
  as soil indicator, 36
white (*Trifolium repens*)
  as dynamic accumulator, 269
  as insectary plant, 252
  intercropping successes, 241, 242
  as soil indicator, 36
yellow, as cover crop, 273
Clover, bur (*Medicago hispida*)
  as cover crop or green manure, 267
  under fruit trees, 285
  as leguminous wildflower, 280
  as nitrogen-fixing bacteria sign, 274
Clover, hop (*Medicago lupulina*)
  as dynamic accumulator, 269
  as soil indicator, 36
Clover, subterranean, as cover crop or green manure, 267
Clover, sweet
  as cover crop or green manure, 267
  soil pH and, 274
  white (*Melilotus alba*)
    as allelopathic, 236
    as insectary plant, 252
    as leguminous wildflower, 280
    nitrogen gathered by, 266
  yellow (*Melilotus officinalis*)
    as cover crop or green manure, 267
    as leguminous wildflower, 280
Clover, white (*Lychnis alba*), as soil indicator, 36
Clover green chop, as cabbage mulch, 240
Clytostoma callistegioides (Violet trumpet vine), Appendix 4

Cobaea scandens (Cup-and-saucer vine), for shade, 73, Appendix 4
Cobalt accumulator plants, 269–70
Cobblestones, for paths, 47
Cockroaches, IPM for, 258
Cocksfoot, nitrogen content and C:N ratio, Appendix 5
Codling moth
  importance of controlling, 256–57
  IPM for, 258, 259
  tillage and, 257
  weather monitoring and, 25
Coffee, Massida's greenhouse-grown, 63
Coffeeberry, California (*Rhamnus californica*), as insectary plant, 252
Coiine, as botanincal insecticide, 259
Cold hardiness, 139–41
Cold protection, for containerized trees, 187. *See also* Frost protection
Cole family, slug or snail problems, 103
Collards (*Brassica oleracea*)
  See also Brassicas
  companion planting studies, 239
  as fruit tree cover crop, 233
  intercropping successes, 242
  in no-till garden, 102
  preventing cross-pollination in, 102
Collins, Major C., 141
Colloidal phosphate
  chemical forms vs., 274
  with clover planting, 103
  cost factors, 229
  for fruit trees, 198, 232
  as phosphorus source, 231
  for sheet composting, 97
Colloids, 29–30
Collops beetles, as beneficial predators, 246
Color, as design element, 1–2, 42, 54
Colorado bean beetle, 239
Colorado potato beetle
  companion planting myths, 238–39
  potato variety resistant to, 260
  tansy and, 240
Colorado river hemp (*Sesbania macrocarpa*), as leguminous wildflower, 280
Coltsfoot
  as dynamic accumulator, 269
  as soil indicator, 36
Comfrey (*Symphytum officinale*)
  for berms, 79
  caution about, 281
  for color, 280
  for compost making, 59, 281
  cover crop problems, 278
  as dynamic accumulator, 269, 280–81
  edible portions, 58, 79, 292
  as fruit tree cover crop, 233
  as mulch, 59
  as multi-purpose plant, 59
  for permanent bed, 281
  planting, 58
  as shade tolerant, 283
  yields, 280–81
Common Sense Pest Control Quarterly, 257
Community, edible landscape as, 92
Compacted soils, fruit trees and, 162, 163
Companion planting, 46–47, 235–43
  allelopathy, 235–36
  climate and, 237
  intercropping vs., 235, 237
  research results, 237, 239–43
Compositae, beneficial insects lured by, 251,

252
Composition, as design element, 42
Compost
  all-vegetable, 108
  in BFI, 115
  comfrey for, 281
  as fruit tree mulch, 232
  for fruit tree planting, 193–95, 198
  hay bales as, 105, 106
  for lawns, 10
  materials for, nitrogen content and C:N ratio, Appendix 5
  as panacea, 38
  planting for, 59, 277, 278, 280–81
  in potting mix, 127, 128
  reducing quantity needed, 108
  running roots in, 97
  sheet composting, 95–98
  for sod culture, 113
  in surface cultivation, 107–8
  weed seeds in, 97
  weeds for, 39
  from windbreak plants, 84
Compost bins, locating, 57, 277, 280
Concrete water tanks, planting near, 83
Conium maculatum (Poison hemlock)
  as insectary plant, 251
  as soil indicator, 36
Construction
  as design element, 43
  drywells, 79–80
  garden use encouraged by, 42
  landscape architecture's emphasis on, 41
  in Mexican-American-style gardens, 63
  swales, 77–78
  thermometer shelter, 25
  waterways and berms, 77–79
  windbreaks, 69
Containers, fruit trees in, 186–87, 198
  espalier pruning for, 221
Convolvulus arvensis (Field bindweed), as soil indicator, 36
Convolvulus minor (Perennial ornamental morning glory), as insectary plant, 252
Convolvulus sepium (Hedge bindweed), as soil indicator, 36
Cooling
  designing for, 67, 73–76
  lawns for, 11
  wind data for, 23, 24
Cooperative extension services, as data source, 141, 155, 255
Copper accumulator plants, 269–70
Coral tree (*Erythrina* sp.), as nitrogen-fixing perennial, 291
Coral vine (*Antigonon leptopus*), for shade, Appendix 4
Corbett, Mike and Judy, 9
Coreopsis, maintenance requirements, 44
Coriander (*Coriandrum sativum*)
  companion planting studies, 239, 240
  as insectary plant, 251, 252
  as multi-purpose edible, 59
Corn
  amaranth and, 237, 242
  azotobacter inoculant for, 126
  BFI unsuited to, 119
  in clover-sod garden, 114
  companion planting myths, 235, 240, 265–66
  as cover crop, 267, 278
  diseases
    host plants to avoid, 287
    insect vectors, 288
  as green manure, 267

ground covers with, 285
  intercropping with, 133, 134, 242, 243
  nitrogen requirements, 231
  nitrogen source, clover-sod, 114
  pest-resistant varieties, 260
  pests, companion planting or intercropping for, 240, 242
  preventing cross-pollination in, 102
  root zones, 135
  surface cultivation vs. single-dug yields, 110
  water use and root depth, 226
Corn borer, 242
Corn chamomile (*Anthemis arvensis*), as dynamic accumulator, 269
Corn earworm
  in corn, 242, 260
  IPM for, 258, 259
  in soybeans, 243
Cornelian cherry (*Cornus mas*), shade tolerance, 284
Cornflower (*Centaurea cyanus*)
  as fruit tree cover crop, 280
  as soil indicator, 36
Cornish Game Hens Stuffed with Garlic and Summer Savory (recipe), **307**
Corn marigold, as soil indicator, 36
Corn salad (*Valerianella locusta*), **303–4**
  cultural guidelines, 303–4
  for no-till gardens, 101
  Salad (recipe), 304
Corn spurry (*Spergula arvensis*)
  intercropping with cauliflower, 242
  as nurse plant, 248–49
  as soil indicator, 38
Cornus mas. See Cornelian cherry
Corylus sp. (Hazelnut), shade tolerance, 284
Cost considerations
  dirt gardening, 54
  drip irrigation, 129
  espalier, 221
  fertilizers, for fruit trees, 231
  genetic dwarf fruit trees, 186, 187
  growing vs. purchasing food, 54
  hay bale gardening, 105
  lawns, 10, 11
  maintenance, 45–46, 54
  path construction and materials, 50
  pea and bean inoculant, 125
  planning for overruns, 54
  spending early to save later, 54, 93
  sulphate of potash, 231
  time saving vs., 54
  TODD® flats, 128
Costmary, as insectary plant, 251
Co-terminal bearing fruit trees, as frost tolerant, 228
Cotton
  azotobacter inoculant for, 126
  water use and root depth, 226
Cotton grasses (*Eriophorum* sp.), as soil indicator, 36
Cottonseed meal, 229, 230, Appendix 5
Cottonwood, for erosion prevention, 78
Cottony cushion scale parasites, 247
Coverage, planning for, Appendix 7
Cover cropping, defined, 273
Cover crops
  allelopathic plants as, 236
  choosing, 267–68

clovers as, corn and, 114
  drip irrigation contraindicates, 130
  establishing, 232, 273–74
  fertilizing with, 261, 265–81
  under fruit trees, 227
  ornamental, 278, 280
  for sandy soils, 273
  slug or snail problems, 103
  soil improvement role, 273
  tilling under, 274–75
Cow manure, nitrogen content and C:N ratio, Appendix 5
Cow parsnip. *See* Wild parsnip
Cow peas
  as cover crop or green manure, 267
  intercropping successes, 242, 243
Coyote bush (*Baccharis pilularis*), as insectary plant, 252
Crabapple
  See also Apple
  chill requirement, 142
  'Whitney,' Linquist on, 65
Crabgrass, compost caution, 97
Crabid beetles, as beneficial predators, 246
Craft materials, weed plants for, 39
Cranberry
  bush (*Viburnum trilobum*), as shade tolerant, 283
  for downspout outlets, 83
  as lawn tolerant, 285
Crataegus sp. (Hawthorn)
  C. douglasii, shade tolerance, 284
  as edible flower, 292
  intercropping with cabbage, 242
Creasy, Rosalind, effort scale by, 295
Creeping thistle. *See* Sow thistle
Creosote bush (*Larrea tridentata*), 236
Cress, for intercropping, 133
Crickets, predators of, 246
Crimson clover. *See* Clover
Crop rotations, 266, 273–75
  five-year plan, 277–78, 280–81
  seven-year plan, 279
Cross-pollination, preventing in no-till garden, 101, 102
Cross vine (*Bignonia capreolata*), for shade, Appendix 4
Crotolaria (*Crotolaria* sp.)
  as cover crop or green manure, 267, 273
  as leguminous wildflower, 280
Croton sp., intercropping with soybeans, 243
Crown divisions, planting in no-till garden, 102
Crown gall, rootstocks resistant to
  almond, 166
  apricot, 168
  cherry, 169
  peach/nectarine, 171
  persimmon, 174
  plum/prune, 175
  walnut, 177
Crown rot (*Phytophthora* sp.)
  diagnosing, 194
  as lawn tree risk, 285
  preventing, 194, 232
    at planting time, 198
  rootstocks resistant to
    almond, 166
    apple, 166–67
    apricot, 168
    cherry, 169
    citrus, 170
    peach/nectarine, 171–72
    pear, 173–74
    plum/prune, 175–76
    walnut, 177
Crucifer flea beetles, 239
Cruciferae. *See* Brassicas

Crusty soil, plant indicators, 36–38
Cucumber
  azotobacter inoculant for, 126
  bush varieties, for compactness, 47
  companion planting studies, 239, 240
  in Flores garden, 64
  growing on trellises, 134
  intercropping with, 133, 134, 242
  pest-resistant varieties, 260
  preventing cross-pollination in, 102
  for quick shade, 73
  as shade tolerant, 133
  with sunflowers, 134
  surface cultivation vs. single-dug yields, 110
  for vertical gardening, 134
Cucumber beetles
  cucumber varieties resistant to, 260
  as disease vectors, 288
  IPM for, 258, 259
  muskmelon varieties resistant to, 260
  on squash, intercropping success, 243
  squash varieties resistant to, 260
Cucumber mosaic virus
  ground cherry spreads, 103
  host plants for, 287
  insect vectors of, 288
Cucurbita sp. (Squash blossom), as edible flower, 292
  in recipe, **296**
Cucurbitaceae (Gourd family)
  as deciduous vines, Appendix 4
  diseases
    host plants to avoid, 287
    insect vectors, 288
  preventing cross-pollination among, 102
Cudweed, low (Gnaphalium sp.), as soil indicator, 36
Cultivated soil, plant indicators, 36–38
Cultivation
  in BFI, 115
  by deep-rooted plants, 77
  double-digging, 115–22
  "natural," 115–16
  no-till methods, 96–111
  plants as indicators of, 35
  pore space and tilth, 117
  surface, 107–10
  tillage methods, 113–22
  tilth vs., 38
  weather watching for, 24
Culture maraîchère, Chadwick and, 115
Cumin, as insectary plant, 251
Cup-and-saucer vine (Cobaea scandens), for shade, 73, Appendix 4
Curly dock. See Rumex crispus
Currants (Ribes sp.)
  blister rust host, 103
  chill requirement, 142
  as lawn tolerant, 285
  as shade tolerant, 283
  yields, 53
Cutworms
  predators of, 246
  sod culture and, 113
  tillage for control of, 257
Cydonia oblonga. See Quince
Cyperaceae sp. (Sedges), as soil indicator, 37
Cyperus esculentus (Nut grass), for berms, 79
Cypress, as windbreak, 69, 71
Cypress vine (Quamoclit pennata), for quick shade, 73

D

Daffodils, ease of care, 54
Dahlias, in Flores garden, 64
Daikon, preventing cross-pollination in, 102

Daisy
  African trailing, as insectary plant, 252
  English (Bellis perennis)
    as edible flower, 292
    as soil indicator, 36
  ox eye (Chrysanthemum leucanthemum), as soil indicator, 36
Damsel bugs, 246
  plants to attract, 252
Dandelion (Taraxacum officinale)
  cover crop problems, 278
  as disease host, 287
  as dynamic accumulator, 269
  edible portions, 59, 292
  as fruit tree cover crop, 233
  as insectary plant, 251
  as multi-purpose edible, 59
  for no-till gardens, 101
  nutritional value, 96
  shade tolerance, 284
  soil builing to reduce, 39
  as soil improver, 59
  as soil indicator, 36
Datura stramonium. See Jimson weed
Daucus carota. See Carrot
Dave Wilson Nursery
  chill zone map from, 141
  miniature tree role, 184
Davis, California, Village Homes, 9–13
Day lily (Hemerocallis fulva)
  as edible flower, 1, 292, 296
  caution about, 291
  as multi-purpose plant, 1, 58–59
  as shade tolerant, 283
DDT, 19, 20
Dead-heading, time required for, 54
Deciduous vines, listed, Appendix 4
Deck gardens, genetic dwarf trees for, 186, 187
Deep-rooted myths, 134, 161–62
Deer fencing, 186, 187
Defoliation, positive role of, 21
de Hart, Robert A., 139
Delayed open center pruning, 213–15
Delphinium, ease of care, 54
Density or mass, as design element, 42
Density of use, 57–58
Derris, as poison, 19
Desert holly (Hymenelytra), as nitrogen-fixing perennial, 291
Design
  See also Form; Planning
  aesthetics of edibles, 44
  basic components of, 42–43, 46–47
  basic guidelines, 91–94
  with chayote, 300
  with Chinese chestnut, 301
  clay models, 87
  climate and microclimate, 23–28
  with comfrey, 280
  compactness, 47
  compost bin placement, 277, 280
  concurrent use, 57–58
  for cooling, 73–76
  with corn salad, 303
  cultural needs and, 284
  deciduous vines, listed, Appendix 4
  density of use, 57–58
  diversity problems, 287–88
  drainage needs and, 284
  edible flowers, 291–92
  for energy conservation, 67–81
  environmental, principles of, 88
  espalier, 221–22
  evergreen vines, listed, Appendix 4
  with fava beans, 303
  fence, for windbreaks, 69
  five-year rotation, 277–81

formal vs. wild, 43–44
  fruit and nut trees and, 139
  perennial mulch, 232
  size considerations, 179–80
  spacing, 191–92
  functional aspects, 42, 46–47
  with garlic, 306
  gravity as part of, 47
  growing before, 28
  with insectary plants, 247, 251–53, 257
  intercropping, 133–38, 238
  with kiwi, 304
  maintenance considerations, 44–47
  with mulch, 227
  multi-layer plantings, 47
  with nitrogen-fixing plants, 291
  with nurse plants, 247, 248–49
  original thinking in, 84–85
  with ornamental kale, 296
  ornamentals as part of, 180
  on paper, 87, 93
  paths, 47
  with persimmon, 305
  for pest control, 247–53, 257
  photographic, 87
  with quince, 307
  with 'Romanesco,' 297
  with rosemary, 298
  scale drawing, 87
  shade plants, 133, 283–84, Appendix 4
  shape, 46
  size considerations, 46, 51–54
    importance of starting small, 93
    standard fruit trees, 179–80
  soil considerations, 29–32
  space considerations, 57–58, 180
  structures as part of, 41, 42
  sunlight as part of, 73–76
  solar charts, Appendix 2
  for synergy, 5–6, 83–85
  traditional, 41
    environmental vs., 88
  usefulness, 42
  vertical space use, 134
  visualizing, 87–88
  wild vs. formal, 43–44
  windbreaks, 67–71
  by zones, 57–58
Desmodium purpureum (Beggarweed), as nitrogen-fixing bacteria sign, 274
Desmodium sp., intercropping with soybeans, 243
Dessert recipes
  Asian Pears Poached in Red Wine, **300**
  Baked Quinces Flambé, **308**
  Chestnut Soufflé, **302**
  Persimmon Ice Cream, **305**
  Persimmon Pudding, **305**
  'Pink Pearl' Apple Tart, **308–9**
Devil's bit. See Veratrum californicum
Diamondback moths
  companion planting studies, 239
  intercropping successes, 242
  IPM for, 258, 259
Dianthus sp. (Carnation; Pinks)
  as edible flower, 292
  under fruit trees, 227
  as soil indicator, 37
Diatomaceous earth, in IPM, 256, 258
Dieldrin, 3, 20
Dill (Anethum graveolens)
  as edible flower, 292, 296
  as fruit tree cover crop, 233
  as insectary plant, 251
  as multi-purpose edible, 59
  for no-till gardens, 101
  for pickling, planning area for, 53
Diospyros kaki. See Persim-

mon, Oriental
Diospyros virginiana. See Persimmon, American
Dioxin, 2
  Fukuoka and, 109–10
"Dirt gardening," 54
Disabled gardeners, 50, 185
Diseases
  See also specific diseases; specific plants
  azotobacter suppresses, 126
  BFI caution on, 121
  drip irrigation reduces, 129
  edible weeds harbor, 103
  fruit and nut trees resistant to, 155–59
  host plant hazards, 287
  insect vectors, 287–88
  in no-till gardens, 103
  planning for sacrifice to, 52
  weather monitoring for spray program, 25
Distictis laxiflora (Vanilla trumpet vine), for shade, Appendix 4
Diversity
  for biological balance, 245
  in gardening methods, 95
  good vs. bad, 247
  host plant hazards, 287
  as part of IPM, 257
Dock (Rumex sp.)
  as dynamic accumulator, 269
  as fruit tree cover crop, 233, 280
  for no-till gardens, 101
  nutritional value, 96
  R. crispus (Curly dock; Dock)
    for downspout outlets, 83
    as soil indicator, 35
  R. obtusifolius (Broad-leaved dock), as dynamic accumulator, 269
  as salad green, 59
  as soil indicator, 36
Dogma, risks of, 109–10
Dolichos lablab (Hyacinth bean; Lablab)
  as leguminous wildflower, 280
  for shade, 73, Appendix 4
Dolomite, in potting mix, 127
Dormancy
  chill requirements, 141–44
  cold hardiness and, 140
Dormant buds, 203
  changing to flower buds, 206–7
Dormant oil spray, cold hardiness and, 140
Double-digging, 115–22
  cautions about, 117
  indications and contraindications, 118–19, 121
  soil layers with, 115–16
  technique, 116, 121–22
Douglas, J. Sholto, 139
Downspouts, planting near, 83
Downy mildew, host plants for, 287
Doxantha unguis-cati (Yellow trumpet vine), for shade, Appendix 4
Dragonflies, as beneficial predators, 246
Drainage
  berms and swales for, 77–79
  drywells for, 79–80
  improving, 77–79
    when planting fruit trees, 193–94, 195
  Kelley garden, 6
  plant indicators, 35, 36–38
Drawing your landscape, 87
Dried Persimmons (recipe), **305–6**
  with Curried Pecan Cream Cheese, **306**
Drip irrigation, 129–33
  for fruit trees, 225–26
Driveways
  locating along windbreaks, 68–69
  weeds barred by, 98
Drought-resistant rootstocks

almond, 166
apple, 166–67
avocado, 168
citrus, 170
Drying, seasonal eating as alternative to, 147
Dry soil, plant indicators, 35, 36–38
Drywells, 79–80
Dugas, Eddy, 140
Dulse, as dynamic accumulator, 269
Dust, windbreaks to filter, 67
Dutch hoe, 109
Dutch iris, ease of care, 54
Dutchman's pipe (Aristolochia durior), for shade, Appendix 4
Dutch white clover. See Clover, Dutch white
Dwarf fruit trees
  for compactness, 47
  harvest expansion with, 147
  pros and cons, 180–81
  pruning, 207, 208, 217
  semi-dwarf vs., 180
  size compared, 179
  yields, 181
Dwarf pyramid (central leader), trees, 217–18
Dyanamic accumulators, 266–70
  comfrey as king of, 280–81
  ornamental, 278, 280
  turning under, 274–75

E

Earthworms, 108
Earwigs
  endemic, as beneficial predators, 246
    plants to attract, 252
  European, as pests, 246
    tillage for control of, 257
Easey, Ben, 107, 108, 109, 110
Eastern bracken (Pteridium aquifolium)
  as dynamic accumulator, 269
  as soil indicator, 36
Eaves, planting under, 83
  fruit tree cold hardiness and, 141
  to protect miniature trees, 185
Eco-agriculture, concept of, 15–16
Ecological gardening, concept of, 15–16
EDB, 2
Edible chrysanthemum, as insectary plant, 251
Edible flowers, 292
  cautions, 291–92
  Ensalada de (recipe), **296–97**
Edible landscaping
  aesthetics and, 44. See also Design; Form
  concept of, 15–16
  guidelines, 91–94
  maintenance time requirements, 54–55
  percent of garden devoted to, 46
  R factor, 91
Edible weeds, 39
"Effects of Soil Amendments and Fertilizer Levels on the Establishment of Silver Maple," 193
Effort scale, 295
  See also Maintenance considerations
  Asian pear, 299
  chayote, 300
  corn salad, 303
  fava beans, 302
  garlic, 306
  kiwi, 304
  Oriental persimmon, 304
  ornamental kale, 296
  quince, 307
  'Romanesco,' 297
  Rosemary, 298
Eggplant
  chayote as substitute for, 58, **300**
  companion planting studies,

356 **INDEX**

238–39
as disease host, 288
root zones, 135
Egyptian top-set onion (*Allium cepa* var. *viviprium*), 58, 59
Elaeagnus angustifolia (Russian olive)
for cooling hedge, 74
as multi-purpose plant, 59, 60
as nitrogen-fixing, 291
as windbreak, 69
Elaeagnus commutata (Silverberry)
as nitrogen-fixing, 291
shade tolerance, 284
Elaeagnus multiflora (Cherry eleagnus), as nitrogen-fixing, 291
Elaeagnus multiflora (Guomi), shade tolerance, 284
Elaeagnus pungus (Silverberry), as nitrogen-fixing, 291
Elaeagnus umbellata (Autumn olive)
as nitrogen-fixing, 291
as windbreak, 69
Elder; Elderberry (*Sambucus canadensis*)
as disease resistant, 155
for downspout outlets, 83
as edible plant, 292
as lawn tolerant, 285
as low-effort perennial, 45
as shade tolerant, 284
Elderly gardeners, as source of wisdom, 63–66, 92, 155
Elecampane, as insectary plant, 251
Eleusine indica (Goosegrass), intercropping with beans, 241
Elm (*Ulmus* sp.), winter shade by, 75
Emerson, Ralph Waldo, on weeds, 95
Emitters, 131, 132
clogging of, 129, 132
complex, or tortuous path, 225, 226
Emitters, 131, 132
Encyrtid parasite, 259
Endive
BFI suitability, 118
blanched, effort ranking, 295
for intercropping, 133, 134
as shade tolerant, 133
Energy, agricultural use of, 2, 3, 16
tree vs. vegetable crops, 139
Energy conservation
with BFI, 116–17
landscape design for, 67–81
English daisy (*Bellis perennis*)
as edible flower, 292
as soil indicator, 36
English laurel (*Prunus laurocerasus*), soil preparation for, 54
Enjoyment, importance of, 91
Environmental design
basic principles, 88
biomass and, 12, 13
lawns as cooling factor, 11
stone paths in, 6
Equisetum sp. (Horsetail)
for berms, 79
cover crop problems, 278
as dynamic accumulator, 269
for erosion prevention, 78, 79
as soil indicator, 35, 37
Erigeron canadensis (Mare's tail), as soil indicator, 37
Eriobotrya japonica. See Loquat
Eriogonum sp. (California buckwheat), as insectary plant, 252
Eriophorum sp. (Cotton grasses), as soil indicator, 36

Erodium cicutarium (Redstem filaree), as soil indicator, 38
Erodium sp. (Filaree), as fruit tree cover crop, 280
Erosion control measures
angles of repose, Appendix 7
berms and swales, 77–79
catch basin, Village Homes, 9–10, *10*
crushed rock paths, 6
drywells, 79–80
fava beans, 110
intercropping, 137
sod culture, 113
street-side plantings, 11–12, *12*
used tires, 84–85
windbreaks, 67
Erwinia amylovora. See Fire blight
Eryngium sp., intercropping with apple, 241
Erysimum cheiranthoides (Wormseed-mustard), intercropping with brassicas, 241
Erythrina sp. (Coral tree), as nitrogen-fixing perennial, 291
Escarole, BFI suitability, 118
Espalier, 221–22
cost factors, 221
effort ranking, 295
genetic dwarf fruit trees for, 185
persimmon for, **305**
'Pink Pearl' apple for, **308**
quince for, **307**
terminal-bearing trees good for, 211
Eucalyptus
as firewood source, 84
windbreak suitability, 69, 70
Euonymus, evergreen (*Euonymus* sp.)
E. fortunei, for shade, Appendix 4
E. japonica, as insectary plant, 252
Euophid wasps, as white fly predators, 259
Euphorbia sp. (Spurges)
as dynamic accumulator, 270
as soil indicator, 38
European corn borers
companion planting studies, 240
intercropping success, 242
IPM for, 258, 259
European red mites, fruit trees mulch for, 242
Evening primrose (*Oenthera laciniata; O. biennis*), as insectary plant, 252
Evergreen grape (*Rhoicissus capensis*), for shade, 73, Appendix 4
Evergreens, design with, 54, 69
Evergreen vines, listed, Appendix 4
Extension services, as data source, 141, 155, 255
Eyebright (*Anagallis arvensis*)
as dynamic accumulator, 269
as fruit tree cover crop, 280

F

Fagopyrum esculentum (Buckwheat)
as dynamic accumulator, 269
as insectary plant, 252
Fall armyworms, intercropping successes, 242
Fall webworms, IPM for, 258
False hellebore. See *Veratrum californicum*
Farallones Institute *Annual Report*, on BFI, 115
Farallones Institute Rural Center
beneficial insects at, 248
century-old pear tree, pruning method, 215
drywells at, 79

host plant experience, 287
leaf fall delay at, 28
Linquist at, 66
Farwell's Tree-Doc™ (Seal and Heal), 209
Fat hen (*Atriplex hastata*)
as dynamic accumulator, 269
as soil indicator, 36
Fava bean (*Vicia faba*), **302–3**
with Artichoke Hearts (recipe), **303**
companion planting studies, 240
as cover crop, 273
cultural guidelines, 302–3
as green manure, 275, 303
for intercropping, 133
as mulch or compost plant, 59
as multi-purpose plant, 59
pests
aphids, 248, 256
insectary plant experiment with, 253
planting before potatoes, 110
as shade tolerant, 133
as soil improver, 59, 110
Feathered maiden fruit tree, 222
Feijoa sellowiana. See Guava, pineapple
Fencing
as design element, 43
genetic dwarf fruit trees, 186, 187
as windbreaks, 69, 71
Fennel (*Foeniculum vulgare*)
for berms, 79
as edible flower, 79, 292, 296
as dynamic accumulator, 269
Florence (*Foeniculum vulgare* var. *azoricum*)
as insectary plant, 251
as multi-purpose edible, 59
as fruit tree cover crop, 233
as insectary plant, 252
for no-till gardens, 101
shade tolerance, 284
Fenugreek, as cover crop or green manure, 267
Fenzau, C.J., 35
Fern, nitrogen content and C:N ratio, Appendix 5
Fertility. See Soil fertility
Fertilization
aphids' role in, 19–20
of fruit trees, ensuring good pollination, 151–53
Fertilizers
See also Fertilizing; Soil amendments
chemical, inoculant need and, 125
compostable materials, nitrogen content and C:N ratio, Appendix 5
cover crops or green manure as, 261, 265–81
dynamic accumulators, 266–70
herbal leys, 280–81
macronutrients, 261–62
multi-purpose plants as, 59
nutrient percentages, 230, 261
perennial legumes as, 291
phosphorus sources, 230, 231
potasssium/potash sources, 230, 231
urine, 105–6, Appendix 5
Fertilizing
See also Fertilizers
basic requirements, 261–62
with BFI, 116
with drip irrigation, 129
fruit and nut trees, 229–33
cold hardiness and, 139
genetic dwarf, in containers, 186
when planting, 194
problems of excess, 286
size and, 191
hay bale garden, 105–6

pest problems and, 255
before sheet composting, 97
for sod culture, 114
Fescues, as fruit tree ground cover, 285
Feverfew, as insectary plant, 251
Ficus carica. See Fig
Ficus pumila (Creeping fig), as evergreen vine, Appendix 4
Field beans, nitrogen gathered by, 266
Field bindweed (*Convolvulus arvensis*), as soil indicator, 36
Field peppergrass (*Cardaria draba*), as soil indicator, 37
Fig (*Ficus carica*)
anchorage promotion, 200
average seasonal growth, 229
chill requirement, 142
as co-terminal bearing, 228
as disease resistant, 155
effort ranking, 295
in Flores garden, 64
as hot-summer tolerant, 144
as low-effort perennial, 45
nitrogen requirements, 230
as nondwarfable, 180
planting locations, separate from lawns, 284
pollination requirements, 151
ripening dates, 147, 148
self-fruitful varieties, 151
standard, height and width, 180
yields, 53
Fig, creeping (*Ficus pumila*), as evergreen vine, Appendix 4
Filaree (*Erodium* sp.)
as fruit tree cover crop, 280
red-stem (*E. cicutarium*), as soil indicator, 38
Filbert
average seasonal growth, 229
chill requirement, 142
as nondwarfable, 180
pollinizer required by, 151
root system, 161
standard, height and width, 179, 180
Filtration, for drip irrigation system, 129, 130, 132
Fingerleaf, as soil indicator, 36
Fire blight (*Erwinia amylovora*)
drip irrigation reduces, 129
host plants for, 287
from overhead irrigation, 285, 286
from overwatering, 285
pear rootstock resistance, 173–74
pruning caution, 208
Firewood, garden sources, 39, 84
Fish emulsion
as fruit tree nitrogen source, 229, 230
nutrient percentages, 230
for seedling water, 128
Fish meal, nutrient percentages, 230
Fish scrap, nitrogen content and C:N ratio, Appendix 5
Five-year plan for soil improvement, 277–81
Flagging, wind direction shown by, 25
Flame pea (*Chorizema cordatum*), as nitrogen-fixing perennial, 291
Flame vine (*Pyrostegia ignea*), for shade, Appendix 4
Flats, TODD®, 127, 128
Flax
azotobacter inoculant for, 126
seed (*Linum usitatissimum*),

as dynamic accumulator, 269
Flea beetles
companion planting studies, 238, 239, 240
as disease vectors, 288
intercropping successes, 241, 242
IPM for, 258, 259
living mulch studies, 240
nasturtium repellent myth, 238
potato variety resistant to, 260
sweet potato varieties resistant to, 260
Fleas, IPM for, 258
Flies
beneficial predators, 237, 246, 247
companion planting myths, 237
parasites of, 246, 247
Florence fennel. See Fennel
Flores, Angelina, 64–65, 133, 307
Flores, Frank, 64–65
Flour, wheat, nitrogen content, Appendix 5
Flower border, 1
cover crop as, 278
Flower buds, 203–4
turning dormant buds into, 206–7
Flower flies, plants to attract, 252
Flowering tobacco (*Nicotiana* sp.)
companion planting studies, 239
as dynamic accumulator, 270
intercropping with collards, 242
pest control problem, 237–38
Flowerpot effect, 193, 194
Flowers
See also specific kinds
as cover crops, 280
under fruit trees, 227
cover crops for, 273
dead-heading, time required for, 54
edible, 58, 79, 292
cautions, 291–92
Ensalada de Flores (recipe), **296–97**
for luring beneficial insects, 251–53
maintenance considerations, 44
planning for, 54
sheet-compost method of growing, 98
synergy with, 84
Flower Salad (recipe), **296–97**
Fluorine accumulator plants, 269–70
Fly parasites, 246, 247
Foeniculum vulgare. See Fennel
Fool's parsley, as disease host, 288
Forest Farming (Douglas and de Hart), 139
Form
See also Design
espalier, 221–22
oblique cordon, 221–22
pruning for, 207
standard form, 179–80
Forsythia, as disease host, 287
Foundation plantings
rosemary for, 298
as windbreaks, 67, 68
Foxglove
ease of care, 54
under fruit trees, 227
Foxtail
as disease host, 287
short awned (*Hordeum jubatum*), as soil indicator, 36
Fragaria sp. See Strawberry
Fraxinus holotricha (Ash), winter shade by, 75
Freeze tolerance. See Frost-

tolerant fruit trees
French intensive gardening.
  See Biodynamic French
  intensive gardening
French sorrel (Rumex scu-
    tatus)
  for berms, 79
  as invasive, 98
  in no-till garden, 102
  shade tolerance, 283
Frost
  data gathering on, 23–24
  planning for sacrifice to, 52
Frost protection
  for fruit trees, 228
  mulching pros and cons,
    292
Frost-tolerant fruit trees, 140–
  41, 228
Fruit buds, 203–4
Fruit flies, intercropping success, 242
"Fruit salad" tree, 63, 63, 64
Fruit spurs, 203–4
Fruit and nut trees
  See also Stone fruits; spe-
    cific fruits and nuts
  alternate bearing, no-
    pruning style exagger-
    ates, 211–12
  average seasonal growth,
    229
  blossom on, chill factor and,
    141–44
  buds, types of, 203–4
  buying, 155, 198
  chill requirements, 141–44
  choosing
    for climate, 139–44
    for disease resistance,
      155–59
    matching rootstocks to
      soil types, 165–77
    sizes, 179–81
  choosing pollinizers for,
    151–53
  for cold climates, 139–40
  for color, 1
    no-pruning style and, 211
  cover crops around, 280
  deep-rooted myths, 134,
    161–62
  disease-resistant, 155–59
  diseases
    brown rot, 257
    crown rot, 194, 198
    defending against, 155
    host plants to avoid, 287
    as lawn planting risk,
      285, 286
    mulch as harbor for, 232
    peach leaf curl, 257
    powdery mildew, 257
    pruning caution, 208
    sanitation importance,
      257
    scab, 257
    shot hole fungus, 257
  dormancy, cold hardiness
    and, 140
  dormant buds, 203
    changing to flower buds,
      206–7
  dormant oil spraying, cold
    hardiness and, 140
  dwarf
    for compactness, 47
    harvest expansion with,
      147
    pros and cons, 180–81
    pruning, 207, 208, 217
    semi-dwarf vs., 180
    size compared, 179
    yields, 181
  dwarfing rootstocks, plant-
    ing for full-size growth,
    199
  early blossom problems,
    143
  espalier. See Espalier
  expanding harvest season,
    147–48
  feathered maiden, 222
  fertilization of, ensuring,
    151–53
  fertilizing, 229–33
    cold hardiness and, 139–
      40
    genetic dwarf, in contain-
      ers, 186

at planting time, 194
  problems of excess, 286
  size and, 191
flavor
  disease resistance vs.,
    155
  genetic dwarf varieties,
    185, 187
  no-pruning style and, 211
  watering and, 211, 225
  in Flores garden, 64
flower or fruit buds, 203–4
frost protection for, 228
frost-tolerant, 228
fruit ripening, chill factor
  and, 141
genetic dwarf (miniature),
  181, 183–89
  for compactness, 47
  pruning, 222, 223
  sizes compared, 179
grafting fruit combinations,
  165
grafting for pollination, 153
ground cover under, 191,
  232–33
growing season, mulch and,
  232
growth patterns, 203–4
hardening-off process, dormant oil spray slows,
  140
harvesting
  extending season, 147–
    48
  no-pruning style and, 211
  sanitation and, 257
heat tolerant, 144
for hot-summer areas, 144
intercropping successes,
  242
keepers, 147
lawns and, 284–86
leaf growth, chill factor and,
  141–44
limiting size of, 191
maintenance considerations
  low-maintenance trees,
    listed, 45
  size and, 180, 191
for mild-winter climates,
  140–44
miniature; see genetic
  dwarf
monitoring for spray pro-
  gram, 25
mulching, 226–27
  drawbacks, 140, 232
  for European red mites,
    242
  perennial mulch, 231–32
nitrogen excess in, 286
nitrogen requirements, 230,
  231
notching, 206–7
painting the trunk, 198–99,
  200
  for chilling, 143–44
pests
  aphids, 286
  borers, 200
  defending against, 155
  European red mites, 242
  mulch as harbor for, 232
  red spider mites, 242
phosphorus deficiency
  signs, 231
pinching, 218
planning considerations,
  52–53
planting, 197–201
  in clay soil, 193–94
  in hardpan, 163
  preventing "walking," 200
  soil amendments pros
    and cons, 193–95
planting locations
  chill requirements and,
    143–44
  for frost protection, 83,
    228
  pollination and, 152
  lawns, 284–86
  maintenance considera-
    tions, 47
  size and, 191
  soil types, 162–63
  spacing requirements,
    191–92
  vegetable garden and, 47

pleaching (living guy wires),
  215
pollen sterile, defined, 152
pollination of, ensuring,
  151–53
potassium/potash deficiency
  signs, 231
productivity considerations,
  180
pruning. See Pruning fruit
  and nut trees
ripening dates, 147–48
rootstocks
  choosing, for soil type,
    165–77
  grafting other fruits on,
    165
  root systems, 161–63
    fertilizing and, 194
    mulching and, 226–27
    responses to environ-
      ment, 162–63
  self-fruitful, 151
  self-sterile, 151
  semi-dwarf, 180
  sharing with neighbors, 51
  size, 179–81
    factors affecting, 191
  size of fruit, no-pruning
    style and, 211
  sizing an orchard, 52–53
  on slopes, root patterns,
    163
  sod culture limitations, 113
  soil types, size and, 179,
    191
  spacing, 191–92
  spreading branches, 205–6
    for central leader style,
      218
  spurs, 203–4
  spur-type, 204
    no-pruning method draw-
      backs, 211
  staking, 197, 199–200
  standard, 179–80
    open center pruning for,
      213
  summer vs. winter pruning,
    74–75, 140, 207, 218
  supporting, living guy wires
    for, 215
  taproots, 161–62
  terminal buds, 203
  terminal-bearing, no-pruning
    method for, 211
  thinning, pruning style and,
    212, 215
  tilling, 229
  trace buds, 203
  trimming low branches
    from, for cold hardi-
    ness, 252
  "walking" by, preventing,
    200
  watering, 199
    cold hardiness and, 140
    with drip irrigation, 225–
      26
    importance of, 225
    after planting, 199
    size and, 191
    yields and, 225
  wind protection for
    mulch and, 227
    when planting, 198–99
    staking, 197, 199–200
    windbreaks, 140
  wrapping trunk, 200
  yields, 53
    central leader pruning
      and, 217
    fertilizing and, 231
    methods of improving,
      205–7
    no-pruning style and, 211
    size and, 180, 181, 184–
      85, 191
    watering and, 225
Fruits, eating seasonally vs.
  preserving, 147
Fuel, multi-purpose plants for,
  59
Fuget, Dick, peach grafting
  result, 183–84
Fukuoka, Masanobu, 109–10,
  211
Fumitory (Fumaria officinalis),
  as soil indicator, 36
Functional design guidelines,

46–47, 58
Fungi, soil depth and, 31
Fungus diseases, as intercropping contraindica-
  tion, 239

G

Galium aparine (Cleavers), as
  dynamic accumulator,
  269
Garbage, green or raw, nitrogen content and C:N
  ratio, Appendix 5
Garden centipedes (Symphylans), tillage for control
  of, 257
Garden clubs, as source of
  wisdom, 63
Garden sorrel (Rumex sp.),
  as soil indicator, 38
Gardena™ speed couplings,
  54
Gardens for All, garden size
  study for, 51
Garlic (Allium sativum), 306–7
  companion planting studies,
    239, 240
  Cornish Game Hens
    Stuffed wih Garlic and
    Summer Savory (re-
    cipe), 307
  cultural guidelines, 306
  designing with, 53, 306
  as dynamic accumulator,
    269
  garlic chives as substitute
    for, 58
  Hot and Sweet Baked
    (recipe), 307
  for intercropping, 134
  juice, for pest control, 256
  as multi-purpose edible, 59
  preventing cross-pollination
    in, 102
  recipes using, 307
  root zones, 135
  as slow-maturing, 138
Garlic, society (Tulbaghia
  violacea), as multi-
  purpose edible, 60
Garlic chives
  in Flores garden, 64
  as garlic substitute, 58
Gaultheria procumbens (Wintergreen), as dynamic
  accumulator, 270
Gaultheria shallon (Salal)
  as disease resistant, 155
  as lawn tolerant, 285
  as low-effort perennial, 45
  as shade tolerant, 283
Gazania, as insectary plant,
  251, 252
Gelsemium sempervirens
  (Carolina jessamine),
  for shade, Appendix 4
Genetic dwarf (miniature) fruit
  trees, 181, 183–89
  borer protection, 187
  climate considerations, 185
  in containers, 186–87
  cost factors, 186, 187
  as early bearing, 184
  extending season with,
    185–86
  fencing ease with, 186
  flavor, 185, 187
  future of, 184
  grafted, 183–84
  history, 184
  life span, 186, 187
  maintenance, 185
  pros and cons, 181, 183–
    87
  protection needs, 186, 187
  pruning, 187, 222, 223
  size compared, 179
  sun protection for, 187
  thinning fruit, 187
  winter protection, containers
    for, 187
  yields, 181, 184–85
Geno, Larry, 139
Geranium (Geranium sp.)
  companion planting studies,
    239
  as edible flower, 292
German chamomile. See
  Chamomile
Ginger, wild (Asarum

caudatum)
  for berms, 79
  as shade tolerant, 283
Gingko (Gingko biloba), winter shade by, 75
Gladiolus (Gladiolus sp.)
  ease of care, 54
  as edible flower, 292, 296
Gleditsia triacanthos (Honey
  locust), winter shade
  by, 75
Glycine max. See Soybeans
Glycyrrhiza lepidota (Wild
  licorice), as leguminous
  wildflower, 280
Gnaphalium sp. (Low cud-
  weed), as soil indicator,
  36
Golden chain tree (Laburnum
  anagyroides), as nit-
  rogen-fixing perennial,
  291
Goldenrain tree (Koelreuteria
  paniculata), winter
  shade by, 75
Goldenrod (Solidago altissima; Solidago sp.)
  as edible flower, 292
  as fruit tree cover crop, 280
  as insectary plant, 252
  intercropping successes,
    242
  as soil indicator, 36
Gooseberry (Ribes divari-
  catum)
  for berms, 79
  as blister rust host, 103
  chill requirement, 142
  as lawn tolerant, 285
  shade tolerance, 284
  wild (Ribes sp.)
    for berms, 79
    for downspout outlets, 83
Goosefoot, oak leaved, as
  soil indicator, 36
Goosegrass (Eleusine indica),
  intercropping with
  beans, 241
Gophers
  comfrey spread by, 280
  drip irrigation and, 130,
    132, 226
  as fruit tree mulch draw-
    back, 232
  hay bale garden protection
    from, 105
  planning for sacrifice to, 52
  protecting fruit trees from,
    197
    aviary wire cost factor, 45
  rootstocks resistant to
    apricot, 168
    cherry, 169
    peach/nectarine, 171
    pear, 173–74
    plum/prune, 175–76
Gosling, Doug, 'Pink Pearl'
  tart recipe by, 309
Gotu kola, as insectary plant,
  251
Gourd family (Cucurbitaceae)
  as deciduous vines, Appen-
    dix 4
  diseases
    host plants to avoid, 287
    insect vectors, 288
  preventing cross-pollination
    among, 102
Grafting
  cold hardiness and, 140–41
  controlling growth with, 191
  in Flores garden, 63, 64
  "fruit salad" tree, 63, 64
  Linquist methods, 65
  miniature fruit trees, 183–
    84
  for pollination, 153
Grain moth parasites, 247
Gramineae (Grasses), pre-
  venting cross-pollination
  among, 102
Granite dust
  under fruit tree mulch, 232
  nutrient percentages, 230
  for sheet composting, 97
Grape (Vitis labruscua, V.
  vinifera)
  average seasonal growth,
    229
  chill requirement, 142

cold-hardy varieties, 140
diseases, insect vectors, 288
in Flores garden, 64
intercropping successes, 242
kale under, 64, 133
nitrogen requirements, 230, 231
pests control measures bordering with blackberry, 259
intercropping, 242
for shade, in cold-winter areas, 73
spray necessity, 73
yields, 53
Grape, evergreen (*Rhoicissus capensis*), for shade, 73, Appendix 4
Grape, mustang (*Vitis mustangensis*), for shade, Appendix 4
Grapefruit, cold hardiness, 140
Grape leafhopper, intercropping success, 242
Grass, quack (*Agropyron repens*), as soil indicator, 36
Grass clippings. *See* Lawn clippings
Grasses (Gramineae)
as disease host, 287
as green manure, 275, 278
as ground covers, 284–85
preventing cross-pollination among, 102
Grasshoppers
IPM for, 258
parasites, 246
Gravel
angle of repose, Appendix 7
as fruit tree mulch, 200
for paths, 47
Gravity, using to advantage, 47
Greasewood (*Sarcobatus vermiculatus*), 236
Great Salt Lake Minerals and Chemical Company, organic potash source from, 231
Greenbelts, edible, 9
Green cloverworms, IPM for, 258
Green Gulch Farm, Alan Chadwick Society at, 118
Greenhouses
bale gardening in, 105
multiple uses of, 57, 58
by old-timers, 63
Green lacewings, 246
design to attract, 5
at Village Homes, 12
Green manure, 273
choosing, 267–70
drip irrigation contraindicates, 130
establishing, 273–74
fava beans for, 303
fertilizing with, 261, 265–81
around fruit trees, 232–33
legumes as nitrogen source, 265–66
for sandy soils, 118
soil improvment role, 273
soil preparation, 273–74
tilling under, 274–75
Green peach aphids (*Myzus persicae*)
companion planting, with peppers, 239, 240
as disease vectors, 287, 288
intercropping successes, 242, 243
potato varieties resistant to, 260
Greens
BFI suitability for, 118–19
chayote for, 59
growing on trellises, 134
for intercropping, 134
for no-till gardens, 95–98, 101–2, 110
shady locations for, 133
Greensand

under fruit tree mulch, 232
nutrient percentages, 230
as potassium/potash source, cost factors, 231
when planting fruit trees, 194
Green stink bug, in soybeans, 243
Grilled Chicken with Rosemary, **298–99**
Grose, Caroline, 140
Ground beetles, as beneficial predators, 247
plants to attract, 252
Ground cherry (*Physalis* sp.)
as disease host, 287
diseases harbored by, 103
as favorite no-till fruit, 96
for no-till gardens, 101
Ground covers
See also Cover crops
with brussels sprouts, 238, 241
clovers as, advantages, 114
corn salad as, 303
for erosion control, 11
under fruit trees, 191, 232–33
grasses as, 284–85
intercropping successes, 241, 242, 243
maintenance considerations, 46
thyme as, 1
weedy. *See* Weedy ground cover
Groundsel (*Senecio vulgaris*)
as dynamic accumulator, 269
as soil indicator, 36
Growing season
finding length of, 23–24
fruit and nut tree choices and, 147–48
Growing techniques, garden size and, 51
Grubs
sod culture and, 113
sweet potato varieties resistant to, 260
tillage for control of, 257
Guar, as cover crop or green manure, 267
Guava, Chilean (*Ugni molinae*)
effort ranking, 295
as shade tolerant, 283
Guava, lemon (*Psidium littorale littorale*)
as disease resistant, 155
as low-effort perennial, 45
Guava, pineapple (*Feijoa sellowiana*)
for cooling hedge, 74
designing with, 1
as disease resistant, 155
ease of care, 44, 45, 295
as hot-summer tolerant, 144
planting locations, 283
shade tolerance, 284
Guava, strawberry (*Psidium littorale*)
for cooling hedge, 74
as disease resistant, 155
in Flores garden, 64
as low-effort perennial, 45
shade tolerance, 283, 284
Guava, true, Massida's greenhouse-grown, 63
Guinea gold vine (*Hibbertia volubilis*), for shade, Appendix 4
Gummosis (*Botryosphaeria*), peach varieties and, 158
Guomi (*Elaeagnus multiflora*), shade tolerance, 284
Guy wires, living (pleaching), 215
Gypsum
in potting mix, 127
when planting fruit trees, 194
Gypsy moths
IPM for, 258
predators and parasites of, 246, 247

H

Hackberry (*Celtis occidentalis*), as windbreak, 69
Hackberry, European (*Celtis australis*), winter shade by, 75
Hairy indigo, as cover crop or green manure, 267
Hairy vetch; purple hairy vetch (*Vicia villosa*)
as cover crop or green manure, 267
as fruit tree cover crop, 280
nitrogen gathered by, 266
Hamburg parsley (*Petroselinum crispum*), as multipurpose edible, 60
Handbook of Afforestation and Soil Melioration, on windbreaks, 68
Handicapped gardeners, 50, 185
Hardenbergia comptoniana (Lilac vine), for shade, Appendix 4
Hardpan or crusty soil, 163
fruit trees and, 163
plant indicators, 36–38
Harmony, as design element, 43
Harris, Donald, with oldest miniature peach, *186*
Harris, Dr. P., on defoliation, 21
Harvesting
expanding fruit season, 147–48
fruit trees, sanitation and, 257
no-pruning style and, 211
Hassett, Rick, 139
Hawkins, Lester, 78
Hawkweeds (*Hieracium* sp.), as soil indicator, 36
Haws oval watering rose, 128
Hawthorn (*Crataegus* sp.)
Crataegus douglasii), shade tolerance, 284
as disease host, 287
as edible flower, 292
intercropping with cabbage, 242
Hay bale gardening, 105–6
Hazelnut (*Corylus* sp.), shade tolerance, 284
HCB, 3
Health
See also Effort scale; Maintenance considerations
antisiphon valve and, 130
BFI and, 117, 118, 121
edible landscaping and, 2–3
Heartnut
root system, 161
as self-fruitful, 151
Hedera helix (English ivy), for shade, Appendix 4
Hedera sp. (Ivy)
as compost problem, 97
as insectary plant, 252
Hedge bindweed (*Convolvulus sepium*), as soil indicator, 36
Hedge-nettle, marsh, as soil indicator, 36
Hedgerows/Hedges
See also Windbreaks
as beneficial insect habitat, 247
for cooling, 74
fruit trees as, no-pruning style for, 212
hiding edible weed patches behind, 97
number of plants needed, Appendix 7
nurse plants in, 248
planting fruit trees along, 143
visualizing effect of, 87
weed seeds filtered by, 98
Heleocharis palustris (Wiregrass), as soil type indicator, 35
Helianthus tuberosus (Jerusalem artichoke), shade tolerance, 284

Hellebore, false (*Veratrum californicum*), as soil indicator, 36
Hemerocallis fulva. See Day lily
Hemlock, poison (*Conium maculatum*)
as insectary plant, 251
as soil indicator, 36
Hemlock, spotted water (*Cicuta maculata*), as soil indicator, 38
Hemlock, water (*Cicuta douglasii*), as insectary plant, 251
Henbane, black (*Hyscyamus niger*), as soil indicator, 37
Henbit (*Camium amplexicaule*), as soil indicator, 37
Heptachlor, 3
Herbal lawns, 10
Herbal ley, 277, 278, 280–81
Herbicides
natural, newspaper or cardboard as, 108
no-till dogma and, 109–10
Herbs
as cover crop, 278
designing with, 284
amount to plant, 53
cultural needs and, 284
drip irrigation for, 225
in Flores garden, 64
as insectary plants, 251
planting locations, 284
vegetables and, 46–47
in salad dressing (recipe), 297
Herb teas or medicines, weeds for, 39
Heterotheca subaxillaris (Camphorweed), as insectary plant, 252
Hibbertia volubilis (Guinea gold vine), for shade, Appendix 4
Hibiscus (*Hibiscus rosasinensis*)
as edible flower, 292
Hickory
as firewood source, 84
as hot-summer tolerant, 144
as nondwarfable, 180
root system, 161
Hieracium sp. (Hawkweeds), as soil indicator, 36
Hilltop Orchards and Nurseries, Inc., pollination charts from, 152–53
Hoes, 109
Hoffmanseggia densiflora (Pignut), as leguminous wildflower, 280
Hollyhock (*Althea rosea*)
as edible flower, 292
as fruit tree cover crop, 233
Hollyleaf cherry (*Prunus ilicifolia*)
for cooling hedge, 74
multiple uses for, 58
for windbreaks, 69, 71
Honeydew, positive role of, 19–20
Honey locust (*Gleditsia triacanthos*), winter shade by, 75
Honey mesquite (*Prosopis chilensis*), as leguminous wildflower, 280
Honeysuckle (*Lonicera* sp.)
around compost bins, 9
as edible flower, 292, 296
for shade, Appendix 4
Hoof and horn meal, nutrient percentages, 230
Hop (*Humulus lupulus*), for shade, 73
Hop, Japanese (*Humulus japonicus*), for shade, 73, Appendix 4
Hop clover. See *Medicago lupulina*
Hordeum jubatum (Short awned foxtail), as soil indicator, 36
Horehound (*Marrubium vulgare*)

as fruit tree cover crop, 280
as soil indicator, 37
Hornet wasps, plants to attract, 252
Hornworms, IPM for, 258
Horse manure, nutrient content, 230, Appendix 5
Horsenettle (*Solanum carolinense*)
as disease host, 288
as soil indicator, 37
Horseradish
companion planting and, 237, 238, 239
root zones, 134, 135
Horsetail (*Equisetum* sp.)
for berms, 79
cover crop problems, 278
as dynamic accumulator, 269
for erosion prevention, 78, 79
field (*Equisetum arvense*) as dynamic accumulator, 269
as soil indicator, 37
marsh, as dynamic accumulator, 269
as soil indicator, 37
Hoses
drip, 131
Gardena speed couplings for, cost vs. time saved, 54
Host plants, 287
Hot-summer areas
BFI contraindicated in, 118
fruit trees for, 144
Hot and Sweet Baked Garlic (recipe), **307**
Houseflies, IPM for, 258
Hover flies. *See* Syrphid flies
Howard, Sir Albert, 261
How to Build Orchard and Vineyard Trellises, 222
How to Grow More Vegetables (Jeavons)
as required reading on BFI, 115
on yields per area, 51
Hubbard, Henry, 41
Huckleberry (*Vaccinium ovatum*)
for berms, 79
as favorite no-till fruit, 96
for no-till gardens, 101
as shade tolerant, 283
Hula hoe, 109
Human manure, nitrogen content and C:N ratio, Appendix 5
Humidity
data gathering on, 24
solar greenhouse and, 83
Humpback flies, as beneficial predators, 246
Humulus. See Hop
Humus, 29–30, 261
cover crops or green manures for, 273
promoting renewal of, 261. *See also* specific methods
water-holding ability, 77
Hyacinth, ease of care, 54
Hyacinth bean (Dolichos lablab), for shade, 73, Appendix 4
Hydrangea, climbing (*Hydrangea anomala*), for shade, Appendix 4
Hymenelytra (Desert holly), as nitrogen-fixing perennial, 291
Hypericum sp. (Saint-John's-wort), as edible flower, 292
Hyscyamus niger (Black henbane), as soil indicator, 37
Hyssop (*Hyssopus officinalis*)
as edible flower, 292
as multi-purpose edible, 60

I

Iberis sp. (Candytuft)
as insectary plant, 252
intercropping with brassicas, 241

Iceland moss, as dynamic accumulator, 269
Ichneumonids, as beneficial predators, 246
plants to attract, 252
Imported cabbage butterflies intercropping successes, 241, 242
weedy ground cover for, 238, 241
Imported cabbageworms, companion planting studies, 239, 240
Indicator plants, 32, 35–39
Indigo, hairy, as cover crop or green manure, 267
Inoculants, 125–26, 274
Insectary plants, 39, 247, 251–53
Insecticides. See Pesticides
Insects. See Pests
"Inspired laziness," 16
Institute for Local Self-Reliance, garden size chart, 51, 52
Integral Urban House, The, on soil testing, 30
Intensive Gardening (O'Brien), 107
Intercropping, 133–38
basic principles, 133, 235
climate and, 237
companion planting vs., 235, 237
as part of IPM, 257, 259
for pest control, 237–39, 241–43, 247–53
root systems and, 134–37
slow- and fast-growing vegetables, 137–38
for space, 133–37
successful scientific trials, 241–43
for sunlight, 133
traditional guidelines tested, 239–40
yields and, 238
International Gardens, Seattle, 134
Invasive wild edibles, avoiding, 98
Iodine accumulator plants, 269–70
IPM (Integrated pest management), 255–60
Ipomoea alba (Moonflower vine), for shade, Appendix 4
Ipomoea sp. (Morning glory) intercropping with sweet potato, 243
for shade, 73, Appendix 4
Iris, Dutch, ease of care, 54
Irish moss, as dynamic accumulator, 269
Iron
accumulator plants, 269–70
comfrey as source of, 281
Irrigation. See Watering
Isogonic chart, 26
Ivy (*Hedera* sp.)
as compost problem, 97
as insectary plant, 252
for shade, Appendix 4
Ivy, Boston (*Parthenocissus quinquefolia*), for shade, Appendix 4

J
Jackson, Paul, 58
Japanese beetles
intercropping success, 243
IPM for, 258, 259
sod culture and, 113
tillage for control of, 257
Japanese bush plum (*Prunus japonica*)
as disease resistant, 155
as low-effort perennial, 45
Japanese hop (*Humulus japonicus*), for shade, 73, Appendix 4
Japanese pagoda (*Sophora japonica*), as nitrogen-fixing perennial, 291
Jasmine (*Jasminum* sp.)
around compost bins, 280
as edible flower, 292
for shade, Appendix 4
Jeavons, John, 115

on BFI garden size, 118
on cultivation time requirements, 55
double-digging method, 116
on spacing, 116, 119, 121
on yields, 51, 116
Jerusalem artichoke (*Helianthus tuberosus*)
as insectary plant, 251
for intercropping, 134
in no-till garden, 102
planting locations for, 57
shade tolerance, 284
for sink-or-swim approach, 101
for vertical gardening, 134
Jimson weed (*Datura stramonium*)
as disease host, 287
for Japanese beetle, 259
Jobb, Jamie, 101, 103
Joe-pye weed, as soil indicator, 37
Johnny-jump-up (*Viola tricolor*), as edible flower, 292
Johnson grass (*Sorghum halepense*)
as disease host, 287
intercropping with grapes, 242
Johnson, Hugh, 42
Jojoba (*Simmondsia chinensis*), for cooling hedge, 74
Juglans sp. See Walnut
Jujube (*Zizyphus jujube*)
as disease resistant, 155
as hot-summer tolerant, 144
as lawn tolerant, 285
as low-effort perennial, 45
as nonwarfable, 180
as self-fruitful, 151
June beetles, sod culture and, 113
June bugs, tillage for control of, 257
Juniper
maintenance requirements, 44
windbreak suitability, 69

K
Kadsura japonica (Scarlet kadsura), for shade, Appendix 4
Kale (*Brassica oleracea*)
closely planting, to deter aphids, 242
as cover crop, 267, 273
under fruit trees, 233
in Flores garden, 64, 133
as green manure, 267, 273, 275
hot-weather protection for, 74
intercropping with, 133, 242
in no-till garden, 102
nutritional value, 96
ornamental (*Brassica oleracea; B. campestris*), 295–96, 295
cultural guidelines, 296
designing with, 1, 296
in Ensalada de Flores (recipe), 296–97
served with 'Romanesco' (recipe), 298
preventing cross-pollination in, 102
Scotch, as cover crop or green manure, 267
as shade tolerant, 284
Kelley, Mr. and Mrs. John. See Kelley garden
Kelley garden, 5–6, 49
concurrent use zones in, 58
maintenance requirements, 54–55
size of, 51
Kelp
as dynamic accumulator, 269
as fertilizer, 231. See also Kelp meal
Kelp meal
nutrient percentages, 230
in potting mix, 127
when planting fruit trees,

194
Kentucky bluegrass, nitrogen content and C:N ratio, Appendix 5
Kernel red streak, insect vectors of, 288
Kidd, Sarah, 38, 108
Kidney beans, root zones, 135
Kiley-Worthington, M., 15
"Kindly use," concept of, 15
Kinosprene, for whiteflies, 259
Kitchen scraps
in bastard trench, before surface cultivation, 107
compost pile for, locating, 57
worm bin for, locating, 57
Kiwi (*Actinidia arguta; A. chinensis*), 304
chill requirement, 142
cultural guidelines, 304
as disease resistant, 155
as hot-weather-damage susceptible, 144
as keeper, 147
Kiwicoladas (recipe), 304
as lawn tolerant, 285
as low-effort perennial, 45
Massida's cultivation of, 63
for shade, 73, Appendix 4
shade tolerance, 284
Kiwicoladas (recipe), 304
Knapweed (*Centaurea nigra*), as soil indicator, 37
Knawel (*Scleranthus annuus*), as soil indicator, 37
Knotweed, prostrate (*Polygonum aviculare*), as soil indicator, 37
Koelreuteria elegans (Chinese flame tree), winter shade by, 75
Koelreuteria paniculata (Goldenrain tree), winter shade by, 75
Kohlrabi
for intercropping, 133
preventing cross-pollination in, 102
as quick-maturing, 138
root zones, 135
as shade tolerant, 133
Kourik, Grandma, 43
Kumquat
cold hardiness, 140, 141
in Flores garden, 64

L
Lablab. See Hyacinth bean
Laburnum anagyroides (Golden chain tree), as nitrogen-fixing perennial, 291
Lacewings (Chrysopidae family), as beneficial predators, 246
plants to attract, 252
Lactuca canadensis. See Lettuce, wild
Lactuca scariola (Prickly lettuce), as soil indicator, 37
Lady's thumb (*Polygonum persicaria*)
intercropping with corn, 242
as soil indicator, 37
Ladybird beetles, as beneficial predators, 247, 248, 256
Ladybugs, as beneficial predators, 246, 247
larva, 245, 246
plants to attract, 252
for scale, 259
at Village Homes, 12
Lamb's-quarters (*Chenopodium album*)
companion plant myth, 235
as disease host, 287
as dynamic accumulator, 269
as favorite no-till green, 96
intercropping with, 133, 242
as nitrogen-lover, 98
for no-till gardens, 96, 101
nutritional value, 96
as shade tolerant, 133
as soil indicator, 37
Landscape architecture

questionable practices, 41–42
traditional, 41
Landscapers, fruit and nut tree disease information from, 155
Larrea tridentata (Creosote bush), 194
Lathyrus odoratus (Sweet pea), for shade, Appendix 4
Lathyrus latifolius (Perennial sweet pea), as leguminous wildflower, 280
Lavender (*Lavandula officinalis*)
companion planting studies, 239
as edible flower, 292, 296
Lawn clippings
as compost material, 108, Appendix 5
as seed-free mulch, 97
Lawns
advantages of, 10
cover crops or green manures as, 273
around fruit trees, 232
fruit trees and, 284–86
green manures as, 278
growing vegetables in, 113–14
maintenance, 10
mowing, with sod culture, 113
positive aspects, 113
separation for, 284
size for, 113
Village Homes, 9, 9–11
Laziness, importance of, 92
LD (toxicity ratings), 19, 20
Leaf beetles, intercropping successes, 242
Leaf curl, peaches varieties to, 157
Leaf diseases, drip irrigation reduces, 129
Leaf fall sequence, data gathering, 27–28
Leaf mold
when planting fruit trees, 197, 198
as seed-free mulch, 97
Leaf spot
drip irrigation reduces, 129
host plants for, 287
Leafhoppers
as disease vectors, 288
intercropping successes, 241, 242
IPM for, 258, 259
predators, 246
Leafrollers, IPM for, 258
Leather meal, for fruit trees, 194
as nitrogen source, 229, 230
Leeks
intercropping with, 133, 134, 137
preventing cross-pollination in, 102
root zones, 135
as shade tolerant, 133
as slow-maturing, 138
Legumes
as corn feeders, 114
as cover crop or green manure, 274
in crop rotation, 277–80
diseases, insect vectors, 288
inoculants for, 125, 126, 274
as nitrogen sources, 265–66, 291
for soil improvement, 291
before potatoes, 110
Leguminous wildflowers, 280
Lemon
blossom as edible, 292
cold-hardy varieties, 140–41
in Flores garden, 64
planting locations, 44
yields, 53
Lemon balm (*Melissa officinalis*)
as dynamic accumulator, 269

as edible flower, 292
as fruit tree cover crop, 280
as multi-purpose edible, 60
for no-till gardens, 101
shade tolerance, 284
Lemon basil, 2
Lemon blossom (*Citrus limon*), as edible flower, 292
Lemon guava. See Guava, lemon
Lemon verbena (*Aloysia triphyllia*)
as edible flower, 292
in Flores garden, 64
Lemquat, in Flores garden, 64
Leptochloa filliformis. See Red sprangletop
Lespedeza (*Lespedeza* sp.)
as cover crop or green manure, 267
as leguminous wildflower, 280
Lettuce
BFI suitability, 118
as compost material, nitrogen content and C:N ratio, Appendix 5
diseases
host plants to avoid, 287
insect vectors, 288
head or iceberg
nutritional value, 96
surface cultivation vs. single-dug yields, 110
hot-weather protection for, 74
intercropping, 133, 134, 137
leaf
for intercropping, 133
as quick-maturing, 138
as shade tolerant, 133
in Malcolm-Neeb garden, 2
nitrogen requirements, 231
ornamental kale among, for color, 1
planting with broccoli, in BFI, 116
as quick-maturing, 138
root zones, 134, 135, 137
Lettuce, prickly (*Lactuca scariola*), as soil indicator, 37
Lettuce, wild (*Lactuca canadensis*)
as disease host, 287
as insectary plant, 252
Leviticum officinale. See Lovage
Lewis and Associates, Solar Site Selector from, 27
Licorice, root, as dynamic accumulator, 269
Licorice, wild (*Glycyrrhiza lepidota*), as leguminous wildflower, 280
Lilac (*Syringa vulgaris*)
as disease host, 287
as edible flower, 292
Lilac vine (*Hardenbergia comptoniana*), for shade, Appendix 4
Lilies, ease of care, 54. See also Day lily
Lillaceae (Onion family), preventing cross-pollination among, 102
Lima beans
diseases, host plants to avoid, 287
root zones, 134, 135
Lime
See also Citrus; Fruit and nut trees
aphids as fertilizing aid for, 19–20
cold hardiness, 140
Limequat, cold hardiness, 140
Lime spray, for cucumber beetles, 259
Liming soil
for calcium, 262
for fruit tree cover crop, 197
for fruit tree planting hole, 197
for legume cover crops or green manures, 274
after potato harvest, 110
to reduce soil acidity, 39
Limnanthes douglasii

(Meadow foam), as insectary plant, 252, 253
Linaria vulgaris (Toadflax)
  as dynamic accumulator, 270
  as soil indicator, 38
Lindane, toxicity of, 20
Linden (*Tilia americana*), winter shade by, 75
Linquist, Emil
  notching technique, 207
  rare fruit evangelism by, 65–66
Linum usitatissimum (Seed flax), as dynamic accumulator, 269
Liquidambar styraciflua (Sweetgum), leaf fall, 28
Liquid measure conversions, Appendix 6
Living mulch
  in BFI, 115
  with cabbage, research on, 240
Loam, angle of repose, Appendix 7. *See also* Soil
Local wisdom, 63–66
Locoweed (*Astragalus* sp.), as leguminous wildflower, 280
Locust eggs, parasites of, 246
Loganberry, cultural hints, 286
London plane tree. *See Platanus acerifolia*
Long-legged flies, plants to attract, 252
Lonicera sp. *See* Honeysuckle
Loquat (*Eriobotrya japonica*)
  as disease resistant, 155
  ease of care, 44, 45, 295
  in Flores garden, 64
  at hot-weather-damage susceptible, 144
  as lawn tolerant, 285
  as nondwarfable, 180
  ripening dates, northern California, 147
  as self-fruitful, 151
Lotus sp. (Trefoils; Bird's-foot trefoil)
  as cover crop, 273
    under fruit trees, 280, 285
  for downspout outlets, 83
  for herbal lawns, 10
  as leguminous wildflower, 280
Lovage (*Leviticum officinale*)
  as insectary plant, 251
  as multi-purpose edible, 60
Luffa (*Luffa cylindrica*)
  as multi-purpose plant, 60
  for quick shade, 73, Appendix 4
Lupine (*Lupinus* sp.)
  as cover crop, 267, 273, 278
    under fruit trees, 233, 280
  as dynamic accumulator, 269
  as green manure, 267
  as leguminous wildflower, 280
  as perennial fertilizer, 291
  as soil indicator, 37, 274
Lychnis alba (Campion), as soil indicator, 36
Lygus bugs, as beneficial predators, 246
  host plants for, 288

M

Macadamia
  as nondwarfable, 180
  as self-fruitful, 151
Macauley, E.D.
Maché. *See* Corn salad
Machines vs. people, 16
Macronutrients, 261–62
Madeira vine (*Anredera cordifolia*), for shad, Appendix 4
Magnesium accumulator plants, 269–70
Magnetic Deviation Chart, 26
Mahonia aquifolium (Oregon grape)

for berms, 79
  as shade tolerant, 283
Mahonia nervosa (Oregon grape), as shade tolerant, 283
Mail-order nurseries, buying trees from, 155, 198, 331–340
Maintenance considerations
  See also Effort scale
  compactness, 47
  designing for, 44–47
  double-dug beds, 121
  drip irrigation systems, 132
  edibles, 54–55
  fruit trees size, 180
  genetic dwarf fruit trees, 185
  old-timers as source on, 63
  ornamentals, 54, 55
  planting locations and, 46–47, 57–58
  time requirements, 54–55
  windbreaks, vines vs. trees, 70
Maize chlorotic mosaic, 287, 288
Maize dwarf mosaic, 287, 288
Malathion, toxicity of, 19, 20
Malcolm-Neeb, Helen, edible landscape by, 1–2
Mallow (*Malva* sp.)
  cover crop problems, 278
  as disease host, 287
  as fruit tree cover crop, 233
  M. neglecta, as edible flower, 292
  as multi-purpose edible, 60
  musk (*M. moschata*), as soil indicator, 36
  as shade tolerant, 283
Malus pumila. *See* Apple
Malva moschata. *See* Mallow, musk
Malva neglecta. *See* Mallow
Malva sp. *See* Mallow
Mandarin orange, cold hardiness, 140
Manganese accumulator plants, 269–70
Manure
  in berm construction, 78
  under fruit tree mulch, 232
  as fruit tree nitrogen source, 229, 230
  as fruit tree soil amendment, 193, 194, 198
  for hay bale garden, 105
  for lawns, 10
  nutrient content, 230, Appendix 5
  planning amount needed, Appendix 7
  as phosphorus source, 231
  as potassium/potash source, 231
  after potato harvest, 110
  for sheet composting, 97
  in sod culture, 114
  sugar beet pest control with, 243
Manure tea, for sandy soils, 118
Maple
  big-leaf, windbreak suitability, 69
  soil amendments study, 193
Mapping the garden, 201
Mare's tail (*Erigeron canadensis*), as soil indicator, 37
Marguerites, maintenance requirements, 44
Marigold (*Tagetes* sp.)
  African, as trap crop, 259
  caterpillars and, 237
  companion planting results, 237, 239, 240
  as cover crop, 273, 278
  dead-heading requirements, 54
  as dynamic accumulator, 269
  under fruit trees, 227
  as insectary plant, 251, 259
  intercropping with, for color, 238
  Mexican (*Tagetes minuta*), as cover crop or green manure, 273

for nematode control, 273
Marigold, corn, as soil indicator, 36
Marin County, "edible" apartments in, 64–65
Marjoram (*Origanum majorana*), as edible flower, 292
Marmalade bush (*Streptosolen jamesoni*), for shade, Appendix 4
Marrubium vulgare (Horehound)
  as fruit tree cover crop, 280
  as soil indicator, 37
Marsh flies, as beneficial predators, 247
Marsh hedge-nettle, as soil indicator, 36
Masking plants from pests, 241–43, 247, 248
Masonry paths, 47
Massida, Joe, 63
Matricaria chamomilla. *See* Chamomile
Matricaria matricarioides (Pineapple weed), as soil indicator, 37
Maypop (*Passiflora incense*; *P. incarnata*), for shade, in cold-winter areas, 73
Mayweed (*Anthemis cotula*), as soil indicator, 37
Meadow foam (*Limnanthes douglasii*), as insectary plant, 252, 253
Meadow sweet (*Astilbe* sp.)
  as dynamic accumulator, 269
  as soil indicator, 37
Mealybugs
  IPM for, 258
  predators of, 5, 246, 247
Measurements, liquid measure conversions, Appendix 6
Meat scraps, as compost material, Appendix 6
Medicago hispida. *See* Bur clover
Medicago lupulina (Black medic; Hop clover)
  as dynamic accumulator, 269
  as soil indicator, 36, 37
Medicago sativa. *See* Alfalfa
Medicines, weeds as, 39
Mediterranean fruit fly, malathion toxicity, 19
Mediterranean umble (*Bupleurum fruticosum*), as insectary plant, 252
Melilotus alba. *See* Clover, sweet white
Melissa officinalis. *See* Lemon balm
Melon
  growing on trellises, 134
  muskmelon, root zones, 135
  preventing cross-pollination in, 102
  as slow-maturing, 138
  surface cultivation vs. single-dug yields, 110
  watermelon, root zones, 135
Melon aphids, muskmelon varieties resistant to, 260
Melon fly, bean variety resistant to, 260
Mentha sp. *See* Mints
Mesquite (*Prosopis glandulosa torreyana*), as windbreak, firewood from, 84
Mesquite; Honey mesquite (*Prosopis chilensis*)
  as leguminous wildflower, 280
  as nitrogen-fixing perennial, 291
Methoxychlor, 2, 20
Mexican-American gardeners, as source of wisdom, 63
Mexican bean beetles

bean varieties resistant to, 260
  companion planting studies, 239
  IPM for, 258, 259
Mexican flame vine (*Senecio confusus*), for shade, Appendix 4
Mexican tea (*Chenopodium ambrosioides*)
  as insectary plant, 242, 252
  intercropping with corn, 242
Mice, 200, 232
  drip irrigation and, 130, 132
  rootstocks resistant to
    apricot, 168
    cherry, 169
    peach/nectarine, 171
    pear, 173–74
    plum/prune 175–76
Microclimate
  in BFI, 115
  companion planting and, 237
  data gathering about, 23–28
  fruit trees and, 141, 143–44
  near house, 83
  intercropping and, 237
Midges, predators of, 246
Mildew
  in fruit trees, from overwatering, 285
  as intercropping contraindication, 239
Milkweed (*Asclepius syriaca*), as soil indicator, 37
Millet
  as cover crop, 267, 273
  as green manure, 267, 273, 275, 278
Milorganite™, nitrogen content and C:N ratio, Appendix 5
Miner's lettuce (*Claytonia perfoliata*; *Montia perfoliata*)
  for berms, 79
  as favorite no-till green, 96
  for intercropping, 133
  as multi-purpose edible, 60
  for no-till gardens, 101
  as shade tolerant, 133
Minerals, as soil component, 29, 30
Miniature (genetic dwarf) fruit trees, 181, 183–89
  borer protection, 187
  climate considerations, 185
  in containers, 186–87
  cost factors, 186, 187
  as early bearing, 184
  extending season with, 185–86
  fencing ease with, 186
  flavor, 185, 187
  future of, 184
  grafted, 183–84
  history, 184
  life span, 186, 187
  maintenance, 185
  pros and cons, 181, 183–87
  protection needs, 186, 187
  pruning, 187, 222, 223
  size compared, 179
  sun protection for, 187
  thinning fruit, 187
  winter protection, containers for, 187
  yields, 181, 184–85
Mints (*Mentha* sp.)
  for berms, 79
  cautions about, 80, 238
  for erosion prevention, 78
  as lawn tolerant, 285
  peppermint (*M. piperita*)
    companion planting studies, 239
    as dynamic accumulator, 270
    as shade tolerant, 283
  planting, 78
  spearmint (*M. spicata*), as shade tolerant, 283
Minute pirate bugs, 246
  plants to attract, 252
Misting
  for cooling, 73–74
  for frost protection, 228

Mistletoe, as dynamic accumulator, 270
Mites
  IPM for, 258
  predators of, 246, 247
  predatory, 246, 247
Moisture content, plant indicators, 35, 36–38
Moisture retention, improving, 77
  berm construction, 78–79
  sod culture for, 113
  swales, 77–79
Molasses, dried granular, in potting mix, 127
Mold, in fruit trees, from overwatering, 285
Moles
  as fruit tree mulch drawback, 232
  as Japanese beetle predators, 259
  protecting fruit trees from, 197
Mollissima sp. *See* Chestnut, Chinese
Mollugo verticillata (Carpetweed), as soil indicator, 36
Momordica balsamina M. balsamina (Balsam apple; Balsam pear), for quick shade, 73
Monarda didyma (Bee balm)
  as edible flower, 292
  as multi-purpose edible, 59
  as shade tolerant, 283
Monilinia laxa. *See* Brown rot
Monstera deliciosa (Split-leaf philodendron), as shade tolerant, 283
Montia perfoliata. *See* Miner's lettuce
Moonflower (*Calonyction aculeatum*), for quick shade, 73
Moonflower vine (*Ipomoea alba*), for shade Appendix 4
Morning glory
  Ipomoea asarifolia intercropping with sweet potatoes, 243
  Ipomoea sp., for shade, 73, Appendix 4
  perennial ornamental (Convolvulus minor), as insectary plant, 252
Morus alba; *M. nigra*. *See* Mulberry
Mosquitoes, predators of, 246
Mosses (*Bryophyta* sp.), as soil indicator, 37
Moths, parasites of, 246, 247
Mountain mahogany (*Cercocarpus montanus*), as nitrogen-fixing, 291
Mountain whitethorn (*Ceanothus cordulatus*), as nitrogen-fixing, 291
Mud-dauber wasps, plants to attract, 252
Muehlenbeckia complexa (Wire vine), for shade, Appendix 4
Mugwort (*Artemesia vulgaris*), as soil indicator, 37
Mulberry (*Morus alba*; *M. nigra*)
  chill requirement, 142
  as disease resistant, 155
  ease of care, 45, 295
  as edible windbreak, 69
  as lawn tolerant, 285
  shade tolerance, 283
  winter shade cast by, 75
Mulch/Mulching
  aphid repellent, 259
  for bare BFI, importance of, 95
  with BFI, in hot summer areas, 118
  compost as, 281
  in surface cultivation method, 107
  with drip irrigation, 226
  for fruit trees, 226–27
  in containers, 186
  drawbacks, 140, 200, 232

growing season and, 232
perennial, 227, 231–32
watering and, 227
white gravel, 185
for hay bale garden, 106
"living,"
in BFI, 115
for cabbage, research on, 240
multi-purpose plants for, 59
nonliving, for cabbage moth control, 238
for paths, 45, 47
pros and cons, 292
for reducing erosion, 95
seed-free materials for, 97
sheet composting, 96–98
slug or snail problem in, 103
before sod culture, 113
sources for, 39
in surface cultivation method, 107–8
water slowed by, 77
Mulch, living. *See* Living mulch
Mullein (*Verbascum* sp.)
as cover crop, 278
for fruit trees, 280
as dynamic accumulator, 270
as edible flower, 292, 296
as soil indicator, 37
Multi-layer planting, design considerations, 47
Multi-purpose design, 5–6
advantages of, 94
multiple-use plantings, 58–60
synergy with, 83–84
Mung beans, intercropping success, 242
Mushrooms, edible, 39
gathering, as growing alternative, 51
Muskmelon
pest-resistant varieties, 260
root zones, 135
Muskmelon mosaic virus, ground cherry spreads, 103
Mustards (*Brassica* sp.)
black (*B. nigra*), as fruit tree cover crop, 233, 280
companion planting studies, 240
as cover crop, 273, 278
as dynamic accumulator, 270
as edible flower, 292, 296
as green manure, tilling under, 275
greens, as quick-maturing, 138
as multi-purpose edible, 60
nitrogen content and C:N ratio, Appendix 5
for no-till gardens, 101, 102
as soil indicator, 37
white (*Brassica hirta*)
as cover crop or green manure, 267
as insectary plant, 252
wild (*B. kaber*)
as disease host, 287
intercropping successes, 242
Myoporum lateum, as windbreak, 70, 71
Myoporum parvifolium, for erosion control, 11
Myrrhis odorata (Sweet Cicely), shade tolerance, 284
Myths
companion planting, 237–40
deep-rooted, 134, 161–62
pest control, 19–21, 237–43, 245

N

NAFEX. See North American Fruit Explorers
Nanking cherry (*Prunus tomentosa*)
as disease resistant, 155
as low-effort perennial, 45
Nasturtium (*Tropaeolum* sp.)
aphids and, 238, 248

for berms, 79
cabbages and, 238
for color, 1
companion planting studies, 239, 240
as edible flower, 292
under fruit trees, 227
for intercropping, 133
as multi-purpose plant, 58, 60
for shade, 73, Appendix 4
as shade tolerant, 133
using flowers in salads, 59, 296
for whiteflies, 259
Nasturtium officinale. See Watercress
Natal plum (*Carissa edulis; C. grandiflora*)
for cooling hedge, 74
as disease resistant, 155
as low-effort perennial, 45
National Garden Bureau, companion plant research by, 239
National Weather Service, 24
Natural farming, concept of, 15–16
Nature and Properties of Soils (Buckman and Brady), 29, 261, 262
Navarretia squarrosa (Skunk cabbage), as dynamic accumulator, 270
Nectarine
average seasonal growth, 229
chill requirements, 142, 143
choosing, by rootstock, 171–72
clay soil problem, 193
cold hardiness, 139, 140; *see also* frost tolerance
crown rot susceptibility, 194
disease-resistant rootstocks, 171–72
'Fantasia'
chill requirement, 143
ripening dates, 148
in Flores garden, 63, 64
frost tolerance, 228; *see also* cold hardiness
fruiting buds, 204
'Garden Beauty,' 1
chill requirement, 143
pros and cons, 188
ripening dates, 148
'Garden Delight'
chill requirement, 143
pros and cons, 188
genetic dwarf, 181, 183
climate considerations, 195
designs with, 1
flavor, 185, 187
future of, 184
pros and cons, 188
pruning, 222, 223
yields, 184–85
grafted on plum, *63*
as hot-summer tolerant, 144
low-chill varieties, 143
nitrogen requirements, 230
pest-resistant rootstocks, 171–72
painting trunk, to prevent borers, 200
planting locations, separate from lawns, 284
pruning
genetic dwarf varieties, 222, 223
open center style for, 213
ripening dates, 148
rootstocks, matching to soil types, 171–72
as self-fruitful, 151
semi-dwarf rootstocks, 171
'Southern Belle'
chill requirement, 143
pros and cons, 188
standard rootstocks, 171, 180
'Sunbonnet'
chill requirement, 143
pros and cons, 188
yields, 53
Neglected soil, plant indicators, 36–88

Neighbors, as information source, 92, 140, 141
Nematodes
controlling, 194
with cover crops or green manures, 273
as disease vectors, 288
marigolds and, 239
sod culture and, 113
Nemophila inignis (Baby blue eyes), as insectary plant, 252
Nerium oleander. See Oleander
Nettle, stinging (*Urtica* sp.)
companion planting studies, 240
for erosion prevention, 78, 79
for intercropping, 133
for no-till gardens, 101
nutritional value, 96
as shade tolerant, 133
U. dioica
for berms, 79
as invasive, 98
U. urens
as dynamic accumulator, 270
as soil indicator, 37
New Alchemy Institute, 125
New Jersey tea (*Ceanothus americanus*), as nitrogen-fixing, 291
Newspaper
ink color importance, 97
as natural herbicide, 78, 96, 97, 108
nitrogen content and C:N ratio, Appendix 5
no-till vegetable planting in, 102
New Weather Observer, The, 28
New York State Fruit Testing Cooperative Association, 155
New Zealand spinach (*Tetragonia expansa*), for berms, 79
New Zealand white clover, intercropping with oats, 242
Nicandra physalodes (Shoofly plant), 237
Nicotiana sp. (Tobacco)
companion planting studies, 239
as dynamic accumulator, 270
intercropping with collards, 242
pest control problem, 237–38
Nicotine, toxicity of, 20
Nicotine sulphate
for leafhoppers, 259
toxicity rating compared, 19, 20
Nightshade
black (*Solanum nigrum*), for no-till gardens, 101
as disease host, 287
Nitrogen
accumulator plants, 269–70
Azotobacter as source of, 19, 108
carbon-to-nitrogen ratios, for sheet composting, 97
clover as source of, 102, 114
comfrey as source of, 281
determining need for, 229
Dutch white clover fixes, 114
for fruit trees, 229–31
green manure for, 274–75
for hay bale garden, 105–6
inoculants and, 125–26
legumes as source of, 265–66
mowing legumes to increase, 114
mulching, and 292
non-animal source of, 108
potatoes as depleter of, 110
problems of excess, 261, 286
role of, 261

in sod culture, 113
urine as source of, 105–6
wild edibles thrive on, 98
Nitrogen excess, 261, 286
Nitrogen-fixing plants, nonleguminous, 291
Nodding thistle (*Carduus nutans*)
as dynamic accumulator, 270
as soil indicator, 38
North American Fruit Explorers (*NAFEX*)
cold hardiness information from, 140
miniature trees boosted by, 184
as old-time fruit source, 155
Norton, Robert, 187
Notching fruit trees, 206–7
No-till gardening
advantages of, 111
area required for, 51
choosing plants for, 101
dogma caution, 109–10
hay bale method, 105–6
health factors, 121
planting, 110
preventing cross pollination in, 101, 102
self-seeding vegetables, 101–3
sheet composting, 96–98
sink-or-swim approach, 101–3
surface cultivation approach, 107–10
Nurse plants, 247, 248–49
Nurseries
as chill zone source, 141
disease information from, 155
mail-order, 155, 165, 331–44
Nut grass (*Cyperus esculentus*), for berms, 79
Nutrient content
of compostable materials, Appendix 5
indicator plants for estimating, 35
Nutrient use, root depth and, 134
Nut trees, as edible windbreaks, 69. *See also* Fruit and nut trees; *specific nuts*

O

Oak (*Quercus* sp.)
bark, as dynamic accumulator, 270
black, winter shade cast by, 75
as disease host, 287
as firewood source, 84
oak-caterpillar symbiosis, 21
pest-repellent features, 139
self-pruning by, 209–10
white, as disease host, 287
as windbreak, 84
winter shade by, 75
Oak leaf caterpillars, positive role of, 21
Oak root fungus, rootstocks resistant to
almond, 166
apricot, 168
cherry, 169
peach/nectarine, 171
pear, 173–74
plum/prune, 175
Oat hay, for bale gardening, 105
Oats
azotobacter inoculant for, 126
as cover crop, 267, 273
for fruit trees, 280
as disease host, 287
as green manure, 267, 273, 278
intercropping success, 242
Oat straw
as dynamic accumulator, 270
nitrogen content and C:N ratio, Appendix 5

O'Brien, R. Dalziel, on surface cultivation, 107, 109
Observation, pest control role, 255, 256
Oenothera biennis; O. laciniata (Evening primrose; Primrose)
as cover crop, 278
as dynamic accumulator, 270
as insectary plant, 252
Ogalla aquifer, 77
Oil spray
Okra, root zones, 135
Olallieberry, cultural hints, 286
Olbrich, Marshall, 78
Olea europaea. See Olive
Oleander (*Nerium oleander*)
as insectary plant, 252, 253
as nurse plant, 248
Olive (*Olea europaea*)
as disease resistant, 155
in Flores garden, 64
as hot-summer tolerant, 144
as low-effort perennial, 45
as nondwarfable, 180
planting locations, separate from lawns, 284
potassium/potash deficiency signs, 231
as self-fruitful, 151
size, 180
as windbreak, 69
Omnivorous leaf roller, weather monitoring for, 25
One-Straw Revolution, The (Fukuoka), 109, 211
Onion
chives as substitute for, 58
companion planting studies, 239, 240
as compost material, nitrogen content and C:N ratio, Appendix 5
Egyptian top-set (*Allium cepa* var. *viviprium*), 58, 59
intercropping with, 134, 242
pest-resistant varieties, 260
planning area for, 53
preventing cross-pollination in, 102
root zones, 135, 136
as slow-maturing, 138
Onion family (Lilliaceae), preventing cross-pollination among, 102
Onion hoe, 109
Onion maggots, 260
Onion thrips, 260
Onobrychis sativa (Sainfoin), as leguminous wildflower, 280
Open center pruning, 213–15
for miniature trees, 222
Opuntia sp. *See* Prickly pear
Orange
See also Citrus; Fruit and nut trees
blossom (*Citrus sinensis*), as edible flower, 292, 296
cold hardiness, 140, 141
in Flores garden, 64
Orchard grass, as fruit tree ground cover, 285
Orchid vine (*Stigmaphyllon ciliatum*), for shade, Appendix 4
Oregano (*Origanum vulgare*)
companion planting studies, 240
as edible flower, 292
in Flores garden, 64
Oregon grape (*Mahonia nervosa; M. aquifolium*)
for berms, 79
as shade tolerant, 283
Organic gardening, 15–16
complexity of, 21
myths and facts, 19–21
soil feeding as part of, 261–62
Organic Gardening, companion planting myth from, 237
Organic insecticides, 19, 20

Organic matter
  for fruit tree planting hole,
    193–95, 197–98
  nutrient content, 230,
    Appendix 5
  as panacea, 30, 38
  for sheet composting, 97
  as soil component, 29, 30
  water slowed by, 77
Oriental fruit moths
  IPM for, 258
  on peach, intercropping
    successes, 242
Oriental gardens
  as source of wisdom, 63
  vertical space use in, 134
Oriental persimmon. See Persimmon
Origanum majorana (Mar-
  joram), as edible flower,
  292
Origanum vulgare. See Oregano
Ornamentals
  for compost or mulch mate-
    rials, 280–81
  cover crops or green manu-
    res as, 273
  edibles as, 1–3, 58
  under fruit trees, 227, 232
  maintenance time require-
    ments, 54, 55
  nitrogen-fixing, 291
  as nurse plants, 248
  windbreaks as, 69
Osage orange, as windbreak,
  firewood from, 84
Owen, Dennis
Ox eye daisy (Chrysanthe-
  mum leucanthemum),
  as soil indicator, 36
Oxalis oregana (Redwood
  sorrel), as shade tolerant, 283
Oyster shell; Oyster shell flour
  for fruit trees, 194, 197,
    198, 232
  in potting mix, 127
  in sheet composting, 97

P
Pacific mites, in grapes, 242
Pacific Northwest
  peach culture in, 185, 187
  solar greenhouse caution,
    83
Pandorea jasminoides (Bower
  vine), for shade,
  Appendix 4
Panicum, as disease host,
  287
Pansy (Viola sp.)
  as edible flower, 292
  under fruit trees, 227
  wild, as soil indicator, 37
Papaver sp. (Poppy), as edible flower, 292
Papaw (Asimina triloba)
  as disease resistant, 155
  ease of care, 44, 45
  as shade tolerant, 283
Paper wasps, as beneficial
  predators, 16, 259
Parasitic chalcids. See Parasitic wasps
Parasitic insects (parasitoids),
  245–47. See also spe-
  cific kinds
Parasitic wasps (Chalcidoidea),
  247, 248, 256
  aphids and, 245
  for Japanese beetles, 259
  plants to attract, 252
  for scale, 259
Parsley (Petroselinum sativa)
  companion planting studies,
    239
  as dynamic accumulator,
    270
  as fruit tree cover crop, 233
  Hamburg (Petroselinum
    crispum), as multi-
    purpose edible, 60
  as insectary plant, 251
  for no-till gardens, 101
  preventing cross-pollination
    in, 102
  root zones, 135
Parsley family (Umbelliferae
  or Apiaceae)

  beneficial insects lured by,
    251
  preventing cross-pollination
    among, 102
Parsnip (Pastinaca sp.)
  as fruit tree cover crop, 233
  as insectary plants, 251
  intercropping with, 133, 242
  as quick-maturing, 138
  root zones, 135
  as shade tolerant, 133
  wild or cow (P. sativa)
    as disease host, 288
    as fruit tree cover crop,
      233
    as insectary plant, 251,
      252
    intercropping with corn,
      242
  wild (Sium suave), as soil
    indicator, 37
Parthenocarpy, 151
Parthenocissus quinquefolia
  (Boston ivy; Virginia
  creeper), for shade,
  Appendix 4
Passiflora incense; P. incarnata (Maypop), for
  shade, in cold-winter
  areas, 73
Passion flower; Passion fruit
  (Passiflora caerulea; P.
  edulis)
  as edible flower, 292
  in Flores garden, 64
  as hot-summer tolerant,
    144
  as lawn tolerant, 285
  for shade, 73, Appendix 4
Pastinaca sp. See Parsnip
Paths
  as design element, 43
  low-cost mulch for, 45
  maintenance considera-
    tions, 47
  multi-purpose, 6
  permanent vs. flexible, 50
  planning considerations, 47,
    50
  between sod culture beds,
    113
  stone, warming effect of, 6
  using garden products for,
    39
  weed control in, mulch for,
    45
  weeds barred by, 98
Patios
  for cooling, 74
  trellising over, cautions ab-
    out, 83
Pattern Language (Alexan-
  der), 47, 50, 57, 61
Pea aphids, varieties resistant
  to, 260
Peach (Prunus persica)
  See also Fruit and nut trees
  'Amsden,' disease resist-
    ance, 157, 158
  average seasonal growth,
    229
  'Babcock'
    chill requirement, 142
    ripening dates, 148
  'Belle of Georgia'
    as bacterial leaf spot re-
      sistant, 158
    as cold hardy, 140
    ripening dates, 148
  'Biscoe'
    as bacterial leaf spot re-
      sistant, 158
    as cold hardy, 140
  'Bonanza'
    longevity, 186
    pros and cons, 188
  'Carmen,' disease resist-
    ance, 157, 158
  chill requirement, 142
  choosing, by rootstock,
    171–72
  clay soil problem, 193
  cling, frost tolerance, 228
  cold hardiness, 139, 140
  for color, 1
  disease-resistant varieties,
    157–58
  disease-resistant root-
    stocks, 171–72

diseases
  bacterial canker, 171–72
  bacterial leaf spot, 158
  brown rot, 158
  crown gall, 171
  crown rot, 171–72, 194
  gummosis, 158
  host plants to avoid, 288
  insect vectors, 288
  oak root fungus, 171
  peach leaf curl, 157, 187
disease-susceptible
  varieties, 157–58
dwarf
  rootstocks compared, 172
  yields, 53
  effort ranking, 295
'Elberta'
  disease resistance, 157,
    158
  ripening dates, 148
extending harvest season,
  with genetic dwarf
  varieties, 185–86
in Flores garden, 64
frost tolerance, 228
fruiting buds, 204
'Garden Gold'
  chill requirement, 143
  pros and cons, 188
'Garden Sun'
  chill requirement, 143
  'Indian Blood' grafted
    onto, 183–84
  pros and cons, 189
genetic dwarf, 1, 181, 183
  borer protection, 187
  climate considerations,
    185
  cost factors, 186
  flavor, 185, 187
  full-size scion on, 183–84
  future of, 184
  as hedge, 11
  history, 184
  life span, 186
  peach leaf curl control,
    187
  pros and cons, 184–87,
    188–89
  pruning, 222, 223
  size, 179
  thinning fruit on, 187
  yields, 53, 184–85
  grafted with almond, 64
'Greensboro,' disease re-
  sistance, 157, 158
'Honey Babe'
  chill requirement, 143
  pros and cons, 189
  as hot-summer tolerant,
    144
'Indian Blood'
  grafted onto 'Garden
    Sun,' 183–84
  ripening dates, 148
'Indian Blood Cling,' pollinizer required by, 151
'Indian Cling,' as gummosis
  susceptible, 158
intercropping success, 242
'J.H. Hale'
  diseae resistance, 157,
    158
  pollinizer required by, 151
low-chill varieties, 142–43
miniature; see genetic
  dwarf
nitrogen requirements, 230,
  231
'Peento,' as brown rot resistant, 158
'Peen-to,' chill requirement,
  143
pest-resistant rootstocks,
  171–72
pests
  borers, 171, 187, 200
  gophers and mice, 171
  Oriental fruit moths, 242
  root-knot nematodes, 171
planting locations
  maintenance considera-
    tions, 47
  separate from lawns, 284
  spacing next to apple,
    191
pollinizer requirements, 151
pruning
  open center style for, 213

  in summer, 218
  'Red Bird,' disease resist-
    ance, 157, 158
  'Redhaven'
    as bacterial leaf spot re-
      sistant, 158
    ripening dates, 148
  'Redskin'
    chill requirement, 143
    as gummosis resistant,
      158
    ripening dates, 148
  rootstocks, matching to soil
    types, 171–72
  self-fruitful varieties, 151
  semi-dwarf rootstocks, 171
  'Sneed,' disease resistance,
    157, 158
  'Southern Flame'
    chill requirement, 143
    pros and cons, 189
  'Southern Rose'
    chill requirement, 143
    pros and cons, 189
    ripening dates, 148
    spacing next to apple, 191
  standard
    rootstocks compared, 171
    size, 180
    yields, 53
    as street tree, 9
  'Sunbeam,' disease resist-
    ance, 157, 158
  varieties, number required
    for area, 52
  water use and root depth,
    226
  yields, 53
Peach borers, 187, 200. See
  also Peach tree borers
Peach leaf curl (Taphrina deformans)
  controlling, in genetic dwarf
    varieties, 187
  from overwatering, 285
  sanitation and, 257
  varieties resistant to, 157
Peach tree borers, rootstocks
  resistant to
  apricot, 168
  cherry, 169
  peach/nectarine, 171
  plum/prune, 175
Peanut (Arachis hypogae)
  intercropping with corn, 242
  nitrogen gathered by, 266
Peanut hull meal, nitrogen
  content and C:N ratio,
  Appendix 5
Pear (Pyrus sp.)
  See also Fruit and nut trees
  Asian. See Asian pear
  'Aurora'
    disease resistance, 156
    pollinizers for, 153
  average seasonal growth,
    229
  'Bartlett'
    disease resistance, 156
    as hot summer tolerant,
      144
    pollinizers for, 153
    ripening dates, 148
    as self-fruitful, 151
  'Bosc'
    pollinizers for, 153
    ripening dates, 148
    choosing, by rootstock,
      173–74
  'Clapp's Favorite'
    disease resistance, 156
    pollinizers for, 153
  cold hardiness, 139
  'Comice'
    chill requirement, 143
    disease resistance, 156
    as good keeper, 147
    pollinizers for, 153
    ripening dates, 148
    as self-fruitful, 151
  as disease host, 287
  disease host plants for, 287
  disease-resistant root-
    stocks, 173–74
  disease-resistant varieties,
    listed, 156
  dwarf
    rootstocks compared, 174
    yields, 53
  for espalier, 222

  espalier effort ranking, 295
'Fan Stil'
  chill requirement, 143
  disease resistance, 156
  in Flores garden, 64
  good keepers, 147
  as hot-weather-damage
    susceptible, 144
'Kieffer'
  as good keeper, 147
  chill requirement, 143
  disease resistance, 156
  low-chill varieties, 143
'Luscious'
  disease resistance, 156
  pollinizers for, 153
'Monterey'
  chill requirement, 143
  as good keeper, 147
'Moonglow'
  disease resistance, 156
  as good keeper, 147
  pollinizers for, 153
  mulching, 226–27
  nitrogen requirements, 230,
    231
  pest control, weather moni-
    toring for, 25
  pest-resistant rootstocks,
    173–74
  pollination requirements,
    151, 153
  pruning, no-pruning style,
    211

  ripening dates, 148
  rootstocks, matching to soil
    types, 173–74
  root zone, 161, 162
'Seckel'
  disease resistance, 156
  pollinizers for, 153
  ripening dates, 148
  self-fruitful cultivars, 151
  as spur-type tree, 204
  standard
    rootstocks compared, 173
    root zone, 162
    size, 180
    yields, 53
  water use and root depth,
    226
  winter, as hot summer toler-
    ant, 144
'Winter Nelis'
  disease resistance, 156
  as good keeper, 147
  ripening dates, 148
  yields, 53
Pear apple. See Asian pear
Pear psyllas, 258
Pear root aphids, 173–74
Peas
  companion planting myth,
    239
  as cover crop or green
    manure, 267
  diseases host plants, 287
  diseases insect vectors,
    288
  field, as cover crop or
    green manure, 267
  growing on trellises, 134
  hot-weather protection for,
    74
  inoculants for, 125, 126
  for intercropping, 133
  as nitrogen fixer, 110
  for no-till gardens, 101
  pest-resistant varieties, 260
  planting before potatoes,
    110
  root zones, 135
  rough, as cover crop or
    green manure, 267
  as shade tolerant, 133
  snap, companion planting
    studies, 239
  surface cultivation vs.
    single-dug yields, 110
  Tangier, as cover crop or
    green manure, 268
Peat moss, in potting mix,
  127
Pecan (Carya illinoiensis)
  See also Fruit and nut trees
  chill requirement, 142
  as disease resistant, 155
  as hot-summer tolerant,
    144

as low-effort perennial, 45
as nondwarfable, 180
root system, 161
self-fruitful cultivars, 151
size, 180
winter shade by, 75
Pelargonium (*Pelargonium* sp.), as edible flower, 292
Pennycress (*Thlaspi arvense*), as soil indicator, 37
Pennyroyal, companion planting studies, 239
People vs. machines, 16
Peppergrass, field (*Cardaria draba*), as soil indicator, 37
Peppermint (*Menta piperita*)
See also Mints
companion planting studies, 239
as dynamic accumulator, 270
as shade tolerant, 283
Peppers
companion planting, 238, 239, 240
as compost material, nitrogen content and C:N ratio, Appendix 5
as disease host, 288
diseases host plants for, 287
disease insect vectors, 288
root zones, 135, 137
Perennial mulch, for fruit trees, 227, 231–32
Perennials
for color, 1, 54
growing annuals as, 101–3
indicator plant suitability, 35
legumes, for soil improvement, 291
multi-purpose, 58–59, 59–60
planting in no-till garden, 102
planting locations, vegetables and, 46–47
Periwinkle (*Vinca* sp.)
avoid in compost, 97
as ground cover, maintenance considerations, 46
Perlite, avoid in potting mix, 128
Permaculture, concept of, 15–16
Persea americana. See Avocado
Persimmon (*Diospyros* sp.)
See also Fruit and nut trees
American (*D. virginiana*)
as disease resistant, 155
as low-effort perennial, 45
as shade tolerant, 283
average seasonal growth, 229
chill requirement, 142
choosing, by rootstock, 174
clay soil problem, 193
disease-resistant rootstocks, 174
ease of care, 44, 45, 295
fruit, sunburned, 144
hot weather problems, 144
nematode-resistant rootstocks, 174
as nondwarfable, 180
Oriental (*D. kaki*), **304–6**
cultural guidelines, 304–5
designing with, 1, 305
as disease resistant, 155
ease of care, 45, 304
'Fuyu,' 148, 305
'Hachiya,' 148, 305
recipes using, 305–6
ripening dates, 148
shade tolerance, 284
as parthenocarpic, 151
planting locations, 283
separate from lawns, 284
ripening dates, 147, 148
rootstocks, matching to soil types, 174
as self-fruitful, 151
standard
rootstocks compared, 174
size, 180

Persimmon Ice Cream (recipe), **305**
Persimmon Pecan Appetizers (recipe), **306**
Persimmon Pudding (recipe), **305**
Persimmons, Dried (recipe), **305–6**
with Curried Pecan Cream Cheese, **306**
Perthane, toxicity of, 20
Pest control
See also Pesticides
backup plans, 257
companion planting for, 237–43
with cover crops or green manures, 273
design for, 247–53
diversity and, 245, 257
insectary plants, 257
integrated pest management (IPM), 255–60
myths, 19, 237–43, 245
nurse plants for, 247, 248–49
pheromone traps, 255–56, 258, 259
predators and parasites for, 245–57
resistant varieties for, 256, 259
sanitation for, 257
spraying, 256, 257, 258, 259
weather monitoring for, 25
trap plants for, 247, 248
Pesticides
See also Pest control
botanical vs. synthetic, 19, 20
homemade, multi-purpose plants for, 59
myths about, 19
organic, 19, 20
residues, 2–3
toxicity ratings (LD$_{50}$), 19, 20
Pesto Vinaigrette (recipe), 297
Pests
See also specific pests; specific plants
climate and, 237
as disease vectors, 287–88
forest tree foliage repels, 139
myths about, 19–21
in no-till gardens, 103
planning for sacrifice to, 52
positive role of, 19–21, 151
in sink-or-swim garden, 103
sod culture and, 113
solar fumigation of, 194
Peter Principle, size of garden and, 93
Petroselinum crispum. See Parsley, Hamburg
Petroselinum sativa. See Parsley
Petunia (*Petunia hybrida*)
companion planting studies, 239
dead-heading requirements, 54
as edible flower, 292
as multi-purpose plant, 58
Pfeiffer, E.E., 35
pH. *See* Soil pH
Phacelia sp., intercropping with apple, 241
Phaseolus acutifolius (Tepary bean), as leguminous wildflower, 280
Phaseolus coccineus (Scarlet runner bean), for shade, Appendix 4
Pheromone traps, 255–6, 258, 259
Philodendron (*Philodendron* sp.), for shade, Appendix 4
Phosphate
See also Phosphorus
chemical forms, for cover crops or green manures, 274
colloidal
with clover planting, 103

rock vs., 231
for sheet composting, 97
when planting fruit trees, 194, 197, 198
rock
nutrient percentages, 230
for sheet composting, 97
when planting fruit trees, 198
super, 274
with clover planting, 103
Phosphate accumulators, 267–68, 269–70
Phosphorus
See also Phosphate
accumulator plants, 267–68, 269–70
cost factors, 229
fruit tree deficiency signs, 231
role of, 261–62
sources, 229, 230, 231, 274
Phoxim, toxicity of, 20
Phyllostachys sp. *See* Bamboo
Physalis sp. *See* Ground cherry
Phytophthora sp., as crown rot cause, in fruit trees, 285
Pickles, Chayote (recipe), **301**
Pierce's disease, insect vectors of, 288
Pig manure, nitrogen content and C:N ratio, Appendix 5
Pignut (*Hoffmanseggia densiflora*), as leguminous wildflower, 280
Pigweed (*Amaranthus* sp.)
A. hybridus, intercropping with corn, 242
A. retroflexus (Prostrate or Red root pigweed)
as disease host, 287
as dynamic accumulator, 270
intercropping with collards, 242
for no-till gardens, 101
as soil indicator, 37
as compost material, nitrogen content and C:N ratio, Appendix 5
as insectary plant, 252
intercropping success, with corn, 242
as invasive, 98
water extract, to attract beneficial predators, 259
Pimpinella anisum. See Anise
Pinching
fruit tree growth, 218
for pest control, 218
Pine (*Pinus* sp.), windbreak suitability, 69
Pine nut (*Pinus* sp.)
as disease resistant, 155
as low-effort perennial, 45
Pineapple guava (*Feijoa sellowiana*)
for cooling hedge, 74
designing with, 1
as disease resistant, 155
ease of care, 44, 45, 295
as hot-summer tolerant, 144
as lawn tolerant, 285
planting locations, 283
shade tolerance, 284
Pineapple sage (*Salvia elegans*), shade tolerance, 284
Pineapple weed (*Matricaria matricarioides*), as soil indicator, 37
'Pink Pearl' Apple Tart (recipe), 308–9
Pinks (*Dianthus* sp.)
as edible flower, 292
under fruit trees, 227
as soil indicator, 37
Pinus. See Pine nut
Pistachio (*Pistacia vera*)
chill requirement, 142
as disease resistant, 155
as low-effort perennial, 45
as nondwarfable, 180
size, 180
winter shade by, 75

Pisum arvensis (Field beans), nitrogen gathered by, 266
Planning
See also Design
drip irrigation system, 130–32
edible landscaping guidelines, 91–94
for fruit and nut trees, 139
goal setting, 50–51
importance of, 93
multiple plants for each function, 58
multiple-use plants, 58–60
on paper, 87, 93
priorities vs. realities, 49–50
size considerations, 51–54
sizing landscape materials, Appendix 7
for the unexpected, 93
using local wisdom, 63–66
windbreak location, 67–69
zones of use, 57–58
Plantain (*Plantago lanceolata; P. major*)
cover crop problems, 247
as disease host, 287
as dynamic accumulator, 270
as fruit tree cover crop, 280, 285
as invasive, 98
for no-till gardens, 101
sea, as soil indicator, 37
shade tolerance, 284
as soil indicator, 37
Planter boxes. *See* Containers
Planting
berms, 78–79
in hay bale garden, 106
in no-till, sink-or-swim garden, 102–3
locations. *See* Planting locations
scheduling, 27
seedlings, 128
windbreaks, 70–71
fruit trees, 197–201
in clay soil, 193–94
soil amendment pros and cons, 193–95
Planting locations
chill requirements and, 143–44
compactness, 47
companion plants, 46–47
fruit and nut trees, 47
for frost protection, 228
size and, 180
herbs, 46–47
integrating home and garden, 83–85
perennial flowers, 46–47
trees, away from south walls, 74, 75
vegetables, near kitchen, 94
zones of use, 57–58
Platanus sp. (London plane tree; Sycamore)
maintenance requirements, 44
winter shade by, 75
Pleaching, living guy wires for, 215
Plum/Prune (*Prunus* sp.)
American wild (*P. americana*)
as cold hardy, 139
as edible windbreak, 69
shade tolerance, 283
apricots, almonds, and nectarines grafted on, 63
beach (*P. maritima*)
as disease-resistant, 155
as low-effort perennial, 45
blossom as edible, 292
'Burbank', pollination, 151, 153
choosing, by rootstock, 175–76
cold hardiness, 139
'Delight'
chill requirement, 142
as self-fruitful, 151
disease-resistant rootstocks, 175–76
dwarf

rootstocks compared, 176
yields, 53
edible flower, 292
'Elephant Heart,' pollination, 151, 153
European
see also specific varieties
average seasonal growth, 229
chill requirements, 142
cold hardiness, 139
frost tolerance, 228
pollination requirements, 151, 153
potassium/potash deficiency signs, 231
in Flores garden, 64
"fruit salad" tree, 63, 64
'Howard's Miracle'
chill requirement, 142
ripening dates, 148
'Italian,' pollinizers for, 153
'Italian Prune,' ripening dates, 148
Japanese
see also specific varieties
average seasonal growth, 229
chill requirements, 142
cold hardiness, 139
frost tolerance, 228
pollination requirements, 151, 153
Japanese bush (*P. japonica*)
as disease-resistant, 155
as low-effort perennial, 45
'Mariposa'
chill requirement, 142
as self-fruitful, 151
'Methely'
chill requirement, 142
pollinizers for, 153
natal. *See* Natal plum
nitrogen requirements, 230
pest-resistant rootstocks, 175–76
pollination requirements, 151, 152, 153
'President,' pollination, 151, 153
pruning, open center style for, 213
'Redheart,' pollination, 151, 153
ripening dates, 148
root zone, 161
rootstocks, matching to soil types, 175–76
'Santa Rosa'
chill requirement, 142
pollination, 151, 153
ripening dates, 148
'Satsuma'
chill requirement, 142
ripening dates, 148
as self-fruitful, 151
self-fruitful varieties, 151
semi-dwarf rootstocks compared, 175
'Shiro'
pollination, 151, 153
ripening dates, 148
'Sprite'
chill requirement, 142
as self-fruitful, 151
as spur-type tree, 204
standard
rootstocks compared, 175
size, 180
yields, 53
yields, 53
Plumbago (*Plumbago auriculata*), for shade, Appendix 4
Plum blossom (*Prunus* sp.), as edible flower, 292
Plum-cot, chill requirement, 142
Pod borers, bean variety resistant to, 260
Podosphaera leucotricha. See Powdery mildew
Poison hemlock (*Conium maculatum*)
as insectary plant, 251
as soil indicator, 36
Pokeweed, as disease host, 287
Pollen sterile, defined, 152

Pollination, assuring, 5–6, 58, 151–53
Polyculture, advantages of, 247
Polygonum aubertii (Silver lace vine)
  as insectary plant, 252
  for shade, Appendix 4
Polygonum aviculare (Prostrate knotweed), as soil indicator, 37
Polygonum persicaria (Lady's thumb; Lady's thumb smartweed; Redshank)
  intercropping with corn, 242
  as soil indicator, 37
Polygonum sp. (Smartweed), intercropping successes, 242
Polyogonum scabrum (Smartweed), as soil indicator, 38
Pomegranate (*Punica granatum*)
  anchorage promotion, 200
  chill requirement, 142
  for cooling hedge, 74
  as disease resistant, 155
  in Flores garden, 64
  as hot-summer tolerant, 144
  as low-effort perennial, 45
  planting locations, separate from lawns, 284
  as self-fruitful, 151
  size, 180
Pomona (North American Fruit Explorers journal), 140, 155
Poncirus trifoliata
  See also Citrus
  in citrange cross, 141
  dwarf rootstock for citrus, 170
Poplar (*Populus* sp.)
  as disease host, 287
  as windbreak, 69, 70, 71
Poppy (*Papaver* sp.), as edible flower, 292
Pore space, 29, 117
Portulaca oleracea. See Purslane
Portwood, Myra, recipe from, 299
Posts, using garden limbs for, 39
Potash, 262
  See also Potassium
  for hay bale garden, 105
  after potato harvest, 110
  when planting fruit trees, 194
Potassium/Potash deficiency signs, in fruit trees, 231
Potassium, 262
  See also Potash
  accumulator plants, 268, 269–70
  comfrey as source of, 281
  sources, 230, 231
Potato
  azotobacter inoculant for, 126
  comfrey and, 281
  companion planting, 237, 239, 240
  as cultivators of soil, 110
  day lily tubers as substitute for, 59
  fertilizing requirements, 110, 231
  harvesting, 110
  in hay bale garden, 106
  for intercropping, 133
  nitrogen requirements, 231
  for no-till gardens, 110
  pest-resistant varieties, 260
  planting, in no-till gardens, 102, 110
  root zones, 135
  as shade tolerant, 133
  for sink-or-swim approach, 101
  as slow-maturing, 138
  tansy and, 239, 240
  tops, nitrogen content and C:N ratio, Appendix 5
  yields
    defoliation increased, 21
    companion planting

studies, 240
  surface cultivation vs. single-dug, 110
Potato aphids, as disease vectors, 288
Potato leafhoppers, bean varieties resistant to, 260
Potato vine (*Solanum jasminoides*), for shade, Appendix 4
Potato virus, insect vectors of, 287, 288
Potentilla argentea Silvery cinquefoil), as soil indicator, 36
Poterium sanguisorba. See Salad burnet
Potter wasps, plants to attract, 252
Potting mix, 127–28
Poultry manure
  See also Manure
  for hay bale garden, 105
  for lawns, 10
  nutrient content, 230, Appendix 5
Powdery mildew (*Podosphaera leucotricha*)
  on apple, 158–59
  drip irrigation reduces, 129
  sanitation and, 257
Practical Organic Gardening (Easey), 107
Praying mantids, 12, 246
Predatory insects, 245–47
  plants to attract, 252
Pressure regulators, in drip systems, 130–31
Prickly lettuce (*Lactuca scariola*), as soil indicator, 37
Prickly pear (*Opuntia* sp)
  as disease resistant, 155
  as low-effort perennial, 45
Primrose (*Oenothera biennis; O. laciniata*)
  as cover crop, 278
  as dynamic accumulator, 270
  as insectary plant, 252
Primrose (*Primula vulgaris*)
  as edible flower, 292
  as shade tolerant, 283
Principles of Gardening, The (Johnson), 42
Privacy, windbreaks for, 67
Productivity, as mixed blessing, 180
Proportion, as design element, 43
Prosopis chilensis (Mesquite; Honey mesquite)
  as leguminous wildflower, 280
  as nitrogen-fixing perennial, 291
Prosopis glandulosa torreyana (Mesquite), as windbreak, firewood from, 84
Prostrate knotweed (*Polygonum aviculare*), as soil indicator, 37
Protozoan parasite, for European corn borer, 259
Prune. *See* Plum/Prune
Pruning cane fruits, 286
Pruning fruit and nut trees, 207–10, 223
  basic guidelines, 207–8
  central leader style, 217–18
  to avoid sunburn, 144
  cold hardiness and, 140
  delayed open center style, 213–15
  dwarf, guidelines, 208
  espalier method, 221–22
  genetic dwarf (miniature), 187, 222, 223
  in containers, 186–87
  no-pruning style, 211–12
  open center style, 213–15
  for miniatures, 222
  Pacific Northwest guidelines, 284
  for pest control, 256
  pinching, 218
  preventing disease spread while, 208

removing diseased wood, 207
  removing suckers, 208
  roots, before planting, 162, 198
  scheduling, 27
  self-pruning, 204
  size and, 191
  for special effects, 221–23
  spur-type, no-pruning method drawbacks, 211
  summer vs. winter, 74–75, 140, 207, 218, 221
  for winter light and summer shade, 74, 75–76
  terminal-bearing, no-pruning method for, 211
  vase pruning; *see* open center style
  where to cut, 208–9
  wound dressings, 209
Pruning shears, disinfecting, 208
Prunus sp.
  See also Plum/Prune
  americana. See Plum, American
  amygdalus. See Almond
  armeniaca. See Apricot
  avium. See Cherry, sweet
  besseyi. See Western sand cherry
  caroliniana (Carolina wild cherry), as windbreak, 69
  cerasus. See Cherry, sour; Cherry, sweet
  ilicifolia. See Hollyleaf cherry
  japonica. See Japanese bush plum
  laurocerasus (English laurel), soil preparation for, 54
  lyonii (Catalina cherry), for cooling hedge, 74
  maritima. See Beach plum
  persica. See Peach
  seratonia (Black cherry), shade tolerance, 283
  tomentosa. See Nanking cherry
  virginiana. See Chokecherry
Pseudomonas syringae. See Bacterial canker
Psidium littorale littorale. See Guava, lemon
Psidium littorale. See Guava, strawberry
Pteridium aquilinum. See Bracken, eastern
Pummelo, cold hardiness, 140
Pumpkin
  for intercropping, 133
  pest-resistant varieties, 260
  preventing cross-pollination among, 102
  root zones, 135
  as shade tolerant, 133
  as slow-maturing, 138
Punica granatum. See Pomegranate
Purslane (*Portulaca oleracea*)
  as compost material, nitrogen content and C:N ratio, Appendix 5
  as dynamic accumulator, 270
  as favorite no-till green, 96
  for intercropping, 133
  for no-till gardens, 96, 101
  nutritional value, 96
  as shade tolerant, 133
Pyracantha, as disease host, 287
Pyrethrum
  companion planting studies, 239
  toxicity of, 19, 20
Pyrostegia ignea (Flame vine), for shade, Appendix 4
Pyrus sp. *See* Asian pear; Pear

Q

Quack grass (*Agropyron repens*), as soil indicator,

36
Quail bush (*Atriplex lentiformis*), as nitrogen-fixing perennial, 291
Quamoclit pennata (Cypress vine), for quick shade, 73
Quamoclit sloteri (Cardinal climber), for quick shade, 73
Queen-Anne's-Lace. *See* Wild carrot
Quercus. See Oak
Quillaja saponaria (Soapbark tree), as insectary plant, 252
Quince (*Cydonia oblonga*), 307–8
  recipe for, 64
  average seasonal growth, 229
  Baked Quinces Flambé (recipe), **308**
  chill requirement, 142
  as co-terminal bearing, 228
  for cooling hedge, 74
  cultural guidelines, 307
  as disease-resistant, 155
  ease of care, 44, 45, 307
  in Flores garden, 64
  with olive oil, garlic, onion, and tomatoes (recipe), 64
  ripening dates, 147, 148
  rootstocks, anchorage promotion, 200
  as self-fruitful, 151
  size, 180
  yields, 53

R

Rabbit foot clover, as dynamic accumulator, 269
Rabbit manure
  for hay bale garden, 105
  nutrient percentages, 230
Rabbits
  multi-purpose plants as feed for, 59
  preventing fruit tree damage by, 186, 187, 200
Raccoons, protecting miniature fruit trees from, 186
Rachel Carson Trust list, 3
'Radicchio,' for color, 1
Radish
  companion planting studies, 239, 240
  as cucumber beetle trap plant, 259
  intercropping with, 133, 243
  as quick-maturing, 138
  preventing cross-pollination in, 102
  root zones, 135, 136
  as shade tolerant, 133
  wild (*Raphanus raphanistrum; R. sativus*)
    as fruit tree cover crop, 233
    as soil indicator, 37
Ragweed (*Ambrosia artemisifolia*)
  as insectary plant, 252
  intercropping successes, 242
Ragwort, nitrogen content and C:N ratio, Appendix 5
Ragwort, tansy (*Senecio jacobaea*), as soil indicator, 37
Rain
  data gathering on, 23, 24–25
  planning for damage by, 52
  predicting maximum rainfall, 80–81
  preventing damage by, 77–81
Rain gauges, 24–25
Raised beds
  double-digging, 115–22
  in hay bale garden, 106
  hot summer climate and, 118
  maintaining, 121
  miniature peach trees in, *183*

Ranunculus acris; R. repens (Buttercup), as soil indicator, 36
Rape (*Brassica hapus*)
  as cover crop or green manure, 267
  as soil indicator, 37
Raphanus raphanistrum; R. sativus. See Radish, wild
Raspberry (*Rubus* sp.)
  for berms, 79
  black (*Rubus occidentalis*), shade tolerance, 283
  chill requirement, 142
  cultural hints, 286
  edible portion, 79
  ripening dates, northern California, 147
  yields, 53
Reality coefficient, 91
Recipes
  Asian Pear Chutney, **299**
  Asian Pear Salad, **300**
  Asian Pears Poached in Red Wine, **300**
  Baked Quinces Flambé, **308**
  Blue Cheese Dressing with Garlic, **297**
  Chayote Parmigiana, **300–301**
  Chayote Pickles, **301**
  Chestnut Soufflé, **302**
  Chestnut Soup, **302**
  Corn-Salad Salad, **304**
  Cornish Game Hens Stuffed with Garlic and Summer Savory, **307**
  Dried Persimmons with Curried Pecan Cream Cheese, **306**
  Ensalada de Flores, **296–97**
  Fava Beans with Artichoke Hearts, **303**
  Grilled Chicken with Rosemary, **298–99**
  Hot and Sweet Baked Garlic, **307**
  Kiwicoladas, **304**
  Persimmon Ice Cream, **305**
  Persimmon Pecan Appetizers, **306**
  Persimmon Pudding, **305**
  Pesto Vinaigrette, **297**
  'Pink Pearl' Apple Tart, **308–9**
  Quince with Olive Oil, Garlic, Onion, and Tomatoes, **64**
  Roasted Chestnuts with Garlic Butter, **301**
  'Romanesco' with Hollandaise, **297–98**
Red clover. *See* Clover
Red scale, parasites, 247
Red spider mites, intercropping successes, 242
Red sprangletop (*Leptochloa filliformis*), intercropping with beans, 241
Red-stem filaree. *See* Filaree
Redbud (*Cercis occidentalis*), as nitrogen-fixing perennial, 291
Redshank (*Polygonum persicaria*), as soil indicator, 37
Redwood sorrel (*Oxalis oregana*), as shade tolerant, 283
Repetition, as design element, 43
Rescue grass, as cover crop or green manure, 267
Research
  .chill zones, 141
  fruit tree cold hardiness, 140
  old-timers as source, 63–66, 92
  riparian habitat, 78
Rest harrow, as dynamic accumulator, 270
R factor (Reality coefficient), 91
Rhamnus californica (California coffeeberry), as insectary plant, 252

Rheum rhabarbarum. See
  Rhubarb
Rhizobium inoculant, 103,
  125, 274
Rhoicissus capensis (Evergreen grape), for
  shade, 73, Appendix 4
Rhubarb (*Rheum rhabar-
  barum*)
  as lawn tolerant, 285
  root zones, 135
  as shade tolerant, 283
Rhus ovata (Sugar bush), for
  cooling hedge, 74
Rhythm, as design element,
  43
Ribes sp. See Currants;
  Gooseberry
Ricard, Dr. David, companion
  plant research by, 239
Rice, defoliation increased
  yield of, 21
Richness, as design element,
  43
Riotte, Louise, 235
Riparian habitat, creating, 77–
  79
Ripening dates, fruit and nut
  varieties, 147–48
Road dust, for cucumber beetles, 259
Roads, locating along windbreaks, 68–69
Robber flies, as beneficial
  predators, 246
Robin, ragged, as soil indicator, 37
Robinia pseudoacacia (Black
  locust), as multi-
  purpose plant, 59, 84
Rock phosphate. See Phos-
  phate
Rock powders
  for lawns, 10
  as potassium/potash
    source, 231
  for sheet composting, 97
Rocks, as design element, 43
Rodale Research Center, on
  inoculants, 125
Rodents
  drip irrigation and, 130, 132
  as fruit tree mulch draw-
    back, 232
Rodia, Simon, 42
'Romanesco' (*Brassica* sp.),
  297–98
  cultural guidelines, 297
  designing with, 1, 297
  with Hollandaise (recipe),
    297–98
  in TODD® planters, 127
Ronnel, toxicity of, 20
Rooftop plantings, miniature
  fruit trees for, 186, 187
Root and collar rot. See
  Crown rot
Root-depth myths, 135
*Root Development of Veget-
  able Crops* (Weaver),
  135
Root divisions, planting in no-
  till garden, 102
Rootfly, intercropping successes, 241
Root-knot nematodes
  persimmon susceptibility to,
    174
  rootstocks resistant to
    almond, 166
    apricot, 168
    cherry, 169
    citrus, 170
    peach/nectarine, 171
    pear, 173–74
    plum/prune, 175–76
    walnut, 177
Root rots
  avocado resistance, 168
  from overwatering, 285
  persimmon resistance, 174
Roots
  azotobacter as stimulus to,
    126
  depth of, nutrient use and,
    134
  fruit tree cold hardiness
    and, 140
  intercropping and, 134–37
  in subsoil, 31

vegetable root zones com-
  pared, 134–37
  water-storage role of, 77
Rootstocks
  citrus, cold hardiness and,
    140–41
  fruit tree, matching to soil
    type, 161–77
  grafting other fruits on, 165
  nondwarfable, 180
Root zones
  fruits and vegetables com-
    pared, 162
  fruit trees, 161, 162, 163
  vegetables, 134–37
Rosa de montana (*Antigonon
  leptopus*), for shade,
  Appendix 4
Rose (*Rosa* sp.)
  See also Rose hips
  companion planting studies,
    239
  as disease host, 287
  as edible flower, 292, 296
  as multi-purpose plant, 58
  wild (*R. californica*), for
    berms, 79
Rose hips (*Rosa rugosa*)
  for cooling hedge, 74
  as disease resistant, 155
  as low-effort perennial, 45
  as multi-purpose edible, 60
  as soil indicator, 37
  as wildlife attractor, 59
Rosemary (*Rosmarinus
  officinalis*), **298–99**
  companion planting studies,
    239
  cultural guidelines, 298
  designing with, 1, 238, 298
  effort ranking, 298
  as edible flower, 292, 296
  in Flores garden, 64
  Grilled Chicken with (re-
    cipe), **298–99**
  as multi-purpose edible, 60
  planting locations, 283
  shade tolerance, 284
Rosy apple aphids, 247, 257
Rotary tilling
  for green manure, 275
  for sod culture beds, 114
Rotation, for soil fertility, 266,
  273–75
  five-year plan, 277–78,
    280–81
  seven-year plan, 279
Rotenone, toxicity of, 19, 20
Rots, as intercropping contraindication, 239
Rubus occidentalis (Black
  raspberry), shade
  tolerance, 283
Rubus parviflorus. See
  Thimbleberry
Rubus spectabilis (Salmonberry), as shade toler-
  ant, 283
Rubus. sp. See Blackberry;
  Raspberry
Rue (*Ruta graveolens*)
  companion planting studies,
    239
  as insectary plant, 252
Rumex acetosella (Sheep
  sorrel)
  as dynamic accumulator,
    270
  as soil indicator, 38
Rumex crispus (Curly dock;
  Dock)
  for downspout outlets, 83
  as soil indicator, 35
Rumex obtusifolius (Broad-
  leaved dock), as dyna-
  mic accumulator, 269
Rumex scutatus. See French
  sorrel
Rumex sp. (Dock)
  as dynamic accumulator,
    269
  as fruit tree cover crop,
    233, 285
  for no-till gardens, 101
  nutritional value, 96
  as salad green, 59
  as soil indicator, 36
Rumex sp. (Garden sorrel)
  as dynamic accumulator,
    270

as soil indicator, 38
Runoff, controlling
  berms and swales for, 77–
    79
  drywells for, 79–80
Rushes, as soil indicator, 37
Russian olive (*Elaeagnus
  angustifolia*)
  for cooling hedge, 74
  as multi-purpose plant, 59,
    60
  as nitrogen-fixing, 291
  as wildlife attractor, 59
  as windbreak, 69
Russian thistle (*Salsola
  pestifer*)
  as dynamic accumulator,
    270
  as soil indicator, 38
Russian thistle (*Salsola kali L.
  var. tenuifolia Tausch*),
  as soil indicator, 35
Rust, from overwatering fruit
  trees, 285
Ruta graveolens. See Rue
Rutabaga
  for intercropping, 133
  root zones, 135
  as shade tolerant, 133
Ryania, toxicity of, 20
Rye; Ryegrass
  azotobacter inoculant for,
    126
  as cover crop, 268, 273,
    280
  for fruit trees, 280
  as disease host, 287
  as fruit tree mulch, 242
  as green manure, 268, 273
  intercropping with soy-
    beans, 243
  as living mulch with
    cabbage, 240

S

Sabadilla, toxicity of, 19, 20
Safer's Insecticidal Soap™,
  256, 257, 258
Sage (*Salvia officinalis*; *Salvia
  sp.*)
  companion planting studies,
    239
  as edible flower, 292
  pineapple (*S. elegans*),
    shade tolerance, 284
Sagittaria latifolia (Arrowhead), for berms, 79
Sainfoin (*Onobrychis sativa*),
  as leguminous wildflow-
  er, 280
Saint-John's-wort (*Hypericum
  sp.*), as edible flower,
  292
Salad beds, crop rotation for,
  277–81
Salad burnet (*Sanguisorba
  officinalis*)
  as dynamic accumulator,
    270
  as fruit tree cover crop,
    280, 285
  for no-till gardens, 101
  for salad garnish, 59
  as soil indicator, 37
Salad dressings (recipes)
  Blue Cheese Dressing with
    Garlic, **297**
  Pesto Vinaigrette, **297**
Salad flowers, 58, **296**
Salad greens, 58, 59
Salad recipes
  Asian Pear Salad, **300**
  Corn-Salad Salad, **304**
  Ensalada de Flores, **296–
    97**
Salal (*Gaultheria shallon*)
  as disease resistant, 155
  as lawn tolerant, 285
  as low-effort perennial, 45
  as shade tolerant, 283
Salep, as soil indicator, 37
Saline soil
  plant indicators, 36–38
  walnut rootstock resistance,
    177
Saline water, drip irrigation
  for, 129
Salix sp. See Willow
Salmonberry (*Rubus specta-
  bilis*), as shade tolerant,

283
Salsify (*Tragopogon
  archangelica*; *Tragopogon* sp.)
  as fruit tree cover crop, 233
  as insectary plant, 251
  for intercropping, 133, 134
  for no-till gardens, 96, 101
  as shade tolerant, 133
  as slow-maturing, 138
Salsola kali L. var. *tenuifolia
  Tausch* (Russian thistle;
  Tumbleweed), as soil
  indicator, 35
Salsola pestifer (Russian
  thistle)
  as dynamic accumulator,
    270
  as soil indicator, 38
Saltbush (*Atriplex* sp.), as insectary plant, 252
Salt damage, drip irrigation to
  prevent, 129
Salt hay, as seed-free mulch,
  97
Salty soil. See Saline soil
Salvia sp. See Sage
Sambucus canadensis. See
  Elderberry
San Jose scale, weather
  monitoring for, 25
Sand
  angle of repose, Appendix
    7
  as seed-free mulch, 97
  when planting fruit trees,
    200
Sand wasps, plants to attract,
  252
Sandy soil, 30
  double-digging contra-
    indicated for, 118
  fruit trees in, soil amend-
    ment debate, 193–94
  increasing water-holding
    capacity, 77
  methods of improving, 118
  plant indicators, 35, 36–38
Sanguisorba officinalis. See
  Salad burnet
Sanicle, as dynamic
  accumulator, 270
Sanitation
  disease hosts and, 287
  for pest control, 257
Santolina, companion planting
  studies, 239
Sapium sebiferum (Chinese
  tallow tree), winter
  shade by, 75
Sapote (*Casimiroa edulis*)
  as disease resistant, 155
  as hot-summer tolerant,
    144
  as low-effort perennial, 45
Sarcobatus vermiculatus
  (Greasewood), 236
Sarsparilla, as dynamic accumulator, 270
Sassafras (*Sassafras
  albidum*)
  as shade tolerant, 283
  winter shade by, 75
Savory (*Satureja* sp.)
  as cover crop, 278 *See also*
    Summer savory
  as dynamic accumulator,
    270
Sawdust
  as compost material, nitro-
    gen content and C:N
    ratio, Appendix 5
  as mulch, 97
  in paths, 45
Sawflies, parasites of, 246
Scab, in fruit trees
  apple, 158–59
  drip irrigation reduces, 129
  hosts for, 287
  from overwatering, 285
  sanitation and, 257
  weather monitoring for, 25
Scale, as design element, 43
Scale, as pests
  IPM for, 258, 259
  predators and parasites of,
    246, 247
  plants to attract, 252
Scale drawings, 87

Scallions, planning area for,
  53
Scarlet kadsura (*Kadsura
  japonica*), for shade,
  Appendix 4
Scarlet Pimpernel (*Anagallis
  arvensis*)
  as dynamic accumulator,
    270
  as soil indicator, 37
Scarlet runner bean
  (*Phaseolus coccineus*),
  for shade, Appendix 4
Scheduling
  bloom sequence, 27
  frost dates, 23–24
  rain prediction, 24
Schultz, Joseph, 193
Scleranthus annuus (Knawel),
  as soil indicator, 37
Scraper, for surface cultivation, 109
Seal and Heal, 209
Sea plantain, as soil indicator,
  37
Season, fruit trees for prolonging, 181, 185–86
Seattle, Washington, International Gardens, 134
Seaweed
  as compost material, nitro-
    gen content and C:N
    ratio, Appendix 5
  as seed-free mulch, 97
  when planting fruit trees,
    197, 198
Sechium edule. See Chayote
*Secrets of Companion Plant-
  ing for Successful
  Gardening* (Riotte), 235
Sedges (*Cyperaceae* sp.), as
  soil indicator, 37
Seedcorn maggots
  bean varieties resistant to,
    260
  soybean intercropping suc-
    cess, 243
Seeding
  cover crops or green
    manures, 232, 273–74
  in hay bale garden, 106
  in no-till, sink-or-swim
    garden, 102, 103
  in TODD® planters, 127–28
Seedlings
  of edible weeds, planting,
    97–98
  for hay bale garden, 106
  for no-till garden, sink-or-
    swim method, 102
  planting in sod, 113
  TODD® system, 127–28
  watering, 128
Seeds. See Seeding
Self-fruitful vs. self-unfruitful
  fruit and nut trees,
  151–53
Self-reliance, tempering, 51
Self-seeding vegetables,
  101–3
Self-sterile, defined, 151
Self-sufficient gardening, concept of, 15–16
  in fertilizing, 266–81
Semi-dwarf fruit trees, dwarf
  vs., 180. See also Fruit
  and nut trees
Senecio confusus (Mexican
  flame vine), for shade,
  Appendix 4
Senecio jacobaea (Tansy
  ragwort), as soil indicator, 37
Senecio vulgaris (Groundsel)
  as dynamic accumulator,
    269
  as soil indicator, 36
Sennas (*Cassia* sp.), as nitrogen-fixing perennial,
  291
Sequence, as design ele-
  ment, 43
Serviceberry (*Amelanchier
  sp.*), shade tolerance,
  284
Sesbania (*Sesbania* sp.)
  as cover crop, 267, 273
  as green manure, 267, 275
  as leguminous wildflower,
    280

Sesbania macrocarpa (Colorado river hemp), as leguminous wildflower, 280

Sewage, nitrogen content and C:N ratio, Appendix 5

Shade
climate and, 283
data gathering on, 26–27, 28
designing with, 73–76
fruit tree chill requirements and, 143
planting fruit trees in, 143, 144
plants tolerant of, listed, 283–84
southern, trees and vines for, 74–75
vegetables for, 133
from windbreaks, 68, 69

Shallots, companion planting studies, 239

Shasta daisy, maintenance requirements, 44

Sheep manure, nitrogen content and C:N ratio, Appendix 5

Sheep sorrel (*Rumex acetosella*)
as dynamic accumulator, 270
as soil indicator, 38

Sheet composting, 96–98
cover crop choice and, 278
edible weeds, 95–98
for fruit trees, 227
as green manuring alternative, 277–78
perennial plants, 98
sink-or-swim approach to, 101–3

Shelterbelt
as beneficial insect habitat, 247

Shelterbelts. See Windbreaks

Shepherd's purse (*Capsella bursa-pastoris*)
as dynamic accumulator, 270
intercropping successes, 241, 242
as soil indicator, 37

Shepherdia canadensis (Buffalo berry), shade tolerance, 283

Shigo, Dr. Alex, 208, 209

Shoofly plant (*Nicandra physalodes*), 237

Shot hole fungus
drip irrigation reduces, 129
on fruit trees, sanitation and, 257

Shredded bark, as fruit tree mulch, 232

Shrubs
for cooling, 73, 74
disease-resistant, listed, 155
evergreen, maintenance requirements, 44
misting, 73–74
nitrogen-fixing, 291
synergy with, 84
visualizing effect of, 87–88
watering, with drip irrigation, 225
as windbreak, 67, 68, 70, 71
buying, 70–71

Siberian pea-shrub (*Caragana arborescens*)
inoculant for, 125
as multi-purpose plant, 59, 60
as nitrogen-fixing perennial, 291
as windbreak, 69

Sicklepod (*Cassia obtusifolia*), intercropping with soybeans, 243

Silene noctiflora (Nightflowering catchfly), as soil indicator, 36

Silica accumulator plants, 269–70, 281

Silverberry (*Elaeagnus commutata*)
as nitrogen-fixing, 291
shade tolerance, 284

Silverberry (*Elaeagnus pungus*), as nitrogen-fixing, 291

Silver lace vine (*Polygonum aubertii*)
as insectary plant, 252
for shade, Appendix 4

Silverweed
as dynamic accumulator, 270
as soil indicator, 38

Silvery cinquefoil (*Potentilla argentea*), as soil indicator, 36

Simmondsia chinensis (Jojoba), for cooling hedge, 74

Simplicity, as design element, 43

Sink-or-swim gardens, 101–3

Sinker roots, on fruit trees, 162

Sium suave (Wild parsnip), as soil indicator, 37

Size of garden
growing techniques and, 51
BFI, 118–19, 121
importance of starting small, 93
lawn, 113
orchards, 52–53
percent of edibles and, 46
planning, 51–54
rectangular shape recommended, 46
for vegetables, 46, 51–52
yields and, 51–52

Skirret, as insectary plant, 251

Skunk cabbage (*Navarretia squarrosa*), as dynamic accumulator, 270

Skunks, as Japanese beetle predators, 259

Sky flower (*Thunbergia grandiflora*), for shade, Appendix 4

Slaughterhouse wastes, nitrogen content and C:N ratio, Appendix 5

Slope gardens
design for, 49
drip irrigation advantages, 129
fruit tree chill requirements and, 141, 143
fruit tree root patterns, 163
sod culture for, 113

Sludge, activated, nitrogen content and C:N ratio, Appendix 5

Slugs and snails
predators and parasites of, 246, 247
in sink-or-swim garden, 103
tillage for control of, 257

Smartweed (*Polygonum* sp.)
intercropping successes, 242
as soil indicator, 38

Smut, insect vectors of, 288

Snack recipes
with dried persimmons, **306**
Roasted Chestnuts with Garlic Butter, **301**

Snails. See Slugs and snails

Snakeflies (*Apulla* sp.)
as beneficial predators, 246
design to attract, 5
identifying, 245, 245

Snakefly, *247*

Snap beans. See Beans

Snapdragon, dead-heading requirements, 54

Snow, windbreaks as protection from, 67

Snowberry (*Symphoricarpos* sp.), as insectary plant, 252

Soapbark tree (*Quillaja saponaria*), as insectary plant, 252

Soap sprays, in IPM, 256, 257, 258

Soapy water, for pest control, 256

Society garlic (*Tulbaghia violacea*), as multi-purpose edible, 60

Sod culture, 113–14

Sodium accumulator plants, 269–70

Soeco Seed Inoculant™, 126

Soft-winged flower beetles, plants to attract, 252

Soil, 29–32
See also Soil mix; Soil type; *specific soil characteristics; soil types*
acidity, plant indicators, 36–38
air component, 29, 30, 31, 115
pore space vs., 117
alkalinity, plant indicators, 36–38
amendments. See Soil amendments
angles of repose, Appendix 7
bacteria, soil depth and, 31
bare, importance of avoiding, 95
bedrock, 30, 31
clay, described, 30
cold hardiness and, 139–40
colloids, 29–30
compacted, fruit trees and, 162, 163
components of, 29, 30
cost of preparing, 54
drainage, earthworms and, 108
erosion. See Erosion control measures
fertility
humus and, 30
improving. See Crop rotation; Fertilizers; Fertilizing; Soil amendments
plant indicators, 36–38
yields and, 51
horizons or profile, 30–31
humus, 29–30
ideal, 30
mineral component, 29, 30
organic matter component, 29, 30, 38
panaceas, 38
pest control and, 255
pH. See Soil pH
planting density and, 117
pore spaces, 29
air pockets vs., 117
sandy, described, 30
silt, described, 30
silty loam, described, 30
solar fumigation of, 194
structure, 30
cover crop or green manure and, 273
drip irrigation and, 129
earthworms and, 108
subsoil, 31
surveys, 31–32
temperature
sod culture lowers, 113
windbreaks raise, 67
testing, 30, 31–32
texture, 30
in no-till garden, 110
tilth, 30
topsoil, 31
water component, 29, 30
water-holding capabilities, improving, 67, 77

Soil amendments
See also Fertilizers; Fertilizing
for exposed subsoil, 273–74
for fruit trees, pros and cons, 193–95
for modifying pH, 39
planning amount needed, Appendix 7
in potting mix, 127
sheet composting, 96–98

Soil Conditions and Plant Growth, on earthworms, 108

Soil Conservation Service, soil surveys by, 32

Soil Enterprise Corporation, azotobacter from, 126

Soil inoculants, 125–26

Soil mix
for fruit trees, 193–95, 197–98

genetic dwarf, in containers, 186, 187
size and, 191
for TODD® planters, 127–28

Soil nematodes. See Nematodes

Soil pH
importance of testing, 38–39
for legume cover crops, 274
modifying, 39
plant indicators, 35, 36–38

Soil preparation. See Soil amendments; Tillage

Soil surveys, 32

Soil type
See also specific types
for fruit trees
hardpan, 163
matching rootstocks to, 165–77
size and, 179, 191
improving, with perennial legumes, 291
inoculant need and, 125
plants as indicators, 32, 35–39
pore space vs. air pockets and, 117

Solanum carolinense. See Horsenettle

Solanum jasminoides (Potato vine), for shade, Appendix 4

Solanum nigrum (Black nightshade), for no-till gardens, 101

Solanums, wild, as disease host, 287

Solar charts, 26, Appendix 2

Solar Card, 26

Solar fumigation, 194

Solar greenhouse
as density of use example, 57
Massida's, 63
synergy with, 83

Solar power, at Village Homes, 9

Solar Site Selector, 26–27

Solar siting, for windbreaks, 68, 69

Solar south, determining, 26

Solar tracking, 26–27

Soldier beetles, 246, *246*, 248, 256
plants to attract, 252

Solidago altissima; Solidago sp.. See Goldenrod

Sonchus arvensis. See Sow thistle

Sophora japonica (Japanese pagoda), as nitrogen-fixing perennial, 291

Sorghum
azotobacter inoculant for, 126
as cover crop, 267, 273
fruit tree mulch success, 242
as green manure, 267, 273, 275
intercropping with cow peas, 242

Sorghum halepense. See Johnson grass

Sorrel
cover crop problems, 278
French (*Rumex scutatus*)
for berms, 79
as invasive, 98
in no-till garden, 102
shade tolerance, 283
garden (*Rumex* sp.)
as dynamic accumulator, 270
as soil indicator, 38
redwood (*Oxalis oregana*), as shade tolerant, 283
sheep (*Rumex acetosella*)
as dynamic accumulator, 270
as soil indicator, 38

Soup, Chestnut (recipe), **302**

Sour cherry. See Cherry, sour

Sour orange, cold hardiness, 140

Southern grasses, as disease hosts, 287

Southern potato wireworm, sweet potato varieties resistant to, 260

Southernwood (*Artemisia abrotanum*)
companion planting studies, 239
for pest control, 259

South-facing slopes, fruit tree problems, 143

South-facing walls
espalier on, 185
shade for, 74–75

Sow thistle; Creeping thistle (*Sonchus arvensis; Sonchus* sp.)
as dynamic accumulator, 270
as nurse plant, 248
as soil indicator, 38

Soybeans (*Glycine max*)
as cover crop or green manure, 267
inoculants and yields of, 125
intercropping successes, 242, 243
nitrogen gathered by, 266
nitrogen requirements, 231

Soybean meal, nitrogen content and C:N ratio, Appendix 5

Spacing plants
in BFI, 115, 116
crop choice and, 119
number of plants required, Appendix 7
soil type and, 117

Space-saving techniques
intercropping, 137
vertical gardening, 134

Spaghetti tubing, 131–32

Spearmint. See Mints

Speedwell (*Veronica* sp.), as soil indicator, 38

Spergula arvensis. See Corn spurry

Spider mites, red, intercropping successes, 242

Spiders, as beneficial predators, 246
plants to attract, 252

Spinach
diseases, insect vectors, 288
hot-weather protection for, 74
intercropping with, 133, 134, 137
nutritional value, 96
pest-resistant varieties, 260
preventing cross-pollination in, 102
as quick-maturing, 138
root zones, 135, 137
as shade tolerant, 133

Split-leaf philodendron (*Monstera deliciosa*), shade tolerant, 283

Spotted cucumber beetles, IPM for, 258, 259

Spotted water hemlock (*Cicuta maculata*), as soil indicator, 38

Spotted wilt, host plants for, 287

Spraying
beneficial insects killed by, 256
fruit tree size and, 180, 185
intercropping and, 238
in IPM, 255–59
tansy study, 240

Spreaders, for fruit trees, 205–6

Sprinklers, for frost protection, 228

Spruce, intercropping with tamarack, 243

Spruce budworms, IPM for, 258

Spurge (*Euphorbia esula; Euphorbia* sp.)
as dynamic accumulator, 270
as soil indicator, 38

Spurs, 203–4

Spur-type fruit trees, 204

Squash (*Cucurbita* sp.)

companion planting studies, 240
edible flowers on, 292, **296**
growing on trellises, 134
intercropping with, 133, 134, 243
luffa, for quick shade, 73
nitrogen requirements, 231
pest-resistant varieties, 260
preventing cross-pollination in, 102
as shade tolerant, 133
summer
preventing cross-pollination in, 102
root zones, 135
winter
compact varieties, 47
in hay bale garden, 106
planting locations, 49, 57
preventing cross-pollination in, 102
for quick shade, 73
root system, BFI suitability and, 119, 121
root zones, 135
as slow-maturing, 138
in small garden, 49
Squash bugs, 240, 260
Squash mosaic virus, 288
Squash vine borers, 260
Squirrels, protecting miniature fruit trees from, 186
Stachys officinalis (Wood betony), as shade tolerant, 283
Staking fruit trees, 197, 199–200
Star jasmine (*Trachelospermum jasminoides*), for shade, Appendix 4
Stark, Paul, Jr., on miniature trees, 184
Stark Brothers Nursery
cold-hardy varieties from, 140
miniature tree role, 184
Starting seeds. See Seeding
Steer manure, nutrient content, 230, Appendix 5
Steiner, Rudolf, biodynamics and, 115
Stellaria media. See Chickweed
Stem pitting, insect vectors of, 288
Stewart's bacterial wilt, insect vectors of, 288
Sticky yellow traps, in IPM, 259
Stigmaphyllon ciliatum (Orchid vine), for shade, Appendix 4
Stinging nettle (*Urtica dioica; Urtica* sp.)
for berms, 79
companion planting studies, 240
gathering, as growing alternative, 51
as nitrogen-lover, 98
for no-till gardens, 101
as nurse plant, 248
as shade tolerant, 283
Stink bugs
IPM for, 258
plants to attract, 252
Stinkgrass, as disease host, 287
Stinkweed (*Thlaspi arvense*), as soil indicator, 38
Stizolobium deeringianum (Velvet bean), as leguminous wildflower, 280
Stone fruit trees
See also Fruit and nut trees
diseases
host plants to avoid, 287
insect vectors, 288
frost tolerance in, 228
phosphorus deficiency signs, 213
pruning, open center style for, 213
Stone paths, landscape warmed by, 6
Stone walls
to protect miniature trees, 185
Storm damage, preventing,

77–81
Storms, wind direction during, 25–26
Straw
for bale gardening, 105
coverage per bale, Appendix 7
in potato planting, 110
as seed-free mulch, 97
slug problems in, 103
as weed-preventive border, 98
wheat, nitrogen content and C:N ratio, Appendix 5
Strawberry (*Fragaria* sp.)
alpine (*F. alpina semperflorens*)
as disease resistant, 155
ease of care, 45, 46
as shade tolerant, 283
chill requirement, 142
disease host plants, 287, 288
for downspout outlets, 83
in Flores garden, 64
as ground cover, maintenance considerations, 46
intercropping with peach, 242
as lawn tolerant, 285
leaves, as dynamic accumulator, 270
ripening dates, northern California, 147
wild
see also alpine
for berms, 79
for no-till gardens, 96, 101
shade tolerance, 284
as soil indicator, 38
yields, 53
Strawberry guava (*Psidium littorale*)
for cooling hedge, 74
as disease resistant, 155
in Flores garden, 64
as low-effort perennial, 45
shade tolerance, 283, 284
Strawberry tree (*Arbutus unedo*)
as disease resistant, 155
as low-effort perennial, 44, 45
as shade tolerant, 283
Streptosolen jamesoni (Marmalade bush), for shade, Appendix 4
Striped cucumber beetles
intercropping successes, 242
IPM for, 258, 259
tillage for control of, 257
Structure, as design element, 43
Stusser, Michael, on BFI, 115
Subsoil, 31
Subterranean clover, as cover crop or green manure, 267
Suburbs
advantages of, 9
ecological diversity in, 12–13
edible landscaping for, 9–13
Suckers, removing, 208
Sudan grass
as cover crop, 267, 273
as green manure, 267, 273, 275
intercropping with grapes, 242
Sugar beets
azotobacter inoculant for, 126
intercropping successes, 243
Sugar bush (*Rhus ovata*), for cooling hedge, 74
Sulfur
accumulator plants, 269–70
to reduce soil alkalinity, 39
Sulfur spray, near house, 73
Sulphate of potash
cost factors, 231
under fruit tree mulch, 232
nutrient percentages, 230
when planting fruit trees,

194
Summer pruning
for central leader style, 218
for espalier, 221
winter pruning vs., 74–75, 140, 207, 218
Summer savory, companion planting studies, 239, 240. See also Savory
Sun charts, 26, Appendix 2
Sun chokes. See Jerusalem artichokes
Sundews, as soil indicator, 38
Sunflower (*Helianthus annuus*)
as allelopathic, 235
azotobacter inoculant for, 126
as cover crop, 267, 273
as green manure, 267, 275
as insectary plant, 251
intercropping with, 133, 134
as slow-maturing, 138
for vertical gardening, 134
Sun protection, miniature fruit trees, 187
Sunscald, painting painting trunk to prevent, 198–99, 200
Sunshine patterns, data gathering, 26–27, 28, Appendix 2
Superphosphate, 103, 274
Surface area formulas, Appendix 7
Surface cultivation, 107–10
Surinam cherry, Massida's greenhouse-grown, 63
Sustainable agriculture, concept of, 15–16
Swales, creating, 77–79
Swards, for slowing fruit tree growth, 285
Sweet cherry. See Cherry, sweet
Sweet cicely (*Myrrhis odorata*), shade tolerance, 284
Sweet clover. See Clover, sweet
Sweet orange. See Orange
Sweet pea (*Lathyrus odorata*), for shade, Appendix 4
perennial (*Lathyrus latifolius*), as leguminous wildflower, 280
Sweet potato
intercropping successes, 242, 243
nitrogen requirements, 231
pest-resistant varieties, 260
planting in no-till, 102
as slow-maturing, 138
Sweet woodruff (*Asperula odorata*), as shade tolerant, 283
Swiss chard
preventing cross-pollination in, 102
root zones, 135
Sycamore. See *Platanus* sp.
Symbiosis, oak-caterpillar, 21
Symmetry, as design element, 43
Symphoricarpos sp. (Snowberry), as insectary plant, 252
Symphylans (Garden centipedes), tillage for control of, 257
Symphytum sp. See Comfrey
Synergy, 5–6, 83–85
Syringa vulgaris (Lilac), as edible flower, 292
Syrphid (hover) flies, as beneficial predators, 246, 248, 256
plants to attract, 5, 252
for scale, 259

T
Tachinid flies, 246
as beneficial insects, 237, 246
for European corn borer, 259
plants to attract, 5, 252
Tagetes sp. See Marigold
'Taiwanica,' 141

Tamarack, intercropping success, 243
Tanacetum vulgare. See Tansy
Tangelo, cold hardiness, 140
Tangerine
'Changsha,' cold hardiness, 141
in Flores garden, 64
Tanglefoot™
guidelines, 257
for scale, 259
Tansy (*Tanacetum vulgare*)
ants and, 237
companion planting studies, 239, 240
cover crop problems, 278
as dynamic accumulator, 270
as insectary plant, 251
as intercrop competition, 238
Tansy ragwort (*Senecio jacobaea*), as soil indicator, 37
Taphrina deformans. See Peach leaf curl
Taproots
in cover crops, tillage vs., 232
on fruit trees, debunking myths, 161–62
Tar, for pruning cuts, 209
Taraxacum officinale. See Dandelion
Taro
in Flores garden, 64
planting in no-till garden, 102
Tarragon (*Artemisia dracunculus*), shade tolerance, 284
TDE, toxicity of, 20
Tea (*Camellia sinensis*), as shade tolerant, 283
Teas, in Flores garden, 64
Temperature
data gathering on, 23, 24, 25
soil, sod culture lowers, 113
windbreaks to raise, 67
Tension, as design element, 43
Tent caterpillars
importance of controlling, 256–57
IPM for, 258
Tepary bean (*Phaseolus acutifolius*), as leguminous wildflower, 280
Terminal bearing fruit trees, 228
Terminal buds, 203
Termites, predators of, 246
Terracing, in Kelley garden, 6
Test plots, in no-till garden, 102
Tetragonia expansa (New Zealand spinach), for berms, 79
Tevis, Grandma, 43
Texture, as design element, 43
Thermometers, 25
Thermopsis (*Thermopsi gracilis*), as leguminous wildflower, 280
Thick-headed flies, as beneficial parasites, 247
Thimbleberry (*Rubus parviflorus*)
for berms, 79
for no-till gardens, 96, 101
as shade tolerant, 283
Thinning wild edibles, 98
Thinning fruit trees
genetic dwarf varieties, 187
with no-pruning style, 212
with open center style, 215
Thistle (*Cirsium* sp.)
Canada (*Cirsium arvense*)
as dynamic accumulator, 270
as soil indicator, 38
as edible flower, 292
as insectary plant, 251
Thistle, nodding (*Carduus nutans*), as soil indicator, 38

Thistle, Russian (*Salsola pestifer*)
as dynamic accumulator, 270
as soil indicator, 38
Thistle, Russian (*Salsola kali L.* var. *tenuifolia Tausch*), as soil indicator, 35
Thistle, sow (*Sonchus arvensis; Sonchus* sp.)
as dynamic accumulator, 270
as nurse plant, 248
as soil indicator, 38
Thistle, creeping. See Thistle, sow
Thlaspi arvense (Pennycress; Stinkweed), as soil indicator, 37, 38
Thrips
IPM for, 258, 259
onion/carrot intercropping for, 242
predators of, 246
Western flower, on squash, intercropping successes, 243
Thunbergia alata (Black-eyed Susan vine), for shade, 73
Thunbergia grandiflora (Sky flower), for shade, Appendix 4
Thyme (*Thymus vulgaris; Thymus* sp.)
companion planting studies, 239
as edible flower, 292
in Flores garden, 64
as groundcover, 1
for herbal lawns, 10
shade tolerance, 284
Thyridopteryx ephemeraeformis (Bagworms), junipers and, 44
Tilia americana (Linden), winter shade by, 75
Tillage, 113–22
clay or wet soil caution, 114
double-digging, 115–22
for fruit trees, 229
for green manure, 274–75
no-till methods, 96–111
for pest control, 257, 259
sod culture, 113–14
taprooted plants for, 232
Tilled soil, plant indicators, 36–38
Tillers, 16, 51. See also Rotary tilling
Tilth, 30
cover crops or green manures improve, 273
indicator plants for gauging, 35
pore space and, 117
tilling vs., 38
Time factors
BFI, 116–17
compost making, 108
cost vs., 54
cultivation, 55
drip irrigation and, 55, 129
flower growing, deadheading, 54
no-till vs. till methods, 95
planning for overruns, 54
resting period after tilling, 114
spending early to save later, 93
surface cultivation method, 108, 109
tree crops, 139
Timothy grass, nitrogen content and C:N ratio, Appendix 5
Tires, for erosion control, 84–85
Toadflax (*Linaria vulgaris*)
as dynamic accumulator, 270
as soil indicator, 38
Tobacco, nitrogen content and C:N ratio, Appendix 5. See also *Nicotiana* sp.
Tobacco budworms, IPM for, 258

Tobacco etch virus
host plants for, 287
insect vectors of, 288
TODD® planters, 127–28
Tomato
azotobacter inoculant for, 126
basil and, 237
BFI and, 119, 121
climbing, for quick shade, 73
companion planting, 237, 238, 239, 240
as compost material, nitrogen content and C:N ratio, Appendix 5
diamondback moths and, 259
diseases
host plants to avoid, 287
insect vectors, 288
preventing, 121
ground cherry as hazard to, 103
growing on trellises, 134
intercropping with, 238, 242, 243
nitrogen requirements, 231
peppers and, as myth, 238–39
pest-resistant varieties, 260
pests
beneficial insects for, 237
climate and, 237
Colorado potato beetles, 238–39
diamondback moths, 243
flea beetles, 243
spider mites, 260
tobacco flea beetle, 260
tomato fruitworm, 237
tomato hornworms, 237, 238
plants stunting growth of, 236
pruning lower leaves, for air circulation, 121
root zones, 134, 135
shoofly plant and, 237
surface cultivation vs. single-dug yields, 110
varieties for compactness, 47
Tomato fruitworms, IPM for, 258
Tomato hornworms
climate and, 237
importance of controlling, 256–57
tillage for, 257
using beneficial insects against, 5
Tomato mosaic virus, host plant, 103
Tools and equipment
double-digging, 117
drip irrigation, 129, 130–32
Dutch hoe, 109
Haws oval watering rose, 128
scraper (onion hoe), 109
for surface cultivaton, 107, 109
TODD® flats, 127–28
Toothpicks, as branch spreaders, 205–6
Toothpick weed (Amni visage), as insectary plant, 251
Topsoil, 31
in berm construction, 78
planning amount needed, Appendix 7
as soil amendment for fruit trees, 194
Trace buds, 203
Trachelospermum jasminoides (Star jasmine), for shade, Appendix 4
Tragopogon archangelica; Tragopogon sp.. See Salsify
Transpiration, cooling effect through, 73–74
Transplant shock, reducing, 127
Transplanting
from TODD® flats, 128
weather watching for, 24
Trap plants, 247, 248

Traps, pheromone, 255–56, 258, 259
Tree crops, choosing for climate, 139–44. See also Fruit and nut trees
Tree of heaven (Ailanthus altissima), as insectary plant, 252
Trees
buying, for windbreak planting, 70–71
as design element, 43
domesticated vs. forest, 139
planting locations, away from south walls, 74, 75
pruning, for winter light and summer shad,e 75–76
soil for, deep-rooted myths, 31
solar cooling drawbacks, 74, 75
synergy with, 84
tube-grown, 70
visualizing effect of, 87
wind data from, 25
for windbreaks, choosing, 70–71
Trefoils (Lotus sp.)
as leguminous wildflower, 280
Trellises
for controlling fruit tree growth, 191
cooling effect of, 73, 74
for espalier, 222
need for, 73
over patios, cautions, 83
for vertical space use, 134
walls as, 83
wire for, 222
Trichogramma wasps, 246, 259
Trickle irrigation. See Drip irrigation
Trifoliate orange rootstock, cold hardiness and, 140–41
Trifolium sp. See Clover
T. hybridum. See Clover, alsike
T. pratense. See Clover, red
T. repens. See Clover, Dutch white
Tristeza virus, citrus resistance, 170
Tropaeolum sp. See Nasturtium
Trumpet creeper, common (Campsis radicans), for shade (deciduous), Appendix 4
Trumpet vine (Campsis radicans), for shade (evergreen), in warm-winter areas, Appendix 4
Trumpet vine, vanilla (Distictis laxiflora), Appendix 4
Trumpet vine, violet (Clytostoma callistegioides), for shade, Appendix 4
Trumpet vine, yellow (Doxantha unguis-cati), for shade, Appendix 4
Tubers, planting in no-till garden, 102
Tubing, drip, 131–32
Tulbaghia violacea (Society garlic), as multi-purpose edible, 60
Tulip (Tulipa sp.), as edible flower, 292
Tumbleweed (Salsola kali L. var. tenuifolia Tausch), as soil indicator, 35
Turf. See Lawns
Turkey manure. See Poultry manure
Turnip
as compost material, nitrogen content and C:N ratio, Appendix 5
defoliation increased yield of, 21
intercropping with, 133, 243
root-maggot-resistant variety, 260
root zones, 135
as shade tolerant, 133

Tussock moths, IPM for, 258
2,4,5–T, 2
2,4–D, 2
Typha latifolia. See Cattail

U

Ugni molinae (Chilean guava)
effort ranking, 295
as shade tolerant, 283
Ulmus sp. (Elm), winter shade by, 75
Umbelliferae (Parsley family)
beneficial insects lured by, 251
preventing cross-pollination among, 102
wild, as disease host, 287
Umble, Mediterranean (Bupleurum fruticosum), as insectary plant, 252
Uncultivated soil, plant indicators, 36–38
United States Department of Agriculture
Forest Service pruning cut study, 208
Soil Conservation Service surveys, 32
United States Weather Bureau, as chill zone source, 141
Unity, as design element, 43
University cooperative extension services. See Cooperative extension services
Unsettling of America, The (Berry), 15
Urban gardens, fruit trees in
espalier pruning for, 221
miniature, containers for, 186–87
Urine
as compost material, nitrogen content and C:N ratio, Appendix 5
as fertilizer, 105–6
Urtica dioca; U. urens. See Stinging nettle
Utah State Agricultural Extension, 211

V

Vaccinium sp. See Blueberry
Vaccinum ovatum. See Huckleberry
Valerian (Valeriana officinalis), as dynamic accumulator, 270
Valerianella locusta (Corn salad). See Corn salad
Vanilla trumpet vine (Distictis laxiflora), for shade, Appendix 4
Varieties, old-timers' experimentation with, 63
Variety
as design element, 43
edible landscaping for, 3
Vase pruning, 213–15
Vectors, 287–88
Vegetables
See also specific kinds
area needed for, 51, 52
compact varieties, 47
companion planting, 237–40
as compost material, nitrogen content and C:N ratio, Appendix 5
cool-weather, protecting during summer, 74
deep- and shallow-rooted, interplanting, 115
density of planting, BFI, 115, 116
soil type and, 117
design for, 46, 57–58; see also planning considerations
disease host plants, 287–88
in Flores garden, 64
green manuring before, 277–81
hay bale method, 105–6
herbs and, planting locations, 46–47
insectary plants as borders for, 257

intercropping, 137–38, 237–40, 241–43
multi-purpose, 58–60
no-till methods, 95–111
hay bale, 105–6
sheet composting, 95–98
sink-or-swim, 101–3
surface cultivation, 107–10
perennials and, planting locations, 46–47
pest-resistant varieties, 256, 259
planning considerations, 46, 51–52, 93–94
planting locations, 57–58, 94
fruit and nut trees and, 47
quick-maturing, listed, 138
root system size, 119–21
root zones compared, 134–37
sink-or-swim approach to, 101–3
size of garden devoted to, 46, 51–52
slow-maturing, listed, 138
sod culture, 113–14
spacing between, in BFI, 115, 116
starting. See Seeding
ten most popular, 51
Velvet bean (Stizolobium deeringianum)
as cover crop or green manure, 267
as leguminous wildflower, 280
Velvet bean caterpillars
IPM for, 258
in soybeans, intercropping for, 243
Venturia inequalis. See Scab
Veratrum californicum (Devil's bit; False hellebore)
as dynamic accumulator, 269
as soil indicator, 36
Verbascum sp. (Common mullein)
as dynamic accumulator, 270
as edible flower, 292
as fruit tree cover crop, 280
as soil indicator, 37
Vermiculite, in potting mix, 127
Veronica sp. (Speedwell), as soil indicator, 38
Vertical gardening, 134
Verticillium wilt
cherry rootstock resistance, 169
host plants for, 287
Vetch (Vicia sp.)
as compost material, 108
as cover crop, 267, 273
as disease host, 287
as dynamic accumulator, 270
as green manure, 267, 273, 275
hairy; purple hairy (V. villosa)
as cover crop or green manure, 267
as fruit tree cover crop, 280
nitrogen gathered by, 266
for hay bale gardening, 105
as leguminous wildflower, 280
as soil indicator, 38
in surface cultivation garden, 108
Viburnum trilobum (Bush cranberry), as shade tolerant, 283
Vicia faba. See Fava bean
Vicia sp. See Vetch
Village Homes, 9–13
Vinaigrettes
for Asian Pear Salad, 300
chayote seeds in, 58
for Corn-Salad Salad, 304
Vinca sp. (Periwinkle)
avoid in compost, 97
as ground cover, maintenance considerations, 46

Vines
for baskets, 30
for cooling, 73–76
deciduous and evergreen, listed, Appendix 4
edible, listed, 73
over patios, cautions about, 83
pruning, 74–75
for quick shade, listed, 73
spraying necessity with, 73
trellised
on house, advantages of, 73–74, 83
as windbreaks, 67
vertical gardening with, 134
as windbreaks, 67, 70, 71
yields, 73
Viola cornuta; V. cucullata (Viola)
in Malcolm-Neeb garden, 2
as multi-purpose plant, 58, 60
shade tolerance, 284
Viola odorata (Sweet Violet; Violet)
for berms, 79
as edible flower, 292, 296
as multi-purpose edible, 60
for no-till gardens, 101
as shade tolerant, 283
Viola sp. (Pansy; Wild pansy)
as edible flower, 292
under fruit trees, 227
as soil indicator, 37
Viola tricolor (Johnny-jump-up), as edible flower, 292
Violet. See Viola odorata
Violet trumpet vine (Clytostoma callistegioides), for shade, Appendix 4
Virginia creeper (Parthenocissus quinquefolia), for shade, Appendix 4
Virus diseases
on fruit trees, pruning caution, 208
host plants for, 287
insect vectors of, 288
Viruses, for pest control, 259
Vitis labrusca; V. vinifera. See Grape
Vitis mustangensis (Mustang grape), for shade, Appendix 4
Volume and liquid measurements, Appendix 6
von Oech, Roger, 84
Vorbeck, Tom, 155

W

Wallace, Henry, on soil, 29
Walls
fruit tree cold hardiness and, 141
as heat retainers, 58
as trellises, 83
Walnut (Juglans hindsii; Juglans sp.)
'Ambassador'
chill requirement, 143
ripening dates, 148
aphid-deterrent ground cover for, 243
average seasonal growth, 229
black (J. nigra)
as disease resistant, 155
ease of care, 45, 295
as hot-summer tolerant, 144
as nondwarfable, 180
plants growing well under, 235–36
chill requirements, 142
choosing, by rootstock, 177
clay soil problem, 193
disease resistance and susceptibility, 177, 159, 194
disease-resistant rootstocks, 177
English (Persian)
as hot-weather-damage susceptible, 144
as nondwarfa ble, 180
self-fruitful varieties, 151
'Franquette'
as blight tolerant, 159

ripening dates, 148
as self-fruitful, 151
'Hartley'
as blight tolerant, 159
as self-fruitful, 151
intercropping success, 243
low-chill varieties, 143
meats, damage to, 144
nematode-resistant root-
stocks, 177
nitrogen requirements, 230
as nondwarfable, 180
'Placentia'
chill requirement, 143
as self-fruitful, 151
planting locations, separate
from lawns, 284
ripening dates, 147, 148
root system, 161
rootstocks, matching to soil
types, 177
self-fruitful varieties, 151
standard
rootstocks compared, 177
size, 179, 180
winter shade by, 75
yields, 53
Walters, Charles, Jr., 35
Warm-winter areas, chill factor calculations, 141
Wasps, beneficial, 245, 246,
247, 248, 256
plants to attract, 252
Water
as design element, 43, 284
as soil component, 29, 30
Water chestnuts, for downspout outlets, 83
Water consumption, with BFI,
115, 116
Watercress (Nasturtium officinale)
for berms, 79
as dynamic accumulator,
270
as favorite no-till green, 96
as soil indicator, 38
Water damage, preventing,
77–81
Water hemlock (Cicuta
douglasii)
as insectary plant, 251
spotted (C. maculata), as
soil indicator, 38
Watering
aphids and, 256
with BFI, 115
cane fruits, 286
for cooling effect, 73–74
drip irrigation, 55, 129–33
for fruit trees, 225–26
energy conserving systems,
77–81
flats, 128
fruit trees, 199
cold hardiness and, 140
with drip irrigation, 225–
26
flavor and, 225
in lawns, 285, 286
miniature, in containers,
186
mulch and, 227
after planting, 194, 199
size and, 191
yields and, 225
Gardena speed couplings,
cost vs. time saved, 54
hay bale garden, 106
lawns, fruit trees and, 285,
286
leaf fall and, 28
location of spigots, 57
moderating flow, 77–79
seedlings, adding fish emulsion to, 128
yields and, 51
Water-loving plants
for berms and swales, 79
for downspouts, 83
Watermelon, root zones, 135.
See also Melon
Watermelon mosaic virus
host plants for, 287
insect vectors of, 288
Water sprouts, removing, 208
Waterways, creating, 77–79
Wattle (Acacia verticillate), as
nitrogen-fixing
perennial, 291

Watts Towers, 42
Waywort, as dynamic
accumulator, 270
Weather
cold hardiness and, 140
data gathering about, 23–
26
local wisdom about, 63
planning for extremes of,
79–81, 93
planning for sacrifice to, 52
Weatherwise, 28
Weaver, John E., 135
Weed control
allelopathic plants, 236
cover crops, 273
around drip tubing, 130
mulching, 292
low-cost methods, 78, 96,
97
in paths, 45
no-till methods, 97
preventing wind-blown
seeding, 98
soil building and, 39
surface weeding, 108–9
Weeds
See also Weed control
as craft materials, 39
diseases harbored by, 103,
287
drip irrigation reduces, 129
edible, 39
as garden alternative, 51
diseases harbored by,
103
growing, 95–98
as herb teas or medi-
cines, 39
list of favorites, 96
nutritional value, 95, 96
sheet composting method
for, 96–98
as insectary plants, 39
intercropping successes,
241, 242, 243
mushrooms, 39
as nurse plants, 248–49
as soil type indicators, 32,
35–39
uses for, 39
as wild plants, 35
as wildlife habitat, 39
Westcape, on cold hardiness,
139
Western chokeberry. See
Chokecherry
Western flower thrips, in
squash, 243
Western Hills Rare Plant
Nursery, 78
Western sand cherry (Prunus
besseyi)
as disease resistant, 155
as low-effort perennial, 45
Western Washington Re-
search and Extension
Unit, 157
Wet soil, plant indicators, 35,
36–38
Whack on the Side of the
Head, A (von Oech), 84
Wheat
azotobacter inoculant for,
126
as disease host, 287
flour, nitrogen content and
C:N ratio, Appendix 5
fruit tree mulch success,
242
intercropping with soy-
beans, 243
straw, nitrogen content and
C:N ratio, Appendix 5
winter, as cover crop or
green manure, 267
Wheat curl mites, as disease
vectors, 288
Wheat streak mosaic, host
plants for, 287
Whitcomb, Carl, 193
White bladder flower (Araujia
sericifera), for shade,
Appendix 4
White bur sage (Ambrosia
dumosa), 236
White clover. See Clover
White latex paint, for fruit
trees, 198–99, 200
genetic dwarf, peach borer

protection, 187
White mustard. See Mustards
White root rot, 287, 288
White spruce, intercropping
with tamarack, 243
White sweet clover. See
Clover, sweet
Whiteflies
on beans, companion planting studies, 239, 240
IPM for, 258, 259
predators and parasites of,
246, 247
plants to attract, 252
shoofly plant and, 237
Wickson, Edward, 214
Wide row gardenings. See
Double-digging
Wild blackberry. See
Blackberry
Wild carrot (Daucus carota)
as disease host, 287, 288
as fruit tree cover crop,
233, 280
as insectary plant, 251
intercropping with veget-
ables, 243
Japanese beetle repelled
by, 243
as soil indicator, 36
Wild celery (Apium graveolens), for berms, 79
Wild cherry (Prunus sp.)
for erosion control, 11
as windbreaks, 69, 71
Wild edible plants. See
Weeds, edible;
Wildflowers
Wildflowers
as dynamic accumulators,
280
leguminous, 280
Wild ginger (Asarum canda-
tum), for berms, 79
Wild lettuce (Lactuca
canadensis)
as disease host, 287
as insectary plant, 252
Wild licorice (Glycyrrhiza lepidota), as leguminous
wildflower, 280
Wildlife habitat
multi-purpose plants, 59
windbreaks, 67
weed plants, 39
Wild mustard. See Mustards
Wild pansy (Viola sp.)
as edible flower, 292
as soil indicator, 37
Wild parsnip (Sium suave), as
soil indicator, 37
Wild parsnip/Cow parsnip
(Pastinaca sativa)
as disesae host, 288
as fruit tree cover crop, 233
as insectary plant, 251, 252
intercropping with corn, 242
Wild plants. See Weeds;
Wildflowers
Wild plum. See Plum, American
Wild radish (Raphanus raphanistrum; R. sativus)
as fruit tree cover crop, 233
as soil indicator, 37
Wild rose. See Rose
Wild strawberry. See Strawberry, alpine; Straw-
berry, wild
Willamette mites, in grapes,
242
Willow (Salix sp.)
beans grown under, 133
black, as soil indicator, 35,
38
as dynamic accumulator,
270
for erosion prevention, 78,
85
windbreak suitability, 69
Wind
data gathering on, 23, 24,
25–26
planning for sacrifice to, 52
as pollinizer, 151
protecting fruit trees from
mulch, and, 227
orienting the graft, 198–
99
staking, 197, 199–200

Wind roses, 23, 24
Wind speed, chill factor and,
67
Windbreaks
designing, 23, 24, 67–71,
87
number of plants needed,
Appendix 7
firewood trees for, 84
for fruit trees, 140, 143
fruit trees as
cold hardiness and, 141
no-pruning style for, 212
instant, 69
maintenance considera-
tions, 70
multi-purpose edibles for,
59, 60
nurse plants in, 248
as nutrient robbers, 68–69,
70
as ornamentals, 69
planting, 70–71
root system drawbacks, 68,
70
shade problems from, 68,
69
structural, 69
weed seeds filtered by, 98
vines vs. trees as, 70
Windmills
gopher control, using for
wind data, 26
siting, 23, 24
Winter chill. See Chill factor;
Chill requirements
Wintergreen (Gaultheria procumbens), as dynamic
accumulator, 270
Winter hardiness. See Cold
hardiness
Winter vs. summer pruning,
74–75, 140, 207, 218
Wiregrass (Heleocharis
palustris), as soil
indicator, 35
Wire vine (Muehlenbeckia
complexa), for shade,
Appendix 4
Wireworms, tillage for control
of, 257
Wisteria, Chinese (Wisteria
sinensis), for shade,
Appendix 4
Wood, white fir, nitrogen content and C:N ratio,
Appendix 5
Wood ash
nutrient percentages, 230
as potassium/potash
source, 231
after potato harvest, 110
when planting fruit trees,
194, 197, 198
Wood betony (Stachys officinalis), as shade tolerant,
283
Wood chips, as mulch, 97,
232
Woodruff; Sweet woodruff
(Asperula odorata)
as edible flower, 292
as shade tolerant, 283
Woolley, Robert, 184, 200
Woolly apple aphids, apple
rootstocks resistant to,
166, 167
World Health Organization,
allowable poison
standards, 2–3
Worm bin, for kitchen scraps,
57
Wormseed-mustard (Erysi-
mum cheiranthoides),
intercropping with
brassicas, 241
Wormwood (Artemisia
absinthium)
as allelopathic, 238
biennial (Artemisia biennis),
as soil indicator, 38
companion planting studies,
239
Wound dressings, 209

X

Xanthium stramonium, intercropping with collards,
242

Xanthomonas campestris.
See Blight
Xanthomonas pruni (Bacterial
leaf spot), peaches re-
sistant to, 158
X disease, 288
Xylosma (Xylosma con-
gestum), for shade,
Appendix 4

Y

Yarrow (Achillea millefolium;
Achillea sp.)
as cover crop, 278
as dynamic accumulator,
270
ease of care, 54
as fruit tree ground cover,
285
as insectary plant, 251, 252
as soil indicator, 38
Yellow jacket wasps, plants to
attract, 252
Yellow sweet clover. See
Clover, sweet
Yellow trumpet vine (Dox-
antha unguis-cati), for
shade, Appendix 4
Yields
aphids and, 20
azotobacter inoculant and,
126
with BFI, 116
defoliation as aid to, 21
drip irrigation and, 129
experience and, 51
fruit trees, 181
central leader pruning
and, 217
genetic dwarf, 181, 184–
85
semi-dwarf, 180
standard, 180
inoculants and, 125–26
intercropping and, 238
no-pruning style and, 211
planning for bugs and disease, 52
single-dug vs. surface cultivation plots, 109–10
size of garden and, 51, 118
sod culture, 113
surface cultivation, 109–10
TODD® system and, 127
watering and, 51
windbreaks and, 68–69, 70
Yucca (Yucca sp.), as edible
flower, 292

Z

Zaiger, Floyd, 184
Zinc deficiency, accumulator
plants to correct, 267
Zinnia
dead-heading requirements,
54
as insectary plant, 251
Zizyphus jujube. See Jujube
Zucchini, chayote as substitute for, 59